Arkansas Biography

Arkansas Biography

A COLLECTION
OF NOTABLE LIVES

EDITED BY NANCY A. WILLIAMS

JEANNIE M. WHAYNE, ASSOCIATE EDITOR

FOREWORD BY SHIRLEY ABBOTT

THE UNIVERSITY OF ARKANSAS PRESS
FAYETTEVILLE · 2000

04   03   02   01   00   5   4   3   2   1

Designed by Ellen Beeler

⊖ The paper used in this publication meets the minimum requirements of the
American National Standard for Permanence of Paper for Printed Library Materials z39.48-1984.

Library of Congress Cataloging-in-Publication Data

Arkansas biography: a collection of notable lives / edited by Nancy A. Williams; associate editor, Jeannie M. Whayne; foreword
     by Shirley Abbott.
          p. cm.
     Includes index.
          ISBN 1-55728-588-8 (alk. paper)—ISBN 1-55728-587-x (pbk.: alk. paper)   1. Arkansas—Biography.   I. Williams, Nancy A.,
     1934–   II. Whayne, Jeannie M.

CT224.W55 2000
920.0767—dc21   99-043732

*This project is supported in part by a grant from the Arkansas Humanities Council and the Arkansas Historic
Preservation Program, an agency of the Department of Arkansas Heritage.*

ACKNOWLEDGMENTS

We are grateful for the partnership of the following donors who made it possible to acquire and edit the biographies in this work: the Roy and Christine Sturgis Charitable and Educational Trust, the Center for Arkansas and Regional Studies, the Arkansas Humanities Council, the National Endowment for the Humanities, the Winthrop Rockefeller Foundation, the Fred Darragh Foundation, and the White Hall High School Social Studies Club.

So many kindnesses have been extended to us over the course of eight years that it is a great pleasure to acknowledge some of them here. The encouragement of well-wishers kept us going. We are grateful to everyone who gave us a name or a list of names; we simply would not have known otherwise about many of the lives presented here. Our thanks go, too, to all the people who gave us information—scraps, bits and pieces, whole volumes—all of it needed and valuable. Over the course of the project we learned that southern hospitality is not mythical but real and freely given. We have been helped materially by Arkansas people who shared books, artwork, homemade bread, guest rooms, meals, and a parking space more precious than pearls.

We will always be grateful to our advisory committee for their gracious and professional counsel: Willard B. Gatewood Jr., Ethel Simpson, Jeannie Whayne, Tom Dillard, Ann Wilson, David Edmark, Jo Bennett, and Eugenia Donovan.

At the University of Arkansas, Fayetteville, our working conditions were never less than pleasant, and we no sooner asked for help than we received it. Our appreciation goes to the Fulbright College of Arts and Sciences and Dean Bernard L. Madison. To the faculty of the history department and its chairmen Tom Kennedy and Daniel Sutherland, thank you all for your patience and generosity. Thanks, also, to the staff of Computing Services.

This work relies heavily on the expertise and good nature of the staff at the University of Arkansas Libraries, Fayetteville; we would like to thank especially John Harrison, Michael Dabrishus, Beth Juhl, Elizabeth McKee, Ethel Simpson, Ellen Shipley, and Andrea Cantrell.

We extend our thanks to John L. Ferguson and the staff at the Arkansas History Commission; the members of the Arkansas Historical Association, especially for their actions in the spring of 1998 when the future of the University of Arkansas Press was in jeopardy; Stephen Recken and the Public History Program at the University of Arkansas at Little Rock; Linda Pine at Archives and Special Collections at UALR; Edwina Walls Mann of the Historical Research Center, UAMS Library; the members of the Arkansas Women's History Institute; and Bob Bailey and the staff at the Arkansas Humanities Council. A word should be said about Arkansas's wonderful museums: they are treasures, and we are glad for their participation in the Arkansas Biography Project.

We share a special relationship with the staff at the University of Arkansas Press. Together we lived through the dark night of the soul in the spring of 1998. Their enthusiasm, encouragement, and courtesy never falter, and to them we trust the bringing of this book into the light of day: Miller Williams, David Sanders, and Ellen Beeler, who are no longer at the Press, and John Coghlan, Brian King, Beth Motherwell, Kevin Brock, Liz Lester, and all the members of the staff. Carolyn Brt is our favorite candidate for sainthood and has our unending gratitude.

To Mary Drake McFeely we owe the meticulous editing of the copy for this book. It was good to have her professionalism and good humor in the service of our contributing authors.

Special thanks go to Amber Mills, Charles Rector, Suz Smith and her staff in the history department, Jean Newhouse, Gretchen Gearhart, Anne and Gus Fulk, Izola Preston, Martha and Bob Douglas, Russell Bearden, James Leslie, Suzanne Maberry, Emily Gregg Pritchard, June Jefferson, and Randy Holder.

To our friends and our dear families, thank you for your patience with such a long project.

Underneath the pleasure of offering thanks lurks the terror of a faulty memory. If we fail to remember someone here, forgive us, it is not from lack of gratitude.

We thank the people of Arkansas for trusting us with part of their history. We have had our share of heartfelt disappointments when we could not obtain certain biographies we wanted to include. But we hope the work is well begun. May *Arkansas Biography* take on its own life and inspire a second volume some not-distant day.

NANCY A. WILLIAMS
JEANNIE M. WHAYNE

CONTENTS

FOREWORD

To know one's history is a great gift, because knowledge of one's past is empowering. Knowing what you've emerged from, you can take pride in what you've accomplished, and you can use your past as a guide to the future. What is true of personal history, of course, is also true of local, state, and national history. We require a past, and for a state or region, it is a handicap to be bereft of it. We require it because the past tells us where we have been and what we might do next. That's why this book was created.

Here, in *Arkansas Biography: A Collection of Notable Lives*, is a past for all Arkansans and a resource for researchers everywhere who are interested in the Arkansas past. It is a source of fundamental information about Arkansas and its people, some born in the state, others who settled here. Each entry is concise; no biographies of living Arkansans are included. Some of the names in this book are famous; others appear as biographical subjects for the very first time. An enormous range of personalities is here, taken from the panorama of Arkansas history and selected from the nominations of dozens of Arkansans.

You may not have heard of Margaret Pittman (1902–1995), but here she is: a microbiologist who helped to develop standards for the safety and efficacy of the whooping cough vaccine. This achievement is all the more impressive since there were so few women scientists in Pittman's time and fewer in Arkansas, perhaps, than elsewhere. Thus her story seems particularly noteworthy. Further on, there's Charles Lee Watkins (1879–1966), parliamentarian of the United States Senate, known as the Senate "ventriloquist" because he so often whispered advice to the presiding officer—a familiar presence to a long list of vice presidents. You'll find Pacaha, a Native American chief born in the early 1550s, an enemy and later friend of Hernando de Soto, the first European to explore what is now Arkansas. (As a token of his hope for a lasting alliance with the Spanish, Pacaha gave de Soto three women as wives.) You'll find that famously rabid anti-Semite and preacher, Gerald L. K. Smith, who was actually from Wisconsin and who began his strange career in Louisiana as a disciple of Huey Long. You'll find balladeers and frontier women, soldiers, aviators, ministers, and enterprising free black farmers. There are heroes, heroines, and just plain folks. You might find your own ancestors. You will certainly find a number of good stories, many of them good enough to read aloud.

The culture that springs to life in this book is rich, colorful, and too little known. Students, teachers, genealogists, historians, librarians, business people, and journalists will find it an essential desk reference. Browsers will find it a treasure house of anecdote and story. Heretofore, those most in need of good tools for Arkansas history—teachers in Arkansas schools, for example—have had little to go on. Much information about our state still lies scattered in old newspapers, periodicals, letters, and other disparate sources.

This new reference book rescues some of what has been obscure. It can do much to inform Arkansans about their history and to raise awareness of a unique cultural history. As the volume ably demonstrates, history is not only a necessity but a pleasure as well.

SHIRLEY ABBOTT

INTRODUCTION

The collection of Arkansas lives offered here represents the cooperative effort of hundreds of Arkansans and others from beyond our borders. It is primarily the work of some 175 contributing authors, all of whom donated their expertise to the project. As they would gladly testify, though these biographies are brief, the time required to research and write one is not brief at all. *Arkansas Biography* is a tribute to their passion for history and their affection for Arkansas.

Arkansas Biography documents lives beginning with the first European to visit this place, Hernando de Soto, and the first inhabitants for whom we have a record, Casqui and Pacaha, who encountered de Soto and his party in what is now northeastern Arkansas. It provides basic, up-to-date, factual information about lives from Arkansas's past. Readers will be able to obtain a brief overview of a life or to quickly locate a fact or date. A list of sources at the end of most entries directs readers to more information about the subject. No living person is included; 1999 is the latest year of death in the book.

During the earliest months of the Arkansas Biography project, which began in 1991, we collected a data base of hundreds of names from which to select entries for the book. A statewide call for names in 1993 brought several hundred responses, affirming that Arkansans revere their heritage and want to pass it on to their children.

We consulted a great many people individually, and we conferred with representatives of such organizations as the Arkansas Historical Association, the Arkansas Women's History Institute, the Arkansas Territorial Restoration, historical museums, and county historical societies, among others. We are proud of the open process we used; the book's vitality comes from the participation of so many Arkansans.

We selected biographies always with reference to Arkansas history. Even in the short space allotted to each entry, contributing authors place their subjects against the background of the times they lived in. We believe this historical point of view will contribute to our understanding of who and what we are as a state.

There is no shortage of Arkansas people worthy to be included in a collection like this. From Henry Shreve, the boatman who cleared the great raft from the Red River, to Thomas Smith, who devoted his life to establishing public education in Arkansas after the Civil War, to Louis Jordan, king of the jukeboxes in the 1940s, Arkansans have served their state and nation with distinction.

To be included a person must have been born here or, no matter where born, must have done something worthy of note while in Arkansas. In practice, defining "Arkansan" was never really an issue; most cases were self-evident, except when we wanted to poach on Missouri territory but thought better of it. The only category for which all members are included is the governors. Their inclusion provides a framework of events important in Arkansas history. Other than the governors, this book does not concentrate on political history.

People were selected for inclusion because they contributed to the good of the state and nation. We emphasized those who made a difference within the state and paid less attention to those who left Arkansas, went to the big city, and made good, though this category is well represented, too. Some people are included not because they led exceptional lives but because they were caught up in historical events or circumstances. One such person is Triphenia Fancher Wilson, who survived the Mountain Meadow Massacre in Utah when she was two years old. There are some others here, very few, whose lives are simply representative of their times: a blacksmith, a farmer. A few criminals here remind us not to sentimentalize the past.

The book reflects the variety of human labor, skill, energy, endurance, faith, intelligence, and heroism that went to make up the Arkansas we know today. It compares favorably with similar works of reference in its coverage of women; even so, we wish it had been possible to include more women. An important determiner of which lives are included was whether or not a writer could be found who had the time to research a given subject. We avoided assigning the writing of a life to anyone closely related to the subject.

We focused on lives that would be of interest to readers statewide, but the line between state, regional, and local interest is not always easy to discern. We hope the publication of *Arkansas Biography* will inspire Arkansans to work with their county and state historical associations to preserve the details of our heritage. We in Arkansas need to do a better job of preservation. The record of family and community slips away very fast, often irrecoverably.

Responsibility for the accuracy of the facts presented here lies with each individual author. The contributing authors have made every effort to ensure the correctness of this material; in fact, they have corrected quite a few errors in published records. But inevitably errors will have crept into this book. If readers will have the kindness to report questionable data to the University of Arkansas Press, the editors will review readers' responses before revised editions are published.

The format of the entries closely follows tradition in reference books and takes the *Dictionary of American Biography* for a model. The subjects are arranged alphabetically, and their lives are presented in chronological order. It is assumed the parents of the subject were married unless the author states otherwise. The mother's name is her name at the time she married the subject's father; for example, the mother of John Gould Fletcher is listed as Adolphine Krause and not Adolphine Krause Fletcher. When the state where the subject was born is not specified, Arkansas is assumed.

For many users *Arkansas Biography* will be a starting point for further research. A source list following most entries directs readers to places where they can find more information than we have space for in this volume. *Arkansas*

Biography does not attempt to be a comprehensive bibliographic resource, however. If a bibliography exists elsewhere, we refer the reader to it. Someone needing information on, say, Roberta Fulbright, is referred to Dorothy D. Stuck and Nan Snow's *Roberta: A Most Remarkable Fulbright*, which has an extensive bibliography. On the other hand, some entries are gathered from scattered sources, perhaps for the first time, and in these cases the source list might be lengthy and detailed.

The only abbreviated title in the source lists is *AHQ* for the *Arkansas Historical Quarterly*.

The following Arkansas reference works are rich in biographical material and may have been consulted by our contributing authors in preparing their entries: the *Goodspeed Biographical and Historical Memoirs* series: *Western Arkansas* (1891; rpt. 1978); *Eastern Arkansas* (1890; rpt. 1978); *Northeast Arkansas* (1889); *Southern Arkansas* (1890); *Central Arkansas* (1889). Also John Hallum, *Biographical and Pictorial History of Arkansas* (1887); Fay Hempstead, *Historical Review of Arkansas: Its Commerce, Industry and Modern Affairs* (1911); Josiah H. Shinn, *Pioneers and Makers of Arkansas* (1908; rpt. 1967); David Y. Thomas, *Arkansas and Its People* (1930); Dallas T. Herndon, *Centennial History of Arkansas* (1922) and *Annals of Arkansas* (1947); Fay Williams, *Arkansawyers of the Years*, 4 vols. (1951–54); *Who's Who in Little Rock–1921* (1921); *Who Is Who in Arkansas*, Vol. 1 (1959), Vol. 2 (1968); John L. Ferguson, ed., *Arkansas Lives: The Opportunity Land Who's Who* (1965); Peggy Jacoway, *First Ladies of Arkansas* (1941); Kitty Sloan, ed., *Horizons: One Hundred Arkansas Women of Achievement* (1980); *Among Arkansas Leaders* compiled by Lex B. Davis, edited by H. F. Barnes (c. 1934); *Bench and Bar of Arkansas, 1935* (1935); E. M. Woods, *Blue Book of Little Rock and Argenta* (1907); Lois Pattillo, *Little Rock Roots: Biographies in Arkansas Black History* (c. 1981); John Hugh Reynolds and David Y. Thomas, *History of the University of Arkansas* (1910); Elizabeth Jacoway, ed., *Behold Our Works Were Good: A Handbook of Arkansas Women's History* (1988).

Readers needing more information about political figures than is provided here might look into the reference books listed above and *The Governors of Arkansas: Essays in Political Biography* (1981; 2d ed. 1995); the *Arkansas Historical Quarterly*; the *University of Arkansas at Little Rock Law Journal*; and the *Arkansas Political Science Journal*, published from 1980 to 1987.

Readers interested in Arkansas history, biography, and culture can consult *Arkansas History: An Annotated Bibliography* compiled by Michael B. Dougan, Tom W. Dillard, and Timothy G. Nutt (1995). An important resource is the Butler Center for Arkansas Studies at the Central Arkansas Library System, Little Rock. The center is a general library for published and unpublished material on Arkansas and has a full-scale genealogy research collection. The researcher might also consult Elizabeth Chadbourn McKee's "Arkansas Reference Sources" in *Arkansas Libraries*, 45 (Dec. 1988): 15–18, and 46 (Mar. 1989): 6–10.

ADKINS, HOMER MARTIN (Oct. 15, 1890–Feb. 26, 1964), pharmacist, governor of Arkansas, was the son of Ulysses Adkins and Lorena Wood. Born on a farm near Jacksonville, Arkansas, he graduated from the Little Rock public schools and Draughon's Business College. In 1911 he completed studies at Hodges Pharmacy School and became a licensed pharmacist.

In 1915 Homer Adkins began studying law, but when the United States entered World War I, he joined the army medical corps. At Camp Beauregard, Louisiana, he met Estelle Smith, a Red Cross nurse from Jackson, Mississippi. They married on December 21, 1921. They had no children.

Adkins's political career began in 1923 when he was elected sheriff of Pulaski County on the Democratic ticket with heavy Ku Klux Klan support. Defeated in the 1926 elections, he returned to private life. In 1932 he worked in Franklin D. Roosevelt's successful campaign for president. As a reward Adkins was appointed collector of internal revenue for Arkansas. He held this post until he ran for governor in 1940. The support he had cultivated during his years as collector helped him defeat his Republican opponent, H. C. Stump, in the general election by a vote of 184,578 to 16,000. In 1942 Adkins was reelected without Republican opposition.

Adkins's election in 1940 made him Arkansas's wartime governor (1941–45) during a period of dramatic economic and social change. The state still suffered from the effects of the Great Depression and the weight of a $137 million highway debt. In his inaugural address Adkins gave refunding of the highway debt first priority. To ensure legislative support without extensive floor debate, he consulted with small groups of legislators, explaining his plan. When the legislature convened in January 1941, Adkins's refunding plan (Act No. 4) was passed unanimously by both houses of the legislature. By law the measure required voter approval. In 1943 Arkansas voters, in a special election, overwhelmingly approved of Adkins's refunding plan.

During World War II some $300 million worth of defense plants and installations were located in Arkansas. The establishment of war plants, increased military spending, growing demand for Arkansas agricultural products, and almost full employment enabled the state to recover from the depression. By the end of the war, the state's treasury surplus had risen from $21 to $45 million.

In addition to improving the state's financial condition, Adkins, a Methodist, attempted to improve the moral climate. In 1942 he authorized the state police to seize gambling equipment in Garland County (Hot Springs) and in Little Rock without benefit of search warrants. His crusade was rebuffed by the state courts, however.

In contrast to his crusade for morality, Adkins showed little concern for the rights of minorities. During World War II approximately twenty thousand Japanese Americans were relocated in Arkansas from the West Coast. When the federal government requested permission to establish two Japanese-American relocation centers in Arkansas, Adkins refused until he was told it was his patriotic duty and was assured that the internees would be kept under military guard and promptly evacuated after the war. To ensure that none of the internees would remain in Arkansas after the war, Adkins pushed for legislation to deny them access to public education and property ownership. In 1943 the state legislature, encouraged by Adkins, enacted a law denying Japanese Americans the right to own property in the state. It mattered little to the governor and the legislature that the internees were loyal American citizens.

Black Arkansans fared little better. They were not denied property rights and educational opportunities (although such opportunities were minimal), but they were denied equal suffrage and employment opportunities. When President Roosevelt issued Executive Order 8802 in 1941 outlawing racial discrimination by industries with defense contracts and in federal job-training programs, Adkins declared that the order violated states' rights and was unenforceable in Arkansas. He was enraged by the Supreme Court's 1944 decision in *Smith v. Allwright* which outlawed the all-white Democratic primary in Texas and prepared the way for black voting in Democratic primaries throughout the South. Adkins declared angrily that the Democratic Party in Arkansas was a white man's party. He sent a letter to the governors of other southern states requesting them to urge their legislatures to petition Congress to call a constitutional convention to repeal Executive Order 8802 and overturn the *Smith v. Allwright* decision. In 1945 the Arkansas legislature, encouraged by Adkins, passed a double primary law providing for separate regular and runoff primaries for state and federal officials. Blacks could vote only in the primaries for federal office.

In 1944 Adkins made a bid for the United States Senate and lost to J. William Fulbright in a spirited contest. Returning to private business, Adkins became something of a political broker for Arkansas politicians aspiring for higher office. In 1948 Governor Sidney S. McMath, an old political ally, appointed Adkins administrator of the Arkansas Employment Security Division, a post he held until 1952.

Adkins spent much of his later life on his 250-acre farm near Malvern. He died in Malvern.

[See C. Calvin Smith, "Homer Martin Adkins, 1941–1945," in *The Governors of Arkansas: Essays in Political Biography,* Timothy P. Donovan, Willard B. Gatewood Jr., and Jeannie M. Whayne, eds., 2d ed. (1995).]

C. CALVIN SMITH

ADLER, SIMON (1832–Oct. 3, 1904), merchant and banker, was born in Bavaria in 1832, according to his tombstone. He first appears on the tax rolls of Independence County in 1856, when he came to Batesville to join his older brother Israel. Israel Adler had arrived in that place about 1853 and had purchased a general store in partnership with Aaron and Samuel Hirsch, immigrants from France.

In 1858 Hirsch, Adler and Company acquired the United States mail contract between Batesville and Jacksonport. The *Arkansas Gazette* noted: "Messrs. Hirsch, Adler & Co. have at last received their new stage, designed for the Batesville and Jacksonport mail line. They have named it the 'Col. Noland,' and it is a very handsome and substantial coach, with ample room for nine passengers."

In the 1860 census Simon Adler is enumerated as a twenty-six-year-old clerk, living in the household of Aaron Hirsch. During the Civil War, according to local and family tradition, Israel Adler moved to Texas with most of the property of the Hirsch, Adler partnership: slaves, stock, and merchandise. Simon Adler is believed to have accompanied his brother to Texas, perhaps even on to Mexico, for the duration of the war. In 1866 Simon returned to Batesville and assumed control of all the Hirsch and Adler holdings, eventually acquiring full ownership. He operated a general merchandise store in the Batesville Institute Building, acted as agent for the Hirsch, Adler land holdings, and as an independent cotton broker.

When the Institute Building burned in 1880, Simon Adler acquired full title to the lot and built his own handsome two-story brick buildling, "Adler Hall." His general store occupied the ground level; offices and a large combination ballroom and opera hall were on the second floor. The building still stands in 1999. The letter *A* can be seen carved in marble high on the facade, and the original tin ceiling of the ground floor remains in place.

In 1891, after a number of years banking "out of his hat"—local tradition holds that he carried bills and notes in his hat as he strolled up and down Main Street—he organized and built the People's Savings Bank. The People's Bank Building is also still standing in 1999.

Simon Adler was the only Jewish resident of Batesville from 1866 until 1877. He had a capacity for sincerity and friendship and earned the respect of the poor as well as that of the most prominent residents of the community. He is mentioned frequently in the Batesville newspapers of the day. On October 27, 1866, the *North Arkansas Times* reported: "The many friends of Simon Adler will be rejoiced to know that he is again located in Batesville." He was so highly respected that people named their children for him. The Independence County census discloses no fewer than thirteen men with Adler or Simon Adler as a given name. When Simon Adler Gill of Bethesda, Independence County, was interviewed in 1980, he was asked about the circumstances of his naming. He replied: "Simon Adler was a friend of my father's even though we were poor."

Simon Adler married Emilie Altschul of New York City on August 1, 1880. A year earlier, on May 15, 1879, the *Batesville Guard* had reported: "What does this mean? Simon Adler received last week from the City of Jerusalem, a commission to marry written in Hebrew. So his friends may expect to hear of his being taken off!" A few days later, on May 20, the *Guard* editor joked: "Simon Adler felt so proud or rich, we don't know which, on receiving that document from Jerusalem that he called us into his store and placed on our needy head one of his best hats. Many thanks, Simon."

Simon and Emilie Adler had two children, Ray (Rachel) and Nathan. After his father's death, Nathan Adler was elected president of the First National Bank of Batesville. Simon Adler died in St. Louis; he and his wife are buried in the Mount Sinai Cemetery there.

[This entry is based on the author's interviews and correspondence with Marie Adler Kessel and Ray Adler Cochran, granddaughters of Simon Adler, between 1980 and 1993; U.S. census records; and deed books in the Independence County Courthouse, Batesville. See Nancy Zilbergeld and Nancy Britton, "The Jewish Community in Batesville, Arkansas, 1853–1977," *Independence County Chronicle* 21 (1980).]

NANCY BRITTON

ALEXANDER, HAROLD EDWARD (Nov. 23, 1909–Sept. 14, 1993), wildlife biologist and water resources scientist, was born at Lawrence, Kansas, and grew up enjoying the hunting and fishing opportunities of rural Kansas. He was the oldest of four sons born to Edward Edwin Alexander, city treasurer of Lawrence, and Ruby Pringle, a homemaker.

Alexander entered the University of Kansas with the goal of becoming a wildlife biologist. He received his bachelor of arts degree in zoology in 1939. He also studied fine arts for two years.

He met Virginia Schooling at the university, and they married in the fall of 1940. They moved to Texas, where Harold earned his master of science degree in wildlife management and ecology from Texas A & M University. He wrote his master's thesis on ducks and geese of the Texas Gulf Coast, illustrating his thesis with watercolor paintings of waterfowl.

The Arkansas Game and Fish Commission hired Alexander as a field biologist. He and Virginia moved to rural Howard County, where Harold worked on game surveys until he was drafted into the army in 1942. His artistic skills earned him a position as a medical illustrator in the U.S. Army Air Corps's Aero-Medical Research Laboratory at Wright Field, Dayton, Ohio. After the war he worked as federal aid coordinator for the Kentucky Department of Fish and Wildlife from 1946 until 1950.

In 1950 Alexander became chief biologist and chief of research for the Arkansas Game and Fish Commission. The Alexanders returned to Arkansas to stay, settling on a hill overlooking Conway and rearing a son, Edward, and three daughters, Ellen, Frances, and Louise.

Alexander was a meticulous field researcher (he is credited with discovering the parasitic "brain worm" in white-tailed deer), but he was also a lecturer, a prolific writer, and an uncompromising advocate of scientific wildlife management as a means to restore depleted game populations.

His 1954 pamphlet, "Deer Problems," replaced myth and folklore with factual information hunters could understand and use to increase and improve Arkansas's deer herd. He instituted a program of live trapping native wild turkeys for restocking in areas where they had been extirpated. He championed wetlands preservation to benefit waterfowl and protection for endangered species as well as for nongame wildlife.

Alexander also was a leader in national and state movements to preserve our nation's dwindling supply of high-quality recreational rivers and streams. He was a friend of the brothers Frank and John Craighead, Montana ecologists who drafted the National Wild and Scenic Rivers Act of 1968. In writing the act the Craigheads used, among other things, a list of candidate rivers compiled by Alexander.

During the sixties Alexander generated support for saving the Buffalo River of northern Arkansas from dams proposed by the United States Army Corps of Engineers at Lone Rock and Gilbert. This was an era when drowning valuable recreational rivers behind "high dams" was still popular among politicians. He encouraged Dr. Neil Compton of Bentonville to form the Ozark Society in 1962; the organization led a successful ten-year campaign to block the dams and place the Buffalo River under protection of the National Park Service as America's first national river.

Alexander is known as Arkansas's "conservation philosopher" because he put the soul in what is often a highly technical business. In a paper presented at a North American Wildlife and Natural Resources Conference in 1965, he wrote: "In the U.S. . . . we have channeled, dammed, polluted, dredged, straightened, silted and altered our waterways and their environs so completely and profoundly, that our forefathers who once crossed them in their westward migrations would no longer recognize the rivers to which they gave names, depicting their beauty and history, and beside which they built their homes, reared their families and structured the concept of a great and free society."

Alexander's advocacy inspired a new generation of sportsmen and conservation professionals who were coming of age in the sixties and seventies. He challenged them, pointing out that "taking from the great outdoors is not enough; you've also got to give something back."

Alexander served as natural resource and recreation specialist and advisor to Governor Winthrop Rockefeller from 1967 to 1968. He then worked for the

Arkansas Department of Planning as natural resources and environmental planning specialist, including outdoor recreation planning, before rejoining the Arkansas Game and Fish Commission in 1977 as an environmental consultant.

He wrote technical papers on wildlife management, stream and wetlands preservation, and the philosophical aspects of conservation that appeared in the conference proceedings of the Southeastern Association of Game and Fish Commissioners; he also published articles in such journals as *Arkansas Game and Fish Magazine* and the *Naturalist*.

His many awards included a presidential citation for water resources conservation in 1970. A consultant to the Arkansas Wildlife Federation, he was named their Conservationist of the Year in 1983. That same year he received the C. W. Watson Award for Conservation from the Southeastern Association of Fish and Wildlife Agencies. In 1993 he was inducted into the Arkansas Outdoors Hall of Fame.

During his final years at the Arkansas Game and Fish Commission, Alexander developed and coordinated research studies of endangered species conducted in Arkansas's colleges and universities. He died at Conway, survived by his wife, four children, and two grandchildren.

[The Harold E. Alexander Papers, including publications, illustrations, field notes, correspondence, and other materials, are housed at Torreyson Library, University of Central Arkansas, Conway.

See Jim Spencer and Joe Mosby, "A Tribute to the Father of Arkansas Conservation," *Arkansas Wildlife Magazine* (Winter 1993); John Heuston, "Arkansas's Greatest Conservationist," *Arkansas Fish and Wildlife Magazine* (Apr. 1993); *Pine Bluff Commercial,* June 3, 1973; and the *Arkansas Democrat-Gazette,* Sept. 15, 1993 (obituary).

Information also came from the author's file of interviews and correspondence with Harold Alexander.]

JOHN HEUSTON

ALTHEIMER, BEN J[OSEPH?] (1877–May 29, 1946), attorney and philanthropist, was born at Pine Bluff, the son of Joseph Altheimer, a merchant and land developer, and Matilda Josaphat. He was a graduate of the Jordan Academy of Pine Bluff and studied law in the firm of F. B. Bridges and Judge W. T. Wooldridge and with N. T. White. He formed the law firm of White and Altheimer with Major Drew White. In 1909 he moved to Chicago, where he established a law firm. He married Belle Mandel, daughter of a pioneer merchant family, and they had one child, Ben J. Altheimer Jr.

During his years in Chicago Altheimer continued his farming interests in the area around the town of Altheimer. (The town had been named for its developers, Ben's father and his uncle Louis Altheimer.) He also maintained a close attachment to prominent Arkansas friends, including United States senator Joseph T. Robinson. In the early 1930s he renovated a plantation house near Altheimer, "The Elms," and used it as his home in Arkansas. When he retired from his Chicago law practice in 1939, he returned to Arkansas and began buying up farmland, eventually acquiring some ten thousand acres.

Altheimer loved Arkansas and its land. He enjoyed walking, riding, or driving through his farms, looking over his crops. He also loved fishing and hunting. He was genuinely interested in the sharecroppers of the area and worked toward improving their lives through educational opportunities for them and their children.

Four years before he died, he established the Ben J. Altheimer Foundation, to benefit Arkansas schools, churches, and civic organizations. In 1951 the foundation established a chair in cotton research at the University of Arkansas, Fayetteville, the university's first endowed chair. Chairs in soybean research and weed science were later established there by the foundation. Altheimer was considered a "real trailblazer" in developing agricultural research and education in Arkansas. The donations to the university were said to enable its agriculture department to move from "mediocre to excellent."

Altheimer ensured that the foundation would benefit his community. It built a clerical and machine trades school, a technical school building, and a Boy and Girl Scout building, and annually donated scholarships to two local students for college. Generous donations were given to churches and public schools, and heart monitoring equipment was donated to the Jefferson County Memorial Hospital, as well as one hundred thousand dollars on a matching-fund basis.

The foundation established the Ben J. Altheimer Law Library in Pine Bluff, donated funds for the renovation and restoration of the Old Federal Building at Second and Center Streets in Little Rock for the University of Arkansas at Little Rock School of Law and, later, supported the construction of its new school.

It supported the Ben J. Altheimer Distinguished Professorship and the Ben J. Altheimer Lecture Series, which brings lawyers and legal scholars of national reputation to the school. In 1993 the UALR School of Law established the Ben J. Altheimer Courtroom as a memorial to his philanthropy. Altheimer died at "The Elms" in Altheimer.

[See the *Arkansas Gazette,* May 30, 1946; *Arkansas Democrat,* June 5, 1960, and Dec. 16, 1986; Dedication Program, Altheimer Laboratory, Agricultural Experiment Station, University of Arkansas, Fayetteville, Oct. 31, 1980; and Dedication Program, Ben J. Altheimer Law Library, Pine Bluff, Apr. 29, 1981.]

CAROLYN GRAY LEMASTER

ANDERSON, GILBERT MAXWELL (Apr. 1880–Jan. 20, 1971), motion picture actor, director, and producer, was born Max Aronson in Little Rock. His father was Henry Aronson, a traveling salesman, and his mother's name was Ester, maiden name unknown. Seven children are listed with Henry and Ester.

Max Aronson grew up in Pine Bluff in the home of an older sister and her husband, Louis Roth. Around the turn of the century he left Pine Bluff never to return, although he did correspond with friends and relatives in his hometown. As late as 1963 he wrote, "Give my regards to old Pine Bluff where I lived quite a few years and made many friends and I hope many of them are with us today."

The names of such cowboy stars as John Wayne, Gary Cooper, and Roy Rogers are well known today. But the first cowboy movie star was an Arkansan known worldwide by the name "Broncho Billy" Anderson. Anderson developed production techniques still in use today. He was awarded a special Oscar by the Academy of Motion Picture Arts and Sciences in 1958 for his contribution to the development of motion pictures as entertainment. From 1900 until 1926, Anderson produced, directed, or appeared in over six hundred motion pictures, everything from the one-reelers of the early days to full-length pictures.

By 1902 Aronson was in New York and was using his professional name, Gilbert M. Anderson. In 1903 he was cast in *The Great Train Robbery,* Edwin S. Porter's classic film in which, for the first time, a western story unfolded on the flickering screen.

From that moment on the film industry began to grow. And Anderson was to grow with it. His contribution was to develop the western film. In the early days of the movies, no one knew much about production. Long shots, medium shots, close-ups, lap dissolves, fades—techniques so necessary to the continuity of the film story—were unknown at the time. Anderson was among the directors who developed these techniques, which are common in movie production today.

In his early films he played various roles under the name G. M. Anderson. For instance, there was *Raffles, the Amateur Cracksman* for Vitagraph in 1904. In 1907 he moved to Chicago to produce films. There he developed the idea that the public would pay to see good western movies. He realized that to be marketable, western movies needed western settings. For a while he produced films in Colorado, but the man for whom he was working could not see the advantage of western scenery in their releases.

Back in Chicago, Anderson began a partnership with George K. Spoor. The two of them established Essanay Studios, the name derived from a phonetic spelling of their two initials. From 1908 until 1915 Anderson made 375 westerns. The most famous of these were the Broncho Billy series. Anderson had read a story in the *Saturday Evening Post* about a character called Broncho Billy. He liked the idea of a series character, and thus Broncho Billy began to ride across the silver screen and into popularity with the American public.

Anderson established a studio at Niles, California, near San Francisco, where he turned out two-reel Broncho Billy stories about every two weeks. The films cost approximately eight hundred dollars to produce and grossed about fifty thousand dollars. The Essanay Studios were in their heyday.

Many of the legendary names of Hollywood began their movie careers at Essanay: Francis X. Bushman, Gloria Swanson, even the great Charlie Chaplin. Anderson signed Chaplin for the unheard of salary of $1,250 per week, plus a bonus of $10,000. But neither Spoor nor Chaplin was happy with the arrangement. Spoor was in shock over the salary, and Chaplin was not happy with either the Chicago or the Niles studios and their regimented way of mass-producing films.

At Niles, Anderson and Chaplin appeared together in Chaplin's thirty-eighth film, *The Champion,* released in March 1915. The Bushman-Chaplin-Anderson movies produced fabulous profits for Essanay, but the days of the studio were numbered. First Chaplin was hired away by Mutual for ten thousand dollars a week. Then Anderson began to realize that the public was demanding more than simple two-reelers.

He approached Spoor with the idea of producing longer, more involved productions. That brought on a change of a different nature: more expense for production. Spoor preferred to continue producing eight-hundred-dollar two-reelers, so Anderson decided to sell his interest in Essanay. The separation contract stipulated that Anderson could not engage in motion picture production for two years and that the Broncho Billy character would remain with Essanay.

For all practical purposes, Anderson retired. Then in 1918, with Essanay gone, he attempted to resume making westerns. But the intervening years were too much. The public had new heroes on the silver screen, and Broncho Billy rode off into the setting sun.

Anderson lived in quiet retirement for most of his remaining years, but surfaced again in the publicity of the special Oscar. He died in Pasadena, California; survivors included his wife, Molly Louise Schabbleman, and a daughter, Maxine.

[Sources include Pulaski County Census Records, June 4, 1880; and the personal files of Freeman H. Owens at the Jefferson County/Pine Bluff Library. See also the *Jefferson County Historical Quarterly* 15 (1987). There is an obituary in the *Arkansas Gazette* on Jan. 21, 1971. Don Cotner of Pine Bluff assisted with the preparation of this entry.]

Dave Wallis

ASHMORE, HARRY SCOTT (July 27, 1916–Jan. 20, 1998), journalist and editor, was born in Greenville, South Carolina, to William Green Ashmore, a merchant, and Nancy Elizabeth Scott.

Just after graduation from Clemson Agricultural College in 1937, Ashmore joined the staff of the *Greenville Piedmont* and was assigned to the courthouse beat. He thus began a career in journalism that would take him to Arkansas, where he won high honors as a courageous editor and became a principal player in a world-riveting chapter in Arkansas history.

In 1939 Ashmore moved to the *Greenville News* and wrote a series on northern "Tobacco Roads" based on his tours of poverty areas above the Mason-Dixon line. That same year he joined the staff of the *Charlotte* (North Carolina) *News,* where he covered South Carolina state politics for two years. He won a Nieman Fellowship to Harvard in 1941.

Ashmore married Barbara Edith Laier of Massachusetts in 1940. They had a daughter, Anne Ashmore.

After World War II erupted, Ashmore enlisted in the army in 1942, attending infantry school and engineer school. He served with the Ninety-fifth Infantry Division, taking part in campaigns in northern France, the Rhineland, and Central Europe and rising from second lieutenant to lieutenant colonel.

He resumed his newspaper career at the *Charlotte News* shortly after the war ended, becoming associate editor and then editor in 1947, writing editorials supporting two-party politics in the South, racial and religious tolerance, the right of blacks to vote, and higher pay for teachers.

In April 1947 he addressed a conference of the American Society of Newspaper Editors, impressing J. N. Heiskell, editor and owner of the *Arkansas Gazette* in Little Rock. Heiskell, the son of a Confederate colonel, hired Ashmore, the grandson of Confederate privates, as editor of the editorial page. Heiskell always retained the title of editor, with responsibility for the *Gazette* news departments as well as for the editorial section.

In 1953 the Ford Foundation commissioned Ashmore to head a team studying biracial education in the United States. Ashmore's report, titled *The Negro and the Schools,* showed statistically that blacks in segregated schools were getting inferior educations and cautioned that school segregation was an explosive issue. The report was published the day before the Supreme Court ruled that school segregation was unconstitutional.

Ashmore took leaves of absence in 1952 and 1956 to serve in Adlai Stevenson's Democratic campaigns for the presidency. He returned to the *Gazette* in the late summer of 1956.

The night of September 2, 1957, Governor Orval E. Faubus of Arkansas, citing the prospect of violence, called out National Guard troops to block integration of Little Rock's Central High School. By the following morning, the guardsmen had occupied the school grounds. Ashmore's lead editorial in the *Gazette* of September 4 began, "Little Rock arose yesterday to gaze upon the incredible spectacle of an empty high school surrounded by National Guard troops called out by Governor Faubus to protect life and property against a mob that never materialized."

That was the first in a two-year series of editorials

that won a 1958 Pulitzer Prize for Ashmore. The *Gazette* itself won a Pulitzer Prize for public service for coverage of integration of Central High and Faubus's confrontation with federal authority, making it the first newspaper to win two Pulitzers in the same year. Under Ashmore's direction, the newspaper won numerous other honors, including the Freedom House Award, the John Peter Zenger Award, and the Elijah Lovejoy Award.

The Little Rock crisis, a confrontation between state and federal authority, commanded newspaper headlines and intense television attention throughout the world. Ashmore waged his editorial crusade amid these developments: a federal court ordered Faubus to comply with its desegregation order; Faubus, somewhat petulantly, removed the National Guard troops, although he was not ordered to do so; a mob that had gathered after Faubus's troop announcement turned violent when nine black students tried to enroll; President Eisenhower federalized the National Guard and sent troops from the 101st Airborne Division; Faubus closed all Little Rock schools after arranging for an election supposedly to support his decision.

Ashmore and the *Gazette* provided a rallying point for the mobilization of concerned citizens, who eventually won a series of skirmishes with the segregationists. The high schools reopened in 1959 with the black students enrolled. Through it all, Ashmore retained equanimity, a keen sense of humor, and a sense of the absurd while he endured a steady barrage of vilification and threats on his life.

Ashmore left the *Gazette* in 1959 to become editor of the *Encyclopedia Brittanica* and to head the Committee for Democratic Institutions, described as a think tank. During the Vietnam War, he traveled to Hanoi with William C. Baggs, editor of the *Miami News*. They met with Ho Chi Minh, reported to the State Department, and wrote a book, *Mission to Hanoi* (1968), which criticized United States peace negotiators. Ashmore's other books included *Epitaph for Dixie* (1958), *Hearts and Minds* (1982), and a history of Arkansas.

He died in Santa Barbara, California. He was memorialized in Little Rock with speeches by old newspaper friends and others.

Robert R. Douglas

ATKINSON, W. EMMETT (Feb. 3, 1874–?), farmer and schoolteacher, was born in a log cabin on the family farm near McNeil, Arkansas. When he was young,

his father died, leaving him to provide for his mother and sister. He taught school in Columbia, Lafayette, and Nevada Counties during the years 1897–1916. He was sometimes the only teacher in schools that enrolled from thirty-seven to eighty students in twelve grades.

Atkinson was involved in Democratic Party politics in Columbia County and was often a delegate to the state Democratic convention. In 1912 he ran for the Democratic nomination for the open position of Columbia County circuit clerk. He finished second in a seven-man field, sixty-four votes behind the winner. Four years later he ran again and defeated the incumbent by 134 votes.

When America entered World War I in 1917, Atkinson supported the war and freely donated his time and money to the cause. He gave money and goods worth about one hundred dollars to the departing soldiers. He also bought eight hundred dollars' worth of war bonds and war savings stamps. These donations were large sums in those days and were significant in light of the fact that there were three persons in his family and that the total value of their property was about two thousand dollars.

In December 1917 Atkinson reportedly was asked by the Red Cross for a donation. When Atkinson offered fifty cents, it was rejected on the grounds that it was too little. Atkinson felt insulted and told several people about his experience.

The incident was trivial; however, these were not normal times. The year 1917 also saw the creation of a new federal agency, the Council of National Defense, which had affiliates at the state and county levels. One of the duties of this organization was to go after "disloyal" individuals.

During the war years, 1917–18, a wave of hysteria swept America, much of which was directed toward persons of German descent. Some of it was absurd, such as calling sauerkraut "liberty cabbage." Some of it could be serious. March 20, 1918, at Altus, Oklahoma, for instance, two German Americans, O. F. Westbrook and Henry Huffman, were dragged from bed, forced to kiss the flag, whipped, smeared with hot tar and feathers, and ordered to leave town. On April 10, 1918, a "slacker" was hanged in effigy at Magnolia, Columbia County, where Atkinson lived. The councils of defense considered the Red Cross and the YMCA to be "war agencies." Citizens who did not donate to them or criticized them were deemed to be disloyal.

In the summer of 1918 the Columbia County Council of Defense sent representatives to Atkinson demanding that he donate one hundred dollars to the Red Cross and the YMCA. Atkinson replied that he could not come up with that kind of money on such short notice. On August 17 the county council issued a resolution stating that Atkinson had "deliberately taken a stand against his people, his government, and the cause of human freedom." The council called on Atkinson to resign as circuit clerk and as the Democratic nominee for the same post. Meanwhile, Atkinson scrounged up the money for the Red Cross and the YMCA, but when he made the donation, the council claimed that he was trying to conceal his disloyalty.

Atkinson tried, without success, to placate the council. On September 5 he appeared before the council and gave a statement detailing his services to the war effort dating back to the previous year. The council ignored this and bought a full-page advertisement in the September 11 issue of the *Columbia Banner*. The ad printed anonymous claims that Atkinson openly wished for a German victory. It distorted Atkinson's statement to the council about his bond purchases and closed with the statement that those who criticized the council's action were guilty of disloyalty.

Atkinson realized that to try to hang on to his position was hopeless. He resigned, and he and his mother entered a hospital in Hot Springs in mid-September. He issued a statement criticizing the council as being "designing political enemies" and promised that as soon as his health improved, he would run for election and so redeem himself. This may seem like bravado, but in 1920 Atkinson ran for circuit clerk, and despite some advertisements by the council, he came within 83 votes of winning out of 2,689 votes cast. In 1922 he was elected to the circuit clerk position and reelected in 1924. In 1926 he won the race for county judge and was reelected in 1928 and 1930. He was defeated in 1932 and settled down on the family farm.

[The Arkansas History Commission maintains a file of Arkansas Council of Defense Papers. Atkinson's activities can be traced through the years 1904–32 in the Magnolia newspapers: the *Banner News,* the *Columbia Banner,* and the *Magnolia News.*]

CHARLES J. RECTOR

BABCOCK, JULIA BURNELLE SMADE (Apr. 28, 1868–June 14, 1962), novelist and founder of the

Arkansas Natural History Museum, was born in Unionville, Ohio, the daughter of Hiram Norton Smade, an engineer, poet, and inventor, and Charlotte Elizabeth Burnell, a musician. Babcock's mother belonged to the Women's Christian Temperance Union, and her maternal grandfather was a Methodist minister with abolitionist sentiments.

The Smade family moved to Arkansas in 1878, and Babcock, who was called "Bernie," spent the rest of her childhood in Russellville and Little Rock. *Arcadian Magazine* says that she began writing "a bit of verse" as early as age five. Because she was one of six children, her parents were unable to provide for her college expenses. She worked as a cook, housekeeper, and baby-sitter for the family of a professor while attending Little Rock College for one year, and she continued to write essays and poems.

At age eighteen she left school to marry William Babcock, an agent for the Pacific Express Company. Eleven years later he died after a prolonged illness. Though hospital and funeral expenses had depleted insurance money and savings, twenty-nine-year-old Babcock turned down a job teaching in public schools in order to stay home with their five children.

When the youngest child started school, Babcock began her writing career as society reporter and book reviewer for the *Arkansas Democrat*. At night she wrote stories, plays, and books. She stayed with the *Democrat* for five years and later worked with a number of small papers in Little Rock.

In 1906 she began the *Arkansas Sketch Book,* a quarterly publication containing poems, stories, photography, art, and articles about Arkansas industry and other state attractions. The publication's purpose was to help Arkansas "become better acquainted with her resources and opportunities in order to more intelligently develop them." After establishing a national and international circulation, the "Sketch Book Lady" resigned as editor in 1910.

In the years just prior to World War I, Babcock worked for women's suffrage, was active in the Women's Christian Temperance Union, served as leader of the Socialist Party in Arkansas, and began her career as a novelist. *The Daughter of a Republican,* the first of more than twenty-five titles to appear during Babcock's lifetime, was published in a temperance paper in serial form and also as a book; it sold one hundred thousand copies within six months.

The Soul of Ann Rutledge (1919) brought Babcock international recognition as a novelist. The first of five novels Babcock wrote about Abraham Lincoln, it tells of Ann Rutledge's life, love, and premature death during the years that Lincoln lived in the frontier settlement of New Salem, Illinois. The novel was translated into several languages and adapted for the stage by Babcock in 1934. In this novel and in all of her historical fiction, accuracy was important to Babcock. In an interview with *Arcadian Magazine* she explained that "sometimes I read carefully through five or six hundred pages of old historical stuff to get three lines."

Within the boundaries of documented history Babcock creates sympathetic and compelling characters. Like the author herself, the Lincoln of Babcock's historical novels never loses sight of the people surrounding him. *The Soul of Ann Rutledge* depicts an awkward, honorable youth, embarking on a career in politics, who sings, reads Shakespeare, takes care of rabbits, travels miles in the snow to attend a family without food, and believes in women's rights and the abolition of slavery. Similarly, *The Soul of Abe Lincoln* portrays a powerful president grieving over the death and destruction of the Civil War and assisting individual soldiers.

During the 1920s Babcock began seeking donations for a natural history museum and in 1927 was given space on the third floor of City Hall in Little Rock. She obtained a collection of stuffed animals from Henry Fairfield Osborn of New York and supplementary acquisitions with her own meager funds. The museum was closed during the Great Depression to provide space for the Works Progress Administration but was reopened in 1942 when Fred W. Allsop, business manager of the *Arkansas Gazette,* offered funds to restore the old Arsenal building. Babcock served as museum director until 1953, adding to the collection and painting murals of vegetation and prehistoric animals on the walls herself.

Serving as supervisor of the Federal Writers' Project in Arkansas from 1935 to 1938, she helped compile a series of guidebooks about Arkansas. She also selected interviewers for the WPA collection of narratives from former slaves. She supplemented the project with her own salary and gave financial assistance to several people whom these interviewers brought to her attention. After stepping down as supervisor, she continued to work for the Federal Writers Project until it was disbanded.

Babcock was the first Arkansas woman to be listed in *Who's Who in America.* Among other honors she received an *Arts et Belles Lettres* medal from the French and in 1951 was awarded an honorary doctor of letters degree from the University of Arkansas. She died at her home on Petit Jean Mountain. In the words of her granddaughter, Alberta E. Bakker, "Bernie Babcock loved Arkansas, and Arkansas loved her."

[The Ottenheimer Library Archives and Special Collections at the University of Arkansas at Little Rock houses the Bernie Babcock Collection, including papers concerning her writings, family, and public career. The Special Collections Division, University of Arkansas Libraries, Fayetteville, also has material by and about Babcock.

See the *Arkansas Gazette,* June 16 and July 2, 1962; *Arkansas Democrat,* Mar. 13, 1927; *Arcadian Magazine* 20 (Jan. 1932); and Netta F. Pyron, "Bernie Babcock, A Twentieth-Century Sentimental Novelist," master's thesis, Iowa State University, 1971.

Special thanks to Cassandra McCraw, Jane-Ellen Murphy, and Burnelle Regnier.]

LORI PETERSON

BAERG, WILLIAM (Sept. 24, 1885–Apr. 14, 1980), entomologist, naturalist and teacher, was born at Hillsboro, Kansas, to Johann Baerg and Margaretha Hildebrand. His parents had left Russia for America in 1874 and settled on a wheat farm. William was the sixth of seven children.

Baerg devoted his life to research on the biology and behavior of black widow spiders, tarantulas, scorpions, and other arthropods, creatures that many people find repulsive or disconcerting.

His distinguished career began humbly enough. He started school at age seven. At fourteen he left school to help his father on the farm. His father was a stern and pious man, who practiced the rule "spare the rod, spoil the child." Aside from the hours of farm work and the many church revivals the family attended, early life for William and his younger brother George was pleasant.

In 1908, after attending preparatory school, he took classes at Tabor College in Hillsboro, Kansas. He spent summers working in the wheat fields. After doing a study of grasshoppers for the entomology department at the University of Kansas, he decided in 1915 to attend Cornell University in Ithaca, New York, to pursue entomology. He enrolled in the spring semester of 1916, but a year later, when his research was not going well and his salary was low, Baerg considered a career in medicine. However, following a five-week bout with tuberculosis, he decided to take a job at the University of Arkansas as the head of the department of entomology. The year was 1918, and Baerg was thirty-three years old.

Things moved slowly during his first year at Arkansas. Only two students (both women) enrolled in his introductory entomology course. Enrollment steadily increased over successive semesters until it often reached one hundred students or more. During the 1918 flu epidemic that swept the country, Baerg volunteered as a night nurse in the university hospital.

Early in his career, he found it inconvenient not having a middle name. He adopted the initial "J" and thereafter published as William J. Baerg. His first publication appeared in 1920 as *Experiment Station Bulletin No. 170*, "Beekeeping in Arkansas," followed in 1921 by "Spraying for the San Jose Scale." After arranging for a temporary department head to replace him in his absence, he went back to Cornell to complete his degree.

Before returning to Arkansas with his Ph.D., he was asked by one Professor Crosby whether the bite of a black widow spider was harmless or poisonous. Since so little was known of these spiders, Baerg devoted much time to this problem over the next few months. Back in Fayetteville he induced a black widow spider to bite him on the hand. During the ensuing twenty-four hours he experienced severe pain in the bitten hand and arm, aching muscles, and sweating and wrote that "breathing and speech are spasmodic." Keeping careful records of the symptoms, he was the first to accurately describe the effects of black widow venom on humans. He published these findings in the *Journal of Parasitology* in 1923 and gained a bit of local popularity for this work.

Over the next several years Baerg became interested in tarantulas and scorpions. He traveled to Panama and Mexico to observe the behavior of these arachnids. His love of the tarantula was such that he often had one at home as a pet and, in 1958, published a small book, *The Tarantula*. His powers of observation and appreciation for nature led to a book, *Birds of Arkansas*, a 1931 publication of the Agricultural Experiment Station. This work was a culmination of five years spent listening to bird songs and observing seasonal changes in their population.

During the Great Depression Baerg met Eloise Ferris. They were married in 1931 and had two children, Gretchen and John.

Baerg endeared himself to students and colleagues with his wit and wisdom. When his laboratory assistant, having been stung by a scorpion during a field trip, asked him what to do for the pain, Baerg recommended profanity.

He retired in 1951 after a thirty-one year tenure as department head. He had published seventy-five papers and a number of books. Before he died he donated a large collection of scientific papers, bound in thirty-six volumes, to the University of Arkansas library. He inspired many students to pursue careers in entomology, and some of them achieved international recognition.

[A memoir, "Dr. William J. Baerg, Entomologist Extraordinary," was published in May 1984 in *Flash Back* (Washington County Historical Society). Other sources include an obituary in *The Journal of Arachnology*, vol. 9, number 115 (1980): 16a–16b; an unpublished history of the Department of Entomology, University of Arkansas, by Lloyd O. Warren; and interviews with Gretchen Baerg Gearhart.

Baerg's books and articles include "The effects of the bite of *Latrodectus mactans Fabr.*," *Journal of Parasitology* 9 (1923): 161–169; "The Black Widow," *Arkansas Agricultural Experiment Station Bulletin* No. 325 (1936); *Elementary Ornithology* (1941); "Birds of Arkansas," *Arkansas Agricultural Experiment Station Bulletin* No. 258 (rev.) (1951); and *The Tarantula* (1958).]

EDDIE DRY

BAILEY, CARL EDWARD (Oct. 8, 1894–Oct. 23, 1948), attorney and Arkansas governor, was born in Bernie, Missouri, to William Edward Bailey and Margaret Elmyra McCorkle. His father was a logger and hardware salesman, his mother a housewife. Carl grew up in Campbell, Missouri, where he graduated from high school. He attended Chillicothe Business College in Missouri but lacked the funds to graduate. He held a series of jobs and read law in his spare time. On October 10, 1915, he and Margaret Bristol were married at Paragould, Arkansas. They raised six children. Bailey passed the Arkansas bar exam in 1922. He moved to Little Rock, where he opened a private law practice in 1924.

In 1926 Bailey worked for Boyd Cypert in a successful campaign for prosecuting attorney of the Sixth Judicial District (Pulaski and Perry Counties). Cypert named him deputy prosecuting attorney. In 1930 he succeeded Cypert.

He gained notoriety in prosecuting A. B. Banks, the owner of a banking empire that collapsed in 1930. Bailey charged Banks with accepting deposits in a bank he knew to be insolvent. The defense counsel, United States Senator Joseph Taylor Robinson, claimed that Banks was being made a scapegoat. In a dramatic trial Banks was found guilty and sentenced to a year in prison, but he received a gubernatorial pardon. While the Banks case garnered Bailey popular acclaim, it also earned him the enmity of Robinson, the state's most powerful political figure.

Although embarrassed by highway scandals and a default on the state debt, the state's political establishment strengthened its position in the early 1930s. Under the New Deal the federal government created scores of new jobs in the state, which Robinson, as Senate majority leader, controlled.

The anti-establishment faction in the early 1930s was led by Brooks Hays and Carl Bailey. With Bailey's support Hays entered the race for the Fifth Congressional District but lost in a controversial runoff to David D. Terry. Terry had the support of a powerful federal-state coalition consisting of Senator Robinson, Internal Revenue Collector Homer Martin Adkins, and Governor Junius Marion Futrell. From this time on a rivalry developed between Bailey and Adkins that dominated Arkansas politics for the next decade.

After four years as prosecuting attorney, Bailey ran for attorney general in 1934 and won by twelve thousand votes. As attorney general he garnered popular support by advocating welfare programs to assist the aged and needy. He also benefited from another sensational criminal case. In 1936 Charles "Lucky" Luciano, a New York gangster, fled to Hot Springs to escape arrest. Luciano was arrested and held for extradition hearings, but Hot Springs officials released him on a token bail. New York Special Prosecutor Thomas E. Dewey appealed to Bailey, who ordered the state police to take Luciano into custody. Bailey was offered fifty thousand dollars if he made sure extradition was denied, but Luciano went back to New York for trial.

In 1936 Bailey was elected governor. His top priority in the legislature was civil service reform; this was a direct attack on the establishment. He also favored reforms in the new Department of Public Welfare to qualify Arkansas for full federal funding.

Bailey had served as governor just over six months when Senator Robinson's death in 1937 threw state politics into turmoil. Bailey jumped at the chance to go to the Senate, and the Democratic state committee, which he controlled, nominated him for the office. The anti-Bailey forces coalesced around Adkins, who recruited Congressman John E. Miller to run as an independent candidate. Miller charged that Bailey had manipulated the Democratic committee. With the endorsement of President Franklin D. Roosevelt and members of his cabinet, Bailey ran as a loyal New Dealer, but Miller, supported by Arkansas's federal officeholders, won easily.

Privately, Bailey was bitter and feared that he might be a one-term governor. In a special legislative session he regained some prestige by pushing through a highway program. In the 1938 governor's race Bailey, admitting he had made mistakes, defeated R. A. Cook, a former Pulaski County judge.

In his second term Governor Bailey faced a tumultuous legislature, which repealed the new, but widely unpopular, civil service system. Bailey quietly favored repeal, since he had come to realize that he could not command support without political patronage to dispense.

Arkansas politics underwent increasing polarization in the late 1930s between Bailey's state-house crowd and the federal crowd. From the safety of his second term, Bailey attacked Floyd Sharp, state director of the Works Progress Administration, for using WPA workers in political campaigns.

In 1940 Bailey broke tradition and ran for a third term. His opponent was Homer Adkins, the leader of the federal faction. At last the two antagonists came out to challenge each other openly. In an acrimonious campaign Adkins won.

Bailey resumed his law practice in Little Rock and founded the Carl Bailey Company, an International Harvester franchise. He and his wife were divorced, and he married Marjorie Compton in 1943. He remained politically active. When Adkins ran for the United States Senate in 1944, Bailey supported his opponent, J. William Fulbright. Fulbright's victory was Bailey's revenge. Bailey died of a heart attack at age fifty-four in Little Rock.

[See Donald Holley, "Carl Edward Bailey, 1937–1941," in *The Governors of Arkansas: Essays in Political Biography*, Timothy P. Donovan, Willard B. Gatewood Jr., and Jeannie M. Whayne, eds., 2d. ed. (1995).]

DONALD HOLLEY

BANDINI, PIETRO (Apr. 30, 1853–Jan. 2, 1917), founder of Tontitown, was born of noble parents in Forli, Italy, and was ordained into the priesthood on September 30, 1878. His interest in Italian immigration to America began in the early 1880s when he joined the Scalabrini Fathers, an organization devoted to protecting Italian immigrants. In 1891 he was sent to New York where he helped establish a Catholic parish in Manhattan and a labor office on Ellis Island to assist newly arrived immigrants.

Bandini believed that the farmers of northern Italy were better suited to the farmland of middle America than to conditions in the cities of the Northeast. This interest brought his attention to the Italian agricultural colony at Sunnyside Plantation, which was founded in 1895 in Chicot County, Arkansas, by a New York industrialist named Austin Corbin. Charges of exploitive labor practices were leveled against Corbin as soon as the immigrants landed in New Orleans. The farmers complained that the overseer system set up by Corbin was corrupt and unmanageable and that the land was prone to floods and deadly diseases. Malaria and yellow fever contributed to the deaths of over one hundred of the colonists in the first few years.

Bandini arrived to assist the immigrants in January 1897, and after struggling for nearly a year against malaria, failing crops, and the breakdown of order in the colony, he persuaded a group of thirty-five families to leave Sunnyside and begin a new colony in the Ozark highlands. They left Chicot County on February 17, 1898, and arrived at Springdale in Washington County on April 6, 1898. Using the money the men had earned on the trip and securing loans from local banks, he purchased eight hundred acres of land located seven miles west of Springdale. The colonists named the settlement for Henri de Tonti, the Italian who established the first European settlement in the state at Arkansas Post.

Even though the immigrants were now free from the peonage and unhealthy conditions of their former home, they were faced with many difficulties during their first years in Washington County. A harsh winter, failing crops, and tornadoes plagued them during 1898. Many of the men traveled to the coal mines of Oklahoma while their wives sought work in local homes in Springdale and Fayetteville to make enough money to keep the town alive.

Besides natural and financial obstacles, the people of Tontitown faced harassment by local citizens who resented the foreigners. Once a gang of hoodlums attempted to burn their newly constructed church. Bandini invited the people of the nearby communities to view the damaged church, where he proclaimed: "We are all Americans and I am warning you that we will use our American rights in our own defense. There are few men among us who have not served in the Italian army. We are familiar with guns. From this moment on I am colonel of our regiment.... Anyone who comes to us intent on evil-doing will be shot." No other attempts were made to run the Italians out of Washington County.

But their financial troubles continued. It was imperative that Bandini establish stability both financially and socially. Support from the Arkansas Diocese faded for a time under Bishop John B. Morris, who questioned Bandini's choice of business partners, with whom he purchased the land for Tontitown, and his continued interest in Italian politics.

Tontitown needed a cash crop familiar to the Italian farmers that could thrive in the Ozark climate. Bandini had soil samples tested and learned that the Concord grape would grow well in this environment. By 1911 he worked with the farmers to establish the Tontitown Grape Growers Association. It was the first plan for a grape market in northwest Arkansas and proved to be a highly profitable venture. By 1921, fours years after Bandini's death, his goal of financial stability was fulfilled when Welch's Grape Company opened a branch in Springdale, assuring the local farmers of a market for their crops.

Even before economic conditions stabilized, Bandini worked for the educational and religious development of the community. He viewed education as essential, especially reading, writing, and speaking the English language. The first school was held in 1903, and the children's attendance was compulsory. He organized St. Mary's Academy, opened in 1906 as a boarding and day school, where he served as director and taught languages and music.

Bandini received many awards from his native land for his work at Tontitown, including a set of vestments from Queen Marguerita of Italy, a visit from the Italian ambassador to the U. S. in 1905, and a Pontifical Award from the Vatican in 1911. His leadership and devotion to his people are remembered every year at the Tontitown Grape Festival, which he himself established in 1898 as a celebration reminiscent of the Pilgrims' first Thanksgiving. Bishop John B. Morris said in his eulogy: "Father Bandini loved his people, and his love for them was so great that he lived with them, sharing their trials and . . . rejoicing with them in their moments of happiness and cheer."

[See Icilio Felici, *Father to Immigrants* (1955); W. J. Lemke, ed., "The Story of Tontitown," *Washington County Historical Society Bulletin Series* 44 (1963); Jeffrey Lewellen, "Sheep Amidst the Wolves: Father Bandini and the Colony at Tontitown, 1889–1917," *AHQ* 45 (Spring 1986): 19–40; Thomas Rothrock, "The Story of Tontitown, Arkansas," *AHQ* 16 (Spring 1957): 84–88; and Jeannie Whayne, ed., *Shadows Over Sunnyside* (1993).]

JEFFREY LEWELLEN

BARNHILL, JOHN HENRY (Feb. 23, 1903–Oct. 21, 1973), college athletic director and football coach, was born in Savannah, Tennessee, to James Monroe Barnhill and Margaret Bryan.

He was elected to the Tennessee Athletic Hall of Fame for his accomplishments as a coach, though he was also an outstanding football player at the University of Tennessee. He was elected to the Arkansas Athletic Hall of Fame primarily for his accomplishments as athletic director from 1946 to 1971 at the University of Arkansas. He was head football coach at Arkansas from 1946 to 1949 and coached the Razorbacks to a Southwest Conference co-championship.

"Barnie" grew up in Savannah. His high school education and early athletic career were interrupted when it was necessary for him to work on his parents' farm. "I did a lot of thinking," Barnhill said about his days on the farm. "I decided I didn't want to spend my life behind a plow."

At nineteen he began attending college at what is now the University of Memphis. He transferred to the University of Tennessee in Knoxville. At Tennessee he was a "running guard" in the single wing on offense and a nose guard on defense from 1925 to 1927. He earned All-Southern honors in 1926 and 1927, playing on 8-0 and 8-0-1 Tennessee Volunteers teams coached by General Robert Neyland. Neyland, regarded as a collegiate coaching legend, became Barnhill's mentor. Neyland's philosophy emphasized a football team's defense, kicking game, and field position. Barnhill maintained that philosophy at Tennessee and brought it to Arkansas.

After earning his degree in 1928, Barnhill became a high school head coach at Bristol, Tennessee. At Bristol Barnhill's teams compiled a three-year ledger of 27-3 before Neyland brought him back to Knoxville in 1931 as the Volunteers' freshman coach. In 1934 Barnhill was promoted to varsity line coach. When General Neyland was recalled to active duty in World War II, Barnhill temporarily took his place as head coach.

In four seasons, from 1941 to 1945 (Tennessee did not field a football team in 1943), Barnhill's Vols went 32-5-2 with records of 8-2, 9-1, 7-1-1 and 8-1. The University of Tennessee capped the 1942 and 1944 seasons with appearances in the Sugar Bowl and the Rose Bowl. Barnhill left Tennessee for Arkansas upon Neyland's return in 1946, but the Volunteers did not forget him. In 1966 a John Barnhill Day was held in Knoxville.

Frank Broyles, successor to Barnhill as Razorback head football coach and later Arkansas's athletic director, recalled what a coup it was for a struggling Arkansas program to land Barnhill as athletic director and head coach in 1946: "John Barnhill surprised everyone coming to Arkansas. He was a hot item with one of the best records in college football—sought after by five schools. But he saw the potential at Arkansas and was architect of a concept copied countless times by other institutions."

Barnhill's first Razorback season was his best. The Hogs rallied from a 3-7 season in 1945 to go 6-3-1 with a Southwestern Conference co-championship and a scoreless tie against Louisiana State during a blizzard at the Cotton Bowl.

The 1946 Hogs were paced by All-American wingback-tailback (and 1948 Olympic track silver medalist) Clyde "Smackover" Scott. Barnhill had recruited Scott the instant the coach learned of Scott's resignation from the Naval Academy. Injuries hit hard the next three seasons, as Barnhill's Hogs went 6-4-1 in 1947, beating William & Mary in the 1947 Dixie Bowl, and 5-5 in both 1948 and 1949.

Late in 1948 Barnhill began to experience the first symptoms of an illness later diagnosed as multiple sclerosis. This contributed to his decision to leave coaching and concentrate on administration. As athletic director he worked despite the debilitating illness, which eventually cost him the use of his right side.

In 1958 Barnhill hired Frank Broyles. Broyles gives credit to Barnhill for providing the tools for his coaching success and the blueprint for the athletic program for which Arkansas became renowned.

Under Barnhill the Razorbacks were among the first football programs to use their statewide radio network as a recruiting tool. He established state and regional Razorback Clubs for fund-raising. Holding the 1947 Arkansas-Texas game in Memphis to make his point, he was instrumental in promoting the 1948 construction of War Memorial Stadium in Little Rock. He oversaw enlarging Razorback Stadium on the campus in Fayetteville and the construction of a fieldhouse, which the University trustees named for him in 1956.

Barnhill Fieldhouse, later called Barnhill Arena, was the Razorbacks' basketball home until Walton Arena's construction in 1993 and 1994. It is still the site of Lady Razorback volleyball games and serves as the Lady Razorbacks' athletic office.

Though visionary and innovative as an athletic director and near-evangelical as a recruiter, Barnhill was strictly old-school taciturn. "A man of few words," his daughter Nancy Barnhill Trumbo recalled. "I remember after he was out of coaching, some man kept complaining about his football tickets. Finally, Daddy said, 'Well, just take mine then.' The man did, bragging he had seats from the A.D. But when he got to the game, the seats were in the end zone. Being an old line coach, that's where Daddy liked to watch to see the holes open up. The man thought he had been done dirty, and Daddy said, 'That's it. I'm out of the ticket business.'"

Barnhill's wife Kathryn died in 1957. Barnhill died in Fayetteville.

[Sources include University of Arkansas Sports Information Department; *The Springdale News* and the *Arkansas Gazette*, 1946–73; Orville Henry and Jim Bailey, *The Razorbacks* (1973); and interviews with Frank Broyles and Nancy Barnhill Trumbo.]

NATE ALLEN

BARRAQUE, ANTOINE (Apr. 15, 1773–Oct. 29, 1858) soldier, fur trader, and planter, was born in the Department of Hautes near the Pyrenees Mountains in France. His parents' names are unknown. He was sent to Paris to be educated and was said to have completed "a full collegiate course." He wrote fluently in French; some of his letters still exist.

After completing his education, Barraque joined Napoleon Bonaparte's army and participated in battles at Marengo, Austerlitz, Jena, Lodi, and Moscow, where

he lost his only brother. After Napoleon's defeat at the Battle of Waterloo, fearing imprisonment, Barraque came to America at the age of forty-two. He landed at Philadelphia and went to New Orleans. Hearing of opportunities for trade with the Indians, he made his way upstream to Arkansas Post.

Obtaining lodging in the home of Joseph Dardenne, a wealthy Arcadian, Barraque began trading with the Quapaw Indians. In 1817 he married his host's daughter, Marie Therese Dardenne, who was part Quapaw from her mother's side of the family. They were parents of eleven children.

With the assistance of Dardenne, Barraque began buying land and established a plantation a few miles below the present location of Pine Bluff. He named his farm "New Gascony" after his former home in France. He was also associated in a number of land transactions with Frederick Notrebe, a wealthy man who had served under Napoleon and had come to Arkansas Post in 1810.

In October 1823 Barraque organized a commercial hunting party to the Red River country and established a camp on a branch of the Red River, within the Osage Indian territory. On November 17, 1823, a war party of eighty to one hundred Osage attacked the camp, killing seven men and either destroying or taking off four thousand dollars worth of pelts, provisions, other goods, and horses. Barraque filed a claim against the government for four thousand dollars, but payment was refused because he had been trespassing on Osage territory.

Barraque's friends, the Quapaw Indians, had ceded to the United States their claims to lands north of the Arkansas River and west into Oklahoma in a treaty signed at St. Louis, Missouri, in August 1818. The tribe retained title to a pie-shaped territory of one and one-half million acres south of the Arkansas River. Once Arkansas became a territory, immediate efforts were started to obtain the rest of the Quapaws' land. On November 15, 1824, at Major John Harrington's home some twenty miles below Pine Bluff, Chief Heckaton and fourteen tribal heads gave away their rights, and Barraque signed the treaty as a witness.

Under the terms of the treaty the Quapaws were to relocate in Caddo country on, or near, the Red River. The tribe delayed their departure, agreeing to leave only if Barraque was appointed as subagent to accompany them. He was not able to get the Quapaws to start the journey until January 1826. He took an assistant with him, Joseph Bonne, the interpreter for the tribe at the 1818 cession. Barraque kept a journal of the trip entitled "The Voyage of the Quapaws." After much suffering due to the harsh winter weather, the Quapaws reached the Red River and found a hostile Indian agent, Captain George Gray. Barraque interceded with Governor George Izard on the Quapaws' behalf, but no relief was given, and an estimated one-third of the tribe died of starvation and disease.

Although Barraque never held elective office, he was a powerful figure in Jefferson County politics during territorial days. In April 1832, after elected commissioners had failed for two years to establish a permanent county seat, he seized the county records and moved them to his home at New Gascony. When the "Town of Pine Bluff" was established as the county seat in October 1832, the first street south of the court square was named "Barraque" in his honor.

Barraque was the impeccable Frenchman all his life, and his home reflected his French background. A family daguerreotype shows him dressed in a fine suit with a white shirt and neckwear of the era and holding what appears to be an ivory-headed cane.

George W. Featherstonhaugh, the English traveler and geologist, visited Barraque's home in December 1835 and described his plantation as the best on the river. When the visitor arrived, Mrs. Barraque, four young daughters, and some friends were all conversing in French. Featherstonhaugh joined in and chatted with the family for an hour. Later, he and Barraque traveled together to Arkansas Post. Because their boat stopped at every landing to load cotton, the trip lasted two days, and the two men spent many hours talking. Featherstonhaugh found Barraque an intelligent and interesting conversationalist.

Barraque sold his New Gascony plantation in 1843 and acquired land in the northern part of Jefferson County near Plum Bayou, on the north side of the Arkansas River. Eventually, he obtained title to 1215 acres. The political township in the northwest corner of Jefferson County was named Barraque in honor of the old settler.

He died in Pine Bluff at the home of his son-in-law, Ben F. Smith, the husband of Eliza Barraque.

[Barraque's letters are in the Gulley Collection at the Arkansas History Commission. The names of his eleven children are listed in Will Book one, 121, Probate and County Clerk's office, Jefferson County Courthouse. Land transactions are recorded in Book D, 98, Jefferson County land records, Circuit Clerk's office, Pine Bluff. See the *Arkansas Gazette,* May 2 and Aug. 22, 1832; and the obituary in the *Arkansas True Democrat,* Dec. 15, 1858.

Other sources include James W. Leslie, *A Pictorial History of Pine Bluff and Jefferson County* (1981); Joseph W. Bocage, "Old and New Pine Bluff," *Jefferson County Historical Quarterly,* Vol. 1, No. 3: 16; Jack Lane, "Federal-Quapaw Relations," *AHQ* 19 (Spring, 1960): 69–72; James W. Leslie, "Barraque, Notrebe Stimulated Early Economy," *Pine Bluff News,* Sept. 27, 1990; Ginger L. Ashcraft, "Antoine Barraque and His Involvement in Indian Affairs of Southeast Arkansas, 1816–1832," *AHQ* 32 (Autumn, 1973): 227–228; David Wallis, "Antoine Barraque and the Voyage of the Quapaws," *Jefferson County Historical Quarterly,* Vol. 3, No. 3, 29–36; and George Featherstonhaugh's *Excursion Through the Slave States* (1844; rpt. 1968).]

JAMES W. LESLIE

BARTON, THOMAS HARRY (Sept. 20, 1881–

Dec. 24, 1960), oil pioneer and philanthropist, was born in Marlin, Texas, to Thomas Killebrew Barton, a saddlemaker, and Mary Estelle Johnson. He moved to El Dorado, Arkansas, January 12, 1921, two days after the famous Busey discovery well blew in.

His formal education consisted of high school at Marlin and a year and a few months at Texas A & M College. He then enlisted as a private in the United States Army and was discharged three years later as a corporal. In 1906 he was commissioned as a captain in the Second Arkansas Infantry, but upon the advent of World War I he resigned his commission and enlisted as a private in the Texas National Guard where he advanced to the rank of colonel by the end of the war.

He held various jobs in timber and banking and the railroad. He became interested in oil when he moved to Dallas, Texas, and lost his last four hundred dollars in a "dry hole." He moved to El Dorado after hearing about the boom and quickly became involved in the hectic struggle to "get rich quick." He managed to acquire the interests of some associates and by 1924 became involved with an eastern corporation that formed the Natural Gas and Fuel Corporation, which produced oil and gas and distributed fuel gas locally.

When the Smackover field came in, "the Colonel" and his associates had already acquired much of the property in that area, resulting in extraordinary expansion. Early in 1928 his company merged with the

Arkansas Natural Gas Corporation which he later sold to Cities Service Corporation. That same year he became a major stockholder in the Lion Oil Refining Company, now known as Lion Oil Company.

After Barton was elected president and director of Lion Oil, the company greatly expanded under his guidance with holdings in Texas, Louisiana, Mississippi, and Arkansas. Lion Oil bought out three large petroleum companies in the Smackover field as well as four hundred service stations from a nationally known company in Arkansas, making Lion a major distributor in the South.

When the Great Depression hit the nation, Barton and Lion Oil Company were faced with saving their company. He felt strongly that their solution was to drill deeper into the existing Smackover field. This gamble paid off when they drilled the deepest well ever drilled in that section—7,200 feet. Although they did not find oil, important information was gathered which later led them to the discovery of oil from a deeper structure in the Snow Hill area a few miles north.

Barton's instincts did not end with this discovery. He still felt oil could be found deeper in south Arkansas. Although Lion Oil's business conditions were none too stable at the time, he gambled again when the company drilled to a depth of 5,559 feet and on April 6, 1937, found the first deep pay sand in the state of Arkansas, the Edna Morgan A-1, an excellent flowing producer of high gravity oil. This exploration led to the Buckner, Magnolia, and Village fields, establishing Arkansas's place in the annals of oil history.

Oil was not the only interest Barton had in Arkansas. Oil was his vocation but cattle was his hobby. He founded the Arkansas Live Stock Association in 1937. In appreciation of his services in the development of the livestock industry in Arkansas the T. H. Barton Coliseum was dedicated in September 1952.

Barton also owned KARK and KARK-TV in Little Rock and KELD in El Dorado; was a director of Southwestern Bell Telephone; was president of Sonbar Corporation, the Barton Corporation, and Real Properties; and was owner and publisher of the *Arkansas Farmer,* a monthly journal.

In 1944 Barton ran for the U.S. Senate with Senator Hattie Caraway, Homer Adkins, and J. W. Fulbright as his opposition. Although Senator Fulbright won, they remained friends for the rest of Barton's life.

On July 13, 1925, Barton married Madeline Mary Lattimer and lived in El Dorado with their two sons, Clark N. and T. Killebrew Barton. Their home was a showplace for the thousands of azaleas, camellias, and hibiscus he grew in their garden. He later owned homes in Coronado, California, and in Gunnison, Colorado.

As a humanitarian Barton contributed as much of himself and his funds to help his state as any other man in the history of Arkansas. His philanthropic gifts include the Barton Library, War Memorial Stadium, the Boys' Club in El Dorado, a wing at the Arkansas Medical Center in Little Rock which held the T. H. Barton Institute for Medical Research, and many scholarships and donations to colleges and universities, among other projects.

[Files at the Arkansas Museum of Natural Resources, Smackover, include newspaper clippings, articles, scrapbooks, and letters donated by the Barton family, as well as oral history resources.]

JEANNE CLEMENTS

BATES, LUCIOUS CHRISTOPHER (Apr. 27, 1901–Aug. 2, 1980), publisher and civil rights activist, was the only son of the Reverend Morris Bates and Lula Brown of Liberty, Amite County, Mississippi. He attended Alcorn A & M in Mississippi and Wilberforce University in Ohio. Over his father's objections, he studied journalism rather than medicine: "As a boy, I worked as a 'printer's devil' ... and I guess the ink must have gotten into my blood at an early age because it seemed like from that time on I knew what I wanted to be."

Bates's early career included working under Roy Wilkins, later president of the National Association for the Advancement of Colored People, at the *Kansas City Call.* In his early twenties, Bates published his own newspaper in Pueblo, Colorado, and then worked as a reporter in California and in Memphis, Tennessee.

When he lost his job during the Great Depression, he moved to Arkansas and sold insurance. He met Daisy Lee Gaston of Huttig, Arkansas, when she was just fifteen and he was selling insurance to her family. They married on March 4, 1942, at Fordyce, Arkansas, and divorced in January 1963. They had one child, Loretta Ann Bates.

In early 1941 Bates purchased some antiquated printing equipment and published the first edition of his newspaper, the *Arkansas State Press,* on May 9, 1941. He believed that owning a newspaper would provide a way to attack political and economic injustice. The *Press*, a weekly paper, achieved a circulation of 10,000 within its first months of operation; its circulation peaked in 1952 at 18,372.

The editorial column, written by L. C. and edited by Daisy, assailed the lack of black employment opportunities, union discrimination, police injustice, opposition to black voting, hostility toward black servicemen, and segregation, especially in education. The weekly columns usually contained three brief essays in a straightforward, plain style. Never radical in tone or message, Bates's editorials promoted even-handedness and practical measures to secure racial justice. The *Arkansas State Press* kept the struggle for justice focused and present before its readers.

As the country retooled for war during 1941, the *Press* called for black employment in defense industries. It also demanded the creation of black unions to circumvent racial discrimination by construction unions. With support from the *Press*, Local 276 of the United Brotherhood of Carpenters and Joiners Union of America, a black local, received its charter in July 1941. After the Japanese attack on Pearl Harbor in December 1941, Bates called for black support of the war effort and justice for blacks in the armed service. Following the apparent murder of a black army sergeant who had been clubbed and shot five times by a Little Rock policeman, Bates demanded the hiring of black police officers. In late 1942 the Little Rock City Council, for the first time since Reconstruction, authorized the employment of black policemen to patrol black sections of the city.

Throughout the 1940s the *Press* continually called for increased federal protection of black voting rights, denouncing the detestable poll tax: "When it comes to giving the Negro a chance to exercise his rights, the south doesn't give a damn about the Constitution or anything else."

In 1949 Bates called for the end of racial segregation in public education and made desegregation of the public schools the premier issue of the *Arkansas State Press* during the 1950s. In 1952 Daisy Bates was elected president of the Arkansas NAACP, a position she held until 1961. L. C. and Daisy worked with Thurgood Marshall, NAACP legal defense counsel, and the Little Rock public school administration to select and assist the first black students to integrate the system, the "Little Rock Nine."

During the Central High School crisis of 1957, L. C.

and Daisy worked with the students, and their home became a hub for out-of-town journalists, especially black journalists, covering the story. Their home was described as "the most dangerous place in Arkansas" because it was periodically targeted for bombings, gunshots, and vandalism. A boycott of the *Arkansas State Press* by white advertisers resulted in an annual loss of ten thousand dollars, and it ruined the paper. With only one major advertiser, Rockefeller Enterprises, remaining, the Bateses published the final edition on October 29, 1959.

At age fifty-eight, his beloved newspaper gone, and his personal finances destroyed, Bates sought a new place to continue his fight against racial injustice. Beginning in 1960 and until his retirement in 1971, he was a national representative for the NAACP, traveling to most of the trouble spots in the South. In 1962 he began working with Governor Orval Faubus, urging increased black employment in state government.

In one of his last public appearances, on February 19, 1977, before some three hundred celebrants of "L. C. Bates Day" in Little Rock, Bates cautioned against complacency: "The days of getting mad are over. Now is the time to get smart so that some day we may be able to say not that we *shall* overcome, but that we *have* overcome." By then a frail-looking man, Bates had earned the accolade "Father of Arkansas Civil Rights." When he died, his body was donated to the anatomy department of the University of Arkansas Medical Sciences in accordance with his instructions.

[Sources include the Daisy Bates Papers in the Special Collections Division, University of Arkansas Libraries, Fayetteville, file 12-9, box 12 and file 5-17, box 5. See the *Arkansas State Press*, Sept. 26, 1941, Nov. 9, 1945, and throughout. See the *Arkansas Gazette*, Oct. 19, 1980, Jan. 25, 1972, Sept. 1, 1942, Aug. 24, 1980; and Daisy Bates's *The Long Shadow of Little Rock* (1962; rpt. 1987).

Other sources include C. Calvin Smith, "Arkansas," in *The Black Press in the South, 1865–1979* (1983), ed. Henry Lewis Suggs; C. Calvin Smith, "From 'Separate but Equal' to Desegregation: The Changing Philosophy of L. C. Bates," *AHQ* 42 (Autumn 1983): 254–70; and Jacqueline Trescott, "Daisy Bates: Before and after Little Rock," *Crisis* 88 (1981): 234.]

DIANE GLEASON

BAXTER, ELISHA (Sept. 1, 1827–May 31, 1899), governor, was born in Rutherford County, North Carolina, to William Baxter and Catherine Lee. William Baxter had emigrated from Ireland in 1789 and settled in western North Carolina. Young Elisha received a limited education; his father forced him to decline an appointment to West Point. In 1847 he entered into business with his brother-in-law, Spencer Eaves. He came to Batesville, Arkansas, in 1852, and went into the mercantile trade with his brother, Taylor A. Baxter. Elected mayor in 1853, he served in the lower house of the state legislature the following year. In 1855 his firm failed. Baxter became a typesetter in the office of the *Independent Balance* newspaper while studying law under Hulbert F. Fairchild. In 1856 he was admitted to the bar, and in 1858 was again elected to his old house seat.

A Whig at the time of his arrival in Arkansas and in the first stages of his political career, by the late 1850s Baxter was siding with extremist states' rights Democrat Thomas Carmichael Hindman. He was elected prosecuting attorney for the Seventh Judicial Circuit.

Baxter claimed in his autobiography to believe that secession was "unjust to the Federal Government." In May 1862 General Samuel Curtis, whose forces had occupied Batesville, offered Baxter command of one of the newly forming Arkansas Union regiments. Baxter declined. After the Union army left and the Confederates returned, he fled to Missouri. He was teaching school when he was captured and carried back to Little Rock for a treason trial. Little Rock friends engineered his escape. Surviving on green corn and berries, he reached Union lines in Springfield and took command of the Fourth Arkansas Mounted Infantry.

In early 1864 the newly installed Union governor, Isaac Murphy, appointed Baxter to the state supreme court. The legislature then selected him as a United States senator, but when he and William M. Fishback attempted to claim their seats, Radical Republicans turned them away, seriously compromising President Abraham Lincoln's plan for restoring states to the Union.

Governor Powell Clayton appointed Baxter judge of the Third Judicial Circuit in 1868. A year later Baxter became, simultaneously with his judicial office, the registrar in bankruptcy for the First Congressional District. In 1872 the Clayton-led "Minstrels" faction of the state Republican Party nominated the "scalawag" (native Unionist) Baxter for governor to oppose the "Brindletail" faction's candidate, carpetbagger Joseph Brooks, whose amnesty for ex-confederates and economic policies had great popularity among white voters.

The close and hotly contested race was decided by the legislature in Baxter's favor. Brooks took his appeal to the courts, but his suit got nowhere until Governor Baxter not only began openly courting Democrats by enfranchising former Confederates but also declared illegal the state's multi-million-dollar railroad aid program. Clayton, by now a United States senator, returned from Washington to organize a revolution. Brooks, armed with a court order, ousted Baxter from the state house. The Brooks-Baxter war that began on March 16, 1874, divided the state into armed and often violent camps, claiming at least fifty casualties before President Grant reluctantly acted to restore Baxter to power. A newly assembled convention drafted a new constitution for Arkansas that the voters then adopted. The Democrats offered Baxter the gubernatorial nomination that fall, but he twice rejected it. In 1878 he sought a Senate seat, but the party rejected him.

Baxter returned to Batesville, practicing law until his death. At that time the *Arkansas Gazette* suggested a monument should be erected to the man who had overthrown Republican Reconstruction; however, nothing came of the scheme.

Baxter and Harriet Patton of Rutherford County, North Carolina, married on August 17, 1849. They had six children: Millard P., Edward A. (a well-known physician of north Arkansas), Catherine M., George E., Hattie O., and Fannie E. His wife preceded him in death by one year. Both are buried in Batesville's Oaklawn Cemetery.

[See Michael B. Dougan, "Elisha Baxter, 1873–1874," in *The Governors of Arkansas: Essays in Political Biography,* Timothy P. Donovan, Willard B. Gatewood Jr., and Jeannie M. Whayne, eds., 2d ed. (1995).]

MICHAEL B. DOUGAN

BENSON, GEORGE STUART (Sept. 26, 1898–Sept. 15, 1991), college president and political activist, was born in Dewey County, Oklahoma Territory, to homesteading pioneer parents, Stuart Felix Benson and Emma Rogers. After two years of teaching elementary school nearby, Benson completed high school and started his college career at Harper College in Harper, Kansas. He planned to become a foreign evangelist. He earned bachelor's degrees in 1925 from Oklahoma A & M and the new Harding College. In 1931 he received a master's degree in East Asian Studies from the University of Chicago.

He married Sally Ellis Hockaday in July 1925, and

they spent the next eleven years as missionaries in Canton, China. When Benson discovered that professional educators were highly respected in the Chinese culture, he centered his missionary work around his Canton Bible School, completed in 1934. Its Chinese students were trained in Christianity while learning to support themselves as teachers. Subsequently in the United States he taught this missionary technique to hundreds of college students who, as missionaries, put his ideas into practice all over the globe.

In 1936 he returned to the United States to become president of Harding College in Searcy, Arkansas. He and the school first gained national notoriety on May 15, 1941, when Benson appeared before the House Ways and Means Committee. His testimony championing fiscal conservatism received front-page headlines in national newspapers. Favorable publicity generated numerous speaking engagements, and Benson made the most of the opportunities to spread his convictions that "creeping socialism" endangered traditional American beliefs in God, constitutional government, and the free-enterprise system.

In 1941 Benson created the National Education Program within Harding College to disseminate conservative Christian social and economic values. The NEP originally functioned as an educational wing of the college; undergraduate students took course work in the American Studies Program and joined in the work of the NEP. They participated in freedom forums on the Harding campus, which were geared to middle-level managers of American industrial giants like General Motors and Republic Steel. Freedom forums focused on such topics as agricultural policies, expanding American markets, and "the Communist Menace." The undergraduates also helped conduct freedom forums emphasizing Benson's theme of Americanism on high-school campuses throughout the nation. After 1954, partly because of pressure from the North-Central College accrediting agency, the NEP was forced to create its own board of directors, which supervised its nation-wide programs from the Harding campus.

The nation's conservative businessmen rallied behind the program. Their contributions not only ensured its financial stability but quickly reduced the college's sizable debt. During Benson's twenty-nine-year tenure as president, big business contributed millions of dollars to the institution.

Benson regarded the perceived threat of increased government control through government spending as the primary battleground of the NEP, and his rhetoric against increasing socialization became its primary text. "If you are going to move Washington to do things it ought to do," he argued, "you have got to move public opinion." His aim was to "move public opinion at the grass roots level in the direction of godliness and patriotism." By 1954 the NEP had compiled a mailing list of over forty-seven thousand people for its bulletins and pamphlets. Its weekly newspaper columns appeared in over four thousand weekly and trade newspapers; it distributed weekly radio programs on tape to 318 stations and produced film series on Americanism distributed throughout America to hundreds of high-school and college film libraries and shown in hundreds of Metro-Goldwyn-Mayer movie theaters. It also produced a syndicated weekly television series, "The American Adventure." The NEP developed and marketed to the armed forces Americanism training programs composed of propaganda literature and films. The freedom forums, perhaps its largest effort, spread from the campus of Harding College to several other Christian colleges around the country. These forums repaid the industrial giants who helped finance them by preaching directly to their employees the merits of Christian morality, constitutional government, and free enterprise. They also provided a workshop environment in which history, comparative economics, and representative government were taught in the context of a virulent anti-Communist message. For twenty years Harding College and its NEP were regarded as the intellectual center for right-wing movements in America. The NEP never had more than fifteen full-time employees, but engaged or coordinated with hundreds of other groups all over the nation serving as "sub-contractors."

As the cold war intensified, so did the rhetoric of NEP propaganda against communism until, in the years before the election of 1964, the NEP's activities were widely criticized in the national media. Branded as an extremist organization, it assumed a somewhat lower public profile, but continued to spread the social and economic ideals which helped to foster a conservative political resurgence culminating in the election of Ronald Reagan in 1980.

Reagan's election rewarded many grass-roots conservative activists like Benson for their years of hard work behind the scenes. While the NEP gradually lost effectiveness, Benson's emphasis on Americanism and the free-enterprise system is carried on through dozens of educational organizations run by his disciples. His fund-raising efforts helped secure the financial stability not only of Harding, but of Oklahoma Christian and Faulkner Universities as well. Contributions solicited by Benson helped support other educational institutions associated with the Churches of Christ, including Pepperdine and Abilene Christian Universities, Columbia Christian, Ohio Valley Christian, Michigan Christian Colleges, and Namwianga Christian School in Zambia.

Benson died in Searcy.

[See L. Edward Hicks, *Sometimes in the Wrong, but Never in Doubt: George S. Benson and the Education of the New Religious Right* (1994).]

L. EDWARD HICKS

BERRY, JAMES HENDERSON (May 15, 1841–Jan. 30, 1913), governor and U.S. senator, was born in Jackson County, Alabama, the son of James M. Berry and Isabelle Orr. The family moved to Carrollton in Carroll County, Arkansas, in 1848. Surrounded by nine brothers and sisters, Berry worked on the family farm and at seventeen enrolled in a private academy at Berryville. His mother's death forced him to leave the academy after one year, ending his formal schooling.

In 1861 he enlisted in the Confederate army; he was elected second lieutenant of Company E of the Sixteenth Arkansas Infantry. He participated in the Battle of Pea Ridge, and in the Battles of Iuka and Corinth in Mississippi. At Corinth he suffered a leg wound and was captured. His right leg had to be amputated above the knee.

After the war Berry taught school at Ozark. There, on October 31, 1865, he married Lizzie Quaile, the daughter of a businessman; the couple settled in Carrollton. In 1866 he was elected to the Arkansas House of Representatives on the Democratic-Conservative ticket. In 1869 he moved to Bentonville and formed a law partnership with his brother-in-law, Colonel Sam W. Peel.

In September 1872 Berry was elected to the legislature again, this time from Benton and Washington Counties, and in 1874 was chosen Speaker of the House. In 1878 he was elected judge of the Fourth Judicial Circuit; he resigned to run for governor in 1882.

Berry's prospects of winning the nomination appeared promising, since he had established political ties throughout the state. His war service enhanced his appeal. An aggressive preconvention canvass lined up so many delegates behind Berry that the other candidates withdrew, permitting Berry to win unopposed. He carried all but eleven counties in the general election.

In his inaugural address Berry pointed to the need for increased taxation on railroads. He also asked for a revenue law requiring assessment of property at its actual value. He urged the legislature to resubmit to the voters the so-called Fishback Amendment, a constitutional amendment repudiating most of the state's bonded indebtedness carried over from Reconstruction. He requested that state and federal elections be held on the same day and asked for increased support for education. Finally, he asked that there be no delay in determining the extent of shortages in the accounts of some state officials.

Berry had mixed success with the general assembly. The lawmakers created a railroad commission to assess railroads. They authorized Berry to employ attorneys to assist in prosecuting state officers accused of mishandling their accounts. They placed the Fishback Amendment on the ballot, but rejected the governor's proposal to consolidate state and federal elections.

When Berry and the railroad commission attempted to increase assessments on railroad property, the companies sought an injunction, claiming that any increase would violate their charters. The commission's stand was upheld in Arkansas courts and in the United States Supreme Court. The Berry administration thereby made good its pledge to increase railroad taxes, but since several classes of railroad property were excluded, the increase in revenue was modest.

The state's efforts to collect claims against former state officials were only partly successful.

Berry promised equal justice and protection to all citizens regardless of class or race. This commitment was severely tested in the summer of 1883, when some Howard County black men killed a white farmer whom they accused of assaulting a black woman. A white posse quickly reacted, killing at least two blacks and jailing more than forty others. A race war appeared imminent. Berry visited Howard County and warned local authorities that he would tolerate no mob action. His firmness defused a dangerous situation, allowing the courts to function.

The prison system inherited by Berry's administration permitted private contractors to lease prisoner labor from the state. Convicts were often brutally treated. Berry denounced the convict-lease system as "uncivilized, inhumane, and wrong," but his efforts to reform it fell victim to the economy-minded legislature.

Berry opposed deficit spending and was pleased when his administration reduced the state's indebtedness. Outstanding scrip was redeemed, short-term loans were repaid, some bonds were retired, and most Reconstruction debt was formally voided.

After one term Berry unsuccessfuly sought a seat in the United States Senate in 1885. A second opportunity for a Senate seat was presented later the same year when Senator Augustus Hill Garland resigned. The legislature selected Berry, a choice generally praised, though some doubted his ability to succeed the distinguished Garland.

As a senator Berry was diligent but not prominent or dynamic, and his voting record was neither consistently conservative nor progressive. He favored tariff reductions, regulation of railroads and trusts, a graduated income tax, increased coinage of silver, expansion of the money supply, and the direct election of United States senators. He opposed extension of the civil service, a law to prevent adulteration of food, a constitutional amendment giving women the vote, and some other progressive measures. He was reelected by the legislature until challenged by Governor Jeff Davis in 1906.

Berry was no match for the colorful and popular Davis, and he lost to him in the primary. His defeat marked the passing of the old order, for he was the last Confederate veteran to represent Arkansas in the Senate.

In March 1907 Berry returned to his home in Bentonville, where he remained active in veterans affairs. He died at his home there, survived by his wife, two sons, and two daughters, and was buried in City Cemetery.

[See Joe Segraves, "James Henderson Berry, 1883–1885," in *The Governors of Arkansas: Essays in Political Biography,* Timothy P. Donovan, Willard B. Gatewood Jr., and Jeannie M. Whayne, eds., 2d ed. (1995).]

JOE SEGRAVES

BINDURSKY, ESTHER (1905?–1971), newspaper editor, was born in Drew, Mississippi, to Meyer Bindursky, a merchant, born in Bessarabia, and Minnie Iskiwitch, a native of Poland. Esther Bindursky attended public school in Drew and had graduated when the family moved to Lepanto, Arkansas, in 1922. As a young woman, she played the piano for the town's movie house. When the great flood of 1927 hit the Mississippi Delta, she became secretary of the local American Red Cross chapter and later was a case worker for the Arkansas Emergency Relief Commission.

During the early 1930s she became a correspondent for the *Memphis Commercial Appeal,* which served as east Arkansas's daily newspaper. She began with reports of natural disasters, man-made tragedies, and obituaries, and progressed to feature stories. In 1937, when the *Lepanto News Record* was established, Bindursky was asked to be its editor.

For thirty-four years Bindursky was the only staff member of the *Lepanto News Record,* which won over two hundred awards from the National Editorial Association (NEA), the National Federation of Press Women (NFPW), the Arkansas Press Association (APA), and the Arkansas Press Women (APW).

She continued writing news and features for the *Commercial Appeal* and the *Arkansas Gazette.* In 1945 she wrote a moving story about a Lepanto congressional Medal of Honor winner, Staff Sergeant Jim Hendrix, which the *Saturday Evening Post* used as a feature. In 1937 the *Literary Digest* devoted a full page to her description of Lepanto's annual fall event, the Terrapin Derby. She promoted this event with stories to newspapers and wire services, and one of those stories made it to the *New York Times Magazine.* She became an accomplished news photographer. Her picture of a nun who was a stunned survivor of a 1955 train wreck in Marked Tree won an NFPW first-place award and gained a Pulitzer Prize nomination.

Bindursky wrote all the news and feature stories as well as society news. She drew up and sold the ads, took the pictures, and wrote a column, "This One's on Me," often subtitled, "Draggin' Main." She once told a group of journalism students, "When I'm pounding the Main Drag for the ads, I run into the news, hear the personals, know who went to the hospital, and who ran off with whose husband. As a 'Mother Confessor,' the country editor carries a burden which might be trying to the casual player at the canasta table.... [S]he must be able to keep secrets and print that which will raise the community's blood pressure, yet not raise Cain."

She often assumed the duties of printer in making up pages. Her mastery was evident in the first-place awards she received in national and state press association contests for feature writing, column writing, photography, advertising, presswork, makeup and typography, general excellence, and community service.

She was a regular attendee at state press group meetings, NFPW annual conventions, and an occasional NEA meeting and developed a nationwide circle of friends and admirers. The University of Missouri made her a featured speaker on the program of its fabled Journalism Week.

In 1960 the NEA was invited to sponsor a group of American journalists on a trip to eight eastern European countries, including Russia, one of the first opportunities for newspaper people to visit behind the Iron Curtain. The people of Lepanto secretly raised $1,575 to send her on the trip and surprised her with the check when they named her "woman of the year" at their annual chamber of commerce banquet.

In Russia she participated in an interview with First Deputy Premier Mikoyan and reported on that and many other highlights of the trip in feature stories and in her column. She wrote she was "more convinced than ever that our American way is best" and told of having her picture made in front of a solid-gold door at the Palace of the Czars. "My father, who once had to serve in Czar Nicholas' army … would have gotten a 'bang' out of that solid gold door picture. Strange, the Russians … who abhor money as a dirty, capitalistic menace, should guard and treasure this golden memento of the past."

Bindursky edited the *Lepanto News Record* until her death in Memphis, a city that knew her well. *Commercial Appeal* columnist Paul Flowers paid tribute to her, saying, "Every newspaper person who ever knew Esther Bindursky envied her for she had tireless energy, could clean up a story in the shortest possible time, and turn in copy that told it like it was." Catherine Kenney, who worked briefly with Bindursky as a college student, remembered her in the *Arkansas Times* magazine: "With a novelist's grasp of character and dialogue, Esther Bindursky could hear a story in the turn of a phrase or the rhythm of an anecdote, and she had the confidence to listen to that sound and record it. She also had the writer's instinctive knowledge that in the most elementary of things there is something profound, while even the grand gesture originates with a finite human being."

[See the *Arkansas Democrat,* Aug. 25, 1957; the *Lepanto News Record,* Apr. 1, 1960; the *Arkansas Gazette,* May 26, 1960; and the *Arkansas Times,* Mar. 1987. See also two pamphlets published by the Lepanto USA Museum, *Tribute to Esther Bindursky* (1986) and *A History of Lepanto,* edited by Gail Jernigan and Sue Chambers; and Carolyn Gray LeMaster, *A Corner of the Tapestry: A History of the Jewish Experience in Arkansas, 1820s–1990s* (1994).]

DOROTHY D. STUCK

BLACK, JAMES (May 1, 1800–June 22, 1872), silversmith and blacksmith, was born in New Jersey. The names of his parents are unknown. His mother died when he was very young. He ran away from home at the age of eight and made his way to Philadelphia. Apparently he was picked up by the authorities and then became indentured to a silversmith named Henderson.

In 1818 James was released from his apprenticeship. Due to British competition in the silversmith trade, he decided not to go into that business but instead to go west to the American frontier to seek fortune and perhaps adventure. When he reached Bayou Sara in Louisiana, he hired on as a deckhand on a steamboat on the Red River. He left the boat at Fulton, Arkansas, and walked to a settlement at what is now Washington, Arkansas.

He was employed as a blacksmith by William Shaw, a man from Tennessee who had a shop there. Black mastered the art of making plows, hoes, wagons, and other farm implements as well as guns and knives.

He became close friends with the older Shaw sons and fell in love with Anne, the oldest of the Shaw daughters. For reasons unknown, William Shaw opposed his daughter's marrying James Black, who evidently became so discouraged that he gave up working at Shaw's shop and moved further west. Daniel Jones, a governor of Arkansas, tells us that James Black selected a location on the Rolling Fork of the Cossatot River where he cleared land, built a cabin, and started to build a dam. Five or six years later, Black was informed that the land had been ceded to the Indians and he must leave.

With no money and no place to live Black decided go back to Washington. It is reported that he worked again for William Shaw, but eventually he opened his own shop, became widely known for his work, and began to prosper. On June 29, 1828, he and Anne Shaw married in Washington. Five children were born to the marriage. Anne Shaw Black died about 1837.

Black was a leader of the community. He was overseer of the road leading from Washington to the eastern boundary of Saline Township and deputy jailer of Hempstead County. In 1834 he was elected trustee of the town of Washington, where he also served on several jury panels. He bought and sold land and slaves, borrowed money, and filed cases in court to recover money owed him. Daniel W. Jones and Augustus Garland, another governor of Arkansas, wrote that Black had an excellent memory of frontier times and in old age was able to settle disagreements about early happenings in the county.

Black lost his eyesight sometime in his forties, perhaps as a result of his craft, which required long attention to fine detail and staring at flames and red-hot metal, or perhaps as a result of a beating by William Shaw. He left Washington to seek medical help for his eyes. While he was away, Shaw went to court and adopted (apprenticed) the five Black children. Shaw also took Black's belongings and sold his entire estate at a public auction on the courthouse steps. About 1845 Shaw, with his wife and family and the Black children, disappeared down the road to Texas.

All Black had left when he returned were his friends, who took care of him through the years. In those days he could have been sent to the poor house to live, but his friends did not want that to happen. Time after time the county court made allowances of money to take care of him, as "he was blind and without means to support himself."

Black is remembered today for the knives he made. On the frontier a knife was essential for survival, and a superior knifemaker was held in high regard. Black never marked his knives with his name or symbol, but the few that remain can be identified by their superb workmanship, the unequaled temper of the blades, and their balance.

In the winter of 1830–31, Black forged a knife for Jim Bowie, a gentleman frontiersman who was a land speculator, a slave trader, and at times an Indian fighter. Bowie used the knife when he participated in the defense of the Alamo at San Antonio, Texas, where he was killed in 1836. His status as a hero gave the Bowie knife special prestige and fame.

According to Bill Moran, a foremost bladesmith, the knives made by James Black are "spectacular knives with all that gleaming silver. They are very different; they have been forged so that the tang tapers towards the blade and also tapers from the back to the edge

side—never seen before in other knives. On earlier blades (ones forged prior to 1820), we've never seen a coffin-shaped handle like these."

Black died in Washington, Arkansas, and is believed to be buried in the Old Pioneer Cemetery, perhaps in the plot of the Jones family, with whom he lived for thirty years.

[The "Carrigan" knife has the best-documented history of owners, back to the time when Black made it. The larger "Bowie Number One" is identical to the "Carrigan" in workmanship. Both are on display at the Territorial Restoration in Little Rock. The "Tunstall" knife is in the Saunders Memorial Museum in Berryville, Arkansas, together with its documentation. At Old Washington State Park there is a reconstruction of Black's shop; also on display are a fireplace fork that Black forged for the Stuart family, documentation concerning his life, and pictures of knives attributed to him. See Charlean Moss Williams, *The Old Town Speaks* (1951).]

LU WATERS

BLACKBURN, WILLIAM JASPER (July 24, 1820–Nov. 10, 1899), newspaper editor, was born on the Fourche de Mau in Randolph County, Arkansas. His parents' names are not known. During 1838 and 1839 he attended Jackson College at Columbia, Tennessee. In 1839 he moved to Batesville, Arkansas, where he became a newspaper printer. He went to Little Rock in 1845 and to Fort Smith in 1846 to continue his career as a printer.

In 1849 Blackburn moved to Minden, Louisiana, where he established the *Minden Herald,* a strong Unionist paper in a region that was becoming secessionist. He expressed his opposition to slavery in his editorials. For instance, in 1856, when Congressman Preston Brooks of South Carolina physically assaulted Senator Charles Sumner of Massachusetts, an outspoken abolitionist, most southern newspapers defended Brooks, but not Blackburn's *Minden Herald.*

In 1859 Blackburn moved to Homer, Louisiana, where he founded the *Homer Iliad.* After southern delegates left the national Democratic convention in 1860 to nominate their own candidate for president, the *Iliad* supported the northern Democratic nominee, Stephen A. Douglas. The *Iliad* opposed secession and was one of the few newspapers in the Confederacy to remain pro-Union.

After the Civil War, Blackburn joined the Republican Party and became active in politics. In 1867 he was a member of the Louisiana state constitutional convention. When Louisiana was readmitted to the Union, he was elected to the United States House of Representatives as a Republican. He served in the House from July 1868 to March 1869. From 1872 until 1878 he served in the Louisiana state senate.

In 1879 Blackburn returned to Little Rock to launch a new newspaper, the *Arkansas Republican,* first published in January 1880. It was originally both a daily and a weekly; however, sharp losses forced Blackburn to suspend publication of the daily edition. The *Republican,* renamed the *Little Rock Republican* in 1885, became one of the most influential journals in the state. Blackburn's editorials were widely quoted and reprinted in other newspapers.

Blackburn became increasingly disenchanted with the Republican Party. He was attracted to the national Republican Party on economic issues, but objected to a state party leadership he perceived as corrupt, which, under the control of blacks and northern white carpetbaggers, pressed a strong civil rights policy over the preference of native Arkansan Republicans (sometimes called "scalawags" by the Democratic press) for gradualism. In an editorial reprinted in the July 20, 1882, *Columbia Banner* (Magnolia) he wrote: "We are in for fair play, and the rights and vindication of the old and well tried members of the party. Men—or fellows—who turn up here in the South only as office holders or seekers, or in order to prey in some way upon the people, are 'no good.' ... The Republican Party of this State, . . . has always been too much 'run' by such elements, and it seems to get worse the farther it goes.... we shall see what good comes of it; but judging from the past the future is not very flattering in this direction."

As time wore on, Blackburn's connection with the Arkansas Republican Party became tenuous. He objected to the party's efforts to establish an alliance with the disaffected radical farmers who were politically active through such organizations as the Brothers of Freedom, the Agricultural Wheel, the Greenback Party, and the Union Labor Party. Blackburn, a Republican economic purist, opposed making any of the compromises necessary to achieve such an alliance. He also disagreed with the Republican Party's efforts on behalf of blacks. During 1889 and 1890, he opposed the Federal Elections Bill (the "Force Bill" to its critics). This was a proposal for federal elections to be supervised by the U.S. Army to prevent election fraud and to protect

the right of blacks to vote in the South. He wrote in 1890 that Negro suffrage was demoralizing to the white race and "the root of all the recent political and social evils of the South." Without the problem of suffrage, the people of the South would "otherwise dwell today together in peace and harmony and fraternal good will." He believed the North meant to "subordinate the white to the black" by means of suffrage and was "wickedly" responsible for "the inauguration of this evil."

In 1888 and 1890 Blackburn supported Democratic candidates at the state level, opposing what he viewed as the "anarchistic" positions held by the Republican-Union Labor ticket. He broke ranks with the Republicans in 1891 and joined the Democratic Party. He renamed his newspaper *Blackburn's Free South.* In his lead editorial in the first issue he stated that the primary purpose of the *Free South* was to fight for white supremacy. His readership did not support his views, and by the middle of 1892, the *Free South* had ceased publication. His career in journalism was over.

After the demise of the *Free South,* Blackburn lived with his son Charles, an editor at the *Arkansas Democrat.* He died at Charles's home in Little Rock. Only a few issues of his newspapers have survived; he is known to us mainly through what was written about him in the editorial columns of other publications. His writings survive only as excerpts and editorials reprinted in other newspapers.

[Blackburn's career can be traced in these newspapers: *Columbia Banner* (Magnolia), July 20, 1882, May 28, 1885, Feb. 28, 1889, Apr. 10 and Nov. 27, 1890; *Lee County Courier* (Marianna), Jan. 10, 1891; *Lonoke Weekly Democrat,* Jan. 1 and 15, 1891; *Monticellonian,* Nov. 24, 1899; *Nashville News* (Nashville, Arkansas), May 25, 1889, May 31, 1890, Oct. 17, 1891, Nov. 15, 1899; *Nevada County Picayune* (Prescott), May 15, 1889; *Osceola Times,* Oct. 4, 1890; *Southern Standard* (Arkadelphia), Aug. 3, 1888, Feb. 1, 1889, Apr. 25, July 25, Aug. 22, 1890, Jan. 23, 1891, July 1, 1892, Nov. 16, 1899; *Wheeler's Independent* (Fort Smith), Jan. 21, 1880.

Biographies of Blackburn appear in *Appleton's Cyclopedia of American Biography,* vol. 1 (1900), and *Biographical Directory of the American Congress,* 1774–1961 (1961).]

CHARLES J. RECTOR

BOCAGE, JOSEPH W. (May 8, 1819–Jan. 14, 1898), judge, Civil War veteran, and entrepreneur, was born to William Bocage and Marrie Ann Lavoisier on the island of St. Lucia in the Caribbean. After the death of William, Marrie and her young son immigrated to the United States. Soon afterward, Marrie died and Bocage was raised by a paternal cousin, Sarah Ann Lillington, of Wilmington, North Carolina. The Lillingtons' wealth provided Joseph an excellent education before he left their care at the age of sixteen.

Bocage journeyed to Philadelphia, Pittsburgh, Cincinnati, and down the Mississippi River to Vicksburg. At the age of eighteen he arrived in Columbia, Arkansas, then traveled to Pine Bluff by the end of 1837. There he entered the law office of General James Yell and was admitted to the bar in 1840. On May 22 of that same year, he and Frances S. Lindsey of Fairfax County, Virginia, married in a plantation wedding. The groom proved his ardor by swimming across the rising Arkansas River to attend the ceremony. He and Frances had thirteen children.

In 1840, four years after Arkansas joined the Union, the first Fourth of July celebration in Pine Bluff took place. The celebration later described by Bocage included a barbecue and "bran" dance. "The cooks and their army of help moved from pit to pit," Bocage wrote, "where roasting, boiling and baking fish, fowl and flesh, steamed and seethed under the skillful manipulation: seeming sufficient to feed half the state." No cannon was on hand to fire a desired salute, "only shotguns and rifles could be had." To remedy the situation, blacksmith James Crisswell built a cannon "of 8 inch caliber 18 inches long, forged out of axe bars and an old mill spindle." The people assembled at the Methodist church where the Declaration of Independence was read by James Yell, and Bocage delivered an address. A marching procession was formed headed by music: "not a brass band with trumpets and drums but two modest violins . . . 'Hail Columbia,' 'The Star Spangled Banner,' and 'Yankee Doodle' were alternately rendered."

The young judge played an active role in politics in his early years in Pine Bluff. He was elected prosecuting attorney for the state for the Second Judicial District from 1844 to 1846. As prosecutor, Bocage rode horseback over primitive trails to attend court held semi-annually at Pine Bluff, Arkansas Post, Columbia, and Scarborough's Landing. According to Bocage, owning a good horse was essential in performing his duties. He also served as county judge of Jefferson County, 1816 to 1848, and was appointed to a four-year term as commissioner of common schools during the 1850s.

A Democrat, Bocage described the factional upheaval in the state prior to the Civil War: "Returning from New Orleans on the 12th of February, I drove to Little Rock on the 13th and was much surprised to find a greatly divided sentiment in relation to the question of secession."

In early 1861, prior to official hostilities between the states, Bocage organized and captained a cavalry company called the Southern Guards, arming himself with a saber and a pair of Colt navy revolvers. In early April 1861 militia companies under Bocage's command fired musket shots across the bow of the steamer *Sky Lark* and removed all of the supplies bound for U.S. forces.

After the Civil War began, Bocage, along with Colonel Thomas Hindman, raised the Second Arkansas Infantry Regiment. Eventually, Hindman was promoted to brigadier general, and Bocage was made colonel. According to Bocage, the regiment saw more than forty pitched battles, including those at Woodsonville and Bowling Green, Kentucky, and Shiloh, Tennessee. Bocage was later transferred to Texas where he spent the rest of his war service building up manufacturing interests for the Confederacy.

Pine Bluff sustained heavy damage in the Battle of Pine Bluff. Many structures were sacked and burned, including Bocage's home. Upon his return to the city, Bocage went into the lumber and brick-making business and formed a partnership with Colonel Marcus Lafayette Bell. Together they worked to repair and rebuild the city. Bocage was involved in the foundry business and manufactured steam engines and cotton presses to process cottonseed oil, which was becoming an important byproduct of the cotton industry. In 1875 Bocage was chosen to act as superintendent and general agent for the Pine Bluff Cotton Oil Mill Company, the first mill of its kind built in the city.

After retirement he was elected mayor of Pine Bluff in 1889. He served a two-year term and received a salary of one thousand dollars. During his term an electric fire alarm system was installed, land was bought for a city hospital, and a sewer system was completed. After his term, Bocage continued to solicit business and agricultural interests to come to the area by working as secretary and general manager for the Jefferson County Exposition, an office he held until his death.

He was a founding member of the Trinity Episcopal

Church, which is still extant. The Bocages' second home, built in 1866, also still exists. Both are named in the Historical Registry.

[See Julia H. Railey, ed., *History of Trinity Episcopal Church* (1953); James Leslie, *Pine Bluff and Jefferson County: A Pictorial History* (1981). See the *Jefferson County Historical Quarterly* for "A Reminiscence of the Fourth of July, 1840, in Pine Bluff," (1962), and "Four Years Service during the Civil War,"(1975). See also James Leslie's detailed articles in the *Pine Bluff Commercial* for Dec. 9, 1973, Mar. 3, 1981, Nov. 1, 1981, and Sept. 12, 1987.]

APRIL L. BROWN

BOGARD, BENJAMIN MARCUS (Mar. 9, 1868– May 29, 1951), Baptist minister and newspaper editor, was born near Elizabethtown, Kentucky, to M. L. and Nancy Bogard, who made a meager living farming tobacco on rented land. From his parents, Benjamin learned hard work and faith in God.

During a revival in February 1885, Benjamin Bogard experienced a conversion by which he was "saved." Despite wintry weather, he insisted on baptism by total immersion. A hole was cut through the ice covering a nearby pond, and he was plunged into the freezing water. He was ordained a Baptist minister in 1889. In 1891 he married Lynn Onida Meacham Owen, a widow with a baby daughter; together they had a son.

From 1892 to 1904 Bogard served as pastor of Baptist churches in small towns in Kentucky, Missouri, and Arkansas. In Fulton, Kentucky, in 1895 he met J. N. Hall, a leader of the Landmark movement within the Southern Baptist Convention, who became a mentor to Bogard.

As a Landmark Baptist, Bogard embraced a conservative theology emphasizing certain "landmarks" of doctrine in the Bible. In 1901 he became the joint editor of the *Arkansas Baptist,* a paper he gained full editorial control of in 1904. Also in 1901 he published *Pillars of Orthodoxy,* venerating the leaders of the Landmark movement. By 1905 Bogard, Hall, and their followers had reached an impasse with the Southern Baptist Convention, and left to form the American Baptist Association, also known as the Missionary Baptists.

From 1903 until 1914 Bogard served as pastor in Argenta (North Little Rock), and in Itasca, Texas, and conducted evangelical revivals on a circuit of seven states. In 1917 his *Arkansas Baptist* newspaper merged with the Texas *Baptist Commoner* to form the *Baptist*

and Commoner. In May 1920 he became pastor of Antioch Missionary Baptist Church in Little Rock, where he remained until his retirement in 1947.

In the 1920s Bogard became a spokesman for the Christian fundamentalist movement, which sought to ban the teaching of evolution in public schools. In 1926 Bogard wrote and published an anti-evolution special edition of the *Baptist and Commoner.* With D. N. Jackson, he expanded this issue into a volume entitled *Evolution: Unscientific and Unscriptural.* Bogard continued to wage his crusade in the *Baptist and Commoner* in 1927 and 1928. He asserted that evolution was not a scientific "fact" but a "theory," reasoning that it had never been directly observed and could not be reproduced through experimentation. He especially objected to tax dollars supporting the teaching of evolution. Evolution undermined the faith of his children, he claimed.

When an anti-evolution bill written by Representative A. L. Rotenberry of Pulaski County came before Arkansas's general assembly early in 1927, Bogard appeared as an expert witness. The Rotenberry bill passed the House by a narrow margin, only to be tabled by the Senate. In response, Bogard circulated a petition to place the bill on the general election ballot, and he collected the requisite signatures. Initiated Act No. 1, the Rotenberry bill, would be decided by the people of Arkansas in November 1928.

During the spring and summer of 1928, Bogard attacked evolution in the *Baptist and Commoner,* linking it to atheism, Bolshevism, and a decline in morals. He joined other conservative Protestant ministers who, though traditional Democrats, denounced the presidential candidacy of Democratic governor Alfred E. Smith of New York, a Roman Catholic favoring the easing of prohibition. Assuming leadership in Arkansas's anti-Smith campaign, Bogard denounced Catholicism as a form of Christianity horribly corrupted by Satan. He said that Smith would bring the "Pope of Rome" into the White House, resulting in the repeal of freedom of religion and the bloody suppression of Protestantism. Finally, he denounced Smith as a "northerner" who would seek to force "Negro Equality" upon the people of the South.

As election day approached, forces gathered to defeat Bogard's ballot initiative. Former governor Charles Brough, University of Arkansas president John Futrall, and *Arkansas Gazette* editor J. N. Heiskell joined others to form the Committee Against Act No. 1.

Initiated Act No. 1 passed by a two-to-one margin. Basking in his victory, Bogard vowed to continue his campaign until every state had a law banning evolution from public schools. But in the pages of the *Baptist and Commoner*, he quietly forgot his anti-evolution crusade and embarked upon a tirade against Catholicism. After a disagreement with the owner of the paper, Bogard was forced to resign as editor in 1931.

He founded a Missionary Baptist seminary in Little Rock in 1934 and started a new paper, the *Orthodox Baptist Searchlight*. In 1937 a new problem captured his attention: the Missionary Baptist Sunday School Committee reported a deficit. Bogard reacted by attacking the committee's manager as incompetent and dishonest. The controversy flared up and died down several times over the next decade, finally driving the manager and his supporters from the American Baptist Association.

Bogard wrote pamphlets detailing Landmark beliefs and was a pioneer in radio evangelism. He belonged to the Ku Klux Klan, probably during its peak in Arkansas in the early 1920s. His dedication earned him an entry in Ripley's *Believe It or Not* for preaching "every Sunday for 61 years without missing a single Sunday."

[*Baptist and Commoner* was published in Little Rock; it is available at the University of Arkansas Libraries, Fayetteville. The Union List created by the Arkansas Newspaper Project has information on other possible locations of this item. Bogard and D. N. Jackson's *Evolution: Unscientific and Unscriptural* was published in Texarkana by the Baptist Sunday School Committee in 1926.

Secondary sources include L. D. Forman and Alta Payne, *The Life and Works of Benjamin Marcus Bogard* (1966); Todd E. Lewis, "Ben Bogard and the Crusade against Evolution, Rum and Romanism in Arkansas, 1926–1928," M.A. thesis, University of Arkansas, 1989; Leo Thomas Sweeney, "The Anti-Evolution Movement in Arkansas," M.A. thesis, University of Arkansas, 1966; James E. Tull, "A Study of Southern Baptist Landmarkism in Light of Historical Baptist Ecclesiology," Ph.D. dissertation, Columbia University, 1960; and Calvin Coolidge Turpin, "A Critique of Ben M. Bogard's Leadership," Th.D. dissertation, Golden Gate Baptist Theological Seminary, Mill Valley, California, 1967.]

TODD E. LEWIS

BOND, SCOTT WINFIELD (1853?–?), was born a slave in rural Madison County, Mississippi, near Canton. His mother, Ann Bond, was a house slave.

According to Bond, his mother married William Bond before Scott was two years old. About 1855 the family moved to Tennessee; they were moved to the Bond plantation in Cross County, Arkansas, around 1860. Ann Bond died after the end of the Civil War. Bond moved with his stepfather to Madison, St. Francis County, at the age of nineteen and remained in his household until 1875.

At the age of twenty-two, Bond began renting a portion of the Allen farm. The next year Bond increased the amount of acreage he rented and hired one man. He established himself as a farmer, then married Magnolia (Maggie) Nash of Forrest City in 1877. Their long-lasting union produced eleven sons.

Having gained respectability, Bond began his singular career as a farmer and businessman. Capitalized by the owner of the Allen plantation (twenty-two hundred acres), Bond managed the property for eleven years. At the same time that he operated the Allen place, he also rented another farm of three hundred acres at Madison on the St. Francis River. Bond decided in 1889 to quit his position at the Allen farm in order to operate the new site. Instead, the owner sold the Allen property to Bond and his partner, T. O. Fitzpatrick. Bond maintained the partnership for approximately five years, then he sold his interest to Fitzpatrick. Said Bond, "I really believe that we could get along as partners in this farm for forty years, but as you have boys and I have boys, after our days, the boys might not get along as well as we have. For that cause I think this is the proper thing to do." Before the turn of the century Bond owned seven other farms adjoining the original three-hundred-acre site.

He also engaged in business opportunities that facilitated his farming. With a reputation for success and prudence, Bond opened a store in Madison in partnership with his stepfather and Abe Davis, with Bond operating the store. Undercapitalized, he closed the store after several months. Eventually, he bought the Madison Mercantile Company as sole proprietor and maintained the store to supply his farms. He also purchased four additional town lots. By 1915 he owned three cotton gin plants, a sawmill, and a gravel pit which supplied the Rock Island Railroad. The number of his farms had increased to nineteen, with a total of five thousand acres. The farm on which the family resided was called "The Cedars."

Scott Bond was a member of the National Negro

Business League (NNBL) established by Booker T. Washington in 1901. Bond addressed the annual meeting of the organization in New York City in 1920 and secured Washington's pledge to visit St. Francis County. The following year the NNBL held its annual meeting in Little Rock. After the conference, Bond was Washington's host on a visit to Madison, Arkansas. The occasion included a public address by Washington and a barbecue in his honor at the Cedars.

[See Dan A. Rudd and Theo Bond, *From Slavery to Wealth: The Life of Scott Bond* (1917; rpt. 1971).]

FON LOUISE GORDON

BORLAND, SOLON (Aug. 8, 1811–Dec. 15, 1864), United States senator, diplomat, was born in Suffolk, Virginia, the youngest of three sons of Thomas Wood Borland, a physician, and Harriet Godwin. Solon attended the University of Pennsylvania Medical School in 1833–34. In 1831 he married Hildah Wright of Virginia. This marriage produced two sons, Harold and Thomas.

Borland moved to Memphis, Tennessee, in 1836, after his wife's death, to set up a medical practice with his brother. On July 26, 1839, he married a Mrs. Eliza Hart, who died just a few months later. Borland eventually entered politics, founding and editing a Democratic paper in January 1839. In 1843 the Arkansas Democratic Party hired him to edit their newly created newspaper in Little Rock.

The *Arkansas Banner* appeared in September 1843, yet Borland did not arrive in Little Rock until late November. In January 1844 he displayed his violent temper when he assaulted Whig editor Benjamin J. Borden and, according to one observer, beat his rival's face "into jelly."

Borland married for the third and final time on May 27, 1845. This union with Mary Isabel Melbourne produced a son and two daughters. Their son, George Godwin Borland, died during the Civil War; Fanny Green Borland and Mary Melbourne Borland were still living by late 1863.

Borland volunteered for military service at the outbreak of the Mexican War. On the morning of January 23, 1847, his unit was captured forty-five miles south of Saltillo, Mexico. Transferred to a prison in Mexico City, Borland escaped to American ranks and participated in the final American attack in September 1847.

Back in Arkansas, the veteran received a major political boost when Senator Ambrose H. Sevier resigned his position. Governor Thomas S. Drew appointed Borland to the United States Senate in March 1848, a post he occupied until fall, when the state legislature would elect someone for a full term. He used his time well. He initiated congressional action on a western branch for the federal court, swampland reclamation, and back pay for prisoners of war. He then successfully blocked Sevier's attempt to reclaim his seat.

His Senate career was neither quiet nor consistent. During the Compromise Crisis of 1850, he belligerently defended southern rights, assaulting a senator in the process. Back in Arkansas he discovered that public opinion did not support his disunionism. In a Little Rock speech in July 1850 he denounced abolitionists and admitted some of the difficulties he had with the compromise. Yet he expressed veneration for the Union. He never returned to Washington to vote on the compromise, and this absence was interpreted as acquiescence to the sectional agreement.

Always an expansionist, he declared in the Senate in 1853 that he had voted against the Clayton-Bulwer Treaty in 1850 because it violated the Monroe Doctrine and restricted U.S. growth. These opinions apparently appealed to the new Pierce administration, which appointed him envoy extraordinary and minister plenipotentiary to Central America, assigned to Nicaragua.

Borland submitted his credentials to the Nicaraguan government in September 1863. As minister, he called for U.S. repudiation of the Clayton-Bulwer Treaty and for American military backing for Honduras in its dispute with Britain. In mid-October he declared that it was his greatest ambition "to see the State of Nicaragua forming a bright star in the flag of the United States." This address, along with his complaints and demands, provoked a reprimand from Secretary of State William L. Marcy, causing Borland's resignation.

In May 1854 Borland interfered with the arrest of an American citizen in San Juan del Norte, Nicaragua. He was almost arrested, and while he was claiming diplomatic immunity, someone threw a bottle in his face. The enraged diplomat reported this incident to his government, whereupon President Pierce sent a naval warship to demand an apology. On July 13, 1854, the U.S. Navy bombarded the town and dispatched marines to burn what remained, an early example of gunboat diplomacy.

Borland returned to Little Rock to become editor of the *Arkansas Gazette,* then the journal of the state's leading American, or Know-Nothing, Party. By the late 1850s he retired from politics to practice medicine in Little Rock and Memphis.

After Fort Sumter, Governor Henry M. Rector appointed him commander of the state militia and ordered him to seize the federal arsenal at Fort Smith, even though Arkansas had not yet seceded. Borland arrived in Fort Smith in April, but the federals had already departed with their military supplies. The secession convention replaced him as head of the state militia the next month. As Confederate commander over northeastern Arkansas, he ordered an embargo of goods to end price speculation. Governor Rector rescinded this, but Borland denied that Arkansas's chief executive could countermand a Confederate officer. In January 1862 Confederate secretary of war Judah P. Benjamin revoked Borland's order.

In June 1862 Borland resumed his medical practice in Little Rock. By October his wife died at the age of thirty-nine. Borland wrote his will in Arkansas's last Confederate capital, Washington, on December 31, 1863.

[Several earlier accounts of Borland's life are in error regarding his date of birth, early education, Civil War career, and date and place of death. For his parents' background, see "Notes and Queries: The Borlands and Godwins," *Virginia Magazine of History and Biography* 17 (1909): 97–98. Some primary material, including copies of Borland's will, is available at the Arkansas History Commission and in contemporary newspapers. Consult the newspapers Borland edited in Arkansas, the *Arkansas Banner* and the *Arkansas Gazette.* See also James M. Woods, *Rebellion and Realignment: Arkansas's Road to Secession* (1987); Margaret Ross, *Arkansas Gazette: The Early Years, 1819–1866* (1969); and for his career in the Mexican War, William W. Hughes, *Archibald Yell* (1988). Also consult James M. Woods, "Expansionism as Diplomacy: The Career of Solon Borland in Central America, 1853–1854," *The Americas: A Quarterly Review of Inter-American Cultural History* 40 (Jan. 1984): 399–415; and Michael B. Dougan, *Confederate Arkansas: The People and Politics of a Frontier State in Wartime* (1976).]

JAMES M. WOODS

BOWMAN, MALCOLM CLEABURNE (Dec. 6, 1926–Mar. 18, 1993), analytical environmental chemist, researcher, and author, was born in Alcedo, Texas, to Clyde C. Bowman, a Cotton Belt Railroad brakeman and conductor, and Lillian McBee, a teacher and a retail clerk. The family moved to Pine Bluff in 1936.

A graduate of Pine Bluff High School, Bowman earned a B.S. degree in chemistry from Arkansas Teachers' College (now the University of Central Arkansas) in 1949. He did postgraduate work in chemistry and mathematics at the University of Arkansas at Fayetteville, Henderson State College (now University), Texas A & M University, and Drexel Institute of Technology.

Except for a brief stint in 1961–62 as a chemist in the pesticide laboratory of Campbell Soup Company in Camden, New Jersey, Bowman served thirty continuous years as a chemist and administrator for the federal government. He began his government career with the army chemical corps at Pine Bluff Arsenal in 1951. Six years later he transferred to the United States Department of Agriculture (USDA), serving in Orlando, Florida, and Tifton, Georgia.

At the USDA Bowman did pioneering studies in pesticide residue analysis. He gained an international reputation for his abilities in developing ultrasensitive methods for the detection and monitoring of toxic chemicals, especially pesticides, in food products and environmental elements. His efforts contributed to more responsible use of agricultural chemicals throughout the world.

In 1972 Bowman joined the Food and Drug Administration (FDA) as chief of its Division of Chemistry's Analytical Methods Branch at the National Center for Toxicological Research (NCTR) in Jefferson, near Pine Bluff. He was promoted to director of NCTR's Division of Chemistry in 1978.

At NCTR he and his associates formulated analytical methods for detecting some of the most toxic chemicals known to man, including some extremely potent, cancer-causing compounds. He and his coworkers developed methods for removal of carcinogens and other toxicants from the facility's wastewater before discharging it into the environment. Because of the diversity of chemicals researched by scientists there, Bowman's division faced a uniquely difficult challenge in the trace-level analysis of the substances. An associate, Charles Nony, described Bowman as the best chemist he had ever known: "He could plan a research method to the finest degree and it never failed to work."

Bowman had "a great sense of designing research never before done" and had an "uncanny talent for solving problems and finding answers to questions by being able to see in new directions." According to one source, "Many of the methods, practices and equipment developed by Malcolm and associates are in such common use that their origin is usually forgotten." He held patents on three instruments used in chromatographic science.

Among the articles and books Bowman wrote or edited were *The Handbook of Carcinogens and Hazardous Substances: Chemical and Trace Analysis* (1982); *Carcinogens and Related Substances: Analytical Chemistry for Toxicological Research* (1979); and "Analysis of Chemosterilants" (substances used to sterilize insects to prevent reproduction) in the *Journal of Chromatographic Science* (1975). He wrote so clearly that a layman with a limited chemical background could understand his articles.

Bowman retired from the FDA in December 1981. During his federal years, he received a number of awards, served on editorial boards of several scientific journals, participated in scientific conferences throughout the world, and was the author or coauthor of over two hundred scientific publications. Among the professional organizations of which he was a member were the American Chemical Society and the Entomological Society of America.

In 1978 he received a special citation from the FDA in recognition of his "analytical chemical development in the field of trace analysis monitoring of chemicals in both animal chow and water for feeding purposes." He was twice a regional nominee for the American Chemical Society's Spencer Award for Outstanding Achievement in Agricultural and Food Chemistry. However, he was said to be motivated not by awards but by his love of chemistry.

Following retirement, he established a private laboratory in Pine Bluff, continuing his research on the analysis and biochemistry of pesticides and animal drugs.

Bowman and Julia Mae Mitchell married in Sheridan, Arkansas, on February 10, 1950. The couple had three sons: David, Robert, and Steven.

Bowman developed cancer and died in Little Rock.

[This entry is based on interviews with Lillian McBee Bowman, 1998; Dr. Robert Bowman, 1998; and coworkers Tom Ashcraft and Charles Nony, 1998. See the *Pine Bluff News*, Mar. 25, 1993.]

RICK JOSLIN

BRANNER, JOHN CASPER (July 4, 1850–Mar. 1, 1922), geologist, teacher, and university administrator, was born at New Market, Tennessee, to Michael T. Branner, a farmer, and Elsie Baker. The Branner family were colonial settlers of the Shenandoah Valley of Virginia.

Branner's early education was supplemented by avid reading and a deep interest in the natural features of the Tennessee countryside. He studied at Maryville College near Knoxville for two years. He went to the newly established Cornell College at Ithaca, New York, in 1870. There he came under the direction and influence of the renowned Charles F. Hartt, professor of geology. Although he had not yet completed his baccalaureate degree, Branner accompanied Hartt to Brazil in 1874 and spent most of his time there for the next nine years. He studied the country's geology, particularly its mineral wealth, but he also searched for vegetable fibers to be used in making incandescent lights at the request of Thomas A. Edison and studied insects adversely affecting cotton plants under a commission from the United States Department of Agriculture. He was awarded the bachelor of science degree from Cornell University in 1882, submitting a thesis entitled "On the Fibro-vascular Bundles in Palms."

In 1883 he was appointed assistant geologist with the Second Geological Survey of Pennsylvania under the direction of J. Peter Lesley. For two years Branner studied the Lackawanna Valley, noted for its anthracite resources. His work involved topographic and geologic mapping as well as analysis of the effects of glaciation on the region, and he acknowledged the influence of that experience and his association with Lesley on his development as a geologist.

In 1885 Branner accepted a position as professor and chairman of the Department of Geology at Indiana University, Bloomington. David Starr Jordan, the president of the university, was an acclaimed icthyologist, and the two established Indiana as a center for natural science instruction and research. Branner received a Ph.D. without dissertation from Indiana University in 1885 and retained his faculty association until 1891.

He was appointed state geologist of Arkansas in 1887, and he organized its first post-Reconstruction geological survey. At that time, central Arkansas teemed with reports of gold and silver discoveries in the Ouachita Mountains; that excitement contributed to the state legislature's interest in establishing a geological survey. T. B. Comstock, assistant geologist, was assigned to examine various claims and mines, mostly in Montgomery and Garland Counties. His report (1888), the first published by the Branner survey, exposed mines with such exotic names as "Golden Wonder," "Silver World," "Mozambique Tunnel," and "Lost Louisiana" as entirely worthless. Branner immediately made this conclusion public in the face of ventures that had been capitalized under the laws of the state at more than $113 million.

Blaming the messenger for the message, his critics burned him in effigy (possibly twice), attacked him ruthlessly in the press, and called for the governor to dismiss him as state geologist. He found allies in Richard P. Rothwell, editor of the *Engineering and Mining Journal;* Edward H. Mathes, a prominent attorney from Ozark, Arkansas; and Governor Simon P. Hughes, among others. Efforts to destroy his professional reputation were successfully challenged; Comstock's report was irrefutable, and all the investments were lost. This episode clouded Branner's tenure as state geologist, however. There was sentiment in the state legislature to do away with the geological survey, although it survived the legislatures of 1889 and 1891. Nevertheless, Branner remained state geologist for only five years. The next geological survey in Arkansas was organized in 1923 by his son, George Casper Branner.

The record of the Branner survey is a remarkable one and a tribute to his skills both as a geologist and as an administrator. The fourteen published volumes on the geology of Arkansas include sixty maps and cover virtually all geological aspects of the state. Of particular significance were reports on coal (1888), manganese (1891), igneous rocks (1891), and the Washington and Benton County reports (1891; 1894). The reports and maps of the Branner survey remain valuable references into the 1990s.

In 1892 Branner joined the faculty of the newly created Leland Stanford Junior University. David Starr Jordan, Branner's colleague at Indiana, was Stanford's first president, and the two men quickly established the institution as a leader in education in the natural sciences. As department head, Branner brought in many of the geologists from his Arkansas survey. He became vice president of Stanford in 1899 and president in 1913, retiring two years later.

Branner published some 371 articles on such subjects as higher education, ants as geological agents, Portuguese grammar, cotton insects, fish taxonomy, glaciation, Arkansas geology, and the geology of Brazil. He was a member of the National Academy of Sciences and founder of the Seismological Society of America. He was a Fellow of the Geological Society of America, serving as its president in 1904. He received several honorary degrees, including one from the University of Arkansas (1897), and he received the Hayden Medal from the Philadelphia Academy of Sciences.

John C. Branner and Susan D. Kennedy of Oneida, New York, were married in 1883; the union produced a daughter and two sons. He died in Palo Alto, California.

[See J. C. Branner, "Incidents in the History of the Geological Survey of Arkansas, and Some Conclusions to Be Drawn Therefrom," in *Outlines of Arkansas Geology* (1920): 15–20; and T. B. Comstock, "Report on the geology of western central Arkansas, with especial reference to gold and silver," *Arkansas Geological Survey, Annual Report,* vol. 1 (1888): 1–320.

This biography draws on memorials by R. A. F. Penrose Jr., *Geological Society of America Bulletin* 36 (1925): 15–44 (which contains a complete bibliography of John C. Branner), and Charles. R. Keyes, *Pan-American Geologist* 37 (1922): 257–66. See D. Yannacci, "John Casper Branner," *Pennsylvania Geology* 19 (1988): 9–10. Most of Branner's papers are in the Stanford University Archives, particularly for the years 1882–1921. There are Branner collections in the Philadelphia Academy of Natural Sciences and the Arkansas Geological Commission, Little Rock. I thank Henry S. deLinde, Joseph A. Ziegler, and Thomas Malefatto for providing information used in this sketch.]

WALTER L. MANGER

BRANTON, WILEY AUSTIN (Dec. 13, 1923– Dec. 15, 1988), civil rights lawyer, was born in Pine Bluff, Arkansas, to Leo Andrew Branton and Pauline Wiley. The Brantons were a prominent African-American family. Leo Branton owned a taxicab company. Wiley's great-grandfather was the Choctaw Indian chief Greenwood Leflore.

After working briefly in the taxicab business, Branton entered Arkansas Agricultural, Mechanical and Normal College (now the University of Arkansas at Pine Bluff), a predominantly black state school. In 1950 he received a bachelor's degree in business administration. In 1953 he graduated from the University of Arkansas School of Law.

Branton returned to Pine Bluff to practice law. Despite his family's relative affluence, he had encountered prejudice at home and in the military during

World War II. Even before entering law school, he had been active in the civil rights movement and in the work of the National Association for the Advancement of Colored People (NAACP). He was a friend and supporter of Silas Hunt, who in 1948 became the first African American to enter the state law school. Branton's early efforts to mobilize black voters led to a conviction on questionable grounds and probably contributed to his decision to go to law school.

By the mid-1950s Branton was traveling throughout Arkansas and Mississippi on behalf of the NAACP's Legal Redress Committee and serving as local counsel for the NAACP Legal Defense Fund. In May 1955 the Little Rock School Board unveiled a plan to desegregate the Little Rock public schools. The plan called for the desegregation of Central High School in September 1957, but did not require desegregation of elementary schools until 1963. To expedite desegregation Branton sued the school district on behalf of thirty-three black children who asked to be allowed to attend their neighborhood schools regardless of the schools' racial composition. Working with future Supreme Court justice Thurgood Marshall, Branton argued the case before a federal appeals court in St. Louis, but lost.

Branton continued his efforts on behalf of black students in Little Rock. After violence broke out in September 1957, when nine black students entered Central High, the Little Rock School Board sought to delay implementation of its desegregation plan for two and a half years. Branton and a team of NAACP lawyers successfully opposed the effort; the 1958 landmark Supreme Court decision in *Cooper v. Aaron* refused to permit delay. He was also involved in successful challenges to state laws authorizing the closing of public schools, or converting them into private schools to avoid integration.

Branton's activities made him a target of militant segregationists. Crosses were burned at his home and at the family burial plot in Pine Bluff. During the height of the Little Rock crisis, he and his family slept under armed guard. Years later Branton recalled, "I used to get threats by letter, by telephone, through intermediaries . . . months on end I would not get in an automobile without checking to see if a little seal on my hood had been broken. I would never take the same way home."

In 1962 Branton moved to Atlanta to direct the Voter Education Project. By 1965 he had helped register six hundred thousand black voters in eleven southern states. From 1965 to 1967 he served in the Johnson administration as a special assistant to the attorney general and as executive secretary of the Council on Equal Opportunity. From 1967 to 1969 he was the executive director of the United Planning Organization, an antipoverty agency in the District of Columbia. He worked briefly as director of the Alliance for Labor Action, a joint endeavor of the United Auto Workers and the Teamsters' Union, before entering private practice in Washington, D.C. In 1978 he became dean of Howard University's Law School, an institution then troubled by a loss of accreditation, its graduates' high failure rate on bar examinations, and a disgruntled faculty. Before leaving in 1983, Branton brought a measure of stability to the school. At the time of his death, he was in private practice with the firm of Sidley and Austin in Washington.

Although, in the words of former NAACP executive director Benjamin L. Hooks, Branton "risked life and limb as a civil rights lawyer in the South," he never became bitter or lost his sense of humor. Effective but unassuming, he did not seek the spotlight. Thurgood Marshall said "he spent most of his time working for free." George Howard, one of Branton's Law School classmates who later became a federal judge, described Branton as "a lawyer's lawyer . . . He wanted to make sure every litigant had his day in court."

Branton married Lucille McKee on February 1, 1948, and they had six children: Toni, Waylene, Wiley Jr., Beverly, Debra, and Richard. Branton died in Washington, D.C., and is buried in Bellwood Cemetery in Pine Bluff.

[Sources include Jack Greenberg, *Crusaders in the Courts: How a Dedicated Band of Lawyers Fought for the Civil Rights Revolution* (1994); Tony Freyer, *The Little Rock Crisis: A Constitutional Interpretation* (1984); and Tom Baskett Jr., ed. *Persistence of the Spirit: The Black Experience in Arkansas* (1986). Material pertaining to the litigation surrounding the Central High School crisis appears in *Race Relations Law Reporter,* vols. 1–4 (1956–59). The Columbia University Oral History Project interviewed Branton in 1973; transcripts are available at Columbia and at the Eisenhower Library in Abilene, Kansas. Obituaries appear in the *New York Times,* Dec. 17, 1988, and the *Arkansas Gazette,* Dec. 17, 1988. See Wiley A. Branton, "The Effect of *Brown v. Board of Education*: A Retrospective View," *Howard Law Journal* 23 (1980): 125–33; and Guerdon D. Nichols, "Breaking the Color Barrier at the University of Arkansas," *AHQ* 27 (Spring 1968): 3–21.]

JEFF BROADWATER

BRECKINRIDGE, CLIFTON RODES (Nov. 22, 1846–Dec. 3, 1932), politician and diplomat, was born in Lexington, Kentucky, to Mary Cyrene Burch and John Cabel Breckinridge, members of prominent political families.

Clifton followed his father, John Cabel Breckinridge, a senator, vice president, and 1860 presidential candidate, into the Confederate military. His Civil War service as an army private and naval midshipman was often near his father, who was a general and the Confederate secretary of war. After the war, Clifton worked in a dry-goods store in Cincinnati for two years. Then he attended Washington College, because General Robert E. Lee had become its president.

In 1870 Breckinridge moved to Pine Bluff, where his older brother had a plantation. He worked with limited financial success for several years as a commission merchant and planter. In 1876 he and Katherine Breckinridge Carson, the daughter of a well-to-do Mississippi family, married in Memphis. The wedding was a noted social event with the son of Jefferson Davis, president of the Confederacy, serving as Breckinridge's best man. The couple had four children.

Breckinridge began a political career in 1876 after Reconstruction had ended in Arkansas. He served as an alderman in Pine Bluff before seeking national office in 1882. The Breckinridge name helped him win election as congressman-at-large from Arkansas. In 1884 he was elected from the Second Congressional District, which he represented for the next decade.

Clifton Breckinridge became a powerful congressional figure. John Carlisle of Kentucky, speaker of the House of Representatives and a family friend, appointed him to the Ways and Means Committee. His influence grew steadily, so long as Democrats were in power, and peaked in 1893–94, early in President Grover Cleveland's second term. He advised the president on congressional matters and had a major role in repealing the Sherman Silver Purchase Act in order to support Cleveland's commitment to the gold standard and in passing the Wilson-Gorman Tariff to lower taxes. He was described in *Harper's Weekly* (June 2, 1894) as "one of the very first men in the House," but one who worked behind the scenes.

A Republican-controlled House voted to unseat him in September 1890 after a lengthy investigation of irregularities in the 1888 election revealed voter fraud and violence in Conway County. These scandalous events were climaxed by the murder, after the election, of Breckinridge's opponent, John M. Clayton. The fact that John Clayton was the brother of the controversial Reconstruction governor and senator, Powell Clayton, intensified emotions. Breckinridge was never accused of misconduct but he paid heavily when, by straight party vote, the House declared Clayton had won the election. Arkansas voters returned Breckinridge to Congress two months later.

Clifton Breckinridge lost his seat for good in 1894. In the wake of a severe economic depression in 1893, Populist demands for "free silver" spread. When Breckinridge refused to bend on the issue and vigorously defended Cleveland's effort to maintain the gold standard, Arkansas Democrats denied him renomination. Cleveland rewarded his loyalty by naming him minister to Russia.

As one of the ablest of the era's amateur diplomats, Breckinridge analyzed world events in dispatches and letters that caught the eyes of secretaries of state under whom he worked. He wrote about deteriorating relations with Russia and urged stronger measures to uphold American interests and ideals. Although his messages were passed along to Presidents Cleveland and William McKinley, they had little impact on policy. The United States in these years remained firmly committed to isolationism.

McKinley, an old friend, appointed Breckinridge to the Dawes Commission to the Five Civilized Tribes in 1900. He worked for several years in Indian Territory, as it prepared to seek statehood as Oklahoma, allotting tribal lands to individual Cherokees. The Indian Rights Association, however, accused Breckinridge and other commissioners of setting up trust companies to obtain the land fraudulently. A federal investigation eventually exonerated the officials. Breckinridge offered his resignation to President Theodore Roosevelt, who refused it. The president wrote Breckinridge that investigators "inform me privately that though they think your actions did not show good judgment in this matter they are convinced of your absolute probity." Roosevelt closed on a personal note: "Permit me to add that any other statement on their part would have astonished me beyond measure." Breckinridge left the Dawes Commission in 1905 and a year later established the Arkansas Valley Trust Company in Fort Smith, heading the business until 1914.

He last served in public life as a delegate from

Sebastian County to the Arkansas constitutional convention of 1917–18. He was named to the Agriculture and Mining Committee and the Taxation Committee, but at the age of seventy-one, he did not play a leading role at the convention. He argued vigorously in favor of a unicameral legislature, a provision adopted but later rescinded. In December 1918 Arkansas voters rejected the proposed constitution.

After his wife died in 1921, Breckinridge was seldom in Arkansas. He moved about the country, visiting his children and grandchildren. He helped his daughter Mary with her Frontier Nursing Service in the mountains of eastern Kentucky and died there at Windover.

[Breckinridge's papers are scattered through the collections of many late nineteenth-century leaders, including those of presidents from Cleveland to Theodore Roosevelt. His letters are also in the Breckinridge Family Papers at the Library of Congress and at the University of Kentucky. Other materials are privately held by his grandchildren.

See James Duane Bolin, "Clifton Rodes Breckinridge: The Little Arkansas Giant," *AHQ* 53 (Winter 1994): 407–27; James F. Willis, "An Arkansan in St. Petersburg: Clifton Rodes Breckinridge, Minister to Russia, 1894–1897," *AHQ* 38 (Spring 1979): 3–31; Kenneth C. Barnes, "Who Killed John M. Clayton? Political Violence in Conway County, Arkansas, in the 1880s," *AHQ* 52 (Winter 1993): 371–404; and Calvin R. Ledbetter, "The Constitutional Convention of 1917–1918," *AHQ* 34 (Spring 1975): 3–40.]

JAMES F. WILLIS

BRINKLEY, JOHN ROMULUS [later Richard] (July 8, 1885–May 25, 1942), medical charlatan, was born in Jackson County, North Carolina, to Sarah Candace Barnett. His father's identity is unclear. Orphaned at age five, he was raised by his uncle and aunt, Dr. John Richard Brinkley and Sally Brinkley, in East La Porte, North Carolina. His early education was occasional and incomplete. Wanderlust evidently led him through the eastern United States as a telegrapher and sideshow doctor. He married Sally Wike in 1907, but the marriage failed in 1913 after producing a son who did not survive and three daughters. He married Minnie Telitha Jones in July 1913.

Brinkley lighted in Chicago and took night classes at the eclectic Bennett Medical College between 1908 and 1910, but poverty forced his withdrawal. He used his omnifarious medical training in practices in Tennessee and North and South Carolina, delving into medical charlatanism as an "Electro Medic Doctor," among other schemes.

After a stay in a Greenville, South Carolina, jail, and practice in Judsonia, Arkansas, he enrolled in the Eclectic Medical University of Kansas City. Seven months and one hundred dollars later Brinkley received a diploma. Arkansas, one of only eight states to recognize the degree, was the first to license him as a physician. Brinkley used license reciprocity between states, weak oversight of the profession, and fraud to obtain diplomas and, at least for a time, medical licenses in several states, Italy, and Great Britain.

The army recruited Brinkley as a medical officer in April 1917. Despite his later claims of heroism, he served only eighty-five days, most of which were spent at the Fort Bliss base hospital after he declared himself unfit for duty.

Brinkley settled in Milford, Kansas, in late 1917 and attracted attention by claiming to restore sexual vitality by transplanting goat gonads into the patient's scrotum. Here he hit upon his gold mine. He advertised copiously, and news of the transplant procedure spread quickly. Aging farmers from near and far sneaked away to Milford to pay $750 for Brinkley's rejuvenating wizardry. The town boomed.

In 1923 Brinkley built a powerful radio station beside his hospital. KFKB broadcasts included homespun religious, agricultural, and musical programming. Brinkley hosted "The Medical Question Box" where he prescribed for listeners' symptoms "special" medications identified by number and available only through his hospital or Brinkley-approved pharmacies.

Claims for the curative value of goat gland implants grew with Brinkley's bank account. Impotence, baldness, prostate trouble, Parkinson's disease, spinal injury, insanity—the "Goat Gland Surgeon" claimed to cure all. Critical scrutiny also grew. Early challenges came from the *Kansas City Star,* but dissatisfied patients found publicity embarrassing. Brinkley's vast popular support and political connections delayed court challenges, but in 1930 the Kansas Medical Association took actions leading to the revocation of Brinkley's license. A month later the Federal Radio Commission revoked KFKB's broadcasting license for not serving the public interest. The resourceful surgeon barely slowed. While the appeals dragged on, his assistants operated at Milford, and Brinkley broadcast by telephone through a Mexican station.

Realizing Kansas was a lost cause, Brinkley relocated to Del Rio, Texas, in 1932. He shifted from gland transplantation to prostate surgery, making similar curative claims, and broadcast from a nearby Mexican radio station (XER) out of federal jurisdiction. The Texas hospital thrived for a time but ultimately succumbed to critical and competitive pressures.

In 1937 Brinkley returned to Arkansas, purchased St. Luke's Hospital at 1924 Schiller Street in Little Rock, and opened the Romulus Drug Store at Wright and Schiller Streets. He bought a former Shriner country club on Arch Street Pike, sixteen miles south of Little Rock, a picturesque stone building surrounded by the former golf course where his Little Rock patients came to recover in comfort.

Brinkley's hospitals boosted the depressed city economy with well-paying jobs. Hotels filled with prospective patients, and farmers gained new markets. Brinkley's staff performed the surgery while he concentrated on administrative, advertising, and legal duties, flying from Del Rio weekly by private plane.

Brinkley's downfall was swift, unmerciful, and self-inflicted. In 1938 he filed a libel suit against Dr. Morris Fishbein, editor of the *Journal of the American Medical Association*, for an article in *Hygeia* which called Brinkley a charlatan. When courts ruled that this was, in fact, the case, Brinkley was inundated with lawsuits. By February 1941 he was bankrupt. The Arkansas properties were lost: the city property was sold in 1944; the country club became a Baptist State Hospital convalescent home and later the Marylake Carmelite Monastery.

Mail fraud indictments against Brinkley's inner circle came in September 1941, but he eluded the charges. His leg was amputated because of a blood clot that month, and he died of heart failure in San Antonio, Texas, the following spring, leaving a wife and son. He is buried in Memphis, Tennessee.

Brash and unapologetic, Brinkley used mass media to take quackery to new depths. His legacy includes tighter regulation of medicine and broadcasting.

[See Gerald Carson, *The Roguish World of Doctor Brinkley* (1960); Clement Wood, *The Life of a Man* (1934); Albert J. Schneider, "'That Troublesome Old Cocklebur': John R. Brinkley and the Medical Profession of Arkansas, 1937–1942," *AHQ* 35 (Spring 1976): 27–46; the *Arkansas Democrat*, 1939–42; and the *Arkansas Gazette*, 1939–42.]

WARD MILLER

BRITT, ELTON (June 27, 1913–June 23, 1972), singer and musician, was born in Zack, Arkansas, to James M. and Martella Baker. James Elton Baker was his real name. The youngest of his mother's five children, he was a sickly child who wasn't expected to live. For that reason he wasn't named until he was over a year old, and then he was dubbed James after his father and Elton in honor of Dr. Elton Wilson, who managed to keep him alive during the first year of his life. Elton was what is now known as a "blue baby" and was plagued with heart trouble all his life.

The Bakers were a musical family, so it is hardly surprising that Elton also acquired a love of music. He started playing guitar at age ten with a $4.95 instrument purchased by mail from Montgomery Ward. Later he was impressed by the records of country singer Jimmie Rodgers, which inspired him to learn how to yodel. Eventually, he became renowned for his ability to sustain his yodel an unusually long time, enabled by breath control he reportedly learned as a kid while swimming submerged for several minutes at a time.

Elton's chance for stardom came in 1930 when he was hired to replace Hugh Ashley, a singer and guitarist from Marshall, Arkansas, who played with the popular country western group, the Beverly Hill Billies. What was intended as a six-week stay in Los Angeles turned out to be the first step in a career that lasted more than four decades.

While with the Beverly Hill Billies, Elton acquired the name Britt, though the exact source of the name is unknown. During this tenure he also entered into the first of his four marriages. His first wife, Margaret, was an eighteen-year-old relative of his brother Vern's wife when they wed in 1933. The following year Margaret was killed in an automobile accident. In 1936 Elton married Jean Kirkpatrick, a Canadian citizen, who died in childbirth in 1940. His third wife, Penny, was a long-time Britt fan whom he wed in 1942. Their marriage lasted almost fifteen years. In 1956 he wed Janet Counts, a woman twenty-five years his junior. Their marriage was dissolved several years before Britt's death. He had children by each wife, except the first, but none followed him into the world of music.

During the first half of the 1930s the Beverly Hill Billies made a number of 78 rpm records and Britt was probably on some of those, but it is impossible to determine which ones. His first documented recordings were in 1933 for the Conqueror label as part of a group called the Wenatchee Mountaineers. In June 1934 Britt's first significant recording, "Chime Bells," was made with this band. This original composition of his would be a big hit for him in 1948, but the earlier version is the superior one.

According to an apocryphal story Britt was offered a lucrative choice in 1935. As the legend has it, two artists were given their choice between a record contract and a movie contract. Elton, being the bigger name, opted for the record deal while the other artist, Gene Autry, took the movie contract. Whatever the merits of the legend, Britt did sign with RCA Victor in 1937 and remained with the company for twenty-two years. During this time he had a number of hit records, including "Someday" (1940), "Born to Lose" (1943), "Detour" (1946), "Candy Kisses" (1949), and "Quicksilver" (1950). But without question, his biggest hit was "There's a Star-Spangled Banner Waving Somewhere," which by 1944 earned the first gold record by a country music star (there had been million-selling country records earlier, but that was before gold records were awarded). There is dispute about how successful the record was; estimates of its sales range from just over a million to four million. Possibly both estimates are correct: the latter number likely reflects total sales over the several years it remained in catalog, while the former number probably reflects sales during the record's initial period of popularity.

Britt appeared in at least three movies but none of them advanced his career. During the 1950s he made a habit of retiring and then unretiring. During one break from show business he did uranium mining in the West. In 1960 he retired once again, this time to wage an unsuccessful campaign for president on the Democratic ticket. He then returned to entertaining and in 1968 had his last major hit with a seven-minute yodeling song, "The Jimmie Rodgers Blues." On June 22, 1972, Britt suffered a heart attack while riding in a car; he passed away the next day. He was buried in the Odd Fellows Cemetery in Broad Top, Pennsylvania. Later, a monument listing his achievements was erected over his grave.

[Old recordings by Elton Britt can sometimes be found in used record stores. His "There's a Star-Spangled Banner Waving Somewhere" is in the *Smithsonian Collection of Classic Country Music*.]

W. K. McNeil

BROOKS, IDA JOSEPHINE (Apr. 28, 1853– Mar. 13, 1939), teacher and psychiatrist, was born in Muscatine, Iowa, the fourth of six children of Joseph Brooks, a Methodist minister, and Elizabeth Goodaugh. The family moved to Arkansas in 1870. In 1872 her father ran for governor of Arkansas against Elisha Baxter. The race was hotly contested, and both candidates claimed victory. This led to an armed conflict called the Brooks-Baxter war, with Baxter the winner.

Ida Jo Brooks was a woman of stately, buxom build, always formally dressed in a lacy blouse, floor-length skirt, pompadour hairdo, and rimless spectacles. Her manner was stern and forceful, at times intimidating, but she was warmhearted.

Brooks was a Methodist and a member of the Women's Christian Temperance Union. She also held membership in all of the elite women's clubs of Little Rock, including the Daughters of the American Revolution and the Women's City Club. Her club connections gave her opportunity for public speaking and association with prominent influential women. She never married, but lived with her sister, Frances B. Kerrott.

Teaching was Brooks's first love. She received her bachelor's degree at old Little Rock University. In 1877 she was elected president of the Arkansas Teachers' Association, the first woman to attain this position. From 1883 to 1887 she taught mathematics at Little Rock University.

In 1887 she applied for admission to the University of Arkansas Medical School and was rejected, leading to one of her ardent campaigns. In a speech before the Columbia Club she said: "I believed Arkansas wanted women physicians, but why send abroad for them? Why not educate them here? Is our medical school not a branch of the state University? Then should it not admit women students? There is one improvement which should be made in our state and I urge the women, by all means, to have the ... legislature make it."

She kept applying to medical schools until she was accepted at a Boston school, probably homeopathic, where she received a degree in 1891. After this she served house staff appointments in five northeastern cities, solidifying her medical knowledge and judgments. Returning to Little Rock in 1900, she established a private practice specializing in diseases of children.

Brooks espoused homeopathy, a system of medicine

that treats illness by administering small doses of remedies that in larger doses would produce symptoms of the disease being treated. She was not accepted warmly by the medical establishment. Records of the county and state medical societies reveal no membership in either. She formed her own group, the Women's Medical Club of Arkansas, and also associated with other homeopaths.

She became more and more concerned about problems in the care of mental patients. She said in a speech before the Columbia Club: "I visited the State Hospital. The genial superintendent kindly showed us through the establishment. He opened the door to the men's wards and said: I can't take you through here. The question in my mind was: Were men physicians stopped at the entrance to women's wards? It is a strange and pitiful fact that when reason has fled, women become more degraded than men. For the sake of propriety, in the name of Christian love, let us give to our sisters who are worse than sick, worse than dead, a woman physician to be near them in their utter helplessness." In 1903 she joined the house staff of Middleborough (Massachusetts) Mental Hospital to specialize in psychiatry. She returned to Little Rock in 1906 to become Arkansas's first woman psychiatrist in private practice.

In 1907 Brooks was hired as assistant medical inspector for the Little Rock school district. In addition to physical exams she administered psychological tests and gave hearing and vision tests. She negotiated with the school board to provide glasses for the indigent. For the mentally retarded she campaigned for a special classroom with a special teacher, resulting in the founding of the Exceptional School in 1913.

In 1914 she received an appointment at the University of Arkansas Medical School as associate professor, lecturing on social hygiene (practical matters pertaining to maintenance of health such as diet, cleanliness, and emotional well-being).

With the advent of World War I, Brooks obtained an appointment as acting assistant surgeon in the United States Public Health Service and served in uniform as psychiatric consultant at Camp Pike, an army post at North Little Rock. After the war she was appointed psychiatrist for the Little Rock school district and for the juvenile court. She held these positions from 1919 until she retired in 1933.

In 1920 Brooks was nominated for state superintendent of public instruction on the Republican ticket, but she was ruled off the ballot. It was the opinion of the attorney general that women could vote but were not eligible to hold office.

Ida Jo Brooks died after a long illness precipitated by a hip fracture and is buried in St. Louis in Bellefontaine Cemetery.

[A file at UAMS archives includes short biographies of Brooks, letters, and other material. See the *Arkansas Democrat*, Apr. 9, 1915, Mar. 13, 1939 (obituary); the *Arkansas Gazette*, June 6, 1920, Mar. 14, 1939; and the *Arkansas News* (Spring 1990).

See also L. B. Kennan, "Three Women," *Journal of Arkansas Education* (Mar. 1957): 8–10; and F. O. Henker, "Ida Jo Brooks," *Journal of the Arkansas Medical Society*, vol. 80 (June 1983–May 1984). This entry is also based on the author's interviews with Elizabeth Fletcher (1984), Mary Burt Nash (1997), and Michael B. Dougan (1997).]

FRED O. HENKER

BROOKS, JOSEPH (Nov. 1, 1821–Apr. 30, 1877), clergyman and politician, was born at Cincinnati, Ohio. His parents' names are unknown. He studied for the ministry at Indiana Asbury University and was ordained in the Methodist Episcopal Church in 1840. He rode circuit in Virginia and then worked in Illinois and Iowa before moving in 1856 to St. Louis. There he became editor of the *Central Christian Advocate*, a Methodist journal with a strong antislavery editorial position, and engaged in business as a cotton merchant.

His career suggests that he not only opposed slavery but also had a real concern with the plight of slaves. When the Civil War broke out, Brooks was appointed chaplain of the First Missouri Artillery, but resigned to take up the chaplaincy of the Eleventh Missouri Infantry. In the summer of 1862 he changed units again when he became chaplain of his brother William's Thirty-third Missouri Infantry.

Brooks believed that abolition should be a major war goal and advocated using freed slaves as soldiers. Extensive efforts to organize African-American regiments began in the Mississippi River region in the spring of 1863, and in the fall Brooks transferred, along with his son Joseph Jr., to the Third Arkansas Volunteers (Fifty-sixth United States Colored Infantry) at St. Louis. He accompanied the regiment to Arkansas and remained with it until he resigned in February 1865.

Brooks left the army to take up a government lease on a seized plantation in Phillips County. Little is known about his career as a planter, but he appears to have established a good rapport with his free workers. In 1867 he became active in the organization of the Republican Party in eastern Arkansas. He gained a reputation as a flamboyant speaker and was popular among freedmen because he advocated equal rights for them. Apparently Brooks hoped to destroy the state's old aristocracy by seizing their lands and dividing it among poor Arkansans. He was elected to the state constitutional convention in 1868; there he supported the writing of a constitution that would have granted African-American freedmen full equality.

In the summer of 1868 he was nearly killed when he and Congressman James Hinds were on the road canvassing for the candidacy of Ulysses S. Grant for president. A group of men attacked them, and Hinds died as a result. The experience may have radicalized Brooks. When he replaced J. C. Tobias in the House of Representatives of the general assembly in 1868, he vigorously supported Governor Powell Clayton's efforts at using the militia to suppress violence directed against the freedmen and their Republican allies.

In 1868 Brooks moved to Little Rock, where he was named revenue collector for the Treasury Department's Second District of Arkansas. The position promised a steady salary and a base for continued political activity.

After 1869 Brooks grew more and more critical of the administration of Governor Clayton and expressed particular concern with its fiscal policies. The fact that he had secured political rewards for his loyalty before suggests that his break with Clayton was based on his ideals rather than personal grudges. For a time he became associated with the state's Liberal Republican Party, organized by many of the wartime Unionists. Increasingly, however, Brooks personally became the focus of those elements within the Arkansas Republican Party who opposed the Clayton (or Minstrel) faction.

In 1871 Brooks announced his candidacy for governor. Promising honesty in office and an end to prescriptive voter restrictions, Brooks quickly developed support from his traditional base of strength among African Americans, Unionists, and some members of the Conservative or Democratic Party who thought his position on voting offered them the quickest way back to power. Brooks's supporters were called "brindletails," supposedly because their leader's speaking style was likened to the voice of a brindletail bull. In November 1872 the regulars ran Elisha Baxter and, following a canvass filled with violence and fraud, election officials controlled by the regular party machine announced that Baxter had won. Brooks and his supporters refused to accept the results.

For two years Brooks appealed the results to the legislature and the state's courts. A break between Governor Baxter and Republican leaders over railroad funding made it possible for Brooks to secure a ruling in the Pulaski County Circuit Court declaring him governor. This time, Baxter's supporters refused to accept the results, and for a time it appeared that only violence would determine the victor. President Grant intervened, urging Brooks to disarm his supporters and step down. This prevented an even more serious confrontation.

Brooks appears to have had no stomach for further conflict following his abandonment by the president. Grant repaid Brooks by naming him postmaster at Little Rock in March 1875. Brooks and his family settled down in their home at the corner of Fourth and Izard Streets to lead a quiet life. He died in Little Rock. His body was returned to St. Louis to Bellefontaine Cemetery.

[There is no biography of Joseph Brooks. His political career may be followed to some degree in James H. Atkinson, "The Arkansas Gubernatorial Campaign and the Election of 1872," *AHQ* 1 (Dec. 1942): 307–21; Earl F. Woodward, "The Brooks and Baxter War in Arkansas, 1872–1874," *AHQ* 30 (Winter 1971): 315–36; and John M. Harrell, *The Brooks and Baxter War: A History of the Reconstruction Period in Arkansas* (1893). Most of the rest of his career can be pieced together from newspaper reports, including his obituary in the *Arkansas Gazette*, May 1, 1877.]

CARL H. MONEYHON

BROUGH, CHARLES HILLMAN (July 9, 1876–Dec. 26, 1935), educator, orator, and governor of Arkansas, was born in Clinton, Mississippi, the son of Charles Milton Brough and Flora M. Thompson. Soon after his birth the family moved to Utah, where a second son, Knight Milton, was born. When their mother's health began to decline, the boys were returned to Clinton in the care of her sister, Adelia Hillman, and her husband, Dr. Walter Hillman, owner and president of Central Female Institute at Clinton. Following Mrs. Brough's death in 1885, the boys remained with the Hillmans.

Charles Hillman Brough attended Mississippi College in Clinton, which, like the Female Institute, was a Baptist institution. He maintained a high scholastic average and excelled in oratorical contests. He graduated with high honors in 1894, and after spending a year with his father in Utah, began graduate work at Johns Hopkins University in Baltimore. In 1898 he received his Ph.D. in history, economics, and jurisprudence. His doctoral dissertation, *Irrigation in Utah*, was published by the Johns Hopkins Press and reviewed favorably.

From 1898 to 1901 Brough taught at Mississippi College. A demanding but popular instructor, he taught a variety of courses, including history, economics, and German, and published several scholarly articles. He also delivered scores of speeches for commencement exercises, Sunday School conventions, memorial celebrations, and the like. Throughout his life he was a leading layman of the Baptist church.

In 1901 Brough resigned to study law at the University of Mississippi. Although he graduated with distinction, he never practiced law. In 1903 he joined the faculty of the University of Arkansas at Fayetteville as professor and chair of the Department of Political Economy. Brough was popular, as he had been in Mississippi, and taught a variety of courses, including economics, sociology, and transportation history. He continued to publish articles, deliver speeches, and support the Baptist church. In 1908 he married Anne Wade Roark, an educated and refined woman from Franklin, Kentucky. No children were born of their marriage.

In 1916 Brough ran successfully for the Democratic nomination for governor and easily defeated his Republican opponent in the general election. He was reelected in 1918. A progressive governor, Brough persuaded the legislature to enact a number of reforms in education, public welfare, prohibition, and road building. Although woman suffrage was not a key plank in his progressive agenda, he supported a measure giving women the right to vote in primary elections and later pushed successfully for Arkansas's ratification of the Nineteenth Amendment. One of his disappointments was the voters' failure to ratify a new state constitution in 1918.

On racial questions Brough was conservative and paternalistic; he supported white supremacy but wanted blacks to achieve a better living standard. During his second term a race riot erupted in Phillips County, resulting in the deaths of five whites and at least twenty-five blacks. After the crisis eased, Brough appointed a special commission charged with finding ways to secure greater harmony between the races.

Brough supported most of President Woodrow Wilson's policies and was an enthusiastic backer of his wartime leadership. During World War I the Arkansas governor delivered hundreds of patriotic speeches, rallying popular support of bond drives and other "home front" efforts.

After his terms as governor ended in 1921, Brough was seriously ill for several weeks. Upon recovery, he began working for the Arkansas Advancement Association, a kind of state chamber of commerce. His job was to advertise Arkansas through speeches, publications, and other means. In addition he followed a busy schedule of lecturing, mostly in summers, for "traveling Chautauqua" agencies, and for a time was billed as a headliner. As publicity director for Arkansas, Brough was doing what he had often done as governor—promoting a positive image of the state and dispelling the "Arkansas hillbilly" stereotype. He boosted Arkansas while on the Chautauqua circuit, prefacing his lectures with remarks extolling the state and its resources.

Between 1928 and 1932 Brough served as president of Central Baptist College in Conway and then as a special lecturer for the University of Arkansas extension program. In 1928 he provoked criticism from some conservative Baptist preachers and laymen by making speeches on behalf of Democratic presidential candidate Al Smith, a Roman Catholic, who favored repeal of prohibition, a position contrary to that of the State Baptist Convention. Fundamentalists also criticized Brough for his opposition to an anti-evolution measure on the ballot in Arkansas in 1928.

In 1932 Brough sought the Democratic nomination for the United States Senate. There were six other candidates, including the incumbent, Senator Hattie Caraway, who had attained the seat in a special election. Senator Caraway, with the crucial assistance of Senator Huey P. Long of Louisiana, won the nomination. Brough subsequently worked briefly as an insurance salesman, and then, accompanied by Mrs. Brough, went to Washington to serve as chairman of the Virginia-District of Columbia Boundary Commission. A few weeks after submitting the commission's report to Congress, he died suddenly from a heart attack. He is buried at Roselawn Memorial Park in Little Rock.

[See Foy Lisenby, *Charles Hillman Brough: A Biography* (1966).]

FOY LISENBY

BROWN, FLOYD B. (Apr. 27, 1891–Sept. 11, 1961), teacher and founder of an agricultural school, was born in Stampley, Jefferson County, Mississippi, to Charley Brown, a tenant farmer, and Janie Brown (maiden name unknown), a housewife.

Floyd Brown was the second oldest of ten children, and schooling for him was limited. He was just a young lad when his father hired him out as a day laborer to help support his younger sisters and brothers. His work took him from the cotton fields of Mississippi to the sugar cane plantations of Louisiana. In 1911 he opened and operated a pressing shop (clothes cleaner) in West Helena, Arkansas, but because of his inability to read and write well, his venture into business failed.

Brown's dream was to get an education. His mother had told him about a person who had founded a school in Tuskegee, Alabama, and who would allow anyone to attend who wanted to learn and was willing to work for an education. At age twenty-one, with no more than a fifth-grade education, he entered Tuskegee Institute, whose founder was Booker T. Washington.

While Brown was at Tuskegee Institute, both his mother and Dr. Washington passed away. In 1915 he was one of several students chosen to sell books on the life of Dr. Washington during the summer vacation. He was assigned the eastern part of Arkansas. In his travels he came across the community of Fargo, where the people were farmers, mostly black and poor, tied to the soil. When the book-selling tour was over, he returned to school, but he never forgot about Fargo. He vowed he would return one day, because that was the place where he wanted to start his life's work.

In 1917 he graduated with a high-school certificate. In August 1918 he was ordained a Baptist minister. He wanted to go to Africa and be a missionary worker, but Fargo stayed on his mind.

In 1919 he returned to Fargo with $2.85, his certificate, and faith in God. He was determined to build a school. The people of Fargo and nearby Zent communities were enthusiastic about his idea and ready to help. He was able to purchase on credit twenty acres of land from a local minister, the Reverend E. M. Garrison, and made an agreement to pay for the land after harvest the next year. On Thanksgiving Day 1919, ground was broken for the first building of the Fargo Agricultural School. The people of Fargo contributed lumber and other supplies as well as labor. The one-room school opened for classes January 1, 1920, with fifteen students and one teacher, Ruth Mahon.

Brown and Lillie Epps married on March 5, 1921; there were no children.

For thirty years Brown maintained the school. He traveled to the northern states seeking donations from white supporters. No student was turned away for lack of funds, because the school was modeled after Tuskegee Institute; students could work and earn an education.

Shaping character was an important part of the school's mission. Brown taught a class in common sense, which he defined as doing the right thing at the right time. He often taught through aphorisms such as "You can make a difference," "Cast down your buckets where you are," "Greatness comes through service," "Service comes through work," and "Work comes through efforts." The school motto was Work Will Win. The boys and girls wore uniforms so that no one would appear less fortunate than another.

The students attended classes eight hours a day. They studied algebra, biology, American and Negro history, English, literature, math, science, physics, civics, psychology, and chemistry. The girls learned sewing, cooking, homemaking, food preparation, and arts and crafts. The boys learned agriculture, carpentry, plumbing, and furniture making. Together they made or grew most of what they needed. All worked to keep the campus beautiful as well as self-sufficient.

Brown educated a generation of rural black boys and girls who would not otherwise have finished high school. Some of them became doctors, nurses, ministers, mayors, lawyers, teachers, principals, professors, and musicians.

During the years the school was open, Brown made many friends. There are letters from governors of Arkansas dating back to 1920, praising him for his dedicated service. He was well liked by everyone who knew him.

Brown's friends often asked, "What will happen to the school when you are old and in poor health?" His reply was, "Let me do my best today, and tomorrow will take care of me." In May 1949 the last graduation was held at the Fargo Agricultural School. Brown sold the buildings and all the land for a modest fee to the state of Arkansas to use as a training school for black girls. In 1919 he had started his school with one building and twenty acres of land; when he sold it to the state, the campus consisted of fourteen buildings and eight hundred acres of land.

Floyd Brown received honorary degrees from

Shorter College, Little Rock (1935); Tuskegee Institute (1940); Arkansas Baptist College (1944); and Arkansas Mechanical and Normal College (1950). He was listed in *Who's Who in Colored America* in 1950 and named Citizen of the Year in Brinkley, Arkansas. In 1958 the state of Arkansas built and dedicated the Floyd Brown Building in Fargo, which stands on the site of the Arkansas Land and Farm Development Corporation. The Fargo Agricultural Museum is there.

Brown served as president of the Arkansas Colored Teachers' Association, founder and president of the Negro Farmers' Conference of Arkansas, and chairman of the Tri-State Farm Day. He founded the Floyd Brown Benevolent Association.

In March 1949, the Wings over Jordan Choir, directed by the Reverend Glenn T. Settle, presented a program in words and music honoring Brown's work on the radio over the Mutual Broadcasting System.

Brown died in Pine Bluff and is buried in P. K Miller Cemetery there.

[The Fargo Agricultural School Museum at Brinkley exhibits and maintains artifacts from the school, including furniture, letters, photographs, and books. The author wishes to thank Elmer C. Burnett for his help in preparing this article.]

GERALDINE PURCELL DAVIDSON

BRYANT, PAUL WILLIAM (Sept. 11, 1913–Jan. 26, 1983), college football coach, was raised on a farm in Moro Bottom, near Fordyce, Arkansas. He was one of twelve children born to Wilson Monroe Bryant and Ida Kilgore.

Bryant was farm tough and big, standing six feet tall by age twelve, when he accepted a dare from his pals to wrestle a carnival bear for a dollar a minute and earned the nickname "Bear," which stuck with him for life. Bryant later said, "Hell, for a dollar a minute I wanted to hold him 'til he died."

He joined the Fordyce Redbugs football team as an eighth grader and later earned All-State honors as a tackle on two state championship teams. He signed a football grant with the University of Alabama and played on the school's 1934 team when it won a national championship at the Rose Bowl, the first of seven such titles he helped to win for the Crimson Tide. In his senior season he played one game with a broken leg.

Bryant joined the Alabama coaching staff and spent four years there before moving to Vanderbilt for two seasons. During World War II he served in the U.S. Navy

in Africa and as a physical training instructor in North Carolina. After the war he was named head coach at Maryland. He started his thirty-eight-year coaching career with a 6-3-1 record.

Following a dispute with the president at Maryland, Bryant moved to Kentucky as head coach where he remained for eight seasons (1946–53), winning sixty games and the school's only Southeastern Conference championship. In 1954 he moved on to Texas A & M, where he earned the reputation of a demanding mentor when about a hundred of his returning players quit during rugged preseason practice. His squad of twenty-seven players managed only one win that year, but his next three teams went 24-5-2 and won a Southwest Conference title.

Bryant returned to his alma mater in 1957, becoming Alabama's head coach after the Crimson Tide had experienced its worst three seasons in history. He turned the team around, going 5-4-1 his first season as he introduced his players to the same gang-tackling, hard-hitting style he had used at A & M. He promised his first freshman class that if they did everything he asked of them, they could win a national championship, and together they delivered, claiming in 1961 the first of six Bryant national titles. Other titles followed in 1964, 1965, 1973, 1978, and 1979. His teams were famous for their quickness, toughness, thorough preparation, perseverance, and discipline. "I try to teach players to show class, to have pride and to display character," he said. "I think football—winning games—takes care of itself if you do that."

Bryant's teams went to a record twenty-four consecutive bowl games. The Crimson Tide averaged 9.3 wins per season and became the first team in history to win more than a hundred games in a decade (103-16-1 in the 1970s). Bryant teams won fifteen conference championships, and Alabama teams won 124 games during his last twelve seasons. Alabama was the nation's college win leader during Bryant's last five seasons (50-9-1), his last ten years (103-16-1), and his entire career at the school (232-46-9).

Bryant's career record of 323-85-17 ranks him the winningest coach in Division I football. He was named national Coach of the Year three times. His six national championships, twenty-nine bowl appearances, and fifteen conference titles are also records. "If anybody has to be the winningest coach, heck, it might as well be me," he said.

Bear Bryant was inducted into the Arkansas Sports

Hall of Fame in 1964, the Alabama Sports Hall of Fame in 1969, and the National Football Foundation College Football Hall of Fame in 1986. He was a member of the *Sports Illustrated* Silver Anniversary All-America team in 1960; Kentucky's Citizen of the Year in 1950; and University Administrator of the Year in Alabama in 1973. He served as president of the American Football Coaches Association in 1972. President Reagan awarded him the presidential Medal of Freedom posthumously in 1983, the same year the American Football Coaches Association recognized his service with the Stagg Award.

Bryant loved football: "Football has never been just a game to me—never.... I knew it from the time it got me out of the Moro Bottom, and that's one of the things that motivated me—that fear of going back to plowing and driving those mules and chopping cotton for 50 cents a day."

He passed along the lessons he had learned, saying, "Football teaches a boy to win, to work for maybe the first time in his life and to sacrifice and suck up his guts when he's behind. It's the only place left where you can learn that." Forty-eight of his former players and/or assistants became head coaches.

Bryant bowed out of coaching on December 29, 1982, as his Alabama team defeated Illinois 21-15 in the Liberty Bowl. He died suddenly of a heart attack a few weeks later.

He and his wife, Mary Harmon Black, had a daughter, Mae Martin Bryant Tyson, and a son, Paul W. Bryant Jr.

[See Paul W. Bryant and John Underwood, *Bear* (1977), and Delbert Reed, *Paul "Bear" Bryant: What Made Him a Winner* (1995). The Paul W. Bryant Museum is on the campus of the University of Alabama, Tuscaloosa.]

DELBERT REED

BUCHANAN, HERBERT EARLE (Oct. 4, 1881–Jan. 17, 1974), astronomer and mathematician, was born in Cane Hill to James A. Buchanan, a farmer, surveyor, and Presbyterian minister, and Susan Clark Williamson. In 1902 Herbert earned a bachelor of arts degree with honors in mathematics from the University of Arkansas, Fayetteville. During his senior year, the death of a professor gave him the opportunity to teach mathematics, launching a career of fifty-two years' service to more than ten thousand students.

His father's apple business was prosperous enough to permit Buchanan to enroll in graduate study at the University of Chicago in 1902. There he came to admire the German mathematician Heinrich Maschke, with whom he studied advanced integral calculus and plane geometry. Later Buchanan became the protégé of the highly regarded teacher Forest R. Moulton, who introduced him to mechanics and astronomy. In 1903 Buchanan completed his master of arts degree at Chicago.

In 1904 Herbert Buchanan married Ada Tilley, his longtime sweetheart and daughter of a well-to-do Arkansas farmer. Four children were born to their marriage.

After teaching for two years, Buchanan returned to Chicago to resume his studies with Moulton, who encouraged his interest in astronomy. In 1908 he moved from the mathematics department to the University of Chicago's Yerkes Observatory, which at the time housed the world's largest refracting telescope. There he gained valuable experience in observational astronomy. The calculations he made as part of his doctoral thesis were published twice by the University of Chicago as *Periodic Oscillations of Three Finite Masses about the Langrangian Circular Solutions* (1909; 1923).

In 1911 he joined the faculty of the University of Tennessee, where he became a full professor after a year. Soon after he arrived he was named chairman of the athletic committee and was asked to clear up a mess in the athletic program's management and finances. He restored order so quickly that he gained a reputation as a sports reformer. He was elected a regional vice president of the new National Collegiate Athletic Association and was one of the founders of the Southern Athletic Conference.

In 1915 Buchanan joined several other noted mathematicians to found the Mathematics Association of America.

After America's entry into World War I, conscription emptied Buchanan's classroom. He followed his students into national service, volunteering to direct the YMCA's program of basic education for American soldiers awaiting transport to France. With A. I. Roehm, he wrote a primer entitled *Camp Arithmetic for American Soldiers* (1917). The YMCA eventually sent him to investigate irregularities in its program in France. As the war ended he stayed on as professor of mathematics in the A. E. F. University at Beaune, where his students were mostly artillery officers preparing to return to universities in the United States.

After the war Buchanan returned to Tennessee for one final year, during which he sent E. P. Lane, one of his brightest students, on scholarship to Chicago. Lane ultimately became head of the mathematics department there. The Lane case established a pattern of mentoring. Eventually he sent more then twenty of his protégés to Chicago, every one of whom became head of a university department. Among them were some of the leading mathematicians in the world.

Buchanan accepted an offer to head the mathematics department at Tulane University in 1920. Soon after arriving he published the first of seven textbooks. This, together with his reputation as a teacher, won the recognition of his old university. Arkansas awarded him an honorary doctor of laws degree in 1928. At Tulane his humor, devotion to students, and reputation for some classic campus pranks won him the nickname "Dr. Buck."

His textbooks—among them *A Brief Course in Advanced Algebra, The Elements of Analytic Geometry,* and *Plane Trigonometry*—were widely adopted in American colleges. He also published twenty-five research papers, which formed the basis of his reputation as a scholar. In 1937 he was honored as Tulane's first Distinguished Professor.

Buchanan's important scholarship lay in the field of celestial mechanics and focused on the stability of the orbits of heavenly bodies. In large part, his work advanced a mathematical understanding of what was called "the three-bodies problem." The issue was whether an orbiting body, if disturbed, would merely oscillate in its orbit or go away and never return.

Buchanan retired twice, once in 1947 and again in 1949. The second time, he said, "finally took." First, though, his devotion to the Presbyterian church led him to accept the interim presidency of the College of the Ozarks in Clarksville, Arkansas. He spent two years restoring the institution's financial and academic foundations.

He devoted much of his retirement to writing his memoirs and to restoring the farm and antebellum house that were the legacy of his wife's family. He was active in civic and church affairs, corresponded with former students, and participated in experimental projects at the University of Arkansas's College of Agriculture. Of his long life, he said he regretted only that the priorities of his retirement made it impossible for him to keep abreast of rapid developments in mathematics. He died at Fayetteville from injuries he suffered in a fall on icy pavement.

[A collection of Buchanan's papers is preserved in the John Tilley House, Prairie Grove, Arkansas, including correspondence, drafts of published works, clippings, and miscellany. Others of his papers are in the Special Collections, Howard-Tilton Memorial Library, Tulane University, New Orleans.

See also H. E. Buchanan, *Memoirs,* ed. Jean Newhouse (Fayetteville, Ark.: *Washington County Historical Society Bulletin* 59, 1974); Thomas Rothrock, "Dr. Buck from Cane Hill," *AHQ* 22 (1963): 332–37; *Newsweek* (June 6, 1949): 78; the *Arkansas Alumnus* (1949): 12–13; and the *Tulanian* 22 (1949): 2.]

EDWARD A. ALLEN

BURNS, BOB (Aug. 2, 1890–Feb. 2, 1956), radio and motion picture comedian whose given name was Robin Burn, was born in Greenwood, Arkansas, to William Robert Burn, railroad civil engineer, and Emma Needham, homemaker. When Burns was three years old, the family moved to Van Buren, Arkansas, where he grew up.

In 1905 the fifteen-year-old Burns created an oddly shaped horn from a length of gas pipe and dubbed it the "bazooka": "I picked up a piece of music and rolled it up and slid it inside the pipe. I found I could make about three fuzzy bass notes. I found another piece of gas pipe and slid it inside the first one and then I soldered a whiskey funnel on the end of it." He later said the name was derived from the word "bazoo," meaning a windy fellow. Sounding like a "wounded moose," the instrument became his trademark as an entertainer, and the term "bazooka" became a part of American lore.

Burns began engineering studies in 1909 at the University of Arkansas at Fayetteville, but dropped out a year later to briefly join the Black Cat Minstrels, a traveling vaudeville show, with his only sibling, his older brother Farrar.

For the next seven years, Burns crisscrossed the South and Midwest in search of success in vaudeville, performing odd jobs along the way as a surveyor, streetcar conductor, steamship purser, and farmhand. Frustrated, he finally landed a full-time job in advertising with the *Chicago Herald* in 1915.

At the beginning of World War I in 1917, Burns joined the U.S. Marine Corps, serving as a top-ranked rifle instructor at Parris Island, South Carolina. After forming the USMC Jazz Band, Burns was sent with his band to entertain Allied troops in France from 1919 to 1921. At war's end he held the rank of sergeant in the Eleventh Regiment.

In 1921 while performing in New York nightclubs, Burns met and married Elizabeth Fisher. They had one child, Bob Burns Jr. Burns teamed up with fellow vaudevillian Claude West to perform blackface minstrel shows under the stage name "Burns and West" during the winter months from 1922 to 1930. To make ends meet in the summer months, Burns operated a traveling carnival ride.

As vaudeville's popularity waned in the early 1930s, Bob and his family headed for Hollywood, California, where he found bit parts in movies. Following some limited success as a radio character known as "Soda Pop," Burns wangled a spot on Paul Whiteman's national radio program in New York in 1935, where he became an instant hit. Returning to Hollywood later that year, Burns joined crooner Bing Crosby's radio show on the National Broadcasting Company's "Kraft Music Hall."

Burns was a national radio star from 1935 to 1940 with his own show on NBC. He was known for his fanciful yarns about the foibles of "Aunt Dutty," "Uncle Hink," and "Grandpa Snazzy" back in Van Buren, fictional characters based loosely on his hometown family and friends. His weekly comedy routines, punctuated with blasts on his famous "bazooka," made Van Buren a household name all across the country.

During this time, Burns starred in a dozen feature films, along with such co-stars as Bing Crosby and the big-mouthed comedienne Martha Raye, as well as actors Joel McRae and Susan Hayward.

From 1941 to 1947 Burns starred in the weekly radio drama series "The Arkansas Traveler."

His wife, Elizabeth, died in 1936; a year later he married Harriet Madelia, with whom he had three more children: Barbara Ann, William Robin, and Stephen Foster.

From 1943 to 1945 Burns appeared in numerous USO shows entertaining World War II recruits at induction centers all across the United States. Around this time a new hand-held rocket weapon was developed for military use. A Marine Corps regiment christened the antitank weapon the "bazooka," because its blunderbuss appearance was similar to Burns's famous musical instrument.

In 1947 Burns retired from show business to devote his attention to his 503-acre ranch in Canoga Park, California: "We raise almost everything we eat, except salt and pepper." He designed the family's twenty-three-room U-shaped home and even built the furniture to go in it. Burns was also an expert machinist, animal breeder, and crop farmer whose interests included astronomy, photography, fishing, and especially skeet shooting.

He spent the last decade of his life quietly working his land: "I've tried the life of a soldier . . . and I've done my share of trouping in show business. But all that couldn't take that hankering out of me to get back and dig in the soil like we used to do when I was a boy in Van Buren." He is buried in Encino, California.

[An exhibit of Bob Burns memorabilia is on permanent display at the Chamber of Commerce, Van Buren, Arkansas. The Chamber of Commerce maintains the William R. Burns family collection of clippings, letters, articles, and photographs.]

MARJORIE ARMSTRONG

BUSEY, SAMUEL T. (1867–Nov. 24, 1962), physician and oil pioneer, was born in Illinois. He came to El Dorado, Union County, Arkansas, in 1920.

Trained as a physician, his early energies were devoted to researching tropical diseases in South and Central America. His ability to speak six languages helped him greatly in his endeavors.

Dr. Busey said, "I was practicing medicine in Old Mexico at the time when the first well was brought in near Beaumont, Texas. I went with some of the boys from Mexico City to Beaumont to see the well and became so enthusiastic over the sight that I determined to learn the business."

He went back to Mexico City, where he interceded with the president of Mexico on behalf of another man who wanted to obtain contracts to build artesian water wells there: "I learned my primary lessons in drilling for oil through drilling for water. Then I took a course in mining at the School of Mines in Mexico City, left my medical practice and have been following the oil trade ever since."

He and fifteen associates brought in an immense gusher near Tuzpan, Vera Cruz. Dr. Busey continued prospecting for petroleum in Mexico until the guerrilla wars of 1905–06 caused him to return to the United States.

In 1920, when the Constantin gasser, the first major gas find in Arkansas, blew in, Dr. Busey rode on horseback from Homer, Louisiana, to El Dorado. He purchased a lease on the Arcade Hotel because he could not find a room at the Garrett Hotel, where most of the oil men stayed. He set up an office in his new quarters, began buying up oil leases and royalties, and started exploring for favorable locations to drill in Union County.

The Mitchell-Bonham Drilling Company, through P. R. Mattocks and Harley Hinton, acquired an eighty-acre lease on the David R. Armstrong property southwest of El Dorado shortly after the Constantin gasser was brought in. The test was carried down to seventeen hundred feet and encountered drilling and financial difficulties. Upon hearing this, Dr. Busey offered them five thousand dollars cash to complete the well in exchange for a 51 percent interest. He went to Ike Felsenthal, a local mercantile store owner, outlined the deal, and asked him to raise the money. Mr. Felsenthal agreed only on condition that Dr. Busey set up a trusteeship and let Mr. Felsenthal and seventeen of his friends come in for a share of the returns. Investing in this well was a large gamble for these citizens. Union and Ouachita Counties were primarily agricultural counties, with timber running a close second in importance. The closest oil field was forty miles away in Homer, Louisiana.

On January 10, 1921, the well came in, first a trickle and then a giant gusher, shooting more than one hundred feet above the wooden derrick. The oil came from 2,223 feet down with estimates of from 3,000 to 10,000 barrels of fluid daily, much of it water, and from 15,000,000 to 35,000,000 cubic feet of gas. By February, this well was producing 1,000 to 1,500 barrels of clean oil daily.

Dr. Busey's name shot around the world as the man who put the state of Arkansas on the oil map. He was even called the "Wildcat King of the Universe." His three secretaries were kept busy returning checks, bills, diamonds, and jewelry sent to him to invest in oil.

The Busey-Mitchell-Armstrong No. 1 gusher, or the Busey No. 1 as it was more commonly called, launched one of the notable United States oil booms of this century and led to the development of more than 150 fields in the state, laying the foundation for Arkansas's multi-million-dollar petroleum and petro-chemistry industry.

Dr. Busey operated in the El Dorado and Smackover areas until about 1928, when he sold out his Arkansas interest. He then wildcatted for oil near Monticello, Arkansas, Shreveport, Louisiana, and elsewhere. On January 10, 1941, the anniversary of the Busey No. 1 well in Arkansas, he brought in a well in El Dorado, Illinois.

Dr. Busey later owned and managed farms in Stevens Point, Wisconsin, and Waterloo, Iowa, as well as several apartment houses in Chicago. In Deerfield, Michigan, he did research on soybeans for Henry Ford.

Dr. Busey died at the age of ninety-five in Elkton, Maryland. Almost blind his last few years, he had lived in semi-retirement in Rising Sun, Maryland. He was survived by his wife, Elsie Transue Busey.

[The research file and the oral history collection at the Arkansas Museum of Natural Resources hold an extensive collection on Busey, including newspaper clippings, an unpublished manuscript, interviews, letters, and a report by the Arkansas Oil and Gas Commission. See also A. R. Buckalew and R. B. Buckalew, "The Discovery of Oil in South Arkansas," *AHQ* 33 (Autumn 1974): 195–238; and Kenny A. Franks and Paul F. Lambert, *Early Louisiana and Arkansas Oil: A Photographic History, 1901–1946* (1982).]

JEANNE CLEMENTS

BUSH, JOHN EDWARD (Nov. 14, 1856–Dec. 11, 1916), politician and businessman, was born a slave in Moscow, Tennessee. In 1862 his owner, fearing advancing Union troops, fled to Arkansas with his slaves. Left an orphan at the age of seven, Bush drifted, eating and sleeping wherever he could.

He worked as a brick molder in Little Rock to finance his education. He became principal of Capitol Hill School in Little Rock and later accepted a principalship at Hot Springs.

In 1879 he returned to Little Rock to marry Cora Winfrey, the daughter of Solomon Winfrey, a building contractor and member of the black aristocracy. Bush had been moving up the social ladder by virtue of his education, hard work, and integrity; his marriage solidified his place in the community. Three children were born to the marriage.

By 1883 he was influential in Pulaski County politics. He saw in the Republican Party a way to fight the Democrats, whom he believed were the party of black oppression. He told a friend: "I am a politician, first for the interest of my race, secondly because I like it."

His prestige was due in part to his relationship with

Powell Clayton, governor and senator from 1868 to 1877 and dispenser of federal patronage. The Bush-Clayton alliance began when Clayton asked him to deliver a speech in "one of the more dangerous sections" of Little Rock. Bush agreed, but declined payment. When Clayton asked what he wanted, Bush replied, "Your influence as long as you have any and as long as I deserve it."

In 1898 he was appointed by President William McKinley as receiver of United States public lands (tax revenue) at Little Rock. He urged Harmon L. Remmel, the leader of the Arkansas Republican Party in 1898, to go to Washington and push for civil service jobs for blacks, but he received no positive response from Remmel. Bush remained receiver for fourteen years until Woodrow Wilson, a Democrat, was elected in 1912, but his tenure was not without opposition. "Lily-white" Republicans opposed all black officeholders. Moreover, a group of Boston-based intellectuals tried to deny Bush's reappointment in 1902 because they distrusted his friendship with Booker T. Washington, whom they viewed as an accommodationist. With powerful city and state support Bush secured reappointment.

In 1906 he faced a threat to reappointment because of a fight brewing between the Lily-whites and regular Republicans. Rumors circulated that the government was considering eliminating his post. Fearing he would be drawn into the fight, Bush called upon Booker T. Washington, a powerful presidential advisor on black patronage, to arrange a meeting for him with President Theodore Roosevelt.

John Bush failed to secure a private audience with the president, however, because Harmon Remmel happened to be at the White House when he arrived and insisted on accompanying him to his meeting with the president. Roosevelt, unaware of the rumors about eliminating Bush's position, promised his reappointment. Bush was unable to express his concerns openly because of Remmel's presence at the meeting.

As the fight between the Lily-whites and regular Republicans grew more divisive in the spring of 1906, Bush called again upon Booker Washington to use his influence to secure his reappointment. Washington immediately contacted Roosevelt. Little Rock rallied with a letter campaign. On April 24 Booker Washington wired Bush that his request had been approved. Later, President Taft reappointed Bush, one of the few to retain a federal post during the "black broom" move-ment under Taft, which removed virtually all blacks from federal office in the South.

Early in his life Bush adopted Washington's philosophy of self-help. He used his position as receiver of public lands to educate blacks about acquiring land, resulting in black ownership of some of the best farmland in the state. He wrote to his friend Washington in 1915: "The development of Negro businesses has been one of my overriding efforts." Booker T. Washington described Bush as the most aggressive of all the men promoting black business in the South.

In 1905 Bush made headlines when he criticized Governor Jeff Davis's plan for funding black schools by taxes collected only from blacks. He organized a campaign which gathered enough support to defeat the Separate Tax Bill.

In 1882 Bush became a founder of the Mosaic Templars of America. The idea for the Templars grew out of an incident in which he and a white businessman were approached on the street by an elderly black woman asking for contributions to the cost of burying her husband. Both men gave money, but the white commented, "whenever a Negro dies or needs help the public must be worried to death by Negro beggars—it is a shame!" Shaken, Bush, with Chester W. Keatts, decided that something had to be done to put "a stop to the public solicitation of funds by Negroes to aid the sick and bury the dead." Thus the Templars were born.

The thirteen charter members combined their resources to pay for organizing, advertising, and renting a building. By 1918 the Templars operated a burial and insurance program, a building and loan association, and a hospital at Hot Springs, and owned a headquarters building in Little Rock. There were chapters in twenty-six states, Central and South America, the Panama Canal Zone, and the West Indies.

John E. Bush died at age fifty-eight. As the *Colored American* expressed it in 1902, he was "the hope of the 'Race' in the Southland, a splendid example for the emulation of aspiring youth."

[Few personal papers of J. E. Bush survive, but ample sources allow for an accurate picture of his career. M. W. Gibbs, *Shadow of Light* (1902); G. P. Hamilton, *Beacon Lights of the Race* (1911); D. B. Gaines, *Racial Possibilities as Indicated by the Negroes of Arkansas* (1898); and E. M. Woods, *Blue Books of Little Rock and Argenta, Arkansas* (1907), contain biographical sketches of Bush. Articles in *AHQ* include John W. Graves, "The Arkansas Separate Coach Law in 1891" 32 (Summer 1973): 148–65; Tom W.

Dillard, "To the Back of the Elephant: Racial Conflict in the Arkansas Republican Party" 33 (Spring 1974): 3–15, and "Golden Prospects and Fraternal Amenities: M. W. Gibbs's Arkansas Years" 35 (Winter 1976): 307–33. The Booker T. Washington Papers in the Library of Congress, manuscript division, contain the Bush-Washington correspondence. See also Aldridge E. Bush and P. L. Dorman, *History of the Mosaic Templars of America* (1924); and Booker T. Washington, *The Negro in Business* (1907).]

C. CALVIN SMITH

BYRNE, ANDREW (Nov. 30?, 1802–June 10, 1862), the first Roman Catholic bishop of Little Rock, a diocese which both then and now encompasses the state of Arkansas. He was born in the town of Navan about forty miles northwest of Dublin, Ireland, the son of Robert and Margery Moore Byrne. According to parish records, he was baptized on December 3, 1802; since his given name was Andrew, he may have been born on November 30, the feast day of St. Andrew the Apostle. While a seminarian in Navan, Byrne heard Bishop John England of Charleston, South Carolina, recruiting prospective priests. Answering the call, Byrne arrived in Charleston in the early 1820s. He completed his priestly formation under Bishop England, who ordained him on November 11, 1827.

Byrne's first assignment was in North Carolina. He returned to Charleston in 1830 to be the pastor of St. Mary's Church. In 1833 he accompanied Bishop England to the Second Provincial Council in Baltimore as vicar general. Byrne's relationship with Bishop England apparently deteriorated, and he left the Charleston diocese in 1836. He transferred to the diocese of New York where he made a name for himself as a preacher-pastor in New York City, becoming the founding pastor of St. Andrew's Church in 1842.

Byrne's proven abilities as pastor, his connection with New York bishop John Hughes, and his southern experience made him a natural choice for a diocese on the southwestern frontier. After Pope Gregory XVI erected the diocese of Little Rock on November 28, 1843, Byrne was consecrated as Arkansas's first Roman Catholic bishop in old St. Patrick's Cathedral on March 11, 1844. He arrived in Little Rock three months later on horseback with just two priests to minister to all of Arkansas.

There was a Catholic church in Little Rock, known as St. Joseph's, built in the early 1840s. The priest who built this structure, however, left the state and sold the deed to a Catholic priest in New Orleans. Byrne needed to raise funds to purchase another lot at Second and Center Streets, where he built his Cathedral of St. Andrew, dedicated on November 1, 1846, and named for his patron saint. Throughout his eighteen years as prelate, Byrne never had more than ten priests at any time. He maintained the diocese with funds from the Austrian-based Leopoldine Society and the French-based Society for the Propagation of the Faith. From this support, Byrne purchased land, sustained his clergy, and started schools. Profits from land sales allowed him to open the College of St. Andrew at Fort Smith in 1849. He traveled to Naas in County Kildare, Ireland, to persuade the Sisters of Mercy to locate a convent in Little Rock. By 1851 sisters opened what became known as Mount St. Mary's Academy, Arkansas's oldest educational institution. Both the convent and school were located at the old church at Seventh and Louisiana Streets. The Mercy Sisters were operating convent schools in Fort Smith and Helena before the Civil War.

During the nativistic, anti-Catholic Know-Nothing uproar of the 1850s, Byrne studiously avoided political disputes, particularly those involving slavery. There is no evidence that he owned slaves, and his correspondence yields no opinion on the subject. Like many Catholic prelates of the period, Byrne probably saw the issue as not one of moral or religious concern.

At first Bishop Byrne was quite dissatisfied with his position. At the Sixth Provincial Council in Baltimore in 1846, he persuaded his fellow bishops to petition the Vatican to abolish the Arkansas diocese so that Byrne could be moved to the newly created diocese of Buffalo, New York. Rome dismissed this recommendation and refused the bishop's later request for a transfer in 1853. In 1850 the Arkansas diocese was attached to a newly created ecclesiastical province of New Orleans. With bishops from Mississippi, Alabama, Texas, and northern Louisiana, Byrne attended provincial councils in 1856 and 1860.

Byrne attempted to attract clergy and laity from his native land during the 1850s, yet Catholics numbered only one percent of Arkansas's population by 1860. His last trip to Ireland in 1858–59 yielded few recruits. The Civil War closed the College of St. Andrew in 1861 by taking almost all of the male students into the Confederate army. The war disrupted some international communications, and this made it more difficult for Byrne to secure funding from Europe. Byrne died in Helena at St. Catherine's Mercy Convent, exhausted by years of mission work. His successor, Bishop Edward M. Fitzgerald, had his remains placed in the crypt of the Cathedral of St. Andrew in 1881. Though he had his share of disappointments and frustrations, Byrne persevered and laid the foundations of the church so securely that even years of civil war and the five years' absence of a bishop did not uproot the Little Rock diocese.

[Letters, documents, and Byrne's personal register, 1844–1850, are in the archives of the diocese of Little Rock, St. John's Catholic Center, Little Rock. Other letters of Bishop Byrne are in the archives of the archdiocese of New Orleans; some material is in archives of the University of Notre Dame. See James M. Woods, *Mission and Memory: A History of the Catholic Church in Arkansas* (1993); Richard N. Clarke, *Lives of the Deceased Bishops of the Catholic Church in the United States,* 2 vols. (1872); and the Diocesan Historical Commission, *A History of Catholicity in Arkansas* (1925). There is an obituary in the *Arkansas Gazette,* June 28, 1862.]

JAMES M. WOODS

CARAWAY, HATTIE OPHELIA WYATT (Feb. 1, 1878–Dec. 22, 1950), United States senator, was born in Bakersville, Tennessee, to William Carroll Wyatt and Lucy Burch. Hattie's father owned a general store in nearby Hustburg. Her introduction to political discourse might have been conversations among her father's customers and cronies in the store.

Little is known about Hattie Wyatt's youth during the first post-Reconstruction generation. Her father apparently achieved some social pretension because he enrolled her in Dickson (Tennessee) Normal College in 1892. She graduated from there in 1896 at the height of populism, almost certainly aware of the political change and racial animosity swirling around her. The precision, economy, and acuity of her written record suggest attainments superior to those of many college graduates of the late twentieth century.

At Dickson she met Thaddeus Horatio Caraway, a bright, ambitious lad who yearned for a career in politics. After they graduated, she became a rural schoolmarm, and he courted her while he went to law school. In February 1902 they married, and later moved to Jonesboro, Arkansas. Their union produced three sons: Paul Wyatt, Forrest, and Robert Easley.

Hattie assumed the traditional roles of wife, mother, and care giver. Thaddeus carved out a successful and colorful career in state and federal government. By 1912 their young brood was ensconced in a historic mansion in Maryland, as Thaddeus went off to serve in the U.S. House of Representatives. Eight years later he was elected United States senator from Arkansas. He died unexpectedly in November 1931.

Hattie Caraway's journal makes it clear that she knew Governor Harvey Parnell's support for her candidacy for her husband's unexpired term was a contrivance cooked up among some of Arkansas's good ol' boys. They planned to warm Thaddeus Caraway's Senate seat until the Democratic primary election of August 1932. Hattie had developed a different plan. She understood the peril of her own financial prospects, the opportunities inherent in the seat she held after her husband's death, and the value of the political prospects Thaddeus had developed. As she wrote in her journal in 1932, "I did not try to wear the pants while Dad lived— yet I'm trying to fit my feet into his shoes. I can well know they are easier on my feet than they'd be on Parnell's or Kirby's."

Senator Huey Long's campaign on behalf of Caraway's candidacy in August 1932 was crucial to her victory in the primary election. By means of Long's acoustically amplified motorcade through Arkansas, she became a candidate in her own right. Charles Brough said it best: "The kingfish made a queenfish in his usual colorful manner." In the hottest week of the worst year of the Great Depression, while six old-fashioned and much-tainted political war horses looked on impotently, Hattie Caraway became visible to serious, hungry, anxious voters. For a brief dozen years, Arkansas elected a woman of the people to sit in the United States Senate.

She preferred to be addressed as "Mrs. Caraway" rather than "Senator Caraway," understanding that it was important for voters to accept her as one of their own kind. In keeping with her keen perception of Arkansas opinion, she chose not to make waves. She made few speeches, claiming that she did not wish to deprive male senators of precious debate time. She was a loyal supporter of President Franklin D. Roosevelt's New Deal agenda, including his Supreme Court-packing bill, National Labor Relations Act, and World Court bill. She was the first woman to preside in the Senate, to chair a subcommittee there, to become a senior senator, and to take part in a filibuster.

Caraway's major defect as a senator was her outspoken and prolonged opposition to the Wagner-Van Nuys Anti-Lynching Bill of January 1938. She also opposed the administration's stingy veterans' bonus bill and the repeal of prohibition.

By 1938 Senator Caraway had cultivated the political support of Homer Adkins, FDR's commissioner of internal revenue. Adkins's statewide patronage, his marshaling of Works Progress Administration employees as campaign workers, and her own solid support of New Deal legislation gave the lie to any notion that the president was neutral toward her reelection. She overcame a serious challenge for the nomination from Representative John McClellan, becoming the first woman to be reelected to a second term in the United States Senate.

Her first years in public life strained her health; she underwent surgery for a perforated stomach ulcer in December 1939. Still, the war years saw her finest hours as a senator.

Caraway often sat silent at her desk during debates. Frequently on such occasions she knitted, wrote verse, worked crossword puzzles, and read newspapers.

She consistently supported internationalism in the great foreign policy debate of 1940–41. She voted for the cash and carry amendment, the arming of American merchant vessels, the conscription bill of 1940, and the lend-lease bill of 1941. She supported the United Nations Organization resolution of 1943 and the GI Bill of Rights in 1944.

Nor did Hattie Caraway forget her constituents. During World War II she was instrumental in securing Camps Robinson and Chaffee, five air bases, two Nisei relocation centers, and defense ordnance and aluminum factories for Arkansas.

In 1943 she cosponsored a version of Alice Paul's equal rights amendment proposal in the Senate, telling the *New York Times* that women should be free to enter the professions, industry, and government and "to work equally with men to build a better world."

Unfortunately for Caraway's political prospects, her alliance with Homer Adkins broke down during the war. By the time a much younger candidate, J. William Fulbright, defeated her bid for a third full term in 1944, she had built a solidly progressive record in the Senate, except in civil rights.

After her loss to Fulbright, Senator John McClellan saw to it that Caraway was appointed to the United States Employee Compensation Commission and later to its appeals board. Her correspondence reveals that she was anxious about her retirement income. In January 1950 she suffered a stroke which left her partially paralyzed. She died at Falls Church, Virginia, and was buried next to her husband at West Lawn Cemetery in Jonesboro, Arkansas.

[Sources include the Hattie Wyatt Caraway Papers, Special Collections Division, University of Arkansas Libraries, Fayetteville; David Malone, *Hattie and Huey: An Arkansas Tour* (1989); G. R. Brooks, "Hattie and Huey: A Re-Examination of the Arkansas Senatorial Primary of 1932," *Arkansas Political Science Journal* 3 (1982): 1–19; and Peter F. Stevens, *The Mayflower Murderer and Other Forgotten Firsts in American History* (1993). There are obituaries in the *New York Times* and the *Arkansas Gazette.*]

LEO J. MAHONEY

CARAWAY, THADDEUS H. (Oct. 17, 1871–Nov. 6, 1931), lawyer, United States representative and senator, was born in Springhill, Stoddard County, Missouri, to Tolbert F. and Mary Ellen Caraway (maiden name unknown). His father was murdered when Thaddeus was an infant. The family was destitute. They moved to Clay County, Arkansas, when he was twelve years old.

Caraway attended Dickson College in Dickson, Tennessee, where he received a bachelor of arts degree in 1896. To pay for his education he worked as a cotton picker, a sawmill laborer, and a railroad section hand. After graduation he taught in country schools in Craighead County, Arkansas.

In 1899 he was admitted to the Arkansas bar. In 1902 he and Hattie Wyatt married. They had three sons, Paul Wyatt, Forrest, and Robert Easley.

He began practicing law in Lake City in 1903. To make money he published legal notices in his weekly newspaper, the *Lake City Sun Times.* Often he would ask his friend Harry Lee Williams, publisher of the *Jonesboro Daily Tribune,* to send a man to Lake City for a week to help print legal notices.

In 1908 Caraway was elected prosecuting attorney for the Second Judicial District of Arkansas. He pursued justice relentlessly, taking little time for leisure. During one court session, he secured eleven hangings for murderers. While he was prosecuting attorney, the crime rate dropped, especially for murders.

In 1912 he sought election to the United States House of Representatives. He defeated the incumbent, R. Bruce Macon. During his campaign, he used the

Memphis Bridge Company as an example of Macon's lack of concern for the common man. The company had been charging eastbound passengers a fee for crossing the Mississippi River into Memphis, Tennessee. Caraway claimed Macon had not tried to abolish the fee. As one of his first acts in office, Caraway persuaded the company to drop the toll.

He served four terms in the House, from 1913 to 1921. He supported President Wilson and believed the United States should remain neutral in World War I. He also supported the Nineteenth Amendment, which gave women the right to vote. He believed in equal rights for women and often consulted his wife on important issues.

In 1919 Caraway obtained for Arkansas fifty thousand dollars from the House of Representatives to build a reform school for girls. Governor Jeff Davis had passed a measure in 1905 to provide for the school, but no one had acted on it until Caraway secured funding.

In 1920 he ran for a Senate seat and again defeated an incumbent, William F. Kirby, a former judge. He was reelected in 1926 and served until his death in 1931. He served on the agricultural and judiciary committees. He had a part in exposing the Teapot Dome oil scandal of the Harding era.

The Department of the Navy had transferred oil reserves to the Interior Department, which subsequently leased the oil to private operators Harry Sinclair and Edward Doheny. In return, Secretary of the Interior Albert Fall received an unsecured loan of one hundred thousand dollars and a gift of more than three hundred thousand dollars. Caraway made a speech on the Senate floor and introduced a resolution canceling the lease.

Caraway was known as a champion of the poor. He favored government loans and price supports for farmers, reform of the cotton exchanges, and old-age pensions. Friends dubbed him "Fighting Thad," but his enemies called him "Caustic Caraway." He had the reputation of not resting until he accomplished his goals.

After his death at Little Rock in 1931, his wife was elected to serve the remainder of his term in the Senate. She went on to become the first woman elected to the United States Senate.

[Sources include C. P. J. Mooney, ed., *The Mid-South and Its Builders* (1920); Harry Lee Williams, *Forty Years behind the Scenes in Arkansas Politics* (1949); Diane D. Kincaid, ed., *Silent Hattie Speaks: The Personal Journal of Senator Hattie Caraway* (1979); and Walter Scott McNutt,

comp., *Great Statesmen of Arkansas* (1954). See also the *Craighead County Historical Quarterly* 2 (Winter 1964): 8; 6 (Autumn 1968): 12; 7 (Summer 1969): 1; 10 (Autumn 1972): 16–17; 13 (Summer 1975): 3–5.]

LICI F. BEVERIDGE

CARR, WILLIAM ARTHUR (Oct. 24, 1909–Jan. 14, 1966), Olympic gold medalist, was born in Pine Bluff, the younger of two sons of William L. Carr and Ann Holmes. He developed extraordinary athletic skills at an early age. No match race, no mud puddle, no front-yard fence escaped his assault. To his friends Bill was "the fastest Carr in town."

From 1927 forward, the "little fella" from Pine Bluff, five feet seven inches tall, made track history. At the state high-school track meet that spring, he gained national attention. He won the high jump with a record leap of 6' 3⁄4" and the long jump at 21' 4 1⁄4" and finished a close second in the 100- and 220-yard dashes. His performance was enough to earn him individual high-point honors. In 1927 these were nationally competitive performances; in the 1990s they are still respectable standards for any high-school athlete.

Carr attended Pennsylvania's Mercersburg Preparatory Academy to prepare to enter an eastern university. During his two years there he became the national schoolboy champion in the long jump and the 100- and 200-yard dashes. To the delight of his friends, he also held the record for not spilling a drop of water while jumping over a dining-room table with a tray of filled water glasses.

Carr attended the University of Pennsylvania. He was elected president of his sophomore class and was awarded the "Golden Spoon" by his classmates for being the outstanding, all-around Penn student. Dubbed the "Arkansas Flyer" by east coast sportswriters, he never lost a 440-yard or 400-meter race while at Penn. With Bill Carr anchoring the mile relay team, the Penn squad never allowed competitors a first-place finish.

In July 1932 Carr competed in the intercollegiate championships at Berkeley, California, against Ben Eastman of Stanford University, who held the world records in the 440-yard and the 880-yard races. Before the race, few gave Carr much chance against the west coast giant. When the rhythmic, effortless Carr swept around Eastman to nip the champion at the tape, officials checked their watches. The time was real: 47.0 for the quarter-mile race.

A few weeks later during the Olympic trials at Palo Alto, California, Carr again overtook Eastman to register 46.9 against 47.1. Later, Lawson Robertson, Carr's track coach and coach of the Olympic track team, suggested to the Stanford coach, Dink Templeton, that perhaps Eastman should switch to the 800 meters for the upcoming Olympics. "Hell no," replied Templeton. "Eastman is still the best quarter-miler in the world."

On August 4, 1932, thirty-six of the world's best quarter-milers assembled at the Los Angeles Coliseum for the preliminary trials of the Olympic 400 meters. By 4:30 the next afternoon, the field had been narrowed to six finalists with Carr and Eastman clocking the best times: 47.2, a new Olympic record, for Carr and 47.6, the previous Olympic record, for Eastman. The stage was set for the "400-meter race of the century."

Seventy thousand spectators cheered as the runners took their staggered positions. Eastman drew a favorable position in the second lane, William Walters of South Africa had the inside lane, Alex Wilson of Canada had the third, Carr the fourth, James Gordon of the United States the fifth, and George Golding of Australia the sixth.

At the gun Eastman took the lead. Walters and Gordon stayed close to Eastman, but Carr, a few yards behind, paced himself. As the runners began to string out in the back stretch, Eastman was still in the lead with Carr a few yards behind. At the curve the Arkansas flyer drew even with Eastman. Eighty yards from the finish, Carr pulled away. He snapped the tape two yards ahead of his foe.

Both runners had smashed the Olympic record. But Carr had established a world record of 46.2 and captured the Olympic gold.

Two days later Carr collected his second gold medal when he substituted for an injured teammate on the 1,600-meter relay. Running the anchor leg, he helped the United States team set a new Olympic record at 3:08.2.

Plagued by a leg injury, Carr recorded lackluster performances during the 1933 indoor track season. On March 17, two days after being awarded the "Class of 1915 Award" as Pennsylvania's ideal athlete, Carr ended his track career. While on his way to a dinner party, he hitched a ride with some friends. Since the seats were occupied, Bill rode on the running board of the automobile. Near an intersection, the car was struck from the opposite side by another vehicle. Bill was hurled to the ground and pinned by the rear fender of his friend's car. He suffered two broken ankles and a fractured pelvis and never raced again.

Before World War II, Bill Carr worked at New York Midtown International Insurance Corporation's Far East division and after the war became its executive director. He served as a naval officer during the war.

In 1954 he was named to *Sports Illustrated*'s all-time Olympic team. In 1964 he was inducted into the Arkansas Sports Hall of Fame. He died two years later in Tokyo. He is buried in Pine Bluff's Graceland Cemetery.

[See Russell E. Bearden, "Arkansas' Double Gold Olympic Medalist: William A. 'Bill' Carr," *Jefferson County Historical Quarterly* 12 (1984): 18–28 and the *Mercersburg Academy Alumni Quarterly* 28 (July 1933): 10. Photocopies of Carr's track records are included in the Willam Arthur Carr Collection, University of Pennsylvania, Archives, North Arcade, Franklin Field E6, Philadelphia. Sources also include the William A. Carr Collection, the Albert M. Swank Library, Mercersburg Academy.]

RUSSELL E. BEARDEN

CASE, SARAH ESTHER (Jan. 28, 1868–May 7, 1932), missionary and teacher, was born in Izard County, the eldest of the thirteen children of Robert Ridgway Case, a merchant, and Ella Byers. The Case and the Byers families had settled in Batesville, Independence County, in the 1840s. Esther, or "Essie," inherited an interest in the work of the Methodist church from her grandmothers, Sarah Ridgway Case and Esther Wilson Byers. Both were leaders in the establishment of women's work at Batesville's First Methodist Church, and both were charter members of the Women's Foreign Missionary Society when it was founded there in 1886. Case herself was also a charter member, even though she was only eighteen years old at the time. As the oldest daughter of a large family, she developed the traits of competence and reliability, along with native intelligence and religious faith. Esther obtained an education beyond that of most girls of her day. She attended the public schools of Batesville, then studied for a time at a private academy in Memphis. Following the death of her fiancé in 1893, she decided to turn her life to Christian service and offered to enter the foreign missionary field.

Her first assignment was to teach at a girls' school in Saltillo, Mexico, where she became fluent in Spanish. She was soon promoted to be the principal of a similar school at Guadalajara, then another one at San Luis Potosi. Finally she became principal of the Mary Keener Institute, a large school for girls in Mexico City. In all these positions she was loved because of her integrity, her sense of humor, and her linguistic and musical abilities. Case probably would have remained at the Mary Keener Institute for many years, but civil war erupted in Mexico in 1911. She continued to work at the school until the building itself was shelled in 1913 and all American missionaries in the area were called home. Within a few months, however, she felt compelled to travel back to Mexico, alone and at considerable risk to herself, to conclude some business affairs for the school and to make sure that her students had safely returned to their homes.

When she returned to the United States, she took advantage of the break in her career to obtain a degree at the George Peabody College in Nashville, Tennessee, and later taught for a time at Scarritt College there.

In 1918 she was elected one of two foreign secretaries for women's work by the General Board of Missions of the Methodist Church. Because of her experience and her familiarity with the Spanish language, she was assigned to Latin America. When mission work was reorganized four years later, she became the first woman ever selected for a full-time position in the church hierarchy. Methodist mission work abroad was curtailed in 1926, and Case was put in charge of all women's work in all foreign fields. Her main responsibilities were to visit and inspect mission schools and to provide counseling and advice to women serving in the mission field. She traveled widely in Latin America, Europe, Africa, and the Orient, adding French to her vocabulary and visiting every field where the Methodist Board of Missions was active. Everywhere she traveled she was comfortable, pleasant, and poised, dealing cheerfully with the discomforts of travel in those days, even when she was trapped briefly by a landslide in Brazil.

While she was visiting the Belgian Congo in 1932, it was discovered that she had a malignancy. She com-

pleted the tour, then returned home for surgery. Continuing with her work, she made another trip to Mexico, her first air travel. Returning home once again, she prepared her report to be given to the Board of Missions at their annual meeting in May, but her condition worsened and she was unable to present the report in person. She died at Batesville and lies buried beside her parents in Batesville's Oaklawn Cemetery.

[See James A. Anderson, *Centennial History of Arkansas Methodism* (1935); Nancy Britton, *The First Hundred Years: First United Methodist Church, Batesville, Arkansas, 1836–1936* (1986); Manon Stark Craig and Robert Andrew Craig, "Sarah Esther Craig," *Independence County Chronicle* 14(3): 2; Marion S. Craig, "William and John H. Byers," and "George Case: Pioneer Merchant," *Independence Pioneers* 1 (1986).]

NANCY BRITTON

CASQUI (1491?–?), Native American chief, was probably born somewhere in northeast Arkansas. He is known only from the four accounts of the Hernando de Soto expedition, in which his name is variously recorded as Casqui, Casquin, or Icasqui.

Casqui was the first Arkansas Native American leader whose dealings with the Spanish explorer Hernando de Soto are recorded in detail in all four accounts, making him the first Arkansan about whom we have written historical information. When the de Soto expedition crossed the Mississippi River in early June 1541, they were attacked by the local Native Americans, but as they moved north, they soon entered the land (or "province") under chief Casqui's control. In contrast to most initial encounters with the de Soto expedition, this one was peaceful, even cordial.

As the expedition made its way toward Casqui's main town (the "capital" of his province), word was sent to the chief from his outlying towns that the Spaniards were approaching. Casqui and a number of his followers walked out some distance from their town bearing gifts of food, clothing, and animal hides to welcome de Soto. As one reads the expedition accounts, it becomes apparent that this gesture was not merely Arkansas hospitality. Casqui had two major problems, and he hoped the Spaniards could help solve them. First, the region had been suffering from a drought for several years, and the people were facing food shortages from crop failure. And second, Casqui was at war with a neighboring chief named Pacaha.

According to the de Soto expedition accounts, Casqui believed that the de Soto entourage had come from heaven. These light-skinned, hairy-faced beings, dressed in strange clothing and many riding bizarre animals (horses), were like no mortals known to the Casqui people. So Casqui asked de Soto to intervene with heaven to end the drought, and two blind men were brought to be healed by him. De Soto was a Catholic and had about a dozen priests accompanying him. He tried to explain Christian beliefs to Casqui and that it was not in his power to grant Casqui's request. He then had his priests conduct a Mass. He also had a great wooden cross made from a tall tree and erected atop the mound where Casqui's house was situated. One of the accounts claims that it rained for the next two days.

Casqui's war with his neighbor Pacaha had probably been going on for years, maybe even for generations. All of Casqui's settlements were fortified, surrounded by moat-like ditches and palisade walls for defense from attack. Pacaha's towns were also fortified, suggesting that warfare had been a fact of life in northeast Arkansas for a long time. The conflict probably consisted of occasional small skirmishes and ambushes in which enemy people were subject to being killed or captured and made slaves. Casqui hoped that de Soto and his soldiers, with their formidable weapons and horses, would help him defeat Pacaha. To Casqui's disappointment, de Soto made a tenuous peace between the two chiefs before moving on to other parts of Arkansas. This peace no doubt quickly dissolved after de Soto left.

A special dinner was held where the peace was agreed upon. The accounts of this occasion provide us some details about Casqui. Casqui noted that he was older than Pacaha (one of the accounts claims he was about fifty years old). In arguing about who would sit next to de Soto, Casqui admitted that Pacaha's ancestors were more "honored" than his and that Pacaha was "a greater lord" (probably meaning he had more people and towns under his control). But Casqui countered that he was a more powerful chief, that he could force Pacaha to stay inside his fortifications whenever he wanted, and he told Pacaha, "You have never seen my land." This suggests that Casqui was more the aggressor in the war. Casqui then gave de Soto one of his daughters as a wife. Not to be outdone, Pacaha gave de Soto one of his wives, one of his sisters, and another woman.

The accounts tell us little about Casqui himself, but provide interesting details about his people and his territory. The town where Casqui lived is described as well fortified and next to a river, with the chief's house upon a man-made mound next to the river. Based on these descriptions, geographical information included in the de Soto accounts, and excavated artifacts, many archeologists believe that Casqui's town was the Parkin archeological site, now part of Parkin Archeological State Park in Cross County. De Soto's personal secretary, Rodrigo Rangel, said that in Casqui's land, "They saw the best towns they had seen up to then, and better palisaded and fortified, and the people of more beauty."

[The firsthand accounts of the de Soto expedition are translated and fully published in *The De Soto Chronicles: The Expedition of Hernando de Soto to North America in 1539–1543* (1993). See Phyllis A. Morse, "The Parkin Archeological Site and Its Role in Determining the Route of the de Soto Expedition," in *The Expedition of Hernando de Soto West of the Mississippi, 1541–1543,* Gloria A. Young and Michael P. Hoffman, eds. (1993).

The Arkansas Archeological Survey and the Arkansas Department of Parks and Tourism cooperate in research and interpretation at the Parkin Archeological State Park in Cross County, where exhibits and excavations reveal evidence that the de Soto expedition visited the site.]

JEFFREY M. MITCHUM

CAULDER, PETER (1795?–?), soldier, joined a South Carolina state militia company eleven days after Congress declared war on Great Britain on June 18, 1812. A mulatto, he joined as a white man's substitute. After three months he received a discharge. Two years later Congress offered land and cash bounties and widened its manpower base to include free men of color. In 1814 Caulder enlisted for five years in the Third U.S. Rifles, which, after mustering in the Tidewater, marched north to Greenleaf Point Barracks, Virginia, for the defense of Washington, D.C.

When the war ended shortly afterward, he stayed in the army, which transferred him to Carlisle Barracks, Pennsylvania, for training that would transform him into a scout and a marksman. He passed rigorous military skills tests and was assigned to a company of riflemen commanded by Captain William Bradford. In 1817 Bradford was selected to build a fort on the Arkansas River. Caulder and sixty-three other riflemen poled flatboats up the river from Arkansas Post in a difficult, but confidence-building journey that created an esprit de corps in the unit. On Christmas Day 1817 they dragged the boats ashore at Belle Point, at the confluence of the Arkansas and Poteau Rivers.

While some soldiers cut trees and hewed logs to build Fort Smith, Bradford dispatched Caulder to scout the Ozarks plateau, which had been opened to Cherokee migrants. Few Americans had traversed the rugged mountains covered by hardwood forests and cut by a thousand rivulets. Caulder bivouacked and hunted game for food while on his first detached duty, which kept him in the field over the winter of 1818. The tall, self-reliant young trooper with "dark hair, dark eyes, and a dark complexion" won the trust of Captain Bradford, who thereafter sent him as far north and east as the White River, with orders to map the terrain, scout Cherokee movements, locate local sources of lead and nitrates for munitions, and track deserters. In 1819, the year that Arkansas became a territory, he reenlisted for another five years. At a sutler's store he bought a pound of tobacco and a quart of whiskey every other month or so, paying his tab in full in 1822.

As his duties drew him into the Ozark mountains, he at some point encountered David Hall, the patriarch of a group of free black people pioneering in Arkansas Territory. Caulder found companionship with the Hall clan along the White River. Meanwhile, two of his friends from South Carolina with whom he had served for seven years decided to leave the army. Moreover, Major Bradford, his long-time patron officer, was replaced by Colonel Matthew Arbuckle.

Caulder's assignments showed that he stood equal in status with other soldiers in his unit. However, though trusted with above-average responsibilities, he was never promoted above the rank of private. To place a soldier with black blood above whites in rank would have challenged antebellum racial attitudes. Even so, Caulder reenlisted in 1824 for his third five-year tour, during which time the Seventh Infantry moved from Fort Smith further west into Indian territory. He accompanied Captain Benjamin L. E. Bonneville, a West Pointer, on an expedition to the Red River. He may have found that increasingly his duties were taking him away from the White River valley he now considered his home.

In 1829 he deserted from the army only a month before his term of service expired. Why he left a few weeks short of an honorable discharge and a pension is a mystery, but apparently no attempt was made to recover Caulder and punish him.

Earlier, he had received a warrant for one hundred sixty acres in present-day Sharp County. He knew that it was too poor to farm, but he pioneered there anyway for a short period. In 1832 he abandoned his stone-strewed military bounty land and moved to the Little North Fork. There, he married sixteen-year-old Eliza Hall and became a part of a substantial free black community in Marion County. Peter and Eliza named their first born son David, after her father, and went on to raise a family of seven children along the banks of the White River, where they preempted the land on which they lived. Caulder farmed, hunted, and tended his cows, a horse, and hounds. Though five free blacks in Marion County patented their farmsteads at the land office in Batesville, Caulder never did. He paid county taxes for three decades, accumulating no more than one horse and two cows at any one time.

As 1850s Arkansas society lurched toward secession, political actions in Little Rock affected the state's free blacks. The general assembly, pressured by plantation men who feared slave insurrection, enacted a law in 1859 that banished free black people from the state. Caulder disappeared from Arkansas records that year when he was about sixty-four. His son David moved to Bollinger County, Missouri, where he married and began a family. David's wife, Matilda, gave birth to a son whom the couple named Peter.

Caulder's achievements in carving out a remarkably independent life for himself and a legacy for his family demonstrated not only his personal integrity, but a tolerance for free black people that existed in yeoman-dominated areas of antebellum Arkansas.

[Sources include War of 1812 Compiled Service Records, Microfilm Series M602, Roll 36 (CAS-CAZZ), National Archives, Washington, D.C.; Returns for Bradford's Company, Rifle Regiment, Dec. 31, 1817, and Feb. 28, 1818, microfilm 40, National Archives; National Archives Bounty Land Files, warrant numbers 24,559 and 24,899; Sutler's Account Book of John Nicks and John Rogers, 1821–1822, Clara Bertha Eno Collection, Arkansas History Commission, 12, 102, 271; Seventh Infantry Return, Jan. 1821–Dec. 1831, National Archives, microfilm 127; Izard County Tax Records, 1829–1866, Marion County Tax Records, 1841–1859, microfilm 66, Arkansas History Commission.]

BILLY D. HIGGINS

CHANDLER, FLORENCE CLYDE (Sept. 28, 1901–June 4, 1987), botanist and plant geneticist, was born in Oliver, Arkansas, to William Festus Chandler and Nannie Charlotte Shannon. Florence excelled in music and science at the University of Arkansas. From 1923 to 1926 she taught biology in the public schools in Pine Bluff.

She moved to New York to study at Columbia University, where she received her Ph.D. degree in botany in 1940. From 1927 until 1943 she worked as a technical assistant at New York Botanical Gardens, where she studied the breeding of flowering plants and the structure, function, and life history of their cells. In 1927 the Gardens published a report she wrote with Arlow B. Stout on iris-breeding experiments.

In the 1940s Chandler worked as a plant breeder in the development of a quinine derivative important to the American war effort in World War II. Quinine was the only effective remedy for malaria. In the early 1940s the Japanese seized control of the Dutch plantations in the East Indies where the source of quinine, the cinchona tree, grew. From the American point of view, the development of a source of quinine was critical, since tens of thousands of United States soldiers were being sent to malarial regions.

From 1944 to 1947 Chandler participated in a large Merck and Company project to cultivate the "fever tree" in Guatemala. She worked primarily at Finca El Naranjo at Chicacacao in the state of Suchitepéquez. There, with two Guatemalan assistants, she studied the flowering habits and fertility of several cinchona species.

Every day she started out by six in the morning astride a mule for the long climb into the mountains. On a typical day she worked on the slopes until noon, returned to headquarters for lunch, then spent the afternoon working in the lab. At the end of the day she walked three quarters of a mile up the mountain to her bungalow, sometimes returning to headquarters in the evening to visit with friends.

In Guatemala the cinchona grows on the slopes of volcanoes or mountains, so the work was all up and down hill, among fragrant blossoms visited by hummingbirds. Small trees were worked from the ground, medium trees from a ladder, and tall trees from a scaffold. Chandler taught her assistants to take samples of bark, to tag trees, and to emasculate flowers to prepare them for pollination. The flowers are small and often had to be tagged individually. Chandler was strict and patient in the work, demanding accuracy, since a mix-up of tags or pollen could ruin an entire study.

The desired result was to produce strong, disease-resistant hybrids with thick bark high in quinine content. Chandler's work was important in the breeding of trees whose bark produced alkaloids from which quinacrine, a quinine substitute, could be synthesized. Her account of her research in Guatemala was published under a masculine form of her name, Clyde Chandler, in 1951, at a time when research by women was less than highly valued in some scientific communities.

Chandler returned to the United States in 1947 to work briefly for the W. Atlee Burpee Seed Company. In 1948 she went to work for the Boyce Thompson Institute for Plant Research at Yonkers, New York, as a geneticist.

There she experimented with inducing polyploidy in several kinds of plants. "Ploidy" refers to an organism's base number of sets of chromosomes. A polyploid has extra sets of chromosomes. Polyploids tend to be more robust plants than diploids and to have fewer mutations or recessive genes.

Chandler studied the plantago plant, whose seed coating is used in pharmaceutical preparations and as a stabilizer in ice cream. Her work included selection and hybridization in an attempt to produce a vigorous plant that could be harvested by machine. She also induced polyploidy in verbenas, an ornamental garden plant, resulting in the patenting of five new verbenas in 1956. She spent years in genetic studies for forest tree improvement, and hybridized lines of larch trees that grew thirty feet in ten years.

One of her associates remembers that Chandler was well known even among scientists for the breadth of her knowledge. She was "not a talker." She enjoyed homemaking, and was a good cook. She made preserves, sewed, embroidered, painted little landscapes, and on holidays made corsages for her friends. She retired in 1966 and moved to Tucson, Arizona, where she pursued her love of music and was a member of Christ Church, United Methodist. She died in Tucson.

[Chandler's "Flowering Habits and Fertility of Some Cinchona Species" is in *Contributions from the Boyce Thompson Institute*, 16(6): 249–59; rpt., No. 699. Her other publications are in *Contributions from the Boyce Thompson Institute* and the *Bulletin of the Torrey Botanical Club*.

This entry is based in part upon correspondence from Chandler's associate Carmen Rademan Ziac and an interview with Anne Shannon Demarest on Oct. 12, 1993. Other primary documents, including patent data and photographs, are in the author's possession.]

Wanda Newberry Gray

CHURCHILL, THOMAS JAMES (Mar. 10, 1824–May 14, 1905), planter, governor of Arkansas, was one of seven children born in Jefferson County, Kentucky, to Samuel Churchill and Abby Oldham. A graduate of Saint Mary's College in Bardstown, he was trained in law at Transylvania University in Lexington.

After service in the Mexican War he settled in Little Rock. On July 31, 1849, he and Ann Sevier, daughter of United States senator Ambrose Sevier and granddaughter of Judge Benjamin Johnson, married. They had six children born between 1854 and 1868: Abbie, Samuel J., Ambrose S., Juliet, Emily, and Matilda. Churchill farmed on a large plantation near Little Rock. He served as postmaster of Little Rock from 1857 until 1861.

In 1874 Arkansas Republicans split in a controversy over who had been elected governor. The quarrel led to the armed confrontation known as the Brooks-Baxter war and was resolved only by the intervention of President Ulysses S. Grant. For all practical purposes Grant's action and a new state constitution, ratified later that year, paved the way for the return of the state to Democratic control.

When the Democrats returned to power, Churchill served three terms as state treasurer. In 1880, after twenty-four ballots at the Democratic state convention, he was nominated for governor. He easily defeated the Greenback nominee, W. P. Parker, by a vote of 84,088 to 31,284.

A proposed constitutional amendment repudiating the state debt was defeated in the 1880 election. It was not an issue in the governor's race. Legislation then passed stating that the state auditor and the state treasurer would not be required "to report the Railroad Aid and Levee Bonds, and what is known as the Holford Bonds, as part of the indebtedness of the State of Arkansas in their biennial reports." Governor Churchill permitted the bill to become law without his signature.

During Churchill's tenure as governor, money was appropriated to build a facility for the insane and to establish a branch normal school of the state industrial university in Pine Bluff. Provisions were adopted for the collection of overdue taxes. A resolution passed stating that Arkansas "should be pronounced in three syllables,

with the final 's' silent, the 'a' in each syllable with the Italian sound, and accent on the first and last syllables."

Allegations of discrepancies in the treasurer's accounts for 1874–80 emerged during the legislative session. Churchill and his friends were inept in defending his record, and anti-administration Democrats, Republicans, and Greenbackers appeared determined to discredit him. After months of investigation a committee fixed the alleged shortage at $233,616. Churchill forwarded the report to the state attorney general for action, but nothing was done until Churchill left office. A suit was filed against Churchill, the former treasurer, and his bondsmen on May 30, 1883. A hearing ultimately reduced the alleged deficit to $23,973 in currency, $56,438 in state scrip, and $110 in swampland scrip. This was affirmed by the Arkansas Supreme Court, and the currency deficit was paid by the defendants. None of the scrip was ever presented for payment or cancellation.

In July 1881 many Perry County citizens were upset about the way the county judge was enforcing the law. The editor of the *Fourche Valley Times* supported the judge; an angry mob burned the newspaper office. When the judge appealed to Governor Churchill for assistance, the governor's special investigator recommended convening a special term of court to try the suspected arsonists. In the meantime, the editor was assassinated. The sheriff requested state aid in apprehending and prosecuting those responsible. Churchill sent the Quapaw Guards from Little Rock to Perryville along with special counsel to assist the prosecuting attorney. Warrants were issued and suspects interviewed and bound over to the court. After about three weeks civil authorities felt able to maintain law and order and the Quapaw Guards returned to Little Rock.

The unwelcome presence of the militia in Perryville further weakened Churchill politically. Disastrous floods in 1881 and 1882 and severe drought conditions in 1881 aggravated agrarian discontent. He served one term as governor and did not hold elective office after 1883. He was a respected private citizen until his death in Little Rock.

[See F. Clark Elkins, "Thomas James Churchill, 1881–1883," in *The Governors of Arkansas: Essays in Political Biography,* Timothy P. Donovan, Willard B. Gatewood Jr., and Jeannie M. Whayne, eds., 2d ed. (1995).]

F. Clark Elkins

CLARK, ALIDA (1822–Mar. 1892), Quaker evangelist, was born in Indiana, the daughter of William Clawson and Keziah Ward, Quakers from North Carolina. In 1844 Alida Clawson married her cousin Calvin Clark, a teacher and farmer. Of the three children born to the couple, only one, Eliza C. (Wright), survived to join them in their evangelical work in Arkansas.

In 1864 the Clarks began their work in eastern Arkansas in a vacated mule stable housing the Helena Orphans Asylum. In 1866 the Fifty-sixth Regiment of the U.S. Colored Infantry donated thirty acres and built a new "colored asylum" nine miles northwest of Helena. Alida Clark received the orphanage on behalf of the Indiana Yearly Meeting, the central governing body of the Society of Friends in the Midwest. She instituted a normal school that eventually developed into Southland College. After the Freedmen's Bureau disbanded in 1869, leaving a five-thousand-dollar debt on the school, Alida added fund-raising to her mission of teaching and preaching.

Clark's evangelical efforts resulted in the establishment of the first black Quaker worship service in America. At the time, black membership within the Society of Friends was virtually nonexistent, despite the Quakers' work in opposition to slavery.

The Society of Friends, or Quakers, was one of the most radical Protestant sects to emerge from the English Puritan Revolution. Guided by an "inner light," Friends vehemently challenged governmental and religious authority in the American colonies during the seventeenth century. Then, after a calming, quietist period, many Quakers embraced nineteenth-century Protestant revivalism.

Immediately following the Civil War, Midwestern Friends became involved in the national Renewal Movement, a legacy of religious fundamentalism and the abolitionist movement. Facing a long-standing decline in membership, Quakers challenged their membership to embrace social reforms and to evangelize among the unsaved. Inspired by the revival, Clark visualized "great *Black Yearly Meetings* all over this benighted and truly heathen land."

Plain in dress and speech, egalitarian toward women, Friends administered their congregations through "yearly meetings" at the regional level down to "monthly meetings" for local congregations. From the earliest days in Helena, the Clarks conducted religious meetings under the auspices of Indiana's Whitewater Monthly Meeting, their home congregation. But not until 1869 was Clark able to convince the meeting to admit fifteen Southland blacks into membership. By 1873 Southland Monthly Meeting, the first virtually all-black Quaker meeting, was established, thanks to her efforts. Even so, her vision of black Quaker worship throughout the South failed to materialize.

As the Southland congregation took shape, Clark's attention was drawn to Daniel Drew, a farmer who had served with the Fifty-sixth Colored Regiment. He had embraced Quakerism and its peace testimony. It took Clark two years to convince the reluctant Indiana Yearly Meeting that he should become Southland's first recorded minister. According to historian Thomas Kennedy, Clark purposely delayed her own application for the ministry until after Daniel Drew was confirmed because she felt it was important for the first recorded minister at Southland to be black. She and Drew often traveled together to offshoots of Southland Monthly Meeting at Hickory Ridge and Beaver Bayou, Arkansas, endeavoring to win souls for Christ.

Under Clark's leadership Southland Monthly Meeting expanded to three locations and four hundred members. Southland College produced three hundred badly needed teachers. However, criticism of the level of education provided by the college and of financial difficulties arising from the Clarks' frequent failure to collect tuition or rents on college lands led to the Clarks' retirement. In 1886 they moved to their "Hillside" farm two miles from the campus, where they maintained an indirect influence over the college.

The Clarks and their extended black family continued their work at the Southland Monthly Meeting. Calvin Clark served as overseer and elder; Henrietta Kitteral, their adopted black daughter, served as clerk and did committee work; and Daniel Drew advanced the work at Hickory Ridge and Beaver Bayou. Alida Clark, up to the day before her death, exhorted Friends in the ways of the Lord.

Alida Clark died at her home in the evening after spending the day preaching a sermon on God's love, eating lunch with Daniel Drew, and walking the campus she loved. After her death Calvin Clark moved to Ohio to live with relatives until his death in 1896. Daniel Drew continued working within the Society of Friends.

Southland College struggled over the next thirty-seven years of its existence. After six different managers in seventeen years, the college's management finally stabilized under the leadership of Henry and Anna Wolford until their departure in 1922. The college closed its doors in 1925.

[Sources include Arkansas Freedmen's Bureau, *Records of the Bureau of Refugees, Freedmen, and Abandoned Lands,* Record Group 105, National Archives, Washington, D.C.; Assistant Commission for the State of Arkansas, *Bureau of Refugees, Freedmen, and Abandoned Lands, Misc. Records,* National Archives, Washington, D.C., microfilm 52; and the Southland College Papers, Special Collections Division, University of Arkansas Libraries, Fayetteville.

Also see *History of Southland College* (1906); Dale P. Kirkman, "Southland College," *Phillips County Historical Quarterly* 3 (Spring 1964): 30–33; and Thomas C. Kennedy, "Southland College: The Society of Friends and Black Education in Arkansas," *AHQ* 42 (Winter 1983): 207–38; "The Last Days at Southland," *Southern Friend* 8 (1986): 3–19; "To Raise This People Up: The Early Years at Southland College," *Reflections* 12, no. 2 (1987): 1–9; and "The Rise and Decline of a Black Monthly Meeting: Southland, Arkansas, 1864–1925," *AHQ* 50 (Summer 1991): 115–39. There is an obituary of Clark in *Friends' Review* 65 (1892): 605.]

LORI BOGLE

CLARK, BENJAMIN (1785?–Nov. 10, 1866), missionary, was born on the southern frontier, probably in the foothills of the Appalachian Mountains. The names of his parents are not known. By 1816 he was living in southeast Missouri and probably was married.

In about 1818 Clark and his family were living alongside the old Southwest Trail, near the crossing of the Fourche-a-Thomas Creek in (then) Lawrence County, Arkansas. There he helped organize his first congregation, the Salem Baptist Church, the first Baptist church, and one of the first Protestant churches, in Arkansas. "The first twenty years of my ministerial labors," Clark wrote, "were spent on the frontiers of Missouri and Arkansas, where there was not arrangement for [any kind of] ministerial support." He supported his family by "laboring."

In 1818 he met the Reverend John Mason Peck, who was touring the western frontier promoting "the cause of Christ" through the use of "modern mission methods." Missionary Baptists like Peck advocated a denomination-sponsored missionary program. They were opposed by the more conservative Anti-Mission (or Hard Shell) Baptists who believed the work of planting new churches should be done by unpaid traveling preachers like Clark. Peck converted Clark to the "Missionary" Baptist persuasion.

Clark's county tax bill was six cents in 1820; he owned no real property and little else.

In 1825 he was the pastor of the Little Flock Church in old Lawrence County, but as families moved down the old Southwest Trail into central Arkansas and beyond, Clark followed his parishioners south. By 1830 he and his family were living in Antoine Township in Clark County, Arkansas, where he was the pastor of another Little Flock Church. The 1830 United States Census lists Elder Clark as about forty-five years old; his wife, name unknown, was about thirty-five. In their household were three sons and four daughters. Soon after this date, Clark's wife died. He found that he could not work for wages and continue preaching and chose to sacrifice income in order to preach.

His son, Green J. Clark, told of years of "toil and privation." Perhaps it was to support his family that Clark once again hit the road. He moved to Pulaski County about 1832. He lived in or near Little Rock and may have preached at its Baptist meeting house. By 1833 he owned an "improvement or town lot" worth eighty dollars.

Clark recalled in the *Texas Baptist* in 1857 that he found it necessary "to make some other arrangement [for a source of income] so that I might live without making such sacrifices.... I sent off and bought a lot of books: hymn books, Sunday school books and Testaments, and supported my family by selling them." Evidently this work took him into central and southwest Arkansas, where he "organized a great many churches."

Around 1833 "things had quite changed over the State of Arkansas." This may refer to the opposition he and other Missionary Baptists faced from Anti-Mission forces. Seeking a reliable income, he went to work for the American Bible Society as a general agent, for the first time receiving a salary for work that indulged his passion for travel and preaching. Soon afterward he became a missionary agent for the Baptist Home Mission Society at a salary of one hundred dollars a year.

He and Mary Ann (Polly) Pierce married about this time. They moved to the Clarksville area of Johnson County, where he set up for "the purpose of being near the school then kept there." In 1836 and 1837 his taxable wealth consisted of horses and cattle, but no land. Polly's first child, Eliza or Elizabeth, was born in 1837.

He moved to Cape Girardeau County in southeast Missouri; there "my family did not suffer want and we had plenty." He reported to the Mission Society that in 1841 he had delivered 244 sermons, baptized five converts, and traveled 1,915 miles in his work and had collected "$27.87 in the field" toward his salary.

Around 1843 Clark's wanderlust was upon him again; this time he set his eyes on Texas, where he and his family arrived in about 1844. By 1850 Clark resided at or near "Clarks crossing of White Oak Creek" in Hopkins County, where he went "about his master's business," preaching and organizing churches. He evidently no longer had a salary from the Mission Society. By some unknown means he suffered a disaster that resulted in the "loss of all of [his] property."

In 1852, at the age of about seventy, Clark moved to Leon County, Texas, where he preached within the "bounds" of the Trinity River Baptist Association. A contemporary recalled that Clark "came [among us] while the sun of life was passing behind the western hills, [and] he reflected back much of the light he had borrowed from Christ." A fall from his horse left him unable to do manual labor. Ill health brought on by "exposure on the trail" left him "feeble and in much need."

In 1859 a visitor to Clark's home found that the family did not have a chair to sit on or enough food to make a meal. The local Baptist association provided the family with a farm of one hundred acres, including a good house and thirty acres under cultivation, at Clear Creek in Leon County. Evidently this is where Clark died.

[The best source for Clark's life is file #686 of the D. D. Tidwell Collection at the Roberts Library of the Southwestern Baptist Theological Seminary in Fort Worth, Texas. It contains copies, not originals, of *Texas Baptist* newspapers, 1856–66. Other newspaper sources include the *Terrell Daily Tribune* (Texas), Sept. 30, 1984, and *The Baptist Banner and Western Pioneer*, Dec. 7, 1843, in the author's collection; and the *Little Rock True Democrat*, Dec. 15, 1858, the *Arkansas Gazette*, Apr. 25, 1832, and the *Arkadelphia Southern Standard*, Oct. 6, 1883 (contains many errors of date) in the Arkansas History Commission.

Accounts of Clark's work are at the Arkansas History Commission in the records of Baptist associations, including Bethel Association of United Baptist Churches of Jesus Christ, 1816–41; Spring River Baptist Association, 1835; and New Cape Girardeau Baptist Association, 1841 and 1842.

The minutes of the seventeenth annual session of the Trinity River Baptist Association are in the *Leon Dispatch* (Texas), 17 (1994): 7–12.

Sources also include *Reports of the American Baptist Mission Society* for 1835–37, 1841, and 1844, in the author's collection.

U.S. Census sources include the 1830 Population Schedule, Antoine Township, Clark County, Arkansas Territory, p. 200B; 1840 Population Schedule, Lorance Township, Cape Girardeau County, Missouri, p. 74B; 1850 Population Schedule, Eighth District, Hopkins County, Texas, p. 159; and 1860 Population Schedule, Leon County, Texas, p. 247.

County records in the Arkansas History Commission include Lawrence County Tax Records for 1820 (incorrectly dated 1831); Pulaski County Tax Records, 1833; and Johnson County Tax Records, 1836 and 1837.

The Arkansas History Commission holds a collection of books relevant to Clark's life, including Z. N. Morrell, *Flowers and Fruits from the Wilderness* (1872; new ed., 1976).]

RUSSELL P. BAKER

CLARKE, JAMES PAUL (Aug. 19, 1854–Oct. 1, 1916), governor of Arkansas, United States senator, was born in Yazoo County, Mississippi, to Walter Clarke, architect, and Ellen White, daughter of a prominent planter. After editing a paper at Yazoo City, Mississippi, James Clarke received a law degree from the University of Virginia in 1878. One of his fellow students recalled him later as "a strong, able, self-willed, determined man."

He moved to Arkansas in 1879, settling first at Ozark but within the year moving to Helena, in Phillips County, where he began a successful law practice. He married Sallie (Moore) Wooten of Moon Lake, Mississippi, on November 10, 1883; they had one son and two daughters. In 1886 Clarke won election to a two-year term as the Phillips County representative to Arkansas's lower house. The next election (1888) saw Clarke elevated to the state senate where he served two successive terms, holding the position of president of the senate and lieutenant governor *ex officio* during his second term (1891). In 1892 he easily won election to the office of attorney general but chose to serve only one term in order to seek the governor's chair. He later followed a similar pattern when he turned down almost certain reelection for governor to launch a campaign for the United States Senate.

At their state convention in July 1894, Arkansas Democrats chose Clarke as their gubernatorial nominee by acclamation. His espousal of the silver cause during the campaign demonstrated a tendency among Democrats to shift to the left in order to undercut the rising strength of agrarian agitators. The Democratic candidate also struck at both the Populist and Republican threats by upholding white supremacy as the keystone of the Democratic Party. "The people of the South," he said in his closing speech of the canvass, "looked to the Democratic party to preserve the white standards of civilization." Clarke easily defeated his opponents.

One of the most dramatic and popular agrarian reforms debated in Clarke's administration concerned regulation of the railroad corporations. Joseph Taylor Robinson, later governor and United States senator, introduced in the Arkansas House of Representatives a bill creating a state railroad commission. On March 5, 1895, in an interview with a reporter from the *Memphis Commercial Appeal*, Governor Clarke charged that the Iron Mountain Railroad had "purchased the defeat of the Railroad Commission Bill." Clarke's statements cast suspicions on those who had voted against the bill. W. R. Jones, chairman of the House Ways and Means Committee, who had led the opposition to the commission bill, took heated exception to Clarke's insinuations of bribery. Governor Clarke's famous temper flared to a white heat on Sunday morning, April 7, 1895. He went in search of Representative Jones. Finding Jones at Gleason's Hotel, Clarke asked him to step into a side room and in Clarke's words took him "by the ear." Jones refused to budge and after an exchange of angry words, the governor spit in Jones's face. When Clarke pulled a pistol from his pocket, his intended victim threw a poorly aimed blow, but bystanders were able to constrain the combatants. In later years, Senator Robinson remembered Clarke as a man whose "physical courage was primitive, at times almost savage." He never avoided conflict and would pursue an enemy relentlessly.

Rather than seek the second term Arkansas traditionally granted its governor, Clarke tried to win the United States Senate seat of Senator James K. Jones in the 1896 primary elections, but was defeated. Before returning to politics, Clarke practiced law in Little Rock. In 1902 Governor Jeff Davis and Clarke formed a political alliance that gave the Davis machine new

strength in the delta region and gained Clarke a powerful advocate in his second attempt to unseat Jones. The state legislature upheld the decision of the primary election and sent Clarke to the Senate. He was reelected in 1909 and again in 1914. In the 1914 primary election, William F. Kirby, an agrarian Radical Democrat, gathered the remnants of the Davis political machine behind him and almost unseated Clarke.

In Clarke the Senate gained an independent-minded and volatile personality. The *Gazette* characterized him as having a "tongue like a scythe blade that can cut and carve." He became president pro tempore of the Senate in 1913 and 1915. He also served as chairman of the Commerce Committee. During his tenure in the Senate, he frequently supported progressive legislation. He voted for the Hepburn bill strengthening the rate-setting powers of the Interstate Commerce Commission and supported the creation of a children's bureau in the Labor Department, the direct election of senators, and the Clayton Anti-Injunction Act. He unsuccessfully proposed a measure to grant independence to the Philippines.

He died at his home in Little Rock.

[See Richard L. Niswonger, "James Paul Clarke, 1895–1897," in *The Governors of Arkansas: Essays in Political Biography*, Timothy P. Donovan, Willard B. Gatewood Jr., and Jeannie M. Whayne, eds., 2d ed. (1995).]

RICHARD L. NISWONGER

CLAYBROOK, JOHN C. (1871–July 21, 1951), lumber man and owner of a baseball team, was born in Florence, Alabama. He ran away to Memphis at age thirteen and began working on the docks along the Mississippi River. He spent four years as a roustabout on riverboats before moving to Mississippi where he worked as a lumber man, cutting and hauling timber.

When he was twenty, Claybrook married Rose (maiden name unknown), who gave him his first lessons in reading and writing. Although he claimed to be literate in the 1920A census, he never learned to read or write very well. But though the lack of a formal education may have affected his literacy, numbers were another matter. He reportedly could compute figures in his head with natural ease. His sharp business sense was apparent in the town he built around his logging and farming operation in eastern Arkansas.

In 1916 Claybrook owned two acres of land in the southern half of Crittenden County in the town of

Topaz. By this time his first wife had died, and he had remarried. His only son, John Jr., was born to his second wife, Emma (maiden name unknown), in 1916.

Claybrook worked hard cutting the area's virgin timber and earned a reputation as a reliable lumber contractor. He could supply millions of feet of hardwood timber on short notice. After clearing the land he planted cotton, which he was successful at as well. He acquired more land and turned his farm into a small community. He owned all the businesses there, including a stone sawmill, a cotton gin, a farm store with rooms for traveling salesmen, and a two-story boardinghouse and honky-tonk for his logging workers. The town of Topaz became known to many as Claybrook.

By 1936 Claybrook had extended his plantation to twelve hundred acres. He was wealthy enough— reputedly he was a millionaire—to have two houses, one in Memphis and the other in Claybrook. He maintained his holdings in Crittenden County until 1940.

Claybrook was a stocky man with a full, gentle face, a self-made man respected by blacks and whites for his industry and character. In 1929 he received a Harmon Award for his accomplishments in business. This was part of a series of achievement awards administered by the Harmon Foundation in cooperation with the Commission on Race Relations of the Federal Council of Churches. His importance in the lumber industry was affirmed when a congressional committee investigating the industry asked him to provide expert testimony.

Claybrook remained a modest man who thrived on hard work and prudence. A woman who delivered mail to the Claybrook farm said he was pleasant and kind, well liked by most everyone, black and white. Even so, he was somewhat proud and pious. The journalist Ernie Pyle met Claybrook in the summer of 1936 and made him the subject of one of his columns. He focuses on Claybrook's determination to mold his son in his own image, saying that Claybrook "considers himself the outstanding example of what a hardworking, right-living Negro can do in this world." Claybrook wanted his son to follow his example by working on the farm, but this did not come about, and John Jr. eventually moved to New York.

Claybrook sponsored an all-black baseball team called the Claybrook Tigers. He bought the team in 1929 for his sports-loving son at a cost of about four thousand dollars. The team played local games on Sunday afternoons at its stadium, Claybrook Park, located on Claybrook's farm. Before long the Tigers became known throughout the South as a solid and respectable baseball team, attracting fans of all races. Some of the players were hired by Claybrook and the rest were his farm workers. During the 1930s the Tigers played teams from the National Negro Baseball League, including the Kansas City Monarchs, the Birmingham Black Barons, and the Memphis Red Sox. In 1935 the Claybrook Tigers finished second in the first National Baseball Congress Tournament held in Wichita, Kansas. That same year a Cuban all-star team traveled to Claybrook only to be swept by the Tigers in a double-header. Around this time future Negro league stars such as John Hundley, Theolic Smith, and Ted "Double Duty" Radcliffe played for the Tigers.

In 1938 Claybrook became the first black citizen since 1888 to serve on a Crittenden County criminal jury. This occurred at a time when whites controlled the jury system, and Claybrook's selection reveals the respect he had earned among both races.

Claybrook left Crittenden County in 1940 and began a logging operation in Lee County near Marianna. Because of poor health, he left there after only a short time and retired to his home in Memphis, where he died, survived by his wife, Emma G. Claybrook, his son, and three daughters. He is buried at Elmwood Cemetery in Memphis.

[Sources include Phil Dixon and Patrick J. Hannigan, *The Negro Baseball Leagues, 1867–1955: A Photographic History* (1992); Thomas O. Fuller, *Pictorial History of the American Negro* (1933); and Margaret Elizabeth Woolfolk, *A History of Crittenden County, Arkansas* (1991). The author's interview with Mrs. Harold Weaver of Edmondson, Arkansas, on June 15, 1995, provided some insight into Claybrook's character. Ernie Pyle's article in the *Memphis Commercial Appeal*, June 18, 1936 (rpt. Aug. 27, 1989), is included in *Pyle's Home Country* (1947). Reports on the Claybrook Tigers are in the *Commercial Appeal*, July 1, 4, 5, 1935. Obituaries are in the *Commercial Appeal*, Aug. 5, 1951, and the *Memphis World*, Aug. 7 and 10, 1951.]

DAVID D. DAWSON

CLAYTON, JOHN MIDDLETON (Oct. 13, 1840– Jan. 29, 1889), Reconstruction official, Republican leader, was born near Chester, Pennsylvania, the son of John Clayton and Ann Glover. During the Civil War he served in the Army of the Potomac and was engaged in several large battles in the eastern United States. In

1867 he migrated to Arkansas to manage his brother's plantation, Linwood, in Jefferson County. His elder brother, Powell Clayton, had commanded the Union regiment in Pine Bluff during the war and afterward settled in the area.

When congressional Reconstruction took effect in 1868, Powell Clayton became governor of Arkansas. John Clayton was elected in 1871 as representative for Jefferson County in the Arkansas General Assembly. In 1872 he was elected state senator to represent Jefferson, Bradley, Grant, and Lincoln Counties, and he served briefly as speaker of the senate, pro tem. The state legislature chose him to serve on the first board of trustees of the University of Arkansas when it was chartered in 1871. Two years later he also helped Pine Bluff secure the Branch Normal College, now the University of Arkansas at Pine Bluff. As Reconstruction ended John Clayton was active in the Brooks-Baxter war, the controversy in 1874 when both Elisha Baxter and Joseph Brooks claimed the governor's office. Clayton raised troops from Jefferson County and marched them to Little Rock to fight supporters of Elisha Baxter. Clayton remained to the end of the conflict one of Brooks's strongest supporters.

After Reconstruction ended and Democrats regained control of state offices in Arkansas, Republicans still prevailed in several counties in eastern Arkansas with large African-American populations. John Clayton became sheriff of Jefferson County in 1876 and held that office for ten years, being reelected to serve five successive terms.

In 1888 Clayton ran as a Republican candidate for the U.S. Congress against incumbent Democrat Clifton R. Breckinridge, representative for the Second District in Arkansas. After a vigorous campaign Clayton lost the election in November by a narrow margin, 746 votes out of over 34,000 votes cast. This election was one of the most flagrantly fraudulent elections in Arkansas history. In one case in Conway County, four white masked men stormed into one predominately black voting precinct and stole at gun point the ballot box which contained a large majority of Clayton votes.

Losing under such circumstances, Clayton cried foul and contested the election. In late January he arrived in Plumerville, where the ballot box had been stolen, to take depositions from mainly black Republicans who had voted for him. On the evening of January 29, someone shot through the window of the boardinghouse where he was staying, killing him instantly.

The press in Arkansas and around the nation condemned Clayton's murder as a vile crime. Thousands thronged his funeral in Pine Bluff. State officials offered a reward of five thousand dollars for information leading to the capture of the murderer. John Clayton's twin brother, William H. H. Clayton, a federal judge in Fort Smith, and his elder brother Powell believed that Democratic authorities in Conway County had planned the murder or at least were sheltering the assassins. They hired Pinkerton detectives to investigate the murder, but despite the reward and investigation, no murderer was ever found. A widower, John Clayton left behind six orphaned children.

[Biographical information about John Clayton may be found in Fay Hempstead, *A Pictorial History of Arkansas from Earliest Times to the Year 1890* (1890); and James W. Leslie, *Pine Bluff and Jefferson County: A Pictorial History* (1981). See Kenneth C. Barnes, *Who Killed John Clayton? Political Violence and the Emergence of the New South, 1861–1893* (1998), and "Who Killed John M. Clayton? Political Violence in Conway County, Arkansas, in the 1880s," *AHQ* 42 (Winter 1983): 371–404.]

KENNETH C. BARNES

CLAYTON, POWELL (Aug. 7, 1833–Aug. 25, 1915), governor of Arkansas, senator, and ambassador, was born in Bethel County, Pennsylvania. The son of John Clayton and Ann Clark, he was descended from early Quaker settlers but was raised a Methodist. Powell was one of ten children, six of whom died in childhood. The four surviving sons all entered politics.

Clayton studied civil engineering and in 1855 moved to Leavenworth, Kansas, where he became city engineer and surveyor in 1857. When the Civil War broke out in 1861, he became captain of Company E of the First Kansas Infantry Regiment.

The First Kansas saw its first action at Wilson's Creek, Missouri, in July 1861. Clayton's service there gained him a promotion. He became lieutenant colonel of the Fifth Kansas Cavalry in December and then was promoted to colonel in March 1862; the Fifth Kansas captured Carthage, Missouri, that same month. Clayton's regiment participated in the occupation of Helena, Arkansas, in July 1862. In August 1863 Clayton commanded a brigade that accompanied Major General Frederick Steele to Little Rock.

Clayton occupied Pine Bluff in October 1863. Later that month, he and a garrison of 550 men defended the city against Confederate brigadier general John Marmaduke's 2,500-man army. Using the services of escaped slaves, Clayton barricaded the streets with cotton bales, preventing the Confederates from overrunning the town. Promoted to brigadier general, he spent the remainder of the war battling guerrillas.

He found personal success in Pine Bluff as well, making money as a cotton speculator. In 1865 he and his brothers, John and William, purchased a large plantation outside of town. In December of that year he married Adaline McGraw of Helena. The couple had five children, one of whom died in infancy. Clayton settled into the life of an Arkansas planter. A lifelong Democrat, he initially supported President Andrew Johnson in the latter's battle with Republicans in Congress over Reconstruction. However, the growing hostility of his ex-Confederate neighbors and escalating violence against Arkansas blacks and Unionists caused Clayton to change his politics. In April 1867 he became one of the founding members of the Arkansas Republican Party.

As dictated by the First Reconstruction Act, Arkansas held a convention in January 1868 to draft a new state constitution. At an election in March, voters ratified the new constitution and elected Clayton as the state's first Republican governor. Scalawag James M. Johnson became lieutenant governor.

Governor Clayton helped secure legislation for state aid for railroad construction; the creation of free (but segregated) public schools, state schools for the deaf and blind, and the University of Arkansas at Fayetteville; immigration incentives to increase the state's population; and a civil rights act. This progress cost money, which meant higher taxes, and that increased opposition to the Clayton administration.

Clayton attracted fierce criticism when he organized the militia to fight Ku Klux Klan violence that erupted across Arkansas in 1868 and 1869. The militia, which consisted of both black and white troops, fought with little support from the federal government, and its existence outraged many white Arkansans. Clayton declared martial law in fourteen counties and rejected voter registration in twelve counties during the 1868 presidential election. By the spring of 1869, the state Klan organization had disbanded, although violence continued at the local level.

Governor Clayton ruled the state Republican Party autocratically. As a result, an opposition movement, led by Lieutenant Governor Johnson, arose within the party. Charging Clayton with corruption and excessive spending, Johnson and his associates formed the Liberal Republican Party of Arkansas in October 1869.

The state legislature elected Clayton to the United States Senate in early 1871. Clayton's Republican supporters still controlled the legislature, but some members of that body voted for him as a means of removing him from the state. Senator Clayton spoke up for the preservation of civil and political rights for African Americans in the South. He continued running the state Republican Party (he served as Republican national committeeman from 1872 to 1913). In the aftermath of the Brooks-Baxter war and the adoption of Arkansas's 1874 constitution, Clayton initiated the creation of the Poland Committee in the Senate to inquire into Arkansas affairs, but the investigation led nowhere. He served one term.

In the 1880s Clayton involved himself in the development of Eureka Springs. From 1897 to 1905, he served as ambassador to Mexico, protecting the substantial financial investments of American business in that country. After leaving his diplomatic post, he moved to Washington, D.C., but continued to control federal patronage in Arkansas. He died in Washington and is buried at Arlington National Cemetery.

[The few of Clayton's papers that have survived are in the Special Collections Division, University of Arkansas Libraries, Fayetteville. His Letterbook, his official gubernatorial correspondence, is at the Arkansas History Commission, and readers may also refer to his book, *The Aftermath of the Civil War in Arkansas*.]

CATHY KUNZINGER URWIN

CLEBURNE, PATRICK RONAYNE (Mar. 16, 1828–Nov. 30, 1864), lawyer, one of two foreign-born officers to become major generals in the Confederate army, was born in County Cork, Ireland, to Joseph Cleburne, a Protestant doctor of modest means, and Mary Anne Ronayne, daughter of a prominent landowning family. Cleburne attended a Protestant school until his father's death in 1843 forced the family on hard times. At fifteen he was apprenticed to a local doctor and learned to mix medicine. He enlisted in the British Forty-first Regiment of Foot just before his eighteenth birthday and served until September 1849.

After his release from the army, Cleburne boarded a ship for America with his two brothers and a sister. He immediately found work at a drugstore in Cincinnati, filling and delivering prescriptions. He did not remain in Ohio for long; he was soon offered the opportunity to become a druggist in Helena, Arkansas. He accepted, and arrived in the frontier town in 1850. His friends there included the lawyer and future Civil War general Thomas C. Hindman, with whom he became identified politically.

Cleburne was a member of the Whig Party until Hindman organized the Phillips County Democratic Association in the mid-1850s. By that time the Irishman had become a naturalized citizen and had been admitted to the Arkansas bar. As a means to attack their political opponents in the Know-Nothing Party, Hindman and Cleburne bought a local paper, the *Democratic Star*, which they renamed the *State's Rights Democrat*.

In May 1856 the two men were in a gunfight with some Know Nothings and both were shot; Cleburne suffered a serious wound. After he recovered he scaled back his political commitments and engaged in land speculation and railroad promotion. When the secession crisis began, he hoped the Union could be preserved, yet he fully believed in the ideals of southern nationalism and was devoted to the Confederate cause. Several months before the 1860 presidential election he was elected captain of the Yell Rifles, a militia company named for former Arkansas governor Archibald Yell. He took this unit to Little Rock, but the Union commander in the capital turned the federal arsenal over to state authorities before there was any violence. After Arkansas seceded, Cleburne was elected colonel of the First Arkansas Volunteer Infantry, later designated the Fifteenth.

Appointed a brigadier general on March 4, 1862, Cleburne fought at Shiloh; at Richmond, Kentucky, where he was wounded in the jaw; and at Perryville, Kentucky, where he was wounded twice. He was promoted to major general in December 1862. He commanded a division at the Stones River and fought at Chickamauga and Chattanooga, as well as in the Atlanta campaign.

Cleburne is best remembered for his controversial proposal to arm slaves. In early 1864 he submitted a plan that would allow the Confederate government to recruit slaves into the army. He believed they would fight in exchange for their freedom. He suggested that the government should also free the slaves' families, sanctify their marriages, and give legal status to their children. He concluded: "If, then, we touch the institution at all, we would do best to make the most of it ... by emancipating the whole race."

When the proposal reached Jefferson Davis's desk, the Confederate president immediately recognized the inflammatory potential of the recommendation and ordered it suppressed. Some historians believe that this document may have killed any chances Cleburne had of further promotion. Others assert that his participation in the anti-Bragg faction (a cabal of officers in the Army of the Tennessee who opposed the commander, Braxton Bragg) was responsible for his failure to achieve a rank higher than major general.

Cleburne was leading his men in a frontal assault at Franklin, Tennessee, when he was mortally struck down as he reached the Union lines. One account claims that he had two horses killed under him before he charged the enemy position on foot. Five Confederate generals died in the attack that took Cleburne's life. After his death, General Robert E. Lee described Cleburne as "a meteor shining from a clouded sky," and Confederate president Jefferson Davis called him the "Stonewall of the West."

Cleburne was originally interred in Rose Hill Cemetery near the battlefield but was soon reburied near St. John's Chapel on Lucius Polk's plantation outside Columbia, Tennessee. The Ladies Memorial Association of Phillips County, Arkansas, raised funds for a monument, but it was eventually decided to return his body to Helena. Even Jefferson Davis joined the public procession in Memphis that accompanied Cleburne's remains to the dock for the trip downriver. On April 30, 1870, Cleburne was buried for a third time in Evergreen Cemetery in Helena; a monument was erected at his grave in 1891.

[Sources include Craig L. Symonds, *Stonewall of the West: Patrick Cleburne and the Civil War* (1997); Mauriel Phillips Joslyn, ed., *A Meteor Shining Brightly: Essays on Maj. Gen. Patrick R. Cleburne* (1998); Irving A. Buck, *Cleburne and his Command* (1908; rpt. 1992); Charles Edward Nash, *Biographical Sketches of Gen. Pat Cleburne and Gen. T. C. Hindman* (1898; rpt. 1977); and Howell Purdue and Elizabeth Purdue, *Pat Cleburne: Confederate General* (1973; rpt. 1987).]

ANNE J. BAILEY

COMPTON, NEIL ERNEST (Aug. 1, 1912–Feb. 10, 1999), physician, regional historian, and environmental writer/photographer, was born at Falling Springs Flats in western Benton County to David Compton, a farmer and county judge, and Ida Wilmoth, a homemaker who instilled a love of nature in her son and her daughter Edra at an early age.

Compton earned degrees in zoology and in geology from the University of Arkansas in 1935, acquiring a background in natural resources that served him well as a writer. He received his medical degree from the University of Arkansas Medical School at Little Rock in 1939. He then began his career as a county health officer in Bradley and Washington Counties. At the outbreak of World War II, he entered the United States Navy's medical corps and served in the South Pacific.

When the long war ended, Compton opened his medical practice in Bentonville, specializing in obstetrics and gynecology. A Presbyterian, he also served his community with the Rotary Club, the Benton County Historical Society, and the National Park Service Regional Citizens' Advisory Committee. He retired from medical practice in 1976. A friend, Joe Clark of Fayetteville, once joked that over the years Compton "delivered enough Northwest Arkansas kids into the world to staff his own Navy."

Compton filled what spare time he had doing what he loved to do most—hiking and photographing the rivers, creeks, bluffs, waterfalls, caves, and pioneer homesteads of the remote Ozark region he loved so well. "For me it was fulfillment of those dreams of homecoming during the long months on Guadalcanal," he wrote after a trip through Boxley Valley along the headwaters of the Buffalo River in Newton County. "I had come to as lovely a vale as could be found on earth … it was Shangri-La, the Shalimar, the Vale of Tralee. It was a place to restore the troubled spirit of any man."

Compton probably would have been content to remain a respected and beloved physician had not the United States Army Corps of Engineers in 1956 revived its plans to flood his cherished "vales" and historical sites along the Buffalo River with high dams at Gilbert and Lone Rock. Various fishing clubs and conservation organizations in Arkansas and elsewhere quickly rallied to oppose these dams in an effort to save this nationally famous float-fishing waterway. They feared these small, wildly fluctuating reservoirs would destroy the Buffalo's lucrative smallmouth bass fishery. However, there was no single statewide organization devoted to saving the Buffalo River. That would soon change.

In October 1961 Compton accompanied a team of specialists from the National Park Service that surveyed the river to see if it merited protection as a unit of the National Park System. The team left Arkansas very impressed with the Buffalo River and with Neil Compton. In May 1962 Harold and Margaret Hedges of the Ozark Wilderness Waterways Club (OWWC) of Kansas City, Missouri, invited Compton to canoe the Buffalo with the club and its guest, United States Supreme Court justice William O. Douglas. An author and internationally known conservationist, Douglas was captivated by the beauty of the Buffalo, and his enthusiastic support for the river attracted national media coverage. Compton and other Arkansans on the trip decided that Arkansas needed an organization similar to the OWWC.

On May 24, 1962, a group of Buffalo River enthusiasts gathered in Waterman Hall at the University of Arkansas and organized the "Ozark Society, Inc., To Save the Buffalo River," later shortened to "Ozark Society."

Compton was elected president of the Ozark Society, and his fervor was contagious. His down-home humor, courtesy, courage, and leadership at home and before Congress attracted people from all walks of life to the campaign to save the Buffalo. Even when the dams seemed inevitable—nobody had ever beaten a Corps of Engineers' dam project—he continued to shower the media with his superb black-and-white photographs of the Buffalo River country, an area largely unknown outside the fishing community. His 16mm movies of canoe trips and his slides of the river landscape captivated civic and garden club audiences throughout the state. Slowly but surely a tidal wave of public support began to build for saving the Buffalo. Compton persevered in this demanding leadership role throughout the Ozark Society's stormy, eventful, and colorful ten-year campaign to have the Buffalo River protected.

Congress passed legislation to create the Buffalo National River, and President Richard M. Nixon signed it on March 1, 1972. The law established the nation's first national river, a unique category within the National Park System. In the 1990s the Buffalo National River attracted some one million visitors annually and was a multi-million-dollar economic asset to the region. The Ozark Society has an international membership and regional chapters in Arkansas, Missouri, Oklahoma, and Louisiana. It continues to be one of the mid-South's most influential conservation organizations and boasts an active recreational, conservation, and educational publishing program.

Compton earned nine prestigious conservation awards and was a charter inductee into the Arkansas Outdoor Sportsmen's Hall of Fame in 1992. He received an honorary doctorate from the University of Arkansas in 1986. He wrote three books, for which he also provided photographs: *The High Ozarks: A Vision of Eden* (1982); *The Battle for the Buffalo River* (1992); and *The Buffalo River in Black and White* (1997).

Compton and his childhood sweetheart, Laurene Putman, were married on September 15, 1935, and she "floated the river of life" with him for fifty-five years. They were the parents of Ellen Compton Shipley, Edra Ann Compton Diaz, and Bill David Compton.

[A collection of Compton's writings and historical records of the Ozark Society is archived in the Special Collections Division, University of Arkansas Libraries, Fayetteville.]

JOHN HEUSTON

CONE, JOHN CARROLL (July 4, 1891–Aug. 12, 1976), promoter of civil aviation, was born in Snyder, Arkansas, to Jesse H. Cone, a salesman, and Annie A. Cone. John attended Ouachita College and worked as an automobile distributor before enlisting in the army. A contemporary of Arkansas's World War I ace Field Kindley, Cone finished ground school and was transferred for flight training to England on October 26, 1917. Although he had three probable, but only one confirmed, combat kills as a fighter pilot, his greater skill proved to be as an instructor. His early claim to fame was discovering and training Eddie Rickenbacker as a combat pilot. Rickenbacker finished the war with the American high total of twenty-six kills.

After the war Cone returned to Arkansas and used his political connections to secure President Calvin Coolidge's approval for the establishment of the 154th Observation Squadron of the Arkansas National Guard. Cone became a lieutenant colonel in the ANG, serving as the first commanding officer of the 154th. The 154th played a major role in surveying damage in the Arkansas river delta and providing relief to isolated people by means of crude air drops of food and other necessities during the great Mississippi River floods of 1927 and 1929.

Cone served two terms as Arkansas state auditor from 1925 to 1929. Throughout his life he managed to combine his political skill and his passion for aviation. This was evidenced when he campaigned for his first term as auditor by touring the state in his single-motor biplane. He held one of the first civilian pilot licenses, No. 4.

Cone initiated the state's first airport development program, and in 1926 spearheaded the Little Rock Air Meet Association, which sponsored the National Balloon Race and Air Race. That same year, Cone and W. F. Moody formed the Arkansas Aircraft Company. The company struggled until it employed a German emigré, Albert Vollmecke, as chief engineer. Soon afterward Cone persuaded Memphis financier Robert Snowden Jr. to buy into the company, forestalling financial problems. With Cone as sales director, Snowden changed the company name to Command-Aire in 1927.

The company quickly expanded to become the top aircraft manufacturer in the South and one of the nation's largest. One of the company's first achievements was the entry of a stock Command-Aire biplane in the 1929 Daniel Guggenheim International Safe Aircraft Competition. The commercial model beat out numerous experimental or hybrid aircraft designed especially for the competition, finishing second to the Curtiss Tanager entry. Among the notables bested by Command-Aire's two-seat biplane was James S. McDonnell's Doodlebug.

Command-Aire capitalized on the biplane's stability and safety after the competition, and by 1929 ranked eleventh in the nation in number of licensed aircraft produced. Unfortunately for Cone and his business associates, a double blow in 1929 crippled the company. The stock-market crash dried up investment capital at the same time that the aviation industry had overbuilt for the fledgling demand of the period. A frantic scramble of mergers and buyouts among the nation's largest aircraft manufacturers ensued. Snowden thought he had positioned Command-Aire to take advantage of the mergers, but instead found his company shut out and forced to cease production in January 1930.

Bankruptcy followed for the company, but not before its greatest achievement. Cone, Snowden, company vice president Charles Taylor, and members of the Little Rock Chamber of Commerce formed a racing association to enter Vollmecke's masterpiece of design, the Command-Aire MR-1, in a national cross-country race. Pilot Lee Gehlbach flew the single-engine monoplane racer, dubbed "Little Rocket," to victory in the All American Flying Derby in July 1930.

Shortly thereafter, Command-Aire was placed into receivership. Cone moved on to a position with the federal Air Commerce Bureau, becoming the assistant director from 1933 to 1936. In 1937 he was hired by Pan American Airlines as the manager of its North Atlantic Division. In this capacity he was supervisor of operations for Pan Am's famous Yankee Clipper seaplane, which inaugurated commercial passenger service across the Atlantic.

He remained politically active through aviation, serving as an advisor on commercial aviation to Franklin D. Roosevelt and Harry S. Truman. He retired from Pan American in 1969 as a vice president. Married twice, Cone had four children. He died in Bethesda, Maryland.

[See the J. Carroll Cone, Robert Snowden, and Command-Aire Files, Arkansas Aviation Historical Association Archives, Little Rock. See also William M. Smith's "The Right Plane at the Wrong Time: A Brief History of the Command-Aire Company," *AHQ* 51 (Autumn 1992): 224–46; and the *Arkansas Gazette*, Nov. 5, 1980. An obituary is in the *Arkansas Gazette*, Aug. 13, 1976.]

WILLIAM M. SMITH JR.

CONWAY, ELIAS NELSON

CONWAY, ELIAS NELSON (May 17, 1812–Feb. 28, 1892), governor, was born in Greeneville, Tennessee, to Thomas Conway, a planter, and Ann Rector, the "noble mother of so many distinguished sons." The ninth of ten children, Elias Conway watched his brothers achieve prominence in public service as delegate to Congress, governor, state supreme court judge, state surveyor general, and physician.

When he was six years old, Conway's family moved to Missouri, where he received his formal education at the school of Alonzo Pearson and at Bonne Femme Academy. Following several of his brothers, he moved to Arkansas in 1833. He was appointed United States deputy surveyor in 1834. In July 1835 territorial governor William Savin Fulton appointed Conway territorial auditor to fill an unexpired term; the territorial assembly elected him to that position later in the year. Upon statehood the general assembly made Conway the first auditor of the state, a position he held from 1836 to 1849. His advocacy of the distribution of forfeited lands to settlers who would live there preceded the national Homestead Act by twenty years.

Conway received the Democratic nomination for governor at the party convention in December 1843, a year after he became old enough to hold the office. He withdrew from the campaign after widespread criticism of the poorly attended convention and of Conway himself. The Conways, with their kin the Rectors and the Johnsons, were called "the Family" or "the Dynasty" because of their domination of pre–Civil War politics in Arkansas. Conway's youth and inexperience suggested to some that the Family had picked one of its own over a more-qualified candidate.

Losing his 1848 bid for reelection, Conway returned to private life as an attorney and land agent. In 1852 the Democratic Party convention again nominated him for governor. He was opposed by Bryan H. Smithson, an independent Democrat whom the Whigs endorsed. Conway was labeled the "dirt roads candidate" for his conservative stance favoring good dirt roads over the uncertain promise of railroads. Conway won the election, garnering 15,442 votes to 12,414 for Smithson. Four years later Conway defeated James Yell, the American Party (Know-Nothing) candidate.

In the 1853 meeting of the general assembly, five railroad companies were chartered, but not until after it adjourned did Congress grant land to the state for railroads. One of the hottest political debates of the decade occurred over competing proposals for terminus locations for the railroads and Governor Conway's hesitation to call a special session to set the conditions for the dispersal of these federal lands. Conway was closely allied with the organizers of the Cairo and Fulton Railroad and felt that the company needed time to proceed responsibly. He also thought that a special session would be a waste of money, and he liked the idea of waiting to call the general assembly to give family member Robert Johnson, whom he had appointed to the senate, time to get established before the legislative body could vote to fill the position.

In the session of the general assembly convened in November 1854, Conway suggested that the eastern end of the congressionally authorized railroad branch to the Mississippi River be located at Hopefield, opposite Memphis. He recommended that the route go through Clarendon, so that it could be shared by proposed railroads to Helena and Napoleon. The general assembly picked Hopefield by one vote, but allowed the Memphis and Little Rock Company to follow the more direct route through DeValls Bluff. In September 1857 the locomotive "Little Rock" carried dignitaries on the first railroad ride in Arkansas.

Conway's greatest triumph came in an ongoing battle with the Real Estate Bank. Created in the administration of his brother James, the State Bank and the Real Estate Bank were thought to be necessary components of a healthy, growing state. The failure of these two entities burdened the state with long-term debt and bad credit. The Real Estate Bank proved the toughest to deal with; it was not a government entity, but the faith of the state was pledged when its bonds were sold. Conway's strategy was to determine the financial situation of the bank and to transfer the bank's assets to a receiver. He persuaded the general assembly to create a new court of chancery in Pulaski County to place the bank in receivership. His success still left the state in debt, because he was unwilling to tax the citizenry to pay it off.

Conway reformed swampland reclamation, improved the prison, successfully promoted the state's assumption of the School for the Blind, and initiated Arkansas's first geological survey. The 1850s saw the population double and the plantation system of the Old South become firmly established. In spite of the cloud of debt hanging over it, the state enjoyed unparalleled prosperity during Conway's term of office. By one analysis, in 1860 Arkansas ranked sixteenth among the thirty-four states of the Union in per capita wealth, a status which it has never since approached.

In 1860 Conway retired to a quiet, nearly reclusive life. He died more than three decades later in Little Rock after falling head first into his fireplace. He is buried in Mount Holly Cemetery.

[See William B. Worthen, "Elias Nelson Conway, 1852–1860," in *The Governors of Arkansas: Essays in Political Biography,* Timothy P. Donovan, Willard B. Gatewood Jr., and Jeannie M. Whayne, eds., 2d ed. (1995).]

WILLIAM B. WORTHEN

CONWAY, JAMES SEVIER (Dec. 4, 1796– Mar. 3, 1855), planter, first governor of Arkansas, was born in Green County, Tennessee, the son of Thomas Conway and Anne Rector. Wealthy by frontier standards, the Conway family grew corn and cotton and raised livestock on their Tennessee plantation. Conway's father employed private tutors to teach his seven sons and

three daughters. In 1818 the family moved to St. Louis, Missouri, where Conway learned the art of land surveying from his uncle Elias Rector.

Appointed as a federal land surveyor in 1820, Conway was assigned to survey the territory of Arkansas's western boundary with the Choctaw Nation and the southern boundary with Louisiana. In 1826 he married Mary Jane Bradley, daughter of a prominent pioneer family in the Red River area. The couple had ten children, five of whom died in infancy or early childhood. In 1832 he was named surveyor general of the territory. His income as a surveyor allowed him to purchase land along the Red River some fifteen miles west of the present-day Bradley. By the mid-1830s he owned more than two thousand acres of land and eighty slaves. Now in the planter class, he built a larger house a short distance from his original dwelling and named his plantation Walnut Hill. His wealth also allowed him to build a summer cottage at Magnet Cove and a bathhouse at Hot Springs.

Entering politics in 1828 he was defeated, then elected in 1831, to represent Lafayette and Union Counties in the territorial legislature. His large family gave him strong kinship ties in Arkansas and with the presidential administration of Andrew Jackson. Using those connections, he was elected the first governor of the state in 1836.

Conway's tenure as governor was a mixture of success and controversy. Under his administration the state's institutional structure took shape, including the banking system, the prison system, and an expanded network of public roads. A rapid increase in population (from 52,240 to 97,574) during his four years in office greatly increased tax collections. That, coupled with turn-back funds from the federal government, allowed the young state to show a surplus in its treasury after only two years of operation.

The early success of the state's finances caused problems for the Conway administration. The newly adopted state constitution prohibited the legislature from levying taxes in excess of the revenue needed for normal operations. When the first year's collection showed income exceeding costs, Conway called the general assembly into special session to revise the tax code. The lower rate of assessment coincided with a national recession and a cutback in federal funds. The state's banking system collapsed, and the state was plunged into economic turmoil.

Conway also found himself caught up in controversy. During the summer of 1836 reports circulated in Little Rock that Indians were gathering in force on the state's western border and threatening to attack local settlements. To meet this threat, Conway assigned a militia unit of battalion strength to federal officials at Fort Towson. Strong disagreement arose over the choice of a commander for the volunteers. In an early election, the troops chose Absalom Fowler, a captain in the Pulaski County militia and Conway's chief opponent in the gubernatorial election. When the troops rescinded their vote and chose Leban C. Howell, an officer in the Pope County unit, Conway supported Howell. Fowler refused to yield and ordered Howell arrested; Conway intervened. Fowler countered by demanding a court of inquiry to investigate the governor's conduct. The court's findings proved less than definitive, but Fowler boasted that his position had been vindicated. Angered by his response, Conway released the court record to the newspapers along with a letter Fowler had written which was highly critical of the governor. Public opinion supported Conway and Fowler dropped his charges, but the incident greatly polarized political opinion.

Much of Conway's tenure as governor was marred by bad health. During the summer of 1838 he became seriously ill and considered resigning from office. He spent several weeks at Hot Springs and at home at Walnut Hill. Because of his health he refused to seek a second term. He returned to his life as a planter. The balance of his life was devoted to farming and local affairs. Long an advocate of education, he led efforts to establish Lafayette Academy in his home county in 1842. He died of pneumonia and is buried in the family cemetery at Walnut Hill.

[See C. Fred Williams, "James Sevier Conway, 1836–1840," in *The Governors of Arkansas: Essays in Political Biography,* Timothy P. Donovan, Willard B. Gatewood Jr., and Jeannie M. Whayne, eds., 2d ed. (1995).]

C. FRED WILLIAMS

CORBIN, JOSEPH CARTER (Mar. 26, 1833–Jan. 1911), educator and writer, was born in Chillicothe, Ohio, the son of William and Susan Corbin. He attended school during the winter months, a common practice at the time. At sixteen he traveled to Louisville, Kentucky, to assist the Reverend Henry A. Adams from whom he received private tutoring while he worked as a teaching assistant.

Corbin graduated from Ohio University in Athens with B.A., M.A., and Ph.D. degrees by 1853. He returned to Louisville where he worked as a clerk in a mercantile company and in a bank as a clearinghouse clerk. Later he taught school for eight years and helped on the *Colored Citizen* newspaper.

In 1866 Corbin married Mary J. Ward, a Kentucky native, in Cincinnati, Ohio. They had six children, two of whom lived. The family moved to Little Rock, where Corbin worked as a reporter for the *Arkansas Republican.* Later he became a money-order clerk in the Little Rock post office.

In 1873 Corbin became Arkansas superintendent of public instruction, and by virtue of that office he was also president of the University of Arkansas Board of Trustees. As president he signed the contract for the construction of University Hall, the first building at the University of Arkansas, Fayetteville, now called Old Main. He served as superintendent of public instruction until the close of the Brooks-Baxter war. That conflict ended in 1874 with a new state constitution and a change in political power from the Republican Party to the Democratic Party. At the end of the Brooks-Baxter war, the Arkansas General Assembly passed an act vacating all trusteeships of the university, forcing Corbin to resign. He then taught for two years at Lincoln University in Jefferson City, Missouri.

Once in control of the state government, the Democrats proceeded with plans for a branch of the university in Pine Bluff. That the Democratic governor, Augustus Garland, persuaded Corbin to return to Arkansas to oversee the establishment of the new school clearly indicates the high regard in which he was held by even his political opponents. In 1875 he was appointed principal of Branch Normal College in Pine Bluff, a position he held until 1901.

Branch Normal trained black teachers for black schools. A five-dollar fee paid to the county judge was the only admission requirement. In 1887 tuition was free to students who signed an agreement to teach for two years in Arkansas.

Corbin conducted teacher training institutes in Arkansas and Oklahoma, believing that such institutes inspired teachers with a spirit of improvement and gave them the opportunity to see exhibitions and new methods of teaching. At an institute in Pine Bluff in 1886, Corbin said, "The demand for well-qualified teachers has been faithfully supplied by the students from the various normal institutions for the education of the colored youth, which are scattered over the South and from the schools of the North."

Corbin and R. C. Childress, a teacher at Branch Normal, formed the Teachers of Negro Youth, the first state teachers' association for black teachers. Corbin was its first president. Twenty years after his death, the organization became known as the Arkansas Teachers' Association. There was a separate association for white teachers.

Branch Normal grew from 7 students in 1875 to 241 by 1894. Under Corbin's leadership a two-story brick building with classrooms and assembly hall was constructed. A dormitory for girls was also built. An industrial department was established with courses in sewing, typing, and printing. Corbin's daughter worked as the sewing and industrial teacher for women, and his wife taught art at the school.

Corbin wrote articles on mathematics and constructed mathematical puzzles. These were published in *Barns' Educational Monthly, School Visitors,* the *Mathematical Visitor,* the *Mathematical Magazine,* and the *Mathematical Gazette.* He spoke and read Greek, Latin, German, French, Spanish, Italian, Hebrew, and Danish. He taught Greek and Latin at the college until the curriculum was modified in 1889. He played the piano, organ, and flute and taught students to play these instruments. He also trained the Normal School choir of forty voices, which was featured at every commencement.

Corbin was also civic-minded. He served as secretary of the Colored Freemen of Arkansas and as vice president of the Colored Industrial Fair. He was a Baptist and a Sunday School superintendent for many years.

Eventually Corbin experienced conflict with the board of trustees of Branch Normal, then still a part of the University of Arkansas. In 1905 he left there to become principal of Merrill public school in Pine Bluff. He died in Pine Bluff.

[Sources include the *Biennial Report of the State Superintendent of Public Instruction of the State of Arkansas, 1873–74, 1885–86, 1891–92;* and deed records, Washington County Courthouse, Fayetteville, Book X (1873): 123–43.

See also D. B. Gaines, *Racial Possibilities as Indicated by the Negroes of Arkansas* (1898); Harrison Hale, *University of Arkansas: 1871–1948* (1948); Robert A. Leflar, *The First*

One Hundred Years: Centennial History of the University of Arkansas (1972); Thomas E. Patterson, *History of the Arkansas Teachers' Association* (1981); John H. Reynolds and David Y. Thomas, *History of the University of Arkansas* (1910); William J. Simmons, *Men of Mark: Eminent, Progressive and Rising* (1970); and the *Arkansas Gazette,* Aug. 23, 1884, July 26, 1886, and Sept. 26, 1886.]

IZOLA PRESTON

CORNISH, HILDA KAHLERT (Jan. 24, 1878–Nov. 19, 1965), founder of the Arkansas birth-control movement, was born in St. Louis, Missouri, to German immigrants Rudolph Kahlert, a carpenter, and Sophie (maiden name unknown).

After earning a high-school diploma, Hilda left St. Louis to work as a milliner in New York. She moved to Little Rock in 1901 and in 1902 married a widowed banker, Edward Cornish. They had six children between 1904 and 1917. Hilda Cornish focused on raising her children during the first two decades of her married life, but she also did volunteer work. She served on the board of managers of the State Farm for Women, a correctional institution, and as an officer of the Arkansas Federation of Women's Clubs. She was appointed by Governor Thomas C. McRae to lead volunteers aiding victims of the great flood of 1927 in Arkansas.

Edward Cornish committed suicide in 1928. Afterward, Hilda devoted much of her time to reform and social work. In the summer of 1930 she met Margaret Sanger, the founder and leader of the American birth-control movement. The two developed a friendship maintained by correspondence and occasional meetings. During that summer Cornish visited Sanger's Clinical Research Bureau in New York. Later the same year she launched the Arkansas birth-control movement.

At Cornish's initiative, a group of physicians, business and religious leaders, and women active in civic work formed the Arkansas Eugenics Association. In January 1931 the association opened the Little Rock Birth Control Clinic, which was housed in the basement of Baptist Hospital. There, poor white women could get contraceptives at a time when men and women urgently sought to limit the size of their families. What motivated Cornish and her fellow birth-control advocates must be understood in the context of economics and the Great Depression.

Until the clinic opened only those women who

could afford a private physician had access to safe, effective contraceptives. African-American women had to wait until 1937 for the clinic to open its doors to them. The Arkansas Eugenics Association reached its immediate goal when several medical units across the state in the late 1930s began to give contraceptive advice to women of limited means.

The success of the Arkansas birth-control movement can be attributed largely to Cornish. She had connections within Little Rock's network of civic volunteers, and she knew who to call on to rally support for a controversial cause. Among the leaders of the medical community who gave their time or lent their names were Dr. Darmon A. Rhinehert, Dr. Joe H. Sanderlin, and Dr. Charles Henry Sr. Religious leaders such as Rabbi Ira Sanders of Temple B'nai Israel and the Reverend Hay Watson Smith of the Second Presbyterian Church were crucial to the success of the movement. Support from business leaders such as the Pfeifer and Cohn families influenced the outcome of the crusade. No significant organized opposition to the movement arose in Little Rock.

Cornish also worked with the National Committee on Federal Legislation for Birth Control. This group, led by Margaret Sanger, was formed to influence legislators and the public to change laws that obstructed free access to contraceptive information. In 1936 in the case of *United States v. One Package,* this legal hindrance was eliminated, and both medical and public opinion became more favorable.

Since many medical units across the state included birth-control services by 1940, the Arkansas Eugenics Association changed direction and limited its work to referrals and education. The name of the association changed to the Planned Parenthood Association of Arkansas in 1942. Cornish spent the following two decades lobbying for the inclusion of contraceptive services in the public health system. In her mind, families should have access to safe, effective contraceptives regardless of their financial resources. This goal was accomplished when, in the mid-1960s, the state health department took on the responsibility of distributing contraceptives to the public.

Cornish was involved in many other community activities. Her leadership in the women's club movement aided her when calling on women to fill the ranks of the birth-control movement. A charter member of the Women's City Club, she served as its president in 1934–35. She was also active in the Democratic Party during the 1940s.

She was busy in civic work until the age of seventy-five, when she was incapacitated after spinal surgery. Two years later she traveled in Southeast Asia. At her death at the age of eighty-five, she still lived in her own house. She was cared for by nurses, a housekeeper, and her daughter Hilda Coates, who lived close by. She was a freethinker well ahead of her time on such issues as birth control and euthanasia. She was not a member of an organized religion but asked for Rabbi Sanders to give a eulogy at her funeral.

[Sources include the files of the Arkansas Eugenics Association and the Little Rock Birth Control Clinic, which are in the History of Public Health in Arkansas Collection, University of Arkansas for Medical Sciences Library, Little Rock. Interviews with Hilda Cornish Coates, Raida Pfeifer, a volunteer for the movement, and Dr. Charles Henry Sr. are at the Oral History Research Office, University of Memphis, Tennessee.

The UALR Archives and Special Collections, UALR Library, has interviews with Rabbi Ira Sanders and Louis B. Hall in its Oral History Collection, and a file on Hilda Cornish in the Arkansas Women's History Institute Collection. An obituary is in the *Arkansas Gazette,* Nov. 20, 1965.]

MARIANNE LEUNG

COUCH, HARVEY CROWLEY (Aug. 21, 1877– July 30, 1941), industrialist, developed the first electric power network in Arkansas. Born at Calhoun, Columbia County, three miles southeast of Magnolia, his parents were Thomas G. Couch, a Methodist minister, and Manie Heard. Couch's early education consisted of a few months in a one-room rural school. Later he entered Magnolia Academy under the tutelage of Pat M. Neff (later president of Baylor University).

Because of his overgrown size, the students taunted Couch. He wanted to quit school, but Neff told him, "A quitter never wins and a winner never quits. Men like you have built empires." He stayed in school and never forgot Neff's advice.

Couch became a railway clerk on a train between McNeil, Arkansas, and Bienville, Louisiana. While riding trains, he conceived the idea of starting a rural telephone company. He raised sufficient funds to build a fifteen-mile telephone line between Arcadia and Bienville, Louisiana, in 1903. With financial assistance from Dr. H. Longino of Magnolia, a former employer, he expanded the system into Texas, Oklahoma, Arkansas, and Louisiana. In 1911 the telephone company owned fifteen hundred miles of line and fifty telephone exchanges. Southwestern Bell Telephone bought the system for $1,200,000, and Couch became a millionaire at thirty-four.

Couch married Jessie Johnson, in Athens, Louisiana, October 4, 1904. They were the parents of Johnson O., Harvey C. Jr., Kirke, William Thomas, and Catherine. Of Couch's early wealth one commentator said Couch "remained the same fine, wholesome character he had always been." His charisma and ability to lead others was a key to his success. He and his wife continued to live simply in an unpretentious house, though they knew two presidents and members of Franklin D. Roosevelt's cabinet.

From early childhood Couch was fascinated with electricity. His dream was to develop a power network similar to his telephone system. In 1911 each city had a power plant, usually part of a factory. In Arkadelphia a flour mill furnished electricity to customers at night. Malvern's power was obtained from two small generators in a chair factory. The service was not dependable. In 1913 Couch bought both plants and connected the towns with a transmission line. New generators were installed in Malvern and run with steam from a lumber mill. The company was incorporated as the Arkansas Light and Power Company (later Arkansas Power and Light Company).

Couch was hampered by the reluctance of Arkansas banks to loan money to power companies; in 1914 he made a trip to New York to seek financial aid. Through Charles McCain, president of Bankers' Trust Company, Little Rock, he met John Watkins of Guaranty Trust Company in New York and was able to make an initial loan of two hundred thousand dollars to continue the power system's expansion. With the financing, Couch was able to buy plants in Camden, Marianna, Newport, El Dorado, Pine Bluff, and other Arkansas cities, as well as the state's first hydroelectric plant, built by Alphonse Brewster of Pine Bluff at Russellville.

Couch was the consummate salesman. He promoted the use of electricity in industry and agriculture, for example, converting rice-farm water pumps to electricity and the Arkadelphia flour mill from steam to electric power. The system's largest steam generating plant was in Pine Bluff, and the company's offices were moved there in 1917.

Flave Carpenter, a riverboat pilot, convinced Couch the Ouachita River was a potential power source. Couch employed Dean William Gladson, a University of Arkansas engineering professor, to study the river and recommend sites for two or three hydroelectric dams. With complete plans and cost estimates Couch was able to obtain financing to build a dam, named for Harmon L. Remmel, who assisted him in securing the required Corps of Engineers permit.

Remmel Dam was completed in 1924, and five years later Carpenter Dam was constructed. While building a power network in Arkansas, Couch was also involved in organizing the Mississippi Power and Light Company and the Louisiana Power Company. A 30,000-kilowatt plant built at Sterlington, Louisiana, connected the three companies by one power grid. The companies merged in 1926 with the Electric Bond and Share Company of New York to become one of the largest power companies in the South.

As a boy Couch had built a track of planks on a hill to coast down in a small box on wheels. In 1928 his dream of a railroad came true. He bought the Louisiana and Arkansas Railroad, a 188-mile line between Hope, Arkansas, and Tioga, Louisiana. In 1938 he purchased control of the Kansas City Southern Railway and merged the two lines.

Couch loved Arkansas and was active in civic affairs. During World War I he was fuel administrator for the state. He was flood relief director for Arkansas in 1927, and President Hoover appointed him a director of the Reconstruction Finance Corporation in 1931. He continued to serve under President Roosevelt. He prevailed on his friend Will Rogers, the humorist, to make a four-day tour of Arkansas in 1931 to raise money for victims of the 1930 drought. Couch was chairman of the Arkansas Centennial Celebration Commission in 1936.

Couch died at his Lake Catherine retreat. The *Batesville Daily Guard* said: "Mr. Couch had an abiding faith in Arkansas and her people and an unfailing interest in his fellow men, humble and great. His vision never wavered even in the depths of the depression and adversity."

[See Stephen Wilson, *Harvey Couch: An Entrepreneur Brings Electricity to Arkansas* (1986); Winston P. Wilson, *Harvey Couch: The Master Builder* (1986); *Arkansas Gazette*, June 15, 1936, July 31, 1941; the *Pine Bluff Commercial*, Aug. 22, 1917, Oct. 4, 1926, Nov. 22, 1926, July 30,

1941, Oct. 12, 1975; the *Pine Bluff Daily Graphic,* Jan. 11, 1914, June 7, 1930; and the *Batesville Daily Guard,* July 31, 1941.]

JAMES W. LESLIE

CRITTENDEN, ROBERT (Jan. 1, 1797–Dec. 18, 1834), first lieutenant governor of Arkansas Territory, was born in Woodford County, Kentucky. He married Ann Innis Morris on October 1, 1822, in Kentucky.

Crittenden, brother of John J. Crittenden, an influential senator from Kentucky, entered the United States Army in 1814 and served through 1818. After military service, he came to Arkansas and joined another brother's law practice in Russellville, after which he was admitted to the Arkansas bar. Primarily through the efforts of his brother the senator, he was appointed first secretary of the territory in 1819 by President James Monroe. General James Miller, appointed as the first governor, delayed in coming to the state, and Crittenden served as acting governor from July until December 26, 1819, when Miller arrived at Arkansas Post.

As acting governor, Crittenden carefully created a political party loyal to him. During the six months before the arrival of the governor, he quickly filled every official post his authority permitted. He also declared Arkansas a territory of the second class, which allowed the territory its own legislature and judiciary. He set the election date of the legislature and judiciary to allow a minimum of campaigning and was able to cause the election of most of the officials loyal to him, thus increasing his power and political prestige.

In 1820 Crittenden used his power to urge the legislature to move the territorial capital from Arkansas Post to Little Rock, where he owned and controlled substantial land. From the beginning, Crittenden was a master politician, forming allegiances and groups of friends in the absence of defined political parties. Soon, after the capital was moved, he established a law partnership with Chester Ashley, another political force in the territory, who also owned and controlled land in the Little Rock area.

From 1823 Crittenden supported the political faction headed by Henry W. Conway. Conway was the public face; Crittenden was the backstage commander. Young and handsome, Crittenden was described as having a tightlipped mouth that bespoke contempt and a chin that proclaimed determination. His detractors described him as flashy, unscrupulous, bold, and determined to succeed by fair means or foul.

In 1824 Governor Miller resigned. Conway, now a member of Congress, recommended Crittenden for the post, but President Monroe appointed George Izard of Pennsylvania as governor. Crittenden remained lieutenant governor. His relationship with Izard was always cool. He was rewarded somewhat for his prominence in the state in 1825 when Crittenden County was named for him.

Crittenden continued his behind-the-scenes control of Arkansas politics until 1827 when he perceived comments by his old crony, Conway, as criticism and challenged Conway to a duel. On a cool October morning the two met on a sandbar on the east bank of the Mississippi River opposite the mouth of the White River. Crittenden fell asleep awaiting the arrival of Conway and his entourage. He wounded Conway with the first shot, and Conway died weeks later from the wound.

Several years afterward Governor Izard died. Crittenden, who resented the repeated appointment of outsiders as governor, again applied for the job; however, in 1829 President Andrew Jackson appointed John Pope, another out-of-state resident. To add insult to injury, Jackson also removed Crittenden from his position. Despite this, Crittenden continued his behind-the-scenes politics. His former law partner, Chester Ashley, referred to him as the "Cardinal Wolsey" of Arkansas politics.

In the congressional election of 1833, Crittenden decided to run against Ambrose H. Sevier, who had been elected in a special election in 1827 to the seat vacated by Conway's death. Crittenden's only campaign for elected office ended in his gaining 36 percent of the vote cast, against Sevier's 64 percent. Clearly in serious decline at that time, Crittenden died a year later of pleurisy in Vicksburg, Mississippi, where he was practicing law.

Crittenden had a profound impact on the first years of Arkansas Territory. His strength of personality, intelligence, and leadership moved the territory forward at a rapid pace, and his decision to declare the territory ready for elected officials, under doubtful circumstances, propelled the territory to statehood earlier than would have occurred without him. His rough-and-tumble style of politics suited the period, and although he killed a political rival and participated in another duel, he was not so unusual, simply more flamboyant and resolute than most of his contemporaries.

[See Farrar Newberry, "Some Notes on Robert Crittenden," *AHQ* 36 (Spring 1977); Edwin Marshall Williams, "The Conway-Crittenden Duel," *Arkansas Historical Review* 1 (Feb. 1934); and Lonnie J. White, *Politics on the Southwestern Frontier: Arkansas Territory, 1819–1836* (1964).]

ALLEN W. BIRD II

DANIEL, THASE CHRISTINE FERGUSON

(Dec. 5, 1907–Sept. 10, 1990), was the daughter of Mr. and Mrs. C. C. Ferguson of Pine Bluff. Thase Ferguson graduated from Ouachita College in 1927 and received a bachelor of arts degree in music from that institution in 1929. While she was there she met John T. Daniel of Arkadelphia, and they were married on June 29, 1930.

The Daniels made their home in El Dorado, where John Daniel was a businessman. They had a daughter, Daphna Ann, in 1937, and began to take family vacations across the country. During these outings, Thase Daniel snapped pictures of scenery and wildlife. After a failed attempt at taking a picture of a Stellers' jay, she began studying works of well-known wildlife photographers. With no formal training in photography, she put technique into practice by taking pictures of birds near her home. As her fascination with outdoor photography grew, she began to apply the same principles of study and discipline to photography that she had brought to her practice of the piano. "Whatever I do," she once said, "a pipe organ or what, I want to do it well." She ultimately came to be recognized as one of the world's leading nature and wildlife photographers.

From her home in El Dorado, she traveled the world recording all kinds of creatures and scenery on film. This took her on numerous adventures. For example, she went on a two-week expedition by dog sled across the Greenland icecap, rode an elephant across a river in India, and suffered a broken ankle when attacked by a six-hundred-pound bull sea lion.

Daniel's photographs appeared in major magazines and publications, spanning a career of over thirty years. Her pictures were featured in *Ranger Rick, Field and Stream, Sports Afield, International Wildlife*, and National Geographic and Audubon Society books, among others. Probably Daniel's best-known photograph is of her husband fishing for trout in a Colorado stream. Kodak placed the poster in practically every camera store in America in the 1950s. The pinnacle of her accomplishments, however, came with the 1984 publication of her book, *Wings on the Southwind,* which featured photographs of southern flora and fauna.

Today, Riley-Hickingbotham Library, Ouachita Baptist University, is the home of Daniel's collection of slides and field notes. The roughly fifty-seven thousand slides, which were donated shortly before her death in 1990, represent the best of almost a quarter-million slides taken during her career.

Daniel died in El Dorado and is buried there.

[The Thase Daniel Collection, Special Collections, Riley-Hickingbotham Library, Ouachita Baptist University, includes slides, field notes, and related materials. See the *Arkansas Gazette,* Sept. 10, 1961, and Apr. 7, 1981; the *El Dorado News,* Nov. 7, 1982; and Ann Guilfoyle and Susan Rayfield, *Wildlife Photography: The Art and Technique of Ten Masters* (1982).]

WENDY BRADLEY RICHTER

DAVIS, JEFF

(May 6, 1862–Jan. 3, 1913), governor and United States senator, was born near Rocky Comfort, Arkansas. His parents, Lewis W. Davis, a Baptist preacher and Confederate chaplain, and Elizabeth Phillips, a native of Alabama, named him after the president of the Confederacy. In 1873 the family moved to the railroad town of Russellville. Jeff Davis spent two years at the University of Arkansas before transferring to the law department of Vanderbilt University in 1880. He completed his degree at Cumberland University. In 1882 he became the junior partner of L. W. Davis and Son, and later in the year married Ina Mackenzie, the stepdaughter of Judge Frank Thach. The marriage produced eight children who survived infancy. After his first wife's death in 1910, Davis and Lelia Carter of Ozark married.

Davis's political career began in 1888, when he served as a Democratic presidential elector, stumping the state for Grover Cleveland, white supremacy, and reform. In 1890 and 1892 he was elected district prosecuting attorney. In 1896 he ran for Congress, but lost. Afterward he became absorbed in the presidential campaign of William Jennings Bryan. Davis's performance, entertaining voters with spellbinding oratory, catapulted him to the state attorney generalship in 1898.

His tenure there was the most memorable in the state's history. By challenging the legality of the Kimbell State House Act, which provided for the construction of a new capitol, and by rendering a highly controversial extraterritorial interpretation of the Rector Antitrust Act, he created a major uproar. According to Davis, the Rector Act prohibited any trust from doing business in Arkansas, regardless of where it had been organized. He filed suit against every fire-insurance company operating in the state, demanding their withdrawal from industry-wide pricing agreements. The companies responded by threatening to cancel all existing policies, prompting outrage from businessmen. Supported by the legislature, Davis refused to back down, but was later overruled by the state supreme court. Styling himself a martyr, Davis took his case to the people in the 1900 Democratic primary. He visited virtually every county, crusading against the "Yankee trusts." "The war is on," he declared, "knife to knife, hilt to hilt, foot to foot ... between the corporations ... and the people ... If I win this race I have got to win it from every railroad, every bank and two-thirds of the lawyers and most of the big politicians." Ridiculed by the state press and branded a demagogue, Davis carried seventy-four of seventy-five counties.

His governorship (1901 to 1907) was marked by bitter factionalism and controversies related to his style of politics. His mastery of invective, his ruthless determination to gain control of the legislature and to create a statewide political machine, his struggle to oversee the building of a new state capitol and the reform of the state prison system, and his periodic battles with prohibitionists, ministers, and other members of "the high-collared crowd" led to increasingly desperate attempts to drive him from power. Several opponents accused him of public drunkenness and had him expelled from the Second Baptist Church of Little Rock. In 1903 legislative leaders brought impeachment proceedings against him. But when the impeachment effort failed, Davis counterattacked with charges of persecution and emerged stronger than ever.

During his third term he gained control of the legislature, which approved several of his pet projects, including an antitrust law and the reorganization of penitentiary management. In his last two years as governor Davis devoted most of his energy to a race for the U.S. Senate. Relying on personal charisma, folksy humor, class rhetoric, and white supremacist demagoguery, he successfully challenged incumbent senator James Berry, an aging Confederate veteran.

The rough-and-tumble political combat that had proved so effective in Arkansas seemed out of place in the Senate. Davis introduced an antitrust bill and delivered a long and impassioned harangue against those President Theodore Roosevelt had called "the malefactors of great wealth." The speech drew sharp criticism from the national press and several senatorial colleagues. Davis claimed that his speech had "swept the cobwebs off the ceiling of the Senate chamber," but in truth he was bitterly disappointed by Washington's refusal to take him seriously. Although he apologized for his intemperate rhetoric, it was too late. The press continued to portray him as a wild-eyed, backwoods buffoon, and he retreated into silence.

A deteriorating power base compounded his problems, and he brooded about his lack of influence. In 1909 he introduced a bill prohibiting speculation in crop futures, but the following year his apparent collusion with east Arkansas land speculators tarnished his reform image. He became increasingly absorbed in his family life and spent less and less time in Washington. In the 1912 primary he fought off a stiff challenge, and reelection seemed to rekindle his interest in public policy. But his comeback was cut short by a fatal stroke two months before the expiration of his first term. His funeral was one of the largest in Little Rock history.

Davis left an ambiguous legacy. He was a college-educated attorney, but he convincingly played the role of a hillbilly. Deeply religious, he battled with preachers and prohibitionists throughout his career. Though passionately egalitarian, he became a ruthless political boss. He tried to reform an inhumane penal system, but he was also a vicious racist who promoted black disfranchisement and defended lynching. He was an agrarian radical who dramatized and personalized the problems of downtrodden farmers, but for the most part he practiced a politics of catharsis that inhibited radical change. He was an innovative politician who knew how to acquire and hold power, but his administrations produced more politics than government.

[See Raymond Arsenault, *The Wild Ass of the Ozarks: Jeff Davis and the Social Bases of Southern Politics* (1984).]

RAYMOND ARSENAULT

DEAN, JAY HANNA (Jan. 16, 1910–June 17, 1974), baseball player and television and radio announcer, was born in Lucas, Arkansas, to Albert Dean and Alma Nelson. Dean created some confusion about the place and date of his birth by giving various stories to various reporters. *The Baseball Enclyclopedia*, the standard reference book for major league baseball, still lists his date of birth as January 11, 1911, but Robert Gregory, in his well-researched biography, *Diz,* states categorically that Dean was born in 1910. Dean also created confusion about his given names. In 1929, having always hated the name "Hanna," he began borrowing the name of his half-brother Herman and became, unofficially, Jay Herman Dean. Later the same year, while playing semi-professional baseball in San Antonio, he took the first name of his catcher, Jerome Harris, and began using the name Jerome Herman Dean. Dean got the nickname "Dizzy," by which he would be known all his adult life, in August 1927 when he was in the army. Sergeant Jimmy Brought was drilling two platoons when he saw Dean behind the barracks hurling peeled potatoes at garbage can lids. Brought called him a "dizzy son-of-a-bitch."

Dean once said, "I never got up to the fourth grade —didn't want to pass my ol' man." His "ol' man" was a sharecropper and migrant laborer. Even by the standards of the time and place the family was very poor. Dean worked until he was sixteen picking cotton for fifty cents a day. Then he joined the army and served three years. Two weeks after leaving the army, Dean was pitching for San Antonio Public Service Utilities, the best semipro team in the area. A St. Louis Cardinal scout saw him pitch and signed him to a contract to pitch for Houston in the Texas League.

In 1932, Dean's rookie season with St. Louis, he won eighteen games, lost fifteen, saved two, and led the league in strikeouts and shutouts. In 1933 he won twenty, lost eighteen, saved four, and led the league in complete games and strikeouts. In 1934 he won thirty, lost seven, saved seven, and led the league in wins, winning percentage, complete games, strikeouts, and shutouts. In 1935 he won twenty-eight, saved five, and led the league in wins, complete games, innings pitched, and strikeouts. In 1936 he won twenty-four, lost thirteen, saved eleven, and led the league in complete games, innings pitched, and saves.

While Dean was pitching in the 1937 All-Star Game, his right big toe was broken by a line drive hit by Earl Averill. A few weeks later Dean permanently injured his throwing arm by pitching before the toe was fully healed. He was traded to the Chicago Cubs in 1938 and pitched for them until 1941, when he appeared in but one game. In 1947 he made a final appearance in a major-league game, pitching four scoreless innings for the St. Louis Browns.

From 1932 until he injured his arm in 1937, Dizzy Dean was baseball's biggest star. In 1934 he was the National League's Most Valuable Player, a rare honor for a pitcher. He was also voted Male Athlete of the Year in 1934. He was the loudest, best, and most devil-may-care member of the Gashouse Gang, the depression-era St. Louis Cardinal teams consisting of such players as Ducky Medwick, Rip Collins, Frankie Frisch, Leo Durocher, Pepper Martin, and Dizzy's younger brother Paul. Just before the 1934 season, Dean promised that he and Paul together would win forty-five games; Dizzy won thirty, and Paul won nineteen. Before the 1934 World Series, a sportswriter asked Dizzy how he expected to beat the powerful Detroit Tigers. "Easy," Dean said. "I'll win two and Paul'll win two." They did precisely that. Accused of being a braggart, Dean said, "It ain't braggin' if you can do it."

From 1941 to 1953 Dean announced baseball games over the radio. From 1953 to 1965, he did play-by-play announcing and color commentary for network television's Game of the Week. His colorful language, poor grammar, and inability to pronounce any name consisting of more than two syllables made him at once popular and controversial. Dean called his language "plain ol' ordinary pinto-bean English." To a critic of his speech, he once responded, "A lot of folks who ain't sayin' ain't ain't eatin'."

Dizzy Dean was elected to Baseball's Hall of Fame in 1953. At the induction ceremony he said, "This is the greatest honor I ever received, and I want to thank the Lord for givin' me a good right arm, a strong back, and a weak mind."

He died of a heart attack in Reno, Nevada, and was buried in Bond, Mississippi.

[Robert Gregory's *Diz: Dizzy Dean and Baseball during the Great Depression* (1992) is the best-written and most thoroughly researched biography, and captures Dean's character. Other sources include Lee Allen, *Dizzy Dean*; (1967); G. H. Fleming, *The Dizziest Season* (1984); Robert Hood, *The Gashouse Gang* (1976); Milton Shapiro, *The Dizzy Dean Story* (1963); and Curt Smith, *America's Dizzy Dean* (1978).]

DONALD S. HAYS

DELLINGER, SAMUEL CLAUDIUS (Jan. 14, 1892–Aug. 12, 1973), zoologist, archeologist, and museum curator, was born at Iron Station, North Carolina, to Robert H. Dellinger and Laura Loftin. He received a bachelor of arts degree in zoology from Trinity College (later Duke University) and a master's degree in zoology from Columbia University in 1917. He married Elsie Adkisson of Conway, Arkansas, the daughter of a prominent businessman. Their one child, Martha, became a professor of architecture at the University of Arkansas.

An early interest in oceanographic fisheries research began in 1913 on and off the Carolina coast and culminated with research at the Marine Biological Laboratory at Woods Hole, Massachusetts, in the summers of 1921, 1923, and 1925. This stream of concern continued with Dellinger's interest in Arkansas wildlife and resource conservation.

His academic career began with an appointment at Hendrix College in 1915–16. He began his tenure at the University of Arkansas in 1921, was appointed head of the zoology department in 1922, and became professor in 1925. In the same year he was appointed curator of the university museum. He held the zoology and museum positions for more than three decades, and he became a dominant figure statewide in zoology and museology.

Dellinger was a leader in advancing the scientific outlook in Arkansas. While a member of the state game and fish commission from 1922 to 1957, he brought a scientific direction to that group, which earlier had been largely political. During this time Arkansas game populations began increasing, so Dellinger's influence may have been critical. He also served as secretary of the state science board. At the university he advised and taught students in the premedical and predental program. Several decades of Arkansas physicians and dentists were subject to his influence early in their careers, and many remained friends as professionals. Since Dellinger taught a conservation course required for degrees in education, his urgent and charismatic teaching in that area affected decades of teachers.

He was outspoken in opposition to the state's anti-evolution law when it passed by popular referendum in 1927. The law forbade the teaching of evolution in public schools. Dellinger intensified the coverage of evolution in his teaching in open defiance of the law. Later in life he championed the Buffalo National River. A fervent New Deal Democrat, he celebrated the Works Progress Adminstration, the Tennessee Valley Authority, and other public works and conservation projects. He was a civil libertarian who sponsored a Jewish fraternity on campus (he was Episcopalian).

Under Dellinger's direction the university museum became the state's primary natural science museum. He is widely regarded as "father" of the museum, although it predated his appointment as curator in 1924. He built collections in zoology, history, ethnology, and geology through gifts and purchases. However, it is the Arkansas archeological collections for which the museum became best known. In 1926 he expressed his idea of what a museum should be: "To a state, a museum is not merely a place for sightseeing but a place for study. Here in the University we have specialists who can make a study of the natural history specimens of the state and at the same time instill in our own boys and girls not only a love for their state but also give them some idea of her wonderful possibilities."

When he joined the museum, he became incensed that out-of-state museums and institutions were excavating prehistoric Indian sites in the state and taking the finds away to their home institutions, robbing Arkansas citizens of access to a part of their heritage. He reacted by combining a museum program of archeological "survey"—excavations to recover artifacts for study and view—with attempts to regulate Arkansas expeditions by out-of-staters. After learning the rudiments of excavation techniques through correspondence with Dr. Carl Guthe, an archeologist on the National Research Council, Dellinger obtained a twenty-thousand-dollar grant from the Carnegie Foundation to do his archeological survey. Over the course of about three years in the early 1930s, he roughly supervised the excavation of over one hundred cave and rock shelter excavations in the Ozarks and the excavations of hundreds of human burials and their associated grave goods from the late prehistoric Indian towns of northeastern Arkansas. Later, during the WPA era of the late 1930s and early 1940s, he was responsible for major excavations of Caddoan culture sites in the Lake Ouachita area of southwestern Arkansas. He also negotiated major gifts and purchases of Arkansas archeological material.

As a result of Dellinger's efforts the university museum became the state's primary archeological repository and agency. The federal government contracted with the museum to do the archeology related to major water reservoirs such as Greer's Ferry, Beaver, De Gray, and Millwood, for the massive Arkansas River Navigation Project and the interstate highway archeological survey and excavation.

The collections which resulted from Dellinger's work remain unsurpassed. While working in the Ozarks, he concentrated on dry deposits in rock shelters and caves in which perishable remains such as sandals, baskets, and plant foods were preserved. These collections have provided recent researchers with valuable information on the evolution of Native American domesticated plants and fiber technology which is absent at most archeological sites because of poor preservation conditions. The approximately eight thousand prehistoric Native American pottery vessels in the museum collections are an important research and artistic resource. The museum collections acquired by Dellinger from the Spiro Mounds site on the Arkansas River just west of Fort Smith are among the best and most studied of materials from that important site.

Dellinger died in Fayetteville.

[Dellinger's papers are in the Special Collections Division, University of Arkansas Libraries, Fayetteville. See the author's profile of Dellinger in "Some Illustrious Educators of Old Main," edited by Thomas Kennedy for the Old Main Rededication Committee (1991); and several articles in the university publications the *Arkansas Alumnus* and the *Arkansas Traveler*.]

MICHAEL P. HOFFMAN

DICKEY, WILLIAM MALCOLM (June 6, 1907–Nov. 12, 1993), professional baseball player, was born in Bastrop, Louisiana, to John Hardy Dickey, a Missouri Pacific Railroad employee and semiprofessional baseball player, and Laura Ann Chapman. The family migrated to Kensett, Arkansas, when Bill was an infant and to Little Rock when he was fifteen.

He was a pitcher and catcher on the Little Rock College (later St. John's Seminary, now defunct) team in 1925. Then he was signed to a contract in the minor-league Southern Association. In 1928 the New York Yankees of the American League purchased Dickey's contract from the Jackson, Mississippi, team. He became a regular with the Yankees in 1929 and batted .324 in his first full season. He averaged over .300 in eleven of his seventeen seasons with the club.

The roommate of first baseman Lou Gehrig, Dickey quickly became valuable as a quiet, courteous team leader. A sports writer of the era, Dan Daniel, wrote, "Dickey isn't just a catcher. He's a ball club. He isn't just a player. He's an influence."

After having all the fingers on his right hand broken, some of them twice, Dickey decided to try catching with one hand. He had seen Mickey Cochrane, backstop of the American League champion Philadelphia Athletics of 1929–31, catch one-handed a few times. Dickey perfected the style and employed it the last ten years of his career. As a coach, he taught his pupils—Yogi Berra, Elston Howard, and Gus Triandos—the one-handed catching skill. Without today's large mitts, this required much practice.

A hard worker and focused competitor, Dickey was at his best during the eight World Series in which he played. The Yankees lost only one Series during his playing years. In the 1932 Series he batted .438. He opened the 1938 Series with a 4-for-4 batting performance and in the 1939 Classic batted in at least one run in every game. His two-run homer in the fifth game of the 1943 Series won the Yankees a championship over the St. Louis Cardinals.

Although he never led the league in an offensive category, he compiled a lifetime batting average of .313 and in 1936 averaged .362, the top mark of the twentieth century by a catcher. He said his career average would have been ten points higher if he had developed his one-hand catch earlier.

Dickey possessed a gentle sense of humor, but he lost his temper once in a costly incident. In a 1932 game, with just one punch, he broke the jaw of the Washington Senators' Carl Reynolds after a collision at home plate. Dickey drew a one-month suspension and a thousand-dollar fine, a considerable figure at the time.

After serving with the United States Navy in World War II, Dickey returned to the Yankees in 1946 as baseball's highest paid player with a salary of twenty-two thousand dollars. Early that season, Yankee manager Joe McCarthy was unexpectedly fired. The team was in second place with a 22-13 record when Dickey was appointed player-manager. Dickey was 57-48 as manager, but the Yankees slipped to third in the final standings. He was dismissed as manager and decided to retire as a player.

The following year he directed the Little Rock Travelers in the Southern Association, but a dismal 51-103 record convinced him managing was not his calling. He rejoined the Yankees in 1949 to coach Berra, his catching replacement, and helped guide the team to five consecutive World Series championships in 1949–53.

The success of Dickey's instruction of Berra was

recognized by the Yankees' retiring of jersey number 8 —the numeral worn by both. Dickey was elected to the Baseball Hall of Fame in 1954, and Berra joined him in 1972.

In the opinion of veteran Arkansas sports writer Orville Henry, "Bill was probably the first Arkansan outside of politicians who left the state and made it big in New York. He was the first person chosen to the Arkansas Sports Hall of Fame . . . and rightly so."

Retiring in 1960, Dickey became associated with Stephens Inc., an investment banking firm in Little Rock. He developed into an avid fisherman and quail hunter and was hailed for his support of youth baseball programs.

Dickey's most amazing statistic as a player was his batting control: he struck out just 289 times in 6,300 plate appearances. Meanwhile, he belted 202 home runs. When he retired, he held career marks for most putouts and the highest fielding average among catchers. His durability in having caught in one hundred or more games in thirteen consecutive seasons was a standard for nearly four decades.

Soon after the 1932 World Series, Dickey married Violet Arnold, a Ziegfeld Follies performer. The couple's only child, daughter Violet Lorraine, was born in 1933.

Dickey's two brothers had some success in baseball: George played for the Boston Red Sox and the Chicago White Sox in the American League; Gus, like their father, was a respected semiprofessional.

Dickey, known as the "Jimmy Stewart of baseball," died in Little Rock. His wife said Dickey was a "quiet Southern gentleman who drank loving whiskey, not fighting whiskey. You never knew he was around."

[This entry is based on interviews with Dickey's niece, Joye Cook. See the *Arkansas Gazette*, Jan. 15, 16, 18, 1959, and Aug. 4, 1974; *Arkansas Democrat-Gazette*, Nov. 14, 1993; the *Treasury of Baseball: A Celebration of America's Pastime* (1994); and Lowell Reidenbaugh and Jo Hoppel, *Baseball's Hall of Fame Cooperstown: Where the Legends Live Forever* (1993).]

RICK JOSLIN

DIERKS, HERMAN (Sept. 24, 1863–Apr. 3, 1946), was born outside Lyons, Iowa, the seventh child of Peter Henry Dierks, a farmer and banker, and Margaretha Dorothea Tauk, who had emigrated from Suderstapel, Denmark (now part of northern Germany) in 1852. It is believed that Herman Dierks attended a business college before joining his older brother Hans in Nebraska. Hans had purchased land along the route of the new Burlington Railroad, near the town of Litchfield, Nebraska.

Herman Dierks and Martha Anne Waters married on May 5, 1887. The couple divorced in 1919.

Herman began his career in Nebraska as a farmer. By the summer of 1887, he owned 320 acres near Litchfield, but he soon gave up the farmer's life. Herman and Hans bought a lumberyard in Litchfield in 1887 and another yard west of Broken Bow in 1888. Soon thereafter, Herman and family moved to Broken Bow. Over the course of the next ten years, Herman and Hans owned a dozen yards in the Broken Bow-Litchfield area.

When the Cherokee strip opened in 1893, Herman moved south, selling his lumber out of a boxcar that often doubled as his bed. Plans to open a permanent yard in Oklahoma never materialized, however, and Herman moved back to Nebraska.

Herman and Hans, along with brothers Peter and Henry, formed a partnership in 1893 to manage these yards. Two years later, Herman and his three brothers incorporated the venture as the Dierks Lumber and Coal Company. Herman was named secretary and treasurer. The following year Hans moved the company headquarters to Kansas City, Missouri, where he spent most of his energy buying lumber for the company. Herman remained in Broken Bow where he and his brother Peter supervised the company's Nebraska operations. By 1900 Dierks Lumber and Coal owned twenty-four yards.

The company entered the lumber manufacturing business in late 1897 when the brothers purchased a sawmill at Petros, in what then was the Indian Territory. Three years later, Dierks Lumber and Coal purchased a large integrated lumberyard near DeQueen, Arkansas, just off the Kansas City Southern Railroad. While Hans remained in Kansas City to direct the finances of the company, Herman moved to DeQueen to manage southern operations. Once there, he assumed the leading role in the acquisition of new timberlands in the southern Ouachitas. He supervised railroad and logging operations and aggressively bought timber.

Dierks Lumber and Coal purchased the Ayers Lumber Company of Florien, Louisiana, in 1906, renaming it the Florien Lumber Company. Herman served as the new company's president until it was liquidated in 1913. During these same years, Herman was also part owner of the Waterman Lumber and Supply Company of Waterman, Texas. The mill there could cut 125,000 feet per day, most of which was shipped north to the Nebraska yards. Once the Oklahoma mills of Dierks Lumber and Coal came on-line, Waterman Lumber and Supply shipped its products to Europe, operating until those markets were cut off during the First World War.

During the next three decades, Dierks Lumber and Coal (including its sister corporation Choctaw Lumber Company in Oklahoma) operated twenty-three lumber-yards in Nebraska, six lumber mills in the Ouachitas (including those at Dierks and Mountain Pine, Arkansas), in addition to the DeQueen and Eastern, and the Texas, Oklahoma, and Eastern Railways. In the process, Herman and his brothers carved out an empire of timber in the midst of the region's last great virgin forest. During that span, the company purchased over 1.2 million acres of timber. Dierks Lumber and Coal became the largest producer of southern pine lumber.

Herman grew less active in the business in the late 1920s. Leadership of the family's holdings was passed to the third American generation of Dierks. Upon Hans's death in November of 1929, Herman became president of the company and remained so until his own death.

Financial troubles caused by the stock-market crash and the depression forced Dierks Lumber and Coal into receivership in 1936. But the company recovered quickly, and all the old debts were paid by 1938. Dierks Forests, Incorporated, as the company was renamed in 1954, sold their assets, including almost 1.8 million acres of timberland, to Weyerhaeuser Company in 1969, thus bringing an end to what had been the single largest family-owned landholding in the United States.

In the 1920s the United States Forest Service and the Dierks companies launched a joint effort to educate the population about modern conservation of forests. The company erected observation towers and helped to develop new firefighting tactics that reduced the damage wrought by forest fires.

[See F. McD. (Don) Dierks Jr., *The Legacy of Peter Henry Dierks, 1824–1972* (1972); and Kenneth L. Smith, *Sawmill: The Story of Cutting the Last Great Virgin Forest East of the Rockies* (1986).]

J. WAYNE JONES

DODD, DAVID OWEN (Nov. 10, 1846–Jan. 8, 1864), known as the boy martyr of the Confederacy, was born in Victoria, Texas, to Andrew Marion Dodd and Lydia Echols.

David's grandfather, Ezra Owen, had been a politician and businessman in Pulaski County and Saline County, Arkansas, before moving to Texas. David's family moved to Benton, Arkansas, in the spring of 1858. David attended school for the first time there. His sister Senhora was sent to Little Rock to live with her aunt, Susan Dodd, and to attend school.

In 1861, or early 1862, David and his parents moved to Little Rock to be closer to Senhora. David enrolled in St. John's College for a short time, but left school after a bout with malaria and worked in the Little Rock telegraph office. He and his father left Arkansas in 1862 and traveled to Monroe, Louisiana, where David took a job in the telegraph office. His father went on to Mississippi, following the Confederate army, possibly supplying food for the soldiers. David joined his father and worked for him near Grenada, Mississippi, for almost a year.

On hearing that Little Rock had fallen to the federal army in the fall of 1863, Andrew Dodd sent David back to get his family out of Arkansas and bring them to Mississippi. Some problem arose which prevented them from leaving. David again took employment in the city, this time possibly as a clerk in a Main Street mercantile establishment. After three months, Andrew Dodd sneaked through Union lines into Little Rock and arranged for his family to slip out of the city and make their way to Confederate-held south Arkansas.

After reaching the safety of Camden, Andrew Dodd asked Confederate general James F. Fagan for a pass to allow David to return to Little Rock to take care of family business there. David returned to the city and is described as being a very popular figure there for the next couple of weeks.

On December 28, 1863, David obtained a pass through Union lines to return to Camden and rejoin his family. South of Little Rock on the Benton Road a Union guard tore up the pass; David was entering Confederate territory and would need it no longer.

He detoured from his route to spend the night with his uncle, Washington Dodd, who lived in the area. The next morning, December 30, when David left his uncle's house he decided to go cross-country back to the Benton Road. That was the fatal decision that placed him in Union territory, where he was stopped by a foraging party.

He was arrested and searched; a book was found with detailed information about the military strength of the Union army in Little Rock. He was tried on January 2 and found guilty of spying for the Confederacy. Who was the Union contact that helped David obtain the information? Who was he gathering the information for? David O. Dodd would not answer. He was hanged on January 8, 1864. Over five thousand people gathered to watch as Union soldiers formed a square around a makeshift gallows on the campus of St. John's College. A monument stands on the Old State House grounds in Little Rock to this "Boy Martyr of the Confederacy."

[Consult the David O. Dodd Collection at the Arkansas History Commission, and Nancy Newell, "The Trial and Execution of David O. Dodd," *Pulaski County Historical Review*, 1992. Most histories of Arkansas that cover the Civil War have information on Dodd.]

LAWRENCE ALLEN SANDERS

DODGE, EVA FRANCETTE (July 24, 1896–Mar. 29, 1990), physician, educator, was born in New Hampton, New Hampshire, to George Dodge, a physician, and Minnie Worthen. As a child Eva enjoyed looking through her father's medical books and bandaging her dolls. In her teens she helped her father with his practice.

In 1920 Eva entered Johns Hopkins Medical School, one of the few in the nation that accepted women. During her third year she encountered actions on the part of the school administration which she believed were designed to keep her from graduating.

She then enrolled at the University of Maryland Medical School, her father's alma mater. The only woman among some eighty-four students, she endured teasing and pranks, but was ultimately accepted by the men in her class. She graduated in 1925, completed an internship at the university hospital, and was the first female resident there. She decided to specialize in gynecology and obstetrics.

Friends and relatives asked her advice concerning birth control. She sought information from the Birth Control League of America and recommended condoms. However, most of the women were unwilling to ask their spouses to purchase them because of a perception that men who purchased such items were cheating on their wives. Dodge, apprehensive, mailed condoms to them in violation of the Comstock Law prohibiting the mailing of contraceptives.

She went on to a residency at the Children's Hospital in San Francisco. In 1928 she went to China as a professor of obstetrics at the Margaret Williamson Hospital and Medical School in Shanghai. After a year she fell ill with meningitis and went to her mother's home in North Carolina to recover. She studied at the University of Vienna during her long recuperation. After a full recovery she returned to North Carolina and started a private practice in Winston Salem. Volunteering for the North Carolina State Board of Health, she set up maternity clinics and conducted prenatal clinics.

Dodge became a consultant with the Alabama State Health Department to help organize prenatal clinics for the twenty-four thousand women a year whose babies were delivered by midwives. Her work there brought her national recognition. She also conducted research with Dr. Thomas T. Frost on the "Relation between Blood Plasma and Proteins and Toxemias of Pregnancy." The study was published in 1938, and Dodge presented the findings at the annual meeting of the American Medical Association.

In 1940 she initiated family planning clinics in Puerto Rico for the federal Children's Bureau. Her work with the Alabama State Health Department brought her into contact with industries which were struggling to improve their health care and maternity policies for women during World War II. In 1943 she joined the Planned Parenthood Federation of America as assistant medical director, traveling extensively to provide advice on women's health care for industries and to assess methods of teaching contraception in medical schools.

In 1944 Dodge attended the first meeting of the American Academy of Obstetric and Gynecology Departments (now the American College of Obstetrics and Gynecology), where she was approached by Dr. Charles Henry, head of the Department of Obstetrics and Gynecology at the University of Arkansas for Medical Sciences, to run the obstetric outpatient department and to teach at the University of Arkansas. Dodge was thrilled by the chance to return to teaching.

As an assistant professor she took a salary cut but felt that "this sacrifice was not too great if I could finally be in a medical school where I could help to produce doctors with a desire to give adequate obstetric care to all pregnant women."

The wartime shortage of teachers led to an overworked and undersupervised staff. Dodge instituted policies that required students to observe regular working hours and insisted that each patient be examined and proper records kept. Other changes included separating the obstetrics and gynecology departments.

In retrospect Dodge claimed that "the nineteen years of my life in academic medicine were certainly fraught with none of the difficulties and frustrations of my early years." In 1947 she was finally appointed associate professor of obstetrics and gynecology. In 1948 she became a Fellow of the American College of Surgeons, one of only six women among nine hundred people chosen for this honor. She also began working with the Arkansas State Board of Health in 1951 as consultant to county maternity clinics and midwife programs throughout the state.

In 1960 Dodge was promoted to professor. In 1964 she retired from the university. She was proud of her years there, where "there seemed to be less difficulties for either women students or women faculty members …than in many medical schools."

During her "retirement" she directed the Detroit Maternal and Infant Care Project, led the National Nutritional Survey in Michigan, and directed the East Arkansas Family Planning Project. She continued to work with the Arkansas State Department of Health as a consultant. In 1975 she became director of the statewide Family Planning Program for the Arkansas Department of Health.

Dodge never married. She never mentioned regret for not having a family. In the early 1980s she moved to North Carolina to be close to her sister. She died in Tarboro, North Carolina.

[The University of Arkansas for Medical Sciences, Historical Research Center, holds personal papers of Eva Dodge and an oral history interview with Dodge by Edwina Walls, June 3, 1980. An oral history interview by Diane Larrison, Mar. 17, 1978, is in the Papers of the Arkansas Women's History Institute, University of Arkansas at Little Rock, Archives and Special Collections.

Dr. Dodge's publications include E. F. Dodge and T. T. Frost, "The Relation between Blood Plasma Proteins and Toxemia's of Pregnancy: Preliminary Report," *Journal of the American Medical Association* 111 (Nov. 1938): 1890–1902; B. B. Austin and E. F. Dodge, "Development and Progress of Maternity Clinic Programs in Alabama," *Journal of the Southern Medical Journal* 33 (May 1940): 537–46; and E. F.

Dodge, "Increasing Health Care Services through Expanding the Role of the Public Health Nurse in Medical Services to the Citizens of Arkansas," *Journal of the Arkansas Medical Society* 70, no. 6 (Nov. 1973): 208–9.

See also Margaret Arnold Leavitt, *Horizons: One Hundred Women of Achievement* (1980); "Eva F. Dodge, First Woman Professor Emerita at the University of Arkansas Medical School," *Journal of the American Medical Women's Association* 19 (Oct. 1964): 872–73; David W. Baird, *Medical Education in Arkansas, 1879–1978* (1979); Judith Walzer Leavitt, ed., *Women and Health in America* (1984); and Regina Markell Morantz-Sanchez, *Sympathy and Science: Women Physicians in American Medicine* (1985).]

CINDY PORTER

DONAGHEY, GEORGE WASHINGTON (July 1, 1856–Dec. 15, 1937), builder, governor of Arkansas, was born in Oakland, Louisiana, to C. C. Donaghey, a farmer, and Elizabeth Ingram, a homemaker. In 1858 the Donagheys moved to Lapile community in Union County, Arkansas. George Donaghey worked on the family farm and spent three years in Texas (1876–79) working at odd jobs including about four months on the Chisholm Trail as a cowboy. He moved to Conway, Arkansas, in 1880 to live with his uncle and stayed there for thirty years.

He became a carpenter and expanded this skill into building and contracting, constructing residences and other buildings in Arkansas and Texas. His formal education was meager; he spent one year at the University of Arkansas. On September 20, 1883, Donaghey and Louvenia Wallace married. They lived in Conway, where Donaghey was a major participant in bringing three colleges (Hendrix, Central Baptist, and State Teachers University of Central Arkansas) to Conway in seventeen years. He was also involved in Conway politics.

Donaghey became wealthy as a railroad contractor in Oklahoma (1899–1903) when the Indian Territory was first opened for settlement. He moved to Little Rock in 1908 and entered the Democratic primary as a candidate for governor in the same year. He defeated a candidate endorsed by Senator Jeff Davis, the first major defeat suffered by the Davis machine.

Donaghey faced a fiscal crisis in 1909 caused by a 1905 reduction in the millage rate for state general operations and state expenditures exceeding state revenues. He had to cut the state budget for the next two years almost 40 percent. Despite this emergency,

Donaghey was able to establish and fund four agricultural high schools, which later became Arkansas State University (Jonesboro), Arkansas Tech University (Russellville), Southern Arkansas University (Magnolia), and the University of Arkansas at Monticello. He supported and the general assembly approved an Arkansas Tax Commission with power to equalize property assessments throughout the state and a tuberculosis sanitarium at Booneville. The 1909 legislature at Donaghey's insistence also passed and submitted to the people a proposed state constitutional amendment that established initiative and referendum. The people ratified the amendment in 1910, and for seventy years Arkansas was the only southern state with any kind of statewide initiative and referendum.

Donaghey ran for a second term as governor in 1910 and was reelected with 69 percent of the vote. His second legislative session saw the creation of a new state board of health with power to regulate sanitation and inspect food and drugs, and a state board of education to supervise the 5,143 school districts in the state at that time.

After saying that he would not run for a third term, he did just that and was overwhelmingly defeated by Congressman Joe T. Robinson. His broken third-term pledge, the unpopularity of some of his fiscal reforms, and the speaking and campaigning ability of Robinson contributed to Donaghey's defeat. Before leaving office in 1913, he pardoned 360 inmates in the state penitentiary, most of whom were serving short sentences. This was 37 percent of the total prison population. He did this to end convict leasing, a system which forced convicts to work under inhumane and barbaric conditions. Donaghey decided to pardon all surplus convicts not needed to cultivate the state farm so that there would be no convicts available for lease. He was severely criticized for his action. Nevertheless, within two months after Donaghey's dramatic action, the Arkansas legislature finally abolished convict leasing.

Another project that bears Donaghey's imprint is the state capitol. While being built, it was plagued by construction problems, legislative scandals, and strong opposition. Donaghey was mainly responsible for pushing the new state capitol to its successful completion.

After leaving the governor's office, he devoted himself to commercial and charitable work in Little Rock. In 1929 the Donagheys transferred ownership of the Donaghey Building and the Federal Bank and Trust Building in Little Rock to Little Rock Junior College. Valued at between $1.5 and $2 million, the endowment was one of the most generous ever given in the state. Little Rock Junior College eventually became the University of Arkansas at Little Rock, bringing to six the number of publicly supported universities that owed their existence to George Donaghey.

Donaghey died in Little Rock and is buried in Roselawn Memorial Park. He served his state well as a progressive and problem-solving politician and as a philanthropist.

[Donaghey's papers are housed in the Special Collections Division, University of Arkansas Libraries, Fayetteville. Calvin R. Ledbetter's *Carpenter from Conway: George W. Donaghey as Governor of Arkansas, 1909–1913* (1993) contains an extensive bibliography.]

CALVIN R. LEDBETTER JR.

DOOLIN, WILLIAM (1858–Aug. 25, 1896), outlaw, was born to Artemina and Michael Doolin, a sharecropper who with six children farmed forty acres near Big Piney River northeast of Clarksville, Arkansas.

In 1881 "Bill" Doolin struck out for Oklahoma Territory, where he worked for Oscar D. Halsell, a rancher who taught him to read and figure. In 1889 he had his first run-in with the law. On the Fourth of July he and some friends were swigging beer at a remote spot when two deputy sheriffs approached them to confiscate the illegal beer. Both were shot. Doolin, the supposed leader of the group, fled to Kansas.

After some restless drifting, he joined the Oklahoma-based Dalton gang, led by Robert Dalton with his brothers Gratton and Emmett. He participated with them in a train robbery at Perry (then Wharton), Oklahoma, on May 8, 1891. The gang escaped uninjured, but a telegraph operator was killed. Over the next year the gang hit trains at Lilleta, Red Rock, and Adair, Oklahoma, with attendant injuries and loss of life.

In October 1892 at Coffeyville, Kansas, the Daltons decided to rob two banks at once. Within minutes after their break from the banks, they were gunned down by the townspeople. Doolin missed the heist, probably because he foresaw the danger and quit the gang beforehand.

After the Coffeyville fiasco, Doolin organized his own gang. Under his tutelage came William Dalton and, from the old Dalton gang, Bitter Creek Newcomb and Charlie Pierce. New recruits were George "Red Buck"

Weightman, whom the men considered homicidal, Roy "Arkansas Tom" Daugherty, William Raidler, Jack "Tulsa Jack" Blake, and Daniel "Dynamite Dick" Clifton, among others. For four years they terrorized southern Kansas and the Oklahoma Territory, robbing trains, banks, and stagecoaches, amassing over $165,000.

By late 1892 the citizens of Oklahoma petitioned President Grover Cleveland to appoint a new federal marshal. In 1893 Evett Dumas Nix, a Guthrie business-man, was appointed United States marshal. Nix quickly brought together one hundred field deputies, the best of whom were Heck Thomas, Chris Madsen, and Bill Tilghman, the "Three Guardsmen." Thereafter, warrants were issued for outlaws "dead or alive."

In July 1893 the Doolin gang drifted into the remote town of Ingalls, Oklahoma, where Bill had earlier met his wife, Edith Ellsworth, daughter of a part-time min-ister and town official. Late in August Marshal Nix dis-patched a posse of thirteen to the town. The Ingalls raid was deadly. After the half-hour fight, three marshals and two citizens lay dead. Only Arkansas Tom was taken prisoner; the rest of the outlaws escaped.

Afterward, the gang began to split up. Desperate for funds, Doolin robbed the postmaster in Payne County, Oklahoma, in January 1894. Later that month, Doolin, Bitter Creek Newcomb, and Tulsa Jack Blake robbed the Farmers' and Citizens' Bank in Pawnee. In March Doolin and Bill Dalton looted $6,540 from the U.S. Army paymaster's office at Woodward. In May the gang hit a bank in McDonald County, Missouri, where Doolin was struck by a buckshot pellet.

Determined to bring the outlaws in at any cost, Marshal Nix directed the Three Guardsmen to scour the southwest for them. In June 1894 Bill Dalton was killed by deputies near Elk, Oklahoma. After a train robbery at Dover in April 1895, Doolin's gang was chased to Hail Creek near Ames, where Tulsa Jack was killed. On May 1, Charlie Pierce and Bitter Creek Newcomb were killed in their sleep. William Raidler was blasted with a load of buckshot and taken prisoner.

With six of his men eliminated from the gang, Doolin decided to lie low for a while. He headed for Eureka Springs, Arkansas, to take the healing waters. Bill Tilghman followed him there and discovered that Doolin was staying at the Davy Hotel under the name Tom Wilson. Tilghman entered the waiting room and positioned himself behind a stove. Noticing that Doolin was reading a newspaper in a corner of the room,

Tilghman drew his revolver and said, "Bill, don't make me kill you." Later he telegraphed Nix: "I have him. Will be home tomorrow. Tilghman."

The marshal and Doolin arrived at the train depot in Guthrie to a crowd of several hundred people. It had taken nearly six years, thousands of dollars, and the lives of several law officers to put Doolin in prison. He was not, however, to stay long.

On May 1, 1896, Doolin was taken to Stillwater where he was indicted for murder in the Ingalls shoot-out. In June Dynamite Dick Clifton was transferred to the Guthrie federal prison where Doolin was, and in no time the two began hatching plans for a break. On the night of July 5, Doolin, Dynamite Dick, and fourteen others escaped. Heck Thomas formed a posse within an hour and sped after the escapees, but found no one. Doolin made his way eastward over the Cimarron Brakes toward Lawson where his wife and son were staying.

An informant told Tilghman and Thomas that Doolin had been riding undetected into Lawson to visit his family. On August 25, learning that Doolin was at his father-in-law's house, Thomas and nine deputies rushed to the farm, took up concealed positions near the house, and waited for him to emerge. Near dusk, Doolin left the house, rifle in one hand, cautiously lead-ing his horse. As he approached, Heck Thomas hollered for him to stop. Instantly, Doolin fired into the darkness toward the voice. A hail of bullets was returned, killing Bill Doolin.

[The William H. and Zoe Tilghman Papers are in the Western History Collection, University of Oklahoma Libraries, Norman. See Bailey C. Haines, *Bill Doolin, Outlaw* (1968); Glen Shirley, *West of Hell's Fringe: Crime, Criminals, and the Federal Peace Officer in Oklahoma Territory, 1889–1907* (1978); and Russell E. Bearden, "Last of the Arkansas Outlaws," *Jefferson County Historical Quarterly* 15 (1979): 10–31.]

RUSSELL E. BEARDEN

DREW, THOMAS STEVENSON (Aug. 25?, 1802–Jan.?, 1879), third governor of Arkansas, was born in Wilson County, Tennessee, and came to Arkansas in 1817. In October 1824 he was appointed clerk of the Clark County Court and three months later became jus-tice of the peace of Caddo Township. On February 2, 1827, Drew married Cinderella Bettis; they had five chil-dren. Her father, a prosperous landowner, gave the couple eight hundred acres of land near present-day

Biggers, Arkansas. Drew spent the next several years developing this property, and by 1832 he was successful enough to own twenty slaves.

In that year Drew was elected judge of the Lawrence County Court, a position he held until 1835. In 1836 he was elected to the Arkansas constitutional convention and served on the judiciary committee. For the next eight years he was active in the Democratic Party; his political connections are elusive but he maintained the trust of the controlling Johnson-Conway-Sevier political dynasty without alienating its opponents. By the early 1840s Drew was widely known and influential within party circles, but he had shown no inclination to run for statewide office.

The Democrats were badly split in December 1843 when they met in the party's first open convention to select nominees for office. It became apparent that the men chosen as candidates for governor and Congress were too weak to face the growing coalition of resurgent Whigs, disgruntled Democrats, and independents. A second convention strengthened the congressional ticket but failed to produce a good gubernatorial candidate. The Democrats, in desperation, returned to the caucus of party leaders to find someone who could unite the badly factionalized party; Drew fit that need exactly. In the 1844 election, Drew, who clearly understood that he had been selected to unite the party, ran as a harmonizer. His opponents attacked him as a nullifier (a supporter of states' rights) and a nominee who was picked behind closed doors by a clique of powerful men. He carried the state in a close three-way race, but, with 47 percent of the vote, Drew was Arkansas's first governor to be elected by a plurality.

As governor, Drew supported a moderate program. He urged the general assembly to create a board of internal improvement with powers to clear rivers and improve the state's abysmal roads, using the proceeds from the sale of federal lands turned back to the states. He asked the legislature to establish a state college. On national matters he endorsed the plan to annex Texas and supported the war with Mexico. Like most southern leaders, he opposed efforts to ban slavery in the territories.

The major issue that Drew faced in his administration was the restoration of the state's financial solvency, which had been wrecked by the panic of 1837. He finally and reluctantly supported a small tax increase to deal with the state's debt, but the revenues were too small to restore the credit of Arkansas. The state continued to teeter on the verge of bankruptcy.

Few of Drew's proposals were adopted by the legislature, but he was well liked by the party faithful. He was easily nominated in 1848 for a second term, and with no formal opposition, he received 15,962 votes out of a total of 16,455 cast in the general election. He was now at the height of his political power and popularity, but the lingering economic crisis and his own speculation in railroads had wrecked his personal finances. Under such circumstances, Drew was reluctant to run for a second term. He did so with the understanding that his supporters would work to get the governor's salary raised. When they failed to carry through with the promise, Drew felt betrayed. He resigned from office on January 10, 1849.

He spent much of the next decade trying to rebuild his personal finances. In 1855 he briefly deserted the Democrats to support the Know-Nothing Party. His last race for public office occurred in 1858, when he waged a halfhearted campaign for Congress as an independent Democrat. Drew's political career was over, and the Civil War destroyed the limited financial recovery he had made in the 1850s. In the early 1870s he moved to Texas to live with his daughter. He died in Lapin, Hood County. In 1923 he was reinterred at Pocahontas, Arkansas.

[See Bobby Roberts, "Thomas Stevenson Drew, 1844–1849," in *The Governors of Arkansas: Essays in Political Biography,* Timothy P. Donovan, Willard B. Gatewood Jr., and Jeannie M. Whayne, eds., 2d ed. (1995).]

BOBBY ROBERTS

DUNCAN, VIRGINIA MAUD DUNLAP (Oct. 22, 1873–Jan. 21, 1958), pharmacist, editor, and mayor, was born in Fayetteville, Arkansas, to Dudley Clinton Dunlap and Catherine Hewitt. After her mother's death when she was an infant, Maud was put in the care of her father's brother, Albert Dunlap, M.D., and his wife. The family lived in Fort Smith until Maud was fourteen.

A brother Rufus also lived with Albert and Virginia Dunlap for a short time. A sister, Lena, and two brothers, Albert and Bertie, were raised by other foster parents.

Maud Dunlap was educated at home by her foster father until she was of high-school age. She attended high school in Fort Smith and the University of Arkansas, and at the age of sixteen she received a teacher's certificate at Cane Hill College. She taught school in the Winslow district and at Mount Pleasant for a short time.

The family moved to Winslow July 12, 1887, and were instrumental in founding the St. Stephen's Episcopal Church and the Helen Dunlap Memorial School. Maud studied pharmacy with her foster father and secured her certificate of registration as a pharmacist in 1906. She was the second woman to register as a pharmacist in Arkansas.

On February 26, 1894, Maud Dunlap married Hallam Pearce, of Milan, Tennessee, who worked for the Frisco Railroad in Winslow. She and her foster father worked together in the M. D. Pearce Pharmacy (M. D. stood for Maud Dunlap). She and Pearce had two daughters. Virginia died in infancy. After Maud had her marriage to Pearce annulled in 1901, Dr. and Mrs. Albert Dunlap adopted Helen.

For a short time in 1905 Maud Duncan was engaged to Dr. T. E. Gray of Winslow, but she broke the engagement. She and Gray remained staunch friends until his murder at the hands of a hitchhiker in 1938. In 1907 she petitioned the court to change her name back to Dunlap. Soon after that she became engaged to a young newspaperman, Gilbert Nelson Duncan, whose family had recently arrived in Winslow. They married June 3, 1908, at the St. Stephen's Church.

While Maud Duncan continued her work at the pharmacy, the couple purchased a monthly newspaper, the *Winslow Mirror*. They changed its name to the *Winslow American* and began weekly publication September 4, 1908. The paper reported local events, but editorials commented on national questions such as women's suffrage and supported United States participation in World War I, urging people to invest in war bonds.

Gilbert Duncan died in the influenza epidemic of 1918. Maud Duncan continued operating the drugstore and publishing the newspaper, but she was an idealist and too generous a philanthropist.

She was greatly interested in women's rights and was active in all civic matters in her town. Winslow in its heyday (1882–1929) was a celebrated resort whose population of four hundred would swell to as many as ten thousand residents during the summer. Flower gardens bloomed beside the train depot and in residents' yards to please the summer visitors.

In 1925 Duncan was elected mayor along with a full slate of women candidates, all business women, for city council. Winslow's "petticoat government" received national attention. They raised money to build a road; the men who did not contribute money contributed labor, and the women brought them meals. They encouraged beautification of the town and home improvement by encouraging merchants to offer low prices on building materials.

Winslow boasted a small jail, but Duncan gave it away, declaring that those who broke the law would come before her and be fined, the money to be used for further improvements to the city. Tough criminals, she said, could be handled by the fine lawmen of the county.

Duncan and her council were reelected to a second one-year term, but declined to run for office again in 1927.

Over the years the *Winslow American* shrank from a four-page weekly to a news bulletin printed on one sheet. Duncan continued to set type by hand in the cold, drafty newspaper office built after the pharmacy burned in 1935. Too stubborn to give up or to accept charity, she would walk the streets, selling ad space in order to buy wood and food. Friends and neighbors did what they could, inviting her in to dine and buying ads they didn't need. Often she was found unconscious by a roadside where she had fallen from exhaustion.

In 1956 friends and neighbors took the frail woman to a retirement home in Fayetteville where she lived her final years. Sometimes she didn't recognize their faces when they visited, but those friends she had always cared so much about never deserted her.

Maud Duncan was a soft-spoken, refined lady who never expressed ill will, resentment, or self-pity. During her lifetime she came to national attention several times, not only as mayor of Winslow and as a prominent woman pharmacist, but for her work in publishing the *Winslow American* long after most would have given up.

She is buried at St. Stephen's Episcopal Cemetery in Winslow near her daughters, her foster parents, and her husband.

[See Robert Winn's books: *The Story of Winslow's Maud Duncan* (1992); *Winslow, Top of the Ozarks* with Lyda Winn Pace (1983); and his column "Recollections" in the *Washington County Observer* (1972–90). Other sources include chancery court records dates Fall Term, Oct. 3, 1901; Washington County Court records Case #170, 1907; and the papers of Tom Feathers of Washington County.]

VELDA BROTHERTON

DUSENBURY, EMMA HAYS (Jan. 9, 1862–May 5, 1941), ballad singer, was born in Georgia, probably in Habersham or Rabun County. She came to Arkansas in 1872, staying first in Crittenden County but eventually settling in Baxter County, near Gassville. Sometime after 1880 she married Ernest Dusenbury, an Illinois man. Two years later she bore her only child, a daughter named Ora. Soon thereafter, in about 1894 or 1895, Emma suffered a serious illness which left her blind.

During this period, and on until about 1907, when they settled near Mena, the family lived an itinerant life, with Mr. Dusenbury working railroad and packing plant jobs and the whole family picking cotton in the summer. Mr. Dusenbury died in 1933. Emma Dusenbury lived at or near poverty her entire life, and when she died in 1941 her funeral cost Polk County $33.10.

And there her story would have ended, but for her fame as a singer. For some years, beginning in the late 1920s or early 1930s, she had been visited and recorded by a number of the best-known folk-song collectors in the region and nation. John Lomax, Vance Randolph, and Sidney Robertson all visited, as did poet John Gould Fletcher and composer Laurence Powell, director of the Arkansas Symphony Orchestra. All were greatly impressed; Lomax wrote in his autobiography that she sang unceasingly for two days and recorded more traditional Anglo-American ballads than any other singer in his experience. In all likelihood the first to call attention to Dusenbury's vast repertoire was F. M. Goodhue, a teacher at Commonwealth College, a nearby radical labor school.

Dusenbury's one brush with notoriety came in 1936, when she was taken to Little Rock to sing as part of celebrations marking Arkansas's statehood centennial. Her photograph appeared in the newspaper, along with a feature article by Powell. Then the moment passed. The collectors went back to Washington with their recordings, the poet wrote an account of his visits and published it in a London literary magazine edited by T. S. Eliot, and the composer based the final movement of his Second Symphony on three of her songs.

But nothing changed for Emma Dusenbury as a result of all this; she was soon back in Mena, as poor as ever. Five years later she died. What is left are her songs—a vast treasure trove that has engrossed and intrigued students of popular and traditional song. For Dusenbury's repertoire was more than simply large—it was remarkably varied, including many rarely recorded songs in addition to the old Anglo-American ballads especially prized by the collectors of the period. "Abraham's Proclamation," for example, a scoffing number denouncing President Lincoln's Emancipation Proclamation and believed by scholars to originate in blackface minstrelsy, has been collected from no other singer.

Emma Dusenbury learned songs all her life, and she spent most of her life in Arkansas. People who visited her described her as "destitute" and "impoverished," and it is said she was offered far too few of the world's goods. But the visitors were nevertheless wrong; Emma Dusenbury's wealth was in her head. And now her place in the state's history is secure. She is Arkansas's outstanding traditional singer, represented by some 116 songs in the nation's leading folk-song archive. Later generations of scholars have studied her songs and marveled at her prodigious mastery. She must, wrote one, have "made a resolution to learn all the songs in the world."

[Dusenbury's legacy is contained on tapes in the Library of Congress, which also issued her performances of "Barbara Allen" and "The Mermaid" on record. The University of Arkansas Library has copies of all the field recordings, as well as a great wealth of manuscript material from Laurence Powell, Vance Randolph, and John Gould Fletcher. A particular highlight is a fine collection of postcards and letters from Emma and Ora Dusenbury to Fletcher. The most extensive biographical study of Dusenbury is Robert Cochran, "'All the Songs in the World': The Story of Emma Dusenbury," *AHQ* 44 (Spring 1985): 3–15.]

ROBERT COCHRAN

EAGLE, JAMES PHILIP (Aug. 10, 1837–Dec. 20, 1904), Baptist minister, governor of Arkansas, was born in Maury County, Tennessee, the son of James Eagle and Charity Swain. The family, of German descent, emigrated to the United States from Switzerland. In November 1839 Eagle's father, a farmer, brought his family to Arkansas and purchased a farm in Pulaski County. In 1857 the family moved to the Richwoods community near Lonoke.

In 1859 Eagle was appointed deputy sheriff of Prairie County. He held that position until the Civil War. In June 1861 he enlisted as a private in the Fifth Arkansas Mounted Regiment and was assigned to Confederate units in Indian Territory. He also saw action in Kentucky and Tennessee, where he was taken prisoner. Released in a prisoner exchange in May 1863, he rejoined his old unit and participated in battles in Tennessee, Mississippi, and Georgia. In the Battle of Atlanta he received a severe abdominal wound but recovered in time to rejoin his unit for campaigns in Tennessee and North Carolina. By the time the war was over he had reached the rank of lieutenant colonel.

His father died during the war, and Eagle inherited most of his estate. He was able to build on his father's holdings and became one of the most prosperous farmers in central Arkansas. By the mid-1880s he owned twenty-four hundred acres of farmland and fourteen lots in Little Rock. Converted to Christianity during the war, he joined the New Hope Baptist Church shortly after his return and was licensed to the ministry in 1868. As a Baptist minister he needed more education, and in 1871 he enrolled at Mississippi College. Illness forced him to drop out of school before completing the first year. He returned to Arkansas, where he began to work with small, rural Baptist churches. He became the best-known member of the denomination and was elected president of the Arkansas Baptist State Convention for twenty-five consecutive years.

In 1872 he was elected to represent Arkansas, Prairie, and Lincoln Counties in the general assembly. He joined the legislature in the midst of the Brooks-Baxter dispute over the governor's office. Eagle supported Elisha Baxter in the dispute, organized six companies of volunteer troops in response to Baxter's call for protection, and served as one of the three commissioners appointed by the legislature to investigate claims growing out of the dispute. He also served as a delegate to the 1874 constitutional convention and continued to represent his district when the new constitution was adopted. Eagle introduced the bill to create Lonoke County and served as representative from that county in the twenty-second (1877–79) and twenty-fifth (1885–87) sessions of the general assembly. During the latter session he served as speaker of the House.

In between those sessions, on January 3, 1882, he married Mary Kavanaugh Oldham, originally from Kentucky, whom he had met during the Civil War. The couple had no children.

After repeated urging from supporters, Eagle sought the nomination for governor in 1888. The Democratic convention of that year was one of the most acrimonious in the party's history. Five candidates appealed for support, and the meeting lasted three days. It took 126 ballots before the delegates chose Eagle as the party's nominee. He won in the general election by a bare 15,000-vote margin; there were widespread charges of election fraud. As governor, he faced a divided party and a disorganized general assembly. He demanded that the assembly appoint a special commission to investigate the fraud charges, but legislators refused. He urged the assembly to reform the prison system and to create an equalization commission to restructure tax rates. Legislators largely ignored Eagle's requests, and for the balance of his first term he spent most of his time trying to restore harmony in the party.

Efforts to reunify the Democratic Party were largely successful, and Eagle won reelection in 1890 by a comfortable margin. But a unified party did not mean a cooperative legislature, and Eagle faced most of the same obstacles in his second administration. The assembly still ignored most of his program, including a new call for a railroad commission, an equalization board, abolition of the convict-lease system used by the state prison system, and a new state penitentiary. Legislators were more interested in "Jim Crow" laws and followed their own agenda. Perhaps the most notorious of the laws that came out of this session was the "separate coach law," which segregated public transportation and accommodations in the state. Eagle refused to endorse the proposal, but he did sign it into law.

He did not seek a third term for governor; he retired from politics. He continued to live in Little Rock and remained active in Baptist church work. He also served on the first State Capitol Commission but was removed from that body by Governor Jeff Davis after a dispute over politics. Eagle died in Little Rock and was buried at Mount Holly Cemetery.

[See C. Fred Williams, "James Philip Eagle, 1889–1893," in *The Governors of Arkansas: Essays in Political Biography,* Timothy P. Donovan, Willard B. Gatewood Jr., and Jeannie M. Whayne, eds., 2d ed. (1995).]

C. FRED WILLIAMS

ELLIOTT, MARION BLANCHE HANKS (Nov. 17, 1901–Dec. 21, 1990), principal founder of the Ozark Arts and Crafts Fair in northwest Arkansas, was born in Johnson, Arkansas, to Maude Mason Hanks, homemaker, and Nathan Hanks, a carpenter and cooper. Elliott grew up in Johnson where she attended public schools. She moved to Fayetteville to live with relatives and attend Fayetteville High School. In 1924 she graduated from the University of Arkansas with a bachelor of science degree in home economics.

During her sophomore year at the university she met and married Lester Elliott. Their daughter Shirley was born in 1937.

Upon graduating from the university, Elliott taught home economics in Tennessee but soon returned to Arkansas, first to Pope County where she began her work as an agent for the Cooperative Extension Service. In 1927 she became the Benton County home demonstration agent. She was proud of her home demonstration work. One of the projects she promoted was the organization of women's rest camps designed to relieve the physically and mentally punishing lives of rural women during the Great Depression. Bringing their own food and bedding, club members assembled at riverbanks and mountaintops to sing, learn home-making skills, and create. Leading these activities fulfilled Elliott's sense of her role as an educator and leader. Prophetically for Elliott, the women of Benton County went, at least twice, to War Eagle.

Admiration for Elliott is revealed in the records of Benton County's Pine Cone and Kilkare Clubs. The 1930 Kilkare album features a portrait of Elliott with this inscription: "Home Demonstration Agent and Friend/ Ever loyal to the End/You're a sponsor well worth the while/and in every way we like your style."

Elliott also became active in the Benton County Rug Weavers' Association, a craft she practiced and promoted throughout her life. She published an article, "Hooked Rugs as an Ozark Craft," in *Farm and Ranch* magazine (October 18, 1930).

In the early 1930s the Elliotts bought a farm near Mount Comfort in Washington County. In 1934 Elliott worked for a while on WPA projects in Fort Smith. A report she wrote at the time describes her attitude toward rural life: "There isn't any place in the world where living can be more satisfying than on the farm if we use our heads as well as our hands, and emphasis on the head." Her definition of a rewarding life for women included the provision of good nutrition, healthy surroundings, and the value of education, music, books, and crafts that spring from rural needs. Elliott worked with agent Mabel King to create the Washington County Farm Women's Market. In December 1932 she published "Arkansas Farm Women in Business," also in *Farm and Ranch.*

In October of 1952 the lives of Elliott and her family took an important turn. During a visit to War Eagle they learned the entire War Eagle Farm might be for sale. Elliott considered the farm "the prettiest place in Arkansas" and had fond memories of the women's rest camps held there. By 1953 the farm and its historic house were theirs.

Elliott was now able to offer a comfortable, beautiful setting for activities and groups to which she belonged. Primary among these was the Northwest Arkansas Handweavers' Guild. In 1954 they invited the public to the last day of their spring workshop. Such a large crowd appeared that the guild determined to sponsor a fair. The first Ozarks Arts and Crafts Fair was held at War Eagle the next October. Elliott encouraged the plan and offered the War Eagle site for as long as it was needed. The 1954 fair was so successful it was continued, and in 1957—thanks to Elliott's efforts with local chambers of commerce—a governing board, the Ozarks Arts and Crafts Fair Association, was formed.

As for Elliott's continued role in all this, Ernie Deane, a longtime board member, wrote, "She is one of the most remarkable citizens in the state. She has never drawn a cent of compensation for the use of her property and time . . . She has an outstanding ability to organize and get things done."

And organize she did. She was elected the fair's executive director and served in that capacity for almost thirty years. In a classic understatement, she called the fair, "my number-one hobby." By the late 1990s an estimated 160,000 to 170,000 fair-goers attended the juried show every October.

Elliott's vision and energy led the association to inaugurate, in the spring of 1962, an annual Back-in-the-Hills Antique Show and Collectors' Fair. In 1970 they began the Ozarks Arts and Crafts Seminar, where participants could learn skills taught by Ozark artisans.

She wrote a regular arts and crafts column for the *Ozarks Mountaineer* magazine and was the War Eagle correspondent for several northwest Arkansas newspapers. She frequently wrote special pieces on local history and families.

Among her papers is a poem saved from 1929 which expresses what Blanche Elliott believed all her life: her work was her blessing and she was the one to make it right.

[The Blanche Hanks Elliott Papers, MC 1272, in the Special Collections Division, University of Arkansas

Libraries, Fayetteville, include articles by or about Elliott. Other sources include Edsel Ford, "An Artistic Bonus for Ozarks Travelers," *New York Times,* Sept. 6, 1967; Clay M. Anderson, "Her Place Is War Eagle," *Ozarks Mountaineer* (Sept.–Oct. 1978): 28–29, and "For the War Eagle Fair, Its the End of an Era," *Ozarks Mountaineer* (Sept.–Oct. 1991): 44–45; Phillip Steele, "War Eagle, Its Legend, History and Fair," printed by the Ozarks Arts and Crafts Association, 1979; Sally Kirby, "The War Eagle Fair," *Arkansas Gazette,* Sept. 9, 1979; and Ernie Deane, "She Planted the War Eagle Acorn," *Morning News,* Dec. 30, 1990. This entry is also based on interviews and correspondence with Shirley Elliott Sutton, Nov. 16–Nov. 25, 1998.]

ELLEN COMPTON SHIPLEY

ELLIS, CLYDE TAYLOR (Dec. 21, 1908–Feb. 9, 1980), advocate for rural electrification, was born in Benton County, Arkansas, to Cecil O. Ellis, a farmer, and Minerva Taylor, a homemaker, and was raised on a farm near Garfield, Arkansas. Like the pioneers before him, Ellis grew up in the Ozarks among modest, backcountry citizens. Two things impressed him when he was growing up. The first was the lack of electricity. The second was the proximity of the Pea Ridge Battlefield: "I grew up on the edge of the Battlefield and I am fairly well familiar with it." Both rural electrification and the battlegrounds at Pea Ridge became lifelong passions.

Ellis attended the University of Arkansas, but left without graduating. (He returned and earned a B.S. in business in 1958.) In 1929 he was appointed a teacher and superintendent of schools in Garfield. His frustration at having no electricity in his classrooms and being unable to get the electric companies to construct a line to his school inspired him to become an advocate for rural electrification.

He won a seat in the Arkansas House of Representatives in 1932. In 1933 he passed the Arkansas bar, and in 1934 he was elected to the state senate. Ellis immediately initiated a plan for rural electrification in Arkansas that became a model for other states. Not satisfied with the snail-paced efforts to bring electricity to rural Arkansas, Ellis ran for United States representative from the Third District in 1938 on a platform that promised cheap electricity, and he defeated the incumbent. A New Dealer, he was an antimonopolist in the tradition of the Progressives.

Once in Congress Ellis devoted his political life to rural electrification. He worked with powerful congressmen such as Sam Rayburn and Lyndon B. Johnson of Texas and George W. Norris of Nebraska. He viewed hydroelectricity as the best source of cheap electricity. His efforts culminated in the careful management of the White River under the Comprehensive Flood Control Act of 1938. Dams on the White were some of the first built under this federal legislation and went a long way in providing farms of northwest Arkansas with electricity. However, Ellis failed to see his dream of an Arkansas Valley Authority modeled on the Tennessee Valley Authority come to fruition.

Ellis worked diligently with northwest Arkansans and Washington politicians to pass legislation creating Pea Ridge National Military Park. He was disappointed that his efforts failed in 1939–41 despite pleas to the secretary of the interior. In the long run the survey and other preliminary work that Ellis conducted proved pivotal and laid the groundwork for the eventual authorization of the park in 1956.

Ellis lost his bid for the United States Senate in 1942, but the following year he was appointed general manager of the National Rural Electric Cooperative Association (NRECA), a New Deal agency designed to "electrify" rural America. He was given a leave of absence to serve in the navy in World War II.

After serving as a gunnery officer, Ellis returned to Washington, D.C., in 1945 to become the director of NRECA. Over the next twenty-five years, he earned a reputation as the greatest advocate of rural electrification in the United States. He regularly testified before Congress in behalf of rural electricity and loans for such projects. His no-nonsense style enabled him to criticize monopolistic utility companies while winning the hearts of average citizens.

He boldly put forward his goals for the agency in a well-received book, *A Giant Step* (1966). He established four major goals for NRECA: to advance the interests of rural electric cooperatives and power districts; to implement the expertise of professionals; to lobby Congress; and to advocate consumer interests over corporate interests. He believed that special-interest lobbying was essential to the political process in America, and he meant to make it work for rural citizens. His goals translated into electricity for rural Arkansas: in 1946, for example, 67,689 rural Arkansans were served by 15,874 miles of lines; by 1960, 317,191 rural folks were served by 57,838 miles of lines.

Ellis's mission for rural electrification took him to Russia in 1959 with a Senate subcommittee to learn how that nation addressed rural power deficiencies. In 1961 he toured rural South America.

Washingtonians recognized his achievements at his NRECA retirement dinner in 1968. Declared "Mr. Rural Electrification," Ellis was honored by more than fifteen hundred attendees. Among the guests was Vice President Hubert H. Humphrey, who commented, "Every time I see a light in rural America, it is a tribute to you [Ellis]."

Three years after leaving NRECA Ellis became an aide to Senator John L. McClellan of Arkansas. In 1977 Ellis took his final assignment as a confidential assistant to the Agriculture Department's director of economics. He retired from public life in August 1979.

Ellis's words illustrate how he felt about his roots and his lifelong commitment to rural electricity: "I could have been born in no better place than Arkansas to see first-hand what an electric power monopoly could do to the people. It was these memories that later, as a Congressman and as general manager of NRECA, made me devote almost my total time and energy ... to the rural electrification program."

[The Clyde T. Ellis Papers, 1933–76, are in the Special Collections Division, University of Arkansas Libraries, Fayetteville. Ellis's publications include *A Giant Step* (1966) and annual reports and regional meeting reports published by the National Rural Electric Cooperative Association, 1950s–1960s. There is an obituary in the *Arkansas Gazette*, Feb. 10, 1980.

See also Clayton D. Brown, *Electricity for Rural America* (1980); Donald H. Cooper, *Rural Electric Facts: American Success Story* (1970); Orval Faubus, "Clyde T. Ellis, Lawmaker, Led Movement to Electrify Rural America," *Arkansas Democrat*, July 23, 1989; Bob Lancaster, "Fifty Who Mattered: Clyde Ellis, Mr. Rural Electrification," *Arkansas Times* (June 1985): 44; and Rebecca R. Wise, ed., *Rural Electric Fact Book* (1965).]

CHRISTOPHER J. HUGGARD

ELLISON, LUTHER (Oct. 10, 1885–Jan. 6, 1935), developer and promoter, was born near Fayetteville, Georgia. He was married on December 25, 1913, at Winfield, Louisiana, to Juanita, last name unknown; they had three children: Juanita, Gertrude, and Luther Jr. Beginning as an economic advocate in Texas, Ellison also worked as a chamber of commerce official in Monroe, Louisiana, and in Florence and Lancaster, South Carolina. He came to Arkansas in 1915 when he was named the executive secretary of the Jonesboro Chamber of Commerce. In the early 1920s he was in Rustin, Louisiana, where he was active in the Pershing Highway Association which built Highway 167 from Louisiana to Little Rock.

Ellison devoted nearly twenty years to Arkansas's economic development. In 1925 he was named executive secretary for the Camden Chamber of Commerce. Camden at that time was benefiting from an oil boom. Ellison saw beyond the boom and persuaded the business community of the importance of developing all of the region's natural resources, building a broad economic foundation for the area, and attracting new industries. He played an important role in locating to Camden the Southern Kraft Company (International Paper Company), the Camden Art Tile and Pottery Company (Camark Pottery), the Rockwell Manufacturing Company, the Camden Furniture Company, and the Houston Oil Refinery.

Realizing that the south Arkansas oil boom was ending, Ellison preached the necessity of reinvesting oil profits in local communities to ensure lasting economic, social, and cultural prosperity. Moreover, the neglected economic potential of timber, livestock, and agriculture as well as associated concerns like consolidated schools, improved communities, transportation, and good roads kept Ellison focused on industrializing the entire state. He participated in local organizations ranging from the Arkansas Federation of Fairs to the Ouachita County Poultry Association, with interests in tick eradication and textile manufacturing.

In the late 1920s Ellison organized several promotional efforts known as the Arkansas Industrial Development Tours. Sponsored by the Camden Chamber of Commerce, these train tours introduced local businessmen to the industries in surrounding states and informed them of new manufacturing concerns and technologies. He also founded the South Arkansas Chamber of Commerce and served as its secretary and manager. A cooperative of business and social leaders, this group successfully organized itself into a vocal instrument for south Arkansas economic development.

In the late 1930s Ellison concentrated on trades campaigns and led the fight for tick eradication and is credited with raising the standard of dairy stock in Ouachita County. In 1932 he ran unsuccessfully for commissioner of mines, manufactures, and agriculture. He was a Presbyterian and served in the church as well as in other civic, business, and secret societies. He died in Camden after a brief illness at the age of forty-nine.

[No collections of papers pertaining to Luther Ellison exist. Since the Jonesboro/Craighead County newspaper is nonextant for this period, there is no record of his activities there. References to Ellison's activities emerge in the *Camden Evening News/Camden News* between 1926 and 1935. An article by Ellison, "Possibilities of South Arkansas," is in the October 5, 1927, issue, and his obituary appears on January 7, 1935.]

DAVID EDWIN GIFFORD

ELLSWORTH, SARAH ELIZABETH VAN PATTEN

ELLSWORTH, SARAH ELIZABETH VAN PATTEN (Nov., 1844–Aug. 17, 1927), civic leader, was born in Washington, D.C., to Dr. C. H. Van Patten and Caroline Harper. Her father's family, led by Claus Frederick Van Patten of Amsterdam, Holland, came to America in 1664. Her mother came from a Philadelphia Quaker family whose ancestors were members of the William Penn Colony.

Sarah Elizabeth was educated in music and languages. She traveled with her father to Central America when she was sixteen years old and was believed to be the first girl from the United States to cross Central America from coast to coast. On November 19, 1863, she sang with a choir at Gettysburg, Pennsylvania, during ceremonies dedicating the Soldiers National Cemetery, and heard Abraham Lincoln present his famous address honoring the men who died in battle.

On January 14, 1873, in Baltimore, Maryland, she married Prosper Harvey Ellsworth, a physician practicing in Hot Springs, Arkansas. The Ellsworths had four children: Bessie, Frank, Elmer, and Ernest, all of whom contributed to the history and culture of Hot Springs.

Throughout her life Sarah Ellsworth preserved family letters, compiled scrapbooks, and logged extensive information into diaries. All these records provide a historical account of life in Arkansas and in the United States during the Victorian era up to the 1920s. Her belief in education and the preservation of historical records and buildings is borne out in activities she carried out throughout her life and the many endeavors that she was involved in or led.

In 1881 Ellsworth, along with other women of Hot Springs, decided that the village needed a library and set about to establish one. In the process the Christian National Library Association was founded.

By appointment of Governor Daniel Jones, on April 27, 1898, Ellsworth was commissioned to represent the state of Arkansas as a member of the Board of Lady Commissioners of the trans-Mississippi Exposition at Omaha, Nebraska. Again, on December 7, 1901, she was appointed by Governor Jefferson Davis to represent the state as an honorary commissioner for the Louisiana Purchase Exposition, St. Louis, 1903.

Through efforts made by Ellsworth and the Arkansas Federation of Women's Clubs (AFWC), the apple blossom was adopted as the state's flower by the thirty-third general assembly in 1901. To commemorate the occasion, Ellsworth painted apple blossoms and an apple tree in oils on a blue silk banner for the AFWC.

As president of the Arkansas Federation of Women's Clubs from 1908 to 1910, she initiated the sale of Christmas seals in Arkansas to benefit the Arkansas Tuberculosis Association. During the first year, sales were very low, but in the years to follow Christmas seals gained popularity, and they are still used today.

In 1908 Ellsworth appealed to the Arkansas Federation of Women's Clubs to preserve the Old State House, which was in danger of being sold or demolished. She addressed the four thousand members who attended the state convention that year: "Believing that Arkansas has not lost the patriotic spirit which was the incentive to the building of her first state house, we hereby appeal to the same spirit which moved those pioneers, some of whom donated the ground . . . and proclaim to the world that Arkansas will honor and forever protect not only the old state house, but every other landmark which has any historic value." The members voted unanimously to have her paper reprinted and sent to all legislators. Through the AFWC's continued efforts, the legislature finally passed a bill in 1921 that designated the building as the War Memorial Building. In 1951 the name was changed to the Old State House. The building provided the dramatic setting for Governor Bill Clinton's acceptance speech on November 3, 1992, after he won election to the presidency of the United States.

In about 1910 Ellsworth started looking for the Arkansas state flag and found that Arkansas did not have a designated state flag. During the 1911 state convention of the General Federation of Women's Clubs, members agreed that something should be done to rectify the problem. Within the following year a campaign was initiated to locate a design worthy to be used as Arkansas's state flag. A state senate resolution and a proclamation by Governor Joseph T. Robinson in 1913 asked the people of Arkansas to submit designs to a selection committee. Ellsworth was a member of this committee, which selected the flag we know today, designed by Miss Willie Hocker of Pine Bluff.

Ellsworth's activities were curtailed in 1906, following an accident, though she seems to have remained remarkably active in view of her injuries. She spent her last days at her home "Wildwood" in Hot Springs. She was laid to rest alongside her husband in Hollywood Cemetery in Hot Springs.

[The Ellsworth Family Papers (MC 1162) in the Special Collections Division, University of Arkansas Libraries, Fayetteville, contain letters, diaries, and other materials. The Mary D. Hudgins Collection (MC 534) in the same place also contains information about Ellsworth. Her "An Appeal for the Preservation of the Old State House" is at the Arkansas History Commission.

Sources include Walter L. Brown, "Arkansas' Flag Is Fifty Years Old," *AHQ* 22 (Spring 1963): 3–7; Clara B. Eno, "Some Accomplishments of the Arkansas Federation of Women's Clubs," *AHQ* 2: 3 (1943): 255–58; and Mary D. Hudgins, "Sarah Ellsworth, Maker of Arkansas History," *AHQ* 11:2 (1952): 102–12.]

JAMA A. BEST

FACTOR, POMPEY (1849–1927), army scout and congressional Medal of Honor recipient, was born in Arkansas to a Biloxi Indian woman whose name is unknown and Hardy Factor, a black Seminole subchief and Indian scout.

The descendants of runaway slaves and Seminoles, many black Seminoles fought against the United States Army in the Second Seminole War (1835–1842). By the end of that conflict, most of them were captured and removed to the Indian Territory. The fear of enslavement, however, drove many black Seminoles to migrate to Mexico in the 1850s.

The black Seminoles remained in Mexico until 1870, when the United States Army recruited them to be scouts. In return, the United States promised land for their families in Texas; they were initially located on a reservation at Fort Clark, near Brackettville.

Factor enlisted in the United States Army with the rank of private on August 16, 1870. As an Indian scout, he performed reconnaissance duties for the army by tracking the movements of American Indians at war with the United States. Scouts were expected to identify any Indian groups they located and determine their

strength. Although the scouts were not expected to fight in any battles, they frequently did.

In the midst of the Red River War (1874–1875) between the United States and the Comanches, Factor distinguished himself in one skirmish on April 16, 1875. On that day, Factor, his commander, Lieutenant John L. Bullis, and two other black Seminole scouts, Sergeant John Ward and Trumpeter Isaac Payne, came upon the trail of a herd of seventy-five horses which they suspected were taken from white settlers. They followed the tracks to the Eagle's Nest Crossing of the Pecos River in southwest Texas where they spotted the horses and twenty-five to thirty Comanches. Factor and his companions took cover within seventy-five yards of the Comanches and opened fire. They ran off the herd twice, killed three warriors, and wounded another within forty-five minutes. By that time, the scouts realized they were about to be encircled by the Comanches and cut off from their own horses. They retreated to their mounts and started to ride away. Then Sergeant Ward noticed that Lieutenant Bullis was not able to mount his frightened horse and was nearly surrounded by the Comanches. He alerted Factor and Payne, and they turned around to rescue their commander. Under heavy fire, Ward pulled Bullis onto his horse while Factor and Payne provided cover. The scouts then quickly rode to safety.

Factor and his fellow scouts were awarded the congressional Medal of Honor on May 28, 1875, for the bravery they exhibited on the Pecos. Less than two years after receiving the medal, Factor left the scouts and returned to Mexico. He had become concerned by the rising tensions between black Seminoles and white settlers in southern Texas. Two scouts, one of whom had also won the Medal of Honor, had been murdered.

He returned to the United States two years later and rejoined the scouts for a short time. He then went back to Mexico, where he remained until 1926. Back in the United States, his request for a pension was denied. He died destitute in 1927. He is buried in the Seminole Indian Scout Cemetery at Brackettville, Texas.

[Sources include John Allen Johnson, "The Medal of Honor and Sergeant John Ward and Private Pompey Factor," *AHQ* 29 (Winter 1970): 361–75; Edward S. Wallace, "General John Lapham Bullis: Thunderbolt of the Texas Frontier, II," *Southwestern Historical Quarterly* 55 (July 1951): 77–85; Thomas W. Dunlay, *Wolves for the Blue Soldiers: Indian Scouts and Auxiliaries with the United*

States Army, 1860–90 (1982); Kenneth W. Porter, *The Black Seminoles: The History of a Freedom-Seeking People*, revised and edited by Alcione M. Amos and Thomas P. Senter (1996); "The Seminole Negro-Indian Scouts, 1870–1881," *Southwestern Historical Quarterly* 55 (Jan. 1952): 358–77; and Frank N. Schubert, *Black Valor: Buffalo Soldiers and the Medal of Honor, 1870–1898* (1997).]

JOSEPH PATRICK KEY

FAUBUS, ADDIE JOSLIN (Oct. 10, 1892–Jan. 26, 1936), farm wife, mother of Orval Eugene Faubus (governor of Arkansas from 1955 to 1967), was born near Combs in Madison County, Arkansas. Her parents, Tom and Sarah Thornberry Joslin, owned a farm at the head of West Greasy Creek.

Addie and Sam Faubus married on December 23, 1908. They homesteaded a 160-acre hillside farm and later added one bottomland field. Orval, their first child, was born in 1910. Addie said, "I started house-keeping with cornbread and meal gravy and borrowed the meal to start with." She owned no prized possessions—not a special comb, a necklace, or even a wedding ring.

Addie was five feet six inches tall and, for most of her life, weighed over two hundred pounds. She had brown hair and dark-brown eyes. Between 1910 and 1925 Sam and Addie had seven children. Infant care, breast feeding, and diaper washing filled Addie's days for many years. Housekeeping was also a regular chore. She swept the floors daily and regularly scrubbed them with soap and hot water, sweeping the water out through the cracks between the planks or under the door. Once each week, she carried laundry to the nearby spring, heated water in a kettle over an open fire, and scrubbed the family's clothing on a rub-board. She cooked on a wood-burning range, sewed nearly all the clothing for the girls in the family on a treadle sewing machine, and made quilts.

The Faubuses participated in most of the social activities in the Greasy Creek community. Addie loved to square dance, and often they gave dances at home. Music was important to her. She sang ballads as she worked and eagerly attended shape-note singing schools held at the Greenwood Schoolhouse.

"She was not a talker like my father," Orval observed. "She would visit with the neighbors . . . She got along all right, but she was not a leader in conversation. She'd talk just enough to get along, be part of the group, be accepted . . . She would sit and listen." He added, "She was very shy."

By any economic measure the Faubuses were poor. In 1929 Addie wrote to her school-teaching son on his twentieth birthday, "Orval dont [sic] spend any more of your money than you have to for we sure must take up that [mortgage] note this year." Each spring they borrowed a few dollars for farm supplies and necessities until crops could be harvested. Orval's sister Connie remembered, "There were times when I wondered whether there was going to be enough food for another meal."

Addie's health was poor. In the early 1930s, she had a tumor removed. She suffered from a gum disease that forced her to get dentures. High blood pressure caused excruciating headaches. She died of a stroke at the age of forty-three.

Orval said, "My mother had a very strong influence on me. She was one of the finest individuals that I have ever known in my life . . . She had so little of the world's pleasures and goods that she was almost as denied as a prisoner. She had family; she had love . . . But . . . she never got . . . to do the laundry without the old rub board, never got to turn on an electric light, never had a refrigerator, never had ice, never had any of the modern conveniences. I've always thought about it with regret, but that's the way things were then. She died about the time these things began to become available to the ordinary folks out in the hills." He concluded, "The strongest impression I have of her is her faithfulness to duty. Work, day by day, year by year, taking care of us youngsters. 'Doing her best,' as they say in the hills, 'to raise us right.'"

[Special Collections Division, University of Arkansas Libraries, Fayetteville, has the Orval Eugene Faubus Papers. The author conducted the following interviews: Orval Eugene Faubus, Jan. 31, Feb. 1, 1986, May 14, 1988; Connie Faubus Tucker, Jan. 14, 1989; Bonnie Faubus Salcido, May 30, 1989.]

TOM WAGY

FAUBUS, JOHN SAMUEL (Oct. 24, 1887–Aug. 24, 1966), farmer, socialist, was born on a farm near Combs in Madison County, Arkansas. His parents were Henry Faubus, a farmer and timber worker, and Malinda (Lindy) Sparks. Henry Faubus died in 1900, leaving thirteen-year-old Sam "to make most of the living for [my] mother and 6 brothers and sisters," he recollected. "We had no such thing as the wellfair [sic][.] [A] family like mine either made their own living or starved." Sam attended Greenwood School, one mile north of Combs on West Greasy Creek, through the fourth grade.

Sam and Addie Joslin were married on Christmas Eve 1908. Seven children were born to them. They homesteaded a 160-acre hillside farm and later added one bottomland field. The harshness of the timber cutting and farm work infuriated Sam. He remembered, "I worked in my younger days as a tiemaker—not the wearing kind, but the kind that railroads use. I made them for 10 cents apiece. That's why I became a liberal. I don't like slave labor, and that's just what it was."

While Sam Faubus and his eldest son Orval hoed, sawed, picked strawberries, or rested at the end of a row, Sam lectured about the world. "He'd talk to me about foreign countries, and I was interested," Orval remembered. "What will Russia do, what will Germany do, and he always had some opinions about it which was kind of interesting, romantic in a way. And he might know what he was talking about and he might not. But as a small youngster, I didn't know the difference . . . I just listened to him."

The Socialist Party of America was an organization through which Sam could express his outrage at the economic status of the working class. "What he always wanted was for the poor man like himself to be able to get ahead a little bit better," his daughter, Bonnie Faubus Salcido, recalled. When he stood by socialist principles in opposing the First World War, authorities arrested him for sedition. His attorney delayed the proceedings, and after the war the government dismissed the charges.

Sam believed that scientific laws should prevail over religious creeds. What he viewed as false piety among churchgoers especially angered him. "The church has more hypocrites than burrs in a mare's tail in [a] cocklebur patch," he claimed. Moreover, he believed that if humans used reason "we would soon get rid of superstition and have a world of free men. Poverty would soon become a thing of the past."

Attracted by Franklin D. Roosevelt's New Deal, Sam became a Democrat in the 1930s and remained loyal for the rest of his life.

Addie Faubus died in 1936. In 1952 Sam and Maudie Jostemeyer Wonder married. They moved to a ten-acre farm about one mile north of his birthplace on Mill Creek and raised chickens.

In 1954 Arkansas voters elected Orval Faubus governor. The key event of Orval's governorship was the Little Rock integration crisis of 1957, in which he used state troops to block the court-ordered integration of Central High School. Initially, Sam believed that Orval handled the incident properly, but he later publicly dissented from his son's policies. He claimed, "I didn't see it [Orval's] way. I've never been opposed to any race myself. I don't hold any race prejudice." He could not explain Orval's action. "I think my son got embittered for some reason or other. I just don't know what it was."

Sam died of Hodgkin's Disease, a lymphatic cancer. An *Arkansas Gazette* editorial proclaimed, "Sam Faubus would have stood out in any time, that of his own father, his father's father, anytime. The Ozark mountaineers needed such a man who could articulate their anger at the exploitative economic system that plagued their lives."

[The Special Collections Division, University of Arkansas Libraries, Fayetteville, has the John Samuel Faubus Papers. Family members hold private papers.

The author conducted the following interviews: with Orval Eugene Faubus, Jan. 31, Feb. 1, 1986; Jan. 30, 1987; Apr. 28, Aug. 22, Mar. 23, 1988; with Bonnie Faubus Salcido, May 30, 1989; with Connie Faubus Tucker, Jan. 14, Mar. 28, 1988; with Betty and Darrow Doyle Faubus, Aug. 28, 1986.

Sam Faubus was featured in stories in the *Arkansas Gazette*, Feb. 16, 1964, and the *Madison County Record*, July 6, 1962, reprinted in Orval Eugene Faubus, *Down from the Hills* (1985): 206–7. See also the *Arkansas Gazette*, Dec. 22, 1963, and Aug. 26, 1966.]

TOM WAGY

FAUBUS, ORVAL EUGENE (Jan. 7, 1910–Dec. 14, 1994), teacher and governor of Arkansas, was born in a rented log cabin on Greasy Creek in southern Madison County in the Ozark Mountains. His parents were John Samuel Faubus and Addie Joslin. A self-educated farmer, Sam Faubus became a fervent opponent of capitalism. He named his three sons for socialist heroes; Orval's middle name was Eugene for Eugene V. Debs.

In his youth at his father's urging, Orval spent three months at Commonwealth College, near Mena, a left-wing, self-help institution. Pragmatism and ambition impelled him toward the Democratic Party as Roosevelt's New Deal took hold. At age twenty-eight, tiring of the poverty of teaching in country schools in the winter and picking fruit in the summer, Orval ran for and was elected circuit clerk and recorder of Madison County. He remained a politician for the rest of his life.

In 1931 he married Alta Haskins, a preacher's

daughter. She became a rural schoolteacher and, in later years, editor and publisher of the *Madison County Record*. They had one son.

Distinguished service in World War II gave Faubus's career a boost. He served as an intelligence officer in five major campaigns in Europe, including the Battle of the Bulge. He attained the rank of major.

Orval Faubus returned to the Madison County seat of Huntsville as postmaster. He and Alta bought the town's weekly newspaper. Orval's editorials on education, health care, and highways caught the attention of Sidney S. McMath, himself a war hero and a leader of Arkansas's "G.I." movement, a campaign that swept away many old-line politicians. Faubus campaigned for McMath for governor in 1948 and was rewarded with an appointment to the state highway commission. That post, along with later service as an administrative assistant in the governor's office, put him in touch with political activists all over Arkansas.

However, he was unknown among the general public. His announcement in 1954 that he would challenge Governor Francis A. Cherry, who had defeated McMath, was seen as quixotic. Nonetheless, he proved himself as a campaigner, attacking electric utility interests and Cherry's political awkwardness. He stood up for old people on welfare, throwing Cherry's unfortunate remarks about "welfare chiselers" and "deadheads" in his face. Faubus forced Cherry into a runoff in the Democratic primary.

Cherry panicked. When his advisors dug up Faubus's old connection with Commonwealth College, he made it public in a way suggesting that his opponent might be a communist. The tactic backfired. Faubus defeated Cherry by almost seven thousand votes.

Arkansas steadily industrialized during Faubus's years as governor. Seizing on the new prosperity, he oversaw numerous improvements in public education, including a large increase in teachers' pay. He initiated an overhaul of an embarrassingly bad hospital for the mentally ill; built the state's first institution for retarded children, the Arkansas Children's Colony; expanded state parks; and forced the Corps of Engineers to abandon plans to dam the Buffalo River.

Highways were important to a man who had walked twelve miles on mountain trails to his first teaching job. He described one hill-country road as "so rough it would shake a cat off a bale of cotton." Hundreds of miles of highways were paved during his tenure.

The defining moment of his life was a constitutional crisis over school desegregation. The Little Rock School Board made cautious plans to place the first black pupils in an all-white school in September 1957, three years after the Supreme Court ruled segregated schools unconstitutional. A federal district court endorsed the board's plans. But growing resistance by segregationists caught the attention of Faubus. He was known as a racial moderate. He calculated, however, that a moderate would stand small chance of reelection in 1958 against a determined white supremacist.

On September 2, 1957, he called out the National Guard to block the admission of nine black pupils to Central High School. His justification was that violence threatened and he had to preserve the peace. A federal judge ordered the guardsmen removed. The black pupils returned to the school but were met by a mob of enraged segregationists. The local police were unable to control the crowd. They spirited the black pupils out of the building. President Dwight D. Eisenhower federalized the National Guard and dispatched army troops to restore order and enforce the court's order. The troops stayed through the school year.

Faubus lost the battle with Eisenhower, but his actions ensured his election as governor four more times. He left office undefeated in 1967.

He accumulated unprecedented power over Arkansas politics. His followers remained loyal even after the race conflict subsided. He was opposed by a substantial coalition of blacks and white liberals and moderates, led by the *Arkansas Gazette*, from 1957 until he left office.

He habitually responded to his critics by sounding shocked and aggrieved. On the campaign trail in 1960, he demanded to know which accomplishments of "Faubusism" his opponents would end. Referring to one of his challengers, the Reverend H. E. Williams, Faubus would shout to the crowds, "Preacher Williams, do you want to close the Children's Colony?"

Catering to the clamors of white supremacists seemed out of character for Faubus, a figure of pronounced country dignity and unusual public reserve. His personal convictions at the time were not virulently racist; indeed, his administration had favored the black minority in several instances. And the voters who repeatedly returned him to office were apparently driven by something more than the obvious motive of racism. They seemed in part to be applauding their governor for standing up to an all-powerful federal government in one last lost cause.

He tried unsuccessfully three times—in 1970, 1974, and 1986—to recapture the governor's office. A new generation of voters and leaders had moved into place.

Faubus's personal fortunes declined after he left office. His only child, Farrell, committed suicide in 1976. Orval and Alta divorced in 1969, and he and Elizabeth Westmoreland married. Elizabeth was murdered in 1983 in Houston, Texas, where she was waiting to divorce Orval.

Faubus spent his last years writing essays and memoirs and commenting on public affairs. He became increasingly conservative and often encouraged Republican office-seekers, although he insisted that he never voted for one. A Republican governor, Frank White, gave him his last political job, state director of veterans affairs.

Faubus and Jan Hines Wittenberg, a teacher, married in 1986. He lived with her in Conway until he died, thirty-seven years after his turbulent encounter with history. He was buried in Combs Cemetery on a hill above Greasy Creek in Madison County.

[See Roy Reed, *Faubus: The Life and Times of an American Prodigal* (1997).]

Roy Reed

FAUCETTE, JAMES PETER (Sept. 28, 1867–Jan. 12, 1956), politician and businessman, was born in Pope Station, Panola County, Mississippi, the second son of James Beard Faucette and Eliza Jane Hubbard.

The elder Faucette moved his family to Dover, Pope County, Arkansas, in 1881. In 1885 James Peter Faucette ("J. P.") moved to Argenta, Pulaski County, a small settlement across the Arkansas River from Little Rock. There he joined his brother W. C. Faucette, who had arrived in the community two years earlier to work on the Little Rock and Fort Smith Railroad.

In 1888 the brothers resigned their positions with the railroad and purchased the Arlington Hotel in Argenta, located near the terminus of the Little Rock and Memphis Railroad. They erected an electric light and power plant in 1896 serving the needs of the northshore settlement. The plant was eventually enlarged and sold to Argenta for fifty thousand dollars. In 1901 they established the Faucette Brothers' Bank, renamed Twin City Bank in 1904.

Alhough W. C. is better remembered as helping to found Argenta, J. P. Faucette was just as much involved as his brother. He participated with W. C. and businessman Justin P. Matthews in a plan by which Argenta was separated from Little Rock and established as a city in its own right. After several changes of name Argenta became known as North Little Rock.

In 1904 W. C. was elected mayor of North Little Rock. Because of an agreement with Little Rock, Argenta relinquished its 1903 tax revenues, leaving no money for the town payroll. J. P., as president of the Twin City Bank, furnished the needed money.

In September 1904 J. P. married Emma May Hogins. The union produced two daughters: Margaret in 1905 and Hallie Laura in 1909.

In 1911 W. C. resigned his position as mayor to serve in the Arkansas House of Representatives. J. P. was chosen to succeed his brother. He was reelected in 1913 and 1915.

The year 1915 was tumultuous for J. P. In early January a bomb exploded at the family house, causing five hundred dollars in damages. A political enemy was suspected, but no one was ever apprehended. In March J. P. and his sister Nanka brought out their homemade medicine Epilol. In July a new city hall opened, whose design and construction had been of special interest to J. P.

J. P. Faucette did not run for reelection in 1917 due to a mental breakdown. That same year he and his family moved to Long Beach, California. While he was there he noticed that property values increased when a smaller city was associated by name with a larger one, as demonstrated by North Hollywood. He proposed a city ordinance changing the name to reflect Argenta's close relationship with the capital city, and the name, which had been changed to Argenta in 1907, was changed once more to North Little Rock. In 1936 J. P. returned home after the death of his wife.

Faucette remained interested in North Little Rock's affairs after his return to the city, but did not participate in its government. Throughout his long life, he was a leader in the development of North Little Rock's businesses. With Justin P. Matthews he developed the North Little Rock suburb of Park Hill. He was also manager of the Rose City Cotton Oil Company, established in 1902.

He died in North Little Rock.

[See the Faucette Brothers Papers, Butler Center for Arkansas Studies, Central Arkansas Library System;

Tim G. Nutt, "Floods, Flatcars, and Floozies: Creating the City of North Little Rock, Arkansas," *Pulaski County Historical Review* 41 (1993): 26–38; and Fay Williams, "'Big Jim' Faucette Is the Daddy of 'Argenta,'" in *Arkansans of the Years* (1953): 57–66.]

TIMOTHY G. NUTT

FAUCETTE, WILLIAM CHESLEY (Aug. 13, 1865– Jan. 19, 1914), politician and businessman, was born in Pope Station, Panola County, Mississippi. "W. C." was the fourth child and first son of James Beard Faucette and Eliza Jane Hubbard. The Faucette family moved to Dover, Pope County, Arkansas, in 1881. W. C. left there in 1883 and arrived at the small settlement of Argenta, across the Arkansas River from Little Rock, where he found work as a locomotive engineer with the recently established Little Rock and Fort Smith Railroad. Three years later he married Lillie Dea Hallows. She died in 1887 at the age of thirteen soon after giving birth to a son, who also died.

In 1888 W. C. and his brother James Peter Faucette ("J. P.") leased the Arlington Hotel located near the Argenta railroad terminus and went into the boarding-house business. In 1901 W. C. and J. P. established the Faucette Brothers' Bank.

From this point W. C. became involved in local and state politics. In 1890 Argenta was forcibly annexed to Little Rock, though the Arkansas Supreme Court decision approving the measure was not issued until three years later. Throughout those three years, Little Rock made little effort to include the citizens of Argenta in city affairs, including council representation. However, when the citizens of the Eighth Ward protested to the point of rebellion, an election was called, and W. C. Faucette was elected to the Little Rock City Council .

During his tenure as a councilman, Faucette worked to secure improvements for Argenta. When the "Argenta Anarchist," as he was known by the other council members, resigned in 1896, he claimed it was because of the substandard services that Argenta received.

With resentment from the annexation lingering, W. C. and J. P. Faucette and businessman Justin P. Matthews worked behind the scenes on a strategy to separate Argenta from Little Rock. Under the guise of creating a school district, the trio bought land adjacent to Argenta and incorporated it as the city of North Little Rock in 1901.

Throughout 1902 W. C. Faucette lobbied state law-makers in an effort to break away from Little Rock. In 1903 he ran an unsuccessful campaign for Little Rock mayor. After this defeat he concentrated his efforts on separating Argenta from the capital city.

During the 1903 general assembly session, Representative John M. Martineau of Pulaski County and Senator David L. King of the Second District, both friends of Faucette, introduced the Hoxie-Walnut Ridge bill. The bill stated that any municipality, or any part thereof, may be annexed by another municipality provided they were less than a mile apart. Little Rock legislators, unaware of the impact the bill would have on the city, voted with the majority and approved the bill, which Governor Jeff Davis signed into law in early March.

The Faucette brothers and Matthews waited until after the general assembly adjourned before acting on the new law. In May petitions were circulated, and the town of North Little Rock ordered an election calling for the annexation of Argenta. Little Rock appealed to the Arkansas Supreme Court questioning the constitutionality of the law and asked that the election be canceled, but the court refused. The election produced a vote of 455 to 44 in favor of annexation. Little Rock was not allowed to participate in the election, which accounts for the small number of votes against the merger. The state supreme court later upheld the constitutionality of the Hoxie-Walnut Ridge Law, validating the election. Little Rock had lost its Eighth Ward.

North Little Rock, now the name of the combined areas, qualified as a first-class city and held its first election in April 1904. W. C. Faucette was elected mayor, and he was reelected in 1905 and 1907. During the 1907 administration, North Little Rock's name was changed to Argenta. Faucette resigned the office in 1909, but was asked to reassume the office a year later. In 1911 he again resigned the office of mayor to represent his district in the Arkansas House of Representatives, a position he held for one term. One achievement of his while in the House was the passage of a bill requiring both cities to agree on annexation, eliminating any chance of Little Rock's re-annexing Argenta.

Faucette remained active in Argenta's government after his retirement, though he was in ill health. He died in Battle Creek, Michigan, while receiving treatment for his illness.

[See the Faucette Brothers Papers, Butler Center for Arkansas Studies, Central Arkansas Library System; and

Tim G. Nutt, "Floods, Flatcars, and Floozies: Creating the City of North Little Rock, Arkansas," *Pulaski County Historical Review* 41 (1993): 26–38.]

TIMOTHY G. NUTT

FITZGERALD, EDWARD MARY (Oct. 13?, 1833–Feb. 21, 1907), second Catholic bishop of Little Rock, was born in the city of Limerick on the west coast of Ireland. His birth certificate does not reveal his exact birthdate; an early account of his life claims October 13, then the feastday of St. Edward the Confessor. His father was Irish, and his mother was of German descent.

He migrated to the United States with his family in 1849. The following year he entered St. Mary of the Barrens Seminary in Perryville, Missouri; two years later he enrolled at St. Mary's Seminary in Cincinnati, Ohio. On August 22, 1857, he was ordained an archdiocesan priest by Archbishop John Purcell of Cincinnati.

Father Fitzgerald's only assignment was St. Patrick's Church in Columbus, Ohio. He brought unity to this divided parish, so Archbishop Purcell allowed him to stay there for nine years. He became an American citizen in 1859.

On June 22, 1866, Fitzgerald received a note from Pope Pius IX informing him that he was to be the bishop of Little Rock. The thirty-two-year-old priest rejected the appointment. In early December he received from the Pope a *mandamus,* an order to accept the Arkansas diocese under holy obedience. In February 1867 Purcell consecrated him Arkansas's second Catholic prelate. He was now America's youngest bishop.

When Fitzgerald arrived in Little Rock, he quickly discovered what a Civil War and five years without a bishop could do to a diocese. (The diocese of Little Rock had been without a bishop since the death of Andrew Byrne in June 1862.) The diocese was almost destitute, with only six priests to serve the whole state.

In 1869 he was summoned to Rome to attend the First Vatican Council. As the council's youngest American bishop, Fitzgerald made a name for himself the following year by being one of only two Catholic prelates in the world to vote against the declaration of papal infallibility. His one negative vote was the first after 491 consecutive votes in favor of the declaration. When the tally ended, this large-framed Irishman knelt before Pontiff and submitted to the council's decision. In a public address later, Fitzgerald stated that while he always believed in the doctrine, he felt its

declaration would hamper Catholic evangelization efforts. His vote did not damage his career. Pope Leo XIII, successor to Pius IX, considered him for the archdioceses of Cincinnati and New Orleans, and three or four other dioceses as well. Fitzgerald stubbornly spurned all offers of promotion or transfer out of his adopted state.

He enjoyed an active episcopal career that spanned three decades, with the diocese of Little Rock experiencing great institutional growth. In 1867 he had only a half dozen priests; by 1900 there were twenty-one diocesan priests and twenty-two priests belonging to either the Order of St. Benedict (Benedictines) or the Congregation of the Holy Ghost (Holy Ghost Fathers). When he came in 1867, he had two seminarians; by 1900 he had twenty-five young men studying for the priesthood at Subiaco Abbey in Logan County. When he arrived there were only nine churches; at century's end there were fifty-one edifices with forty chapels and missions stations attached to parishes. Where once there had been about 20 sisters and one religious order in Arkansas, thirty-three years later there were four women's religious orders and 150 sisters ministering in schools and hospitals.

Under his administration the main Catholic medical facilities were established. Fitzgerald opened Arkansas's first Catholic hospital, St. Vincent's Infirmary in Little Rock in 1888, staffed by the Sisters of Charity of Nazareth. By 1900 St. Vincent's was joined by two other Catholic hospitals which are still operating: St. Joseph's in Hot Springs, conducted by the Sisters of Mercy, and St. Bernard's in Jonesboro, served by the Olivetian Benedictine Sisters. In 1905 the Mercy Sisters in Fort Smith opened St. Edward's Hospital, named for his patron saint.

Bishop Fitzgerald attempted to attract Catholic foreign migration into the state, while also trying to convert African Americans to Catholicism. These efforts yielded few results as the percentage of Catholics in the state by 1900 amounted to just less than one percent of the population, an incremental increase from the time he became Arkansas's Catholic prelate. Fitzgerald established Arkansas's oldest black Catholic parish in Pine Bluff in 1895, and a year later he had six black Catholic schools opened, yet only two were left a decade later.

Fitzgerald continued to play a major role within the American church. He delivered the opening sermon for the Third Plenary Council in Baltimore in 1884.

Throughout much of 1893 he lived in Texas, administering the newly created diocese of Dallas. He also represented Archbishop Francis Janssens of New Orleans at a conference of archbishops held in Philadelphia in 1895.

On January 17, 1900, Bishop Fitzgerald's years of ministry came to an end; he suffered a stroke in Jonesboro and spent the rest of his life confined to St. Joseph's Hospital. He celebrated his fortieth anniversary as bishop on February 3, 1907, eighteeen days before his death. A funeral Mass was celebrated on February 27 in Little Rock; he is buried under the Cathedral of St. Andrew.

[The most complete collection of Bishop Fitzgerald's letters, business documents, sermons, and other primary material is in the Archives of the Diocese of Little Rock, St. John's Catholic Center. Other primary material can be found in the Archives of the Archdiocese of New Orleans and the Archives of the Archdiocese of Baltimore. Bishop Fitzgerald between 1867–1894 wrote annual reports to the Society for the Propagation of the Faith in Paris and Lyon, France; microfilm copies are found in the Archives of the University of Notre Dame. For his efforts on evangelizing blacks into the Catholic church, see his reports to the Catholic Commission for Catholic Missions to the Colored People and Indians (1887–1907) in the Sulpician Archives, Baltimore, Maryland.

See also James M. Woods, *Mission and Memory: A History of the Catholic Church in Arkansas* (1993).]

JAMES M. WOODS

FLANAGIN, HARRIS (Nov. 3, 1817–Oct. 23, 1874), governor of Arkansas, was born in Roadstown, Cumberland County, New Jersey, to James Flanagin, a cabinetmaker and merchant, and Mary Harris. James had emigrated from Ireland in 1765. Harris Flanagin was educated in a Quaker school and became a professor of mathematics at Clermont Seminary in Frankfort, Pennsylvania, at age eighteen. He next opened his own school at Paoli, Illinois, where he also began the study of law.

Flanagin moved to Arkansas in 1839, settling in Greenville in Clark County before relocating to Arkadelphia, where he established his law office on the town square. He also speculated in land. A Whig in politics, in 1842 he was elected to the state house of representatives, serving one term. Although he volunteered for the Mexican War, his company seems not to have completed its organization. In 1847 he was elected captain of a militia company. Flanagin won a spirited contest in

1848 against Democrat Hawes H. Coleman for a state senate seat, again serving one term. After the collapse of the Whig Party in the 1850s, his political activity was limited to Arkadelphia city politics.

He reentered politics in 1861 when he was elected to the state secession convention. A reluctant secessionist, he left the convention after the passage of the ordinance of secession on May 6 in order to accept the captaincy of Company F of the Second Arkansas Mounted Rifles. He participated in actions at Wilson's Creek (Oak Hills) and Pea Ridge (Elk Horn Tavern). After the death of Colonel James McIntosh and the reorganization of the regiment, Flanagan was elected colonel. He was serving in the Army of Tennessee at the time of his election as governor.

During the summer of 1862, Flanagin's name was put forth as a gubernatorial candidate in a public letter by a strong coalition of ex-Unionists (mostly ex-Whigs) and Democrats who wished to supplant the inept incumbent, Henry Massie Rector. The secession convention had contrived to shorten Rector's term by scheduling elections for the fall of 1862. A story that Flanagin had no knowledge of his nomination is evidently false, but all the campaigning was done by his friends in Arkansas. A pro-Rector paper tried to stir up anti-Irish sentiment by claiming Harris's last name was O'Flanagin, but the colonel outpolled Rector by more than a two-to-one margin.

Sworn in on November 14, 1862, Governor Flanagin called on the legislature for action on shortages of salt, impoverished soldiers' families, profiteering, liquor production, and state finance. Some laws were passed, but Flanagin took a passive attitude toward executive responsibilities and failed to offer effective leadership. In contrast to many southern governors, he did not oppose the imposition by Confederate authorities of conscription or endorse an extreme states' rights position. He worked strongly to get Confederate authorities to take seriously the defense of Arkansas, accompanying the army on its futile assault on the Union-held port of Helena in July 1863. He also made two efforts to raise state troops for defense, once after the fall of Arkansas Post in January 1863. In August when a federal column began marching on the capital, Flanagin offered to lead a company of old men.

With the fall of Little Rock on September 10, 1863, Flanagin went home to Arkadelphia, apparently assuming that the war was over. Confederate authorities prevailed on him to reestablish the state government at Washington, where the legislature met in 1864 to hear that the state war effort had collapsed. Flanagin failed to attend the first Trans-Mississippi Department governors' conference, made limited use of his executive powers, and did little to retard the rising peace sentiment among the masses. He did participate in another conference held in 1865 after the news of General Robert E. Lee's surrender. Opposed to continuing the war or conducting guerrilla operations, Flanagin returned to Arkansas and suggested to federal authorities that he be allowed to summon the old legislature, repeal all acts of secession, and then resign. Federal authorities, having installed a loyal governor, Isaac Murphy, under the Constitution of 1864, ignored this proposal but did allow Flanagin to return the state archives and retire unmolested to Arkadelphia.

During the Reconstruction period Flanagin tried to reestablish his law practice and participated little in state affairs. His correspondence indicates he opposed violence and took the same high legal and moral tone that had marked his gubernatorial career. In 1872 he was selected as a delegate to the Democratic National Convention. After the Brooks-Baxter war, he was elected to the state convention that wrote the Constitution of 1874, serving as chairman of the judiciary committee. He died before final ratification, but he had signed an early draft.

Flanagin had been raised a Baptist, but after he and Martha Elizabeth Nash of Hempstead County married on July 3, 1851, he affiliated with the Presbyterians, his wife's church. He was the father of two sons, Nash and Duncan, and a daughter, Laura. Despite his gloomy countenance, his friends and former slaves were devoted to him.

[See Michael B. Dougan, "Harris Flanagin, 1862–1864," in *The Governors of Arkansas: Essays in Political Biography*, Timothy P. Donovan, Willard B. Gatewood Jr., and Jeannie M. Whayne, eds., 2d ed. (1995).]

MICHAEL B. DOUGAN

FLETCHER, ALBERT LEWIS (Oct. 28, 1896–Dec. 6, 1979), fourth bishop of Little Rock, the Catholic diocese for Arkansas, was born in Little Rock. His parents, Thomas Fletcher and Helen Wehr, were converts to Catholicism, and Albert was their first child. Months after his birth, the family moved to Paris, Arkansas; Albert spent his boyhood there and at Tontitown. He graduated from Little Rock College with a degree in chemistry in 1917 and then entered St. John's Seminary to study for the priesthood. He was ordained by Bishop John B. Morris on June 4, 1920.

Fletcher served two decades as a priest in central Arkansas. He earned an M.A. in chemistry from the University of Chicago in 1922. He taught at Little Rock College and became its president in 1923, a position he held for two years until he became vice chancellor. In 1926 he became chancellor and then vicar general seven years later. Upon Bishop Morris's request, the Pope granted him the title of Monsignor in 1934. Five years later, with Bishop Morris's recommendation, Fletcher was named auxiliary bishop. On April 25, 1940, Albert L. Fletcher was raised to the hierarchy of the American Catholic Church, the first native Arkansan to be so honored.

As auxiliary bishop he ran the day-to-day operations of the diocese for the growingly incapacitated Bishop Morris. When Morris died in 1946, it was not automatic that Fletcher would become his successor, since his position was only that of auxiliary bishop. On December 11, 1946, Fletcher was informed that Pope Pius XII had named him bishop, and on February 11, 1947, Fletcher was consecrated the fourth bishop of Little Rock at St. Andrew's Cathedral.

Bishop Fletcher was a tall, soft-spoken, courtly gentleman, who happened to be bishop during a turbulent era. His first decade was relatively quiet. A Catholic bookstore opened, the seminary expanded, and the number of Catholics in the state topped 2 percent of the population in 1960 for the first time since Arkansas was a European colony.

A major storm erupted, however, over the integration of Little Rock schools in 1957–59. Bishop Fletcher, though often cautious and slow, always believed that racist bigotry was wrong and that integration should proceed. In 1960 Bishop Fletcher wrote *An Elementary Catholic Catechism on the Morality of Segregation and Discrimination* in which he stated that racial discrimination and segregation are immoral, since they violate justice and charity. He oversaw the integration of Catholic schools and hospitals. One consequence of this policy was the closing of four black Catholic schools and seven black Catholic parishes between 1962 and 1972.

Bishop Fletcher attended the Second Vatican Council which met between 1962 and 1965. He served on the committee to advise the council on faith and morals. He never addressed the council, yet he wrote thirteen interventions or amendments into the documents, and nine were accepted by the council. While he agreed with the council's pronouncements, he reflected later that so many decrees were issued that it was difficult to implement them all.

Another difficulty for the bishop was the turmoil within the diocesan seminary. St. John's Seminary was expensive to maintain for a small diocese, and tensions existed between a younger and an older group of faculty members. In the summer of 1967 one of the leaders of the younger priests, in a series of articles in a local newspaper, challenged the church's ban on artificial birth control. He mistakenly predicted that the Pope would lift the ban, leading to a "demythologizing" of papal office. Bishop Fletcher demanded that this faculty member repudiate these assertions; when he did not, Fletcher suspended him. A week later, Bishop Fletcher announced that St. John's Home Mission Seminary would close due to the difficulty of obtaining "adequate teaching staff." The old seminary now became the home of a new chancery building and Arkansas's Catholic newspaper.

Like Bishop Morris, Bishop Fletcher asked for an auxiliary bishop in his latter years. On April 25, 1969, twenty-nine years after Fletcher's consecration as auxiliary bishop, Lawrence P. Graves was consecrated as auxiliary bishop at St. Andrew's Cathedral, the second native Arkansan to be named to the hierarchy. This led to speculation that history would repeat itself, that Auxiliary Bishop Graves would eventually succeed Bishop Fletcher.

New rules required bishops to retire at age seventy-five, so Bishop Fletcher submitted his resignation in January 1972. News came the following summer that Monsignor Andrew J. McDonald from Savannah would become the fifth bishop of Little Rock; Auxiliary Bishop Graves later became bishop of Alexandria, Louisiana.

Bishop Fletcher continued to live at his home until his health began to fail by the fall of 1979. He was moved to the new rectory next to the cathedral. On December 6, 1979, the retired bishop traveled to the chancery on an errand. On returning, he stopped in at a local diner. There he collapsed and was rushed to St. Vincent's Infirmary where he died. Five days later he was buried under St. Andrew's Cathedral in the crypt he had built in 1962 for the remains of all his predecessors.

[Bishop Fletcher's unpublished account of his life, "Reminiscences," is in the Archives of the Diocese of Little Rock, as are his official papers, his personal correspondence, and his book on the morality of segregation. Also consult the Archives of the Archdiocese of New Orleans. See the *Guardian* for the years 1940–79. Also see James M. Woods, *Mission and Memory: A History of the Catholic Church in Arkansas* (1993).]

JAMES M. WOODS

FLETCHER, JOHN GOULD (Jan. 3, 1886–May 10, 1950), poet, was born in Little Rock to Adolphine Krause and John G. Fletcher. The Fletcher ancestors had migrated from Tennessee to Arkansas by 1815 and eventually became prosperous slave-owning farmers in Saline County. Following the Civil War John G. Fletcher and fellow Confederate veteran Peter Hotze formed a cotton brokerage firm with offices in Little Rock and New York. Wealth and prominence followed, although Fletcher's three campaigns for the governor's office were unsuccessful. In 1877 the forty-six-year-old financier and politician married twenty-three-year-old Adolphine Krause, the daughter of German immigrants.

Adolphine Krause had abandoned the prospect of a musical career to tend to her ailing mother and likely centered her artistic ambitions on her only son. John Gould was reared and early educated by tutors in the company of his two sisters, Adolphine (born 1882) and Mary (born 1890). As a child John Gould was rarely permitted to leave the grounds of the shadowy antebellum mansion built by Albert Pike and purchased by the Fletchers in 1889. Distanced from the outside world, young John Gould developed a dense imaginative life nurtured by reading Poe, Coleridge, and Goethe.

In 1903, following a year at Phillips Andover Academy, Fletcher enrolled in Harvard. He made little progress toward his father's goal that he study business and law, but instead adopted his mother's assumption that artistic accomplishment was superior to mercantile success. He wrote his first poems during a 1905 train journey through the American West and quickly determined that he had discovered his lifework. His father's death and an estate settlement allowed Fletcher to leave Harvard without a degree and in 1908 sail for Italy. The family fortune gave the poet an independent income and the freedom to write full time throughout his life, although the regular checks from a trust fund did not assuage his anxieties about his livelihood. These anxieties resulted from cyclical episodes of depression which first became evident during his college years.

By 1913 Fletcher's settling in London allowed him to strengthen his relationship with the American poet Ezra Pound. Pound promoted Fletcher's free-verse experiments to Harriet Monroe, editor of *Poetry: A Magazine of Verse,* and invited him to join the Imagist group. Resisting Pound's advice on editing his poems, Fletcher became identified with the Imagist movement only when Amy Lowell supplanted Pound as its leader.

In 1914 Fletcher journeyed to America. He wrote incessantly during his tour, enjoyed the critical attention given to his newly published *Irradiations* (1915), and participated in the literary politics associated with the publication of *Some Imagist Poets, 1915.* Despite Lowell's objections, Fletcher recrossed the Atlantic to resume a liaison with the recently divorced Florence Emily Arbuthnot in her spacious home located near Kent in England. Their marriage on July 5, 1916, produced no children, but "Daisy" Arbuthnot Fletcher's son and daughter lived with the couple.

The end of the First World War was a turning point in Fletcher's career. His early poetry as represented in *Irradiations* and *Goblins and Pagodas* (1916) was characterized by heightened emotion and prosodic innovations. Throughout the 1920s he crafted works intended to employ the unique visionary authority of the poet to renew a society corrupted by the excesses of industrialism and mass politics. Fletcher's work, which owed much to nineteenth-century Romanticism, placed him at odds with T. S. Eliot and Pound's High Modernist tenet that the poetic personality was anachronistic. His most significant contribution in this mode was the epic *Branches of Adam* (1926) with its echoes of the prophetic works of William Blake.

In early spring 1927, toward the end of another American sojourn, the expatriate poet met John Crowe Ransom and Donald Davidson at Vanderbilt University and their fellow Fugitive poet Allen Tate in New York. These southerners were beginning to form the Agrarian movement, and Fletcher willingly enlisted. His overwrought essay in the Agrarian symposium, "I'll Take My Stand" (1930), laden with anti-democratic invective, signaled the onset of a depressive crisis. Following a suicide attempt in late 1932 and committal at Royal Bethlehem Hospital, Fletcher permanently left his English family and took up residence in Little Rock. His return to native ground did not quell Fletcher's

psychic storms. Within two years he had bitterly seceded from the Agrarians, and throughout the rest of his life he frequently made plans to live in urban locales far from Arkansas. Fletcher's primary source of stability was the talented writer Charlie May Simon, whom he married on January 18, 1936, on the heels of the divorce from his first wife. Simon's book royalties bolstered their income as Fletcher found publishers less willing to bring out his work. Even the 1938 Pulitzer Prize for Poetry did not gain him a new readership. Thus *The Burning Mountain* (1946), his last and finest collection, was not widely recognized for containing vital, well-crafted poems. His intuitive, original history, *Arkansas* (1947), was similarly ignored.

The knowledge that he was falling into obscurity coupled with his worsening arthritis ignited more debilitating bouts with depression. Early one morning in May 1950, Fletcher drowned himself in a shallow pond near Johnswood, his home on the western edge of Little Rock. Though his dramatic, restless imagination and energetic, discursive intellect produced notable individual achievements in poetry and criticism, Fletcher's volatile psychology prevented the sustained legacy necessary to grant him a clear identity in modern literary history.

[See Ben F. Johnson, *Fierce Solitude: A Life of John Gould Fletcher* (1994).]

BEN F. JOHNSON

FLOWERS, WILLIAM HAROLD (Oct. 16, 1911– Apr. 7, 1990), lawyer and civil rights activist, was born in Stamps, Arkansas, to Alonzo Williams Flowers, a businessman, and Beuhlah Lee (?), a schoolteacher.

Flowers found an early vocational calling, gaining his first glimpse of trials on trips with his father to the courthouse at Little Rock. On one of these occasions in 1927 Flowers witnessed the burning of lynching victim John Carter on the main downtown thoroughfare. This graphic demonstration of lawlessness convinced Flowers to enter the legal profession. After passing the Arkansas bar examinations in 1935 he graduated from Robert H. Terral Law School in Washington, D.C., setting up practice in Pine Bluff in 1938.

He and Margret Brown married in the 1940s.

From the outset Flowers was determined to fight for African-American rights. When the National Association for the Advancement of Colored People (NAACP), the leading civil rights organization of the day, proved reluctant to help, Flowers founded his own Committee on Negro Organizations (CNO) at Stamps on March 10, 1940. The fundamental aim of the CNO was to raise political consciousness and increase the number of African-American registered voters in the state. To this end, Flowers set off on an extensive speaking tour in 1941, talking to church, civic, fraternal, and social organizations, imploring them to use their influence to encourage voter registration. As a result the percentage of African Americans in Arkansas registered to vote rose from 1.5 percent in 1940 to 17.3 percent by 1947.

This growing political participation provided a backdrop for increased civil rights activism. In 1942 African-American teachers in Little Rock launched a successful suit to equalize salaries with their white counterparts. The case attracted NAACP assistance and led to the organization of an Arkansas State Conference of Branches in 1945. Flowers was promptly instated as its chief recruitment officer.

Flowers also blazed a path for African-American rights in the courts. In the landmark 1947 *Wilkerson* case he won commutation of the death sentence for two brothers accused of killing two white men. At the same trial he demanded and received the appointment of African Americans on the jury for the first time in the county since Reconstruction. Wiley Branton, a protégé of Flowers who later became a nationally renowned civil rights lawyer, remembered the case as having "a major impact on the view of black people . . . that maybe there is justice after all."

In 1948 Flowers played an instrumental role in the desegregation of the University of Arkansas Law School, acting as counsel to the first successful African-American applicant, Silas Hunt. The year after, Flowers launched the first suit for the equalization of school facilities at DeWitt, Arkansas. Along with several other similar suits, the case paved the way for later attacks on racial discrimination in schools, which proliferated after the United States Supreme Court's 1954 *Brown v. Board of Education* school desegregation decision.

Flowers's successes earned him election as president of the Arkansas NAACP State Conference of Branches in 1948. However, the office proved his downfall. As bureaucratic matters of paperwork remained undone at the expense of other activities, accusations of mismanagement led to Flowers's removal from office. The decision raised a storm of controversy, with only the intervention of leading national NAACP figures preventing an en masse defection in Arkansas.

Nevertheless, Flowers's legacy remained indelibly marked on the NAACP's future activities. In 1951 local members succeeded in electing a dynamic new leader, Daisy Bates. Daisy and her husband Lucious Christopher Bates, who together ran the *State Press* newspaper in Little Rock, were old friends of Flowers. Daisy Bates built upon his groundwork, particularly in the area of school desegregation, culminating in the infamous showdown of the 1957 Little Rock school crisis.

During the 1950s and afterward disagreements with other leaders, coupled with a troubled personal life, meant a lowering of Flowers's civil rights profile. Nevertheless, he continued to make a valuable contribution to the struggle as one of Arkansas's most respected lawyers. In 1977 he was named special circuit court judge in Jefferson County, the first African American in the state to hold such a position. In 1980 Governor Bill Clinton appointed him as associate justice in the state court of appeals. A year later, the Arkansas Black Lawyers' Association was renamed the W. H. Flowers Lawyers' Association in his honor.

In 1971 Flowers was ordained as a Methodist minister and remained active in the church until his death in Pine Bluff. He was survived by five sons and three daughters.

Flowers is still largely overlooked for his part in Arkansas's early civil rights struggles, principally because his endeavors came at a time when such activism remained out of the national spotlight. Yet it was the work done by figures such as Flowers that paved the way for later civil rights victories. In 1942 the *State Press* printed his photograph with the caption "He Founded a Movement." From today's perspective, this remains a perceptive and befitting accolade.

[Sources include the William Harold Flowers Papers privately held by his daughter, whose assistance in this research is gratefully acknowledged. See also John A. Kirk, "'He Founded a Movement': W. H. Flowers, the Committee on Negro Organizations and Black Activism in Arkansas, 1940–1957," in Brian Ward and Tony Badger, eds., *The Making of Martin Luther King and the Civil Rights Movement in America* (1996); "Black Activism in Arkansas, 1940–1970," thesis, University of Newcastle upon Tyne, United Kingdom, 1997; and "The Little Rock Crisis and Postwar Black Activism in Arkansas," *AHQ* 56 (Autumn 1997): 273–93.]

JOHN A. KIRK

FORD, EDSEL (Dec. 30, 1928–Feb. 19, 1970), poet, was born in Eva, Alabama, to Nora and James Ford. His early years were spent in Eva and in Roswell, New Mexico. In 1939, when he was eleven, Ford moved with his family to Avoca, Arkansas, where his father raised broiler chickens. The Ford farm was located near the site of the Civil War battle of Pea Ridge. Ford's poem, "Return to Pea Ridge," was read at the 1962 dedication of Pea Ridge National Battlefield Park and today is inscribed on a plaque located in the park.

In 1948 Ford won an Arkansas Poets' Roundtable award. He entered the University of Arkansas at Fayetteville the same year. Two mentors there, W. J. Lemke and Rosa Zagnoni Marinoni, befriended Ford for life. Professor Lemke and Ford wandered the backwoods of northwest Arkansas looking for ancient cemeteries. Marinoni was surrogate mother, wise confidante, and critic. Rosa, as Ford called her, flattered his youthful vanity. Ford was able to avoid Marinoni's worst poetic extremes: an intellectual snobbishness, a distorted sense of uniqueness, and a superiority over less-gifted individuals. In spite of these traits, he remained her friend.

Ford graduated from the University of Arkansas in 1952. His two-year military deferment having expired, he was drafted into the United States Army during the Korean War. Private Ford, serial number U54068113, sent his last will and testament to a friend. Ford turned down officer training because he believed no individual should have authority over another.

While on military duty in Hanau, Germany, he submitted so many poems to *Stars and Stripes* magazine that a soldier's letter was published which read: "I am getting bored/with the works of Edsel Ford." The hardness and boredom of army life gave his poems a realistic edge. Whereas his college poems describe physical death, his army poems describe spiritual death, with which he was more familiar. In "Memento Mori" he described children playing in the still-visible ruins of World War II. The army poems were published under the title *This Was My War.*

In 1956 Edsel Ford was working at the Phillips Petroleum Company in Hobbs, New Mexico, when his manuscript, "The Manchild from Sunday Creek," won the Kaleidograph Book Competition from a field of 131 entries. A Phillips vice president turned a company celebration into a fete honoring Ford. This generous act made Ford realize that his vocation was writing.

Ford quit Phillips in February 1957, but he was not able to support himself by writing, so he returned to the family farm in February 1958. In that month, he took over Professor Lemke's column, "The Golden Country," in the *Ozark Mountaineer* magazine. Reacquainting himself with the region, he produced *One Leg Short from Climbing Hills* in 1959.

From 1960 until 1970 Ford was closely associated with the War Eagle Fair. Since some of his most touching poems describe Ozark flora and fauna, he was ideally suited to promote the War Eagle Fair in national magazines. At the 1961 War Eagle Fair, in a brilliant October setting, Ford met his companion and patron Hank Spruce.

In late 1961 Ford moved to Fort Smith to be with Spruce. The years of their friendship from 1961 to 1970 were among Ford's best. During this time his work matured enough to win national poetry awards. Commercial sale of his works improved greatly. His increasing prominence gained him honor throughout Arkansas and beyond, and his service to poets and poetry gained him many friends.

Ford published in 1963 his series of Civil War poems entitled *Return to Pea Ridge.* This led to a commission from *Boy's Life* magazine to rewrite Clement Moore's "Visit from St. Nicolas" in the original meter from St. Nicolas's point of view. The poem, "St. Nicolas Rides Again," was printed in the Christmas issue of 1963, netting Ford the largest amount he ever received for a single poem, 750 dollars.

Nineteen sixty-five and 1966 were good years. Ford published a book of love poems called *Love Is the House It Lives In.* The Library of Congress asked him to record some of his poems, and the Poetry Society of America awarded him the Alice Fay di Castagnola Award. This $3,500 award was for a work in progress, "A Landscape for Dante," in which he transferred some of Dante's subjects from the *Inferno* to a contemporary small town in the Ozarks. In June of 1966 Ford was chosen one of three distinguished alumni of the University of Arkansas.

Throughout his life Edsel Ford was mistaken for the Edsel Ford of automobile fame. The doctor who delivered Ford and suggested the name to Mrs. Ford, who thought the name would "in a wistful sort of way tie the two families together." As his fame grew, his name attracted requests for money, which he did not have. Far from being angry, Ford met the challenge with characteristic humor.

He died at the age of forty-two in the Veterans' Hospital in Little Rock of a brain tumor. He was buried in Rogers, Arkansas, and saddled with the inscription on his tombstone, "Edsel Ford: Poet Immortal." He would not have approved the "immortal" part, but perhaps it rings true.

[The Edsel Ford Papers are in the Special Collections Division, University of Arkansas Libraries, Fayetteville. The Walter John Lemke Papers in the same collection also contain information concerning Ford. Ford's books include *Two Poets* (1951); *This Was My War* (1955); *One Leg Short from Climbing Hills* (1959); *Return to Pea Ridge* (1963); *Love Is the House It Lives In* (1965); and *Looking for Shiloh* (1968).

Other sources include the author's interviews with Hank M. Spruce, Feb. 11 and Apr. 30, 1978, and Miller Williams, May 1, 1978. See Marcus Clyde Woodward, "Edsel Ford: Poet Immortal," thesis, University of Arkansas, Fayetteville, 1979; *Arkansas Democrat Magazine* (May 17, 1959): 4; and the *New Yorker* (Nov. 14, 1959): 46–47.]

MARCUS CLYDE WOODWARD

FORDYCE, SAMUEL WESLEY (Feb. 7, 1840–Aug. 3, 1919), was born in Senecaville, Ohio, the son of John Fordyce and Mary Ann Houseman.

Fordyce became a station agent on the Central Ohio Railroad at the age of twenty. Soon thereafter he enlisted as a private in the First Ohio Volunteer Cavalry. His record in the Civil War is distinguished. He quickly rose to officer status and participated in the Battles of Murfreesboro, Chickamauga, and Shiloh, among others.

At the end of the war, he moved to Huntsville, Alabama, where he established the banking house of Fordyce and Rison and played a leading role in the development of northern Alabama.

He and Susan E. Chadick of Huntsville married on May 1, 1866.

Injuries he sustained in the war affected his health, and he moved to Hot Springs, Arkansas, in 1876 to obtain the benefits of the healing waters there. He immediately recognized the possibilities of Hot Springs as a health resort and worked to turn those possibilities into reality. He financed the town's leading hotels; the opera house; water, gas, and electric systems; the street railway system; and many other public enterprises, including several bathhouses. Hot Springs's transition from a village to a cosmopolitan spa between the end of the Civil War and the turn of the century owes as much to Samuel Fordyce as to any other individual. Today, the Fordyce Bath House on Bath House Row remains one of the most elegant structures of its kind anywhere in the world.

Fordyce also became the builder and leader of many railroads, not only in Arkansas, but throughout the South and Southwest. Active in St. Louis, Missouri, as well as in Hot Springs, he helped build or finance many thousands of miles of railway during his career. Fordyce led the effort to build the first railroad through Arkansas from Missouri to Texas, which became known as the Cotton Belt Route. Cutting a northeast-southwest diagonal across the state, it opened up to agriculture the swamps and prairies of northeast and east-central Arkansas and created the modern timber industry of southern and southwest Arkansas. The railroad opened the vast pine forests to sawmillers who followed the rails through the region. Completion of the line in 1883 changed Arkansas permanently, making major railroad towns out of cities like Pine Bluff and Texarkana. New communities sprang up along the line, including Fordyce (named for Samuel Fordyce) and Rison (named by Fordyce for his former banking partner in Alabama). The *Arkansas Gazette* described Fordyce as "one of the empire builders, one of the men whose vision, energy, and ability have made America."

Samuel Wesley Fordyce never sought public office, but he was one of the most significant figures in the politics of his day. He enjoyed friendships with Presidents Hayes, Harrison, and McKinley, all of whom asked his advice on matters concerning appointments and other area issues. He was often mentioned as a potential candidate for governor and United States senator, but always declined political honors, choosing to channel his energies into the development of the region.

Samuel Fordyce was a lover of the outdoors and a sportsman. His declining years were spent primarily at his home on the outskirts of Hot Springs. "The Cabin," as it was known to his family, remains today in a forested area landscaped so as to preserve the natural beauty of the grounds. Fordyce died in Atlantic City, New Jersey, and was buried in St. Louis.

[The Fordyce Papers, including the business records of Samuel W. Fordyce and John R. Fordyce, are housed at the Arkansas History Commission, Little Rock. The "Autobiography of Samuel Wesley Fordyce" is on microfilm there. See the *Arkansas Gazette*, Aug. 4 and 5, 1919, and the *Fordyce News-Advocate*, May 25, 1977.

See also Bob Lancaster, "Samuel W. Fordyce: Railroad Man," *Arkansas Times* (June 1985): 70; W. J. Lemke, "Men Who Made Arkansas History," *Arkansas Gazette*, June 6, 1937; and Wendy Richter, "Samuel Wesley Fordyce: 1840–1919," *Record* (1989): 1–5.]

WENDY BRADLEY RICHTER

FREEMAN, THOMAS JEWEWL (Jan. 22, 1904– Feb. 25, 1986), professional boxer who briefly held the world welterweight championship, was born in Garland County, Arkansas, to Hunter Freeman, a farmer and woodcutter, and Flora Sangster.

"Tommy" Freeman engaged in 197 recorded prize fights from 1920 to 1938, with 159 victories (seventy-eight by knockout), nineteen losses, twelve draws, and seven "no-decision" bouts. He possibly had twenty or more other matches that went unrecorded. Bob Sangster, his uncle, turned him pro at the age of sixteen and managed him throughout his career.

"If I had grown up any place except around Hot Springs, I might not have ever boxed," Freeman said once. "But Hot Springs was a big sporting town in those days, one of the few places in the South except for New Orleans where they had pro boxing on a regular basis. It seemed like the natural thing for me to do."

As a beginner in Hot Springs, he was billed as the "Bear Mountain Bearcat" or the "Lumberjack from Bear Mountain," although he said he "really didn't come from Bear Mountain—I was raised a few miles from there."

By the time Freeman was nineteen he was boxing fifteen-round main events in New Orleans. From February of 1923 until March of 1926, he went undefeated in forty-three consecutive bouts, vaulting from a promising regional fighter to a world-rated contender in his division. He made his debut in New York's Madison Square Garden on January 1, 1926, with a seventh-round knockout of Sammy Baker, an outstanding contender. His winning streak was broken on March 1, 1926, by a technical knockout loss to future welterweight champ Joe Dundee in Madison Square Garden. The match was stopped in the fourth round with Freeman bleeding profusely from cuts around the eyes.

The welterweight title changed hands eight times from 1926 to 1932, passing from Pete Latzo to Dundee to Jackie Fields to Young Jack Thompson to Freeman to Thompson again to Lou Brouillard to Fields again. The key to Freeman's opportunity was a ten-round decision he won over Thompson at Detroit in January 1930.

When Thompson defeated Fields for the championship four months later, Freeman's recent victory over Thompson made him the logical next challenger. Freeman was extremely popular in Cleveland at that time, so the match was made in League Park, the Cleveland Indians' baseball stadium, for September 5, 1930.

A crowd of 11,448 paid gate receipts of $46,861 to see Freeman win the championship in a close fifteen-round decision. He stayed busy winning eight nontitle bouts, including two in Hot Springs, before a rematch with Thompson at Cleveland on April 14, 1931. Unable to come out for the twelfth round, Freeman lost on a technical knockout. He never offered excuses for his showing, though others believed he had weakened himself by the task of sweating down to the 147-pound class limit. He had outgrown the welterweight division and campaigned as a middleweight the remainder of his career. His purses of $5,000 and $10,000 for the two title bouts were his largest.

After leaving the ring, Freeman worked twenty-five years for the Hot Springs Fire Department, served in the navy during World War II, and worked with at least two generations of Hot Springs boys as a teacher of amateur boxing. In 1946 he joined the "GI Reform" political ticket of returning war veterans out to unseat a long-entrenched Hot Springs political machine. The movement was headed by future governor Sidney McMath, then a candidate for prosecuting attorney. A candidate for constable, Freeman was the ticket's only loser.

In 1967 Freeman became the first boxer inducted by the Arkansas Sports Hall of Fame.

[Sources include *Everlast Ring Record Book* (1931), *The Ring Record Book and Boxing Encyclopedia*, various annual editions, 1949–87; the *Cleveland News*, Sept. 6, 1930, and Apr. 15, 1931; the *Arkansas Gazette*, Sept. 6, 1930, and Dec. 18, 1966; the *Arkansas Democrat*, Mar. 1, 1986; and unpublished interviews with Steve Gable (1967) and Thomas Freeman Jr. (1999).]

JIM BAILEY

FRENCH, ALICE (Mar. 19, 1850–Jan. 9, 1934), a writer, was born in Andover, Massachusetts, to George Henry French and Frances Morton. In 1856 the family moved to Davenport, Iowa. French studied at Vassar College and Abbot Academy.

Her first published work was a sentimental story,

"Hugo's Waiting," printed in the *Davenport Gazette* in 1871. A few years later she finished "Communists and Capitalists, A Sketch from Life," inspired by a strike against the railroads. It was published in October 1878 in *Lippincott's Magazine,* which paid her forty-two dollars, the first money she earned from writing. Under the pseudonym "Octave Thanet," French published stories, essays, and novels until 1911 in such national periodicals as the *Atlantic Monthly, Harper's, Scribner's Magazine,* and *Century Magazine.*

Early in her career, French published stories with philosophical or political themes, such as "Schopenhauer on Lake Pepin: A Study." She also published nonfiction along similar lines, such as "The English Workingman and the Commercial Crises" in *Lippincott's* in 1880 and "A Neglected Career for Unmarried Women" in *Harper's Bazaar* in 1882.

She drew on travel experiences as well. For example, the "Schopenhauer" piece arose from a trip to the upper Mississippi Valley. Following a three-month coach tour of Great Britain with industrialist Andrew Carnegie, she published "A Day in an English Town" and "Through Great Britain in a Drag" in *Lippincott's.*

French launched her career by exploiting the new interest in local color writing. The American popular magazine was coming into its own, and her location in the Midwest provided her with subject matter, the laborers and capitalists in the growing towns and cities of that region.

Her career took another turn after 1883, when French and Jane Allen Crawford set up a permanent winter home at Clover Bend Plantation in Lawrence County, Arkansas. They lived there for several months each year until 1909. Arkansas provided material for French's fiction as well as time to write uninterrupted by obligations to her family and to her membership in the Colonial Dames, the Society of Mayflower Descendants, the American Red Cross, and other organizations. "Thanford," as she and Crawford called their house, was also the setting for their literary and social events. French exercised other talents at Thanford: she had a workshop where she built shelves and simple furniture and a darkroom where she developed and printed photographs with chemicals she mixed herself, an experience she described and illustrated in *An Adventure in Photography,* published by Scribner's in 1891.

Octave Thanet's Arkansas stories are squarely in the local color tradition. The reading public wanted romance and moral uplift garnished with realistic details of speech, setting, and character types. Stories about southern black people were popular. Thanet collected lists of curious dialect phrases and pronunciation, folklore, and superstitions, and retold Lawrence County legends about conjurers, ghosts, and family feuds. Her evocative descriptions of the swamp vibrate with overtones of Romanticism. Her characterizations, however, are based on the ideas of class and race she held all her life. The planters she describes are intelligent, brave, shrewd, and successful; her farmers are shiftless, sickly, and lacking foresight or ambition. She portrays blacks, for whom "Negroes" is the politest word she uses, as merely ridiculous.

French did not accept the tenets of literary realism or naturalism with their more pessimistic or deterministic view of human nature and divine providence. Her New England background and her New West experience put her on the side of business and capitalism and those who succeeded in those areas—white, Protestant, Republican Americans. In holding these opinions, French was not very different from many other successful writers of her time. Moreover, the racism and xenophobia that underlie French's black characters and her foreign-born labor agitators were unquestioned assumptions of most of her readers.

Fortunately for present-day readers, French also had narrative skill and a wry sense of humor. In her Arkansas stories the narrator is the superior outsider, reporting the shocking, amusing, or irritating ways of people clearly her—and her reader's—inferiors. In 1891 the *Atlantic Monthly* published two of her nonfiction pieces, "Plantation Life in Arkansas" and "Town Life in Arkansas," in which she presented a generally positive picture of the state. In these pieces, she poses as a member of the group she describes: "We have the virtues of our vices in Arkansas." French defends those aspects of southern life that make good stories and says that life in Arkansas is "more attractive than anyone who does not live in the state will believe."

Octave Thanet was acclaimed by critics and editors. She was financially successful as a writer, though her investments in banks and railroads provided most of her income. In the 1890s French published ten books. Between 1896 and 1900 fifty of her stories were published, and four different publishers collected five volumes for reprinting. An Octave Thanet Society was formed in 1899 in Iowa City.

In 1909 French and Crawford gave up their house at Clover Bend. French traveled widely in the United States, speaking for the conservative causes she embraced, adding to them her opposition to woman suffrage. Her point of view remained fixed in the era of her youth. After the first year of the twentieth century, she lost touch with the literary and social developments in America. She developed diabetes. As a result of its complications, she became virtually blind and had a leg amputated. She died in Davenport, impoverished and forgotten.

A resurgent interest in American local color in the late twentieth century has revived Thanet's work. The women's movement has found in some of her Arkansas stories a degree of sympathy for the conditions of poor southern women, black and white. Several of these stories are among her best, which "is surprising, considering that French opposed suffrage and other popular women's causes" and that her views on race were based on the pseudoscientific theories held by most white Americans of her day. The best of her Arkansas fiction demonstrates her skills: she could render the speech of common people; she had an eye for the colorful, arresting details of the southern landscape; and she presented a view of Arkansas that was popular with the American people. One of her reviewers wrote, "There is but one Arkansas, and Octave Thanet is its prophet."

[The Alice French Collection at the Newberry Library, Chicago, includes letters, diaries, literary and business papers, and memorabilia. It also includes an unpublished work, "Octave Thanet, A Biography of Alice French," by Ruth Tucker, a microfilm copy of which is in the library of the University of Arkansas, Fayetteville.

French wrote three novels with an Arkansas setting: *Expiation* (1890), *We All* (1891), and *By Inheritance* (1910). An exhaustive chronological list of her published and unpublished works is in George McMichael's biography, *Journey to Obscurity: The Life of Octave Thanet* (1965). McMichael's list includes her short stories set in Arkansas and articles about Arkansas.

The standard work on American magazines of the period is Frank Luther Mott, *A History of American Magazines* (1938–1968). See also Michael B. Dougan and Carol W. Dougan, *By the Cypress Swamp: The Arkansas Stories of Octave Thanet* (1980); Linda Elizabeth Rushton, "The Arkansas Fiction of Alice French," thesis, University of Arkansas, Fayetteville (1982); Josiah H. Shinn, "Miss Alice French of Clover Bend," *Publications of the Arkansas Historical Association* 2 (1906): 344–51; Ethel C. Simpson, "Octave Thanet of Clover Bend," *Arkansas Libraries* 34, no. 4 (1977): 17–24; and Sandra Ann Healey Tigges, "Alice French, A Noble Anachronism," thesis, University of Iowa (1981).]

ETHEL C. SIMPSON

FULBRIGHT, JAMES WILLIAM (Apr. 9, 1905– Feb. 9, 1995), United States senator, was born in Rothville, Missouri. When he was three years of age, his parents, Jay and Roberta, moved the family to Fayetteville, Arkansas. His father made a successful career as a banker while his mother published and wrote a column for the *Northwest Arkansas Times*. Fulbright graduated from the University of Arkansas in 1924 and then attended Oxford University as a Rhodes scholar. After earning a degree in modern history, he returned to Arkansas to run the family businesses. In 1932 he married Elizabeth Kremer Williams of Philadelphia, in the process earning a law degree from George Washington University. In 1939 he was named president of the University of Arkansas, the youngest college executive in the country at the time. Ousted two years later by his mother's bitter political enemy, Governor Homer Adkins, he decided on a career in politics.

During his thirty-two years in Congress, fifteen of them as chairman of the Senate Foreign Relations Committee, the former Rhodes scholar appealed to the peoples of the world but particularly to his countrymen to appreciate and tolerate other cultures and political systems without condoning armed aggression or human rights violations. At the close of World War II and the dawn of the cold war, Fulbright perceived the central problem of United States foreign policy to be how to preserve Anglo-American civilization from destruction. Appalled by the bombing of Hiroshima and Nagasaki, he decided that the world was far too dangerous a place for the members of the Atlantic community to simply go their own way. In 1943 he cosponsored the Fulbright-Connally resolution putting Congress on record as supporting membership in a collective security organization—the United Nations. Three years later, following his election to the Senate, he introduced legislation creating the academic exchange program that bears his name. He was convinced that the exchange of students and scholars would increase understanding generally and breed political elites capable of pursuing enlightened foreign policies.

Confronted with the reality that neither his country nor its wartime allies were willing to relinquish their freedom of action within the context of a United Nations, Fulbright turned his attention to rehabilitating Western Europe and defending the Atlantic community from the scourge of Stalinism. Thus did he support the Truman Doctrine, the Marshall Plan, and NATO, and he defended executive prerogatives in foreign policy against isolationists who wanted to retreat within Fortress America.

For Fulbright the greatest threat to America's republican form of government and its civic culture came not from the political left but from the right. He understood that the confrontation with the Soviet Union coupled with the dawn of the atomic age had bred in America a virulent anticommunism that threatened civil liberties at home and peace abroad. This realization led him to confront McCarthyism, defending the exchange program from its ravages and playing a major role in the movement to censure the Wisconsin demagogue. So, too, did he combat the John Birch Society, the Christian Crusade, H. L. Hunt, Strom Thurmond, and the other organizations and personalities that made up the radical right of the early 1960s.

Frightened by the resurgence of the radical right and greatly impressed by Nikita Khrushchev's conciliatory visit to the United States in 1959, Fulbright moved beyond competitive coexistence and embraced the concept of détente (a lessening of tension or hostility). He was well pleased with the Kennedy administration's flexible response to the communist threat and, following the Berlin and Cuban missile crises, with its willingness to make a fresh start with the Soviet Union. During the 1964 presidential election, Fulbright took the point in the foreign policy debate with Senator Barry Goldwater and his conservative followers.

Fulbright fell out with Lyndon Johnson because he believed that his longtime political comrade in arms had sold out to the very forces that he, Johnson, had defeated in 1964. The decision to intervene in the Dominican Republic and to escalate the war in Vietnam signaled to Fulbright the triumph of the nationalist, xenophobic, imperialist tendencies that had always lurked beneath the surface of American society. Only months after Richard Nixon's election, Fulbright concluded that, like Johnson, the new president had become a prisoner of the radical right, the military industrial complex, his own psyche, and other forces of which he was only dimly aware and which he could not control. Using the Constitution as a rallying point, he aligned conservatives and liberals behind his national commitments resolution, which required specific congressional approval of any agreement by the United States to provide military or nonmilitary aid to another country.

A central enigma in Fulbright's public career was his stance on civil rights. He signed the Southern Manifesto and did not vote for a civil rights bill until 1970. His racism had much more to do with class than skin color, however. To the manor born, he lived in milieus in Fayetteville and Washington that allowed him to escape contact with sharecroppers and ghetto dwellers. And yet he played a key role in toning down the manifesto in 1956, and, deeply affected by the killing of four African-American girls in the Birmingham church bombing of 1963, he provided behind-the-scenes help on civil rights measures to the Kennedy and the Johnson administrations. During Nixon's tenure in office Fulbright led the way in defeating the nomination of G. Harold Carswell, an outspoken opponent of the civil rights movement.

Fulbright was defeated in the Senate race of 1974 by Governor Dale Bumpers. For the next twenty years he spoke and wrote on foreign affairs. When Fulbright died in Washington, D.C., his memory was honored at a ceremony at the National Cathedral by President William Jefferson Clinton, a former Fulbright employee.

[This entry is based on my *Fulbright: A Biography* (1995). The voluminous J. William Fulbright Papers are in the Special Collections Division, University of Arkansas Libraries, Fayetteville.]

RANDALL WOODS

FULBRIGHT, ROBERTA WAUGH (Feb. 14, 1874–Jan. 11, 1953), businesswoman and newspaper publisher, was born in Rothville, Missouri, to James Gilliam Waugh, a farmer, and Martha Stratton.

Roberta grew up in north-central Missouri where farming was subject to the vagaries of weather, and life was an uncertain experience. She attended the University of Missouri for two years to qualify for a teacher's certificate. She taught briefly before her marriage to Jay Fulbright, also of Rothville, in October 1894. They were the parents of six children: Frances Lucile, Anna Waugh, Jay (Jack) Jr., James William (Bill), Helen Stratton, and Roberta Empson.

Jay Fulbright was a banker and entrepreneur. In 1906 he and Roberta, in search of new business ventures and educational opportunities for their children, moved to Fayetteville, the home of the University of Arkansas. Here Jay's holdings grew to include a variety of businesses. Although Roberta had worked alongside him in Missouri, she now turned her attention to family, social, and civic activities. Her back-yard garden became a showplace; to her, gardening ranked "almost on a par with religion."

Jay died suddenly in 1923. Shocked and grieved by his death, Roberta had no time to indulge her sorrow. Immediately, her husband's business enterprises were threatened by legal challenges from anxious partners and other claimants. These enterprises included two Fayetteville banks; a hotel; a publishing company; a number of lumber, mercantile, and grocery businesses; and a small railroad.

As Roberta Fulbright fought to hold on to these enterprises, she encountered opposition from those who believed that a woman had no place in business. She prevailed and solidified the family holdings under the umbrella of the Fulbright Investment Company. For some businesses, she relied upon managers; in others she assumed management. At various times she served as an officer of Phipps Lumber Company, Fayetteville Ice Company (holder of the local Coca-Cola franchise), Fayetteville Mercantile Company, Citizens' Bank, and the Bank of Elkins. In 1936 she was one of three women bank presidents in Arkansas.

A solidly built woman with a determined jaw and stern gaze, Fulbright gave the appearance of someone to be reckoned with. Her fine hair, accented by an ever-present hat, her often plain dress and sensible shoes added to her air of authority. Those who opposed her regarded her as aggressive and domineering. Others saw her as garrulous, a marvelous raconteur, and the rightful center of attention at any gathering.

Her most active role was as publisher of the *Fayetteville Daily Democrat*, later the *Northwest Arkansas Times*. Under her management the newspaper became the chronicler and conscience of the town. "It is a fallacious notion," she wrote, "that a newspaper should or could be an isolated affair. Its life-blood should flow in the veins of the community in which it lives." In its pages she campaigned for a new hospital, a boys club, and a library, and kept a watchful eye on local government.

In the 1930s she took on corrupt local politicians in Fayetteville and Washington County. Along with her editor, Lessie Stringfellow Read, she undertook a campaign to dislodge the entrenched politicians who harbored "moonshine" operations and an automotive theft ring and who engaged in election fraud. Joining forces with the Good Citizenship League, she spoke for change through her column, "As I See It." Despite threats of reprisal to Fulbright-owned businesses, hints at physical violence, and nuisance lawsuits, she remained steadfast. By 1936 election fraud was eliminated, and local government was largely in the hands of the reformers.

With each economic and political battle won, Fulbright became more influential. The broad base of family businesses, her public voice expressed through newspaper columns, and her own affinity for a wide circle of friends made her a power in local business, government, and university affairs, an unusual role for a woman of her era.

She was never shy about expressing her opinions about her hometown and its citizens, politics, equality for women, religion, philosophy, travel, gardening, and her family. When outraged she did not hesitate to express her anger in print. Yet she once confessed, "I never write about anything that I'm not possessed of a lurking fear that perhaps I don't know what I'm talking about."

Her support for Governor Carl Bailey is widely credited with influencing Bailey's decision in 1939 to appoint her son Bill Fulbright as president of the University of Arkansas. By the same token, her opposition to Governor Homer Adkins contributed to her son's firing from the post. Ironically, this led to Bill Fulbright's defeat of Adkins for a United States Senate seat in 1944. A Democrat, Roberta twice considered running for Congress herself, but did not do so.

In 1946 she was named Arkansas Mother of the Year, and in 1949 she founded the Arkansas Newspaper Women (later the Arkansas Press Women). Upon her death in Fayetteville, she was eulogized by the *Arkansas Gazette* as "a tireless, strong woman who had created for herself the role of matriarch in the town of Fayetteville." Two Fayetteville buildings bear her name: a women's dormitory on the university campus and the Fayetteville public library.

[See Dorothy D. Stuck and Nan Snow, *Roberta: A Most Remarkable Fulbright* (1997).]

DOROTHY D. STUCK
NAN SNOW

FUTRELL, JUNIUS MARION (Aug. 14, 1870–
June 20, 1955), attorney, governor of Arkansas, was
born in the Jones Ridge community in Greene County.
He attended the University of Arkansas, Fayetteville. He
returned to eastern Arkansas, taught school, entered
the timber business, and was admitted to the Arkansas
bar in 1913. He and Tera A. Smith married in 1893. The
couple had six children: Nye, Prentiss, Byron, Ernie,
Janice, and Daniel.

In 1896 he was elected state representative from
Greene County, a position he held until elected circuit
clerk for Greene County in 1906. He served in that post
until the voters of the First District (Greene, Clay, and
Craighead Counties) elected him state senator in 1912.

After leaving the Arkansas senate, Futrell returned
to his home in Paragould and practiced law until
appointed circuit judge for the Second Judicial District
in 1921. Two years later he was elected chancellor of the
Twelfth District; he was reelected in 1930. He ran for
governor in 1932, easily defeating his Democratic challengers in the primaries and his Republican opponent
in the general election by a vote of 123,920 to 13,121.

In January 1933 when Futrell was sworn in, Arkansas was on the verge of bankruptcy and in danger of
losing its national credit due, in part, to its failure to
make payments on a $146,000,000 highway debt. In
his inaugural address Futrell pledged his administration to the reduction of state employees and salaries; to
the elimination of duplicated services; and to the expul-
sion of graft, waste, and mismanagement. He also
promised to pay off the state's debts and put Arkansas's
government on a cash basis.

His debt-reduction plan called for the consolidation
of highway debts with all claimants to highway revenues having equal status. Increased fees on the sale of
oil and on gas, truck, and auto licenses would finance
debt payment. The 1933 legislature failed to enact the
governor's plan, but a special session of the general
assembly passed the proposal as the Highway
Refunding Act. Futrell considered its passage his greatest achievement.

To put Arkansas on a cash basis, he proposed two
amendments to the state constitution. The Nineteenth
Amendment limited legislative appropriations to a
fixed amount; required the approval of voters in a general election or a two-thirds vote in each house of the
legislature before state taxes could be increased; and
required a majority vote in each house for enactment of

new tax laws. The Twentieth Amendment required
voter approval before new state bonds could be issued.
The legislature adopted both measures, and they were
approved by the voters in the 1934 general election.

Futrell was reluctant to take action to aid the state's
impoverished public education system or assist the
aged, the poor, and those on relief rolls. He believed
poverty to be the result of lack of individual initiative.
He blamed the huge unemployment rolls on the use of
unnecessary labor-saving machinery. He argued that
public education was not necessary beyond the primary grades (grades 1–8), and in 1935 asked the legislature not to fund education beyond that level. He was
content to let the Federal Emergency Relief Administration (FERA) shoulder the cost of education and
poor relief in Arkansas, but FERA officials disagreed. In
1934 Harry Hopkins, FERA director, informed Futrell
that Arkansas would lose all federal funds on March 1,
1935, if the legislature did not appropriate $1,500,000
for relief and education. Futrell and the legislature
began work on three measures to raise the required
revenue: sales taxes, prohibition repeal, and legalized
gambling.

The sales-tax bill, which levied a 2 percent tax on all
retail sales except specified foods and medicines, passed
the senate. In the house the bill was held up beyond the
March 1 deadline, resulting in the loss of FERA funds.
Futrell urged passage of the measure only after FERA
funds were terminated. The bill passed on March 17. Of
the $250 million the tax was expected to generate,
$1,500,000 was set aside for public education.

The liquor and gambling measures easily made
their way through the legislature. The liquor bill
repealed prohibition on a local option basis and
included an excise tax. To provide relief for the poor, the
legislature established the Arkansas Department of
Public Welfare and passed two controversial gambling
measures permitting parimutuel betting on dog racing
at West Memphis and on horse racing at Hot Springs.
The passage of these measures satisfied the FERA, and
funds were restored.

Destitute tenant farmers and sharecroppers in eastern Arkansas had formed the Southern Tenant
Farmers' Union (STFU) in July 1934 to protest their
wholesale eviction by landlords who wanted to avoid
sharing Agricultural Adjustment Administration cotton
parity payments. The STFU campaigned to increase the
wages of cotton pickers from forty cents to one dollar

per hundred pounds. Landlords and law enforcement officials responded with mass arrests and mob violence. The governor's sympathies lay with the landlords, but the nationwide sympathy aroused by the plight of evicted tenant farmers and sharecroppers forced him to appoint a state commission to investigate farm tenancy in eastern Arkansas. The commission did little to improve the situation.

In 1937 Futrell's second term expired. He left the state's financial condition improved. He died in Greene County.

[See C. Calvin Smith, "Junius Marion Futrell, 1933–1937," in *The Governors of Arkansas: Essays in Political Biography,* Timothy P. Donovan, Willard B. Gatewood Jr., and Jeannie M. Whayne, eds., 2d ed. (1995).]

C. CALVIN SMITH

GAINES, HELEN FOUCHÉ (Oct. 12, 1888–Apr. 2, 1940), cryptographer, was born in Hot Springs to Abner Gaines and Virgie (maiden name unknown) and grew up in Lake Village. In 1906 Helen graduated from Central High School in Little Rock, "half valedictorian . . . since two of us . . . tied for the honors." This was the end of her formal education.

Gaines devoted her life to the art of writing and deciphering messages in code. She defined the term cipher as "a method, or system, of secret writing."

Several clues point to her having worked as a cipherer for the United States Navy during World War I. In a sketch of her own life she wrote that after graduating from high school she loafed for a year, taught school in Hot Springs for three years, and taught two "other" years. "Beginning at that point, I begin to forget a lot—perhaps with reason?" Among the details she "forgets" is the year when she went to live in Washington, D.C. She must have gone there shortly before the war, in 1912 or 1913, and she remained there until the end of the war.

Dr. Dorothy Bernstein, late professor of mathematics at Goucher College and a cryptographer for the U.S. Navy during World War II, knew of Helen Gaines. Bernstein stated in conversation that Gaines had worked for the navy during World War I and had written a manual used by the navy. The attribution of a now unknown handbook would be consistent with Gaines's authorship of a handbook of cryptography later in her life. Both Bernstein and a distant kinswoman of Gaines believed that Gaines continued to work for the navy after the war into the 1920s.

Gaines wrote about codes in wartime. In the introduction to her book *Elementary Cryptanalysis* she states that when war is declared, "The cryptographic service . . . is suddenly expanded to include a large number of new men, many of whom know nothing whatever of *cryptanalysis,* or the science of decryptment. Many of these are criminally careless through ignorance, so that, entirely aside from numerous other factors (including espionage), it is conceded by the various War Departments that no matter what system or apparatus is selected for cipher purposes, the enemy, soon after the beginning of operations, will be in full possession of details . . . and will have secured a duplicate of any apparatus or machine. For that reason, the secrecy of messages must depend upon a changeable key added to a sound basic cipher."

How did Gaines come by her knowledge of war departments and ignorant recruits? She could have got it out of books, but the energy, directness, and confidence of her tone suggest otherwise. Has she given us enough clues to deduce that her knowledge was based upon experience?

In 1919 she left Washington to return home "and to be with my invalid mother. I took her to El Paso, and there married. In 1925, I returned to Lake Village, where I have lived ever since." She returned without a husband, a "grass widder," she said. The residents of Lake Village knew her as reclusive in the extreme. She took little part in the life of the town, but revealed her individuality in letters to friends, sometimes writing in an Arkansas dialect.

She joined the American Cryptogram Association a few years after its founding in 1929. Members of the association adopt special names; hers was Piccola. From 1933 through 1939 she published thirty-four articles in the ACA's publication *The Cryptogram.* She loved puzzles and liked to help people with them and was considered one of the best solvers in the organization.

In the middle 1930s she began work on *Elementary Cryptanalysis,* now a standard elementary and intermediate text for people seriously interested in the subject. She did not have enough money to buy a typewriter when she started; the ACA helped her to buy one. She spent months of relentless labor typing and retyping to produce the book, with its page after page of columns and blocks of letters and numbers.

Elementary Cryptanalysis offers representative types of ciphers in order to bring out principles like concealment, substitution, periodicity, and transposition. It makes use of geometry, abstract algebra (especially group theory), combinatorics, and recurrence relations. However, Gaines seems less interested in theory than in solving puzzles.

Evidently the ACA underwrote the book. Within three months of its publication in 1939, it had earned back the expenses of production. Gaines was surprised at "this soonness": "I took it for granted we should be stuck with a thousand unsold copies." According to David Shulman, author of *An Annotated Bibliography of Cryptography* (1976), "The book became the best ever published for beginning cryptographers and in my opinion still remains the best. It is the official book of the ACA."

Gaines was a modest woman. She did not tell her friends in the ACA about her service in the war, though her family seems to have known about it. An obituary in the *Cryptogram* mentions her brilliant mind and remembers "our Piccola" with genuine affection. She died in Lake Village.

[*Elementary Cryptanalysis* was reissued in 1956 under the title *Cryptanalysis: A Study of Ciphers and Their Solution.* Gaines's sketch of her life is quoted in an obituary in the *Cryptogram,* June 1940. Sources include correspondence with Dr. Mary Jane Gates, July 8 and 19, 1993; with David Shulman, Aug. 10, 1993; and a copy of a letter from "Piccola" to "Ayemache," Jan. 15, 1940. The American Cryptogram Association archives are at the Department of Special Collection and Archives, Libraries and Media Services, Kent State University.]

NANCY A. WILLIAMS

GARLAND, AUGUSTUS HILL (June 11, 1832–1877), governor of Arkansas, United States senator, attorney general of the United States, was born in Tipton County, Tennessee, the son of Rufus and Barbara Hill Garland. Rufus Garland died when Augustus was an infant. Barbara Garland remarried in 1836, and the family relocated to Washington, Arkansas. Augustus Garland attended college in Kentucky, graduating from St. Joseph's in 1849.

Before beginning his legal career, Garland briefly taught school in Sevier County. Then, in 1853, he and his stepfather, Thomas Hubbard, formed a law practice, and Garland began his life as an attorney. That same year, Garland and Sarah Virginia Sanders married. Over the course of the next seven years, he became one of the state's eminent attorneys and a force in state politics.

He was elected to represent Pulaski County at the 1861 secession convention in Little Rock. As the sectional crises unfolded, he had consistently remained a unionist and advocated Arkansas's continued allegiance to the United States. He had campaigned for John Bell, the nominee of the Constitutional Union Party, in the election of 1860 and, true to form, he opposed secession at the convention's first session. It was only after President Abraham Lincoln issued his call to arms that Garland reluctantly chose to support the secessionists.

During the Civil War Garland served in the Confederate House of Representatives and Senate. Pardoned by President Andrew Johnson in July of 1865, he returned to Washington, D.C., to practice law. Perhaps his most significant case was *ex parte Garland,* argued in 1865. When the war was over, the United States Supreme Court changed its rules to prevent former members of the Confederate government and military from arguing cases before the Court. The requirement, Garland argued, was unconstitutional. By a margin of 5–4 the Court agreed.

Garland was elected governor of Arkansas in 1874 and played a significant role in the ratification of the new state constitution. In 1875 Arkansas faced a crisis of insolvency as the result of a $17 million debt. Over the course of the next two years, Garland's financial policies significantly reduced the state's debt.

In 1876 he was elected to the United States Senate. During his tenure there, he served on the Judiciary Committee and worked to bring about tariff reform, internal improvements, federal aid to education, and civil service reform. Garland resigned from the Senate on March 9, 1885, to accept the position of United States attorney general in President Grover Cleveland's administration, the first Arkansan to serve in a cabinet position.

When Cleveland lost the election of 1888, Garland retired from politics. He continued to live in Washington, D.C., and resumed his legal practice before the Supreme Court. In 1899, while arguing a case before the Court, he suffered a stroke and died a few hours later. His body was returned to Arkansas and buried in Little Rock's Mount Holly Cemetery.

In the last decade of his life, he wrote several tracts on American jurisprudence. His publications include *Third-Term President* (1896), *Experience in the Supreme Court of the United States* (1898), and *A Treatise on the*

Constitution and Jurisdiction of the United States Courts (1898).

[See Beverly Watkins, "Augustus Hill Garland, 1874–1877," in *The Governors of Arkansas: Essays in Political Biography,* Timothy P. Donovan, Willard B. Gatewood Jr., and Jeannie M. Whayne, eds., 2d ed. (1995); and "Augustus Hill Garland, 1832–1899: Arkansas Lawyer to United States Attorney General," dissertation, Auburn University, Auburn, Alabama, 1985. See also Farrar Newberry, "A Life of Mr. Garland of Arkansas," thesis, Arkadelphia, Arkansas, 1908.]

. *J. WAYNE JONES*

GERARD, MOTHER PERPETUA (Sept. 19, 1879–July 10, 1964), prioress, was born Sophia Gerard in Maxville, Missouri, to Julius Gerard and Modesta Wester. Her parents relocated to Arkansas, first to Little Rock, then to Altus. Sophia Gerard entered the novitiate of the Benedictine Sisters of Shoal Creek at Saint Scholastica's Convent in Logan County on September 20, 1895.

She made her first vows on May 16, 1897, and her final vows on June 24, 1905. As Sister Perpetua, her first teaching assignment was in Indian Territory in what are now the towns of Lehigh and Colgate, Oklahoma. In 1898 she was reassigned to Saint Edward's School in Little Rock, where she taught for the next twenty-two years. In 1920 she was elected prioress of her community. She served in that capacity for twenty-seven years.

As prioress, Mother Perpetua was the superior of this teaching and nursing community, responsible for finances, assignment of duties, and other aspects of administration, and for reporting to the bishop of Little Rock. During her time in office, the Benedictine Sisters experienced a number of challenges. The motherhouse at Shoal Creek, established in 1879, proved to be too small for the community, and so in 1922 the Chapter decided to relocate to Fort Smith. By the time Mother Perpetua received approval from Rome for the endeavor, she and Monsignor Winand Aretz, the diocesan chancellor, had already taken out a loan and laid the cornerstone (which contained a copy of *The Rule of Saint Benedict,* medals of Saint Benedict and the Blessed Virgin Mary, photographs of Bishop John Morris and the prioresses who had served at Saint Scholastica, and a list of government officials: President Calvin Coolidge, Arkansas governor Thomas McRae, and Fort Smith mayor David Ford). On May 17, 1925, the formal transfer of the motherhouse from Shoal Creek to Fort Smith was made.

The 1920s were years of prosperity for the community, which numbered over two hundred sisters and had established thirty missions in Arkansas, Texas, and Oklahoma by the close of the decade. This prosperity ended with the onset of the Great Depression. Most of the sisters taught in Catholic and public schools, and many pastors and school districts were unable to pay them for their services. The community was not able to meet the payments on the building loan and had to borrow additional money to pay the interest. Mother Perpetua faced a financial catastrophe. In 1929 she wrote to Monsignor Aretz, describing her difficulties with the banks, but also showing tremendous faith: "I am certain that the Sacred Heart and good Saint Joseph will not go back on us. I have asked the Sisters to pray." Already in poor health, she offered to resign her position and allow another sister to be elected. Albert Fletcher, who succeeded Monsignor Aretz as chancellor, wrote on behalf of Bishop Morris: "The wholehearted approval which you have from the Sisters shows that your bad health . . . is more [than] compensated by many advantages. In saying this, the Bishop has good reasons to know that he is but voicing the almost unanimous conviction of the Sisters."

The sisters themselves discussed the possibility of sending the novices home and disbanding. Mother Perpetua refused to yield. Her courage during this crisis became legendary, and several sisters later remembered that she often made late-night vigils in the convent chapel for the success of the community.

She did not restrict her efforts to prayer. At one point, denied entry at the bank, she continued to knock until she was admitted. Then she threatened to take her business elsewhere unless the bank president agreed to a further loan. The loan was granted. Through Mother Perpetua's perseverance and the community's frugal sacrifices, the Benedictine Sisters survived the depression, and by 1948 the debt had been completely erased.

Mother Perpetua sought to be excluded from consideration for reelection in 1943, but Bishop Morris replied that had God not desired her to be prioress, he would not have allowed her to accomplish so much during her tenure. The community reelected her that year; she was finally permitted to resign her position three years later. Upon her resignation, she was appointed superior of Saint Joseph's Hospital in Boonville, Missouri (1947–53). Later she served as superior of Clarksville Hospital in Clarksville, Arkansas.

She retired in 1961 to Saint Joseph's Orphanage in Little Rock. She returned to Clarksville shortly before her death.

[The Mother Perpetua Gerard Papers are in the Saint Scholastica Monastery Archives in Fort Smith. See also Sister Louise Sharum's *Write the Vision Down* (1979); and obituaries in *The Guardian* (Diocese of Little Rock), July 13, 1964, and the *Arkansas Gazette,* July 11, 1964.]

SCOTT JONES

GERSTÄCKER, FRIEDRICH (May 10, 1816–May 31, 1872), adventurer and writer, was born in Hamburg, Germany, to opera singers Karl Friedrich Gerstäcker and Luise Frederike Gerstäcker.

As a child he immersed himself in tales of foreign adventures, ranging from DeFoe's *Robinson Crusoe* to Fenimore Cooper's *The Pioneers.* Intended for a career in commerce, Gerstäcker proved constitutionally ill-equipped for such a bourgeois existence. He found German society with its social strictures and traditionalism too restrictive and fancied America to be a land of unbridled freedom. In 1837 at the age of twenty-one, he left Germany for the United States, drawn by the prospect of adventure.

After three months in New York City, he began a journey west, indulging his wanderlust. Traveling largely on foot, by early 1838 he finally entered Arkansas. He traveled through the state to Texas and Louisiana, and then to Cincinnati, Ohio, by steamboat. He returned to Arkansas in 1839 and lived for some nine months in Poinsett, Independence, and White Counties, where he worked for local farmers and devoted much of his time to his favorite pursuit, hunting.

In 1840 he returned to Cincinnati, and later cut cane in Louisiana, fattening his purse sufficiently to allow him to return to Arkansas, which he had sized up as having excellent hunting. In early 1841 he stayed in the Fourche La Fave valley and then wandered north of the Arkansas River into Madison County. Again he exchanged his labor for a place to sleep in the homes of local farmers. Finally in 1842 Gerstäcker left Arkansas for Louisiana, where he worked for a year to earn the passage home. Though he relished the unfettered existence of a vagabond, he was also wracked by homesickness for his family.

Once back in Germany in 1843, Gerstäcker was surprised to learn that he was already a published author. He had been sending lengthy diary entries home to his mother in lieu of letters, and she had taken them to the editor of the literary magazine *Die Rosen.* The initial encouraging reception of these vignettes and his lack of other employment led Gerstäcker to transform his diary into a book. *Strief- und Jagdzüge durch die Vereinigten Staaten Nord-Amerikas* (published in 1846 in English as *Wild Sports in the Far West*) appeared in 1844, and there followed a flood of works from his pen. Although the book chronicles his entire trip to the United States, Arkansas figures prominently in the account. This was even more the case with his second book, a novel entitled *Die Regulatoren in Arkansas* (*The Regulators in Arkansas*), published in 1845.

The popularity of these works made Gerstäcker one of the most widely read popular writers of his time. Financial success gave Gerstäcker the means to indulge his fascination with the exotic. Between 1849 and his death in 1872, he was able to make four long trips abroad, traveling to North and South America, Africa, and Australia and the Pacific. Each of these trips provided material for his literary output, some of it in the form of travelogues, some of it fictional.

His first wife, Anna Aurora Saurer, the daughter of a Dresden artist, died while he was on one of these trips. In 1863 he married a woman twenty-eight years his junior, Marie Louise Fischer van Gaasbeck, the daughter of a Dutch colonial official he had met in Java over a decade earlier. While planning yet another trip to Japan, China, and India, Friedrich Gerstäcker died in 1872 in his hometown of Braunschweig of a stroke brought on by an altercation with a police officer. He left behind his widow and five children.

Gerstäcker's importance for Arkansas is his literary legacy. He wrote seventy books and 425 articles and short stories, many of which were set wholly or in part in the state. In contrast to such early observers of the state as George Featherstonhaugh, Gerstäcker was not condescending toward the backwoods residents whose hospitality he had enjoyed. He was a keen observer and he included his insights on a wide range of matters in both his fiction and nonfictional works. Many, though not all, of the characters in his novels, stories, and sketches can be verified from census and tax records of the period or accepted as actual historical persons on the basis of his diaries. He was not only accurate with regard to individual persons, he also described the material culture of antebellum Arkansas with some precision. Gerstäcker explained with considerable accuracy how log houses were constructed and how corn was planted and how the open-range system functioned. In one of his short stories he described the interior of a backwoods store and tavern, including what goods it carried and how alcoholic beverages were dispensed. In other works he touched on women's roles, the backwoods legal and postal systems, social relations, and religion. Taken together Gerstäcker's works provide some of the best descriptions of life among the common people of backwoods Arkansas in the early nineteenth century.

[Gerstäcker's papers are in the municipal archives of the city of Braunschweig, Germany (NachlaB Friedrich Gerstäcker, GIX23). Additional archival material may be found in the Clarence Evans and Friedrich Gerstäcker collections of the Archives and Special Collections, UALR Library, University of Arkansas, Little Rock. The best biography of Gerstäcker is Thomas Ostwald, *Friedrich Gerstäcker—Leben und Werk* (1976). For English language treatments of his Arkansas work, see Clarence Evans, "Gerstaecker and the Konwells of White River Valley," *AHQ* 10 (Spring 1951): 1–36, and "Friedrich Gerstäcker, Social Chronicler of the Arkansas Frontier," *AHQ* 6 (Winter 1947): 440–49; Evan Bukey, "Friedrich Gerstäcker and Arkansas," *AHQ* 31 (Spring 1972): 3–14; James William Miller, ed., *In the Arkansas Backwoods: Tales and Sketches by Friedrich Gerstäcker* (1991); Edna and Harrison Steeves, introduction to *Wild Sports in the Far West: The Narrative of a German Wanderer beyond the Mississippi, 1837–1843* (1968).]

JAMES WILLIAM MILLER

GIBBS, MIFFLIN WISTAR (Apr. 17, 1823–July 11, 1915), was a Little Rock businessman, a politician, and the first elected black municipal judge in America. He was born in Philadelphia, Pennsylvania, the eldest child of Jonathan and Maria Gibbs. His father, a Methodist minister, died when Mifflin was a child, and his mother worked as a laundress.

Gibbs learned carpentry through an apprenticeship. He read widely and attended debates at the Philadelphia Library Company of Colored Persons, soaking up the sights and sounds of well-read black men discussing the issues of the day. He had a chance to practice his own oratory in the 1840s when Frederick Douglass invited him to help conduct an abolitionist lecture tour.

Journeying to California soon after the gold rush of 1849, he became a successful retail merchant and a leader of the growing black population. He was a founder of the first black newspaper west of the Mississippi River, *The Mirror of the Times*. He left San Francisco in 1858 to escape growing racial prejudice on the California frontier.

Always on the alert for new opportunities, Gibbs settled in Victoria, Vancouver Island, British Columbia. Once again, he found grand business opportunities and was soon among the colony's black elite. In 1866 he became the first black man elected to the Victoria City Council.

It is unclear why Gibbs abandoned British Columbia, where his economic fortune was assured and where he had found a modicum of political success. In 1869 he returned to the United States and settled in Oberlin, Ohio. But he was restless, and the placid college town (where he had sent his daughters to Oberlin College) must have been a disappointment after the heady days in San Francisco and Victoria. In 1871 he headed south to a different type of frontier.

His brother Jonathan C. Gibbs was serving as secretary of state in Reconstruction Florida, where Gibbs visited him. Then he attended a freedmen's convention in South Carolina. There he met William H. Grey, Arkansas's state commissioner of immigration and lands. At Grey's urging Gibbs set off for Arkansas.

Gibbs crossed the Arkansas River into Little Rock one bright Sunday morning in May 1871. He liked the city and settled in quickly. He read law with some local white Republican lawyers, and as soon as he had passed the bar examination, he opened a partnership with Lloyd G. Wheeler, a well-known black attorney and leader in the Pulaski County Republican Committee.

In October 1873 Gibbs accepted the Republican nomination for Little Rock police judge. He was allied with the "regular" Republicans, the faction controlled by United States senator Powell Clayton. Gibbs won the election in a tight race, and served as police judge from November 1873 to April 1875, when he was defeated by the Democrats at the end of Reconstruction.

The restoration of Democratic hegemony in 1874–75 did not end black political participation. Gibbs continued to be a power in the Republican Party, serving for a decade as secretary of the state GOP central committee. He was often a delegate to national conventions.

His success within the GOP reflected his close affiliation with the iron-willed Powell Clayton, who used Gibbs and a number of other black leaders to keep the black party leadership pliant and dependable. This "clientage politics" resulted in Gibbs's selection for patronage jobs. In 1877 President Rutherford B. Hayes named Gibbs registrar of the Little Rock district land office; President Benjamin Harrison named him receiver of public monies in Little Rock in 1889; and President William McKinley named him United States consul to Tamatave, Madagascar.

During these years Gibbs kept his eye on economic opportunities. He started a real estate agency in his law office, and he invested widely, using profits from his California and Canadian ventures. In 1903 Gibbs, eighty years old, commenced his most ambitious business effort, the creation of the Capital City Savings Bank.

It was the second black-owned bank in Arkansas. Organized with a capital stock of ten thousand dollars, by 1905 its deposits reached one hundred thousand. Shortly after the bank opened, a health insurance division, the People's Mutual Aid Association, was added.

On June 18, 1908, when it appeared the bank might be in trouble, scores of angry depositers waited to withdraw their funds. The bank failed to open that morning. Efforts to save the bank were fruitless, and the chancery court appointed a receiver. It became public knowledge that the bank had been miserably managed, and its records were in shambles. A grand jury began investigating the bank management.

In January 1909 Gibbs and other bank directors were indicted for knowingly accepting deposits in an insolvent bank. In May 1909 Gibbs reached a settlement in an out-of-court decision on the twenty-eight thousand dollars in claims against him. The amount of the settlement was not announced, but it is clear he was able to save the bulk of his personal fortune.

For a man as well known as M. W. Gibbs, little is known of his personal life. He married Maria Alexander Gibbs in 1859, and they had five children: Donald Francis, Ida A., Horace, Wendal, and Harriet. In his autobiography Gibbs barely mentions his family. He died at his home in Little Rock; his body was interred in the Fraternal Cemetery on Barber Street in Little Rock.

[See Mifflin W. Gibbs, *Shadow and Light: An Autobiography with Reminiscences of the Last and Present Century* (1902) and Tom W. Dillard, "'Golden Prospects and Fraternal Amenities': Mifflin W. Gibbs's Arkansas Years," *AHQ* 35 (Winter 1976): 307–33.]

TOM W. DILLARD

GILLAM, ISAAC T. (1839?–1905?), politician and blacksmith, was born a slave in Hardin County, Tennessee. Nothing is known of his life until September 15, 1863, when he enlisted in the Union army at Little Rock five days after the city fell to federal troops.

Gillam served for three years, first in Company I, Second Regiment, Arkansas Infantry. Later the unit was renamed Company I, Fifty-fourth Regiment, U.S. Colored Infantry. The twenty-four-year-old volunteer immediately attained the rank of sergeant, probably in recognition of his leadership qualities, and possibly because he might have been at least minimally literate. After a three-year stint Gillam was mustered out of the army, having attained the rank of first sergeant.

About the time he left the army, Gillam married Miss Cora Alice McCarrall, a fifteen-year-old native of Mississippi. By 1869 they had their first child, a son named Matthew. Later the Gillams had seven more children.

To provide for his growing family the young veteran turned to blacksmithing and horse breeding. Blacksmithing seems to have been a relatively open trade for blacks in postbellum Little Rock. Slavery had been a good training ground for smiths. Gillam's widow remembered late in her life that race horse owners in Texas "took our colts as fast as they got born."

Gillam became active in Reconstruction politics, and by 1872 he held the political job of city jailer and later, city policeman. When the Reconstruction Republican Party fell into bitter internal bickering, like most blacks Gillam sided with the faction led by Joseph Brooks. When the violent Brooks-Baxter war erupted in 1874, Gillam was commissioned a captain in the Brooks militia.

Gillam entered elective politics in April 1877, when he won election to the Little Rock City Council. A Republican, he represented the heavily black Sixth Ward. Another black Republican, Green Thompson, also served on the council at the same time. A surprising aspect of Gillam's tenure on the council was his appointment by the Democratic mayor, John G. Fletcher, to the Ways and Means Committee. Green Thompson was also on the three-member panel, so Gillam's appointment gave blacks a majority on the committee that oversaw municipal spending.

Mundane administrative matters, such as street paving and construction of water cisterns, occupied much of Gillam's time. Partisan political bickering occasionally enlivened things. Often Gillam and his fellow Republicans allied with the Greenback Party councilmen in opposition to their common enemy, the Democrats. In April 1879, for example, Gillam nominated George Counts for city police chief. The Democrats put forth the name of J. H. Plunkett. An incredible 102 ballots were required before the Republican-Greenback coalition finally received a majority.

In 1878 Gillam successfully ran as a Greenbacker for the Arkansas House of Representatives. The Greenback Party, a popular third party which attempted to improve the economic condition of farmers and laborers through an inflation of the currency, swept the 1878 municipal elections in Little Rock. For a brief time Gillam was serving simultaneously as a Republican alderman and a Greenback legislator; however, he was defeated for reelection to the city council in April 1879. His defeat reflected the discord within the Greenback Party in the Sixth Ward, which resulted in the nomination of two rival tickets and the eventual triumph of the Democratic nominee.

Gillam's tenure in the legislature was similar to his aldermanic service in its concentration on the day-to-day workings of the body. Since the conservative Democrats held a lopsided majority, it was easy for them to stifle the Greenback-Republican minority. However, occasionally Gillam rose to fight. On one occasion he nominated a prominent black cleric for the post of house chaplain, noting that black citizens deserved more than the house janitor's job.

Though he began his political career as a traditional Republican, Gillam's career as a Greenback signaled his dissatisfaction with the GOP. In 1882 he switched to the Democratic Party and served two terms as Pulaski County coroner as a Democrat. Later, in 1890, Gillam switched parties again and supported the Populist Party, an agrarian reformist movement. In that year he was the Populist nominee for county coroner, but he lost. This defeat ended his elective political career, but it did not stop his search for a political home. Later he completed the circle of party affiliation by returning to the party of Lincoln.

Gillam died around the turn of the century. His widow, Cora Alice, when interviewed during the depression, recalled: "He has been dead over 30 years. He had been appointed on the Grand Jury; had bought a new suit of clothes for that. He died on the day he was to go, so we used his new suit to bury him in." He was probably buried in the black Fraternal Cemetery in Little Rock, though his tombstone is not to be found in the family plot.

Gillam's heirs were numerous and prominent in Little Rock. His widow died in 1947 at the age of 101.

[No body of Gillam papers survives. His service on the Little Rock City Council can be traced through the pages of the *Arkansas Gazette* and the city council minute books for 1877–80. See also Tom W. Dillard, "Isaac Gillam: Black Pulaski Countian," *Pulaski County Historical Review* 24 (1976): 6–11; and Dillard, "The Gilliam [sic] Family, Four Generations of Black Arkansas Educators," *Journal of Arkansas Education* 45 (1973): 19, 22. The WPA interview with Cora Gillam is in George P. Rawick, ed., *The American Slave: A Composite Autobiography,* vol. 9, pts. 3 and 4 (1972).]

TOM W. DILLARD

GILLILAND, CHARLES LEON (May 24, 1933–Apr. 25, 1951), congressional Medal of Honor winner, was born in the Colfax community of Baxter County, Arkansas, to Leon Carl Gilliland, a farmer and construction worker, and Evangeline Margarite Martin, a nurse's aide.

He was posthumously awarded the Medal of Honor, the nation's highest military honor. A month shy of his eighteenth birthday, a mortally wounded Gilliland single-handedly covered the overnight withdrawal of army Company I, Third Infantry Division, as it was being overrun by Chinese army units near Tongmangni, Korea.

"I've come to think that was his purpose in life," said his sister, Dale Shelton. "It seemed like everything in his life was leading up to that night."

Gilliland was the second of nine children and the oldest son. His family moved from Baxter County to neighboring Marion County when he was a teenager. He was a country boy who loved to be outdoors hunting and fishing. He also was fascinated with law enforcement and the armed services. "Mama said she would save badges and buttons from cereal boxes" for him, Shelton said. Pictures of ships and planes decorated the walls of his bedroom. His drawers were full of magazines about the military and about police work.

He worked hard to build his muscles, using whatever

weights he could improvise. He lifted rocks, an anvil, and even trudged around with the younger children hanging from his shoulders.

Gilliland was six feet tall, bigger than most of his classmates. His childhood friend Harold Mears said he was fun but not frivolous. "He was solid. He never fooled around like the rest of us. We were glad to have him around when we'd go to the next town as kids. Nobody would mess with us" with him around.

He tried to join the marines at sixteen, but the recruiter sent him home, advising him to get an education first. He sent off for a mail-order correspondence course and badgered his parents to let him enlist. They finally relented, giving their permission for him to join the army on his seventeenth birthday, May 24, 1950. The Korean War began one month later.

In a letter to his parents from Fort Riley, Kansas, where he underwent basic training, he wrote on May 28, 1950, "Well, I am in the Army now. I like it all right. How is everything at home? Tell Billy [a brother] he can have my fishing tackle."

Shelton said his letters often resemble those of a boy writing home from summer camp. In one letter from Korea, he mentioned in passing that he had been wounded. A December 30, 1950, telegraph from Tokyo read, "Loveing [sic] wishes for Christmas & New Year. Am well and safe. Please do not worry."

His body building paid off when he carried to safety a soldier whose legs had been blown off. He talked about the harrowing experience in a letter urging Billy to stay in school. "I would give my right arm if I could be back now. I get to think about walking across the fields. Their [sic] is no shells falling around [or] someone in a hole with a machine gun fireing [sic] at you. If you have a flat on the car be thankful that the work you put in fixing it isn't the work of carrying your buddy down a mountainside with no legs."

According to his Medal of Honor citation, "Cpl. Gilliland, facing the full force of the assault, poured a steady fire into the foe which stemmed the onslaught. When two enemy soldiers escaped his raking fire and infiltrated the sector, he leaped from his foxhole, overtook and killed them both with his pistol." He suffered a serious head wound but refused medical treatment.

"His unit was ordered back to new defensive positions but Cpl. Gilliland volunteered to cover the withdrawal and hold the enemy at bay," the citation read. "His heroic actions and indomitable devotion to duty

prevented the enemy from completely overrunning his company positions."

His remains were never found. His family was notified by the army in 1952 that he had been recommended for the Medal of Honor but that an announcement would be delayed in case he was a prisoner of war. The army said things could go much worse for him if his captors knew he was a war hero. He was declared dead in 1954, and his family was presented with the Medal of Honor at a ceremony at the Pentagon in December of that year.

On May 24, 1997, which would have been his sixty-fourth birthday, the navy christened the USNS *Gilliland* at Newport News, Virginia. The ship was the first of about twenty military sealift ships designed to transport tanks, trucks, and other large pieces of army equipment to areas of conflict around the world. The USNS *Gilliland* was one of five sealift ships named for Medal of Honor winners.

[This biography was based on private scrapbooks and the author's interviews with Gilliland relatives and friends. See the *Arkansas Democrat-Gazette*, May 24, 1997; *Harrison Daily Times*, May 26, 1996; *Baxter Bulletin*, Sept. 27, 1979; *Evening Star*, Sept. 17, 1954.]

JULIE STEWART

GOVAN, DANIEL CHEVILETTE (July 4, 1829–Mar. 12, 1911), Confederate general, was born in Northampton County, North Carolina, the son of Andrew Robison Govan and Mary Pugh Jones. The father had represented South Carolina in the United States House of Representatives. Govan spent his youth on his family's "Snowdown" plantation in Marshall County, Mississippi, and attended the University of South Carolina.

At twenty Govan joined his kinsman Benjamin McCulloch and headed for the California gold fields. He returned to Mississippi two years later to become a planter. In December 1853 he married Mary F. Otey, daughter of James H. Otey, Tennessee's first Episcopal bishop. The newlyweds established a plantation in (then) Phillips County, Arkansas.

Following the surrender of Fort Sumter, Govan raised a company of volunteers at Hopefield. He was elected captain, and his unit was mustered into Confederate service as Company F, Second Arkansas Volunteer Infantry. On December 17, 1861, he first saw combat at Rowlett's Station near Bowling Green, Kentucky.

In January 1862 he was promoted to colonel. He commanded the Second Arkansas on the retreat from Bowling Green to Corinth, Mississippi, and in April 1862 led his regiment, a unit in Colonel R. G. Shaver's brigade, into the Battle of Shiloh (Tennessee), the first in which the loss of life on both sides was staggering. Exhausted by the flu, he was unable to take the field on the battle's second day. Even so, Colonel Shaver reported that the Second and Seventh Arkansas "both did good, effective service, and were well fought by their respective commanders."

Govan participated in the invasion of Kentucky by General Braxton Bragg in the fall of 1862. Back in Tennessee under General Patrick R. Cleburne of Arkansas, he led his regiment at Stones River at the close of the year. In the summer of 1863 the federals maneuvered Bragg's army out of middle Tennessee.

Govan, now in command of the brigade, fought in the terrible struggle at Chickamauga, September 18–20, 1863. The Confederates had the city of Chattanooga under siege until late November when Union forces, under General U. S. Grant, broke out in a series of crucial battles. At Missionary Ridge, November 25, Govan led his fellow Arkansans in the brigade that held off the savage attack of Union troops, but in the end, the Confederate forces were driven back.

The Confederate defeat at Chattanooga made possible the Union invasion of Georgia. Govan, now a brigadier general, participated, with his Arkansas brigade, in the desperate efforts to stop General W. T. Sherman, most notably at the Battle of Resaca, May 14, 1863. Govan was in the forefront of the Confederate onslaught on July 22 at the Battle of Atlanta, and he claimed the capture of seven hundred Yankees, many of them from the Sixteenth Iowa, in the first charge. He reported that when the tide turned, his men "brought off 8 pieces of artillery, several wagons loaded with ammunition and with intrenching tools." The cost was terrible: half of the one thousand men Govan took into the fight were casualties.

September 1 was another terrible day. Having been rushed to Jonesboro, south of Atlanta, on August 31, Govan's troops helped hold a salient angle in the Confederate line. They beat off one attack, but were overwhelmed by a second, and Govan, six hundred of his men, and eight cannon were captured. Govan remained a prisoner for three weeks, then was exchanged for Major General George Stoneman.

Govan rejoined his brigade to participate in General John Bell Hood's ill-fated middle Tennessee campaign, November 20–December 28, 1864. He was with Cleburne at Spring Hill and in the charge at Franklin, in which six Confederate generals, including Cleburne, were killed or mortally wounded. Govan was wounded at Nashville on December 16, but recuperated. By early April 1865 he had rejoined the Army of Tennessee, then camped in and around Greensboro, North Carolina, and returned to the command of his depleted Arkansas brigade, consolidated with a Texas brigade. Govan and his troops were among those who, under J. E. Johnston, surrendered to Union general Sherman on April 26, 1865.

Govan returned to Arkansas and resumed life as a planter near Marianna. In 1878 he wrote a "Brief History of Cleburne's Division," published in 1911 as an article in the first volume of Fay Hempstead's *Historical Review of Arkansas.* He was named by President Grover Cleveland as agent for the Tulalip Indian Agency in the state of Washington. His wife died there in 1896. The widowed general moved to Tennessee in 1898 and resided there and in Mississippi with one or another of his fourteen children until his death in Memphis. His comrade, Captain Irving A. Buck, wrote, "I regard him as one of the best soldiers it was my good fortune to know—a true Christian gentleman, a noble patriot, a loyal and uncompromising friend." Govan is buried in Holly Springs, Mississippi.

[See the *Memphis Commercial Appeal,* Mar. 13, 1911; *War of the Rebellion: A Compilation of the Official Records of the Union and Confederate Armies.* 70 Vols. in 128 Parts and Atlas (1880–1901); Irving Buck, *Cleburne and His Command* (1908); John M. Harrell, *Arkansas,* vol. 10 in Evan, *Confederate Military History;* and Ezra J. Warner, *Generals in Gray: Lives of the Confederate Commanders* (1959).]

EDWIN C. BEARSS

GREGG, LAFAYETTE (Feb. 6, 1825–Nov. 1, 1891), a lawyer and a founder of the University of Arkansas, was born in Lawrence County, Alabama, to Henry Gregg and Mary Murrill. In 1835 the family moved to Arkansas Territory, settling on a farm north of Fayetteville. In 1849 Lafayette Gregg moved to Fayetteville to study law in the office of W. D. Reagan. He taught in the county schools to support his studies and later established a private law practice in Fayetteville. In 1852 he married Mary Ann Shreve. They had four boys and two girls; one daughter died in infancy.

In 1855 he was elected to the state House of Representatives, where he participated in the 1855 and 1856 sessions. In 1856 he became prosecuting attorney of the Fourth Circuit, a position he held until 1861.

A lifelong Republican, Gregg opposed secession and, as was not uncommon in northwest Arkansas, remained loyal to the Union during the Civil War. Initially excused from military service due to a medical condition, he enlisted in the Union army in December 1864. He was assigned the rank of colonel and placed in command of the Fourth Regiment of Arkansas Cavalry which saw sporadic action, mostly involving the capture of bushwhackers. After the war he served as chancellor of the Pulaski Chancery Court from 1867 to 1868 and as an associate justice of the Arkansas Supreme Court from 1868 to 1871. Refusing a second term on the court, he returned to his law practice in Fayetteville.

Gregg is perhaps best known for his role in the establishment of the University of Arkansas. In response to legislation passed in 1868 and 1871 authorizing the creation of an Arkansas Industrial University, he worked to have the university located in Fayetteville. Together with Judge David Walker, he organized a campaign for the approval of bond issues to support the proposed university, passage of which was considered a prime factor in the decision to locate the university in Fayetteville. The collaboration between Gregg and Walker, who had been a prominent supporter of the Confederacy, provided evidence that postwar political factions in Fayetteville were united in their desire to see the university located there. Gregg drafted the legislation establishing the university at Fayetteville.

He was appointed to the university's building committee and assumed primary responsibility for overseeing the construction of the school's first permanent building, University Hall or "Old Main." In 1874 he was appointed to the university's board of trustees on which he served until 1883. In 1890 the university established a department of law with Gregg as professor of constitutional and international law, a position he held until his death the following year.

In 1871 Gregg undertook the construction of a large Georgian-style brick home adjacent to the university. It has long been rumored, and occasionally taught to Fayetteville schoolchildren, that the house had served as a way station for the underground railroad. This legend holds that a tunnel connected the house to the nearby railway and was used to smuggle escaped slaves aboard northbound trains. Contrary to legend the house was not built until after the war, and the first railway line did not reach Fayetteville until 1881. The house, which shares several architectural features with Old Main, still stands in 1999.

Gregg once again entered politics in 1886, receiving the Republican nomination for governor to oppose the incumbent Democrat Simon P. Hughes. Gregg apparently did not view himself as a politician and seems to have entered this campaign reluctantly. As the *Arkansas Gazette* observed on August 24, 1886, "He had been astonished when he was called upon to be the standard bearer ... He could not account for the choice unless the gentlemen who presented him wanted a man who knew nothing about political tricks." The Republican Party was still burdened with the perceived abuses of reconstruction, and Gregg lost the election. However, he ran ahead of others on the Republican ticket and was spared the vitriolic attacks aimed at Republican candidates by the state's Democratic press. This is typical of his public career, throughout which he was characterized as honorable and fair-minded even by those politically opposed to him.

During the final years of his life, he remained active with his law practice and managed a four-hundred-acre farm outside of Fayetteville. He was a founder and president of the Bank of Fayetteville. He donated land to the American Missionary Society for the construction of a school for black children. He was an advocate for Arkansas's participation in the 1893 Columbian Exposition in Chicago and was the Arkansas representative on the Exposition Commission at the time of his death.

Gregg died at his home. On the day of his funeral, banks and businesses in Fayetteville were closed, the circuit court adjourned, and classes at the university were suspended in his honor.

[Gregg lived a public life chronicled by state and local newspapers, including obituaries in the Fayetteville and Little Rock press. See the Gregg Family Papers in the Special Collections Division, University of Arkansas Libraries, Fayetteville, and the Fayetteville history files at the Fayetteville public library. See also Albert W. Bishop, *Report of the Adjutant General of the State of Arkansas for the Period of the Late Rebellion, and to November 1, 1866* (to the U.S. Senate, 1867). A detailed description of Gregg's home, including construction specifications, is in *Flashback*, Aug. 1973, published by the Washington County Historical Society.]

RUSSELL C. GREGG

HALE, MAMIE ODESSA (1911–1968?), public health nurse and midwife educator, was a new graduate of the Tuskegee School of Nurse-Midwifery for Colored Nurses when she arrived in Arkansas in 1942 to begin her work as a public health nurse with the Crittenden County health department. Her arrival coincided with the United States' entry into World War II and the departure of many of the state's physicians and registered nurses to assist in the war effort. By the end of 1941 there were 1,819 licensed physicians in Arkansas, yielding a ratio of one physician to 1,113 people, drastically lower than the national ratio of one per 750.

In July 1945 Hale was appointed to the position of midwife consultant for the Arkansas Department of Health. The position required her to provide the educational programs necessary to assure that "granny" midwives (older women with experience, but no formal training) were competent to attend deliveries. With funding from the Children's Bureau, a statewide training program was started to supplement classes taught by local health units.

More than half of the live births in the United States, but less than 25 percent of the births in Arkansas, occurred in hospitals. Sixty-six percent of the state's population, black and white, lived in rural areas which lacked adequate health services. Racial barriers kept many Arkansans from seeking health care. Except for twenty-three beds at the University Hospital of Little Rock, there were practically no hospital beds for black women in Arkansas as late as 1947.

Prior to Hale's appointment, the state's attempts to educate and regulate granny midwives had been ineffective. The medical community was appalled that in 1941 there were 142 deaths in childbirth among black women, of which 107 could have been avoided. Babies less than a year old accounted for one-tenth of all deaths in Arkansas in 1943. The state could not do without the granny midwife because there were not enough physicians to attend some eight thousand home births annually.

By 1946 Hale was conducting classes in midwifery, often in local churches, in four counties. Community support for these programs was overwhelming. She capitalized on this support to publicize the notion that a granny midwife with a permit meant better health care during pregnancy and childbirth. This publicity encouraged these midwives, on average between sixty and eighty years of age, to obtain the prestigious permit.

Hale commanded respect from the black midwives and from white public health nurses across the state. Since it was not socially acceptable in the 1940s to address a black woman by the title "Miss," blacks as well as whites bestowed the title "Nurse Hale" upon her.

A seven-week training program was developed to train midwives across the state. Because three-quarters of these midwives were illiterate, they failed to complete birth certificates for about 25 percent of the babies born in Arkansas. Incomplete statistics resulted in fewer federal dollars to the state's health department. This simple but crucial task must be learned. Midwives were taught by rote memory and encouraged to get assistance from family members or neighbors to complete birth certificates.

Hale employed a thirty-pound mannequin as a demonstration tool. She acted out every procedure related to the childbirth, from hand washing to the placement of newspapers to catch the baby, to the tying and cutting of the cord. She also used songs and films to convey important information to the midwives. At the conclusion of the seven-week program, the midwives were required to have a medical examination, a pledge card, a midwife bag equipped according to Hale's specifications, and an application for a midwife permit. Graduation exercises took place in local churches, and communities turned out for the event. Dr. Frances Rothert, director of the state Board of Health's Maternal and Child Division, addressed the midwives and presented their certificates.

During 1948 almost twenty-five hundred women received medical services from the Arkansas health department. That year, some six hundred granny midwives received annual permits. They had delivered over five thousand babies during the year. By 1949 more than 50 percent of the counties in Arkansas had some type of maternity clinic. After almost five years of classes, licensed midwives attended 75 percent of the births attended by midwives. In less than two decades, the program produced dramatic results. The number of deaths among blacks due to pregnancy and childbirth fell from 128 in 1930 to 43 in 1950.

Hale's contributions to the state during the 1940s were significant against the backdrop of a global war and racial prejudice. She and her "army" of granny midwives made great strides on the home front to assure that women and children had access to maternity care.

She returned to her home in Pennsylvania in 1950. She later married a physician and worked with the World Health Organization. Her later life, like her background, is unknown.

[Sources include the Arkansas State Board of Health, *Annual Report of the Arkansas State Board of Health,* 1949–1950, 1950–1951; *Requirements for Midwife Permits* 19 (Sept. 1940); and *Arkansas Health Bulletin* 8 (Feb. 1951). Sources also include Mamie Hale, "Arkansas Teaches Her Midwives," *Child* 2 (Oct. 1946) and "Arkansas Midwives Have All-Day Graduation Exercises," *Child* (Oct. 1948); Claire Moody, "State's Midwife Schools Win U[nited] N[ations] Recognition," unidentified news clipping (c. 1951) in the archives of the Arkansas Department of Health; J. Price, W. Martin, and T. Jones, "Report of the Committee on the Study of Midwifery," *Journal of the Arkansas Medical Society* 43 (June 1946): 20–21; Sarah Hudson, "Thoroughly Modern Midwives; Black Granny Midwives and Public Health in Arkansas 1920 to the Present 1984," in Special Collections, University of Arkansas for Medical Sciences library; Matilda Tuohey, "Train Midwives to Aid Work of Health Division," *Arkansas Gazette* (Nov. 1950); and interviews with Marguerite Burt, retired public health nurse (Sept. 1991), and Dr. Frances Rothert (Sept. 1991).]

PEGGE L. BELL

HALL, DAVID (1782?–1859?), described as a "colored" and "exceedingly stout man," settled along the White River bottoms some seven miles below the mouth of the Little North Fork in 1819, the year that Congress created Arkansas Territory. The North Carolina-born Hall and his light-skinned wife, Sarah, a Tennessean, built a cabin, raised corn, horses, and cows, made whiskey in one of the first stills to be seen on the upper White River, and, not least of all, tended to their growing family. An 1840 surveyor's map shows the Hall farm, which was located twenty miles west of today's city of Mountain Home, with forty acres under cultivation, a larger operation than any other in his township. Hall paid county and state taxes for thirty years, and these records document his relative prosperity. His ownership of a number of horses and cows kept his assessments continually well above the county average and enabled him to supply starter livestock to his off-

spring who married and set up homesteads. The patriarch's sons Willoghby, Joe, and James, and his daughters Margaret Hall Turner and Eliza Hall Caulder established families that expanded the free black population in Marion County. These pioneer farmers lived in semi-isolation and in harmony with whites, a situation that attracted other free mulattos who settled in the vicinity, forming antebellum Arkansas's largest free black community.

United States censuses of 1830, 1840, and 1850, categorized David and Sarah Hall as free colored people or free mulattos. An Arkansas statute defined mulatto as "a person one fourth or more Negro." Chronicler Silas Turnbo, writing around the turn of the century about early settlement days on the White River, includes several hunting and "long time ago" stories that he heard from Joe Hall and refers to Dave, Sarah, and Joe Hall, as "free Negroes."

Hall and his son-in-law Peter Caulder, despite state laws to the contrary, kept hounds and firearms essential to their frontier life. The Marion County sheriff never recorded any objections to these practices, apparently following a leave-well-enough-alone policy. Traveling about by any conveyance was legal in the territory and after statehood, but risky for free blacks since they were under the jurisdiction of any white man who cared to exercise that authority. Despite the risk, the Halls and their neighbor John Turner occasionally traveled outside the county by horse and by boat to attend to their business affairs.

Landownership was one of the few legally recognized rights of Negroes in slave states such as Arkansas. During the winter of 1849, David Hall and John Hall (possibly a brother) traveled one hundred miles to the United States government land office at Batesville to pay cash for and later receive patents on their White River valley acreage. Subsequently, at least six mulattos came to own property in Marion County via purchase of government land. Others such as Peter Caulder and Henly Black preempted or squatted on land where they farmed and raised families.

The settlement lasted until the Arkansas General Assembly passed a law in February 1859 entitled, "An Act to Remove the Free Negroes and Mulattos from the State." Penalties included seizure and sale into slavery, emancipation already having been made illegal in Arkansas. The enormity of the threat was enough to overcome the tenaciousness of folks in the free Negro community. More than one hundred of them abandoned good farms and departed Marion County and the state of Arkansas, a gut-wrenching turn of events, without doubt.

Today the land patented by David Hall lies beneath Bull Shoals Lake. With the exception of weathered and nameless wooden markers placed atop a stone wall alongside the Promised Land Cemetery by the Corps of Engineers before the valley was flooded, no physical trace remains of the free black community that thrived along the banks of the White River near the Missouri border. Hall disappeared from the tax and census records in 1859 when he would have been seventy-six years old. According to Turnbo, Hall was buried near where he had settled. For five decades a substantial number of black farmers, following the example set by David Hall, had shared with white counterparts amidst the mountain valleys of north Arkansas the yeoman values of family, landownership, and independence. But for an ill-conceived slavocracy law which placed continuation of those values in jeopardy, the presence in Marion County of a stable and mutually respectful society of blacks and whites might have offered a valuable example for reconstruction Arkansas.

[See Elbert H. English, ed., *A Digest of the Statutes of Arkansas, 1846* (1848); John Steele and James McCampbell, comps., *Laws of Arkansas Territory, 1835* (1835); Theodore Branter, *Black Codes of the South* (1965); Seventh Census of the United States, Arkansas, Marion County, 1850; Eight Census of the United States, Arkansas, Marion County, 1860; National Archives, Batesville Track Book, 2-2-34, pt. 1, vol. 7,43, cash file 3213; Marion County Tax Record, 1841–1865, Arkansas History Commission; Turnbo Manuscript Collection, Springfield-Greene County Public Library, Missouri; *New York Weekly Anglo-African*, Feb. 4, 1860; Acts of the General Assembly of the State of Arkansas, 1859.]

BILLY D. HIGGINS

HANCOCK, ARCHIBALD REX JR. (July 6, 1923–July 8, 1986), conservationist, was born in Laddonia, Missouri, to A. R. Hancock, a dentist, and Alma Bothmann Klein. He attended Westminster College in Fulton, Missouri, but his education and semi-pro baseball career there were interrupted by World War II. During the war he served as a pharmacist's mate in the U.S. Seventh Fleet's Amphibious Division. After the war he finished up at Westminster College and then earned a D.D.S. degree from the University of Missouri School of Dentistry at Kansas City.

He chose to locate in Arkansas because of its reputation as a hunting and fishing paradise. In the early 1950s he moved to Huntsville where he and a neighbor, future governor Orval E. Faubus, cared for each other's hunting dogs when either was away. In 1951 Hancock settled permanently in Stuttgart, which is renowned for its waterfowl hunting.

He was a competent dentist active in the Arkansas Dental Association, but his passion was hunting and fishing. His mission was saving wildlife habitat, for which he received national acclaim. In these endeavors he was known for intensity, energy, organizational skills, salty language, and perseverance likened to that of a pit bull terrier.

At home Hancock hunted anything that was legal—squirrels, deer, duck, and quail. During treks to Alaska and British Columbia he took polar, grizzly, Kodiak, black, and brown bears; a record-class dall sheep; caribou; and a moose ranked second in North American records. By the late 1960s he had switched almost exclusively from gun to bow and arrow, explaining, "I feel the odds are more even when I use a bow; a big game animal doesn't stand a chance against a modern scopesighted high power rifle."

In 1958 Hancock realized Arkansas was not represented in the whitetail deer listings of the Boone and Crockett Club's Records of North American Big Game. That had to be corrected, he said, because "We have a hell of a lot of big deer in this state." He became certified as an official scorer for the club, then scoured the state for record-book heads. They were everywhere, stored in barns and hanging in barbershops, living rooms, and country stores. He measured hundreds of superb heads, and by 1964, Arkansas had jumped from none to first place in Boone and Crockett Club records.

Hancock searched with equal thoroughness for the source of fish kills on the nearby Bayou Meto, and documented in 1964 what the federal government did not acknowledge until 1979—that an old pesticide plant at Jacksonville was discharging TCDD (dioxin) into the stream. Known as Vertac, the site became Arkansas's most notorious toxic cleanup case.

Hancock served five consecutive terms as president of the Grand Prairie Chapter of the Wildlife Federation, and brought its membership roster to more than five hundred. In 1968 he was the Arkansas Wildlife Federation's Conservationist of the Year. He then became AWF president and served from 1975 to 1979 as a regional director of the National Wildlife Federation.

In the early 1970s Hancock began leading one of Arkansas's foremost environmental crusades, the fight to save 232 miles of the Cache River and its tributary, Bayou DeView, from being channelized. The Cache meanders through northeast Arkansas from the Missouri boot heel to the White River at Clarendon. Bayou DeView parallels the Cache about eight miles to the east for much of its length. Together they are the winter resting place for an estimated 800,000 migrating ducks.

A plan to straighten and deepen the streams to improve the drainage of surrounding lands was proposed as early as the 1920s. After soybean prices soared in the 1960s, U.S. representative Bill Alexander (Democrat of Arkansas) got Congress to allocate $60 million for the work.

As attorney for a group of environmentalists, Richard S. Arnold filed suit in federal court, challenging the adequacy of the U.S. Army Corps of Engineers' twelve-page Environmental Impact Statement on the project. After District Judge J. Smith Henley ruled for the Corps, it began dredging the Cache near Clarendon even though the case had been appealed to the U.S. Eighth Circuit Court of Appeals and Governor Dale Bumpers had asked for delay.

"I couldn't stand by and watch a bureaucratic federal agency thumb its nose at Arkansas," Hancock said, explaining why he single-handedly organized the Citizens Committee to Save the Cache River Basin in October 1972. The committee eventually included thirty-five national organizations and eight states in the Mississippi Flyway. Hancock challenged the Corps at every turn, spending hundreds of hours and thousands of his own money.

The battle raged until Congress cut off funds in 1978 after a U.S. Fish and Wildlife Service (USF&WS) study called the plan "the single most damaging project to waterfowl in the nation," and the Environmental Protection Agency refused to grant a necessary permit to the Corps in 1979. In 1980 the USF&WS announced plans for a thirty-five-thousand-acre Cache River National Wildlife Refuge, which has since been established. Only seven-plus miles of the Cache near Clarendon ever were "ditched."

National plaudits rolled in to Hancock, including the prestigious *Outdoor Life* award in 1973, Winchester's National Conservation Award in 1975, and a Westminster Alumni Achievement Award in 1976. He was inducted posthumously into the Game and Fish Commission Foundation's Arkansas Outdoor Hall of Fame in 1993.

Hancock married his dental assistant Jan Hagaman in 1963, and they had three daughters and two sons. He died of cancer two days after his sixty-third birthday. His ashes were placed in the Cache River bottoms of the Rex Hancock/Black Swamp Wildlife Management Area in Woodruff County.

[Sources include scrapbooks, articles, and documents owned by members of the Hancock family. Obituaries are in the *Stuttgart Daily Leader*, July 8, 1986, and the *Arkansas Gazette*, July 9, 1986.]

CAROL GRIFFEE

HARRIS, MARQUIS LAFAYETTE (Mar. 8, 1907– Oct. 7, 1966), bishop, president of Philander Smith College, was born in Armstrong, Macon County, Alabama, to William Eugene Harris and Estelle Marie Glenn. He became an ordained minister in the Methodist Episcopal Church in 1929.

Harris earned a bachelor of science degree in 1928 from Clark College (now Clark Atlanta University), with a major in chemistry and minors in physics and mathematics. A football player, he was All-American in 1926. He earned a bachelor of divinity degree from Gammon Theological Seminary in 1929, and a master of sacred theology degree from Boston University in 1930. He entered Ohio State University to study philosophy and received a Ph.D. in 1933.

Harris loved learning, and he loved to teach. From 1927 to 1929 he taught chemistry and mathematics at Clark College. He taught physics and religion and coached football at Claflin College in Orangeburg, South Carolina.

Marquis Harris was appointed dean and professor of sociology at Samuel Huston College (now Huston-Tillotson College) in Austin, Texas. Even after becoming president of Philander Smith College in Little Rock in 1936, he continued to teach classes, philosophy and religion. He has been described as an exemplary teacher who inspired students to realize their potential. In a tribute to him James P. Brawley wrote, "Many young men and young women lighted their intellectual torches from the flame of this great teacher and went on to earn higher degrees, following his example."

During Harris's twenty-four-year tenure as president of Philander Smith College, academic programs were evaluated and strengthened, leading to accreditation by the North Central Association of Colleges and Schools on March 30, 1949. Enrollment began to rise, and eventually increased from 381 to 1,130. The campus was significantly expanded and enhanced. Old buildings were renovated, property acquired, and new buildings developed. The value of the college increased from $125,000 at the beginning of Harris's term to well over $3 million when he retired.

In July 1948 the college purchased the site of Little Rock Junior College, adjacent to the south end of the campus. This site comprised one city block on which was located a building containing classrooms, a library, a gymnasium, and a chemistry laboratory. Kelly Hall, the present home of the president, was completed and a new science building was erected in 1952.

In March 1958 Harris launched a $3.5 million capital funds campaign after a study revealed that substantial financial outlay was needed to sustain a high-quality undergraduate program at the college. Harris completed construction on new dormitories, a student union, and a cafeteria, and began construction on a library and fine arts center which was named in his honor.

Harris was elected to the Methodist episcopacy and assigned to the Central Jurisdiction of the Atlantic Coast area on July 15, 1960. He served as chairman of the boards of trustees for Methodist institutions in his jurisdiction, including Bethune-Cookman College, Claflin College, Clark College, Rust College, and Gammon Theological Seminary, and was a board member for Atlanta University and the Interdenominational Theological Center. He was also was a thirty-third-degree Mason.

He received several honors, including the honorary doctor of divinity degree from Gammon Theological Seminary in 1941, the honorary doctor of law degree from Clark College in 1959, and the doctor of humane letters from Southwestern College in 1960.

Harris wrote several books, too, among which are *Voice in the Wilderness* (1941), *Our Tomorrow's World* (1945), and *To Magnify My Power* (1948). *Life Can Be Meaningful* (1951) is a collection of the weekly addresses that he delivered on campus. In the intro-

duction, Harris expressed appreciation to the students and faculty of the 1949–50 school year for serving as "sounding boards." Well respected on campus and in the community, he was known for his wide interests and thirst for knowledge. His advice for daily living was treasured by those with whom he shared it. In *Life Can Be Meanigful* he said, "Everyone must bear in mind at all times that the greatest sin is FEAR ... that the greatest invention of evil which man has contrived is the evil of ill will and war ... the greatest need in this life is Common Sense on the part of each person, and an attitude of love and respect toward every person."

Harris retired from Philander Smith College in 1960. At a program held in his honor, a speaker described him as a deeply spiritual man who always conveyed a positive attitude: "He never became antagonistic, impatient or discouraged—no matter what difficulties he faced."

Harris married his college sweetheart, Geneva Nelson, on September 6, 1931. They had a son, Marquis Lafayette, and a daughter, Erseline.

Marquis Lafayette Harris died in Atlanta. He is buried in South View Cemetery there.

[Sources include obituaries in the *Arkansas Gazette* and *Arkansas Democrat*, Oct. 8, 1966; James P. Brawley, "A Tribute to Bishop Marquis Lafayette Harris," *Mentor* (Clark College newsletter), Winter 1966–67; Philander Smith College Catalog, 1997–98; and *Encyclopedia of World Methodism*, vol. 1, edited by Nolan B. Harmon.]

DELIA MOORE

HARRISON, MARCUS LARUE (Apr. 1, 1830–Oct. 27, 1890), military leader and business promoter, was born at Groton, New York, to Marcus Harrison and Lydia House. The elder Harrison, a Presbyterian minister who supported the temperance and antislavery movements, served churches in New York and Michigan. LaRue Harrison grew up in Michigan. By 1850 he was in Nashville, Illinois, where he married Rebecca Axley. From this first marriage, which ended in Rebecca's death in 1861, came two sons. One son, Edward, became a physician in Fort Smith.

During the decade before the Civil War, Harrison practiced civil engineering and was employed for several years by the Chicago, Burlington, and Quincy Railroad. In September 1861 he enlisted as an infantry private in the Thirty-sixth Illinois Volunteers and later transferred to a cavalry company. By late fall he was an acting lieutenant of engineers. The next spring, after the Battle of Pea Ridge, Harrison was working as an engineer out of Cassville, Missouri. Aware that a large number of Union loyalists were fleeing from Arkansas into Missouri, he asked for and received permission to organize a regiment of these men. The First Arkansas Cavalry was mustered in at Springfield, Missouri, on August 7, 1862, with Harrison as colonel. The First Arkansas remained under Harrison's command throughout the war. The unit fought in battles at Prairie Grove and Fayetteville and at numerous other sites in northwest Arkansas. Its responsibilities included keeping communications and supply lines open. From his headquarters in Fayetteville, Harrison directed the Union occupation of the region, tried to neutralize the activities of looters and raiders, and sought to restore order.

Pacification of the countryside and protection of the civilian population, Harrison claimed, were his motives when he embarked on his most controversial wartime project, the establishment of post colonies. Begun in early 1865, these communities were agricultural colonies organized as homeguard militia under the auspices of the First Arkansas Cavalry. Harrison planned to establish twenty to forty colonies throughout the region. At least fourteen colonies became operational and planted crops on abandoned lands. Harrison argued that these families enjoyed greater personal safety and were more likely to harvest crops than if left on their own farms.

However, many people, especially those who had Confederate leanings, saw the colonies not as protective but as punitive. Reports reached Harrison's superior, General Cyrus Bussey, that Harrison had tried to force "all the people in Northwest Arkansas to join colonies" and was preventing those who would not join from growing "any crops." Moreover, Bussey had heard that Harrison's policy was to "burn the house and kill any man who would not join a colony." Other complainants charged that Harrison's goal was to ensure that the seven-county area yield a Republican majority in the next election. Bussey, who described Harrison as "a good talker [who] writes a good letter," ordered the colonel to rescind any orders which made participation in the colonies mandatory. Harrison could, however, continue to encourage agricultural colonies with voluntary participation. The conclusion of the war just as the colonies became operational ended the experiment.

During the war, Harrison married Medora Bigby of Springfield, Missouri. When they were divorced in 1873, the judge granted him custody of their only child, Grace.

After the war ended, Harrison was honored with the brevet rank of brigadier general. He remained for a few years in Fayetteville and served as mayor for a short time in 1869. Almost immediately after he took office, a group of dissatisfied citizens petitioned the state legislature to rescind the city's charter. The legislature agreed and thereby eliminated Harrison's office. Issues bearing on the controversy included taxation, the establishment of public schools, and the restriction of alcoholic beverages at polling places. When a new city government was created under authority of a general statute, Harrison was not an official.

During his final years as an Arkansas resident, Harrison served as chief engineer for the Pacific and Great Eastern Railroad Company, which proposed to build an east-west line across northern Arkansas. He promoted the project and traveled the state with the surveying team. While surveying in the Crooked Creek area of Boone County in 1869, Harrison was approached by a group of citizens who asked him to lay out a new town for them. He complied, and in return the citizens named the town for him. In early 1870 a nearby post office was renamed "Harrison."

In the early 1870s Harrison left Fayetteville for Washington, D.C., where he received an appointment as a money order inspector in the post office department. He continued with the money order bureau, and by the time of his death had become its chief inspector. In 1873, a few months after divorcing his second wife, Harrison married Mollie Merrill, a Baltimore widow, with whom he had one son, Bruce.

Harrison died at his Fort Meyer, Virginia, home from a chronic respiratory ailment that he and his physicians claimed resulted from his war service. He was buried in Arlington National Cemetery.

[Files in the National Archives and the Department of Veterans Affairs Regional Office, North Little Rock, clearly indicate that Harrison's first name was Marcus.

Sources include Roger V. Logan Jr., "General M. LaRue Harrison," *Boone County Historian* 2 (1979): 2–3; and obituaries in the *Washington Post*, Oct. 30, 1890, and the *Fayetteville Democrat*, Nov. 7, 1890.

For Harrison's activities with the Thirty-sixth Illinois Volunteers, see his military file in the National Archives. See Wendell P. Beall, "Wildwood Skirmishes: The First

Federal Arkansas Cavalry," thesis, University of Arkansas, Fayetteville, 1988. For the post colonies, see Leo E. Huff, "Guerrillas, Jayhawkers and Bushwhackers in Northern Arkansas during the War," *AHQ* 24 (Summer 1965): 127–48; Edwin C. Bearss, "General Bussey Takes Over at Fort Smith," *AHQ* 24 (Autumn 1965): 220–40; Michael A. Hughes, "Wartime Gristmill Destruction in Northwest Arkansas and Military-Farm Colonies," *AHQ* 46 (Summer 1987): 167–86; and Lloyd McConnell, "The Colony at Union Valley," *Flashback* 26 (1976): 4–15. The principal primary source on the colonies is *Official Records of the War of the Rebellion* (1880–1902), Series 1, vol. 48, pt. 1, 305, 1120–21, 1139, 1167–68, 1177–79, 1293–94, and especially 1302. See also the *Fort Smith New Era*, Mar. 18 and 25, 1865.

See the *Boone County Historian* 5 (1982): 172; and Ralph Rea, "Sidelines on Boone County History," *AHQ* 16 (Spring 1954): 72.]

RICHARD A. BLAND

HARVEY, WILLIAM HOPE

HARVEY, WILLIAM HOPE (Aug. 16, 1851–Feb. 11, 1936), lawyer and promoter, was born on a farm near the village of Buffalo in what is now West Virginia, the son of Robert Trigg Harvey and Anna Hope. After attending Buffalo Academy, Harvey taught school for three years while studying law. In 1870 he was admitted to the West Virginia bar.

Harvey began his law career in West Virginia, but soon moved on to Ohio. In Gallipolis Harvey met Anna R. Halliday, whom he married on June 26, 1876. The Harveys were constantly on the move. In Cleveland two of their children, Mary Hope and Robert Halliday, were born. Thomas W. was born during a return to Gallipolis.

In 1884 Harvey moved to Colorado, where he operated the Silver Bell, one of the best-producing silver mines in the Red Mountain district. Here a fourth child, Annette, was born. In 1888, following a steady decline in the price of silver, Harvey took his family to Pueblo, Colorado, where he resumed the practice of law and began a real estate career.

While there Harvey became one of the major developers of Pueblo's Mineral Palace, an ornate exposition hall designed to promote Colorado's mining resources. He moved on to Ogden, Utah, where he formed the Order of Monte Cristo to promote the city. The organization held an extravagant carnival, which was a financial failure for Harvey and the town.

In 1893, as the nation entered a period of deflation, bank failures, bankruptcies, and farm foreclosures, Harvey turned his attention to the "free silver" issue.

Along with other western business leaders, Harvey believed that prosperity could be restored by abandoning the gold standard and returning to the free coinage of silver, which had been discontinued in 1873. Harvey moved his family to Chicago to devote his time to the cause, calling for the U.S. Treasury to buy all silver offered at a set price and issue silver certificates backed by the deposits.

Harvey's 1894 book, *Coin's Financial School*, brought him fame and his nickname, "Coin." Other publications followed, and Harvey became a spokesman for the free silver cause. During the 1896 presidential race, he campaigned for William Jennings Bryan, the Democratic free silver candidate. Though Bryan lost the election, Harvey was named to the Democratic National Committee.

Harvey moved his family to northwest Arkansas, where he had campaigned for Bryan. In 1900 he purchased acreage around what was then called Silver Springs five miles southeast of Rogers. He developed his property as a luxurious resort called Monte Ne. Soon after the Harveys moved to Monte Ne, their house burned. Anna Harvey, perhaps exasperated by years of moving, returned to Chicago. Having obtained a divorce in the 1920s, Harvey married his secretary of many years, May Leake, in 1929.

In 1913 Harvey formed the Ozark Trails Association. Although the association's stated purpose was the promotion of better roads, Harvey's goal was the promotion of Monte Ne. The OTA marked routes, published route books, and at major junctions erected obelisks which were lettered with the distance and direction to Monte Ne.

Unfortunately, the association did little for Harvey's resort. The formality and strict schedules of resort life had been ideal for the railroad traveler, but automobile travelers tended to avoid resorts in favor of cross-country travel and camping. Like many resorts, Monte Ne suffered with the growth of automobile travel.

By 1920 Harvey was convinced that the fall of civilization was imminent, and he wanted to leave an explanation and a warning for future generations. He announced plans for the construction of a "pyramid," a 130-foot-tall obelisk to contain a message written by him. He exhausted his funds and was unable to complete the project, but he did construct the amphitheater which was to have been the pyramid's "foyer."

"Coin" Harvey appeared in the national spotlight

again in 1931 when he ran for president of the United States. He was the candidate of the Liberty Party, which he had formed the previous year. Monte Ne hosted the party's national convention. Harvey, then eighty years old, was the only candidate the delegates would support. The party platform was based on Harvey's writings and called for government ownership of utilities and heavy industry, strict limits on land holdings and personal wealth, and, of course, "free silver." When the votes were tallied, he was in sixth place, with 53,434 votes, of which 1,049 were from Arkansas. Nearly all his support came from the western states.

Harvey developed a reputation for eccentricity and irascibility. He was known for his checkered suits and red neckties and was said to talk with a Harvard accent until angered, when he would revert to his West Virginia dialect. C. W. Henninger, the Liberty Party national chairman, defended Harvey in a letter to the party's national committee: "I deny that Mr. Harvey is unbearable." Yet even Harvey's critics admitted he was sincere, dedicated, and single-minded in his pursuit of policies he felt would benefit the ordinary people of the nation.

Harvey died at Monte Ne and was buried beside his son Robert Halliday. Today most of Monte Ne is beneath the waters of Beaver Lake, but in 1962, before the lake was filled, the tomb of Harvey and his son was moved up the hillside.

[The most reliable accounts of the life of Harvey are the introduction by Richard Hofstadter, ed., *Coin's Financial School* (1963), and Jeanette P. Nichols, "Bryan's Benefactor: Coin Harvey and His World," *Ohio Historical Quarterly* 67 (4) (Oct. 1958): 299–325. See also Harry A. Stokes, "William Hope Harvey: Promoter and Agitator," thesis, Northern Illinois University, 1965.

On Harvey's life in the West see the Works Progress Administration's *Colorado: A Guide to the Highest State* (1941): 187–88, and the WPA's *A History of Ogden* (1940): 55. There is a manuscript on the Mineral Palace in the collections of the El Pueblo Museum, Colorado.

Harvey's role in the free silver movement is mentioned in most treatments of the Populist movement and the election of 1896. See William Jennings Bryan, *The First Battle* (1896): 153–54, 290–93, and Laurence Laughlin, "'Coin's' Food for the Gullible," *Forum* 19 (1895): 572–85. See also the *Chicago Daily Tribune*, May 18 and July 17, 19, 21, 23, 24, 26, 27, 28, and 30, 1895.

Also see Clifton E. Hull, "Monte Ne: Coin Harvey's Town Only a Memory," *Arkansas Gazette*, July 21, 1968; the *Arkansas Gazette*, Apr. 9, 1924; the *Rogers Daily News*, June 18, 1938; and Nan Lawler, "The Ozark Trails Association," M.A. thesis, University of Arkansas, (1991).

The Special Collections Division, University of Arkansas Libraries, Fayetteville, has materials relating to Harvey, Monte Ne, and the Ozark Trails Association. The collections of the Rogers Historical Museum include issues of the *Monte Ne Herald* and the *Liberty Bell*, Liberty Party manuscripts, various publications by Harvey, materials relating to the Ozark Trails Association, and photographs, postcards, and archival material relating to Monte Ne. The research library of the Rogers Historical Museum includes extensive files on Harvey and Monte Ne.

Harvey's writings in addition to *Coin's Financial School* include *A Tale of Two Nations* (1894), *Coin on Money, Trusts and Imperialism* (1899), *The Remedy* (1915), *Paul's School of Statesmanship* (1924), *The Pyramid Booklet* (1928), and *The Book* (1930).

Obituaries appear in the *Arkansas Gazette* and the *Rogers Daily News*, Feb. 12 1936.]

GAYE KELLER BLAND

HAVIS, FERDINAND (Nov. 15, 1846–Aug. 25, 1918), Pine Bluff's "colored millionaire" and a leader of the Arkansas Republican Party, was born a slave in Desha County. His father John Havis was a white slave owner who owned Ferdinand's mother. In 1859 John Havis moved his operations to Jefferson County. Growing up there Ferdinand received a little common school education and learned the barbering trade. Later he owned a profitable barbershop on West Court Street in Pine Bluff, which was later moved to Barraque Street.

Ferd Havis began his political career in the 1870s. He served as an alderman, representative, and assessor. In 1871 he was elected Pine Bluff's Third Ward alderman along with a white man named H. King White. In 1872 Havis served one term as a representative for the Twentieth District to the Arkansas Legislature. The Twentieth District included Jefferson, Bradley, Grant, and Lincoln Counties. In 1873 he was again elected third ward alderman along with H. King White.

Havis supported Governor Elisha Baxter during the Brooks-Baxter war, a conflict over the Arkansas gubernatorial election of 1874. Baxter commissioned him a colonel in the Arkansas militia in April 1874. After the Brooks-Baxter conflict, in 1874, Havis again was elected third ward alderman.

For about twenty years Havis served as chairman of the Jefferson County Republican Party. Starting in 1880 he served as a delegate to several national Republican conventions. At the 1880 Republican National Convention he was one of the 306 delegates who supported Ulysses S. Grant in his fight for the presidential nomination. In 1888 Ferd Havis became the vice president of the Arkansas Republican Party.

In 1882 he was elected Jefferson County circuit clerk and held this position for five terms (ten years). In 1883 the grand jury investigated the county clerk's office. Havis had presented an unlawful account against the county for $195.50 which was disallowed. The same account was later presented for credit upon an account due by him to the county. Evidently Havis had received double pay for his service. The grand jury was made up of ten white and six black Pine Bluff citizens, who did not indict him.

As a businessman he was often under scrutiny. He told the *Pine Bluff Press Eagle* that while in the tavern business he never allowed his saloon to be opened on Sunday. Technically, this was true; that is, he opened the tavern, a popular meeting place for the black society of Pine Bluff, on Saturday night. It closed sometime in the wee hours, not to open again the rest of the day on Sunday. On the police court docket of Pine Bluff in 1882, every Monday morning from July 4 until November, a certain F. Harris pled guilty to "Sabbath breaking" and paid a weekly fine of five dollars. "F. Harris" and Ferd Havis were apparently one and the same man, and the fine represented one of his costs of doing business in the town. Two years later Havis was arrested for selling whiskey on the Sabbath, to which he pled guilty and was fined ten dollars and costs.

In 1889 he was a Republican nominee for the U.S. Senate. In 1898 President McKinley nominated him for the position of Pine Bluff postmaster. Pine Bluff citizens, along with the local newspaper, opposed his nomination.

The United States Senate Committee on Post Offices and Post Roads had to consider charges of gambling, immorality, and Havis's having been investigated by a grand jury. Some opposition to his appointment was clearly racist, for that was the climate of the time. However, a good many prominent black citizens thought Havis's appointment would be detrimental to the best interests of the colored race. Some people thought the charges raised at this time were based upon his record keeping while in office and not upon his race. The furor created by his nomination no doubt played a part in the decision of the Post Roads Committee to turn down his nomination.

Besides owning a barbershop and his own home, Havis owned about two thousand acres of land, several tenement houses, and was a part owner of a local tavern. He belonged to the A.M.E. Church, Masonic Fraternity, Grand United Order of Odd Fellows, Knight of Pythias, and the United Brothers and Knights of Friendship.

He married three times. His first wife, Dilsa, died in 1870. His second wife, Geneva, died in 1886 from "consumption." He married his third wife, Ella Cooper, in 1887. He had four kids: Ferda, Viessy, Alma, and Felton. He is buried in Bellwood Cemetery at Pine Bluff.

Havis was unquestionably one of the dominant black political figures in Arkansas's Republican Party during the period following the Civil War. And yet, slightly more than a century later, he is little remembered by the Republican Party or the people of Arkansas whom he once served so faithfully.

[See John William Graves, "Negro Disenfranchisement in Arkansas," *AHQ* 26 (Autumn 1967): 224, and "The Arkansas Negro and Segregation," M.A. thesis, University of Arkansas, Fayetteville. See also C. Calvin Smith, *War and Wartime Changes* (1986); James Leslie, "Ferd Havis, Jefferson County's Black Republican Leader," *Jefferson County Historical Society* (1978); Marian B. Morgan and Izola Preston, *The Arkansas African-American Quizbook*, Fayetteville, Arkansas (n.d.); the *Pine Bluff Press-Eagle*, Dec. 16, 1884; and the *Weekly Graphic*, May 19, 1906.]

MARIAN BERNETTE MORGAN

HAYS, GEORGE WASHINGTON (Sept. 23, 1863–Sept. 15, 1927), attorney, governor of Arkansas, was born at Camden, Arkansas, to Thomas Hays, a farmer, and Parthenia Jane Ross.

Hays farmed until he was twenty-five years old, worked as a store clerk for six years, and taught school for three months. He received a legal education at Washington and Lee University in Lexington, Virginia, and, after studying with the firm of Gaughan and Sifford at Camden, he began his own law practice there in 1894. On February 20, 1885, Hays married Ida Virginia Yarbrough. They had two sons.

Hays was probate and county judge for Ouachita County from 1900 to 1905. He returned to his law practice in Camden until October 31, 1906, when he became judge of the Thirteenth Judicial District. Reelected in 1910, he resigned before completing his second term when he was elected governor in 1913.

Hays looked to remnants of former governor Jeff Davis's faction for support. His opponent, Stephen Brundidge, drew his support from the towns and cities. Hays allied himself with the politically powerful Eugene Williams, treasurer of the St. Francis Levee District Board, a major influence in delta-region politics. Brundidge accused Hays of backroom dealings with the levee board. Despite charges of vote manipulations in eastern Arkansas, Hays easily won the election.

He came to the governor's chair at a time of rising reform sentiment in the state and nation; Woodrow Wilson's crusades for antitrust, banking, and tariff reform all occurred during Hays's election campaign and tenure as governor. But Hays showed much less interest in the goals of the Progressives than one of his recent predecessors, George Washington Donaghey, or his successor, Charles Brough. He did not actively press for change; critics charge him with inactivity, irresolution, and vacillation. His major preoccupation seemed to be creating a loyal political machine by gaining control of the board of charities and the levee board.

Hays had no opposition in the Democratic gubernatorial primary election held in March 1914. Andrew L. Kenney, the Republican candidate, described Hays as a "man of high character" but condemned him for spending too much time "building up or attempting to build up a political machine." Hays called for a rigid economy to keep the state solvent. He enjoyed an overwhelming victory at the general election on September 14, 1914.

Prohibition was a major issue in Hays's administration. Under the Going Law of 1913, liquor licenses could not be granted in a community unless a majority of the white voters signed a local-option petition. Arkansas had become an almost totally dry state by 1915. The liquor forces determined to abrogate the Going Law by submitting the prohibition question to the people at a general election. Hays flip-flopped on the prohibition issue several times. During his campaign he joined forces with prohibitionists who favored a statewide prohibition law, and in his inaugural address he vigorously assailed the evils of liquor. Later he aligned himself with the wets by asking the legislature to resubmit the question to the voters and by supporting the wet candidate for president of the senate, but the senate rejected his advice and chose a strong prohibitionist.

The governor expressed his embarrassment for supporting the wets and promised to call for a strong prohibition measure. With his support the legislature passed the statewide prohibition bill making it illegal after January 1, 1916, to manufacture or sell liquor in Arkansas. After some waffling, Hays also vetoed a bill to legalize parimutuel betting at Hot Springs.

In another controversial veto, Hays struck down a bill to make the membership of the St. Francis Levee Board elective. He preferred to keep appointive power intact despite pressure from delta-area legislators to reform the board. Hays helped to bring about the defeat of a primary-election reform bill designed to end the vote manipulation that had often occurred in eastern Arkansas.

During the 1915 session the legislature passed a number of significant progressive measures that received Hays's approval. The Alexander Road Improvement Act provided for creation of road-improvement districts governed by commissions with power to issue bonds. The legislature also enacted a "blue sky law" to protect investors from stock and bond fraud, a law to regulate chiropractors, and an act to regulate the methods of weighing coal at mines. Women achieved important gains during the Hays administration. Their working day was restricted to nine hours, with a six-day maximum week. The legislature gave women the right to enter into contracts and to own property and submitted to the voters a woman-suffrage amendment.

After Hays left office in January 1917, he practiced law in Little Rock and Camden. He died in Camden.

[See Richard L. Niswonger, "George Washington Hays, 1913–1917," in *The Governors of Arkansas: Essays in Political Biography,* Timothy P. Donovan, Willard B. Gatewood Jr., and Jeannie M. Whayne, eds., 2d ed. (1995).]

RICHARD L. NISWONGER

HAYS, LAWRENCE BROOKS (Aug. 9, 1898–Oct. 12, 1981), congressman and Baptist lay leader, was born in London, Pope County, Arkansas, the only child of Adelbert Steele Hays, lawyer and political operative, and Sarah Tabitha Butler, homemaker. He served eight terms as United States Representative of Arkansas's Fifth Congressional District (1943–1959) and was president of the Southern Baptist Convention for two one-year terms (1957–1959). While holding those offices, he was drawn into the 1957 controversy over the integration of Little Rock Central High School.

Hays attended the University of Arkansas from 1915 until graduation in 1919, despite an absence of several months to serve stateside in World War I. He earned his LL.B. degree from George Washington University School of Law in 1922, the year in which he married Marion Prather of Fort Smith, passed the Arkansas Bar, and began the practice of law with his father in Russellville.

From his mid-twenties Hays loved and practiced politics and eventually began referring to it as his "parish" for service to God and man. In 1922 he managed his father's unsuccessful campaign for Congress. In 1924 he managed the successful campaign of H. W. Applegate for Arkansas attorney general and was invited to move to Little Rock to serve as Applegate's assistant. Certain that he would run for office himself, Hays took every opportunity to plead cases before the Arkansas Supreme Court and to hone his oratorical skills in public Democratic rallies.

In 1928, although at the time of the primary he was not yet the thirty years of age required to serve, Hays ran for governor. He placed second in the Democratic primary, both that year and again in a second run two years later. In 1933, in what he always called "the most fraudulent election in Arkansas history," he lost a special election to fill the Fifth District's congressional seat. With a family to support—a wife, a son, and a daughter—he accepted an appointment with the National Recovery Administration; and for nine years he addressed southern economic problems with what observers described as the devotion of a Christian social worker.

In 1942, when the congressman who had beaten him in 1933 ran for the Senate, Hays finally won the Fifth District's House seat and was reelected seven times before losing in 1958. In Congress he was famous for his dedication to social reform, his engaging oratory, and his great sense of political humor. For example, he liked to tell about an Arkansas politician named Strange, who asked that on his tombstone be inscribed just these words: Here Lies an Honest Politician. When someone said people would not know who was buried there, he said, "Yes they will. When they see those words they'll say, 'That's Strange.'" His favorite committee assignment was Foreign Affairs, where he exercised great influence during the World War II and Cold War eras. Here, too, he considered his work a form of Christian ministry, part social, part missionary.

Hays was a devoted Baptist, a popular Sunday School teacher in Little Rock and in Washington churches, and a lay preacher. Despite some conservative reservations about allowing a layman (especially a politician, and a "liberal" one at that) to exercise denominational influence, Southern Baptists elevated Hays to the chairs of several of their key committees and finally in 1957 to the office of president of the Southern Baptist Convention. In 1958, having won over with warmth and humor those who had questioned his credentials, he was elected to a second term.

That year saw Hays reach both the apex and the nadir of his career. When Governor Orval Faubus was unable or unwilling to guarantee civil order during the integration of Little Rock Central High School, Hays, who represented Little Rock in Washington, felt a responsibility to mediate between state and federal authorities. His moderate actions caused many of his constituents to conclude that he was too willing to bow to the demands of the Supreme Court. After winning the Democratic nomination for reelection, he was fell victim in November to a Faubus-supported write-in campaign and was turned out of office.

From age sixty, when he left Congress, until his death in his Washington home, Hays remained an active and influential public figure. He served during the last two years of the Eisenhower administration on the executive board of the Tennessee Valley Authority; he was assistant secretary of state for congressional affairs under President John F. Kennedy; and he was special assistant to President Lyndon B. Johnson during the passage of Great Society legislation. He even returned to Arkansas in 1966, at age sixty-eight, to make one last unsuccessful run for governor. And while serving as director of the Ecumenical Institute at Wake Forest University, at age seventy-four, he ran unsuccessfully for a North Carolina congressional seat, enlivening a hopeless campaign and preparing for a Democratic victory in a Republican district in subsequent elections.

[Hays wrote four books: *A Southern Moderate Speaks* (1959), *A Hotbed of Tranquillity* (1968), *This World: A Christian's Workshop* (1968), and *Politics Is My Parish* (1981). His papers are at the University of Arkansas at Fayetteville, the Southern Baptist Sunday School Board Archives in Nashville, the John F. Kennedy Presidential Library at Harvard, and the Wake Forest University in Winston-Salem, North Carolina. Especially helpful for research are a series of interviews with Hays by Ronald

Tonks, available in typeset at the Sunday School Board Archives. James T. Baker's biography *Brooks Hays* (1989) addresses the major issues and achievements of Hays's career.]

JAMES T. BAKER

HAYS, LEE (Mar. 14, 1914–Aug. 26, 1981), songwriter, folk singer, was born in Little Rock, the son of the Reverend William Benjamin Hays and Ellen Reinardt. Lee Hays spent much of his life rebelling against his father's hardback fundamentalism. He replaced religion with an equally strict set of political principles.

Hays first gained notoriety at Commonwealth College, a radical "labor" school located in Polk County, Arkansas, near Mena. He transformed hymns and black spirituals into union organizing songs, sometimes, as one observer noted, "replacing the word 'union' for the word 'Jesus.'" The songs pleased his radical colleagues so much they raised a few dollars to send him to New York to gain a larger audience. Hays left Arkansas in 1940 with a batch of songs that lifted the hearts of sharecroppers and miners and labor organizers, songs that pushed unions on throughout the nation.

In New York Hays met another young political singer named Pete Seeger, who became his lifelong friend and collaborator. Together they pursued the dream of using folk music—the traditional melodies of the rural working class—to achieve their political goals. This dream remained the bedrock principle of Hays's life for the next forty years.

Along with Seeger, Millard Lampell, and Woody Guthrie, Hays was a charter member of the Almanac Singers, who lived in a commune, first used the word "hootenanny," and made wonderful music together. Hays, a burly man with a thick shock of sandy hair, provided the wonderful, rolling, church-house bass voice for the group as they traveled across the country in 1940 and 1941. They sang in front of college groups, union rallies, and picket lines, improvising lyrics to fit the occasion. It was the first income Hays had ever made from singing.

World War II broke up the Almanac Singers, as Pete Seeger joined the military (Hays suffered from diabetes which exempted him from service). After the war Seeger and Hays tried to revive the group, but failed. In 1948 Ronnie Gilbert, Fred Hellerman, and Lee Hays joined Seeger in creating the "Weavers." They made their debut in New York's Village Vanguard and became a legendary group in folk-music history. The Weavers brought folk-music to a mass audience for the first time. They achieved a national reputation in 1950 with the highly successful song "Goodnight Irene." The Weavers' hits continued with "On Top of Old Smokey," "So Long, It's Been Good to Know Ya," and "Kisses Sweeter Than Wine." Their popularity soared as they appeared in nightclubs, concert halls, on radio and television, and on college campuses. There were moments of brilliance. Hays and Seeger wrote "If I Had a Hammer" by passing a notepad between them at a political meeting.

The Weavers did not hide their social commitment. Ronnie Gilbert said they stressed "songs of hope, . . . hoping it would make a difference." The poet Carl Sandburg noted, "When I hear America singing, the Weavers are there." The Weavers sang about civil rights, equality, and peace. The Weavers' fans knew deep down that the Weavers meant what they sang about, whether the music was anti-fascist, political, pro-labor, or protest songs.

"Songs are dangerous," commented Hays. The Weavers' successes came during the McCarthy Era, and they were Red-baited nearly out of existence. Anti-leftist sentiment caught up with the Weavers before the fifties were very old. The United States House of Representative's Committee on Un-American Activities became a familiar sight on television (along with Senator Joseph McCarthy's Senate hearings), as they searched for "communist subversions" in every facet of American life. Both Hays and Seeger were called to testify before the committee, and Hays later remarked, "It was a frightening experience. Pete actually got handcuffs clamped on him and got hauled off for a few hours."

The Weavers were blacklisted and were put under surveillance. They were picketed, canceled, barred, and black-balled. The Weavers disbanded in 1952, reunited in 1955 at a sold-out performance in Carnegie Hall, and had a farewell concert in December 1963, at Chicago's Orchestra Hall.

In his last years Hays wrote stories for magazines as his health declined, losing both legs to his diabetes. In November 1980 a final concert was held at Carnegie Hall. What a time it was! Although Hays was almost unrecognizable in a wheelchair, the Weavers' magic filled the hall. Nine months later Hays died of a heart attack at his home in Tarrytown, New York. He was survived by his brother Ruben.

Following Hays's wishes, his friends gathered at his home and mixed his ashes into his compost pile. Some of Lee's friends and neighbors then took scoops of the compost to add to their own piles, hoping thus to have him with them forever.

[See Kristin Baffelarr and Donald Milton, *Folk Music: More Than a Song* (1986); John S. Wilson, "Weavers Reunited after Twenty-two Years," the *New York Times* Biographical Service (Nov. 1980); Doris Willens, *Lonesome Traveller: A Biography of Lee Hays* (1988); "The Weavers: Wasn't That a Time," MGM/UA Home Video (1981); and Harold Coogan, "The Ballad of Lee Hays," *Arkansas Times* (July 1988): 40–44. This entry is also based on a taped interview with Eli Jaffe (Dec. 24, 1987).]

HAROLD COOGAN

HEISKELL, JOHN NETHERLAND (Nov. 2, 1872–Dec. 28, 1972), editor of the *Arkansas Gazette*, was born at Rogersville, Tennessee, the son of Carrick White Heiskell, a judge, and Eliza Ayre Netherland. J. N. Heiskell attended schools at Memphis, where his parents moved shortly after the Civil War. A bookish youth who briefly published a neighborhood newspaper, he graduated from the University of Tennessee at Knoxville at the head of his class. His career included jobs with Knoxville and Memphis newspapers and with the Associated Press.

On June 17, 1902, Heiskell, his younger brother Fred Heiskell, and their parents bought control of the *Arkansas Gazette*. J. N. Heiskell became editor, with responsibility for the editorial page; his brother became managing editor. The paper was struggling, but under the Heiskell brothers circulation nearly doubled in four years. They made it a seven-day-a-week publication in 1906, and modernized the newspaper and its plant.

Heiskell kept the *Gazette* neutral in Democratic primaries and faithfully supported Democratic nominees against all others.

He never went looking for fights; however, beginning in 1903, he found himself in one with Governor Jeff Davis. It began after Davis branded the newspaper "a Republican sheet" and implied that it took money from politicians. In a series of editorials Heiskell commented critically on Davis's misrepresentations, political tactics, and campaign antics. On April 1, 1906, Heiskell published seven and a half columns analyzing Davis's demagogic style, an essay still considered one of the better contemporary commentaries on Davis. "He tells one side of a matter and counts on the public not

knowing the other side. And the public seldom fails him," Heiskell observed. He noted that one of Davis's opponents had complained he was making a circus of their political race. "But everybody likes to go to a circus," Heiskell wrote, suggesting why Davis's foes were no match for him.

In 1913 Heiskell was appointed by Governor George W. Donaghey to the United States Senate where he served for twenty-two days, fulfilling the unexpired term of his old nemesis Jeff Davis.

In 1907 he participated in an effort to build the city's first public library and served on the library board from 1910 until his death. Considered "the father of city planning" in Little Rock, he joined the city's first planning commission in 1928.

Though pro-business, Heiskell saw the need for fundamental changes in Arkansas's agriculturally based economy, including less dependence on the "tyrant" crop, cotton. In 1935 he testified against a proposed state law, aimed at farm labor organizers, that established a crime of sedition. He saw plantation owners not as oppressive landlords but as victims in common with their tenants and sharecroppers due to the problems inherent in cotton farming.

Heiskell supported the government's decision to enter World War I, opposed pacifist activities, and condemned draft resistors, but also opposed a decision by the Little Rock School Board to drop German from its curriculum.

He favored immigration curbs so that newly arrived foreigners could be assimilated. He defended conventional morality and supported prohibition, but split with religious fundamentalists by opposing a law that forbade the teaching of evolution.

Under Heiskell the *Gazette* editorial page steadfastly supported states rights, the poll tax, and measures to bolster racial segregation under the "separate but equal" doctrine. He was paternalistic toward blacks, urging them to trust in white leaders to further their interests. He campaigned editorially against lynching.

A reserved, sometimes shy, and unfailingly polite man, Heiskell was nonconfrontational and generally left the unpleasant tasks of newspapering to subeditors. His editorials avoided personal attacks and focused on issues. He was quick to defend the state against critics.

On June 28, 1910, Heiskell married Wilhelmina Mann, daughter of a prominent architect. From the marriage came two daughters, Elizabeth and Louise, and two sons, John N. Jr., who died young, and Carrick, who was groomed for leadership of the *Gazette*. However, Carrick Heiskell was killed November 29, 1943, while flying for the army.

At age seventy-one, a distraught Heiskell began a search for "a 'big' man, or a man who could become 'big,'" to assist him. He chose Harry S. Ashmore, who joined the newspaper in August 1947 as editor of the editorial page. The possibility of maintaining family control of the *Gazette* had arisen in 1943 when Heiskell's daughter Louise was married to Hugh B. Patterson Jr., who became national advertising manager.

With Heiskell's approval, Ashmore and Patterson expanded their responsibilities. Ashmore was appointed executive editor and Patterson publisher. Heiskell, still nominally editor, continued writing some editorials, including the short, witty "paragraphs" for which he was renowned, but left most decisions to the two younger men.

However, when Governor Orval E. Faubus called out the National Guard to block court ordered integration of Little Rock Central High School in 1957, it was left to Heiskell to give the final approval of an editorial stand calling for law and order and obedience to the federal courts. In so doing he nevertheless insisted the *Gazette* was not advocating integration, and continued to believe a gradualist approach by the courts would have been best in dismantling segregated schools.

A consequence of Heiskell's decision was a boycott inspired by segregationists and a loss of 17,000 subscribers as circulation dropped from 100,000 to 83,000. Some small advertisers withheld their business but major advertisers did not, and the lost circulation was subsequently regained. The *Gazette*'s financial loss was estimated at $2 million.

Among honors Heiskell received for his stand were an award for "singular journalistic performance in the public interest" from Columbia University, the Elijah Parish Lovejoy Award from Colby College, and the John Peter Zenger Freedom of the Press Award from the University of Arizona. The *Gazette* won two Pulitzer Prizes in 1958.

In November 1972 Heiskell observed his one hundredth birthday. On December 28, after asking that the *Gazette* be read to him, he died of congestive heart failure. He had served as editor of the *Arkansas Gazette* for seventy years.

[Heiskell's personal papers are maintained by the Archives and Special Collections, University of Arkansas Libraries, Little Rock. No biography of Heiskell exists. Useful articles are Harry S. Ashmore, "J. N. Heiskell," *American Library Association Bulletin* 51 (1957): 691–92, and "Mr. J. N. at 91," *American Society of Newspaper Editors Bulletin* 470 (1963): 13–15; and Wesley Pruden, "Mr. J. N. and a Legend at the *Gazette*," *National Observer*, Sept. 28, 1964. See also a special section on Heiskell's one hundredth birthday, Nov. 2, 1972, published by the *Arkansas Gazette*. James Street gives a colorful impression of Heiskell in *James Street's South* (1955).

Two unpublished works cover parts of Heiskell's career: John A. Thompson, "Gentlemen Editor: Mr. Heiskell of the *Gazette*, the Early Years: 1902–1922," M.A. thesis, University of Arkansas, Little Rock, 1983; and William K. Rutherford, "*Arkansas Gazette* Editor J. N. Heiskell: Heart and Mind," M.A. thesis, University of Arkansas, Little Rock, 1987.

For Heiskell's journalistic philosophy, see the *Gazette*, June 28, 1952. He published no books and only a few articles, two of which illustrate his style: "Bringing Up Father Mississippi," *Liberty* 5 (1928), and "Apes and Atheism in Arkansas: Another State Outlaws Evolution," *Liberty* 6 (1929).

His editorials in the *Gazette* were not signed. The period during which he can be considered to have set daily editorial policy seems to begin with an introductory editorial on July 1, 1902, and extends to the coming of Harry S. Ashmore in August of 1947. However, Heiskell continued to have some influence on editorial policy until his death.

His obituary appeared in the *Gazette* and the *New York Times*, Dec. 29, 1972. The *Gazette* also published an obituary editorial that day.]

JOHN A. THOMPSON

HILL, ROBERT LEE (June 8, 1892–?), sharecropper, founder of a farmers' and laborers' union in eastern Arkansas, was born in Dermott, Chicot County, Arkansas. From the fall of 1919 through the fall of 1920, Robert L. Hill was public enemy number one in the minds of many white Arkansans because of his leadership of the Progressive Farmers and Household Union, a black labor union formed to combat racism and economic injustice in the Delta. Upon learning of Hill's efforts to confront their power, Phillips County planters and mill owners reacted violently, triggering the events that came to be known across the nation as the Elaine Race Riot.

Since Arkansas sharecroppers of the period moved frequently and public records on rural African Americans were not well maintained, Hill's early years remain shrouded in mystery. Although Hill did read and write, his handwriting and grammar suggest a limited formal education. He did complete a detective training correspondence course offered by a St. Louis–based company, after which he referred to himself as "Robert L. Hill, U.S. Detective."

By 1918 he had moved just twenty miles from his birthplace to Winchester, Drew County. He was married with two children and worked as a sharecropper for the Valley Planting Company. While living in Winchester, he organized a group of men to form an association that borrowed goals and approaches from the growing national trade union movement, black fraternal organizations, and Booker T. Washington's National Negro Business League. The early plans of Hill's Progressive Farmers and Household Union included seeking legal assistance to secure fair crop settlements and purchasing land to build an office and establish union-owned farms.

During the summer of 1919, Hill persuaded hundreds of African-American farmers and sawmill workers to join his campaign. Black veterans, empowered by their participation in the Great War and embittered by their mistreatment at the hands of their employers, particularly resonated to the union message. By the end of the summer, Hill had organized local chapters in Ratio, Hoop Spur, Elaine, Old Town, Countiss, Ferguson, and Mellwood.

In September sharecroppers from the Ratio and Hoop Spur chapters decided to hire a lawyer to obtain fair settlements from area plantation owners. Hearing of the plans through black informants, Phillips County whites moved to counter the union. On the night of September 30, outside a church near Elaine where the Hoop Spur local was meeting, gunfire broke out between union sentries and a small group of law officers. While it is not clear who fired first, the shootout served as the pretext local whites needed to crush the growing union. Over the next three days, Phillips County whites, led by the Helena American Legion and assisted by six hundred federal troops and posses from Mississippi and Tennessee, murdered between twenty-five and one hundred African Americans. Three hundred more African Americans throughout the Delta were arrested on suspicion of involvement with the union. Four white posse members and a United States soldier were killed during the melee.

In nearby Ratio on the morning of October 1, Hill narrowly escaped arrest when a white mob broke up a meeting he had arranged between sharecroppers and an attorney's representative. Hill fled to Kansas and then moved around several midwestern states over the next several weeks. As Phillips County officials began convicting union members for rioting and murder, public pressure mounted to find Hill, who was believed to be the mastermind behind an alleged plot to murder plantation owners.

On January 20, 1920, he was arrested in Kansas by local authorities after Arkansas officials intercepted a letter home to his wife arranging a meeting in Kansas City. Arkansas authorities charged Hill with murder as an accessory to the fact and demanded his extradition. To ensure that Hill would be returned to Arkansas to face charges, federal authorities in Little Rock indicted him for inciting a riot and impersonating a federal officer. But intense lobbying from the local National Association for the Advancement of Colored People convinced Kansas governor Henry J. Allen to refuse extradition on the grounds that Hill's safety and a fair trial could not be guaranteed in Arkansas. The Justice Department dropped the federal charges following a similar NAACP campaign, and Hill was freed on October 11, 1920.

According to both his defenders and his enemies, Hill was a shrewd organizer who adeptly fused religious imagery, music, and patriotic appeals to recruit members into his union. Despite claims that Hill used the union for his own economic benefit there is no evidence that he was motivated by anything other than a desire to "advance the interests of the Negro, morally and intellectually, and to make him a better citizen and a better farmer," as the Progressive Farmers and Household Union constitution stated. In a letter to the union's attorney Hill also denied the allegations that he encouraged members to kill white planters. "It seems it would be awful foolish for me to go to Phillips County only to plan killing whites of that county and there was local Unions in about 25 or 30 Counties."

Much of what happened to Hill after the Phillips County events is unknown. In June 1921, after sustaining an injury in a packing plant in Topeka, Hill wrote to NAACP secretary James Weldon Johnson offering to work for the association in appreciation of their efforts on his behalf. Johnson recommended to Hill that he might best support the work of the NAACP by joining the local Topeka branch, but nothing further is known.

[The "Articles of Incorporation of the Farmers and Laborers Household Union of America" (Aug. 7, 1919) are in the bar docket book, Drew County, Arkansas. See Richard C. Cortner, *A Mob Intent on Death: The NAACP and the Arkansas Riot Cases* (1988); Arthur L. Waskow, *From Race Riot to Sit-in, 1919 and the 1960's* (1966); B. Boren McCool, *Union, Reaction, and Riot: A Biography of a Rural Race Riot* (1970); and Bessie Ferguson, "The Elaine Race Riot," M.A. thesis, George Peabody College for Teachers, Nashville, Tennessee, 1927.]

KERRY TAYLOR

HINDMAN, THOMAS CARMICHAEL (Jan. 28, 1828–Sept. 28, 1868), lawyer, soldier, was born in Knoxville, Tennessee, to Thomas Hindman, a planter and federal agent for Indian affairs, and Sallie Holt. In 1841 the family moved to a plantation near Ripley, Mississippi. Hindman received the educational advantages of his parents' planter-officeholding class, including high school at the Classical and Commercial High School at Lawrenceville, New Jersey.

In 1845 he enlisted in the Second Mississippi Volunteer Infantry for service in the Mexican War. He was brevetted lieutenant for bravery in battle. When he returned to Mississippi, he was admitted to the bar, practiced law in Ripley, and became active in Democratic Party politics.

In 1856 he moved to Helena, Arkansas, and opened a law office. He was immediately embroiled in local politics and, recognized as a superb stump speaker, he campaigned for Democratic candidates in the 1856 election. In 1857 he married Mary Watkins Biscoe, daughter of Henry L. Biscoe, a wealthy planter and land speculator with political connections. In 1858 Hindman was elected to Congress where he championed states' rights and came to believe that the only solution to the North's attack upon southern slave property was disunion.

At home Hindman participated in a growing political revolution against the domination of state politics by the Johnson-Conway-Sevier clan, known as the "Family," whose control over political offices may have thwarted his own ambitions. His rebellion may also have been prompted by the growing interest on the part of Governor Elisha N. Conway in settling the state bank question. This potentially threatened the assets of those indebted to the bank, a group that included Hindman's father-in-law. In the 1860 gubernatorial campaign Hindman supported the successful candidacy of Henry M. Rector, who avoided the bank issue.

Local issues were supplanted quickly by national concerns in 1860 when the Republican candidate, Abraham Lincoln, won the presidential race. In December South Carolina responded with secession. Long an advocate of disunion, Hindman joined Senator Robert Ward Johnson in urging Arkansans to join South Carolina. The attack upon Fort Sumter and Lincoln's call for troops to suppress rebellion secured Arkansas's secession on May 6, 1861.

Hindman resigned from Congress and turned his attention to efforts to raise a regiment of infantry. This unit was enrolled in the Confederate army as the Second Arkansas Infantry, and Hindman was named its colonel. In September 1861 he was promoted to brigadier general and placed in command of a brigade in the corps of William J. Hardee. At Shiloh on April 6–7, 1862, he showed vigorous leadership and was promoted to major general on April 14.

In May 1862 Hindman was named to command the newly established Trans-Mississippi Department. He arrived to find Arkansas on the verge of falling to a Federal invasion force under General Samuel R. Curtis. Hindman took draconian measures, pushing his authority beyond its constitutional limits, in his efforts at stopping Curtis. His effort, plus low water on the White River, turned Curtis from Little Rock, but Hindman's methods produced such opposition that the War Department at Richmond replaced him with General Theophilus H. Holmes (who ultimately approved much of what Hindman had done).

Hindman was left in command of the district of Arkansas and the army in the field. In the autumn of 1862 he led that army into northwestern Arkansas to drive out federal forces that had moved into the region. At the battle of Prairie Grove on December 7, 1862, he was able to secure a tactical draw with his opponent, but strategically the battle was a defeat and he was forced to pull his army back to the Arkansas River. On the retreat to Fort Smith the units, poorly fed and clothed, fell apart and pursuing federals were able to push the remnants of Hindman's troops back toward Little Rock.

After the failed campaign in northwestern Arkansas, Hindman asked to be reassigned to the Army of Tennessee. Here his career quickly came under a cloud when he became associated with the clique of General

William J. Hardee, his old commander, which was antagonistic toward General Braxton Bragg, the army's commander. Hindman continued to demonstrate his bravery and leadership. He was seriously wounded at Chickamauga in September 1863, but he rejoined his brigade in time for the Battle of Chattanooga on November 24–25, 1863. Through the spring of 1864 he continued to serve in the Army of the Tennessee in the Atlanta Campaign. At Kennesaw Mountain on June 27, 1864, he was partially blinded. He never returned to his command.

At the war's end Hindman fled to Mexico, where he tried to grow coffee, but he had little success. In 1867, prompted by his wife, he returned to Helena, where he was an opponent to the Republican regime. He was killed by an unknown assailant who shot him through the window of his home. No one was able to determine the cause for the attack, but politics, settlement of a personal grudge, or domestic problems were considered possible explanations. He was buried at Maple Hill Cemetery.

[Two good biographies offer insights into Hindman's life: Diane Nea, *Lion of the South: General Thomas C. Hindman* (1993), and Bobby L. Roberts, "Thomas C. Hindman, Jr.: Secessionist and Confederate General," M.A. thesis, University of Arkansas, 1972.]

CARL H. MONEYHON

HOLMES, THEOPHILUS HUNTER (Nov. 13, 1804–June 21, 1880), lieutenant general in the Confederate army, commander of the Trans-Mississippi Department, and commander of the District of Arkansas, was born into a rich North Carolina family in 1804. He graduated from West Point forty-fourth out of a class of forty-six in 1829. Assigned to the infantry, he proved a better soldier than student. He earned a brevet for bravery during the Mexican War. During the late 1850s he was stationed in New York City as the director of national recruiting for the United States Army.

In 1841 he and Laura Wetmore married. They had four sons and two daughters. Laura died in 1859.

When North Carolina seceded from the Union in 1861, Holmes resigned his commission and took up the colors for his native state. Initially he was a colonel in the North Carolina state army, but in June 1861 President Jefferson Davis appointed him to the Confederate States Army as a brigadier general. Most of Holmes's first year was spent in the Army of Northern

Virginia, where he first commanded a brigade, then a division. He also served as commander of the Department of North Carolina where he reorganized defeated rebel forces and halted a Union advance in eastern North Carolina.

In August 1862 Holmes was sent to Arkansas where he took command of the newly established Department of the Trans-Mississippi. He established his headquarters in Little Rock and immediately began confronting the problems facing his command. Among other things, the troops had not been paid for ten months, and the Confederate government owed the army's civilian suppliers in the region about thirteen million dollars. Holmes was also confronted with shortages of medicine, weapons, and ammunition. Over a fourth of Holmes's troops did not possess guns, and many were armed with civilian shotguns. Virtually all of Holmes's troops, as well as their commanders, were "green." Finally, the Confederate high command at Richmond had not created a strategy for the Trans-Mississippi Department.

Holmes took stock of the situation and began trying to correct it. He saw to the construction of facilities to manufacture arms and ammunition for his troops. He persuaded Richmond to redeploy a veteran infantry brigade from Mississippi to Arkansas and to send three experienced combat leaders: Brigadier Generals Thomas J. Churchill and James M. Hawes and Major General John G. Walker.

Holmes has been faulted for not having a strategy and for scattering his troops around his command without rhyme or reason. However, a strategy can be inferred from the pattern of his deployments and his actions as departmental commander.

Holmes concentrated the majority of his troops in Arkansas, with headquarters in Little Rock. He undertook to defend the rich agricultural lands of eastern Arkansas that provided much of the food for the army and the civilian population. He stationed half of his troops in eastern Arkansas mainly between the White River and Little Rock, while the other half was placed in the Fort Smith area. The eastern force remained on the defensive while the western force undertook limited offensive operations with a view toward distracting Union attention away from eastern Arkansas.

This strategy did not work, mainly because of Holmes's problems with Major General Thomas C. Hindman. In September 1862 Hindman initiated an offensive action in northwestern Arkansas and southwestern Missouri. Holmes agreed with Hindman's plan, but he halted operations because he believed that Hindman was opening the campaign prematurely. One month later Hindman reignited combat operations in his area, intending to attack federal troops at Springfield, Missouri. Holmes disapproved and ordered Hindman to call off the operation. Hindman ignored Holmes's orders, and his offensive culminated in defeat at Prairie Grove, Arkansas. Shortly thereafter, the federals captured the garrison at Arkansas Post.

These setbacks proved Holmes's undoing. In March 1863 he was demoted to the command of the District of Arkansas. Lieutenant General Edmund Kirby Smith gained the departmental command, and soon ordered the transfer of many of Holmes's troops to Louisiana. This left Holmes with a depleted force to defend Arkansas while he was also under orders to try to help the beleagured Confederate garrison at Vicksburg. Toward this end, on July 4, 1863, he launched an attack upon the federal garrison at Helena, which was repulsed.

Soon after, he came down with a serious illness and was temporarily replaced. During this period the federals captured Little Rock. In late fall 1863 he resumed command, but recurrent health problems caused him to relinquish command in Febrary 1864. Later that year he was appointed to the command of the North Carolina Reserves, which he held to the end of the war. Following the South's defeat, he retired to his farm in North Carolina where he died at the age of seventy-six.

[Sources include the U.S. War Department, *The War of Rebellion: A Compilation of the Official Records of the Union and Confederate Armies* (1880–1901). See Anne J. Bailey, "The Abandoned Western Theater: Confederate National Policy toward the Trans-Mississippi Region," *Journal of Confederate History* 5 (1990): 35–54; Albert Castel, "Theophilus Holmes—Pallbearer of the Confederacy," *Civil War Times Illustrated*, July 1977; Mark Mayo Boatner III, *The Civil War Dictionary* (1966); and Daniel O'Flaherty, *General Jo Shelby: Undefeated Rebel* (1954).]

CHARLES J. RECTOR

HOWELL, CHARLES MILTON (June 2, 1892–Sept. 18, 1971), farmer, was born in the Holla Bend Bottoms of Pope County to Jesse R. Howell and Minnie Hamilton. Land along the Arkansas River near Norristown, including much of Holla Bend and New Hope bottoms, had been in the family since 1840. By the time Charles Milton was born, it had been cleared and was producing abundant crops, especially cotton.

When Charles was six years old he witnessed the great flood of 1898. The following year, the family moved to Russellville, a small farm town with good schools. When Charles was not in school, he rode with his father in a buggy out to the farm, where he helped chop and pick cotton.

In 1909 he enrolled in Russellville High School, which offered three years of Latin, plane and solid geometry, trigonometry, German, two years of algebra, three years of history, and four of English. Charley, as he was called, was "steady at his work," according to the school yearbook, and was the "best athlete and biggest flirt."

Howell and Lexie Henry married on March 24, 1914. Shortly after their marriage, Howell's father gave them a mule and twenty acres of bottomland at New Hope and a house on a rise overlooking their land. Three of their children reached maturity: Milton, R. D., and Charles F.

Along with other farmers, Howell prospered during World War I, when prices and production soared. Cotton reached thirty-five cents per pound in 1918 and by 1919 reached forty cents. When prices dropped after the war, Howell expanded ginning and cottonseed oil operations.

Many farmers did not fare as well as Howell did and were forced to abandon their holdings. Five of these displaced families moved to Howell's New Hope farm. Howell provided a four-room cottage for each family, with vegetable gardens, clothes lines, and chickens.

In 1922 Charles and Lexie built a Craftsman style house on a lot adjoining his father's house in town. Now Charles rode to work in a horse-drawn buggy as his father had done. Fortunately, he had a dependable horse that delivered him to his door if he fell asleep coming home.

The stock market crashed in October of 1929. Cotton fell to five cents. Howell responded to the Great Depression energetically. He replaced profits from farm products by increasing cotton ginning and vigorously marketing its by-product, oil. He owned outright, or in partnership, three gins, one at New Hope, one at Cotton Town in northern Yell County, and one at Fowler in Carden Bottoms between the river and Petit Jean Mountain. To have time for the ginning enterprise he relegated the cultivation and harvest of crops to sharecroppers or farm hands.

The economic downswing caused some farmers in the river bottoms to retrench or sell out; Howell, however, added to his holdings. He purchased land and reclaimed land on sandbars deposited by the flood of 1898. In 1931 he inherited from his father two hundred and forty acres of bottomland and considerable property in Russellville.

He further improved his situation by cooperating with federal New Deal programs designed to help farmers. He accepted subsidies from the Agricultural Adjustment Administration for reducing crops and for planting soybeans to improve animal nutrition and to put nitrogen back into the soil.

In the fall of 1937 Howell's New Hope gin burned to the ground. The *Russellville Courier Democrat* reported, "All five buildings of the New Hope plant, the gin, seed house, cotton house and store building were destroyed." Howell estimated the loss at fifteen thousand dollars. He said he could build a modern gin for eighteen thousand dollars and have it ready by the following season.

The new gin created wide interest since it was the first electric gin in Pope County, perhaps in the state. On opening day, photographers, merchants, and farmers gathered, along with Harvey Couch, president of the Arkansas Power and Light Company. As a gesture of appreciation for Howell's cooperation, Couch extended electric lines to Howell's house and to his tenants' cottages.

Beginning with the depression, Howell witnessed many changes in farming. Cotton production declined as profits fell, and machines began to replace laborers. Drought years and floods increased, putting more stress on the farmer. But Howell, as usual, was prepared to meet the new challenges.

For one thing, Howell owned enough acreage to justify purchasing machines. And he was a natural machinist, able to invent or repair them. For example, he once welded together a couple of two-row planters to form the first four-row planter in the Arkansas River Valley. Equally important to his survival as a farmer, he knew and believed in success. As cotton gradually lost its place in Pope County, he adapted to growing beans and grain.

He served on the school board and was president of the Western Arkansas Ginners' Association and the Farm Bureau. His eight years as mayor of Russellville saw the constructions of an auditorium, a city hall, and a gymnasium.

Charles Howell continued to operate the farm with his son Milton until his death in Russellville. He had lived by his belief that good land is the measure of all things.

[Sources include privately held family papers. This account relies on the author's interviews with Charles M. Howell, Milton Howell, and R. D. Howell between June 11, 1995, and Nov. 3, 1995; and with Rhea Putman, U.S. Army Corps of Engineers, Oct. 10, 1995. See also the *Russellville Daily Courier Democrat*, 1937–44; and the Russellville High School yearbook, *Crisis*, 1911, 1912 and 1913. Other useful sources are Gerald T. Hanson and Carl H. Moneyhon, *Historical Atlas of Arkansas* (1989); and Charles S. Bolton and others, *Documentary History of Arkansas* (1989).]

LOIS LAWSON MORRIS

HUDGINS, MARY DENGLER (Nov. 24, 1901– Oct. 18, 1987), a native of Hot Springs, was the only child of Ida Dengler and Jackson Wharton Hudgins. After completing high school at Hot Springs, she enrolled at the University of Arkansas, where in 1924 she received a B.A. in English. Her interest in writing was developed during those formative years, in part as a reporter for the student newspaper, the *Arkansas Traveler*.

After graduation she taught English and social studies at Waldo, Arkansas, high school from 1924 to 1925. Then, she resumed her formal education at Rice School of the Spoken Word, in Massachusetts. Her stay there lasted less than a year. The next fourteen years were spent researching, free-lance writing, and collecting Arkansiana. And while Arkansas music and composers were keen research interests, they were by no means her sole areas of interest. The history of the state of Arkansas, as well as that of Hot Springs—for which there was no greater authority at one time—intrigued her. This background served her well when she worked for Bernie Babcock on the Arkansas volume of the American Guide Series, a project of the federal Works Progress Administration during the Great Depression. As a free-lance writer she submitted articles, reviews, or verses to newspapers, historical journals, popular magazines, greeting card publishers, and radio stations. The *Arkansas Historical Quarterly* and the Garland County Historical *Record* were among her favorite publishers.

Her interest in books was such that she enrolled at the University of Chicago to pursue courses in library science, a field that she also studied at the University of Wisconsin in 1941 and at Emory University in 1952. She was librarian at Hot Springs Library from 1939 to 1943, and medical and post librarian at the United States Army and Navy Hospital at Hot Springs from 1943 to 1959. For several years she had a weekly radio program on KTSS. Her programs were usually devoted to discussions about books or historical vignettes. Regardless of the topic, it provided her with another outlet for expounding on her interests while, at the same time, placing her listeners on the alert as "lookouts" for potential books and historical papers.

Her passion for collecting books, manuscripts, photographs and postcards, scrapbooks, pamphlets, sheet music, and other materials pertaining to the history of Arkansas encompassed the better part of fifty years. Practically every room in her house at 1030 Park Avenue held something that she had collected. Her collection of books numbered over three thousand volumes. More than a few were autographed and inscribed by the author, frequently thanking her for all of the help that she had provided during the author's research. Those books that couldn't fit into the handsome, custom-made bookcases in her living room, or on other smaller bookcases in the house, were carefully indentified and stored in her attic.

Promoting interest in the state's history was never far from her mind. To encourage students at the University of Arkansas, Fayetteville, to pursue historical research on Arkansas subjects, Hudgins created an endowment through the Department of History. She established another endowment shared by the Department of Music and the Special Collections Division of the University Libraries, which encourages the performance and preservation of Arkansas music. The endowment also supported the publication of *A Directory of 132 Arkansas Composers*.

She once wrote: "When I'm being pompous I call myself an Arkansas musicologist. My collection valuable? Not in terms of money. When I'm gone, or too tired to research and write, it will go to some institution in the state. Meanwhile, I have fun researching, collecting and writing. Financially rewarding? Not especially. I give away too many of my features. But in the heady joy my hobby brings, I'm a millionare."

Miss Hudgins—which is how most people addressed her—was a longtime member of the Arkansas Historical Association and served on its board for nineteen years. In 1980 the association presented her with its highest form of compliment, the Distinguished Service Award. She is included in numerous editions of *Who's Who of American Women* and *Who's Who in the South and Southwest*.

[Hudgins donated most of her collection to the University of Arkansas, Fayetteville, where it is available for use in the Special Collections Division. And her handsome maple bookcases now grace the division's reading room.]

MICHAEL J. DABRISHUS

HUNT, SILAS HERBERT

HUNT, SILAS HERBERT (Mar. 1, 1922–Apr. 1948), pioneer in the integration of the University of Arkansas, was born in Ashdown, Arkansas, and lived briefly in Oklahoma with his parents, who were quite poor, before returning to Texarkana, Arkansas. He attended Texarkana's Washington High School, where he was a member of the debate team and student council president before graduating in 1941 as class salutatorian. He attended the Agricultural, Mechanical and Normal College at Pine Bluff, one of Arkansas's black colleges. During his first year, he worked at a number of jobs, including work on the construction of the Pine Bluff Arsenal. Still, Hunt excelled in his classes. His exceptional academic abilities earned him financial aid for the rest of his undergraduate career.

His education was interrupted when he was drafted into the army. He served with the construction engineers in the European theater for twenty-three months before being seriously wounded at the Battle of the Bulge (December 1944–January 1945). After recovering from his injuries, he returned to AM & N, graduating in 1947. After graduation, he was employed at the college, working in the dean's office while he applied to various law schools throughout the country. He was accepted at the University of Indiana School of Law and was prepared to attend there until he became interested in the attempt of Ada Lois Sipuel, a former classmate, to gain admission to the University of Oklahoma Law School. Sipuel was waging a legal battle to overturn the university's policy of refusing to admit black students. It was standard practice, until federal courts found it illegal, for southern states to pay the tuition of African Americans at black institutions like Howard University rather than admit them to their own state universities. No black students were allowed to attend any of the traditionally white southern universities at this time. At the urging of his friend Wiley Branton and others, Hunt consulted Lawrence Davis, president of AM & N College, and after much deliberation, decided to apply to the University of Arkansas Law School.

University of Arkansas officials, observing the legal battles at other southern universities, formulated a policy to avoid legal battles and bad publicity. In January 1948 they announced that they would accept qualified African-American graduate students. This would make the university the first southern state university to admit black students. They fully expected Clifford Davis, a native of Arkansas who was attending Howard University Law School, to be the first African American to attend the university since Reconstruction. He had been corresponding with Robert A. Leflar, dean of the Law School, about admission. Davis was informed of the new policy and offered admission, but declined because of the stipulation that African-American students attend segregated classes.

On February 2, 1948, Silas H. Hunt, accompanied by his friend Wiley Branton, Pine Bluff attorney Harold Flowers, and Gelieve Grice, photographer for the AM & N College newspaper, arrived at the University of Arkansas to meet with Dean Leflar and gain admission to the Law School. After a brief perusal of Hunt's stellar academic record, Dean Leflar admitted him. He was the first black student to be admitted to a traditionally white southern university.

Hunt attended classes that spring in the basement of the Law School. These were intended to be segregated and to deal primarily with portions of the law relating to blacks, but nothing barred white students from the classes, and three to five white students usually attended. Hunt achieved straight Bs. He got along well with other students; his easygoing nature helped. Although there were the occasional racial slurs and epithets to deal with, he handled himself with dignity, and there were no major protests or incidents. There is little doubt that Hunt would have been the first black student to graduate from the university had he lived. Shortly after completing his first term, he suffered a recurrence of his old war injuries, and after a three month stay at the veterans hospital in Springfield, Missouri, he died. He blazed the trail for integrated education at southern state universities.

[Sources include the *Arkansas Traveler* 42 (Feb. 3, 1948); the *Northwest Arkansas Times,* Feb. 2–3, 1948; the *Arkansas Gazette,* Jan. 30–Feb. 3, 1948; Benin Goodwill, "Silas Hunt: The Growth of a Folk Hero" (May 20, 1957) in the Special Collections Division, University of Arkansas

Libraries, Fayetteville; Cathy C. Gottsponer, "Campus Honors First Black Student," *University Reflections* (Spring 1993): 1–3; Tammy Williams, "UA Integrated for Fifty Years," *Arkansas Traveler* 92 (Feb. 11, 1998): 1, 3.]

RICHARD BUCKELEW

HUTSON, DONALD ROY (Jan. 31, 1913–June 26, 1997), professional football player, was born in Pine Bluff, Arkansas, the son of Roy B. Hutson, a conductor on the Cotton Belt Railway, and Mabel Clark. Hutson was a "late bloomer" who did not play football until his junior and senior years in high school. Sportswriter George Heister described his actions on the field: "In spite of North Little Rock defenders clustering around Hutson, the sure-fingered lanky Pine Bluff player caught passes from every angle, once or twice he took the ball out of the hands of a defender." Hutson kicked the extra points for the team as well as playing defense.

The University of Alabama was interested in recruiting Robert Seawall, Hutson's teammate and neighbor, who informed the recruiters he would not go to Alabama unless they took Hutson, too. At Alabama Hutson made All-American his junior and senior years. He ran the 100-yard dash in 9.7 seconds, an exceptionally fast speed in those days, and was noted for his elusiveness in the open field. He was nicknamed "the Alabama Antelope."

Undefeated in 1934, Alabama played Stanford University, the West Coast champions, in the Rose Bowl on New Year's Day 1935. Hutson caught six passes for 165 yards and made two touchdowns as Alabama defeated Stanford 29 to 13. When asked about his performance, Hutson, who was known as timid and shy, said, "I just ran like the devil and Dixie Howell (the Alabama quarterback) got the ball there."

Hutson's showing in the Rose Bowl game impressed "Curly" Lambeau, coach of the Green Bay Packers. He signed Hutson for three hundred dollars per game, a top salary for the National Football League. It was paid by two checks on different banks, evidently because Lambeau did not want other players to know what he was paying Hutson.

Hutson is credited with changing the pro football game with his style of play. Because of the way he played left end, the position became known as "wide receiver."

No longer a skinny youth, Hutson retained his running speed. In his first game with the Packers he turned a quick over-the-middle pass from quarterback Arnie Herber into an 83-yard touchdown. Working with the

147

quarterback, Hutson devised pass routes with many variations, enabling the quarterback to throw to a designated place on the field; the receiver would race to be at that spot when the ball arrived. Today's receivers use many of the routes Hutson created.

Jim Benton, a 1937 University of Arkansas All-American, played against Hutson as a member of the Cleveland Browns NFL team. He said Hutson's speed was deceptive and when he caught a pass he simply outran his opponents: "He had wonderful change of pace. He'd lull guys and then turn it on. They were the first club to use timing passes, which are common now. Arnie Herber would throw the ball to a spot and Hutson would be there."

During his years at Green Bay (1935–1945) Hutson led the way to a team record of 120 wins to 29 losses, five division championships, and three national football championships. His defensive play almost matched his aggressiveness on offense. In 1940 he was the league's leading pass interceptor. His devastating blocking and bone-crushing tackling were known throughout the league. He also excelled as place kicker. When Hutson retired in 1945, he was the NFL's leading scorer with 838 points, 99 touchdowns, 7 field goals, and 172 extra points. His record for touchdowns stood for forty-four years until Steve Largent of the Seattle Seahawks broke it in 1989. Hutson led the NFL as a receiver for eight of the eleven years he played.

Hutson was inducted into the Arkansas Hall of Fame in 1960, and the Pro-Football Hall of Fame in 1963. He was selected for the NFL All-50-Year Team in 1970 and its seventy-fifth anniversary team in 1994. A half century after his retirement, Hutson still held eleven NFL records.

After his death, Green Bay Packer general manager Ron Wolf said: "He was the greatest player of this franchise. In the era he played, he was *the* dominant player in the game, not just as a receiver, but as a kicker and with his defensive ability."

Hutson and Julia Kathleen Richards married at Fayette, Alabama, December 16, 1935; they were the parents of three daughters.

Don Hutson retired from his automobile business at Racine, Wisconsin, in 1984 and moved to Rancho Mirage, California, where he died.

[Sources include the Pine Bluff City Directory for 1910, 1917–18, 1920–21, 1936; U.S. Census, Jefferson County, Jan. 29, 1920; Marriage License Records, vol. F, p. 419, Probate Clerk, Fayette County, Alabama; and the *Pine Bluff Commercial*, Sept. 24, 1943, Dec. 6, 1972, and June 28, 1997. The author also relied on a letter from Raymond Hutson, Sept. 29, 1997; and interviews with Emil Mitchell, a Hutson family friend, Sept. 5 and 6, 1997; and William T. Seawell, Oct. 29, 1997. See also Richard Whittingham, *What a Game They Played* (1987), and *National Football League: The First Fifty Years* (1969).]

JAMES W. LESLIE

HYTEN, CHARLES DEAN (Mar. 14, 1877–Sept. 6, 1944), potter and co-founder of the Niloak Pottery Company, was born in Benton, Arkansas, the third son of John Franklin Hyten and Harriet Elizabeth Brown. Charles, who from childhood was called "Bullet," followed in the family tradition of pottery making started by his father in Boonesboro, Iowa. The Hyten family moved from Iowa to Saline County, Arkansas, where John Hyten started making pottery in the late 1870s. The business produced common utilitarian wares such as crocks, jugs, and churns. Charles Hyten, together with his two brothers, took over the family business in the mid 1890s and operated it as Hyten Brothers Pottery.

He and Cora Zella Caldwell were married on February 5, 1901, in Benton, Arkansas.

Hyten assumed ownership of the stoneware business at the turn of the century and renamed it the Eagle Pottery Company. Like most other local businesses, Eagle Pottery served a local market. In 1909 he started working with a partner, Arthur Dovey, who had worked for the Ouachita Pottery Company of Hot Springs from about 1905 to 1908. They began experimenting with Dovey's concept, which he had used at Ouachita Pottery, of using swirled, colored clays thrown into art pottery wares.

The manufacture of American art pottery gained prominence during the late 1890s and continued to prosper with great art pottery manufacturers in the Midwest, particularly in Ohio, and on the Eastern seaboard. An extension of the American Arts and Crafts Movement, art pottery production lasted for over thirty years.

Niloak Pottery was a successful manipulation of artificially colored clays hand-thrown to produce a swirling effect. It derived its name from kaolin, a type of fine clay, spelled backward. This art pottery, introduced in March 1910, was marketed nationally as

"Missionware." Unlike most other art pottery, whose aesthetic design derived from either applied decorations or the application of glazes, Niloak's art pottery achieved aesthetic value from the swirling patterns of these clays themselves.

The company utilized local capital and achieved some immediate success throughout the 1910s. Hyten gained complete control of the company in 1918 and steered it through a period of prosperity and recognition. Connecting with various booster organizations in the early 1920s, Niloak achieved a level of renown when Arkansas was noted as the "Home of Niloak Pottery." Sales increased further as Niloak standardized "Missionware" and found outlets in established department stores across the country. Hyten acquired a trademark for Niloak in 1925 and a patent for the technique in 1928.

Over-optimism in the mid-1920s led Hyten to borrow heavily and invest in the Niloak Pottery and Tile Company, organized in 1928, with a new sales and showroom on Old Military Avenue in Benton. However, serious financial trouble developed with the onset of the Great Depression in 1929, and Hyten had to accept financial assistance in 1934, when he neared bankruptcy.

He continued with the company as a board member and traveling salesman throughout the 1930s. The company's production changed radically during this time, as it reduced the manufacture of "Missionware" and increased production of industrial castware. These molded items were mass produced, sold to a variety of gift and florist shops, and had little aesthetic value. The company continued until 1947, when it became the Winburn Tile Company of Little Rock. Hyten sold his interest in it in 1941. He became an agent for Camark Pottery of Camden and briefly operated a retail gift store in Benton.

Involved in many civic organizations as well as businesses, Hyten served the Benton community with his participation in area Boy Scout chapters, the Presbyterian Church, and several businesses, including the Bank of Benton, of which he was a director. He lost his life at the age of sixty-seven, when he drowned in the Saline River during a church outing. He is buried in the Rosemont Cemetery, Benton, Arkansas.

[Hyten's role at Niloak Pottery and the history of the business have been confused by a lack of primary research combined with a heavy reliance on local traditions. Several uncritical articles and biographies on Hyten and the Niloak Pottery Company exist; these include the *Arkansas Democrat*, April 17, 1921, and the *Arkansas Gazette*, July 19, 1926; Dallas T. Herndon's *Centennial History Of Arkansas* (1922); and *The Saline II* (June 1987). References to Hyten appear in the *Benton Courier* from 1914 into the early 1930s. David Edwin Gifford's *Niloak: A Reference And Value Guide* (1993) offers a critical but incomplete history based on primary sources.]

DAVID EDWIN GIFFORD

JACKSON, TRAVIS CALVIN (Nov. 2, 1903–July 28, 1987), professional baseball player elected to the Hall of Fame, was born at Waldo in Columbia County, Arkansas, to William Calvin Jackson, a storekeeper, and Etta Farrar.

Jackson spent his full major-league career, from 1922 until 1936, with the New York Giants, earning widespread recognition as the National League's best shortstop of the 1920s. Late in his career he switched to third base. With a career major-league batting average of .291, including six seasons in which he batted above .300, he became an offensive as well as defensive force.

He was such a baseball prodigy he spent two summers of his early teens playing for Marvell in a fast "semi-pro" league in eastern Arkansas, where most of the players were adults and, in some cases, former pros. He was discovered there by Norman "Kid" Elberfeld, manager of the Little Rock Travelers of the Southern Association. Jackson always thought his uncle, Clyde Donavan, recommended him to Elberfeld. Donavan operated a Little Rock drugstore, and the Travelers' manager was one of his frequent customers. At any rate, the Travelers signed Jackson during the summer of 1921, several months before his eighteenth birthday.

"Because he was only seventeen, his father had to sign for him," said Jackson's daughter, Dorothy Fincher. "And because his mother was a staunch Baptist, they wouldn't go through with it unless they were sure he wouldn't have to play on Sundays. Apparently some towns had Sunday baseball then and some didn't, but Elberfeld had to come down and do some fast talking to get the signature."

Before Jackson turned nineteen, he had been purchased by the Giants, then the National League's premier franchise. He never played another game in the minors until, as manager of Jersey City in the International League in 1937–38, he put himself in the lineup a few times when he found himself short of infielders.

In 1922, his only full season with the Travelers, he made 73 errors in 147 games. Most of them were on wild throws; he had a powerful but unpredictable arm. "When I was a kid with Little Rock," Jackson said once, "it took some brave souls to sit in the stands behind first base when I was playing shortstop."

He joined the Giants, then in the process of winning four straight pennants, in time to appear in three games during September of 1922. He stuck with the team as a utility infielder in 1923 and became the regular shortstop in 1924. John J. McGraw, the Giants manager from 1902 to 1932, and considered one of the game's more exacting taskmasters, made Jackson team captain while he was still relatively young.

Jackson played in four World Series (1923, 1924, 1933, 1936) and served the Giants as a coach in 1939–40 and 1947–48 under managers Bill Terry and Mel Ott, two of his former teammates. In a 1960 interview, Jackson said he liked everyone he ever knew in baseball. Then the reporter mentioned the abrasive, aggressive Leo Durocher, who moved over from the archrival Brooklyn Dodgers to replace Ott as Giants manager during the 1948 season. "I told you wrong a few minutes ago," Jackson said. "I guess I meant I liked almost everybody. I don't like Durocher." Jackson left as a coach at the end of the year.

Jackson married Mary Jeannette Blackman on January 24, 1928, and they had two children. Waldo was always the Jacksons' permanent home, no matter where his career sent him during the summers.

He was out of baseball from 1940 to 1946, a period of time spent recovering from tuberculosis. He spent fourteen years as a manager of minor-league teams before retiring from baseball in 1960, the year he was inducted to the Arkansas Sports Hall of Fame.

In 1982, quite unexpectedly from Jackson's standpoint, he was informed of his election to the Baseball Hall of Fame at Cooperstown, New York. Symbolically he joined many old friends. Thirteen of his Giants teammates have been inducted over the years, as well as manager McGraw.

[Sources include *The Sporting News Hall of Fame Book* (1983), *The Baseball Encyclopedia,* seventh edition (1988); Frank Graham, *The New York Giants* (1952); the *Arkansas Gazette,* Jan. 18, 1960, and July 29, 1987; and an interview with Dorothy Jackson Fincher (1998).]

JIM BAILEY

JOHNSON, BENJAMIN (Jan. 22, 1784–Oct. 2, 1849), Arkansas jurist, was born in Scott County, Kentucky, to Robert and Jemima Johnson. The Johnsons were one of the most prominent families of early Kentucky. Robert Johnson was active in political and military affairs and was instrumental in the creation of several educational and religious institutions in the Bluegrass State. Jemima Johnson was the mother of eleven children and was renowned for her heroism at the siege of Bryant's Station in the state's long and bloody Indian wars.

Five of Benjamin's eight brothers served in the War of 1812, and one, Richard M. Johnson, gained fame as the man who killed the great Shawnee leader Tecumseh at the Battle of the Thames in 1813. Richard Johnson used the celebrity gained from that exploit to launch a political career which included terms in both the U.S. House of Representatives and the U.S. Senate. In 1836 he was elected vice president of the United States on a ticket with Martin Van Buren. Benjamin's younger brother Joel moved to the Arkansas delta in the early 1830s and became a prominent Chicot County planter.

Benjamin Johnson married Matilda Williams in September 1811, and the union eventually produced eight children. Johnson chose to pursue a legal career and gained admittance to the bar in the Lexington Circuit, where, one early historian noted, "his ability and popularity soon marked him for the high station of jurist." He later served as a circuit judge and a district judge in the Lexington area.

In 1821 President James Monroe appointed Johnson to be one of three judges of the Superior Court for the Arkansas Territory. He was reappointed by Presidents John Quincy Adams and Andrew Jackson and served in that capacity until 1836. His tenure on the territorial bench was the longest in Arkansas history. Until 1828 the state was divided into two circuits with one judge assigned to each and the third judge assisting in both. In 1828 a fourth judge was added, and the territory's sixteen counties were divided into four circuits. Johnson's circuit consisted of Pulaski, Conway, Crawford, and Washington Counties. Superior Court sessions were held in Little Rock, and Judge Johnson took up residence there.

He was apparently a man of some means when he arrived in the territory, and his tenure on the territorial bench seems to have done nothing to diminish his standing. In 1830 he was reputed to be the second largest slaveowner in Pulaski County with twenty-one slaves. In 1832 he purchased a large home which became a Little Rock landmark.

When Arkansas became a state in 1836, President

Jackson appointed Johnson to be the state's first federal district judge. In addition to his judicial duties, Johnson was active in Arkansas politics. His family had long been associated with the Democratic-Republican Party in Kentucky, and Johnson was a staunch Jacksonian Democrat. In Arkansas he allied himself with the Conways and the Seviers to form a Democratic political dynasty known as "the Family." This political union was solidified in 1827 when Johnson's oldest daughter Juliette married Ambrose H. Sevier, an aspiring Arkansas politician who was also related to the Conways. The Johnson-Conway-Sevier dynasty dominated Arkansas politics until the time of the Civil War.

Politics in early nineteenth-century Arkansas was a rough-and-tumble affair, and Judge Johnson's tenure was not without controversy. In 1827 his decisions in favor of the holders of some dubious Spanish land grant claims, including a number of prominent members of the Arkansas bar, were strongly criticized and tarnished the image of the territorial court. The decisions were later overturned by a higher court. In 1832 some of the Family's political opponents brought impeachment charges against Johnson. Territorial governor John Pope and a hosts of other state officials and members of the bar rushed to Johnson's defense, and the House of Representatives' Judiciary Committee exonerated him of any wrongdoing. These controversies notwithstanding, Johnson's career was a distinguished one.

In July 1849 his granddaughter, Ann Sevier, married Thomas Churchill, a Mexican War veteran and a native Kentuckian who later became Arkansas's thirteenth governor. Three months after the wedding, Benjamin Johnson died at the family home in Lexington, Kentucky. At the time of his death, Johnson could rightfully claim to have been Arkansas's greatest jurist. Albert Pike remarked, "There never lived a more honest, upright, honorable or generous man than Benjamin Johnson," and his court reporter wrote, "He died full of judicial honors, beloved by all; admired for the purity of his public life and private character, and for his devotion as a citizen; respected for unbending integrity and for a heart full of kindness to all."

Benjamin Johnson's legacy was carried on by his son, Robert Ward Johnson, who served as a United States senator and, after secession, as a senator of the Confederate States of America. Benjamin Johnson is buried in Mount Holly Cemetery in Little Rock. Johnson County, Arkansas, is named in his honor.

[Sources include John Hugh Reynolds, *Makers of Arkansas History* (1905); O. E. McKnight and Boyd W. Johnson, *The Arkansas Story* (1955); and Thomas A. DeBlack, "A Garden in the Wilderness: The Johnsons and the Making of Lakeport Plantation, 1831–1876," Ph.D. dissertation, University of Arkansas, 1995.]

THOMAS A. DEBLACK

JOHNSON, LYCURGUS LEONIDAS (Mar. 22, 1818–Aug. 1, 1876), a planter, was born the eldest of nine children to Joel Johnson and Verlinda Offutt of Scott County, Kentucky. He was descended from one of the most powerful families of early Kentucky. His paternal grandfather, Robert Johnson, was a political, educational, and religious leader. One of his uncles, Richard Mentor Johnson, served as vice president under Martin Van Buren. Another uncle, Benjamin Johnson, became a distinguished Arkansas jurist and a leading figure in the state's Democratic political dynasty known as "the Family."

Lycurgus's father, Joel, came to Chicot County in the southeasternmost reaches of the Arkansas delta in 1831 to establish a plantation called Lakeport along the banks of the Mississippi River. Within fifteen years Joel transformed Lakeport into one of the most prosperous cotton-growing operations in the delta, and he became one of the wealthiest and most influential men in the state. Like many early planters, he spent only part of the year in Arkansas, returning to his family in Kentucky for about half the year.

Sometime in the late 1830s while he was still in his teens, Lycurgus left the family home in Kentucky to join his father in Arkansas. He established his own plantation down river from Lakeport.

In January 1842 he and Lydia Taylor married. The union produced eleven children, six of whom lived to adulthood.

Following Joel's death in June 1846, a lengthy legal battle prevented the Johnson heirs from establishing a clear title to Lakeport. A favorable court decision in 1858 allowed Lycurgus to gain control of Lakeport and consolidate it into his holdings.

By 1860 Lycurgus owned more than 4,000 acres of rich delta land and 150 slaves. That same year his lands produced some 1,300 bales of cotton and 10,000 bushels of corn. The total value of his taxable property exceeded $200,000.

To crown his plantation, he constructed a two-story, seventeen-room mansion. The house, still standing in

1996 and on the National Register of Historic Homes, was built in a modified Greek Revival style. It was an imposing L-shaped structure measuring sixty-six feet long by forty-four feet wide. The front of the house had a two-story portico with a triangular pediment gable and centered rose windows. With its tapered white columns and wrought iron, lace work grill in an oak leaf and acorn design, it was a showplace of the state's "cotton aristocracy."

The Civil War caused a dramatic decline in Lycurgus's fortunes, as it did for most delta planters. Chicot County was the scene of heavy fighting and suffered great physical devastation. But Lycurgus retained control of his house and land, adjusted to the new realities of the postwar South and began to rebuild his Lakeport operation. By 1870 Johnson was again the leading cotton producer in the county.

His conduct during this difficult period demonstrated the qualities that had earned him the admiration and respect of his neighbors in the years before the war. The local agent of the Freedmen's Bureau, a man not favorably disposed to planters, remarked that Johnson "works one hundred hands and does them the fullest justice" and referred to him as a "model man of Chicot County."

In May 1874 Johnson was elected to represent Chicot County in an extraordinary session of the state legislature. Appointed to the Committee on Agriculture and the Committee on Cities and Towns, he sponsored bills to remit the penalty for the nonpayment of taxes in Chicot County and to empower aliens to acquire, hold, and devise real estate. This latter measure laid the groundwork for the importation of Italian immigrant workers into Chicot County in the 1890s.

Aside from this, he seems to have lived out the turbulent Reconstruction years in the peaceful surroundings at Lakeport. A chronicler of the county referred to him as "a good citizen and able business man" and "a gentleman of superior education ... noted for hospitality, dignity and social culture." In his fifty-eighth year he suffered from a severe gastrointestinal disorder that eventually took his life. He died in Wilmington, Delaware, where he had apparently gone for medical treatment.

[Sources include Chicot County deed records and tax records; Manuscript Census Returns; U.S. Census, 1850, 1860, 1870; and the National Register of Historic Homes. See Thomas A. DeBlack, "A Garden in the Wilderness: The Johnsons and the Making of Lakeport Plantation, 1831–1876," Ph.D. dissertation, University of Arkansas, 1995.]

THOMAS A. DEBLACK

JOHNSON, ROBERT WARD (July 22, 1814–July 26, 1879), political leader, was born in Scott County, Kentucky, to Benjamin and Matilda Williams Johnson. His family was politically powerful in Kentucky: two of his uncles won election to the U.S. House of Representatives, while another, Richard Mentor Johnson, served in Congress and became vice president of the United States.

Johnson was a member of the "Dynasty," or the "Family" which dominated Arkansas government from 1833 to 1860. His father, Benjamin, was placed on the Arkansas Territorial Superior Court in 1821; President Andrew Jackson appointed him the first federal district judge for the new state of Arkansas in 1836. Benjamin Johnson became associated politically and through marriage with the emerging Democratic leadership. One daughter married Ambrose H. Sevier, head of the state Democratic Party and an early U.S. senator. Sevier was cousin to the Conway family, whose members included two governors. The Johnson, Sevier, and Conway alliance controlled Arkansas government for nearly thirty years.

Robert W. "Bob" Johnson earned a law degree from Yale. In 1836 he married Sarah S. Smith of Louisville, Kentucky. The marriage produced six children, three of whom lived to adulthood. When Sarah died in 1862, he married her younger sister Laura; their union yielded no offspring.

Arriving in Little Rock in 1835, Johnson became county prosecuting attorney in 1840. Two years later, he was elevated to state attorney general, and then won election in 1846 as Arkansas's only member of the United States House of Representatives.

In Congress he assumed the most pro-southern, pro-disunionist positions. He opposed the Wilmot Proviso and the Compromise of 1850, voting only for that part of the compromise which supported a new Fugitive Slave Act. His Whig opposition labeled him a disunionist and used this charge against him in 1851. He tempered his association with southern radicalism enough to win reelection, and his disunionism remained dormant throughout the 1850s. He fought hard for swampland reclamation, which provided land to those who drained the swamps or built levees. Government grants for such projects were beneficial to his political supporters, especially to wealthy planters.

On July 6, 1853, his relative by marriage, Governor Elias N. Conway, appointed him to the U.S. Senate, a position made vacant by the resignation of Solon Borland. Winning election to a full term the following year, he served from December 1853 until March 1861.

Senator Johnson sought federal land grants for railroad construction in Arkansas, with little success. He voted for the Kansas-Nebraska Act of 1854 and backed efforts to pass a homestead act until the Kansas question became prominent. After 1854 Johnson opposed all homestead bills, believing such legislation was now associated with those who sought the abolition of slavery.

After Sevier's death in 1848, Johnson and Governor Conway led the Democratic Party during the 1850s. Senator Johnson had the loyalty of his brother Richard H. Johnson, who edited the Family's main newspaper in Little Rock. By 1860 Bob Johnson was one of the wealthiest lawyer/planters in Arkansas. His estate in Jefferson County was assessed in that year at more than $800,000, and he possessed 193 slaves.

His political dominance appeared to be finished by 1860. That year the Dynasty attempted to rotate leadership, giving Governor Conway the U.S. Senate seat Johnson was vacating, while putting editor Richard H. Johnson in the governor's office. Such in-family maneuvering prompted a revolt among Family members, such as Thomas C. Hindman, who fielded an insurgent ticket that swept the state. The Family lost control of the governor's office and both seats in the U.S. House.

Southern secession, however, gave new life to Johnson's political career. Now working with Hindman, Johnson successfully carried the state into the Confederacy. He was one of the five men elevated to the Provisional Confederate Congress in May 1861. When the Provisional Congress became a bicameral assembly, the Arkansas legislature selected Johnson as one of the state's two Confederate senators.

Johnson was one of the richest men in the Confederate Congress. He supported the Davis administration, served on the powerful Military Affairs Committee, and chaired the committee on Indian Affairs. He faced a reelection challenge from Augustus H. Garland in 1862, but retained his seat. He never attended the final Confederate congressional session from November 1864 to March 1865, perhaps realizing that the cause of southern disunionism was now lost.

The South's defeat destroyed Johnson's political career and his wealth. He traveled to Galveston, Texas, to flee the country, but changed his mind and returned to Little Rock to practice law with Albert Pike, an old political enemy and ex-Confederate general. Johnson attempted to regain a U.S. Senate seat in 1878, but lost to fellow Democrat James D. Walker. Johnson died in Little Rock.

Known for his courtly manner and political ability, Johnson vigorously defended slavery and the South as he and his relatives maintained their dominance of Arkansas politics from statehood through the Civil War.

[Robert Ward Johnson left no papers; much of the material on his life comes from public sources: newspapers, the *Congressional Globe,* and his published addresses. These are in the Arkansas History Commission in Little Rock. See James M. Woods, *Rebellion and Realignment: Arkansas's Road to Secession* (1987), and "Devotees and Dissenters: Arkansans in the Confederate Congress, 1861–1865," *AHQ* 38 (Autumn 1979): 227–47. See also Elsie Mae Lewis, "Robert Ward Johnson: Militant Spokesman of the Old South-West," *AHQ* 13 (Spring 1954): 16–30, and "From Nationalism to Disunion: A Study of the Secession Movement in Arkansas, 1849–1861," Ph.D. dissertation, University of Chicago, 1947; Dewey Allen Stokes, "Public Affairs in Arkansas, 1836–1849," Ph.D. dissertation, University of Texas, 1966; and Michael B. Dougan, *Confederate Arkansas: The People and Policies of a Frontier State in Wartime* (1976).]

JAMES M. WOODS

JONES, DANIEL WEBSTER (Dec. 15, 1839–Dec. 25, 1918), attorney and Arkansas governor, was born in Cleburne, Texas, to Dr. Isaac N. Jones, a physician and member of the Texas Republic Congress, and Elizabeth W. Littlejohn. In 1840 the family moved to Washington, Arkansas, and Dr. Jones purchased a large plantation in LaFayette County. After graduating from Washington Academy, Daniel Jones began studying law under John R. Eakin in January 1860, but when Arkansas seceded from the Union in April 1861, he enlisted in the Third Arkansas Regiment. He fought at Corinth and Vicksburg, was wounded, became a prisoner of war, and rose to the rank of colonel.

Jones and Margaret P. Hadley of Ashley married on February 9, 1864. They had two daughters and three sons. He returned to Washington to resume his study of law and in September 1865 was admitted to the bar. The following January Governor Isaac Murphy appointed him prosecuting attorney for Hempstead County. During the 1870s he practiced law in partnership with James K. Jones, a boyhood friend and future United States senator. Dan Jones was elected prosecuting attorney for the Ninth Judicial Circuit in 1874, served as a presidential elector in 1876 and 1880, and won the office of attorney general in the 1884 and 1886 elections. After practicing law in Little Rock for several years, in 1890 Jones was elected to serve in the state house of representatives for Pulaski County.

In 1896 he entered the county primaries as a candidate for the Democratic gubernatorial nomination. Despite his image as a planter class, Bourbon Democrat and railroad attorney, he set out to champion those causes most dear to the rising agrarian agitators. The last Civil War veteran to serve as governor, the last of the conservative Democrats, he came to be a moderately Populist and reform-minded governor. His administration set the stage for the more demagogic and less respectable agrarian reformism of Governor Jeff Davis (1901–1907).

Silver became the leading issue in the 1896 campaign in Arkansas, and Jones, establishing himself as the most aggressively pro-silver candidate, won the state primary. He easily won the September state elections. In his inaugural address on January 18, 1897, he called on the general assembly to reform the election laws to provide fairer treatment for the minority (Republican) party. The assembly rejected this and most of the other reform measures suggested by Jones. The assembly did enact a mild antitrust measure, created county normal institutes, and allowed farmers to establish mutual insurance organizations.

Disappointed with the regular legislative session's lack of productivity, Jones called a special session to meet on April 26, 1897. The extraordinary session accepted the Populist plan for a state-owned railroad by passing the Bush Bill. Actually, Arkansas never built a state-owned railroad, and the 1899 legislature repealed the Bush Act. The most important railroad measure from the governor's viewpoint was the commission bill, a regulatory measure, but the pro-railroad forces, continuing their domination of the senate, killed it.

In April 1898 the United States entered into armed conflict with Spain. Jones called for the creation of two new regiments of volunteers. Although the state responded with enthusiasm, the fighting came to an end in August before the Arkansas troops had completed their training.

In the fall of 1898, Jones easily defeated the Republican H. F. Auten and won a second term. He won a major victory when the legislature finally enacted the railroad commission bill in March 1899. Some shippers actually experienced higher rates, but by 1901 the commission claimed it had achieved an overall lowering of rates.

The general assembly responded to the state's antitrust sentiment by passing the stern Rector Antitrust Act. Newly elected attorney general Davis so vigorously prosecuted the trusts that many insurance companies fled the state. Jones considered Davis's behavior demagogic and excessive. A serious rift developed in the administration.

The Jones administration generated another controversy that raged for a decade. The governor repeated former governor James P. Clarke's request that the old state house be replaced by a new capitol; the old building had grace and charm, but insufficient space. Davis initiated a frenzied legal campaign in May 1899 to obstruct the project, which he viewed as a boondoggle. Jones did manage to lay the cornerstone in November 1900, but the construction site remained inactive for two years.

On January 29, 1900, Jones announced his candidacy for the United States Senate. He argued for an imperialist policy; Puerto Rico and the Phillipines should be retained but given a large degree of self-government. In his expansionist sentiments he stood squarely in opposition to his opponent, Arkansas senator James K. Jones. Dan Jones lost the primary election.

He turned his energies toward the practice of law in Little Rock. His political star was rapidly eclipsed by Jeff Davis's meteoric rise. After his wife's death in 1913, the old veteran returned briefly to active political office as Pulaski County representative in the 1915 assembly.

The *Arkansas Gazette* once descibed Governor Jones as tall and slender, with iron gray hair and a "courtly manner." He was an Episcopalian, a Confederate veteran, and one of the last Arkansas politicians from the old patrician class. He died at Little Rock.

[See Richard L. Niswonger, "Daniel Webster Jones, 1897–1901," in *The Governors of Arkansas: Essays in Political Biography,* Timothy P. Donovan, Willard B. Gatewood Jr., and Jeannie M. Whayne, eds., 2d ed. (1995).]

Richard L. Niswonger

LOUIS JORDAN, "King of the Jukeboxes," in the 1940s. *Image courtesy Martha Jordan; artist, Jana Frost.*

ALICE FRENCH. Her stories appeared in the popular magazines of the late nineteenth century. Her Arkansas stories are in the local color tradition. *Courtesy Special Collections Division, University of Arkansas Libraries, Fayetteville.*

SCIPIO JONES, the Little Rock attorney best remembered for his successful defense of twelve black sharecroppers sentenced to death in the wake of the Elaine riots in 1919. *Courtesy Special Collections Division, University of Arkansas Libraries, Fayetteville.*

PIETRO BANDINI, priest, led immigrants out of peonage in Chicot County to Northwest Arkansas, where they grew grapes and established a community, church, and school. *Courtesy Special Collections Division, University of Arkansas Libraries, Fayetteville.*

CARRIE SHEPPERSON STILL, a teacher and civic leader in Little Rock. *Courtesy Special Collections Division, University of Arkansas Libraries, Fayetteville.*

SCOTT BOND, entrepreneur. In 1915 he owned three cotton-gin plants, a saw mill, and nineteen farms totaling five thousand acres in eastern Arkansas.

SIMON ADLER, early merchant and banker, once owned a stagecoach line to carry mail and passengers between Batesville and Jacksonport. *Courtesy Lyon College, Regional Studies Center.*

BROOKS HAYS served as United States Representative of Arkansas's Fifth Congressional District (1943–1959) and as president of the Southern Baptist Convention (1957–1959). He saw his political career as a Christian ministry. *Courtesy Special Collections Division, University of Arkansas Libraries, Fayetteville.*

FIELD KINDLEY, aviator and World War I ace pilot. *Courtesy Special Collections Division, University of Arkansas Libraries, Fayetteville.*

LESSIE STRINGFELLOW READ, newspaper editor and spiritualist who helped clean up a corrupt political machine in the 1930s. *Photo courtesy Bill and Cindy Long.*

SAMUEL LEE KOUNTZ, pioneer of organ transplant surgery. *Courtesy University of California at San Francisco, The Library, Special Collections.*

JOHN GOULD FLETCHER won the Pulitzer Prize for Poetry in 1938. His book *Arkansas* (1947) takes an original approach to the state's history. *Courtesy Special Collections Division, University of Arkansas Libraries, Fayetteville.*

LENA LOWE JORDAN founded the Lena Jordan Hospital in the 1930s. *Courtesy Historical Research Center, University of Arkansas for Medical Sciences Library.*

JOHN C. BRANNER, Arkansas state geologist. His post-Reconstruction geological survey exposed as worthless various reports of gold and silver in the Ouachita Mountains.

CHARLES E. TAYLOR was mayor of Little Rock from 1911 until 1919. Under his leadership the city took on "a new municipal life." *Courtesy Special Collections Division, University of Arkansas Libraries, Fayetteville.*

ROBERTA FULBRIGHT, publisher of the *Northwest Arkansas Times*, scanning teletype in 1935 with her son Bill, later a United States senator. *Courtesy Special Collections Division, University of Arkansas Libraries, Fayetteville.*

MARY HUDGINS, a librarian whose passion for collecting books, manuscripts, photographs, sheet music, and other materials pertaining to the history of Arkansas encompassed the better part of fifty years. *Courtesy Special Collections Division, University of Arkansas Libraries, Fayetteville.*

WILBUR MILLS, chairman of the Committee on Ways and Means of the United States House of Representatives, "Mr. Chairman" was proudest of his work on the Medicare Act of 1965. *Photo courtesy Kay Goss.*

SILAS HUNT (seated) with Wiley Branton (left) and Harold Flowers, on the occasion of Hunt's registration at the University of Arkansas School of Law, February 1948. *Photo courtesy of Geleve Grice.*

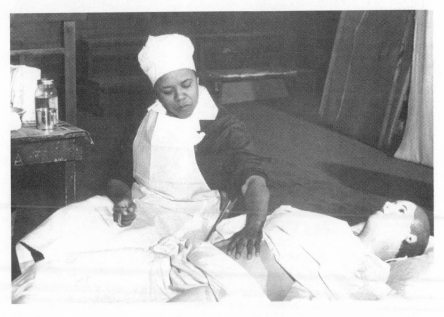

MAMIE ODESSA HALE, shown with a mannequin, was a public health leader whose work helped to reduce infant mortality in the 1940s. *Photo courtesy Historical Research Center, University of Arkansas for Medical Sciences Library.*

Senator Joe T. Robinson (left) with comedian Bob Burns *circa* 1935, admiring the famous bazooka, a horn that sounded like a wounded moose. *Courtesy Special Collections Division, University of Arkansas Libraries, Fayetteville.*

URIAH M. ROSE, regarded as the "ablest lawyer in the state," was a founder of the Rose Law Firm and the American Bar Association. *Courtesy Special Collections Division, University of Arkansas Libraries, Fayetteville.*

HATTIE CARAWAY, United States senator (1932–1944). "Silent Hattie" was a loyal supporter of Franklin Roosevelt's New Deal agenda. *Courtesy Special Collections Division, University of Arkansas Libraries, Fayetteville.*

IDA JO BROOKS at age twenty. A physician and a civic leader in Little Rock, she began private practice as a psychiatrist in 1907. *Photo courtesy Historical Research Center, University of Arkansas for Medical Sciences Library.*

LOGAN ROOTS. Congressman, U. S. marshal, businessman, and booster, he negotiated Little Rock's acquisition of what is now McArthur Park. *Courtesy Special Collections Division, University of Arkansas Libraries, Fayetteville.*

BERNIE BABCOCK, novelist and founder of the Arkansas Natural History Museum. *Courtesy Special Collections Division, University of Arkansas Libraries, Fayetteville.*

AL SMITH, columnist for the *Chicago Defender,* founded the Capital Press Club and was a member of Franklin Roosevelt's "black cabinet." *Courtesy Special Collections Division, University of Arkansas Libraries, Fayetteville.*

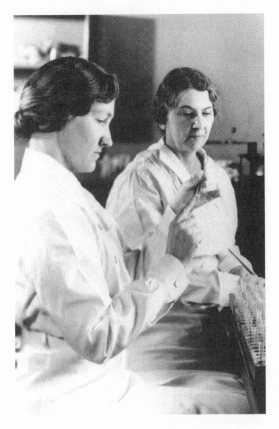

MARGARET PITTMAN (left), microbiologist, with an assistant in the 1930s. She was the first woman to head a laboratory at the National Institutes of Health. *Photo courtesy of the National Institutes of Health Historical Office.*

EDWARD DURRELL STONE, architect. His designs include the Kennedy Center for the Performing Arts in Washington, D.C., Busch Memorial Stadium in St. Louis, the University Medical Center in Little Rock, and the Pine Bluff Civic Center. *Photo courtesy Special Collections, University Arkansas Libraries, Fayetteville.*

FLORENCE SMITH PRICE, composer whose symphonic works were performed by major American orchestras of the 1930s. *Courtesy Special Collections Division, University of Arkansas Libraries, Fayetteville.*

RUTH POLK PATTERSON, teacher and author of *The Seed of Sally Good'n,* an acclaimed family history in which she portrays family members "as actors in the drama of life in pioneer Arkansas." *Courtesy Special Collections Division, University of Arkansas Libraries, Fayetteville.*

ESTHER BINDURSKY, prize-winning editor of the *Lepanto News Record. Courtesy Special Collections Division, University of Arkansas Libraries, Fayetteville.*

FLOYD BROWN founded the Fargo Agricultural School in 1920. *Photo courtesy Fargo Agricultural School Museum.*

VIRGINIA WILLIAMS. A biochemist, she
researched the nature of enzymes and the basic
chemistry of rice. *Photo courtesy Hulon
Williams.*

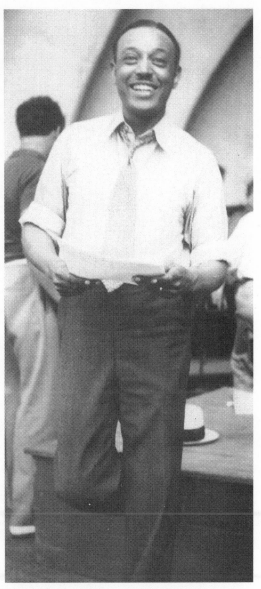

WILLIAM GRANT STILL, composer, at the
Hollywood Bowl. *Courtesy Special Collections
Division, University of Arkansas Libraries,
Fayetteville.*

CARL MOOSBERG, cotton breeder, developed "Rex," a leading strain of cotton in the United States in the 1950s. *Photo courtesy Pearlie Moosberg.*

FREEMAN OWENS, a photographer and inventor who held patents to approximately two thousand improvements in photography. *Courtesy Jefferson County Historical Museum.*

HUGH D. MISER, geologist, was involved with mapping in Arkansas for the United States Geological Survey. He became an authority on manganese deposits and diamonds in Arkansas.

CLYDE ELLIS. "Mr. Rural Electricity" was director of the National Rural Electric Cooperative Association in the 1940s and 1950s. *Courtesy Special Collections Division, University of Arkansas Libraries, Fayetteville.*

JANE STERN, conservationist and naturalist. She was a leader in the struggle to preserve natural waterways and migratory bird habitat in Arkansas. *Courtesy Ellen Stern.*

SAM DELLINGER (left), a leader in saving the state's archeological heritage and advancing science in Arkansas. *Courtesy Special Collections Division, University of Arkansas Libraries, Fayetteville.*

NEIL COMPTON, physician and author, was instrumental in winning congressional legislation to create the Buffalo National River. *Photo courtesy Ellen Compton Shipley.*

LOUISE THADEN, pioneer during the golden age of aviation, set world performance records in altitude, endurance, and speed. *Courtesy University of Arkansas at Little Rock Archives and Special Collections.*

ROSA MARINONI, poet, campaigned for women's
suffrage in Arkansas, published many books of
poems, and encouraged young writers. *Courtesy
Special Collections Division, University of
Arkansas Libraries, Fayetteville.*

JAMES McDONNELL, engineer and aircraft
designer, formed the McDonnell Aircraft
Corporation in 1939, merging it in 1967 with
Douglas Aircraft to form the McDonnell-
Douglas Corporation. *Photo courtesy Special
Collections Division, University of Arkansas
Libraries, Fayetteville.*

JONES, SCIPIO AFRICANUS (1863?–March 28, 1943), attorney, was born in southwest Arkansas to nineteen-year-old Jemmima, a slave of Dr. Sanford Reamey of Tulip, Arkansas. As Union troops advanced into southern Arkansas in 1863, Reamey, like many slave owners, fled toward Texas hoping to avoid the liberation of his slaves. During or shortly after this flight, Jemmima gave birth to Scipio.

Following the Civil War Jemmima and her husband Horace took the surname of Jones and returned to Tulip, in Dallas County, an area dominated by large cotton plantations. Scipio Jones attended an all-black school; he was listed in the 1870 census as the only literate member of his family.

Shortly before his twentieth birthday, Jones moved to Little Rock, where he worked as a farmhand and enrolled in college preparatory courses at Bethel University (now Philander Smith College). He completed the four-year program in three years, then went on to receive a bachelor's degree from Shorter College, in North Little Rock, in 1885. After teaching for two or three years in the public schools of nearby Sweet Home, he applied for admission to the Law School at the University of Arkansas. His application was rejected because African Americans were denied admission to the university. Jones then offered his services as a janitor, hoping to acquire some legal education by working in the Law School. This request, too, was denied, so Jones began studying law in the Little Rock offices of various white attorneys. In June 1889 Jones passed the bar examination and was authorized to practice law in Arkansas.

Jones quickly gained a reputation among Little Rock attorneys as a formidable courtroom opponent, combining a terrific memory with considerable oratorical skills. Among his chief clients were black fraternal societies, including the Shriners, the Arkansas Knights of Pythias, and the Mosaic Templars of America, whose headquarters were in Little Rock.

Throughout his legal career, Jones fought to improve the condition of African Americans, combating discrimination in the selection of juries and participating in the effort to strike down the Arkansas grandfather clause, which prevented blacks from voting. As Jones's reputation grew, he was frequently appointed by the courts to defend African Americans who were without counsel. In 1924 he was elected as a special judge of the chancery court of Pulaski County.

The high point of Jones's career was his defense of twelve black sharecroppers wrongly convicted of murder during the race riots in Phillips County, Arkansas, in 1919. Jones's work on the case, which lasted more than four years, culminated in a landmark United States Supreme Court decision greatly expanding the rights of the accused.

In the fall of 1919, upon learning that black sharecroppers had formed a union to address grievances, white cotton planters in Phillips County had provoked a shootout as a pretext to suppress the budding labor organization. With the help of federal troops, white posses organized by the planters crushed the union, imprisoned hundreds of black sharecroppers, and summarily tried, convicted, and sentenced twelve black men to the electric chair.

Jones's quick intervention after the initial trials delayed the men's scheduled executions and allowed for the organization of a legal appeal. For the next four years, he led the legal defense and local fund-raising efforts on behalf of the sharecroppers. With attorneys from the National Association for the Advancement of Colored People, he filed a series of appeals calling for new trials for the defendants. These maneuvers concluded when the case reached the United States Supreme Court in January 1923. The Supreme Court, in *Moore v. Dempsey*, 261 U.S. 86 (1923), ruled in favor of the sharecroppers, finding that the mob spirit prevailing at the time of the initial criminal trials prevented the defendants from receiving the due process to which they were entitled under the Fourteenth Amendment. Previous to this historic decision, the Court had declined to referee the states' conduct of criminal trials.

Jones was a longtime Republican Party activist, serving as a Pulaski County party official and as a delegate to several national conventions. He also participated in the ongoing intraparty fight against the "lily-white" Republicans who sought to exclude blacks from official positions within the organization. After 1920 the "lily-whites" controlled the state party, but Jones remained faithful, even serving as a delegate to the national convention in 1940.

In 1896 Jones and twenty-five-year-old Carrie Edwards married. She died young, leaving Jones with one daughter, Hazel. Hazel also died young, leaving Jones to care for three grandchildren. In 1917 Jones and Lillie M. Jackson of Pine Bluff married. Jones died at home in Little Rock. A large, and segregated, funeral was held at Bethel African Methodist Episcopal Church, to which Jones had belonged for over fifty years. The *Chicago Defender* reported that at the time of his death, Scipio Jones was the second oldest African-American lawyer in the nation.

[See Mary Ovington White, *Portraits in Color* (1927); Tom W. Dillard, "Scipio A. Jones," *AHQ* 31 (Autumn 1972): 201–19; Richard Cortner, *A Mob Intent on Death* (1988); and the *Chicago Defender*, Apr. 3, 1943.]

KERRY TAYLOR

JORDAN, LENA LOWE (Apr. 6, 1884–Sept. 30, 1950), nurse and hospital founder, was born in Georgia, the daughter of Hollin and Martha Lowe. She trained in nursing at Charity Hospital in Savannah, Georgia. She graduated from the United Friends Hospital nurses' program in Little Rock in March 1930 and was licensed in Arkansas that same year.

Little Rock became Jordan's home in the early 1920s. She was the head nurse at the Mosaic State Templars Hospital, which opened in 1927, and worked there until 1932 when she opened her hospital. She was the wife of Peach H. Jordan Jr., the grand master and president of the Mosaic Templars of America, a black fraternal insurance organization based in Little Rock.

In May 1932 Jordan established a hospital at 1500 Pulaski Street, the Arkansas Home and Hospital for Crippled Negro Children, later known as the Lena Jordan Hospital. It was the only institution in Arkansas which cared for crippled Negro children at the time. Jordan mortgaged her own home in 1936 to continue the operation of the hospital. An appeal for funds to repay the fifteen-hundred-dollar mortgage was made in the *Arkansas Gazette* of August 6, 1936. When asked how she kept the hospital in operation, she answered, "The Lord provides." In addition to her administrative duties at the hospital, the indefatigable Jordan began training nurses. In 1934 she taught a course in home nursing sponsored by the American Red Cross. Ninety-one women completed the course and graduated at the First Baptist Church at Seventh and Gaines Streets.

Her program for providing nurses for the hospital was an innovative one. She brought black girls from the country, and while they worked at the hospital, they attended school. They received clothes, board, and a small salary. They earned a practical nursing certificate for their work at the hospital, and some also went to business school.

On May 12, 1950, as an observance of National Hospital Day, Lena Jordan was honored on her sixty-sixth birthday and her fortieth anniversary in the nursing profession. The occasion was celebrated at the hospital. Included in the program was a letter from Eleanor Roosevelt, regretting that she could not attend the event. Lena Jordan's philosophy was "helping others to help themselves." She was a champion for and pioneer of health care for blacks in Arkansas. Only a few months after the celebration Jordan died at her home of a cerebral hemorrhage. She was survived by her husband, a granddaughter, two great grandchildren, three sisters, and a brother. She is buried at the Haven of Rest Cemetery in Little Rock.

[See the *Arkansas Gazette*, Aug. 6, 1936, Apr. 26, 1950, and Oct. 1, 1950 (obituary); and Edwina Walls, "Some Extinct Black Hospitals of Little Rock and Pulaski County," *Pulaski County Historical Review* 34 (Spring 1986): 2–13.]

EDWINA WALLS MANN

JORDAN, LOUIS THOMAS (July 8, 1908–Feb. 4, 1975), band leader, was born in Brinkley. His father, James Aaron Jordan, studied with W. C. Handy and directed the Brinkley Brass Band. His mother, Adell (maiden name unknown), died in her twenties; afterward Louis's grandmother, Maggie Jordan, and his aunt, Lizzie Reid, helped to raise him. He began studying music with his father at age seven. In time he could play the saxes from soprano to baritone, as well as other horns. His first known professional gig, at age fifteen, was at Hot Springs's Green Gables Club with Ruby "Junie Bug" Williams.

In the late 1920s Jordan briefly attended Arkansas Baptist College in Little Rock and later became a benefactor of the school. He worked with Jimmy Pryor's Imperial Serenaders and married a woman named Julie (surname unknown) from Arkadelphia. One source lists Jordan's recording debut on June 14, 1929, on "Dog Bottom" backed with "Jungle Mama (Brunswick 4450)" by the Jungle Band.

In 1930 he moved to Philadelphia where he found work with the Charlie Gaines Band.

In 1932 Jordan married Ida Fields, a singer and dancer who helped his career with money and encouragement.

The Charlie Gaines Band was gigging at the Apollo Theatre in Harlem when the booking agent for the Apollo convinced Jordan to form a quintet. This he did, but only for two years until 1936, when he joined Chick Webb's Savoy Ballroom Band, one of the leading black bands in the country. Each year they played several engagements at the Savoy in Harlem, and toured a theater circuit the rest of the year. Ella Fitzgerald was the featured singer. Jordan handled alto sax and did some vocals, including "Rusty Hinge (Decca 1273)," "It's Swell Of You (Decca 1213)," and "Gee, But You're Swell (Decca 1115)."

In 1938 Jordan again embarked as a band leader and formed his Tympani Five. He signed with Decca Records, a major label, beginning an often wildly successful fifteen-year recording relationship. He led the Tympani Five, with many changes of personnel and instrumentation, for three decades. The group began at the Elks' Rendezvous in Harlem and toiled in the club circuit. In 1941 they recorded "Knock Me a Kiss," "I'm Going to Move to the Outskirts of Town," and others, and the group began to catch on. In 1942 they recorded "Five Guys Named Moe," which became a signature song.

The short, mustachioed Jordan was a perfectionist, said to be one of the strictest leaders in the business, demanding punctuality and long rehearsals. Though he paid his musicians well, he could be aloof and moody, in contrast to the joking, jiving hipster he portrayed on vinyl and on stage.

In 1942 Jordan married a childhood friend, Fleecie Moore, a Brasfield-born businesswoman given cowriting credit on several Jordan records.

During World War II, Jordan appeared in several USO tours, and with hits like "Ration Blues"(1943) and "G.I. Jive" (1944) he won a huge following among U.S. troops. Health problems barred his own military service.

During the 1940s he had twenty-one number-one hits on *Billboard*'s rhythm and blues, country, and pop charts, and recorded with Bing Crosby, Ella Fitzgerald, and Louis Armstrong. In 1946 the Tympani Five enjoyed a million-record seller with "Choo-Choo Ch'Boogie." Jordan became "king of the jukeboxes," noted for his frantic and funny lyrics in such hits as "Saturday Night Fish Fry," "Is You or Is You Ain't (My Baby)," and "Open the Door, Richard."

In 1945 he starred in several movies based on, and named after, his songs, like Astor Pictures' "Reet, Petite and Gone" and "Caledonia." In "Beware!" he warns against chicks who "are looking to hook you." An equal opportunist, Jordan recorded an answer song addressed to women, called "Look Out." Another movie, "Look Out, Sister," soon followed.

After a decade of often wild popularity, his record sales stalled with the rise of rock and roll. When bookings in larger venues slowed, Jordan began performing in clubs in California and Nevada. In the late 1940s he bought a house in Phoenix, Arizona, where the climate eased his arthritis. In 1951 he married Vicky Hayes, a dancer. His longtime deal with Decca ended in 1953. He continued to tour, and to record for Aladdin, Mercury, and X Records. He returned to Brinkley in 1957 for "Louis Jordan Day." In 1960 he and Hayes separated. In the late 1960s he toured England and Asia. In 1966 he married Martha Weaver, also a dancer. He played regularly around Los Angeles until his death there in 1975. He was buried in St. Louis.

The beat and personality of Jordan's horn-driven music were moving toward rock and roll before there was even a name for it. He was an innovator. When big bands were all the rage, he became famous with a small combo, as most rock musicians later did. He was one of the first to join electric guitar and bass with horns, and his over-the-beat monologues are a prototype of rap music. His songs have been recorded by dozens of artists. A host of musicians, including James Brown and Chuck Berry, have acknowledged Jordan's influence. Joe Jackson's *Jumping Jive* album (1981) was a tribute. In 1991 Cameron Mackintosh staged a musical revue, "Five Guys Named Moe," which played on Broadway and London's West End and toured the United States.

[In 1992 Germany's Bear Family Records released a nine-disc set of Jordan's Decca recordings from 1938 to 1954. MCA and Rhino Records have also released reissues of his material. His LPs and 78s may be found in used record stores and specialty shops.

Written resources include John Chilton's *Let the Good Times Roll: The Story of Louis Jordan and His Music* (1994); Leonard Feather, *Encyclopedia of Jazz* (1955); Gérard Herzhaft, *Encyclopedia of the Blues* (1992); Henry T. Sampson, *Blacks in Black and White* (1977); Bill Jones, "Jordan Jive," *Little Rock Free Press* (Sept. 2–15, 1994); S. Koch, "Louis Jordan Gets His Due," *Little Rock Free Press* (Feb. 24–Mar. 9, 1995); *The New Rolling Stone Encyclopedia of Rock and Roll* (1995); and Wayne Janick and Tad Lathrop, *Cult Rockers* (1995).]

S. KOCH

KAYS, VICTOR CICERO (July 24, 1882–Jan. 20, 1966), educator and administrator, was born in Magnolia, Illinois, to John Kays, a farmer, and Mary Alice (maiden name unknown).

Kays grew up on the family farm, which had been worked by the Kays family since the 1830s. He attended a one-room grammar school. He completed high school in three years at Henry, Illinois.

In 1902 he graduated from Northern Illinois State Teachers College in DeKalb. After graduation he taught math and coached at Savannah Township High School. He then continued his education at the University of Illinois in Urbana, where he earned a bachelor of science degree. He also earned bachelor of science and master of science in agriculture degrees from the State College of Agriculture in Las Cruces, New Mexico.

After completing his education Kays worked as a chemist at the agricultural experiment station in Mesilla Park, New Mexico. He was the agricultural director of the Agricultural School in Wetumpka, Alabama, in 1910, when he was asked to be the principal of the State Agricultural School in Jonesboro, Arkansas. On June 1, 1910, he was appointed principal of the school that later became Arkansas State University.

"Tex" Plunkett, a member of the faculty when Kays was president, talked about Kays's involvement in campus activities in *Voices from State: An Oral History of Arkansas State University.* "He spent about three hours a day being president," Plunkett said, "and the rest of the time he was out on the campus putting in a sewer line or a water line or doing some kind of work."

In 1915 the legislature appointed a committee to review the agricultural schools, and Kays received high marks for the school's and his own work. According to *The ASU Story,* the committee recommended that he receive a raise. The report stated, "We find Professor Kays a most excellent gentleman, of indispensable value as the head of such a school. The only deplorable fact in regard to his service to the state is that he is paid a mere pittance for his services."

On June 12, 1917, he and Bertie Hale of Paragould, Arkansas, were married. They had one son, V. H. Kays, who was born in 1919.

In 1918 the school became a junior college as well as a high school, and Kays was named president. In 1925 the school's name was changed to First District Agricultural and Mechanical College. In 1933 the school received the name of Arkansas State College.

The Great Depression caused problems for the college, and Kays worked to get assistance from the government to keep the school going. He was known to make personal loans to students to keep them in college.

Kays was an athlete as well as an academic and humanitarian. When he was an undergraduate at Illinois Teachers College, he started the school's first football team. In 1903, under Kays's leadership, the Savannah High School basketball team won the Illinois State Championship. His athletic leadership continued at New Mexico A & M College. He not only started the first basketball team, but also led them in an undefeated season and a Southwest championship.

His enthusiasm continued at Arkansas State College. He often traveled with the athletic teams and assisted the coaches. Fred Barnett, a member of the basketball team, recalled in *Voices from State* a time when Kays had sacrificed his own railroad pass so that Barnett could make it to a road game in Little Rock.

Kays resigned in January 1943 after nearly thirty-four years of service. He did not leave the college, but remained as its business manager. When the next president, Horace Thompson, resigned unexpectedly in June 1945, Kays took his place until a permanent replacement could be found. He left the presidency for good in 1946, when William J. Edens was appointed.

The board of trustees awarded Kays an honorary doctor of laws degree on May 25, 1956. The school he led for more than thirty years became Arkansas State University on January 17, 1967, one year after his death.

[Sources include Larry D. Ball and William M. Clements, *Voices from State: An Oral History of Arkansas State University* (1984); News and Information Services Office at Arkansas State University; Arkansas State College Board of Trustees minutes; Lee A. Dew, *The ASU Story* (1968).]

GRETCHEN HUNT

KEY, VERA ESTELLE (Sept. 16, 1893–Mar. 16, 1987), nurse and civic leader, was born at War Eagle, Arkansas. Her father, Charles W. Key, had been the first postmaster at the Key community southeast of Rogers. Her mother, Hettie Blackburn, was the daughter of William Jasper Blackburn, a two-term legislator. Vera's great-grandparents, Sylvanus and Catherine Blackburn, founded the community of War Eagle in the 1830s; her uncle, J. A. C. Blackburn, was prominent in the region.

Always proud of these antecedents, Vera Key maintained a strong interest in history throughout her life.

Key spent her earliest years at War Eagle, where her father ran a store and gristmill. In 1897 Charles Key went into business for himself and moved his family to Rogers, where he opened a general mercantile store. He died three years later at the age of forty-two, when Vera was seven years old. After graduating in 1908 from the Rogers public schools, she entered the Centenary Hospital School of Nursing in St. Louis, graduating in 1911 as a registered nurse.

For the next few years Key was a private duty nurse in St. Louis and in Rogers. When World War I began, she volunteered for the army nurse corps. On September 28, 1918, she set sail for France. Influenza struck on the way over, and she herself was ill for much of the time she was in France. After a stint at Fort Sam Houston in Texas, she returned to Rogers in June of 1920, one of the last Benton County volunteers to be released from duty.

During the 1920s Key continued her career, working first at the Public Health Service Hospital at Colfax, Iowa, a facility for merchant seamen and servicemen. She then returned to Rogers and private duty nursing for a time before accepting an appointment as school nurse at Hendrix College at Conway, Arkansas, in 1925.

In 1924 Key joined the First Church of Christ, Scientist, in Rogers, where she served as Sunday School superintendent and as chairman of the board. While in Rogers she participated in the annual Apple Blossom Festivals held there from 1923 through 1927. She is credited with designing the official flag of that event, a tri-color in which pink represented the flowers, white the streams, and green the mountains of northwest Arkansas.

In the summer of 1928 Key enrolled in the home economics program at the University of Missouri, but her studies were cut short by the news that a former patient, the author Tom Morgan, was seriously ill. She returned to Rogers to care for Morgan, who died soon after her arrival. Morgan left his house and the bulk of his estate to Key in appreciation for her care.

From 1928 through the 1950s Key operated her home as the Woodbine Guest House. An avid gardener, she first entered civic affairs in 1929, when she became one of the founders and the first president of the Rogers Garden Club. That organization inaugurated yard contests and in the 1940s was responsible for the planting of thousands of colorful maples in Rogers and vicinity.

Key remained a member of the Garden Club all of her life, but in the 1950s she turned her attention to history. She was a founder and president of the Benton County Historical Society, organized in 1955. She wrote articles for the society's publication, *The Benton County Pioneer,* and was the co-chairman of the Pea Ridge Memorial Association. This group erected historical markers and planned for the commemoration of the 100th anniversary of the Battle of Pea Ridge. In 1965 the American Association for State and Local History awarded the Benton County Historical Society a Certificate of Commendation for the work of the Memorial Association. Key remained a member of the society until her death.

In the 1950s Key received a bequest from a long-term boarder which allowed her to travel and to indulge her love of antiques. In 1960 she traveled to Europe, and in 1962 she took a two-month trip around the world.

In August of 1974 the city council of Rogers authorized the use of five thousand dollars in revenue sharing funds to establish a city museum. Key was appointed the first chairperson of the museum commission. For the next several years she devoted much of her volunteer time to the Rogers Historical Museum. In addition to serving as a commissioner until 1981, she arranged exhibits and gave guided tours.

In 1978 Key was recognized for civic leadership by the Rogers Chamber of Commerce. In 1981, her health failing, she was made an honorary member of the museum commission.

In 1983 she entered a Christian Science care center in Springdale, where she died. Her estate was divided equally between the Rogers Historical Museum and the First Church of Christ, Scientist, of Rogers. An endowment fund for the museum was established with the Key bequest, and the museum's new wing, opened in 1988, was named in her honor.

[Key's wartime diaries and photograph albums, family photographs, and personal papers are in the collections of the Rogers Historical Museum. The museum maintains files of clippings, an oral history collection, and other materials relating to the Key and Blackburn families. See Key's articles in the *Benton County Pioneer,* 1955–57, 1963, 1973; *Rogers Daily News,* Aug. 13, 1980; and *Northwest Arkansas Morning News,* May 26, 1986. Also see the *Benton County Pioneer* from 1955 through 1987. An obituary can be found in the *Northwest Arkansas Morning News,* Mar. 18, 1987.]

GAYE KELLER BLAND

KIMPEL, BEN DREW (Nov. 5, 1915–Apr. 21, 1983), author and teacher, was born in Fort Smith to Ben D. Kimpel, an attorney, and Gladys Crane. He earned a bachelor's degree from Harvard University. To satisfy his mother he studied law for one semester, but then chose to pursue a master's degree in literature. He received his Ph.D. from the University of North Carolina at Chapel Hill, specializing in American literature and writing his dissertation on Herman Melville. Immediately after his graduation in 1942, he enlisted as a private in the United States Army. He was sent to intensive language school and then served with a civil affairs unit in France and was commissioned as a second lieutenant before leaving the army in 1946.

Joining the state department soon after, he served as first secretary and public affairs officer in Vienna from 1946 to 1950. A lover of rich food, music, and dancing, he reminisced that he often waltzed from ten in the evening until three or four o'clock in the morning without stopping except to sip a glass of champagne. After being transferred to Washington and finding bureaucracy not to his liking, he did postdoctoral work in medieval literature at Harvard until 1952.

He traveled to Fayetteville that year to visit Duncan Eaves and agreed to begin teaching at the University of Arkansas, where he remained for more than thirty years. He taught a range of courses from Anglo-Saxon and Beowulf through the modern novel. He told his teaching assistants that a lecturer's knowledge of the subject matter of a course should be like an iceberg, with only one-eighth showing above the surface. On three occasions he taught "New Developments in Twentieth-Century Thought" with Dr. Lothar Schaffer of the chemistry department. Although many students found his vast knowledge intimidating at first, many came to regard him as a wise and sympathetic counselor who could help with problems. He enjoyed student parties and continued to be a graceful dancer in spite of his great weight. In a public lecture delivered three months before his death, he said that he appreciated being paid for teaching, but would pay the university, if necessary, to let him continue. In 1961 he was the recipient of the university's first Distinguished Teaching Award.

At the age of eleven Kimpel indicated his determination to travel. He had planned to attend a lecture by the visiting travel writer Richard Halliburton, but was in bed with pneumonia during a winter storm. His doctor, after anxious consultation with his mother, announced that it would be better to allow him to attend the lecture than to try to keep him in bed. The following year his mother paid for an uncle to travel with him to Europe. He later visited every continent, including Antarctica. One of his favorite trips was a sailing voyage in the South Seas as a passenger/crew member, appropriately serving as a cook. He was an energetic traveler, sometimes seeing three plays in a day in London and catching up on scientific reading while in transit.

He spoke German, French, Italian, Greek, Russian, and Chinese, and had a reading and writing knowledge of several other ancient and esoteric languages. It was his habit at one time to translate one hundred lines of ancient Greek before breakfast.

He is best known for his biography of the eighteenth-century English novelist Samuel Richardson, written with Duncan Eaves. He and Eaves researched a wealth of new material on Richardson's life as a printer and novelist, and included general chapters on his personality and opinions, and a list of his numerous correspondents. *Samuel Richardson* was immediately accepted by scholars as definitive. Critics praised their close and exact reading of various texts of the novels *Pamela, Clarissa,* and *Sir Charles Grandison,* and their sympathetic regard for them in their contemporary context. The English novelist Angus Wilson said, "I wish that I had written it."

The next major project was a line-by-line explication of the *Cantos* of Ezra Pound. Kimpel and Eaves worked together almost daily on this task for more than ten years. They published twenty-three articles concerning Pound's sources for the *Cantos,* his "Ideogrammic Method" and major forms, his anti-Semitism, his view of Hitler's economic policies, and his experiences in prison. The work was never completed.

Kimpel died sitting in his favorite arm chair, the lamp beside him illuminated by a 200-watt bulb (one of his complaints about traveling was the lack of proper light in hotel rooms), preparing for his evening conference with Eaves. In his lap was a volume of Pound's *Cantos,* on the table beside him a Chinese dictionary, and in his hands an unlighted Camel cigarette and a pack of matches.

[This entry is based on conversations the author had with Kimpel from 1954 to 1983; a telephone interview with his sister Betty Warner, Apr. 10, 1993; and an interview with Juliet Eaves, May 9, 1993. Kimpel and Eaves edited *The*

Informal Reader (1955) and Richardson's *Pamela* (1971); translated Goethe's *Torquato Tasso* (1956); and wrote *Samuel Richardson: A Biography* (1971). Their articles on Ezra Pound appeared in such journals as *Paideuma, American Literature, and Philological Quarterly,* and others from 1977 to 1983. See Leighton Rudolph, "Ben Drew Kimpel," in "Some Illustrious Educators of Old Main," edited by Thomas Kennedy for the Old Main Rededication Committee (1991); a copy is in Special Collections Divisions, University of Arkansas Libraries, Fayetteville. See also Paul H. Williams, "In Memoriam: Ben Kimpel," *Arkansas Times,* July 1983.]

CATHY BOYD

KINDLEY, FIELD E. (Mar. 13, 1896–Feb. 2, 1920), aviator, World War I ace, was born near the Civil War battlefield at Pea Ridge, Arkansas, to George C. and Ella Kindley. After Ella's death in 1898, George accepted a teaching position in the Philippines, leaving young Field to be raised by his grandmother, Cynthia Kindley of Bentonville. At seven Field rejoined his father in Manila for five years, then in 1908 moved back to Arkansas to live with his uncle in Gravette. After high-school graduation, he moved to Coffeyville, Kansas, to become a partner in a motion picture theater.

From Coffeyville Kindley enlisted in the Kansas National Guard after America's entry into the First World War. Originally posted as a foot soldier, he volunteered for transfer into the aviation branch of the Army Signal Corps, and was sent to the School of Military Aeronautics at the University of Illinois. His natural talents moved him into the first class of American pilots to be transferred from ground school to England for flight training in September 1917. He was commissioned a first lieutenant in the American Air Service on April 15, 1918.

His first assignment was as a ferry pilot moving aircraft from England to the western front. His first assignment nearly became his last on May 5, 1918, when in a heavy fog he crashed his Sopwith Camel biplane into the famous white cliffs at Dover, England. After he recovered from his injuries in an English hospital, his first combat assignment was to the Royal Air Force's 65th Squadron. It was with the 65th Squadron that he scored his first kill: on June 26, 1918, over Albert, France, he shot down Lieutenant Wilhelm Lehmann, commanding officer of the German Jagdstaffel 5.

In July 1918 the Americans formed the 148th Squadron, which was assigned to serve in the British sector of the western front. Kindley was one of the first pilots posted to the new unit. On July 13 he earned the 148th's first victory by shooting down a German Albatros D-3 over Ypres. The win earned Kindley brief celebrity on the British front, and he soon became the commanding officer of the 148th, a position he held until the end of the war. He was later promoted to captain. His twelve confirmed kills ranked third in aircraft shot down during the war behind Captain Eddie Rickenbacker and Major Raoul Lufbery.

Kindley's most stunning day of combat was September 27, 1918. He led his patrol of Camel biplanes out on a bombing mission just before 9:00 A.M. He dropped four small bombs on a group of German transports, leaving them in flames. Climbing from the attack, he spotted an observation balloon which he riddled with gunfire and forced down. Minutes later, he strafed a German infantry column, then took out a machine-gun nest which had pinned down a British infantry advance. He climbed back to two thousand feet searching for targets of opportunity, and found another German machine-gun emplacement. As he focused on the ground, a German Halberstadt two-seat biplane fixed on his tail. He wheeled to the right upon hearing machine-gun fire and opened up with his guns beneath the German. The Halberstadt burst into flames, his eleventh kill. He continued to strafe German infantry until he ran out of ammunition. On his way back to his home base at Baizieux, he noticed two Germans attacking an Allied plane. He jumped into the dogfight without ammunition in hopes of scaring off the two Fokker biplanes. The bluff worked. For this furious period of just over two hours' combat, Kindley earned his Oak Leaf Cluster and the British Distinguished Flying Cross. His final action came on October 28 with his twelfth kill, a Fokker near Bapaume, France.

After the war Kindley was posted in December 1919 to the 94th Aero Squadron at Kelly Field near San Antonio, Texas. As a member of the "Hat-in-the-Ring" 94th, he was assigned to take part in a demonstration for General John J. Pershing in February 1920. His flight of SE-5 biplanes was scheduled to perform strafing and bombing runs. On February 1, the day before Pershing's visit, Kindley rehearsed the bombing run. Diving into his target, he discovered that a group of enlisted men had wandered into the area. In an attempt to warn the troops, Kindley buzzed the area. When he pulled up, the engine stalled, the SE-5 fell from an altitude of almost one hundred feet, and he was killed. The subsequent inquiry found that support wires broke from the strain of his maneuver to warn the soldiers. Kindley's body was returned to Gravette for burial. Several monuments remain to the World War flying ace: Gravette's city park, a high school in Coffeyville, Kansas, and a Second World War air base in Bermuda are named for him.

[Sources include the Field Kindley Files, Arkansas Aviation Historical Association Archives, Little Rock; and the Field Kindley Files, Arkansas Aviation Museum, Fayetteville. See also James J. Hudson, "Air Knight of the Ozarks: Captain Field E. Kindley," *Journal of the American Aviation Historical Society* (1959): 233–60; and *Hostile Skies: A Combat History of the American Air Service in World War I* (1968).]

WILLIAM M. SMITH JR.

KING, HELEN MARTIN (Sept. 20, 1895–Dec. 11, 1988), artist and businesswoman, was born at Powhatan in Lawrence County, Arkansas. She was the only child of John William Martin, lumberman and manufacturer of wagons, and his wife, Clara Isabelle Norment. In 1903 the family moved to Batesville in canvas-covered wagons, and there Helen spent most of the rest of her life. She attended the preparatory academy at Arkansas College. In 1913 she married Fitzhugh Hail, who died a short time later.

Helen then returned to school. She attended the Cincinnati Conservatory of Music, studied art at the Cincinnati Art Museum, then enrolled at Sophie Newcomb College in New Orleans. On December 31, 1916, she married the Reverend Harry King, a Methodist minister and teacher. They had two daughters. The Reverend King served from 1920 to 1933 as professor and dean at Galloway College in Searcy. In 1943 the family moved to Batesville where the Reverend King served as professor and dean at Arkansas College.

While the couple was living in Searcy, Helen King became interested in designing and working hooked rugs. She organized classes and wrote a book, *How to Hook Rugs*. She sold pre-stenciled rug kits of her own designs to friends, complete with instructions, burlap backing with stamped design, and yarns dyed to her own specifications. Interest in her work led her to develop a full-scale "cottage industry," designing the rugs, stenciling and assembling the kits, experimenting with dye colors, and improving tools for cutting and hooking the wool. Eventually, according to *Life* magazine, she made over twenty-five hundred different patterns available to rug hookers, some copied from rare museum pieces.

She came to employ a number of people in the business, and her kits were marketed all over the United States. She was invited to lecture, to exhibit her rugs, to give instructions, and to sell her patterns and kits in museums, department stores, at ladies' club meetings, rug-hooking parties, and church circles across the South, culminating in an appearance at the Smithsonian Institution. Her work was featured in a number of national magazines and in newspapers, including the *Washington Post*. *National Geographic* stated that between 1935 and 1946 King and her staff had stenciled and assembled twenty-five thousand rug kits.

She continued to work after her husband's death. She built a small studio behind her family home in Batesville, where she taught classes and continued to design patterns. Her rugs were mostly of floral design, usually with a border of flowers, leaves, or scrolls, and a floral bouquet center. She rarely used abstract designs. Her favorite colors were shades of rose and green. One dye color she devised and particularly liked was a deep burgundy which served as the background of her "Cambridge" rug, now on permanent display at Morrow Hall, First Presbyterian Church, Batesville. Among her favorite designs were the "Broken Wreath," the "Daisy Scroll," the "Laurel Wreath," and her most original creation, the "Arkansas" rug. All of the floral motifs of the Arkansas rug depict flowers and crops of her native state, including cotton blossoms and the David O. Dodd rose.

Mrs. King's rugs are displayed at the Powhatan Courthouse State Park Museum, Powhatan; the Decorative Arts Museum, Little Rock; and Morrow Hall, Batesville.

[This sketch is based largely on the author's conversations with Helen King and her daughter, Cecilia King Butt, 1973 to 1988; and on clippings in Mrs. King's personal scrapbook, a photocopy of which is in the Regional Studies Center, Lyon College, Batesville. A collection of her papers and correspondence is at Lyon College. See *National Geographic*, Sept. 1946; *Life*, Jan. 29, 1940; and *Holland's: A Magazine of the South* (June 1949).]

NANCY BRITTON

KOUNTZ, SAMUEL LEE (Oct. 20, 1930–Dec. 23, 1981), international leader in transplant surgery, was born in Lexa, Phillips County, Arkansas, to J. S. Kountz, a farmer and Baptist minister, and Emma Montague. His parents were sharecroppers for a time, but when the children were born they acquired a housestead of their own. Samuel Kountz may have acquired his love of medicine early in his life. When he was little he accompanied his mother to midwifery activities, and he was once impressed by the way a doctor eased the suffering of an injured friend.

He attended segregated schools in Lexa. After he graduated from Arkansas AM & N College at Pine Bluff in 1952, he discovered that he needed more schooling to qualify for admission to medical school. He attended the University of Arkansas, Fayetteville, where he earned a master's degree in chemistry. Later, he prized this "scientific grounding," believing "it would have been tragedy" if he had not had it. He is remembered as an unusually ambitious student with an inquiring mind, rather quiet, determined not to let racial barriers stand in the way of his goals. He received an M.D. degree from the University of Arkansas School of Medicine in 1958.

He married Grace Akin, a teacher, on June 9, 1958, in Chicago. Three children were born to the marriage.

The same year he was appointed to an internship at the Stanford Service at San Francisco General Hospital. He spent three years as a junior resident in the department of surgery at Stanford University. In 1962 he received the Bank of America Giannini Fellowship in Surgery, which he spent at Hammersmith Hospital in London. He was appointed senior resident at Stanford in 1963 and chief resident in 1964–65. In 1965 he joined the faculty at Stanford. The same year he was Visiting Fulbright Professor in the United Arab Republic.

During his residency at Stanford, he assisted Dr. Roy Cohn; together they performed the first kidney transplant in which a near relative of the patient was the donor (instead of an identical twin donor).

In 1967 Kountz was appointed to the faculty of the University of California at San Francisco, where he was chief of the kidney transplant service. There, with Dr. Folkert Belzer, he developed a technique of preserving kidneys from donors for later transplantation. Kountz's biographer, Dr. Claude H. Organ, states that two of Kountz's contributions "deserve special mention: the discovery of the effectiveness of prednisolone in reversing acute rejection of the transplanted kidney; and the advocacy of earlier reimplantation, *i.e.,* the implantation of a second kidney at the earliest sign of first kidney rejection ('Better to save the patient and sacrifice the graft')."

A bold surgeon who expected the best outcome, Kountz performed some five hundred transplants with a "phenomenal" survival rate. Transplants posed difficult ethical problems, however; for that reason, Kountz established the Center for Human Values at UCSF, a group of residents, doctors, and ministers who met weekly to explore the ethical dilemmas generated by transplant surgery.

He worked to make the public aware of the need for donated organs, believing organ donation was "a great act of altruism." To gain a large public audience he once performed a kidney transplant on live television. A colleague said that "what he did to help get transplantation off the ground will always be remembered."

He was close to his patients: "Every surgeon has to fall in love with his patient to effect a cure. In this service, we marry 'em." A former patient recalled: "Every time I saw him, he was happy. He cared very much for his patients."

In 1972 he became professor and chair of the department of surgery at the State University of New York, Downstate Medical Center, Brooklyn, and surgeon-in-chief at King's County Hospital. Downstate was in a black community where life was hard. He told friends that an important reason why he moved to Brooklyn was to improve medical care for the black community. There he strengthened the transplant program, improved the quality of the residency program, and established research priorities. His purpose, he said, was "to train people who have to be reckoned with."

In the summer of 1977 at the height of his career he was felled by an illness, never diagnosed, that left him severely disabled. He was never able to return to medicine, but died four years later at the age of fifty-one. He was interred in All Saints Church Cemetery in Great Neck, New York.

He is remembered as a precise clinician and diligent scientist who had great warmth of personality. He was governor of the American College of Surgeons (1975), president of the Society of University Surgeons (1974), and a member of such organizations as the National

Academy of Sciences and the American Surgical Association. He served on the editorial boards of such publications as the *Journal of Nephrology,* the *Journal of Hypertension and Renal Diseases, Surgery,* and the *New York State Journal of Medicine.* He contributed many articles, often jointly, to such journals as the *Journal of Nuclear Medicine, Surgery, Surgical Forum,* and the *New England Journal of Medicine.*

He received honorary degrees from the University of San Francisco, the University of Arkansas, and Howard University. The Kountz-Kyle Building at the University of Arkansas at Pine Bluff is named in his honor, as is the Kountz Pavilion at Harlem Hospital in New York City.

[See Claude H. Organ and Margaret M. Kosiba, eds., *A Century of Black Surgeons: The U.S.A. Experience,* vol. 2 (1987); Claude H. Organ, "Samuel Lee Kountz, 1930–1981," *Surgery* (1982): 609–10; and J. K. Robinson, "In Memorium, Dr. Samuel Lee Kountz," *UCSF Journal* 6 (2): 2–3, May 1982. See also the obituary in the *New York Times,* Dec. 24, 1981. Mrs. Virgie Kountz supplied information about the Kountz family; Arthur Fry provided insights about Kountz's student days.]

GORDON D. MORGAN
NANCY A. WILLIAMS

LAMB, THEODORE LAFAYETTE (Apr. 11, 1927–Sept. 6, 1984), businessman and lawyer, was born in Detroit, Michigan, the son of Foster Lamb and Theodosia Braswell. The family moved to Arkansas in the early 1930s, and Ted Lamb attended Little Rock schools. He briefly attended Little Rock Junior College before entering the army. He graduated from officer candidate school and the army language school where he became proficient in Japanese. He was in the army until 1947, serving as a Japanese linguist in the Counterintelligence Corps. Upon his discharge, he attended Yale College, graduating with a B.A. in 1950. He worked for General Electric Company until 1952, when he returned to Little Rock and established an advertising agency, Ted Lamb and Associates. Between 1952 and 1958 the business grew into a large and successful agency specializing in advertising for financial institutions, with offices in Little Rock, Dallas, Princeton, New Jersey, and Milford, Connecticut.

The Little Rock school crisis of 1958–59 resulted in the closing of all four Little Rock high schools. At the time Lamb was considered an up-and-coming businessman, a reputation he risked when he was elected to the school board on a platform of immediately reopening the schools. From 1958 until he stepped down in 1964 (he was reelected handily in 1961, despite strenuous opposition from segregationist forces), he led the liberal wing of the school board in the fight to reopen the schools, which was accomplished in August 1959.

Lamb could be outspoken. When he won election to the school board he stated publicly that "our victory is the beginning of the end for Orval E. Faubus ... his entire political empire, founded as it is upon deceit, misrepresentation and bigotry soon will be crumbling," and added that Faubus was "an unscrupulous demagogue."

Lamb devoted as much as forty hours a week to seeing that the plan to reopen the schools would succeed. He enjoyed recounting an incident in 1959 in which segregationists on the board held that reopening the schools would unnecessarily expose Little Rock children to the possibility of a polio epidemic. "I thought long and hard about what I could do to overcome this threat that had put natural fear in the hearts of mothers and fathers," Lamb said. His solution was to persuade Dr. Jonas Salk, developer of the Salk vaccine, to send a telegram to the board to the effect that reopening the schools would not endanger children's lives. The telegram "brought a stillness and hush to the ... proceedings, and the matter of the polio epidemic was never again raised."

Lamb's activities in connection with the school closings, and his public castigation of Governor Faubus and the segregationists, had the effect of almost closing down Ted Lamb and Associates. The agency lost twenty-one of its twenty-six accounts in Little Rock and started running a deficit. Instead of forcing Lamb to back down from his support for school integration, the business pressure made him more adamant. With a family of four children and a drastic drop in family income, he began commuting to Dallas to maintain as much of his business as possible.

Following his two terms on the school board, he decided to become a civil rights lawyer. Because he still had some advertising accounts in Dallas, he attended Law School there at Southern Methodist University. Later he transferred to the University of Arkansas at Fayetteville. For the next two years, he commuted between Little Rock, Fayetteville, and Dallas, attending to classes in Fayetteville and to business in Little Rock and Dallas.

In 1967 Lamb began practicing law in Little Rock, at first with Jim Youngdahl, a union attorney, and then on his own. He had been appointed chairman of the Arkansas Advisory Committee to the U.S. Commission on Civil Rights while still in Law School. As chairman he was a strong voice for school integration throughout Arkansas, so strong that he was not reappointed in 1967. His "sin" was criticizing the commission when it refused to recommend the cutting off of federal funds for seven Arkansas school districts that still operated segregated schools.

From the late 1960s until his death Lamb built a successful labor law practice in Little Rock. For seven of those years, he was general counsel for the Teamsters Union in Arkansas, Oklahoma, and eastern Texas. He also was instrumental in forming the Arkansas affiliate of the American Civil Liberties Union in 1968. He was the first chairman of the legal panel for the ACLU of Arkansas, and he litigated several civil liberties cases for the ACLU as a volunteer attorney.

He had a strong interest in helping the schools in his community. He served as president of the Yale Club of Arkansas, helping promising young Arkansans get admitted to Yale University. He also served as statewide publicity chairman for U.S. Savings Bonds and Muscular Dystrophy and county publicity chairman for the American Cancer Society.

During the last several years of his life, he lived on and maintained a farm owned by his father in Bryant. At the time of his death, he was survived by his first wife, Ardella Bullard, four children, his second wife, Deanna Jones Dudley, and two stepchildren.

[This biography is based on personal acquaintance, the archives of the American Civil Liberties Union of Arkansas, and communications with family members in February 1995 and September 1996. See the *Pine Bluff Commercial,* Jan. 10, 1968, and an obituary in the *Arkansas Gazette,* Sept. 7, 1984.]

MORTON GITELMAN

LANEY, BENJAMIN TRAVIS (Nov. 25, 1896– Jan. 21, 1977), governor of Arkansas, was born in Jones Chapel, Ouachita County, the son of Benjamin Travis Laney and Martha Ellen Saxon.

He attended Hendrix College and Arkansas Teachers College (A.B., 1924), and served in the United States Navy during World War I. He worked in business and banking from 1925 to 1926 in Conway, where he and Lucile Kirtley were married on January 19, 1926; the couple had three sons. In 1927 Laney returned to Ouachita County where his activities included oil, banking, farming, cotton gins, and retail stores.

He was the mayor of Camden from 1935 to 1939 and a member of the Arkansas Penitentiary Board (1941– 44). His activity on behalf of John L. McClellan's 1942 United States Senate bid solidified a friendship and political alliance.

A relative unknown when he ran for the 1944 Democratic gubernatorial nomination, he had the support of conservative business and financial interests. His runoff opponent withdrew ten days before the election amidst accusations of a negotiated deal; a token Republican opponent was easily defeated in the general election. Laney's 1946 renomination and reelection were effortless.

The governor's work on behalf of efficiency, economy, and consolidation in state government and his encouragement of industrialization and broadly based economic development earned him the nickname "Business Ben." These activities and his opposition to organized labor strengthened his ties with Arkansas business conservatives.

Laney's greatest achievement was the 1945 Revenue Stabilization Law, which combined flexibility in funding state programs with a priority mechanism to prevent deficit spending. Before 1945 fractions of taxes were allotted to more than one hundred separate accounts; this prevented shifting of resources as conditions and needs changed. The new law created a single general fund from which all state appropriations are made and prohibits departments and institutions from spending if cash is not available.

In 1947 he successfully urged the legislature to create a legislative council to provide research and bill-drafting assistance for Arkansas's part-time legislators.

Laney is remembered less for his streamlining of governmental structure and finance than for his opposition to proposals that would alter existing racial relationships and weaken or end segregation. He spoke out against federal initiatives dealing with lynching and the poll tax and quietly but firmly worked to prevent desegregation of state professional and higher education programs. Although Laney was Arkansas's last committed and philosophically consistent segregationist governor, it was on his watch that in 1948, the University of Arkansas Law School became the first public, all-white institution in the South to admit black students.

In 1948 Laney broke with the Truman administration (which he had enthusiastically welcomed in 1945) over Truman's use of federal law to require fair employment practices and end racial discrimination. The governor was a leader in the States' Rights Democrats ("Dixiecrats") movement and was seriously considered for a presidential or vice presidential nomination by the Dixiecrats.

Laney claimed that his actions were based on constitutional principles and states' rights philosophy and not on racial considerations, but he had praised Arkansas and Arkansans as being close to what he described as good and pure Anglo-Saxon stock.

Sidney S. McMath, elected governor in 1948, was a vigorous supporter of Truman and helped hold Arkansas in the Democratic column in the presidential election. Governor Laney had campaigned for the Dixiecrat ticket (Strom Thurmond and Fielding Wright) despite his doubts about the success of a third party in the South. In 1950 Laney challenged Governor McMath and sought a third term (a feat accomplished only once previously in Arkansas). McMath, with the support of the black electorate and organized labor, swamped the former governor.

Laney remained a spokesman for states' rights but disapproved of Governor Orval E. Faubus's actions during the 1957 Little Rock Central crisis. Laney believed that Faubus was less a defender of southern traditions on race and states' rights than a demagogue interested in immediate political gain.

Laney, who had earlier railed against what he called the "socialistic" Truman administration, was convinced that the national Democratic Party had been captured by the forces of liberalism, integration, and big labor. He supported the third-party candidacy of George Wallace in 1968.

Laney embraced the economics of a post-World War II "New South" and toiled to attract industry and investment capital to Arkansas. A gracious and articulate spokesman for the state, he traveled throughout the nation promoting a new image for Arkansas. However, regarding race, Laney clung to an old southern style of benign paternalism. The successful linking of economic growth with a more enlightened view of racial integration was left to Laney's successors.

In 1969 Laney served as a delegate to the Arkansas Constitutional Convention. He was active in the reelection campaigns of Senators John L. McClellan (1972) and J. William Fulbright (1974), two close friends whom he supported in spite of their Democratic affiliation.

He managed the rice farm of Winthrop Rockefeller in the 1960s and spent his last years in Magnolia looking after his own business affairs. He died at Magnolia and was buried in Camden Memorial Cemetery.

[The Laney papers are to be placed in the library at University of Central Arkansas, Conway. See Tom Forgey, "Benjamin Travis Laney Jr., 1945–1949," in *The Governors of Arkansas: Essays in Political Biography,* Timothy P. Donovan, Willard B. Gatewood Jr., and Jeannie M. Whayne, eds., 2d ed. (1995).]

TOM FORGEY

LEE, BURWELL (Oct. 20, 1809–May 28, 1877), Methodist preacher, was born in Davidson County, Tennessee. His parents are believed to have been Braxton and Polly Hunter Lee, who were married in northern Arkansas. Lee served briefly on two circuits in what was then part of the Missouri Conference—the White River and the Spring River—then went on to the Cherokee Mission at Adair, where he taught and preached to the Indians for three years. On July 2, 1831, he was present at the organization of a Temperance Society at Batesville, and one week later he solemnized the marriage of William Porter to Martha Bateman. This was the first of many marriages he performed in Independence County over the next forty-six years. He married Ann Maria Smith in about 1835, place unknown. To them were born Henrietta in 1836, Richard H. in 1840, and Julia in 1842. Ann Maria died sometime before 1850, and Lee next married Susan Serena Brownfield, in Little Rock on January 9, 1851. Lee settled permanently in Independence County about 1835. He is mentioned in early Methodist records as presiding over the organization of a Methodist Society in Batesville in that year, and one year later, in the year Arkansas achieved statehood, the Batesville Society hosted the first meeting of the new Arkansas Conference of the Methodist Episcopal Church, with Burwell Lee as the first presiding elder. In 1839 Lee "located," meaning that he retired from the active ministry to farm north of Batesville. He continued to perform marriages and funerals, however, and often filled the pulpit of the Batesville church. In 1849 he was one of the founders of Ebenezer Methodist Church near Moorefield. This church was later renamed Lee's Chapel in his honor. Between 1850 and 1854 he also served as Independence County treasurer. During the upheaval of

Civil War and Reconstruction, he accepted several conference appointments—as pastor of the Batesville church and as presiding elder of the Batesville district. He was listed as a member of the Batesville City Council in 1873, and was still performing marriages as late as 1877.

Lee's death followed what his obituary in the *Batesville Guard* called "a long and painful illness." He was only sixty-eight, but he must have been marked by hard work and poor health; the newspaper expressed surprise that he was not much older. "The last active labors of his long and useful life," wrote the editor, "were mainly spent as a colporteur, in the supplying of Scriptures to the people of an adjoining county [Izard County] at their own doors." The obituary gave him credit for organizing the first Bible society west of the Mississippi, and remarked that through his zeal and exertions, the first church was built in Batesville, and the first Methodist society organized in north Arkansas. The small one-horse cart, in which he had delivered Bibles and religious tracts to rural settlers, was used to transport his coffin for burial in Batesville's Oaklawn Cemetery. A plaque commemorating his service was placed in the wall of the First Methodist Church sanctuary in Batesville. When the present church was built in 1913, the plaque was moved to a prominent location near the chancel of the sanctuary. It reads: Sacred To The Memory of Rev'd. B. Lee/Founder of the First Methodist Church/In Batesville and Who Remained/In The Ministry 43 Years/Born Oct. 20, 1809/Died May 28, 1877.

[Sources include James A. Anderson, *Centennial History of Arkansas Methodism* (1935); Horace Jewell, *History of Methodism in Arkansas* (1892); Walter Vernon, *Methodism in Arkansas 1816–1976* (1976); Nancy Britton, "Burwell Lee" in the *Independence County Chronicle* 18(4): 19; and Duane Huddleston, "Early Religious Activities in Independence County, 1816–1836" in the *Independence County Chronicle* 11(4): 8. See also obituaries in the *Batesville Guard*, May 30 and June 7, 1877; a booklet commemorating the centennial of First Methodist Church, Batesville (1936); U.S. Census Records; Deed Books and Marriage Records, Independence County Courthouse; and the *Arkansas Annual Conference Minutes* of the Methodist Church.]

NANCY BRITTON

LINEBARGER, CLARENCE A. (Aug. 17, 1889– Aug. 8, 1978), real estate developer and resort owner, the youngest of three sons of Samuel Linebarger and Mary Pearson, was born in West Union, Indiana. When Mary's health worsened from tuberculosis, Samuel, Mary, and young Clarence, known as "C. A.," moved to Bentonville, where she had earlier found relief. Mary died in 1906, and Samuel moved to south Texas, where his older sons were involved in town siting. C. A. Linebarger graduated from Bentonville's Ouachita Academy before joining his family in Texas.

In 1912 Clarence Linebarger went to work for his brothers F. W. and C. C., who had pooled their resources and purchased the town of Tomball, Texas, at the north end of Houston's Harris County. By targeting the types of businesses needed to create a stable and enduring community and offering them incentives, Linebarger Bros. Realty attracted many buyers. They marketed all the land in the original town site, acquired surrounding acreage, and continued to expand. Linebarger gained valuable experience in public relations, sales, and construction at Tomball and was keen on self-improvement. He married Regina Agnes Naylor from Orange, Texas, and they set up housekeeping in Tomball. Their only child, C. A., was born there in June 1914.

Linebarger Bros. Realty sold out its inventory in Tomball and set its sights on Bentonville with its good water supply and pleasant climate. In January 1917 they purchased an undeveloped community of summer homes called Bella Vista together with adjoining land. C. A. Linebarger and his brother F. W., the idea man, designed and constructed a summer resort. They opened their first season that June with a dining hall, thirty-five guest rooms, a hydroelectric plant, a fresh water system, and improvements to the lake. Roads were laid out, summer home lots plotted, and sales brochures written, printed, and distributed. Their brother Clayton Linebarger (C. C.) stayed in Dallas, where he promoted sales.

Bella Vista was not on a railroad line, but the Linebargers had faith in 1917 that private ownership of an automobile was going to be common and they were right. In less than ten years Bella Vista was enjoying tremendous success. Linebarger Bros. continued building facilities for their summer vacationers, added two more guest-room buildings, a lakeside dance pavilion, an underground nightclub, and a nine-hole golf course. Their efforts resulted in the sale of over eight hundred lots with over five hundred summer cottages built by their own construction crews.

Cottage owners and guests enjoyed swimming, tennis, golf, and horseback riding by day, and spent their evenings dining at the Lodge and dancing at Moonlight Gardens or Wonderland Cave. Card parties and socials were organized and run by the Linebarger Bros. staff. The Linebargers controlled all of the activities at Bella Vista, including ice delivery and dairy and food vendor sales. C. A. Linebarger bought into his brothers' partnership in 1925. He continued to supervise the building crews. He was responsible for finishing owners' cottages to their liking. Records indicate that he designed the cottages and worked with the new owners to produce bungalow-style cottages of native wood integrated into the landscape so as not to destroy the beauty of the place. He achieved and maintained a high standard while meeting the customers' deadlines.

Owning and operating Bella Vista was challenging and the Linebarger boys thrived on it. Their lives belonged entirely to Bella Vista from April through September, but the rest of the year they escaped to recharge their batteries. C. A. Linebarger and his wife spent the winters in Florida for many years.

Bella Vista's high times began to wind down when the stock market crashed in 1929. Unfortunately, the Linebargers had just built a sixty-five-room hotel when hard times brought fewer vacationers. Many cottage owners did not return for the entire summer as they had in the past. The Linebargers were not hurt severely since they had almost sold out their inventory, but times were changing. As hard times eased up and people started traveling again, World War II started and Bella Vista lost even more returning families. They continued to have a band in residence to play for the dinner hour at the Sunset Hotel and later at the lakeside pavilion or the cave, and everyone enjoyed the swimming and hiking, but in time the golf course was abandoned.

After the war ended, Americans spent vacations differently. Families no longer encamped at their cottages from Memorial Day until Labor Day. Bella Vista was sold in 1950. Linebarger managed property he had acquired over the years in Bentonville and rural Benton County. He continued an active life after his wife's death in 1968 and enjoyed seeing Bella Vista's rebirth after its purchase by Cooper Communities in the mid-sixties. Cooper's new project encompassed the old Bella Vista (less than a thousand acres) and extended over an area of about forty square miles. By the time of his death C. A. Linebarger saw year-round residents enjoying this special place the brothers had described as "Nature's Gem of the Ozarks" sixty years earlier.

[The Linebarger Brothers Papers (ms. collection number 946), including business and personal papers, are in the Special Collections Division, University of Arkansas Libraries, Fayetteville. There is an obituary in the *Bentonville Daily Record*. See also George Phillips, ed., *The Bella Vista Story* (1980); and Gilbert C. Fite, *From Vision to Reality: A History of Bella Vista Village, 1915–1993* (1993).

CAROLE WESTBY

LISTON, CHARLES L. (Jan. 8, 1932?–Dec. 30, 1970?), professional boxer and world heavyweight champion, was born in St. Francis County, Arkansas, to Tobe Liston, a sharecropping farmer, and Helen Baskin.

Most students of ring lore rank Liston, called "Sonny," among the all-time top-ten heavyweights. Historian Herbert G. Goldman places him second behind Muhammad Ali, his nemesis, and ahead of celebrated champions Larry Holmes, Joe Louis, Jack Johnson, Jack Dempsey, Rocky Marciano, George Foreman, Joe Frazier, and Mike Tyson.

The circumstances of Liston's life and career were so controversial and mysterious that even his birth and death dates are open to speculation. Many people still question the authenticity of his two losses to Ali. Some think he may have been murdered, although the official finding was natural causes.

In a 1962 interview, Liston's mother told an *Arkansas Gazette* reporter her son was born January 8, 1932. Other sources quoted her giving the date as January 18. In 1967, annoyed by rumors he was several years older than he claimed to be, Liston produced a birth certificate showing May 8, 1932, as his date of birth.

Tobe Liston reportedly fathered twenty-five children in two marriages. Helen Liston, much younger than her husband, was mother of the younger ten. Tobe Liston's family originated in Mississippi and moved to eastern Arkansas about 1916, settling near Forrest City. "The boll weevils drove us out," Helen said. "They chased us across the Mississippi River and followed us." The Listons started to scatter during World War II. Helen Liston left her husband and several children on the farm and found a job in a St. Louis shoe factory. Sonny joined her at St. Louis in 1945, when he was thirteen. He said he knocked pecans off a neighbor's trees and sold them to buy a bus ticket.

Liston grew up illiterate. His father's child-rearing philosophy, according to his mother, was, "If they're big enough to go to the dinner table, they're big enough to go to the fields." In St. Louis Liston adapted to a ghetto environment by running with a street gang that graduated from petty thefts to mugging to armed robbery. In 1950 he was sentenced to concurrent five-year terms in the Missouri State Penitentiary at Jefferson City. It was here he was introduced to boxing.

Father Alois Stevens, the prison chaplain and recreation director, was so impressed by Liston's ring abilities that he contacted St. Louis sportswriter Robert Burnes, who in turn informed St. Louis boxing insiders that a possible heavyweight prospect was confined at Jefferson City. Frank Mitchell, a newspaper publisher and sometime manager of boxers, took trainers Monroe Harrison and Tony Anderson to the prison to watch Liston spar with a capable, experienced St. Louis heavyweight they brought with them. Liston passed the test with flying colors; the visiting fighter quit after two rounds.

In October 1952 Liston was paroled to Mitchell and Harrison. In a single amateur season, he dominated the national heavyweight field. He turned professional on September 2, 1953, with a one-round knockout of Don Smith at St. Louis. His rapid climb in the rankings was interrupted in 1956, when he was sentenced to a nine-month jail term after an altercation with a St. Louis policeman in which Liston reportedly took the officer's gun and broke his leg. At some point, control of the fighter passed from Mitchell to "underworld" figures, most notably Frank "Blinky" Palermo of Philadelphia. Because of questions about unsavory connections, Liston was never granted a license to box in New York, then the boxing industry's center.

From 1958 through 1961, Liston overpowered a succession of well-known heavyweights including Zora Folley, Eddie Machen, Cleveland Williams, Nino Valdes, and Roy Harris, and became number-one contender for the championship, then held by Floyd Patterson. Cus D'Amato, Patterson's manager, stalled until Patterson, out of pride, insisted on meeting Liston's challenge. On September 25, 1962, at Chicago, Liston won the title by knocking out Patterson in the first round. The contract mandated a return match, so Liston again knocked out Patterson in the first round at Las Vegas on July 22, 1963.

The most attractive challenger in the field was brash, colorful young Cassius Clay, soon to be called Muhammad Ali. As a 7-1 favorite, Liston quit in his corner, claiming a shoulder injury, before the start of the seventh round at Miami Beach on February 24, 1964. He had not been able to cope with Clay's superior speed, even during the fifth round when the challenger was temporarily blinded by an astringent solution that somehow got in his eyes. In a return match at Lewiston, Maine, on May 25, 1965, Liston went down and out in the first round from a short, chopping punch half the crowd didn't see.

From then until 1970, Liston won 15 of 16 bouts but was never again taken seriously as a contender. His overall record is 50-4 with 39 knockout victories. He moved from St. Louis to Philadelphia to Chicago to Denver before settling in Las Vegas. It was there his wife, Geraldine Liston, returning from a lengthy holiday, found him dead in their home. Date of death was estimated as December 30, but the precise cause was never determined.

[Sources include the *Arkansas Gazette*, Mar. 16, 1962 (Helen Liston interview); A. S. "Doc" Young, *Sonny Liston: The Champ Nobody Wanted* (1963); Nigel Collins, *Boxing Babylon* (1990); *The Ring Record Book* and *Boxing Encyclopedia*, various annual editions, 1972–87.]

JIM BAILEY

LITTLE, JOHN SEBASTIAN (Mar. 15, 1851–Oct. 29, 1916), congressman and governor of Arkansas, was the son of Jesse Little and Mary Elizabeth Tatum. He spent his childhood on the family's farm near Greenwood in Sebastian County. Known as "Bass," he attended Cane Hill College in Washington County for a single term (1871–72), then settled in Greenwood where he taught school and studied law. Admitted to the bar in 1873, he established his practice in Paris, Arkansas, where he and Elizabeth Jane Erwin married. The couple had five children.

He was elected prosecuting attorney of the Twelfth Judicial Circuit on the Democratic ticket in 1877, and reelected to three additional two-year terms. Elected in 1894 to represent Sebastian County in the general assembly, he served a single term (1885) and the following year was elected judge of the Twelfth Judicial Circuit Court, a position that he held until 1890. Impeccably attired in a Prince Albert coat, and armed with two derringers, the affable Judge Little "rode the circuit" in a buggy along the rough and lonely roads of his four-county jurisdiction. In 1890 he entered the race for Congress but withdrew because of "nervous exhaustion." In 1894 he waged a successful campaign for a seat in the United States House of Representatives, a victory that began a dozen-year tenure in Congress.

Closely associated with William Jennings Bryan, a House colleague from Nebraska, he was an ardent champion of "free silver," prohibition, and antitrust legislation. He focused special attention on matters relating to Indians and the Indian Territory that bordered his district, working to introduce into the territory more homesteaders, railroads, and business enterprises. Despite his concern for government economy, Little regularly sought expensive federal projects for his congressional district. His close attention to the needs and demands of his constituents, coupled with his penchant for small courtesies and for "treating everyone as his equal," endeared him to voters. The *Arkansas Gazette* described him as "the Great Commoner."

In 1906 Little decided to seek the Democratic nomination for governor of Arkansas. The incumbent governor, Jeff Davis, was attempting to unseat Senator James H. Berry. Little's chief rival for the gubernatorial nomination was Robert L. Rogers, the state's independent-minded attorney general who had alienated Governor Davis. Davis threw the weight of his political organization behind Little, who won the gubernatorial nomination and was elected. Although Little and Davis had much in common ideologically, they were radically different in style and personality. Little projected the image of a moderate who would restore harmony, decency, and cooperation to public life in Arkansas. His major liability was his health. A recurrence of "nervous exhaustion" caused him to attempt to withdraw from the gubernatorial race, only to be persuaded by Davis to carry on.

At his inauguration on January 18, 1907, Little outlined an impressive legislative program that called for free public school textbooks, the establishment of a textile school, greater support for the state university, a "fellow servant" law that would compensate the "laboring people" for job-related injuries, additional legislation to restrain corporations, the abolition of the convict-lease system, and a variety of internal improvements. Although legislators may not have been enthusiastic about all items on his agenda, they agreed that Little would pursue his goals with tact, civility, and moderation.

Immediately after his inauguration the new governor suffered a physical and mental collapse. He returned home to Greenwood, leaving his son, who served as his secretary, in charge of the governor's office. Failing to respond to treatment, he surrendered his office to the president *pro tempore* of the state senate in May. He died in the State Hospital for Nervous Diseases. At his funeral hundreds of mourners paid their last respects to one whom they considered a steadfast defender of the plain people.

[See Freed S. Little, *John Sebastian Little, 1851–1916: The Great Commoner* (1994).]

WILLARD B. GATEWOOD JR.

LONG, ISAAC JASPER (Feb. 23, 1834–Dec. 10, 1891), Presbyterian minister and educator, was born in Anderson District, South Carolina, the son of Isaac and Lettie Hamilton Long. Orphaned at fourteen, he supported himself as a laborer and tutor, and obtained an education at the Thalian Academy in South Carolina. Under the sponsorship of Reverend David Humphreys, he was able to attend Centre College in Danville, Kentucky, where he graduated in 1858. He then pursued his theological studies at Danville Seminary and at Columbia Seminary in South Carolina. In 1859 he married Callie P. Kennedy, daughter of the Reverend J. Leland Kennedy, principal of the Thalian Academy. He was ordained to the Presbyterian ministry in 1861 and became the pastor of Concord Church in Sumter District, South Carolina.

In 1866 he was sent by the Committee of Domestic Missions of the Presbyterian Church to collect information on the condition and needs of Presbyterian churches in Arkansas. Among the towns he visited was Batesville, and the congregation of the First Presbyterian Church there called him as their minister in 1867. He was at the time the only Presbyterian minister in fifteen counties, and served the Batesville church and several others in the area. He also taught school, eventually becoming principal of the Batesville Academy.

In 1872 he was instrumental in the founding of Arkansas College, the oldest independent college in Arkansas still operating under its original charter. He became its first president, also serving as professor of moral sciences and ancient languages. In an article for the *Arkansas Presbyterian* in 1891, he described his early days at the college: "It would have been, from a human standpoint, a more hopeful undertaking at the time ... to have started to build a railroad from White River to the Pacific Ocean with a pick and shovel and fifty dollars to start on. . . . The board had elected a president of the opening college, and two additional professors who had accepted, and announcements had been sent out. Within three weeks of the time of opening they both sent in their declinations, leaving the college with a president, who was also ex-officio professor of whatever no one else wanted ... on a prospective salary of about $750 or $800. As to the spare time, this witness can testify that from sixteen to eighteen out of every twenty-four hours were filled to overflowing seven days of each week, for months in succession, and as to the exchequer, by the blessing of the Lord, he, nor any member of his family ever went to bed hungry."

Long remained both college president and pastor until 1883, when he left the pulpit to devote his full energies to the college. His classroom experience resulted in the publication of his *Outline of Ecclesiastical History, for the Use of Colleges, High Schools, and Theological Classes* in 1888.

Among the four of his seven children who survived infancy were Eugene R. Long (born 1862), who followed his father as president of Arkansas College, and Mack H. Long (born 1873), longtime Little Rock banker.

[Sources include James P. Coffin, "Biographical Sketch of Rev. Isaac Jasper Long, D.D.," in *The History of Presbyterianism in Arkansas, 1828–1902* (1903); Alfred Nevin, *Encyclopedia of the Presbyterian Church in the United States of America* (1884) and *Biographical and Historical Memoirs of Northeast Arkansas* (1889). An obituary was published in the *Arkansas Gazette* on Dec. 11, 1891. Eugene R. Long's "Historical Sketch of Arkansas College" (1908) and A. C. McGinnis's "Arkansas College," *AHQ* 31 (Autumn 1972) include information on Long and the early days of Arkansas College. The archives there contain family scrapbooks, photos, and other memorabilia.]

NANCY SNELL GRIFFITH

LOUGHBOROUGH, LOUISA WATKINS WRIGHT (Jan. 23, 1881–Dec. 10, 1962), historic preservationist, was born in Little Rock to Louisa Watkins and William Fulton Wright, a Confederate veteran, and took pride in her family lineage through such leaders as Arkansas Supreme Court justice George Claiborne Watkins and United States senator William Savin Fulton. Her family was much attuned to history, and as a child she heard stories about the importance

of several houses on the east half of Block 32, Original City of Little Rock. These houses eventually became the core of the Arkansas Territorial Restoration.

Louisa Wright, who was called Louise, was educated in Little Rock schools. In 1902 she married J. Fairfax Loughborough, an attorney in the Rose law firm. The couple moved to the new Pulaski Heights suburb and Loughborough engaged in civic activities. She was a charter member of the Little Rock Garden Club and a member of the National Society of the Colonial Dames of America. She served as vice regent of the Mount Vernon Ladies Association of the Union, the organization which restored and maintains the home of George Washington. She later served on the board of Kenmore, the home of George Washington's sister, Betty Washington, in Fredericksburg, Virginia.

Loughborough's interest in historic structures in Little Rock began when the Little Rock Garden Club sought to improve the appearance of the War Memorial Building (Old State House). The grounds were littered with signs and monuments, and the roof of the Greek Revival building sported figurative statues of Law, Justice, and Mercy which had been salvaged from the Arkansas exhibit at the Philadelphia Centennial of 1876. To take the facade back to its original appearance, Loughborough had the statues removed without the permission of the War Memorial Commission, which had legal authority over the building. Rumor had it that to ensure that the statues would not be reinstalled they were dropped into the Arkansas River.

In 1935 Loughborough was appointed to the Little Rock Planning Commission, and it was in this role that she heard about the plan to condemn the half-block of houses on Cumberland and East Third Streets which she remembered from her youth. Fearing the loss of several historic structures, one of them thought to be Arkansas's last territorial capitol, she mobilized a group of civic leaders to save them. She enlisted the aid of the prominent architect Max Mayer and coined the term "town of three capitols" to try to capture the imagination of potential supporters. In the midst of the Great Depression, she approached one of the New Deal agencies, the Works Progress Administration, to finance the saving of the structures. Floyd Sharp, the WPA administrator in Little Rock, promised that he would help but informed her that the project needed at least thirty thousand dollars to get started and had to be owned by a government agency. Sharp figured that

Loughborough would be deterred from her goal by the WPA requirements.

Instead, she turned to the general assembly. Through her own dogged but genteel persistence (and the help of the good contacts of the other committee members and her husband's law firm) she got her thirty thousand dollars and the creation of the Arkansas Territorial Capitol Commission. When she returned to Floyd Sharp, he had a difficult time remembering her. He later explained what happened after he was reminded of his promise: "There was nothing I could do except reluctantly call in Capt. Limerick and other construction officials and tell them what I had done ... It was necessary that we withdraw or withhold from other projects, a portion of their material funds and reallocate to this project in order to keep my promise."

A private fund-raising campaign brought in the remaining money for the completion of the project. The Arkansas Territorial Restoration opened on July 19, 1941, a historic site museum with four museum houses on their original half-block in downtown Little Rock. This was a great step forward for historic preservation in Arkansas. With this worthy model, eventually museum houses, preservation organizations, and historic districts would spring up all over Arkansas. The project was also a milestone for the state's relationship with its own history. Some state funding had gone to preserve old buildings, but never before had the government created an agency committed to both the restoration of structures and the interpretation of their history. Finally, the Arkansas Territorial Restoration garnered national attention for the state. At the same time that such institutions as Colonial Williamsburg were gaining prominence as pioneering preservation projects, Arkansas could point with pride to its own accomplishment. In 1960 the National Trust for Historic Preservation honored the complex as one of twelve outstanding museum communities in the country.

As founding chairman of the Arkansas Territorial Restoration Commission, Louisa Loughborough provided daily direction for the museum house complex through the first twenty years of its existence, yielding her authority only as her health began to fail. She died in Little Rock and is buried at Mount Holly Cemetery.

[Sources include obituaries in the *Arkansas Democrat* and the *Arkansas Gazette,* Dec. 11, 1962, and other articles, especially in the *Arkansas Gazette,* Mar. 16, 1950, and Mar. 18, 1955. See William B. Worthen, "Louise Loughborough and Her Campaign for 'Courage and Fineness,'" in the *Pulaski County Historical Review,* Summer 1992. The Arkansas Territorial Restoration files and scrapbooks cover Loughborough's involvement in the museum. A copy of a critical essay by Jamye Landis on her preservation philosophy is at the museum. The museum, which features the state's premier Arkansas-made collection, is open to the public most days of the year.]

WILLIAM B. WORTHEN

LOVELY, PERSIS (July 1, 1770–Jan. 18, 1842), pioneer and frontier wife, was born in Stow, Massachusetts, to Thomas Brown and Persis Gibson. Thomas Brown, a blacksmith, served in a company of Minutemen which fought the British at Concord and Lexington in 1775. He removed his family to Henniker, New Hampshire, in February 1785.

Persis married Joshua Goodrich of Sharon, Connecticut, March 24, 1793; her second marriage was to Major William Lewis Lovely at Kingston, Tennessee, February 15, 1807. Twenty years Lovely's junior, she removed with him to the lands of the Arkansas Cherokees in the spring of 1813. After a three-month journey by keelboat, she helped establish their primitive log home and agency on the eastern bank of the Illinois Bayou, one mile above the Arkansas River (now the campground at Lake Dardanelle State Park) in Pope County, Arkansas. Childless and lonely for civilized comforts, calling her situation "the inhospitable gloom of the savage wilderness," Persis assisted her husband in his duties with the Cherokees, who referred to her as "Mother." At the death of Major Lovely in 1817, she fixed his grave on the grounds of the agency and continued to live in her log home with her servants.

A few months later she convinced the government to allow her to remain on her property in spite of an impending treaty. Signed July 8, 1817, it granted to the Cherokee exclusive occupation of lands north of the Arkansas River in compensation for lands relinquished in Tennessee and Georgia; all citizens of the United States must leave the treaty area. Persis, with support from the tribal leaders, wrote to Return J. Meigs, Cherokee agent in Tennessee, pleading her "attachment to the place where is deposited the mortal remains of her deceased husband," and asked to remain. Meigs, General Andrew Jackson, and Secretary of War George Graham granted her request.

Her home became well-known to travelers in the

region. The first territorial governor of Arkansas, James Miller, became acquainted with her hospitality due to his frequent trips between Arkansas Post and Belle Point (Fort Smith) as he worked to bring peace between the warring Osage and Cherokees. The "Little Osage Captive," Lydia Carter, was placed by Governor Miller at Persis's home for safekeeping in February 1821, after a failed prisoner exchange between the two tribes at Belle Point. Lydia, taken captive in 1817 at age seven, had been in school at Brainerd Mission in Cherokee-occupied Tennessee under the direct order of President James Monroe. Suffering from dysentery and "malarial fever" contracted during the long trip from Tennessee, Lydia died a few weeks after arriving at Persis's home and was buried near the grave of Major Lovely. When Cephas Washburn, missionary and founder of Dwight Mission, appeared on her doorstep also suffering from "malarial fever" in the summer of 1820, Persis gave him a room until he was well enough to meet with Cherokee leaders and select a location for the new school.

In early 1828 Persis again faced the prospect of losing her home as rumors circulated that the Arkansas lands of the Cherokees would soon be open for settlement by United States citizens. The Cherokee Treaty of May 1828 validated the rumors as the tribe agreed to move further west, relinquishing their Arkansas tract. The "for life" status of her home on the Illinois Bayou was not addressed in the new treaty, and she faced possible homelessness. In July 1828 she wrote James Barbour, secretary of war, detailing that property granted her in the Treaty of 1817 was now included in the lands to be settled by whites. She requested title to the section of land she and her husband settled upon in 1813. Her request was forwarded to Thomas McKenney of the Indian Office in September 1828. McKenney, who either misunderstood or ignored her request, wrote E. W. DuVal, agent of the Arkansas Cherokees, directing that Persis "who is old, and the land of but little value from its extreme poverty, the shortest, and no doubt most acceptable mode of satisfying her will be to pay her a proper value for it."

Outraged, she wrote a scathing letter to Congress in December 1829, demanding redress: "The former Compact [Treaty of July 1817] is entirely forgotten, her name not even mentioned [in the new Treaty], and herself disposed of as though she was a Cherokee." Her home "has been sold and become private property, and she now finds herself a tenant at will to an individual,

instead of being sheltered under the wing of Government." Her property was valued at five hundred dollars, which she called "an inconsiderable sum."

In the meantime, she obtained permission to move into the home of Alfred Finney (on Mill Creek in Pope County), a former missionary at Dwight Mission. Reverend Finney had died a few months earlier, and the school had recently moved west with the Cherokees. In January 1830 she wrote President Andrew Jackson requesting his direct intervention on her behalf. But a year later she still had not received compensation for her former home and farm. Amazingly, upon inquiry to the government land office by a delegate to Congress from the Territory of Arkansas, A. H. Sevier was told that there was "no such name on the list returned by the [Arkansas] assessor [in 1828]."

Finally, through the efforts of Sevier and others, an Act of Congress for the benefit of Persis Lovely was approved on March 3, 1831. This granted her a one-half section of land, including her present residence on Mill Creek, and the amount (five hundred dollars) at which her original property had been valued in 1828.

Persis continued to live at her Mill Creek home until her death and was buried by friends next to her husband on the Illinois Bayou.

[See "Vital Records of Stow, Mass." (Church of Latter Day Saints, Salt Lake City); L. W. Cogswell, *History of the Town of Henniker* (1880); S. E. Roberts, *Roots of Roane County, Tennessee 1792–* (1981); the Foreman Collection, Thomas Gilcrease Museum of History and Art, Tulsa; G. R. Turrentine, "Early Pope County History," *Arkansas Valley Historical Papers*, Oct. 15, 1954; E. Cornelius, *The Little Osage Captive, an Authentic Narrative* (1822); A. Finney, "Arkansas Mission: Journal of the Missionarys," *Missionary Herald*, May 1821; Letters Received by the Secretary of War Relating to Indian Affairs, 1800–1823 (Record Group M271) and Letters Sent by the Secretary of War Relating to Indian Affairs, 1800–1824 (Record Group M15) in the National Archives (Washington, D.C.); obituary in the *Arkansas Gazette*, Feb. 16, 1842.]

BRENT G. BERGHERM

LOVELY, WILLIAM LEWIS (1750–Feb. 24, 1817), teacher, Indian subagent, was born in Dublin, Ireland, and emigrated to western Virginia shortly before the Revolutionary War. He lived briefly in the household of President James Madison's father, James Madison Sr.

He began his military career in 1774 as assistant to the commissary general of the army at the Battle of

Point Pleasant. In the Revolutionary War he served in the Fourth and Eighth Virginia Regiments, seeing action in major battles. He attained the rank of captain, and for his service was granted a military warrant of four thousand acres in Kentucky.

He made his way to eastern Tennessee a few years later, teaching school in the State of Franklin during its brief existence. By 1792 he was a major in the Washington County Tennessee militia under General John Sevier, protecting white settlers from hostile Indians. From 1792 to 1799 he served as sheriff and town commissioner in Greene County and Roane County.

He married Mrs. Persis Goodrich at Kingston, Tennessee, on February 15, 1807, and may have had at least one child (Robert Lewis Lovely).

Major Lovely became known as a friend by the Cherokee tribal leaders, who developed great confidence in him. In 1801 a prominent chief, James Vann, requested that Lovely be chosen as subagent under the new agent, Return J. Meigs. In this role Lovely resided among the Cherokees, attended their councils, and was accessible for immediate advice.

Upon President Jefferson's approval in 1809, Cherokees began emigrating west of the Mississippi River because of white encroachment on their lands in Tennessee and Georgia. In 1813 Meigs assigned Lovely to relocate his subagency to the Cherokee settlements along the Arkansas River. Lovely, with his wife, Persis, made the three-month journey by keel boat down the Tennessee, Ohio, and Mississippi Rivers, and then up the Arkansas River. He established his wilderness home and subagency in May 1813 in the heart of the Cherokee settlements, at a former Osage Indian campsite on the eastern bank of the Illinois Bayou, one mile above the Arkansas River. As a result, he became the farthest west, and most isolated, official of the young United States Government for that time. In a letter to Meigs, he called his wilderness home a "handsome situation" complete with "a plumb orchard of fifty acres and the finest I ever eat [sic]." Specifically, his subagency was located in what later would be Lake Dardanelle State Park (S2-T7N-R21W) just west of Russellville, Arkansas. The Arkansas River region, Lovely said, was the "Garden of the World" and "the most valuable as to soil and valuable minerals that belongs to the whole [Louisiana] Purchase."

Soon after his arrival, he attempted to set a boundary between whites and Indians, angering squatters and land speculators, who complained to government officials. Seemingly unaware of Lovely's subagency, William Clark, of Lewis and Clark fame and superintendent of Indian Affairs at St. Louis, was caught off guard by the complaints and wrote to Lovely, criticizing his acting without Clark's knowledge and consent. Clark asked Lovely to send a copy of his appointment by the secretary of war and his instructions as sub-agent to the Arkansas Cherokees. Lovely complied, writing, "I am here without a cent, among the worst banditti [who] have made their escape to this country guilty of the most horrid crimes and are now depredating on the Osage and other tribes."

The biggest problem facing Lovely was the conflict between the Osage Indians under Chief Clermont and the emigrating Cherokees. The Osage were unhappy to see their recently ceded hunting grounds settled by another tribe. They were also angered over the ever increasing Cherokee hunting parties competing for game on Osage lands. Reports of horse stealing and murder by the Osage were frequent, as were reports of retaliation by Cherokees. Lovely wrote about the conflict to Meigs in Tennessee and Clark in St. Louis, urging as early as 1814 that a military post in the region was necessary to keep peace between the two tribes. (Fort Smith was established for this reason, but several months after Lovely's death.)

In order to prevent a full-scale war, Lovely held a conference at the mouth of the Verdigris River (Oklahoma) in July 1816 with leaders from both tribes. He proposed to the Osage that the government would pay all claims by Cherokees and whites against them if they would relinquish a tract of over seven million acres lying between the Verdigris River in Oklahoma and the home of the Arkansas Cherokees. It was Lovely's intention that Osage abandonment of this area would leave it free for the Cherokees to hunt over in peace. The Osage agreed to this proposition, and the tract became known as "Lovely's Purchase," because Lovely acted without official authority to make such an offer.

In 1815 due to isolation, danger, and a meager salary, Lovely wrote President Madison, whom he had known forty years before in Virginia, requesting a transfer to a civilized location where he could "pass the evening of my life with comfort." When the Arkansas Cherokee leaders learned of this request, they assembled around his log home and declared that if he left, the tribe "would re-cross the Mississippi and never return." Lovely remained at his wilderness station, helping the Indians he loved.

In the winter of 1816, he contracted an unknown illness from which he never recovered. When he died, Persis buried him on the grounds of their home. A historical marker, on the shore of Lake Dardanelle, has been placed on the approximate location.

[See F. B. Heitman, *Historical Register of Officers of the Continental Army during the War of the Revolution* (1893); Goodspeed Publishing Co., *History of Tennessee, Containing Historical and Biographical Sketches of Thirty East Tennessee Counties* (1887); W. Hutcherson, *Marriage Record of Roane County, Tennessee, 1801–1855* (1973). See also S. E. Roberts, *Roots of Roane County, Tennessee, 1792* (1981); P. E. Allen's article "Leaves from the Family Tree" in the *Chattanooga Sunday Times Magazine*, Apr. 25, 1937; the Foreman Collection, Thomas Gilcrease Museum of History and Art, Tulsa; Records of the Cherokee Indian Agency in Tennessee, 1801–1835 (Record Group M208) in the National Archives (Washington, D.C.); and G. R. Turrentine, "Early Pope County History, William Lewis Lovely," *Arkansas Valley Historical Papers*, Oct. 15, 1954.]

BRENT G. BERGHERM

LUCAS, JOHN GRAY (Mar. 11, 1864–Oct. 27, 1944), attorney and legislator, was born in Marshall, Texas. Official records list his father's name as unknown; his mother's name is listed as "Bettie." As a youth Lucas moved to Pine Bluff, where he attended public schools, then entered the Branch Normal College of Arkansas Industrial University (now the University of Arkansas at Pine Bluff), "where he remained up to a few months of his graduation." Afterward, he "remained in the merchandising business two years, when he graduated with the Degree of A.B."

Lucas moved to Massachusetts, where in October 1884 he entered the Boston University School of Law. He was graduated in 1887, the only African American in a class of fifty-two students, and one of seven students graduating with honors.

In December 1886 he was interviewed by the *Boston Daily Globe* and asked about racial conditions in his hometown of Pine Bluff. Lucas responded with enthusiasm. He observed that in Pine Bluff three of the eight city councilmen were African American and that African Americans held the offices of county coroner and county circuit clerk. African Americans comprised half of the members of the local police force and half of the local justices of the peace and often served on juries. In addition, a black entrepreneur owned the city's principal streetcar system. He also noted that on public carriers throughout Arkansas "there was neither distinction nor separation [by race]." Contrasting the lot of Massachusetts blacks with conditions in Arkansas, he wondered why "more colored young men from the North did not make Arkansas their home. It is an inviting field for them and a grand opportunity to make something of themselves."

Lucas followed his own advice. He returned to Arkansas and was admitted to the state bar. Soon afterward, he was named assistant prosecuting attorney for Pine Bluff and Jefferson County. His abilities brought him to the attention of Judge H. C. Caldwell, who appointed him United States commissioner for the United States Circuit Court, Eastern District of Arkansas. He was also elected to the Republican state and county central committees and served on the Republican Eleventh Judicial District Central Committee. In the fall of 1890 he was elected as a state representative from Jefferson County.

His service during the following year in the Arkansas General Assembly earned him a permanent place in the annals of Arkansas history. Entering the legislature at the very time that a new wave of racial reaction was inundating the American South, he emerged as a leader among the legislature's twelve African-American lawmakers. He is especially remembered for the trenchant and eloquent address he delivered in February 1891 against a Jim Crow separate-coach bill that would mandate racial segregation on Arkansas's railroads. Although the measure was passed easily by the legislature's white Democratic majority, Lucas's address against it won praise from white adversaries. The *Arkansas Gazette* and the *Arkansas Democrat*, the state's most important Democratic newspapers, characterized Lucas as "a fluent debater," "unquestionably the ablest and most brilliant representative of his race in the state, and it might truthfully be said (for his age) in the South," "a born leader of his people" for whom in 1891 there was "certainly a bright future in store."

The same legislature adopted a series of measures that effectively disfranchised a majority of black voters and removed virtually all blacks from public office in the state during the next four years. By 1893 Lucas had left Arkansas and relocated in Chicago, where he established a lucrative law practice, conducted from his spacious suite of offices at 88 Dearborn Avenue in the downtown Chicago Loop. He gained a reputation as an expert in criminal law and on four occasions appeared before the United States Supreme Court. By the early twentieth century, the local African-American press was referring to him as "a black millionaire." He became active in Republican politics and obtained appointments as assistant corporation counsel and first assistant recorder of deeds in Cook County. During the Great Depression he, like so many African Americans, left the Republican Party and became a Democrat. In 1934 he was appointed assistant United States attorney in Cook County, a position he was still holding in the year of his death. He died in Chicago and was buried in that city's Lincoln Cemetery. He was survived by his wife, Olive Gulliver Lucas, and his daughter, Elaine Louise Lucas Henderson. His only son, John Gray Lucas Jr., predeceased him.

Lucas's life was emblematic of broad changes in patterns of race relations occurring in Arkansas and the South during the latter half of the nineteenth century. From the end of the Civil War until the early 1890s, African Americans could obtain an education and then enter politics as independent, forthright champions of their race's interests. After that point, as historian J. Morgan Kousser has observed, "most blacks would have to emigrate to the North, choose other professions, or settle for the role of white-appointed race leader, with all the constraints that role imposed on their statements and actions." Lucas's decision to move from Pine Bluff to Chicago in 1893 was understandable. For an intelligent, articulate, and militant black leader like himself, Arkansas had ceased to be a land of opportunity.

[Sources include Willard B. Gatewood Jr., *Aristocrats of Color: The Black Elite, 1880–1920* (1990) and his editions "Negro Legislators in Arkansas, 1891: A Document," *AHQ* 31 (Autumn 1972): 220–33, and "Arkansas Negroes in the 1890s: Documents," *AHQ* 33 (Winter 1974): 293–325. Sources also include James N. Simms, ed. *Simms Blue Book and National Negro Business and Professional Directory* (1923); J. Morgan Kousser, ed., "A Black Protest in the 'Era of Accommodation': Documents," *AHQ* 34 (Summer 1975): 149–78; and John William Graves, *Town and Country: Race Relations in an Urban-Rural Context, Arkansas, 1865–1905* (1990), "The Arkansas Separate Coach Law of 1891," *Journal of the West* 7 (Oct. 1968): 531–41 and (revised) in *AHQ* 32 (Summer 1973): 148–65, and "Jim Crow in Arkansas: A Reconsideration of Urban Race Relations in the Post-Reconstruction South," *Journal of Southern History* 55 (August 1989): 421–48.]

JOHN WILLIAM GRAVES

LYON, AARON W. (July 11, 1797–Oct. 23, 1888), pioneer educator, was born in Elizabeth, New Jersey, the son of Aaron Lyon and Joanna Hatfield. During the war of 1812 he served in Captain Altman's Pennsylvania Militia. In 1824 he graduated from Union College in Schenectady, New York. He entered Princeton Theological Seminary in 1825 and completed the full three-year course. After completing his studies in 1828, his health forced him to move south; he accompanied Major Edward Duval to Arkansas, where Duval was in charge of the Cherokee agency.

In 1829 Lyon married Elizabeth Agnew of Princeton and made plans to open a private academy at what had been the Dwight Mission in Pope County, Arkansas. The academy opened in 1830, offering Latin, Greek, and the "higher branches of English Education" in addition to a more basic curriculum. In 1833 Lyon and his wife moved to Batesville, where he again opened a school. This school, the Batesville Academy, was the first such institution to be chartered by the Arkansas legislature. It is unclear just how long Lyon was in charge of the academy. Contemporary records show that by 1835 he was the receiver in the Batesville land office, and as early as 1838, he was involved in various commercial ventures in the area. In the early 1840s, he and John Ringgold became partners in a mercantile business; he later owned a drugstore in partnership with Dr. John F. Allen, and still later with E. R. Goodwin. Along with Noadiah Marsh, he was instrumental in the development of Elizabeth, the first seat of Jackson County.

Lyon was a lifelong Presbyterian, serving as an elder in the First Presbyterian Church in Little Rock, and then as a founding elder of the First Presbyterian Church in Batesville. He was active in Presbyterian affairs, served several times in the general assembly, and was active in the Sunday School movement. He was on the original board of trustees of Arkansas College and served as its vice president from 1872 to 1882.

Lyon's first wife died in 1857; in 1862 he married Carra J. Hutchins. They had four children: Mary Clarence (born 1863); Elinor Bryan (died in infancy); Sarah Wildey (born 1867); and Aaron Woodruff (born 1869). In 1882 the family moved to Fresno, California.

Here again, Lyon was active in church affairs, participating in the establishment of the First Presbyterian Church of Fresno. He died of pneumonia.

[Little information is available on Lyon. This entry was gleaned from census records, newspapers, and other contemporary records. Obituaries for Lyon appeared in the *Arkansas Gazette*, Nov. 29, 1888, and the *Fresno Evening Expositor*, Oct. 24, 1888. An obituary for his first wife appeared in the *Batesville Independent Balance*, Apr. 17, 1857.]

NANCY SNELL GRIFFITH

MADDEN, OWEN VINCENT (Dec. 18, 1891–Apr. 24, 1965), gangster and underworld boss, was born in Leeds, England, to Irish parents, Francis Madden and Mary (maiden name unknown), who had migrated looking for work. "Owney" spent his early childhood in Wigan and Liverpool, where his father worked in textile mill sweatshops until his death in 1902. Mary then took her family to New York, settling in a crime-ridden westside Manhattan district known as Hell's Kitchen. She worked as a scrubwoman, while Owney sporadically attended St. Michael's Parochial School on West 33rd Street.

But Owen Madden got his real education on the sidewalk. According to his own account, he committed his first crime at age fourteen, clubbing a man and stealing five hundred dollars. Wily and tough, he rose to lead the area's most violent gang, the Gophers. In 1911 Madden married and briefly lived with Dorothy Rogers, by whom he had a daughter, Margaret, his only known child. His vocation was gunman and killer, and he was wounded many times. In 1915 he was tried for manslaughter and sent to the New York State Correctional Facility at Ossining (Sing-Sing). He was paroled February 1, 1923, in the midst of prohibition. The Volsted Act, which implemented the prohibition of alcohol, had been in effect three years.

Now in his element, Madden made fast profits in bootlegging, nightclubs, and show business. Among other enterprises, he turned a failing Harlem nightspot at Lenox Avenue and 142nd Street into the Cotton Club, the fabled showcase for black musical talent in the Jazz Age. Downtown, his partner was Texas Guinan, the speak-easy queen who ran New York at night, it was said, as Mayor Jimmy Walker ran it by day. Madden also bankrolled the Hollywood careers of George Raft and Mae West, both Hell's Kitchen alumni. "Sweet but oh so vicious" was how West later described her longtime boyfriend and protector.

By the late 1920s Madden was a millionaire, chief of an underworld empire that included real estate, boxing, gambling, bootlegging, breweries, and entertainment. With Frank Costello, Lucky Luciano, and other mob figures, he organized a "crime commission" or syndicate, whose objective was high profits, a businesslike operating style, and a minimum of bad publicity. Street shootouts were passé; murder and terror were henceforth to be managed with discretion.

In 1930 New York governor Franklin Roosevelt was seeking a presidential nomination, and a crackdown on corruption in New York City was essential to his plans. On July 7, 1932, Madden went back to Sing-Sing for parole violations. In 1933 he was released, and prohibition was repealed later that year.

Now in his forties and in chronic ill-health from old bullet wounds, Madden emerged in a new world. His presence in New York had become intolerable not only to politicians but no doubt to other racketeers. He went or was sent into exile to Hot Springs, Arkansas, which had for many years been a center of gambling, prostitution, and bootlegging. For some time Madden had been romancing a Hot Springs gift-shop clerk, Agnes Demby, daughter of the local postmaster. They were married November 26, 1935, and settled down in a modest house on West Grand Avenue. Contrary to myth, she was no ingenue at thirty-four, and she was well acquainted with her husband's racketeer friends, his prison record, and his way of living.

The terms of Madden's exile to Hot Springs will never be known; important New York politicians and criminals may have struck the deal, possibly with Frank Costello as broker. Confined to Arkansas, Madden was not a passive "retiree." Hot Springs mayor Leo P. McLaughlin and Judge Vern Ledgerwood ran their own syndicate, the so-called "Little Combination," which controlled gambling and prostitution, paid bribes, rigged elections, skimmed profits, evaded taxes, and kept the peace. Madden probably furnished the wire service that brought racing results to bookmakers; he was thought to own controlling interests in the Southern Club and other lucrative gaming establishments. A Who's Who of gangland chiefs—Costello, Luciano, Meyer Lansky, Joe Adonis—visited Madden regularly and openly.

In 1946 the McLaughlin machine was voted out, but

local rackets continued to flourish. Under constant FBI surveillance, Madden played godfather to local charities and became a familiar, even beloved, figure in his trademark cap and scarf. In 1961 he was summoned before the Senate Judiciary Committee, where he repeatedly invoked the Fifth Amendment. But the Hot Springs Jazz Age was running out; in 1964 the state government took its first decisive steps to shut down the rackets. A year later Madden died of emphysema.

Madden may not have seen himself as a patron of the arts, but his claim, if any, to immortality may be the Cotton Club and the great musicians it employed, including Duke Ellington and Cab Calloway. The idea that big crime should model itself after big business is another of his lasting contributions to American life.

[Graham Nown's *The English Godfather* (1987), the sole biography of Madden, is disorganized and filled with conjecture and with conversations the author cannot have heard. However, Nown investigated the sources that exist for Madden's life and interviewed Agnes Madden and others who knew him. Other sources include newspaper clippings in the Garland County Historical Society, as well as the taped oral history project the society carried out in 1980 on the McLaughlin era. To a small extent I also relied on personal recollections.]

SHIRLEY ABBOTT

MAGUIRE, HOSEA M. (Apr. 18, 1813–July 23, 1888), general store owner, postmaster, congressman, was likely born in Simpson County, Kentucky. His parents, Owen and Mary McGuire (the family spelled the name both McGuire and Maguire), had migrated from Buncombe County, North Carolina. No information is available on Hosea Maguire's early years. The family, including four sons and one daughter, came to Arkansas Territory sometime during the 1830s before statehood was granted in 1836. The family first appears in land certificates dated 1836 and 1838 for property near present-day Elkins, Arkansas. Their single-pen log home, though modified, was still occupied in 1996.

From about 1836 to 1840 Owen McGuire owned one to two slaves who helped in the fields. Tax records indicate that the family owned horses and cattle and 120 acres of land. The nearest commercial center was Fayetteville, about nine miles distant; the McGuires would have visited there infrequently to purchase sugar, coffee, and other goods not produced on the farm.

The family had to clear the land, a slow process. Larger trees were girdled with axes and left to die; undergrowth was rooted up with hoes and burned. Stumps left in the ground took six to ten years to rot away. Bull-tongue plows were used to open up the tough virgin lands. Labor was generally shared by all family members. Women worked in the fields, and men assisted women in the house. Many shared tasks were gender neutral during the early years of establishing a farmstead.

Following the death of Owen McGuire in about 1845, Hosea began buying his brothers' shares of the family land. By 1848 he owned the entire familial farm, and he continued to deal in land for the rest of his life.

Maguire married Sara Louisa Tramell on May 18, 1850. He belonged to the Cumberland Presbyterian Church, a pioneering denomination in the area; from 1853 to the 1880s, the local congregation met at the Maguire house. Sarah's obituary notes that she joined the church "for the sake of being associated with her husband."

Maguire owned four slaves from the 1850s to 1861. During the early 1850s he purchased the land where he built a large Greek Revival style home and a three-story brick store, which stood as a landmark in the area until it burned in 1976. Bricks for the store were probably made on the farm. One full story was largely underground, the ground floor served as the store, and the second story was used by the Masonic Lodge.

Hosea Maguire is listed as a postmaster at Maguire's Store in 1853, indicating that his commercial venture was established by then. The store was apparently operating during the War between the States; Confederate general Thomas C. Hindman writes in a letter dated October 26, 1862: "I moved toward Fayetteville, intending to take position at McGuire's Store, which would enable me to get subsistence and forage for a few days, there being considerable wheat and forage and two mills in that vicinity." Even though Hosea was a southern sympathizer, his assets would have been threatened by Hindman, who seized foodstuffs and supplies, restricted travel, and established price controls.

Tax records suggest that Maguire came through the war without major adverse personal consequences. During 1867 he still owned more than two hundred acres, and by 1868 he owned more than five hundred acres of land, ownership indicating his stature in an agricultural society. He was an elder of his church and a member of the Masons, a group which wielded considerable political influence during the nineteenth century throughout the nation. In 1869 Maguire's Store was listed in the Dun, Barlow, and Company credit reference for Arkansas. The store probably was at its commercial and social peak during the 1870s and 1880s.

Hosea and Sarah Louisa had eight children; two of them died as infants, and all except one daughter were deceased by 1889. Sarah Louisa died in 1875. Hosea married again on June 28, 1877; his second wife, Mary Smith, was a sister of Sarah and a widow.

Maguire is listed as a farmer in the 1880 census. His wife is listed as "keeping house," a considerable burden, which would have included sifting flour, shelling nuts, drying herbs, killing and plucking chickens, among numerous other tasks necessary to prepare even a simple recipe. Livestock on the farm included horses, cattle, mules, sheep, and hogs. Crops grown were corn, oats, wheat, and apples. The census also records poultry and bees.

In 1886, at the age of seventy-three, Maguire ran from Washington County as a Democratic candidate and took a seat in the Arkansas House of Representatives, where he served on the House Ways and Means Committee. Two bills were introduced by him; neither passed. He was running for reelection when he became sick and died at his home. He is buried in the Stokenbury Cemetery in Washington County.

His house was occupied after his death, but Maguire's Store declined. In time the school and Masonic Lodge moved to Elkins and the buildings in Maguire's Store were demolished. The only structures that remain are the Owen McGuire home and the Hosea Maguire home, the latter now restored as a bed-and-breakfast inn.

[See John N. Edwards, *Shelby and His Men: Or, The War in the West* (1867); Tom Feathers, "Maguire's Store," *Flashback* (Washington County Historical Society: 1952) vol. 2, 1–5; and *War of the Rebellion,* Series 1, vol. 13 (Washington: 1885) 46–51. Tax records for Richmond Township, Washington County, 1836–1888, are in the Washington County Courthouse. Census records for Washington County, 1840–1880, are in the Fayetteville public library; before the Civil War, Census of the United States, Arkansas, Free Population Schedule, and Slave Population Schedule; after the war, Census of the United States, Arkansas. Also see Census of the United States, Arkansas: Agricultural, 1860 and 1880.]

LAWRENCE GENE SANTEFORD

MANNING, VANNOY HARTROG (July 26, 1839–Nov. 3, 1892), soldier and lawyer, was born in Edgecombe County, North Carolina, to Reuben S. and Dorothy Howell Manning. He grew up in Mississippi and studied law at the University of Tennessee. On May 3, 1859, he married Mary Zilephro Wallace of Holly Springs, Mississippi, and the following year moved to Hamburg, Arkansas. By 1861 he was a lawyer and farmer with eight slaves, a town house and lot in Hamburg, and six hundred and forty acres of good land.

After Arkansas's secession from the Union, Manning and Dr. William H. Tebbs of Portland raised two companies under Manning's command. Manning arranged for their transportation to Vicksburg, Mississippi, where his offer of service was rejected due to the small size of his command. He appealed to his friend Albert Rust, a senator from Arkansas in the Confederate Congress. Rust interceded on Manning's behalf with Secretary of War Leroy P. Walker, and Manning's two companies were accepted for service.

Albert Rust had also decided to enter military service, and at Manning's urging he returned to Arkansas to raise eight more companies. A rendezvous was arranged at Lynchburg, Virginia, and there on July 3, 1861, the Arkansans enlisted "for the war." In the election of regimental and company officers, Albert Rust was elected colonel, and Manning, major. The Confederate War Department conferred the title of Third Regiment of Arkansas Infantry (Volunteers). This was the only Arkansas regiment to fight under General Robert E. Lee in the Army of Northern Virginia. On March 11, 1862, Manning was promoted to the rank of colonel and to the command of the Third Arkansas.

Colonel Manning led the regiment through several battles in Virginia. They fought at White Oak Swamp, from June 25 to July 1, 1862. On September 17, 1862, at the battle of Sharpsburg, Maryland, Manning was wounded by rifle fire and carried from the field. In December 1862, he led the regiment at the Battle of Fredericksburg. Here the Army of Northern Virginia was reorganized, and regiments were brigaded by states. The Third Arkansas was brigaded with Hood's Texas Brigade, considered the most famous unit in the army.

Manning was wounded at the Battle of Gettysburg in Pennsylvania on July 2, 1863, in an area known as the Devil's Den. An artillery shell exploded in his face.

He was knocked senseless and suffered a large gash on his forehead and a bad cut on the bridge of his nose.

In September 1863 General James Longstreet's Corps of the Army of Northern Virginia was ordered west to support General Braxton Bragg's Army of Tennessee during the Chickamauga Campaign in Tennessee. The Texas Brigade and part of five brigades of General Longstreet's Corps boarded trains to Tennessee and by September 18, 1863, had reinforced General Bragg at the Battle of Chickamauga. Manning led the Third Arkansas in assaults on Union positions on both days of the battle. He was struck by flying metal and knocked down on the first day of fighting, but was not seriously hurt. Casualties suffered by the Third Arkansas included twenty-five dead, one hundred and twenty wounded, and twelve missing, the heaviest losses in the Texas Brigade.

In April 1864 the regiment returned to Virginia, where they received a new issue of uniforms. Together with the rest of General Longstreet's Corps they stood inspection by General Lee, who, though pleased to see his veterans, was shocked by their diminished force. The Third Arkansas numbered fewer than three hundred men.

In May 1864 the Union Army of the Potomac, under General Ulysses S. Grant, moved into an impenetrable, marshy tract of land in Virginia known as the Wilderness; from May 4 to 7 the armies were locked in combat there. On May 6 Colonel Manning was wounded in the right thigh and was left on the field. He spent the rest of the war a prisoner.

After his capture he was taken to a field hospital at Fredericksburg, Virginia, and later was admitted to the Lincoln U.S. Army General Hospital at Washington, D.C. After his release from the hospital he was moved from prison to prison in Washington, D.C., Delaware, South Carolina, and Georgia. At Morris Island, South Carolina, he was placed in solitary confinement for cutting the buttons off the coats of officers who had taken the Oath of Allegiance to the United States.

At Fort Delaware he was one of several officers who refused to take the Oath of Allegiance, and he made at least one fiery speech urging his fellow prisoners to continue to resist. He finally took the oath, and was released by order of the president on July 24, 1865, four months after the surrender at Appomattox Courthouse. At the time he took the oath he was described as having a dark complexion, dark hair, and black eyes and being five feet seven inches tall.

After his release Manning returned to Holly Springs, Mississippi, where he opened a law office and was elected to the U.S. Congress from 1877 to 1883. Afterward, he opened a law office in Washington, D.C., where he remained until his death. He is buried in Glenwood Cemetery in Washington, D.C.

[Manning's military records are located in the National Archives and Records Administration, Washington, D.C. A brief account of his service and one of two known wartime photographs are in Robert K. Krick, *Lee's Colonels: A Biographical Register of the Field Officers of the Army of Northern Virginia* (1992). An account of his activities in Ashley County, Arkansas, and two of his wartime letters are in *Reflections of Ashley County* (1988), compiled by Robert A. Carpenter and Mary Imogene Noble Carpenter. Calvin L. Collier's *They'll Do to Tie To!: Hood's Arkansas Toothpicks* (1959) contains several rosters of the Third Arkansas.]

HOWARD R. BRANDES

MARINONI, ROSA ZAGNONI (Jan. 5, 1888– Mar. 26, 1970), poet laureate of Arkansas, 1953–1970, was born in Bologna, Italy. She came to the United States in 1898 with her parents, Maria Marzocchi, a poet and artist, and Antero Zagnoni, a newspaper war correspondent and drama critic. Marinoni's maternal uncle Frederico Marzocchi was one of the leading Italian poets of his time.

Rosa Zagnoni married Antonio Marinoni in Brooklyn, New York, on July 30, 1908. She moved with him to Fayetteville, where he was head of the Department of Romance Languages at the University of Arkansas. He died in 1944. In 1946 Rosa Marinoni and L. A. Passarelli were married. Passarelli, an author and professor, died in 1953.

Marinoni was one of the first women to campaign for women's suffrage in Arkansas. During World War I she supported the Liberty Loan Drive, and after the war she worked to establish chapters of the American Red Cross and the YMCA.

Beginning in 1922 the Marinonis organized and led summer tours of Europe for several years. In 1925 Marinoni fell in her kitchen and sustained a severe injury to her knee. While in the hospital she overheard her doctor saying that she might not walk again. In the midst of dealing with her feelings about this possibility, she was brought to a further awareness of the human condition when the woman in the bed beside her began to sing a lullaby for her infant who had died. Marinoni is said to have taken up her pen at that time and rarely set it down again.

According to family archivists, in her first sixteen months of writing, her work was accepted by sixty-eight publications. In her lifetime, she produced over one thousand short stories in seventy magazines, printed poetry in some nine hundred publications in the United States and abroad, published fifteen books, and wrote more than five thousand poems.

Her work was published in eight languages. *Radici Al Vento (Roots to the Sky)* (1956) was published by the Mario Bazzi company, Milan, Italy. These poems and epigrams of hers were selected by Italian critics and translated by Marinoni. The book featured a biographical sketch of her by the poet Alberto Marzocchi, and the Italian and English versions of each poem were printed on facing pages. It is not surprising that the Italian government recognized Marinoni as its most widely known poet abroad. In 1960 and 1961 she was honored with expositions of her work in Turin and Milan.

She once said that "as a housewife and mother, I find writing a rest from my housework and housework a rest from my writing." To relieve the isolation inherent in writing, she founded the University-City Poetry Club, which met regularly at her home, Villa Rosa, just a step away from the university campus. Members fostered the writing, reading, analysis, and publishing of poetry. The group met for forty-five years. Collections of their poetry can be found in the public and university libraries in Fayetteville. Their meeting place, Villa Rosa, was designed by Marinoni after a fire destroyed the family's original home in 1924. In 1990 it was placed on the National Register of Historic Places for "its unique architectural characteristics" and its association with the poet Marinoni.

In 1948 Governor Ben Laney's proclamation of the first Poetry Day in Arkansas culminated an effort spearheaded by Marinoni and sponsored by the National League of American Pen Women. State committees were formed to promote interest and involvement in poetry by schools, women's clubs, home demonstration and 4-H groups, newspapers, literary magazines, and similar organizations. A flier announcing the proclamation read: "With PRIDE let us honor our poets of yesterday! With CONFIDENCE let us present our poets of today! With FAITH let us inspire our poets of tomorrow!" This dynamic and positive presentation

was a Marinoni hallmark. The sponsor of many contests for young and new writers, she also selected three outstanding Arkansas poets every year for recognition on Poetry Day as poets of the past, present, and future.

The support and encouragement of writers was a primary lifetime aim for her. Several of her books are dedicated to her adopted Ozarks and its people. She advocated the development of Arkansas's cultural richness. Whenever she submitted her writing she asked that Fayetteville, Arkansas, be written under her name, "Not because I want the town to be proud of me, but because it's my hometown and I'm proud of it." In 1954 she was commissioned by the governor as an Arkansas Traveler to be an "Ambassador of Good Will" from the state to the people of other states and nations.

She was named poet laureate of the Arkansas Federation of Women's Clubs in 1928, of the Ozarks in 1936, and of Arkansas in 1953. In 1969 Governor Winthrop Rockefeller proclaimed October 15, Poetry Day in Arkansas, as Rosa Zagnoni Marinoni Day.

Charles J. Finger, an Arkansas author and 1925 Newbery Medal Winner, wrote this of Marinoni: "There's such a thing as being a very fine exponent of one's age, of being sound-minded and clear-headed, of being truthful and genuine, of being vigorous, of hating tyranny and injustice in no uncertain manner. To dwell with joy on the beautiful is well enough, but to see the life about one, to say something that causes reflection—that's something, too. Mrs. Marinoni has the admirable gift of bringing her readers up all standing and making them think. She is an influence."

Marinoni died in Fayetteville.

[Much of this entry is based on communications with members of Marinoni's family, 1995–99. See the *Northwest Arkansas Times*, Oct. 4, 1995; Mar. 27, 1970 (obituary); and Aug. 15, 1998. Charles Finger's words are from the dust jacket of Marinoni's book *Side Show* (1938).]

JUNE BAKER JEFFERSON

MARTINEAU, JOHN E. (Dec. 2, 1873–Mar. 6, 1939), governor of Arkansas, federal district judge, was born in Clay County, Missouri, to Gregory Martineau, a farmer recently arrived from Quebec, and Sarah Hetty Lamb. Four years later they moved to a farm near Concord, Arkansas (northwest of Lonoke), where his parents reared ten children. There, John began a lifelong friendship with a future United States senator, Joseph Taylor Robinson.

Martineau received his bachelor of arts degree in 1896 from the University of Arkansas. He served as principal of the Chicksaw Male Academy in Tishomingo, Indian Territory. After graduating from the University of Arkansas Law School in Little Rock he was admitted to the Arkansas bar in 1899.

In 1902 and 1904 Martineau won election as Pulaski County's state representative. In 1907 Acting Governor Xenophon Overton Pindall appointed him to fill a First Chancery Court vacancy (Pulaski, Lonoke, and White Counties). He subsequently won election unopposed to three six-year terms on the bench.

As chancery judge, Martineau earned a reputation for fairness and liberalism. His most notable case concerned the 1919 race riots in Elaine, Phillips County. Martineau signed a *habeas corpus* petition blocking the execution of twelve African Americans sentenced for their alleged participation in the riots. The United States Supreme Court eventually upheld his decision.

In 1909 Martineau married Ann H. Mitchell of Pine Bluff, who died six years later. In 1919 he and Mabel Irwin Thomas of Des Arc married.

In 1912 the mayor of Little Rock, following a national trend, appointed a vice commission and named Martineau to its chair. The commission recommended ending police tolerance of brothels and creating a special police agency to combat prostitution.

In 1924 Martineau sought the Democratic gubernatorial nomination, finishing third in a field of five. In 1926 he again entered the race. The incumbent, Thomas Jefferson Terral, had been charged with mismanagement. Martineau proposed reorganizing Arkansas's highway system and initiating a road-building program. Terral countered that this would mire the state in debt. He further accused Martineau of supporting Sunday baseball and the repeal of prohibition, labeling him the candidate of "Booze and Bonds."

Martineau won a close Democratic primary in August 1926, becoming the first person since Reconstruction to defeat an incumbent Arkansas governor running for a second term. The lack of a competitive second party assured his victory in the November general election.

As governor, Martineau restored state honorary boards, created the Confederate Pensions Board, and issued bonds to cover the pension program's cost. His greatest trial was the April 1927 flooding of the lower Mississippi Valley. President Calvin Coolidge named Secretary of Commerce Herbert Hoover to head relief efforts. Louisiana and Mississippi joined with Arkansas to form the Tri-State Flood Commission with Martineau as president. Martineau worked closely with Hoover, making several trips to Washington to brief the president.

Martineau's most lasting achievement as governor was laying the foundation for Arkansas's highway system. The state had paid for an earlier road-building program by taxing land through local improvement districts. This caused skyrocketing property taxes and heavy indebtedness for road districts. Martineau proposed the state assume the districts' debts and issue highway bonds for road construction. Instead of taxing land to pay the bonds, Martineau urged user-related taxes, such as automobile license fees and gasoline levies. The 1927 Arkansas General Assembly authorized his proposals. These and associated measures, known as the "Martineau Road Plan," inaugurated Arkansas's commitment to modern transportation.

Critics repeatedly challenged the plan in court. Martineau himself ruled on several of the suits, for on March 2, 1928, fourteen months after taking office, he resigned as governor to become United States district judge for the Eastern District of Arkansas. Herbert Hoover, who had come to know Martineau during their collaboration on flood relief, strongly urged President Coolidge to appoint him. Martineau's lifelong friend, Senator Joseph Taylor Robinson, also lobbied hard for him, and the Senate confirmed his appointment on the same day the president announced it. On March 14, 1928, Martineau was sworn in and began his second judicial career.

After almost nine years on the federal bench, Martineau died of influenza. He was buried in Roselawn Memorial Park in Little Rock.

[The Arkansas History Commission preserves an incomplete set of Martineau's papers. The Joseph Taylor Robinson Papers at the Special Collections Division, University of Arkansas Libraries, Fayetteville, might have been an important resource had the correspondence between Robinson and Martineau not been so circumspect. See Leon C. Miller, "John E. Martineau, 1927–1928," in *The Governors of Arkansas: Essays in Political Biography*, Timothy P. Donovan, Willard B. Gatewood Jr., and Jeannie M. Whayne, eds., 2d ed. (1995).]

LEON C. MILLER

MASSEY, MARY ELIZABETH SMITH (Aug. 21, 1900–Dec. 24, 1971), businesswoman and civic leader, was born in Marshall, Arkansas, the daughter of Union Civil War veteran Martin Charles Smith and Rebecca Jane Heard. Her parents came to Searcy County in 1885 from Overton County, Tennessee. Her father was a farmer, a trader, and a storekeeper.

She was not over five feet tall, but size did not restrict her outdoor activities driving a tractor, hunting, and fishing. At age fifteen she began growing garden vegetables and, traveling with her mother by horse and buggy, peddled her produce to the miners and their families at the Evening Star Mine, six miles north of Marshall. Through the next two summers she earned three hundred dollars, enough to pay her way to business school. After graduating from Marshall High School, she taught one term in 1918 at the Nubbin Hill School in Searcy County, then attended business school in Harrison.

Mary Smith's first marriage on November 25, 1919, to James Albert Henley of St. Joe, Arkansas, ended in divorce. On October 14, 1923, she married Aud Tillman Massey of Bruno, Marion County, who was then living in Marshall. She had no children.

In 1920 she went to St. Louis to work with Searcy County banker Ed Mays, who had just opened the Missouri National Bank (later incorporated with the Grand National Bank). She served as Mays's secretary and office manager for three years.

In 1923 Mary Elizabeth Massey returned to Marshall and bought the Guaranty Abstract Company, with offices in the courthouse. She also served as deputy county and circuit clerk, chairman of the county board of education, and commissioner of county accounts. She was admitted to the Arkansas bar in 1927 and won her first court case in 1929. As city attorney in 1935 she completed plans for the city water system, drafted the ordinance, and steered a bond issue to completion to finance the installation. In 1934 she ran for county and circuit clerk on the Republican ticket, won, and served three terms.

In 1937 Massey became manager of the newly formed Citizens Banking Exchange. Citizens Banking Exchange fulfilled the requirements for a state bank charter and opened its doors March 4, 1940, as the Citizens Bank, with Mary Massey as president and cashier. The *Arkansas Banker* in 1942 commented, "There are few lady bank presidents. And a combina-tion of the two is almost unheard of." She served as the Citizens Bank's president and chief executive officer until 1956.

Mary Massey and her husband operated several businesses in Marshall: a building materials and lumberyard, several sawmills, a locker refrigeration plant, and a Hereford cattle ranch. She was active in securing Reconstruction Finance Corporation and other government assistance to develop Searcy County resources and served as first president of the Marshall Chamber of Commerce. Massey was also president of the Marshall Business and Professional Women's Club, chairperson of the Searcy County Board of Education from 1929 to 1931, matron of the Marshall Chapter of the Order of the Eastern Star, and in 1959, state worthy grand matron. She was an aggressive businesswoman and civic leader. She died in Marshall.

[See the *Marshall Mountain Wave*, Apr. 5, 1929, June 29, 1934, Feb. 6, 1942, and Dec. 30, 1971. See also the *Arkansas Democrat Magazine*, Mar. 14, 1948; and the *Arkansas Banker*, Jan. 1942.]

JAMES J. JOHNSTON

MCALMONT, JOHN JOSEPHUS (Dec. 19, 1824–Sept. 24, 1896), physician, was born at Hornellsville, New York, eldest of seven children of Daniel McAlmont and Samantha Donham. When John was seventeen years old, his father died and he left home, earning his way by teaching school. By age twenty-one he had saved enough to enter Geneva Medical College, New York, for their one semester course in medicine. He completed this in April 1843 and immediately set out on horseback to Kendall Creek, Pennsylvania, to begin his practice. The place proved to be a company-owned lumber town not to his liking, so in June 1845 he moved to Waymouth, Ohio, near where his grandmother lived. He built a thriving practice and was able to return to New York to marry Martha J. Gregg, a former pupil, on October 1, 1845. To this union were born two daughters, Myra and Cresida, the latter dying in infancy. The winter of 1848–49 found McAlmont in Western Reserve Medical School; he graduated in the spring of 1849.

John McAlmont believed rural Ohio winters were bad for his health so he spent the winter of 1849–50 in Cincinnati. There he met a man supervising the publication of a map of Arkansas. So great was the appeal of Arkansas as presented by the printer that John decided to move there.

Traveling by steamboat, accompanied by his wife, Martha, daughter Myra, and sister Julia, John arrived at Little Rock in March 1850. He decided the city was too big for his delicate health and continued southwest to Benton, where he practiced two years. When he felt more secure about his health, he returned to Little Rock, opening an office "one door west of Tucker's Corner on Markham Street." He became known as "Dr. John." He was joined by his brother Corydon, "Dr. Corey." John McAlmont was honor-bound to make house calls, sometimes out of town on horseback. Trails were rough, crooked, steep, muddy or dusty, bridgeless, and devoid of direction signs, often no more than dim paths. He was frequently lost; when overtaken by darkness he would tether his horse, fashion a bed from his longcoat, position his saddle for a pillow, and sleep until dawn. He always carried a pouch of green tea leaves, which he chewed to stave off exhaustion.

In 1854 he and a partner, former United States senator Solon Borland, acquired a drugstore on the northeast corner of Markham and Main Streets. He staffed it with employees, participating himself only when health limitations prevented active medical practice. He opened another drugstore in 1884. Active in pharmaceutical politics, he was a member of the American Association of Pharmacists and the first president of the Arkansas Association of Pharmacists.

As North-South tension developed, McAlmont cast his lot with the Confederacy. He did not believe in slavery, yet he had five "servants." He was against secession, but when it occurred, he hoped desperately for negotiated settlement. Joining the local militia, he was appointed to the rank of major. He participated in the surrender of federal facilities at Little Rock Barracks and Fort Smith and served as enrolling officer for Little Rock. In May 1861 he moved his family six miles out of town on the Old Military Road. They took in sick and wounded soldiers. McAlmont spent long hours in town tending to his practice and drug business.

Late one night came a knock at the door; it was Corydon, with his children, a black nursemaid, and three slaves. He had been ordered out with King's regiment as unit surgeon. He asked John to care for the children and sell the slaves and his house to cover their expenses. Several months later Corydon died of dysentery and fever (typhoid).

After the war ended, the McAlmonts moved back into town where John continued his practice. During the late 1870s he became associated with a group of progressive physicians dedicated to the establishment of a medical school for the state of Arkansas. On October 8, 1879, their effort culminated in the gathering of six students, eight faculty members, and local dignitaries for a formal ceremony marking the opening session of the Arkansas Industrial University Medical Department. McAlmont was made professor of pharmacology and therapeutics and became treasurer of the school. He held these positions the rest of his life.

He was a member of the First Methodist Church and steward and trustee for over forty years. He carried a little booklet of sixty-five rules of conduct, one of which was to read the entire book twice a week. He was a trustee for St. John's College and served on the board of directors of Arkansas Female Academy and the Arkansas School for the Blind. He was mayor of Little Rock in 1866–67.

John McAlmont was interred at Mount Holly Cemetery. In his memory the street before the old medical school was named McAlmont.

[See Fred O. Henker, "John J. McAlmont, Physician, Druggist, Benefactor," *Pulaski Country Historical Review* 46 (4): 83–86, Winter 1998. There is a biography file on McAlmont in the Historical Research Center, University of Arkansas for Medical Sciences Library.]

FRED O. HENKER

MCCLELLAN, JOHN LITTLE (Feb. 25, 1896– Nov. 28, 1977), was born on a farm near Sheridan, Arkansas, the son of Isaac S. McClellan and Belle Suddeth. The McClellans were staunch Democrats and named their son for Congressman John Little.

Educated in public schools, McClellan became interested in law and studied in his father's law office when not busy on the family's farm. He was admitted to the Arkansas bar in 1913 at the age of seventeen, one of the youngest lawyers in the United States. That same year, he married Eula Hicks of Sheridan and practiced law with his father in Grant County. In August 1917 he joined the army and served as a first lieutenant in the aviation section of the Signal Corps. Following his discharge from the army and a divorce from his wife, he opened a law office in Malvern.

His political career began in 1920 when he was chosen city attorney of Malvern, a post he held until 1926. During this time he married Lucille Smith of Malvern. At age thirty he was elected prosecuting attorney for the

Seventh District of Arkansas. Elected to Congress in 1934, he served two terms (1935–38) in the House of Representatives. Lucille McClellan died suddenly in 1935. McClellan married Norma Myers Cheatham in 1937.

In 1938 McClellan challenged Senator Hattie Caraway for her seat, losing a close Democratic primary. He resumed the practice of law in Camden, then ran for Arkansas's other Senate seat in 1942, which he won easily. He was reelected in 1948, 1954, 1960, 1966, and 1972, serving until his death in 1977. He represented the people of Arkansas in that capacity longer than anyone in the state's history. McClellan earned the highest committee rank ever attained by an Arkansan in the Senate, the chairmanship of the Committee on Appropriations.

McClellan advanced to prominent positions of leadership in the Senate. The McClellan-Kerr Arkansas River Navigation System is a prime example of his leadership in providing opportunity and progress in Arkansas and the Southwest. Numerous dams, lakes, drainage and flood control projects, wildlife habitats, forest preserves, and recreational facilities bear the stamp of his endeavor.

McClellan served for twenty-two years as chairman of the Committee on Government Operations. He served as chairman of the Senate Permanent Subcommittee on Investigations for eighteen years (1955–73), and no other chairman of a congressional investigating committee in the history of the United States Congress has approached McClellan's record for the number of investigations conducted or the results achieved. As chair of that subcommittee and two other investigative committees—the Committee on Improper Activities in the Labor or Management Field and the Special Committee to Investigate Political Activities, Lobbying and Campaign Contributions—he conducted more investigations than any other member.

He first emerged as a national figure during the Army-McCarthy hearings of 1954. He led a Democratic walkout of the Republican-controlled subcommittee because of objections to Senator Joseph McCarthy's witch-hunting conduct. In 1955 McClellan assumed chairmanship of the Subcommittee on Investigations and hired Robert F. Kennedy as chief counsel.

Under McClellan's leadership, the committee probed into corruption and criminal activities in the labor-management field, organized crime, the TFX aircraft contract, profiteering in defense contracts for missile procurement, and the riots that erupted in cities and college campuses in the late 1960s. Probes into the activities of teamsters Dave Beck and Jimmy Hoffa, the so-called "Valachi hearings," and investigations surrounding the affairs of Texas financier Billie Sol Estes kept McClellan in the public eye. As a vigorous, relentless, and effective investigator, he won a reputation for judicial impartiality and fairness which brought him the respect of his colleagues.

As a member of the first and second Hoover Commissions, McClellan authored many of its recommendations to reorganize the federal government, resulting in savings of hundreds of millions of dollars to taxpayers. Prominent among these was his sponsorship of legislation which created the General Services Administration, the business arm of the federal government. He was also the coauthor of the bill which in 1976 resulted in the first complete revision of the U.S. copyright laws since 1909.

A leading advocate of law enforcement, McClellan was key figure in winning congressional approval for the landmark Omnibus Crime Control and Safe Streets Acts of 1968 and 1970, and the Organized Crime Control Act of 1970. In his thirty-five years as a senator, he introduced over 1,000 bills of which 140 were signed into law.

For many years McClellan, Senator J. W. Fulbright, and Representative Wilbur D. Mills gave Arkansas one of the nation's most powerful congressional delegations.

Paralleling his successful political career was a series of tragic deaths within his family. After losing his second wife to spinal meningitis in 1935, his three sons died within a relatively short period of time: Max died of spinal meningitis in Africa while serving in World War II; John L. Jr. died from injuries received in an automobile accident; and James H. died in a plane crash in 1958. McClellan also had two daughters, Doris and Mary Alice.

McClellan died in Little Rock and is buried in Roselawn Memorial Park. At the time of his death, he ranked second in seniority in the Senate and was one of its most powerful members.

[The John L. McClellan Collection is housed at Ouachita Baptist University, Arkadelphia. See John Little McClellan, *Crime without Punishment* (1962); the *Arkansas Gazette,* Nov. 29, 1977; the *New York Times,* Nov. 29, 1977; and the *St. Louis Post-Dispatch,* Apr. 13, 1913.]

WENDY BRADLEY RICHTER

MCCURRY, MAMIE SMITH (July 27, 1879–Aug. 2, 1952), an oil operator, was born on her family's farm three and a half miles east of El Dorado in Union County to David Carroll Smith and Nannie Everett. She attended what is known today as Ouachita Baptist University and the University of Central Arkansas.

McCurry married W. B. Coffey on November 22, 1896; he died in June of the following year. On August 14, 1898, she married Dr. William Thomas McCurry. They had one child, Ruth. For twelve years they lived in Texarkana, where Thomas McCurry attended medical schools, and Mamie McCurry studied anesthesia in order to administer anesthetics for him. They moved to Little Rock in 1912. They were in Berlin on an extended European tour when World War I was declared.

McCurry made a name for herself as the state's first woman oil operator. On a cold, misty day in January 1921, a dark cloud appeared over El Dorado and poured black rain, marking the beginning of the town's oil boom days. The boom has been described as the last unbridled oil boom in United States history. The first gusher came in at about 4:30 P.M. just west of the city, with an initial flow of from three thousand to ten thousand barrels a day. The well was named for Dr. Samuel T. Bussey, who owned 51 percent of it. Among his partners was Mamie McCurry.

Her involvement in oil production began about three years before the 1921 discovery when she helped Bruce Hunt, a Tulsa speculator, secure leases. Her father is credited for her interest in oil. Before he died, he told her he thought there was oil beneath their land. After his death McCurry returned to Union County, where she found two government survey maps indicating that the area could be productive. While she began her search for oil, her husband remained in Little Rock where he was a doctor at the Arkansas School for the Blind.

After the Bussey well blew in, McCurry directed her interests east of town to her family's property. The well drilled on her property became McCurry No. 1. Drilled by Hensy and Zoda Contractors, it produced about seventy-five barrels of oil and 25 million cubic feet of gas at its initial test at a depth of 2,149 feet in the Nachitoches sand. The gusher was completed in May 1921 (to "complete" a well or gusher means to drill it and discover oil).

After McCurry No. 1 was drilled, McCurry's homeplace took on a new look. She expanded the dogtrot house with additions reflecting the popular Craftsman style of architecture. The Smith-McCurry house is today the best example of a Greek Revival-style frame house in Union County. Clad with weatherboard and featuring a gable roof, recessed front porch, and box columns, it is on the National Register of Historic Places.

Following the completion of McCurry No. 1, McCurry drilled one other well on her family's 280 acres. Both wells were abandoned in the 1920s. She said in an interview with the *El Dorado Daily News* in 1941 she would one day drill farther into her property, but she never followed through with that plan.

The completion of McCurry No. 1 led to the founding of the Hunt, McCurry, and Zoda Company, formed to launch other explorations. G. W. Zoda was the drilling contractor, Bruce Hunt negotiated the leases, and McCurry kept the books. The company was active for about five years. The partners drilled the discovery well in the Urania field in Louisiana, and completed fifteen producing wells in that area.

McCurry was the only woman to be actually engaged in the oil production business during the early years of the 1920s boom. She was an oil operator, which meant that she looked for oil, acquired the property where oil was located, either by purchase or lease, and drilled until she struck oil.

She was active in the East Side Oil and Gas Company, serving as secretary-treasurer and as a board member. She also had a financial interest in the Shuler field in El Dorado, a productive field. The last well she was in charge of was near Bay Minette, Alabama. She was made an honorary member of the Mobile Chamber of Commerce, and the Bay Minnette Lions Club passed a resolution expressing their appreciation of her arousing interest in the well. McCurry also drilled in Texas, Tennessee, Florida, and Mississippi.

For all that she participated in a rough business, she was, according to her granddaughter, very much the southern gentle lady, poised and proper. But when it came to the oil business, she was adventurous, smart, and enthusiastic.

Dr. McCurry died February 19, 1925. At about the same time, the activity of the Hunt, McCurry, and Zoda Company began to slow down. In 1931 Mamie McCurry took a trip around the world with an international universities group. She retired to the family farm where she raised cotton and corn. She died in Little Rock.

[Sources include A. R. Buckalew and R. B. Buckalew, "Discovery of Oil in South Arkansas," *AHQ* 33 (Winter 1974): 195–238; *El Dorado News-Times,* Nov. 4, 1990; *El Dorado Daily News,* June 17, 1941, special edition, "Twenty Years of Oil"; and an interview with Mamie Ruth Williams, Dec. 13, 1993. The form nominating the Smith-McCurry house to the National Register of Historic Places is located at the Arkansas Historic Preservation Program, Little Rock.]

SHEA HUTCHENS WILSON

MCDERMOTT, LILLIAN DEES (Oct. 4, 1877–Apr. 30, 1965), social worker and community leader, was born about ten miles north of Little Rock, the daughter of Hardy Scott Dees, a farmer and merchant, and Mary F. Pace. She was educated in the Little Rock public schools and at Galloway College of Searcy, which was later merged with Hendrix College of Conway. She married William Pryor McDermott, a salesman, in 1895. They lived in Little Rock most of their married life and had two children, William Dees and Lucy Kendrick. William Pryor McDermott died in 1941.

In 1918 Lillian McDermott was appointed assistant probation officer for the Pulaski County Juvenile Court; in 1921 she was promoted to chief probation officer. Between 1922 and 1924, in order to gain greater competency in her work, she attended law classes in the evenings at the Arkansas Law School and studied social work at the University of Southern California. Except for two years as financial secretary for the Children's Hospital (1929–31), McDermott served as chief probation officer until 1941; for most of that period she also was referee of the court. During her tenure, a survey of public and private social work agencies for the Greater Little Rock area called the juvenile court the most important children's agency in the county, and the National Probation Association recognized the court as one of the nation's best.

In the depression years McDermott participated in a number of federal activities and programs. She was Arkansas's representative to the President's White House Conference on Children and Youth, served as chairman of the women's division of the National Recovery Administration re-employment campaign in Arkansas, and was a member of the advisory committee for the United States Children's Bureau. She was active in professional organizations, serving three terms as president of the Arkansas Conference of Social Work and one term as president of the Little Rock

Council of Social Agencies. In 1935 she was a speaker at the annual meeting of the National Conference of Social Work in Montreal.

In 1941 her tenure as chief probation officer and referee of the Pulaski County Juvenile Court ended, and she accepted a position as special coordinator in the professional and service division of the federal Works Progress Administration. In this capacity she worked with the Civilian Military Council and other agencies in developing a program of "off post" activities for soldiers training at Camp Robinson.

In 1942 McDermott became executive secretary of the newly organized Little Rock Family Service Agency, which was supported by funds from the Greater Little Rock community chest and whose functions included marriage counseling, advising on parent-child relations, and working with the elderly. She served as head of the agency until her retirement in 1964. She was the first woman in central Arkansas to become a certified social worker, a title indicating recognition by the National Academy of Social Workers.

McDermott had a distinguished record of service in school and church activities. In 1922 she was elected to the Little Rock School Board, having been nominated by her friends and fellow members of the City Federation of Women's Clubs. She served for twenty-four years, including three terms as president of the board. In 1932 she was named a member of the Hendrix College Board of Trustees, and in 1937 the college awarded her an honorary LL.D. degree. Among the many accolades given her for community service was the title "Woman of the Year" (1961) in an *Arkansas Democrat* annual poll.

She was a devoted and seemingly tireless leader in church work, serving as general secretary of the First United Methodist Church, South, of Little Rock, taking a role in the Women's Missionary Society, and teaching the Elizabeth Remmel Bible Class for Women for thirty-five years. Her class was popular and well attended. As might be expected her lessons often focused on the role of the church in the amelioration of social problems. In 1945 the class honored her by establishing the Lillian McDermott Educational Fund to provide scholarships for Hendrix College students.

McDermott died at her Little Rock home and is buried at Oaklawn Cemetery.

[The Hendrix College Archives contains the best collection of materials on McDermott, including clippings from the *Arkansas Gazette* and the *Arkansas Democrat*. Information on her church activities is found at Robert E. L. Bearden History Room at the Little Rock First Methodist Church. The Arkansas History Commission has a number of helpful sources. Incomplete files of a newsletter, "Arkansas Probation Bulletin," issued during the early 1930s, are in the Special Collections Division, University of Arkansas Libraries, Fayetteville. Other sources include Walter N. Vernon, *Methodism in Arkansas, 1816–1976* (1976); and interviews with Nellie Reid, Dick Butler, and others who knew McDermott.]

FOY LISENBY

MCDONNELL, JAMES SMITH JR. (Apr. 9, 1899– Aug. 22, 1980), was born in Denver, Colorado, to James Smith and Susie Belle McDonnell. James and his two brothers were raised in the Little Rock area. McDonnell spent his childhood in Altheimer where his father, a cotton merchant and mercantile store owner, had one of the two family stores. The other was in Little Rock, where McDonnell graduated from Central High School. A 1921 graduate of Princeton, McDonnell received his master's in aeronautical engineering from the Massachusetts Institute of Technology in 1925 and earned a second lieutenant's reserve commission as an Army Air Service pilot.

McDonnell designed and built his first aircraft in 1929 for the Daniel Guggenheim International Safe Aircraft Contest. His low-winged monoplane, the "Doodlebug," crashed when the rear stabilizer failed during the competition. One of his main competitors in the contest was the Arkansas-built Command-Aire.

He worked as an engineer for several companies, most notably the Glenn L. Martin Company, until 1939 when he formed the McDonnell Aircraft Corporation. He sought a midwestern base due to his concern for building an aircraft factory away from the east or west coasts, which he thought were vulnerable to attack. His close ties with Little Rock financiers nearly resulted in the location of the company in Arkansas; however, the incentives provided by St. Louis were more substantial, encouraging his decision to build the factory there.

The demand for aircraft during the Second World War was a boon for McDonnell's company. The majority of its work was contracting for other manufacturers, but one project became extremely significant for the company. In 1942 McDonnell was awarded the navy's contract to develop the first carrier-based jet airplane.

The twin-engined Phantom was the first of a series of McDonnell jet fighters which became integral to the navy, including the F-2 Banshee, the F-101 Voodoo, the F-4 Phantom II, the F-15 Eagle, and the F-18 Hornet.

The company merged with the bankrupt Douglas Company on April 28, 1967, taking over that company's popular line of commercial transports. Through this merger McDonnell was able to achieve his goal of a balance between commercial and military production. The new company became a mainstay of commercial passenger travel with continued production of the Douglas DC-8 and the DC-9. As Douglas changed the propeller age of transport aircraft with the DC-3, similarly the McDonnell-Douglas Corporation produced one of the handful of aircraft which broadened the airline industry from the relative exclusivity of the jet set 1960s into the age of mass air travel with the introduction of the tri-engined DC-10.

A key to McDonnell's success was his rapid expansion from strictly aviation into aerospace. His company began development of space vehicles well ahead of the requests by the U.S. Government and received the contract to produce America's first spaceship, the Mercury capsule, in 1959. McDonnell's most-prized possession was an autographed photograph from John Glenn, the first American to orbit the earth, which carried the inscription: "To Mr. Mac—from a very satisfied customer." McDonnell followed its space success by providing the Gemini capsule and stages for the Saturn launcher used in the Apollo program and by serving as the major contractor for NASA's Skylab.

McDonnell headed his corporation from its beginnings and continued as chairman of the board and CEO of McDonnell-Douglas Corporation from the 1967 merger until 1972 when he relinquished the CEO position to his brother, Sanford N. McDonnell. He remained chairman of the board until his death in 1980. The year prior to his death, McDonnell's company had grown to over 125,000 with earnings of $199 million in sales, $5.3 billion in back orders, and $10.9 billion in pending orders.

McDonnell married Mary Elizabeth Finney in 1934. She died in 1949. He and Mary had two sons, John S., III, and John Finney. He married Priscilla Forney in 1954. McDonnell died in St. Louis. Among his numerous honors are his enshrinement in the Aviation Hall of Fame in Dayton, Ohio, and the Arkansas Aviation Historical Society Hall of Fame.

[Consult the James McDonnell File, Arkansas Aviation Historical Association Archives, Little Rock; Rene Francillon, *McDonnell Douglas Aircraft since 1920,* vol. 2, Naval Institute Press, 1990; the obituary in the *Arkansas Gazette,* Nov. 6, 1980; and the *Arkansas Gazette,* Nov. 6, 1980.]

WILLIAM M. SMITH JR.

MCLAUGHLIN, LEO PATRICK (June 5, 1888–May 5, 1958), was born in Hot Springs, Arkansas, the son of John Henry McLaughlin and Bridget Russell. There are conflicting reports concerning his marriages; the mystery surrounding them adds to his legend. He had no children.

McLaughlin's political career began in 1910 when he was elected to the state legislature. The following year he was elected Hot Springs city attorney, a position he held for thirteen years, with the exception of the time he spent in the Army Signal Corps during World War I.

He ran for mayor in 1926 on a platform that promised Hot Springs would be an "open town" with gambling permitted under official supervision. He also pledged to improve city streets, and he kept his promises. He directed work that paved miles of Hot Springs streets. And, most notably, he opened the town for gambling.

During the two decades McLaughlin held the office of mayor, only one person ran against him. As mayor he became the undisputed boss of Hot Springs and Garland County politics. For example, prior to each election during his administration, a "pink slip" named the candidates favored by the McLaughlin regime. Those candidates appearing on the slip were assured of favorable support, even though the names of many voters were rumored to be found only on cemetery headstones. McLaughlin's ability to deliver votes made him a power in state politics. All he asked in return was that Hot Springs be left alone to operate as an open town.

McLaughlin was a showman. Among his best-known activities was a daily ride down Central Avenue in a sulky pulled by his horses, Scotch and Soda. Always attired in riding costume with a red carnation in his lapel, he drew the attention of tourists and locals alike. This showmanship also surfaced in his political speeches. A natty dresser, he would shed his coat and roll up his sleeves as a speech intensified.

Underworld characters frequented Hot Springs during the McLaughlin administration. Men like Al Capone, Lucky Luciano, and Frank Costello visited the spa with the understanding that they would exhibit only their best behavior. Local people managed the town's gambling operations under the watchful eyes of McLaughlin and his associates. The owners and managers appeared in municipal court regularly and paid fines considered to be license fees for their operations. The funds collected were important in financing city government and in McLaughlin's ability to direct the development of Hot Springs, which reached its peak as a health resort during his tenure as mayor.

McLaughlin remained the boss of Garland County politics until Sid McMath, a young war veteran who later became governor, led a group of G.I.s in the "revolt" that put the McLaughlin machine out of office. In March of 1947, after a grand jury began an investigation of his administration, the mayor announced that he would not seek reelection. He was indicted on fourteen charges, ranging from accepting bribes from gamblers to misuse of public funds. He was never convicted.

His business was politics. His family, his social life, his home, and even his horses are all a part of his political legend. He was one of Hot Springs's most memorable personalities: just the mention of his name continues to stir the emotions of longtime residents.

A Roman Catholic, he was buried in Calvary Cemetery in Hot Springs.

[See Wendy Richter, "The Death of Leo P. McLaughlin," *Record,* Garland County Historical Society (1988); Nancy Russ, "Life and Times of Leo P. McLaughlin," *Record* (1983); and Shirley Abbott, *The Bookmaker's Daughter: A Memory Unbound* (1991). Some thirty interviews with contemporaries of McLaughlin are available on audio cassette at the Garland County Library and the Garland County Historical Society Archives.]

WENDY BRADLEY RICHTER

MCRAE, THOMAS CHIPMAN (Dec. 21, 1851–June 2, 1929), governor of Arkansas, was born in Mount Holly, Arkansas. He was the oldest of five children born to Duncan L. McRae and Mary Ann Chipman. In the fall of 1871, with less than two years of formal education, he entered the Law School of Washington and Lee University in Lexington, Virginia, graduating the following year. He was admitted to the Arkansas bar two years later, and established a lucrative practice in Prescott, Arkansas. On December 17, 1874, McRae and

Ameria Ann White married; their union lasted nearly fifty-five years and produced nine children.

McRae had a long and successful public career before he was elected governor of Arkansas, holding a variety of posts in state and local government. In 1884 he was elected United States Representative from Arkansas's Third Congressional District, an office he held for eighteen years. In 1903 he returned to Prescott to practice law and engage in banking. His peers elected him to serve first as president of the Arkansas Bankers Association (1909) and subsequently as president of the Arkansas Bar Association (1917).

In 1920 the sixty-eight-year-old McRae agreed to run for governor of Arkansas only because of the constant importunities of his friends. His platform called for better schools, an honest road-building program, a fairer system of taxation, and economy in government. He won the primary and general elections easily despite the landslide victory of Republicans on the national level. McRae's legislative proposals were modest: the abolition of useless commissions and boards, increased support for the state's educational program, a state purchasing system, and appointment of women to state office. He also advocated consolidation of all highway construction under the auspices of the state highway department. The general assembly, however, virtually ignored the governor's recommendations.

During his second term McRae redoubled his efforts to win approval of his legislative agenda. The assembly did enlarge the tax base (income, severance, and gasoline), but national press accounts about "Arkansas road scandals" and threats of federal officials to withhold all highway subsidies to the state could not induce members to embrace highway construction reform laws. Subsequently, federal officers made good on their threat and withdrew both highway construction funds and technical personnel from the state.

Governor McRae responded to the escalating crisis by calling the general assembly into a series of special sessions. In September 1923 he persuaded the legislature to make the state rather than local districts responsible for highway construction. In March 1924 he won approval of a new tobacco tax to fund public education. When the state supreme court ruled the tax unconstitutional, he cajoled the legislature to rewrite the tobacco tax law in June 1924 so as to make it acceptable to the court.

McRae made three notable contributions to Arkansas during his four years as governor. He managed to reform the highway construction program, to place the burden of taxation on intangible rather than tangible wealth, and to infuse state funds into the public school system. Upon the completion of his term as governor, McRae returned to Prescott, where he resumed pursuit of his legal and banking interests. He died at Prescott and was buried in De Ann Cemetery there.

[See W. David Baird, "Thomas Chipman McRae, 1921–1925," in *The Governors of Arkansas: Essays in Political Biography*, Timothy P. Donovan, Willard B. Gatewood Jr., and Jeannie M. Whayne, eds., 2d ed. (1995).]

W. DAVID BAIRD

MILLAR, ALEXANDER COPELAND (May 17, 1861–Nov. 9, 1940), Methodist educator and publisher, was born in McKeesport, Pennsylvania, to William John Millar and Ellen Caven. Describing himself as a "practical idealist," Millar graduated from the Methodist-affiliated Central College in Fayette, Missouri, in 1885 and earned a master of arts degree in 1889. Honorary doctorate degrees were conferred upon him by Wesleyan College (Kentucky) in 1907, the University of Arkansas in 1922, and Hendrix College in 1940. He married Elizabeth Harwood on June 27, 1887; they had three children. After Elizabeth's death in May 1924, Millar married Susie McKinnon, a professor and author from Jacksonville, Texas, on October 15, 1925.

Millar began teaching in 1885 at Grove's High School in Dallas, Texas. Returning to Missouri in 1886, Millar accepted a professorship at Neosho Collegiate Institute, where he soon became one of the nation's youngest college presidents. In 1887 he accepted the presidency of Central Collegiate Institute at Altus, Arkansas, where he played a major role in changing the school's name to Hendrix College and moving it to Conway.

In 1889 Millar toured American colleges and universities to examine ways to improve instruction. The tour shaped Millar's ideas about higher education as evidenced by his book, *Twentieth-Century Educational Problems*. He promoted uniform ideals among the state's institutions of higher education. He was elected to the presidency of the Arkansas Education Association in 1911.

He was ordained into the Methodist ministry in 1888. Throughout his ministry, he supported overseas missions and moral behavior and opposed Sunday baseball, liquor sales, gambling, and divorce. He only nominally supported efforts to prohibit the teaching of evolution. Although he never held a pastorate in an Arkansas church, he served in church offices including presiding elder of the Morrilton, Little Rock, and Arkadelphia districts; delegate to Southern Methodism's General Conference; and delegate to the commission that selected the name and the site of the Western Methodist Assembly at Mount Sequoyah in Fayetteville. In 1934 Millar was elected to the Judicial Council of the Methodist Episcopal Church. As a member of the executive board of the Federal Council of Churches, he supported the reunion of the southern and northern branches of the Methodist Church.

At the turn of the century, Millar advocated the conservation and development of Arkansas's natural resources and improvements in the state's railroads and highways. He was chairman of the state's first Good Roads Convention. His activities helped lead to the state constitutional amendment authorizing counties to levy road taxes. Later, he was appointed to the state forestry commission, where he helped to establish a permanent forestry commission.

In 1902 Millar left Hendrix to accept a professorship at Central College, where he wrote his most notable poem, "Together, Yes, Together." Two years later he returned to Arkansas and bought the *Arkansas Methodist* in partnership with his friend Dr. James A. Anderson of Little Rock. For nearly ten years he was the paper's associate editor and business manager. During this time he composed "My Own Loved Arkansas," a song approved for use in the public schools. In 1908 he was appointed by the Arkansas Penitentiary Board to conduct an investigation of conditions at the Cummins prison farm. Many of his recommendations were enacted into law by the general assembly. His close friend, Governor George W. Donaghey, appointed him to the first executive board of the Arkansas History Commission.

In 1910 Millar celebrated his return to the presidency of Hendrix College by composing "Hendrix, O Hendrix." In 1914 he accepted the presidency of the newly created Oklahoma Methodist College to be located in Muskogee, but the college never opened its doors. In late 1914 he returned to Little Rock and became the editor-in-chief of the *Arkansas Methodist*, a position he held until his death. He was twice elected president of the Southern Methodist Press Association. By 1930 he was known as the senior editor of *American Methodism*.

An organizer of Arkansas's Anti-Saloon League, Millar served as its president from 1925 until his death. In 1928 he briefly sought the state Democratic nomination for lieutenant governor. However, he dropped out of the race after the Democrats nominated Governor Alfred E. Smith of New York, an Irish Catholic, anti-prohibitionist whom Millar could not support for president. He helped organize the Arkansas anti-Smith Democrats in their bid to defeat the ticket of Smith and Arkansas's senator Joseph T. Robinson. Five years later he helped lead the fight against the repeal of prohibition.

In the final years of his life, Millar tried to raise public support for the adoption of one of his compositions, "America, Our Fatherland," as the national anthem. He died at Little Rock and is buried in Oak Grove Cemetery in Conway.

[The Alexander Copeland Millar Papers are in the Arkansas Methodist Church Archives, Bailey Library, Hendrix College. Other sources include the *Arkansas Gazette*, Nov. 9 and 12, 1940; *Arkansas Methodist; Minutes of the Seventy-fifth Session of the Little Rock Annual Conference, Methodist Episcopal Church, South* (Little Rock, Nov. 14–18, 1928); *Journal and Minutes* (Little Rock Annual Conference of the Methodist Church, Second Session, Texarkana, Nov. 12–17, 1940); and the Joseph T. Robinson Papers, Special Collections Division, University of Arkansas Libraries, Fayetteville.

See also James A. Anderson, *Centennial History of Arkansas Methodism* (1935); James Lester, *Hendrix College: A Centennial History* (1984); Robert Meriwether, *Hendrix College: The Move from Altus to Conway* (1976); J. H. Riggin and W. F. Evans, *Lest We Forget; or Character Gems Gleaned from South Arkansas* (191–); Thomas Rothrock, "Dr. Alexander Copeland Millar," *AHQ* 22 (Fall 1963): 215–23; and Michael Richard Strickland, "'Rum, Rebellion, Racketeers, and Rascals': Alexander Copeland Millar and the Fight to Preserve Prohibition in Arkansas, 1927–1933," master's thesis, University of Arkansas, Fayetteville, 1993.]

MICHAEL RICHARD STRICKLAND

MILLER, ASBURY MANSFIELD (Feb. 4, 1893– Sept. 14, 1982), educator, was born in Perla, Hot Spring County, Arkansas. His parents were Randal Miller Jr., a sawmill laborer and a native of Mississippi, and Pollie Miller (maiden name unknown), who was born in Alabama. At the time of the 1900 census, his grandparents Harriett and Randal Miller were living near the younger Millers in Perla. Asbury Miller graduated from Arkansas Baptist College and did graduate work at the

University of Arkansas at Pine Bluff. He served in World War I. Afterward, he became coach at Arkadelphia and went to Batesville in 1924 as principal of the black school. His wife, Ethel O. Miller, was employed as a teacher at the same school.

Miller found the school building in Batesville, which had been built in 1905, in deplorable condition. At that time the school employed four teachers and educated children only until the ninth grade; a senior high school for blacks was added in 1947. As late as 1950, however, an article in a local newspaper described the Negro school building as "dismal" and went on to say: "This drab structure, with its broken window panes and peeling paint, presents an ugly picture of American education, whether it be an isolated case or not.... Lack of room is the major problem facing Principal A. M. Miller. Classes for his first and second grade pupils are conducted in the basement of the Negro Baptist church a short distance from the school. He needs at least two more rooms and a home economics building or room. At present, home ec. classes are held in an improvised basement ... Athletic facilities are practically nonexistent." A new school, named for Mrs. Miller, was opened in 1952.

Willene Harper, in a reminiscence published in a local newspaper, remembered both Mr. Miller and his first wife, Ethel: "Mrs. Miller taught primer through third grade. Boy, she was tough and I was scared of her. Not only did she teach, she organized and directed the Rhythm Band, the Glee Club, the acrobat team at school but she was also the pianist, director of her church's choir. Mrs. Miller was the motivator that pushed our principal A. M. Miller, whom we all called Professor ... not only was Professor the principal, he taught grades seven and up. He acted as coach, too, having one time won the black schools' state tournament ... Our school, Batesville Junior High, had three rooms and a basement. Folding doors separated two rooms, and when there was a play or special event the doors folded back and there was our auditorium. One room had a step up stage and three light bulbs hanging from long wires from the high ceiling. Whatever we did, we did our best, thanks to Mrs. Miller ... when Ethel Miller taught you something, then you never forgot it."

Professor Miller retired in 1966 after forty-two years in the Batesville schools. The first three grades of the schools were integrated during the 1967–68 term; the process was completed for all grades the next year.

Much of the credit for this smooth transition was given to Theodora Waugh Miller, Miller's second wife.

A school yearbook describes Professor Miller as devout and cheerful but not austere. He was also active in community development and was a deacon of the Bethlehem Baptist Church, and a 33d-degree mason. Following the death of his first wife, he had two subsequent marriages, to Theodora Waugh and to Annie Mae Williams, both of whom were teachers.

[Almost nothing has been published about Professor Miller. His obituary appeared in the *Batesville Guard* on Sept. 16, 1982.]

NANCY SNELL GRIFFITH

MILLER, WILLIAM READ (Nov. 23, 1823–Nov. 29, 1887), attorney and the first native Arkansan elected governor of the state, was born and reared on a farm near Batesville, Arkansas Territory, one of seven children of Clara Moore and John Miller. His father was register of the United States Land Office at Batesville.

Educated in local schools, Miller early showed an interest in politics and law. Two historians, Josiah H. Shinn and Dallas T. Herndon, recount an incident from Miller's youth when, in the course of the 1836 presidential campaign, he exchanged shouted remarks with the Whig notable C. F. M. Noland, but their interpretations of this altercation differ. Herndon offers it as an instance of political precocity, but Shinn sees it as evidence that Miller was "a holy terror as a boy." There seems, however, to be no reason to think of Miller as anything other than an ambitious and studious youth.

Although his father questioned his decision to study law, Miller was admitted to the Arkansas bar in 1868. In the meantime, he served from 1848 to 1854 as clerk of Independence County. He left to accept Governor Elias Nelson Conway's appointment to fill the unexpired term of state auditor C. C. Danley, who had resigned. The legislature named the Know-Nothing candidate, A. S. Huey, to the auditor's office in 1855, and Miller was appointed by Conway to be accountant of the State Real Estate Bank. He and William M. Gouge prepared a *Report of the Accountants ... to Investigate the Affairs of the Real Estate Bank of Arkansas* (1856). In 1856 the legislature returned him to the auditor's office.

On January 27, 1849, Miller married Susan Elizabeth Bevens, the daughter of Judge William C. Bevens. The couple had seven children, four of whom grew to maturity: Louisa, Effie, William R., and Hugh.

Reelected state auditor in 1858, 1860, and 1862, Miller served until April 1864. Two years later he again became auditor but was removed during Reconstruction in 1868. Admitted to the bar in that year, he returned to Batesville where he apparently practiced law. Family tradition had it that his home was sold for nonpayment of the direct tax levied on officials of the Confederate state governments. With the victory of the conservative Democrats, he was returned to the auditor's office in the election of 1874; during this term he published a seventy-three-page *Digest of the Revenue Laws of the State of Arkansas* (1875).

In anticipation of Governor Augustus Hill Garland's elevation to the United States Senate, several newspapers in early 1876 proposed Miller as a successor likely to continue Garland's policies as governor. He was nominated by the Democratic convention in June, winning over a distinguished field that included Simon P. Hughes, Thomas Fletcher, and Grandison Royston. Miller campaigned on a reconciliation platform and offered assurances to black voters, winning by a substantial margin in September over a divided Republican opposition. He earned a reputation for personal probity and sound financial management. Because he was reluctant to grant pardons to individuals convicted by jury trials and given death sentences, he was sometimes referred to as "the hanging governor." Notwithstanding outbreaks of violence in some counties, his tenure in office was marked by general good feeling, by a continuing commitment to public education and the state university, and above all by a constant effort to redress and establish the state's credit. A movement was afoot to repudiate much of the state's indebtedness by submitting the so-called Fishback Amendment to a popular vote. Miller, Garland, and U. M. Rose led the opposition to debt repudiation but were only temporarily successful in forestalling eventual passage of the amendment. Despite rising Greenback sentiment, however, Miller was easily renominated and reelected in 1878 without Republican opposition. A bid for renomination for a third term failed in 1880.

Described by an acquaintance as "a charitable, public-spirited, plain, unassuming gentleman," William Miller stood almost six feet tall and possessed "a business rather than a professional manner." He served on the governing board of the University of Arkansas and received that institution's honorary doctorate. He was named president of the Kansas City and New Orleans Railroad Company in 1880 and was associated with other railroad enterprises, but he did not become a wealthy man. After serving as deputy treasurer of the state in 1881–82, he was returned to his old office of state auditor in the election of 1886, defeating the incumbent for renomination in what was described as an exciting contest. It was said that "he needed the position." He died in Little Rock and was buried in Mount Holly Cemetery in a grave that remained unmarked until after his widow's death in 1905.

[This entry is taken from William McDowell Baker, "William Read Miller, 1877–1881," in *The Governors of Arkansas: Essays in Political Biography*, Timothy P. Donovan, Willard B. Gatewood Jr., and Jeannie M. Whayne, eds., 2d ed. (1995). —*Editor.*]

MILLS, WILBUR DAIGH (May 24, 1909–May 2, 1992), was born in Kensett, White County, Arkansas, the first of three children of Ardra Pickens Mills and Abbie Lois Daigh. Ardra was chairman of the bank in Kensett, president of the school board, member of the city council, and owner of a general store, a cotton gin, and hundreds of acres of farmland. Wilbur Mills graduated from Hendrix College in 1930 and attended Harvard University Law School from 1930 to 1933, studying under Felix Frankfurter. Mills and Clarine Gertrude Billingsley, who had known one another since childhood, married on May 27, 1934. They had two daughters, Martha Sue and Rebecca Ann Mills.

In 1934 Mills was elected county and probate judge in White County. During the Great Depression he instituted a revolutionary system of medical care. To meet the needs of the people there, he persuaded the hospital administrator to charge only $2.50 per day for hospital rooms, the pharmacies to provide drugs at cost, the doctors to see unemployed, needy patients without charge, the quorum court to appropriate $5,000 to cover costs for those in need, and the county doctor to coordinate the model program.

In 1939 Mills, a Democrat, was elected to the Congress of the United States, where he served for thirty-eight years, most notably as a member and later chairman of the Committee on Ways and Means of the House of Representatives. The jurisdiction of Ways and Means covers reciprocal international trade, management of the federal debt, Social Security, Medicare, Medicaid, unemployment compensation, income tax, and other taxes. When Mills was there, the Democratic members also constituted the Democratic Committee on Committees, making committee assignments for all Democratic members of the House. With the power to raise revenue and make committee assignments, Ways and Means was the most powerful committee in the House.

Mills, usually called "Mr. Chairman," compiled a legendary record. He felt closest not to his colleagues, but to his constituents back home. When asked if he ever voted contrary to his own convictions to please his constituents, he replied, "No, I was so close to my people that I thought as they did." He was known for integrity: he took a standard deduction on his tax forms to avoid the appearance of conflict; he never traveled overseas at government expense; he never kited a check; he never accepted honoraria.

As Speaker Sam Rayburn's protégé and upon his instruction, Mills became thoroughly knowledgeable about his committee's work, memorizing the tax code and the Social Security laws. Elected chairman in 1958, he hired a small, gifted staff who reported directly and only to him, centralizing decisions; abolished subcommittees, centralizing information; and usually took legislation to the floor under a "closed" rule, limiting opposition. He cultivated a close relationship with the leading Republicans on the committee and in the House. He tried to compose the committee of a cross-section of the House and the country, so that when a consensus for a bill could be constructed, it could pass the House and then the Senate with widespread public support.

Though he exercised tight control, Mills was regarded as an open and fair chairman who provided an atmosphere in which all members, freshman or ranking, could participate comfortably. He never had a rigid personal agenda, but maintained the flexibility needed to draw passable bills. He missed few House votes. He was an attentive listener, kept in close touch with his district back home, and knew his constituents' concerns. Thus, with solid information astutely gleaned, he crafted sound legislation.

He preferred to develop legislation in committee, rather than to consider bills proposed in an already drafted form. He himself never introduced a bill to the committee; instead, he worked with committee members to get a bill. "It's much easier to develop a bill in the committee than it is to defend a bill in the committee. Well, they shoot at everything when you give them

advance notice." Working this way, committee members had a stake in the outcome of a bill: "You ask this one to offer an amendment, to put a part in; you ask another one to do it, it's part their bill there."

Mills presented his legislation to the House himself, offering a well-organized, moving, and convincing summation of his proposals. His skills of persuasion were such that he could change members' votes on the very day of a vote by the eloquence of his presentation. He said of himself, "I was persuasive at times, but I never forced anybody to do anything."

Mills sponsored bills which instituted investment tax credits for plant expansions; encompassed the principle that increases in federal income taxes should be tied directly to decreases in federal spending; repealed excise taxes adopted during the Korean War; removed 5.5 million low-income taxpayers from the rolls; liberalized child and dependent expense deductions; and repealed excise taxes on passenger cars and light-duty trucks.

His hallmark trade bills authorized the Dillon Round of trade negotiations; gave the president broad powers in trade negotiations; modernized the entire schedule of U.S. tariffs; and established U.S. initiative in new trade negotiations.

Wilbur Mills's work on Social Security doubled the Old Age Survivors Insurance program benefits, lowered the age at which benefits could start, broadened coverage by double, and increased disability coverage.

Other legislation led by Mills provided for trust funds for highways; unemployment compensation; the exemption of fringe benefits from income tax; Individual Retirement Accounts and reform of private pension systems; revenue sharing for cities and counties; the creation of the Office of Budget; the Office of U.S. Trade Representative; and the inclusion of libraries in the federal budget for the first time.

Of all his work, Mills was proudest of Medicare, which he called "a cornerstone in the social progress of our nation." Medical assistance for the aged was a priority because many retirees had no regularized access to group insurance and had a diminished ability to pay. Mills crafted a pragmatic solution based on universal access, designed to make family life and old age more stable.

The Medicare Act of 1965 provided Americans sixty-five years old or older substantial assistance with the costs of hospital, physician, and nursing home care.

The plan can be seen as highly developed federal version of the system Mills had instituted in White County thirty years earlier. He was concerned from the first to develop a comprehensive program: "I wanted to do a complete job once we started in that direction."

A fiscal conservative, Mills for years opposed health care initiatives he considered inadequate or unsound, to the point where he was considered by some the main obstacle to a health care program. He wanted a tax rate that would make Medicare fiscally healthy, one that was not dependent upon tax increases from future congresses. His mastery of the complicated actuarial bases of estimating financial needs made him sensitive to Medicare's financing mechanisms.

On March 2, 1965, the committee spent the day reviewing the health bills pending before it. Chairman Mills directed testimony back and forth over all the alternatives. Three major proposals—put forward by the Johnson administration, by John Byrnes, the ranking Republican member of the committee, and by the American Medical Association—had been presented, analyzed, and discussed for several hours. Suddenly, in a historical moment, Mills asked that the three be combined. It was a coup nobody had seen coming, and it left the opposition dumbstruck. The resulting bill was not an administration bill, nor an AMA bill, nor a Republican or Democratic bill, but a congressional bill. Derived from three competing plans, it gave virtually all members of the committee and Congress some reason for satisfaction. It passed the House by a vote of 263 to 153.

Wilbur Mills worked with eight presidents. He was fondest of President Kennedy, who was greatly reliant on Mills. In 1962 President Kennedy had an ambitious legislative program, with Mills as its chief strategist. After passage of major tax reform and Social Security expansion, the president confided to Mills that he wanted to seek an extension of international trade through legislation, but that his cabinet thought such legislation would not pass Congress. Mills replied, "Well, Mr. President, I don't know what the Senate will do, but I do know the House will support you on it." Kennedy responded, "Let's try for it." Mills introduced the legislation; it was referred to Ways and Means and reported out favorably almost immediately. The Senate followed suit. As the president signed the Trade Reform Act into law, he called it "the Mills Act," and Mills joked, "Nothing is impossible until you try it."

With the Legislative Reorganization Act of 1946, Congress regained some of the strength it had lost in the shadow of Theodore Roosevelt, Woodrow Wilson, and Franklin Roosevelt. For some thirty years until the passage of the Congressional Reform Acts of the 1970s, Congress was at a crest of its power. Thus, Wilbur Mills served as chairman of the most powerful committee in Congress during a period when Congress itself was powerful, making him the most influential committee chairman in the twentieth century. In 1962 it was rumored that President Kennedy had offered to nominate Mills to the Supreme Court. Mills declined to comment except to say, "The House is my home." He loved the trading and cajoling necessary to achieve unity. In Alton Frye's words, Mills's genius lay in "deriving workable and constructive accommodations from the welter of claims and pressures."

In 1974, after a history of increasing alcohol consumption, Mills was involved in a widely publicized incident in Washington. While driving late at night, he was stopped by police, whereupon one of his four companions, whose stage name was Fanne Foxe, jumped out of the car and into the water at the Tidal Basin, evidently in an effort to divert attention from Mills. Despite embarrassing publicity, Mills was reelected.

In 1975 he underwent intensive treatment for alcoholism, and afterward abstained from alcohol for the remaining seventeen years of his life. During those years he helped others who suffered as he had: he counseled alcoholics, attended twelve-step meetings, spoke in every state, and raised money for treatment programs.

In 1976 he decided not to seek reelection. The seniority system had been weakened. No longer chairman of Ways and Means, he was not particularly comfortable in a lesser role. He was tired after thirty-eight years in Congress and did not know whether he could maintain his sobriety in the midst of a tough campaign.

He then worked as tax counsel at the Washington office of the law firm Shea and Gould. When he retired in 1991, he and his wife, Clarine, returned to their home in Kensett, where he dictated correspondence, managed investments, paid bills, helped people get jobs, counseled alcoholics, raised funds, read, and signed autographs. He took long drives in the counties he had served during his tenure in Congress. He worked crossword puzzles, watched his favorite television programs, and remained a fan of the Washington Redskins and the Arkansas Razorbacks.

Wilbur Mills died suddenly at his home in Kensett, apparently of a heart attack.

[The Wilbur D. Mills Papers are at Hendrix College in Conway, Arkansas, along with a replica of his congressional office, at the Wilbur D. Mills Center for Social Studies. Ways and Means Committee Papers are at the National Archives and are under the control of the committee. The Sam Rayburn Library in Bonham, Texas, and the presidential libraries of John F. Kennedy and Lyndon B. Johnson have extensive materials on Mills. *The Committee on Ways and Means: A Bicentennial History, 1789–1989* by Donald R. Kennon and Rebecca M. Rogers contains a detailed chapter on "The Mills Era." John Manley's *The Revenue Committees* and *The Politics of Finance* discuss Mills's leadership in insightful detail. See Alton Frye, *A Responsible Congress: The Politics of National Security* (1975), p. 175. See also Kay Goss, "Wilbur D. Mills' Influence on Social Legislation," *AHQ* 54 (Spring 1995): 1–12; and "Wilbur D. Mills," in *The Encyclopedia of the United States Congress* (1995).]

KAY GOSS

MISER, HUGH DINSMORE (Dec. 18, 1884–Aug. 1, 1969), geologist, was born at Pea Ridge, Washington County, Arkansas, the third child of Jordan Stanford Miser, a farmer, and Eliza Caroline Webb. The Miser family were of German and English descent. Miser's ancestors moved from Tennessee to northern Arkansas early in the nineteenth century.

Miser attended Pea Ridge Normal School, an early academy whose principal, Benjamin Harvey Caldwell, was renowned in the community as an inspiring teacher. Miser entered the University of Arkansas at Fayetteville in 1903. In the summer of 1907 the United States Geological Survey employed Miser, still an undergraduate, as an aide on a project mapping and interpreting the geology of the DeQueen and Caddo Gap quadrangles in the western Ouachita Mountains of Arkansas. This experience began his lifelong interest in the Ouachita Mountains and Arkansas geology. He received a master of arts degree in geology in 1912 and became an associate geologist with the USGS soon afterward. His first assignments involved field mapping in Arkansas, Tennessee, and Virginia.

Most of Miser's career, 1912 to 1969, was spent with the United States Geological Survey except for two year-long stints in the 1920s, first as acting professor of geology and acting state geologist at the University of Arkansas, and then as acting state geologist of Tennessee.

Miser's career with the USGS was distinguished, and with each promotion the breadth of his geological experience increased and with it his reputation. He was involved with mapping in Arkansas that resulted in publication of the Eureka Springs and Harrison quadrangles (U.S. Geol. Surv. Folio 202, 1916), the Hot Springs quadrangle (U.S. Geol. Surv. Folio 212, 1923) and the DeQueen and Caddo Gap quadrangles (U.S. Geol. Surv. Bull. 808, 1929). During this time he became an authority on manganese deposits and diamonds in Arkansas. He was promoted to the position of geologist in 1919.

During the field season of 1921 he participated in a remarkable three-month expedition in southeastern Utah. He and his party traversed approximately 140 miles of the San Juan River to map the river and describe its hydrology and the geology of the rocks forming its gorge.

In 1923 Miser was assigned the compilation of the first geologic map of Oklahoma on a scale of 1:500,000, which was assembled largely from confidential materials contributed by major oil companies and independent geologists. It is a measure of his reputation and ability that he was given access to this material and was able to see publication of the map only three years after the project began. In 1928, at the age of forty-four, Miser was appointed chief of the Fuels Branch, the largest entity in the USGS. He oversaw investigations of strategic and critical minerals during World War II and governmental support of petroleum exploration and production. The latter effort led to the establishment of the Oil and Gas Preliminary Maps and Charts publication series of the USGS. At his own request, he stepped down as chief of the Fuels Branch on July 1, 1947. Following the war, the USGS had cooperative arrangements with some state geological surveys, and Miser was assigned as staff geologist with the Oklahoma Geological Survey from 1948 to 1954 to compile a revision of his 1964 state geologic map.

Miser retired in 1954 at the mandatory age of seventy, but from 1955 until his death, he held appointment as scientific staff assistant in the office of the director of the USGS in Washington, D.C. In that capacity, he reviewed and approved maps and reports for publication. Miser was awarded the Distinguished Service Medal by the United States Department of the Interior in 1955. During those latter years, he was able to renew his association with Arkansas geology by spending one month each year with the Arkansas Geological Commission in Little Rock advising their staff on the mapping of the Ouachita Mountains for revision of the Geologic Map of Arkansas.

Miser published eighty-five articles on topics including diamond-bearing periodotites; Ouachita Mountain structure; geology of manganese deposits; mineralogy, particularly quartz; and petroleum geology, among others. In 1950 he was honored by the naming of "Miserite," an unusual potassium silicate mineral discovered at Potash Sulphur Springs, Arkansas, by Waldemar Schaller. Miser was a member, and often an officer, of at least fifteen professional societies, and many conferred honorary membership upon him, among them the American Association of Petroleum Geologists. He was awarded an honorary doctor of laws by the University of Arkansas in 1949.

His hobby was collecting quartz crystals from Arkansas, and he assembled a large collection of beautiful and unusual specimens. He donated some of these crystals for the manufacture of radio equipment during World War II and presented large collections of crystals to the University of Arkansas and University of Oklahoma upon his retirement from the United States Geological Survey.

Miser and Mary Kate Goddard of Fayetteville, Arkansas, were married in 1910; they had one daughter. Hugh Miser died at his home in Washington, D.C.

[A complete list of Miser's publications can be found in a memorial by George V. Cohee in the *American Mineralogist* 55 (1970): 583–91. Other sources include memorials by Thomas A. Hendricks, *Geological Society of America Bulletin* 1 (1971): 57–62; George V. Cohee, *American Association of Petroleum Geologists Bulletin* 53(12) (1969): 560–62; and Malcolm C. Oakes, *Oklahoma Geology Notes* 29 (1969): 129–30. Details of Miser's early life can be found in L. G. Henbest, *Symposium on the Geology of the Ouachita Mountains,* vol. 1 (Arkansas Geological Commission, 1977): 4–5. I thank Norman F. Williams, former state geologist of Arkansas, and Kenneth S. Johnson, associate state geologist of Oklahoma, for some of the information included here.]

WALTER L. MANGER

MITCHELL, HARRY LELAND (June 14, 1906– Aug. 1, 1989), union organizer, was born in Halls, Tennessee, to Maude Ella Stanfield and James Young Mitchell, a barber and sometime preacher.

H. L. Mitchell began farm work when he was eight years old, attending school during the off-season. In December 1917 he witnessed a lynching at the nearby Dyer County Courthouse. He ran from the spectacle, and for the rest of his life he held the image of the lynching in his mind.

Mitchell made his first sharecrop in Ruleville, Mississippi, in 1919. He had to support his family periodically when his father left them for extended periods. His jobs included sharecropping, working in a clothing store, and running a one-pump gas station. Attending school sporadically, Mitchell eventually graduated from Halls High School. His dream of becoming an attorney fell by the wayside as he took employment to support his family.

Lyndell Carmack and H. L. Mitchell were married in 1925; they had two sons and a daughter.

In 1927 Mitchell's parents were living in Tyronza, a rural eastern Arkansas community, where James Mitchell was operating a successful barbershop. The senior Mitchell persuaded H. L. to take over a clothing press located in his shop. The dry-cleaning business became prosperous and expanded, allowing H. L. to be financially secure for the first time in his life.

H. L. Mitchell was an avid reader, especially of "Little Blue Books" which could be ordered through the mail. These books presented the tenets of various political parties and offered commentary on social issues. After extensive reading, he became a Norman Thomas socialist and achieved prominence in the Socialist Party of Arkansas.

One of Mitchell's closest friends, Clay East, owned one of the three gas stations in Tyronza. East thought of a plan by which each of the three stations would operate two days a week, and all three would be open for business on Saturdays. He believed his plan would save time and effort and would divide profits equally among the owners. Mitchell told him it sounded like a good Socialist plan, and soon East was reading Mitchell's "Little Blue Books." The corner of town where their two businesses were located became known as "Red Square."

The renowned socialist Norman Thomas visited Tyronza in 1934. He suggested that Mitchell and East begin a sharecroppers' union to protect the interests of the workers against the wealthy planters. Living in an agricultural community had rekindled the empathy Mitchell had always felt for sharecroppers and poor farmers. Jonathan Daniels wrote that Mitchell "brooded over the fate of the sharecroppers while he cleaned the clothes of the planters." After witnessing the way landowners treated their tenants, Mitchell took the advice of Norman Thomas.

Sharecroppers and tenant farmers worked the hardest jobs for the lowest pay in agriculture. President Roosevelt, in his attempts to help the United States recover from the Great Depression, created an even more dismal situation for farm workers in the form of the first Agricultural Adjustment Act. Planters who owned land were awarded federal subsidies to plow up crops and kill livestock, while their tenant families were starving and going further into debt. The majority of tenants did not receive compensation for their labor.

Mitchell and East decided to organize the farmers in hopes that a united front could accomplish what individuals could not. In July 1934 eleven white men and seven black men met at the Sunnyside Schoolhouse in Poinsett County, Arkansas. There was a mention of segregating the union, but it was quickly dismissed. The Southern Tenant Farmers' Union (STFU) was born. The union was a radical notion at the time, largely because it was one of the first racially integrated unions in the South.

The organization of the STFU led to a life of union work for Mitchell. He constantly lobbied wealthy and politically powerful people who could help his cause. Evelyn Smith Munro, longtime friend of Mitchell and STFU employee, described him as "the Man with the Hoe, Billy the Kid and Abraham Lincoln, with a little of Jesse James thrown in." He became a reformer who dreamed of helping as many disenfranchised farmers and other workers as possible.

Mitchell served as the executive secretary of the STFU from 1934 to 1939 and 1941 to 1944. He married Dorothy Dowe, an STFU officer, in 1951. At its largest in 1938, the union had thirty-one thousand members. According to Mitchell, one of the important differences between other unions and the STFU was that "We were probably the only organization that ever encouraged its workers to leave." If members were offered work in another area, the STFU encouraged them to leave farming and attempt to better their lives.

The National Farm Labor Union and the National Agricultural Workers' Union were successors to the STFU. Mitchell went on to serve as a national labor organizer and made appearances at colleges and universities throughout the United States. He also maintained an active role in the Historic Southern Tenant Farmers' Union, a group that organized reunions, pension funds, and various activities for former STFU members. Harry Leland Mitchell died in Montgomery, Alabama.

[The personal and professional papers of H. L. Mitchell are in the Archives and Special Collections of the Ottenheimer Library, University of Arkansas at Little Rock. The Southern Tenant Farmers' Union Papers are in the Southern Historical Collection, Wilson Library, University of North Carolina at Chapel Hill.

See also Harry Leland Mitchell, *Mean Things Happening in This Land: The Life and Times of H. L. Mitchell, Co-founder of the Southern Tenant Farmers' Union* (1979); and *Roll the Union On: A Pictorial History of the Southern Tenant Farmers' Union* (1987).]

MARCI BYNUM

MITCHELL, JAMES (May 8, 1833–June 26, 1902), professor and journalist, was born at Cane Hill, Washington County, Arkansas, to James Mitchell, a farmer, and Mary Ann Webber. James was the third of ten children of parents who had moved their family from Indiana to the Arkansas Territory about 1830.

The Mitchell children grew up on the family farm; James assisted his father and attended the common schools during the winter seasons. In 1850 he entered Cane Hill Collegiate Institute, later named Cane Hill College. He spent a five-month term there and then taught school in the Choctaw Nation to finance his return to the institute in 1854 and 1855. Although he did not complete a degree, he received a conferred bachelor of arts while a member of the Cane Hill College faculty after the Civil War. His special interests were Latin, rhetoric, and history, areas from which he later drew heavily as a teacher, a writer, and a public speaker. In an address he said that "whatever prosperity I have enjoyed at home and abroad, I attribute to Cane Hill College."

In 1856 he was appointed a United States deputy surveyor for Kansas and Nebraska. A journal he kept that year, in which he attacked the anti-Catholic, anti-immigration positions of the Know-Nothing Party, offers insight into his character and beliefs. A Protestant, he wrote that "toleration in matters of faith is the grand distinguishing feature in the Constitution of the United States . . . it makes us different from, and exalts us above, every other nation under heaven." He went on to query, "What right have you or I to oppose foreign emigration when we remember that foreigners battled for the liberties which we now enjoy?" The journal exemplifies views that remained constants in Mitchell's life.

Mitchell returned to Arkansas in 1858, and the next year opened a school at Evansville in Washington County. In January of 1860, he and Sarah Elizabeth Latta of nearby Vineyard married. The couple had eight children, the first of whom died soon after she was born in 1861. In 1860 Mitchell also began a term in the state legislature. With the outbreak of the Civil War, he enlisted in the Confederate forces; he was mustered out in 1865. To escape hardships caused by the war, in January 1865 Sarah Elizabeth and the Mitchells' daughter, Mamie (born in 1863), took refuge in Bonham, Texas. Mitchell joined them when the war ended and taught school in Bonham for a year. The family returned to Cane Hill in 1866. In 1868 Mitchell became a professor at Cane Hill College, where he taught for the next six years.

In 1874 he was elected to the chair of history and English literature at Arkansas Industrial University in Fayetteville, later named the University of Arkansas. He remained there until 1876, when he moved to Little Rock to become editor-in-chief of the *Arkansas Gazette*. To accommodate his growing family, Mitchell purchased a residence at 1421 Spring Street, which remained the family's home from that time on.

Within two years of the move to Little Rock, Mitchell left the *Gazette* to join William Durbin Blocher in the purchase of the *Arkansas Democrat*. Mitchell served as president and editor-in-chief of the *Democrat* until shortly before his death. Blocher died in 1879; financial hardships for the paper followed. Management as well as editorial duties fell on Mitchell. During that same period, the *Democrat* supported David Walker's candidacy for the United States Senate against the *Gazette*'s choice, Robert W. Johnson. Walker's win, credited to the *Democrat*, aided subscriptions and expanded advertising.

Mitchell believed that his mission as a journalist was to teach. Politically, he guided the paper along conservative Democratic lines. As a journalist and public speaker, he promoted the beauty and riches of Arkansas. He faithfully supported a strong system of public schools, improved pay for teachers, and effective college-level instruction, insisting that college "should be the nursery of patriotism." He editorialized on the need for economic diversification in order for the state to prosper. In these ways, Mitchell made the paper a leading voice in the state and gained the reputation of a "fearless and outspoken" editor.

He strongly advocated rights for women. In addressing inequities in teacher salaries, he argued that merit, not gender, should determine compensation. He believed "in the absolute equality of opportunity in the race of life, the opening of avenues of employment to women in all professions . . . and in the policy of co-education in school, college and university."

Mitchell was postmaster at Little Rock under Grover Cleveland from 1893 to 1897. He was appointed by Governor James Eagle to the Arkansas commission to plan the Columbian Exposition in Chicago in 1893 and was elected president of the state board. He served as chairman of the Pulaski County Bureau of the State Immigration Board in 1888 and was a member of the Little Rock Public School Board, which named one of its schools the James Mitchell School. He served terms as orator and as president of the Arkansas Press Association and was a Mason. Mitchell maintained his civic involvement until shortly before his death in Little Rock.

[Mitchell's thinking can be traced through his editorials in the *Arkansas Gazette*, 1876–78, the *Arkansas Democrat*, 1878–1902, and his "Kansas-Nebraska Journal, 1855–56." See Frances Mitchell Ross, ed., "Civil War Letters from James Mitchell to His Wife, Sarah Elizabeth Latta Mitchell," *AHQ* 37 (Winter 1978): 306–17, and "James Mitchell, Spokesman for Women's Equality in Nineteenth-Century Arkansas," *AHQ* 43 (Autumn 1984): 222–35. An obituary appeared in the *Arkansas Democrat* on June 27, 1902.

Other sources include Fred W. Allsopp, *History of the Arkansas Press for a Hundred Years and More* (1922); Robert Harold Basham, "A History of Cane Hill College," dissertation, University of Arkansas, 1969; and John Hugh Reynolds and David Yancy Thomas, *History of the University of Arkansas* (1910). A Mitchell family history was published in 1952.]

FRANCES MITCHELL ROSS

MONTANA, PATSY (October 30, 1914–May 3, 1996), country singer, was born in Hot Springs, the eleventh child and only daughter of farmer Augustus Blevins and his wife, Victoria. Patsy Montana is a stage name, of course—Augustus and Victoria named her Ruby. Raised on church songs, fiddle music, and Jimmie

Rodgers, Ruby headed to California with her older brother Ron and his wife in 1930, and soon added showbiz panache to her name by changing the spelling to Rubye. A victory in a talent contest in 1931—she yodeled and sang Jimmie Rodgers songs—led to her own radio show. Soon thereafter she dropped Ruby Blevins altogether and became Patsy Montana, a name pinned on her by singer/songwriter Stuart Hamblen while she was performing with the Montana Cowgirls on a show Hamblen hosted with cowboy star Monte Montana.

In 1932 Montana returned to Arkansas, where she got a break when Jimmie Davis heard her on KWKH in Shreveport and invited her to back him up at his next Victor recording session. She cut four songs, her debut recordings, on the same trip. A bigger break came in 1933 when she moved to Chicago and landed a job with the Prairie Ramblers on WLS. She then appeared regularly on the pioneering *National Barn Dance* show and recorded for the American Record Corporation. She also toured steadily, even after her marriage to Paul Rose, who worked with WLS's touring shows, in 1934. Her biggest hit, "I Want to Be a Cowboy's Sweetheart," composed by Montana herself, was recorded in 1935 and went on to become the first million-selling record by a female country artist.

After this Montana was an established star with a clearly defined image. She was a "cowboy pal" who yodeled and dressed in the full cowboy drag favored by 1930s country stars, complete with gun and holster. Additional efforts in the same vein followed—"Rodeo Sweetheart," "Shy Anne from Old Cheyenne," "I Want to Be a Cowboy's Dream Girl," "Sweetheart of the Saddle," "I Wanna Be a Western Cowgirl." In all of these Montana's role is remarkably independent for the day, and country music historians have credited her with opening the way for Dolly Parton, Loretta Lynn, Tammy Wynette, and other stars. Even more spirited, however, are numbers like "The She-Buckaroo" and "A Rip-Snortin' Two-Gun Gal"—in the former she comes on as a "man-hatin' lassie." Montana also appeared in several films, the best known being *Colorado Sunset* (1939) with Gene Autry. In 1946–47 she had her own network radio show, "Wake Up and Smile," on ABC, which featured her trademark "Hi, pardner! It's Patsy Montana" greeting, accompanied by the thunder of horses' hooves.

Montana returned to Arkansas in 1948, raising her children, doing radio shows on KTHS in Hot Springs, and appearing on Shreveport's *Louisiana Hayride.* Her husband's work eventually took the family back to California, but Montana continued to tour and make records into the 1990s, adding to her reputation as a hard-working professional entertainer. Between 1934 and 1992 she made over seven thousand personal appearances in the United States, Canada, and Europe. In the fall of 1995, just before her eighty-first birthday, Montana played concerts in Hope and Little Rock. She was frail and tiny, even in her boots and cowboy hat, but she sang and yodeled vigorously, closing as always with her signature "I Want to Be a Cowboy's Sweetheart." Then she sat at a table and signed autographs until the last fan left happily. She ended her career as she started it, a trouper. Patsy Montana died at San Jacinto, California.

[No full-length biography of Montana has yet been published. Good brief treatments include Mary A. Bufwack and Robert K. Oermann, *Finding Her Voice: The Saga of Women in Country Music* (1993), and the entries in *Definitive Country* (1995), by Ivan M. Tribe, and *The Encyclopedia of Country Music* (1998), by Mary A. Bufwack. It's easy to find reissues of "I Want to Be a Cowboy's Sweetheart," but there are few collections of Montana's work available. One of the best is Columbia's *Patsy Montana and the Prairie Ramblers* of 1984. For the truly dedicated there are several good 1980s reissue collections on the German Cattle Records label.]

ROBERT COCHRAN

MOORE, ELIAS BRYAN (Jan. 23, 1842–May 20, 1897), newspaper editor and politician, was born in Sparta, Tennessee, to William Ward Moore, a tailor, and Isabella Bryan, the third of eight children surviving to adulthood. In 1858 the Moore family moved to Fayetteville, Arkansas, where Elias apprenticed himself as a compositor for the *Arkansian,* a newspaper founded by James R. Pettigrew and Elias Boudinot in 1859. By the following spring, he had learned enough of the printer's trade to establish his own newspaper.

In partnership with his brothers James and William and T. J. Usrev, Moore established the *Democrat* in June 1860. The political controversies of the time allowed a brief competition between the *Arkansian* and the *Democrat* to flourish. Moore supported Stephen A. Douglas for the presidency, a position that placed the

Democrat behind the *Arkansian,* which, together with a plurality of local voters, supported John C. Breckinridge.

Shortly after secession Moore abandoned his paper to his younger brother and father to enlist in Gratiot's regiment of the Arkansas State Troops. Bidding farewell to his readers, he wrote: "We have felt it our duty to drop the pen and the composing stick and to leave home, friends and all that is near and dear to us, and shoulder our rifle and march foreward [*sic*] to defend our common country against an invading enemy."

In August 1861 at the Battle of Wilson's Creek in southwest Missouri, Moore was shot in the right thigh. The wound never healed properly and troubled him for the rest of his life. He returned briefly to Fayetteville to recuperate during the winter of 1861–62, then accepted a Confederate appointment as postmaster. By the following year he was back in the rebel army as a partisan ranger in Captain Palmer's company and participated in General William Cabell's ill-fated attack on Fayetteville, April 18, 1863. Aside from another period of convalescence with his refugeed family in Texas, Moore finished the war under Cabell's command.

After the surrender of the Confederate Trans-Mississippi forces in May 1865, the Moore family returned to Fayetteville. Elias Moore joined his brothers and father to reestablish their newspaper, the *Fayetteville Democrat,* in August 1868. The newspaper business had changed following the war. Personal invective and the reliance on state and national politics for news gradually gave way to a more restrained reporting on local affairs. The Moores successfully competed with all the other sheets established in the town during Reconstruction. As editor Moore maintained civil relations with Pettigrew when the two men found themselves rival editors once again after Pettigrew founded the *Arkansas Sentinel* in Fayetteville in 1874. Moore and Emma Jane North, the daughter of an old army comrade, married February 9, 1869. The couple had four children: Fred, Cora, George, and Sallie.

The *Fayetteville Democrat* prospered with the town during the postwar years, championing such causes as the establishment of the Arkansas Industrial University in Fayetteville and railroad connections for economic growth.

Following the ratification of the 1874 state constitution, Moore discovered, as did many other former Confederates, that his prewar support of the moderate course in Democratic politics had become irrelevant in the post-Reconstruction political arena and so took an active role in the party. He served three terms in the state legislature from 1878 to 1884. By 1884 he was so well known that he was elected secretary of state. All of his brothers eventually followed him to Little Rock when he sold the *Fayetteville Democrat.* After serving two terms, Elias remained in Little Rock and tried a number of business ventures, including a life insurance and private investigation agency.

Following the death of his oldest son in 1889, his wife in 1890, and his brother James in 1892, Moore's own health began to deteriorate due in part to the constant pain he endured from his war wound. He accepted a brief appointment as warden of the Arkansas State Penitentiary in 1895, but he began thinking about a return to his home in Fayetteville and a peaceful retirement in the newspaper business. In 1896 he returned to Fayetteville to join forces with his youngest brother, Dillard, to establish the *Mountain City Gazette.* Taking advantage of the newest innovation in newspapering, the ready-print sheets available from syndicates that allowed him the leisure of composing only two pages of reading matter a week, he quietly worked at his paper until his death. Elias Moore died at Fayetteville.

[Materials on Moore are largely restricted to the public record, including those from his years as secretary of state, nineteenth-century biographical works, and traces he left in his newspapers. Two issues of his first and one issue of his last newspapers have survived. The May 30, 1861, *Democrat* contains his farewell to his readers. Other sources include the *Fayetteville Democrat,* Nov. 12, 1896, Nov. 19, 1896, Feb. 11, 1892, and May 27, 1897; the *Arkansas Sentinel,* Feb. 9, 1892; the *Arkansas Gazette,* Nov. 15, 1886, and May 22, 1897; and *Mountain City Gazette,* Dec. 5, 1896.

See also Kim Allen Scott, "The Arkansas Newspaper Project and the Legacy of Elias Moore," *Flashback* 37(4) (1987): 28–30; and "Window on the Frontier: The Early Newspapers of Washington County, Arkansas, 1840–1862," *Flashback* 39(3) (1989): 7–21; and Millard Fillmore Stipes, *Genealogy and History of the Related Keyes, North and Cruzen Families* (1914): 122–55.]

KIM ALLEN SCOTT

MOOSBERG, CARL AVRIETTE (Aug. 24, 1905–Mar. 27, 1990), cotton breeder, was born at Tyler, Texas, to Frank Olaf Moosberg and Anna Trofast, who had migrated separately from Sweden in the late 1800s. Carl graduated from high school at Wills Point, Texas, in

1923 and went to work for the United States Department of Agriculture at Greenville, attending Texas A & M intermittently.

Later he worked for the USDA at Sacaton, Arizona, where he became interested in Indian artifacts at a nearby excavation. After conferring with scholars at the University of Arizona, he began digging. The artifacts he uncovered and his manuscripts documenting his finds are in the Arizona State Museum at the University of Arizona, Tucson, and the museum at Casa Grande Ruins National Monument, Coolidge, Arizona.

After graduating from Texas Tech with a degree in agronomy, Carl Moosberg returned to Greenville, Texas, as a cotton breeder. During World War II he was a supply sergeant in the United States Army Air Force, "flying the hump" into China, Burma, India, and Pakistan. After the war he returned to Texas, where he married Pearlie Hagler on November 22, 1945; they had three daughters.

Moosberg was associated with the Cotton Branch Station of the University of Arkansas (Marianna) from 1948 to 1972, working first for the USDA and later for the state. His first assignment there was to develop a cotton of unusual fiber strength. In the years right after World War II, cotton mills were still making denim for jeans according to military specifications, which required heavy fiber that wore like iron. Americans came to prefer comfort to indestructibility, however, and the cotton market changed.

By 1950 there was an urgent demand for an earlier maturing cotton. Growers had been using full-season cottons and depended on a cotton crop to keep going until frost. However, insecticides developed to control the boll weevil and boll worm were expensive to apply, making a long growing season very costly. Expense, together with low cotton prices and the anticipation of a mechanical stripper (cotton was still picked by hand), created a critical need for an early maturing variety. Moosberg worked with B. A. Waddle to develop an early strain that could stand up to machine harvesting. He had brought some strains from Texas that were resistant to bacterial leaf blight, and he crossed these with a delta type. The result was an early maturing cotton having a potential for high yield in addition to being resistant to thrips, fusiliam wilt, leaf blight, and storm loss.

Called Rex, this new strain was released in 1957. "Rex cotton is Moosberg's baby," the journal *Progressive Farmer* declared. It was grown generally in Arkansas and from Texas to the Atlantic seaboard. For a brief period it was planted in 60 percent or more of Arkansas's cotton acreage and was the second leading cotton variety in the United States. Rex proved that it was possible to grow an earlier maturing cotton equal in quality to older varieties, thereby affecting the economics of growing cotton.

Moosberg had a gift for looking at a few plants and telling which of them were worth looking at again. Prior to the electronic age, breeders were self-taught, not university trained. Moosberg could feel cotton bolls with his fingers and discard useless material by touch: his fingers knew what to keep and what to throw away.

He brought these talents to bear in the field in the long, careful work of the cotton breeder. On a typical day he was in the field between dawn and daylight to wrap newly opening cotton blossoms with copper wire to keep them from being pollinated and to force them to self-pollinate. Controlled cross-pollinations would be done next, since the pistil of the flower is not receptive to pollination until the sun warms it up. The rest of the day was spent collecting data in the field, data on fruiting, disease symptoms, and, importantly, the absence of disease symptoms. Tagging done earlier in the day was double-checked, because one wrong pollination by an errant bee could ruin an entire experiment.

It takes ten years to develop a variety of cotton, fewer if seeds are grown alternately here and in Mexico to produce two crops in twelve months. Either way, the introduction of a new variety amounts to years of exacting attention to detail in field conditions. Since it was not possible to register a patent for a cotton variety until the 1970s, Moosberg did not benefit financially from the products of his creativity. He later developed Quapaw cotton, a strong, beautiful variety suitable for harvest by stripping machine. Quapaw was still planted in Texas in 1998.

When he retired from the university, he went to work for Growers Seed Company in Lubbock, Texas, developing new strains. Growers had invested time and money trying to breed hybrid cottons successfully, but Moosberg believed that this could not be done and refused to take over their hybridizing efforts.

Moosberg was named the *Progressive Farmer* "Man of the Year in Service to Arkansas Agriculture" in 1966. He participated in church and civic work. Wherever he lived he enjoyed improving his land with grasses, fruits, windbreaks, lakes for waterfowl, and flowers. He died at Duncan, Oklahoma, and is buried at Center, Texas.

[Sources include an interview with B. A. Waddle, Sept. 8, 1997; correspondence with Pearlie Moosberg, Dec. 2, 1998, and Dale A. Hinkle, May 1, 1997; F. M. Bourland and B. A. Waddle, "Cotton Research Overview: Breeding," *Arkansas Farm Research* (July–Aug. 1988): 7; *Progressive Farmer*, Mid-South edition (Jan. 1967): 19; and Stephen Strausberg, *A Century of Research: Centennial History of the Arkansas Agricultural Experiment Station* (1989).]

NANCY A. WILLIAMS

MOREHART, HENRY (Oct. 30, 1841–Jan. 14, 1911), legislator and agrarian leader, was born near Greencastle, Fairfield County, Ohio, the son of Henry Morehart and Mary Plotner. After spending his youth on his parents' farm, he left home to fight for the Union during the American Civil War. He enlisted in Company C, 114 Ohio Volunteers, and, along with the rest of his regiment, saw action in General John McClernand's successful attack on Arkansas Post on January 10–11, 1863, and, later that year, in General Ulysses S. Grant's Mississippi campaign and siege of Vicksburg. After the fall of Vicksburg, Morehart's regiment was transferred to the Acadian country of south Louisiana and later to Alabama, where Morehart was mustered out at the end of the war. While in Alabama, he suffered a wound from a shell shot to his left leg at the Battle of Fort Blakely, April 8, 1865.

Morehart returned to Fairfield County, Ohio, and on October 18, 1866, married Catherine Solt. To their long and apparently happy marriage nine children were born. Morehart and his family lived in Michigan for several years after the war. In 1881 they traveled to Arkansas, making part of the journey by steamboat, and homesteaded land on Sardis Road near the Mabelvale community in southwest Pulaski County.

Morehart is primarily remembered in Arkansas history for his campaign for the office of Pulaski County state representative in 1888 and for the role he played in the Twenty-seventh Session of the Arkansas General Assembly in 1889. Faced with hard times in southern agriculture and falling cotton prices and incomes, as early as the late 1880s and early 1890s discontented white farmers threatened to bolt the Democratic Party and join third-party agrarian insurgencies, such as the Union Labor and Populist Parties. In 1888 Morehart was nominated as a Union Labor Party candidate for Pulaski County state representative, running on a joint Union Labor-Republican fusion ticket.

Encountering their most formidable political challenge since the end of Reconstruction, some Democrats in panic turned to desperate measures. On the night following the state and local races in Pulaski County, burglars entered the courthouse in Little Rock, broke open a safe, and made away with several ballot boxes from what unofficial tally sheets showed to be heavily Union Labor-Republican precincts. This sensational incident was highlighted in newspapers throughout the state and was universally denounced. John Gould Fletcher, president of the German National Bank and former mayor of Little Rock, expressed the general sentiment: "My verdict in matters of this kind is that no condemnation can be too severe."

The Union Labor-Republican claimants went before the county's election board, but that body ruled that the unofficial tally sheets could not be used in computing the voting returns. The decision, complained the *Arkansas Democrat*, "was one of those cases where the law and justice part company." The *Arkansas Gazette* urged the Democratic candidates in question voluntarily to resign, and their refusal to do so evoked much criticism. Encouraged by the public response, Union Labor-Republican nominees for state representative carried their appeal to the general assembly. Spurred on by the popular indignation, the lawmakers were induced to act; on February 18, 1889, Pulaski's Democratic representatives unwillingly surrendered their seats in the House, their places being taken by Morehart and his fellow contestants.

During his term in the legislature, a bill was introduced to establish a state board of election commissioners, with authority to appoint the election officials at each polling place in the state. In one stroke the bill would have given the Democratic Party total control over the election machinery of Arkansas, even in those counties where Union Laborites or Republicans constituted a majority of the voters. Other features of the proposal would have discouraged voting by poor and illiterate persons, both white and black.

Joining with Speaker of the House B. B. Hudgins and other leaders, Morehart helped to create a coalition of Union Laborites, Republicans, and western Arkansas Democrats that, against all odds, defeated the bill.

For unknown reasons Morehart chose not to seek a second term. During the next session of the general assembly, in 1891, a similar centralized election bill was introduced and passed. Within four years there was a one-third decline in voter participation, causing the collapse of the agrarian insurgency and an almost complete removal of African Americans from public office in the state. More than any other single measure, the bill established one-party rule and white supremacy as the central motif of Arkansas politics for almost three-quarters of a century to come.

Morehart never again sought elective office but remained active in local and civic affairs until the year of his death. He is buried in the Martin Cemetery, the oldest cemetery in Pulaski County, located near the Mabelvale community in southwest Little Rock. Little Rock's Morehart Park is named in honor of the Morehart family.

[See John William Graves, *Town and Country: Race Relations in an Urban-Rural Context, Arkansas, 1865–1905* (1990); "Negro Disfranchisement in Arkansas," *AHQ* 26 (Autumn 1967): 199–225; and "A Question of Honor: Election Reform and Black Disfranchisement in Arkansas," University of Virginia *Essays in History,* 15 (1969–71): 9–26. Sources also include Garland Erastus Bayliss, "Public Affairs in Arkansas, 1874–1896," Ph.D. dissertation, University of Texas, 1972; Joe Tolbert Segraves, "Arkansas Politics, 1874–1918," Ph.D. dissertation, University of Kentucky, 1973; and the author's conversations with Henry Calvin Lewis, page boy to Morehart in the Arkansas General Assembly.]

JOHN WILLIAM GRAVES

MORGAN, WINFIELD SCOTT (Aug. 25, 1851– Aug. 27, 1928), populist, author, was born in Columbus, Ohio. At fourteen he moved with his family to Chillicothe, Missouri. When he turned eighteen he married Retta Gilliland, and together they had five children. He passed the Missouri state bar examination in 1884 and moved his family to West Plains, Missouri, where he expected to practice law.

Morgan's law career did not go quite as he expected. As soon as he arrived in West Plains, he went into the business of supplying ties to the Frisco Railroad. He purchased ten thousand acres of land from the federal government, mostly in Sharp County, Arkansas. Then he established an office and shipping point at Ravenden and hired many crews of men to make ties. Later he developed farms in Sharp County and started a lumber mill with his son Claude.

From 1885 to 1891 Morgan lived and worked in Hardy, the seat of Sharp County, at that time a village of six hundred people, half of them involved in some sort of farming. Here he became involved in the Populist movement and began promoting it in lectures and pamphlets. He wrote informational pamphlets about the Arkansas Agricultural Wheel, an organization of small farmers, sharecroppers, and tenants founded in Arkansas in 1882. He often opened his home to prominent Populists on lecture tours. He began a newspaper, the *National Reformer,* later called *Morgan's Buzzsaw.*

His weekly column in the *Buzzsaw,* "Tobe Spilkens" or "Uncle Tobey," written in country dialect, expressed agrarian grievances from the point of view of the poor farmer: "Them dad burn Rebublikins and Democrits maks us pur wurkin people look a phool, wurkin for ther food, yet gettin nothin in return. I don think dat they is listin much to pur ole Tobe, but pur ole Tobe helps to feed them dad burn politicans."

The Populist movement brought together various agrarian organizations and early farmers' alliances in opposition to the exclusionary practices of American politics. Morgan became an important voice in this mass reform effort. He presented "A Pure Creed: A Vindication of Populist Principles" at the first national convention of the Populist Party in 1892. The convention adopted a platform calling for government ownership of telephone, telegraph, and railroad systems, a graduated income tax, free silver, the direct election of United States senators, immigration reform, public education, and a subtreasury plan.

In his book *The History of the Wheel and Alliance and the Impending Revolution* (1891), Morgan describes the leaders of the Wheel movement, where they came from, their reasons for joining the effort, and how the effort got started. He outlines the various abuses that farmers suffered from the government and criticizes government monopolies and what he terms the "anaconda mortgage" problem. Before his book was published Morgan sent circulars advertising it to every state in the nation. He intended his book not only for those already involved in the Wheel movement but to promote the goals to new people and urge them to join together.

In 1898 Morgan ran for the office of governor of Arkansas, seeing the race as an opportunity to speak to more people about Populism and tell voters how the Democratic Party continued to cheat Arkansans. He seized every chance to speak about Populism in those areas where his pen did not reach. In his race against

H. F. Auten, Republican, and Governor Dan Jones, Democrat, Morgan fired heavily at both parties but saved most of his criticism for the Democrats. At Benton he brought up the subject of campaign frauds. He asked Governor Jones why he could so easily find and jail hog thieves but had yet to jail one ballot thief, and went on to say that hog thieves go to the penitentiary while ballot thieves go to the governor's church.

The Democrats won the election of 1898 and Populism seemed to have lost all its support, but Morgan continued to fight for his ideals. In 1905 he published *The Red Light,* a fictional version of events that took place in Conway and Crittenden counties in the 1888 election. In it he describes the corruption of the Democratic Party and gives details of how the party used fraud, ballot theft, and even murder to defeat the alliance of black Republicans and poor white farmers.

By the 1920s the Populist movement was virtually over; the support once given by rural farmers to the mass agrarian movement was gone. But Morgan never gave up on it, continuing to speak and write about Populism long after his newspaper had gone out of business. He died at his son's home near Hardy.

[The W. Scott Morgan Papers, 1871–1929, are in the Special Collections Division, University of Arkansas Libraries, Fayetteville, Ser. 5, Box 2.]

LORRIE MCCLURE

MORRIS, JOHN BAPTIST (June 29, 1866–Oct. 22, 1946), third Roman Catholic bishop of Little Rock, was born near Hendersonville, Tennessee, the son of John Morris and Anne Morrissey, Irish immigrants. Morris received his first formal education at St. Mary's College in Lebannon, Kentucky. Receiving a degree in 1887, he returned to Nashville to live with his family, who had moved there. He decided to enter the priesthood and Bishop Joseph Rademacher of Nashville sent him to seminary in Rome. Ordained there on June 11, 1892, he returned to Nashville to serve at St. Mary's Cathedral. In 1894 the new Nashville bishop, Thomas S. Byrne, appointed him his personal secretary, and then rector of the cathedral the following year. He became vicar general of the diocese in June 1900, and six months later Pope Leo XIII granted him the title of monsignor. Six years later Pope Pius X named him Arkansas's third Catholic bishop, consecrated in Nashville on June 11, 1906, the first native of Tennessee to be raised to the American Catholic hierarchy.

Morris's position was that of coadjutor bishop, serving as auxiliary bishop for Bishop Edward M. Fitzgerald, with right of succession upon his death. When Bishop Fitzgerald died in 1907, Morris became bishop of Little Rock. A bishop through two world wars and the Great Depression, Bishop Morris also headed the diocese during a resurgent anti-Catholicism in state and nation just before and after World War I. The bishop's strong patriotic stands during the national conflicts and his political connections helped him blunt some anti-Catholicism.

Another way this stocky, bespectacled bishop hoped to ward off prejudice was to build up Catholic institutions. He founded St. Joseph's Catholic orphanage in North Little Rock in 1909, which lasted more than sixty years; St. John's Home Mission Seminary in Little Rock in 1911, which lasted for fifty-six years; and a weekly English-language Catholic newspaper in 1911, which still operates in 1998. Some institutions did not outlive his episcopacy. He started Little Rock College in 1908. The Great Depression closed that facility in 1930, yet the high-school department continued as Catholic High. During the depression Bishop Morris opened a black Catholic orphanage near Pine Bluff named St. Raphael's. Unfortunately, this missionary experiment failed. Black Arkansans were unwilling to place their children in an institution run by whites and operated by a church to which they did not belong. Morris reluctantly closed it by the end of 1937; it operated as a trade school until 1961.

Institutionally, the church grew tremendously. In 1906 there had been 60 priests and 200 sisters; four decades later, there were 154 Catholic priests and 582 religious sisters in Arkansas. Where once there were about twenty-nine schools with 2,702 students, by 1946 there were eighty schools with 7,710 students. From 1905 to 1945 the number of Catholic hospitals increased from four to nine, with a bed capacity of over a thousand. The number of Catholics grew from 20,000 in 1906 to 35,196 in 1946, going from a overall population of less than one percent of the population in 1900 to 1.7 percent by 1940. The diocesan departments of education and social services have their origin during the episcopacy of Bishop Morris.

One of his proudest achievements was his mission work among African Americans. When he came to Arkansas, he found only two fledgling black Catholic parishes in Pine Bluff and Pocahontas. By 1946 there were nine black Catholic parishes throughout the state, and all but two of them had Catholic schools.

Bishop Morris was a gifted orator in demand for speaking engagements. At the National Eucharistic Conference in New Orleans in 1937, he presented a discourse on the Holy Father. One of his last major addresses was an attack on Nazi anti-Semitism after *Kristallnacht* in November 1938. Even though his remarks did not receive distant notice or reaction, no other American Catholic bishop made such an attack on Nazism at that time.

Due to his advancing age, Bishop Morris petitioned Rome for an auxiliary bishop. The Vatican agreed and named Vicar General Monsignor Albert L. Fletcher. Fletcher became the first native Arkansan ever raised to the rank of a Catholic bishop. While day-to-day operations were handled by the Auxiliary Bishop Fletcher, Bishop Morris maintained control over major appointments, naming a new rector for the seminary in the fall of 1944. The growingly incapacitated prelate marked the centennial of diocese in November 1943, but he did not live long after the close of the Second World War. He died at the rectory at St. Andrew's and is buried under the cathedral.

[Papers pertaining to the life and career of Bishop John B. Morris can be found in the Archives of the Archdiocese of New Orleans. See James M. Woods, *Mission and Memory: A History of the Catholic Church in Arkansas* (1993); the Diocesan Historical Commission, *History of Catholicity in Arkansas* (1925); and Thomas Stritch, *The Catholic Church in Tennessee* (1987).]

JAMES M. WOODS

MURPHY, ISAAC (Oct. 16, 1799–Sept. 8, 1882), teacher, attorney, and governor, was born and raised near Pittsburgh, Pennsylvania. After graduating from nearby Washington College he moved to Clarksville, Tennessee, where he taught school and practiced law. There he met and married Angelina Lockhart; the couple produced six daughters.

In 1834 Murphy moved to Fayetteville in the Arkansas Territory. He resided in Fayetteville for twenty years and held a number of local public offices. Always more interested in education than law, he operated a grammar school and was a founder of the board of visitors of Far West Seminary, the first college in the state. Washington County voters elected Murphy, a Jacksonian Democrat, to the legislature in 1846 and 1848.

In 1854 he moved to Huntsville where he and his eldest daughters operated a grammar and a secondary school. Two years later the voters of Madison and Benton Counties returned him to the legislature.

In 1861 Murphy was one of two men selected by Madison County residents to represent their strong Unionist feelings at the secession convention in Little Rock. Unionists were in the majority at first, but secessionist sentiment swelled after Fort Sumter. On May 6, 1861, the convention approved secession by a vote of sixty-five to five. The five Unionist delegates were asked to change their votes so that the resolution might be unanimous. Four did so but Murphy declared: "I have cast my vote after mature reflection, and have duly considered the consequences, and I cannot conscientiously change it." He remained steadfast despite appeals and threats. He returned to Huntsville, but in early 1862 he was forced to flee to the protection of Union military forces operating in southern Missouri and northern Arkansas.

The Confederates were compelled to abandon Little Rock in September 1863, and Arkansas became the third secessionist state to come under some degree of Union control. In accordance with Abraham Lincoln's Proclamation of Amnesty and Reconstruction, an election was held to choose delegates to a Unionist constitutional convention. Because of chaotic wartime conditions, only counties in the central and northern parts of the state were represented. In January 1864 the convention met in Little Rock and, at Lincoln's urging, chose Murphy as provisional governor and Calvin C. Bliss as provisional lieutenant governor. Murphy, Bliss, and a rump Unionist legislature were formally elected in March. At his inauguration on April 18 Murphy made an eloquent plea for expanded public education and urged all Arkansans to work together to repair the ravages caused by the war.

Murphy faced enormous problems as governor: the treasury was empty, the southern half of the state was under Confederate control, and the northern half was plagued by anarchy. To make matters worse, Murphy's isolated government in Little Rock was entirely dependent for its survival on Major General Frederick Steele, the conservative Union military commander in Arkansas who had little sympathy for southern Unionists, emancipation, and reconstruction policies. Murphy's personal survival also was in doubt. Without a salary or any means of his own, he subsisted for months on handouts from supporters and relatives. Under these circumstances relatively little was accomplished. The high point of this first phase of Murphy's administration came in April 1865 when the legislature approved the Thirteenth Amendment to the Constitution, which prohibited slavery in the United States. Throughout this difficult period, Lincoln and his successor, Andrew Johnson, steadfastly recognized the legitimacy of the Unionist state government.

In the postwar election of 1866 Unionist legislators were replaced by former secessionists and Confederates. Now began the second phase of Murphy's administration. Murphy urged the legislature to comply with national policies so that the state could be restored to the Union as quickly as possible. The legislature refused to cooperate. It rejected the Fourteenth Amendment to the Constitution, which guaranteed equal rights for all citizens, and passed racially repressive laws which distressed Murphy and infuriated the Congress. On the positive side, at Murphy's request the legislature established the first statewide public school system, albeit for whites only, and approved the 1862 Morrill Land Grant Act which led to the establishment of the University of Arkansas.

In 1867 an angry Congress passed the Reconstruction Acts which placed the recalcitrant south under military supervision. Because of Murphy's reputation as a staunch Unionist, he was allowed to administer the state government in a relatively normal manner without interference by military authorities. Arkansas was readmitted to the Union on June 18, 1868, four days before the end of Murphy's term. Murphy, now sixty-nine, did not run for reelection. He returned to Huntsville where he lived in very modest circumstances and farmed, practiced law, and occasionally served as a judge.

Murphy was a frontier educator thrust into the governorship during the most difficult period in Arkansas history. His wartime election was questionable, his administration was buffeted by powerful forces over which he had no control, and he had to work with Unionists, ex-Rebels, and military occupation forces. Despite his sometimes controversial and unpopular opinions, he gained widespread respect for his integrity, sound judgment, and good intentions. His most important contribution to Arkansas was the establishment of a firm foundation for public education.

[For more detail and bibliographic information, see William L. Shea, "Isaac Murphy, 1864–1868," in *The Governors of Arkansas: Essays in Political Biography*, Timothy P. Donovan, Willard B. Gatewood Jr., and Jeannie M. Whayne, eds., 2d ed. (1995).]

WILLIAM L. SHEA

NANCARROW, SAMUEL CONLON (Oct. 27, 1912–Aug. 10, 1997), composer, was born in Texarkana, Arkansas, to Samuel Charles Nancarrow, a businessman and mayor of Texarkana from 1927 to 1931, and Myra Brady. He attended Cincinnati College-Conservatory and while in that city married Helen Rigby in 1932. They moved to Boston in 1934. There Nancarrow studied composition with Walter Piston, Roger Sessions, and Nicolas Slonimsky and conducted a Works Progress Administration orchestra. In 1937 he went to Spain as a member of the Abraham Lincoln Brigade to fight with the Loyalists in opposition to Franco's fascist government. While he was out of the country, his wife divorced him.

When Nancarrow returned to the United States in 1939, he learned that Slonimsky had arranged to have two of his compositions published. Nancarrow settled in New York and associated with other composers of new music, including Elliott Carter and Aaron Copland. Because the State Department, citing his radical background, refused to give him a passport, he moved to Mexico City in 1940 and resided there the rest of his life, taking out Mexican citizenship in 1956. His only return visit to Arkansas was in 1992.

His second marriage, to Annette Stephens, a painter, in 1948, ended in divorce five years later. In 1970 he and Yoka Seguira, a Japanese anthropologist, were married and the following year had a son, David Makota.

As a child Nancarrow escaped from hated piano lessons by taking up trumpet. He continued to play the trumpet in Cincinnati and returned to that instrument in 1936 for a tour of Europe with a jazz group. He was fascinated by the player piano in his home when he was growing up, but it was a performance of Igor Stravinsky's "Le Sacre de Printemps," which he heard when he was in his late teens, that opened up a new world of possibilities for him. Later he read Henry Cowell's treatise, *New Musical Resources*, in which Cowell suggested that certain rhythms too complex for live performers could easily be cut on a player-piano roll.

In 1947 Nancarrow traveled to New York to find a player piano and a punching machine. Back in Mexico he began the Studies for Player Piano, which established his reputation. As he composed the Studies, he was always experimenting. In his book, *The Music of Conlon Nancarrow,* Kyle Gann wrote that "there is not a piece in Nancarrow's mature output that does not contain some new idea or twist he had never tried before." In an interview the composer identified a pervading idea: "Almost all of my music is canonic. Quite a few [of the Studies] are strict canons, but they all have canonic passages." (In a canon a melody is imitated note for note in one or more other parts. A round is a type of canon.) His canons are tempo canons; that is, transpositions of the same melody played in different tempos at the same time. Composing for player piano gave him the freedom to hear his rhythmical complexities without waiting for a performer to be willing to play them.

Nancarrow considered his studies unplayable by humans. But musicians who have found ways to surmount the difficulties by multi-tracking and arranging the music for two pianos and string orchestra have shown that the human element brings added nuances and warmth to the music. Nancarrow's obituary in the *New York Times* quotes composer Gyorgy Ligeti, who wrote in the 1980s that Nancarrow's music is "utterly original, enjoyable, constructive and at the same time emotional" and "the best music by any living composer."

Fame, however, was slow in coming. Merce Cunningham choreographed six of the Studies in 1960 and in 1964 his dance company performed them on a world tour. Columbia issued the first commercial recording of the Studies in 1969. Only in 1977, though, did Nancarrow become well known, even to the devotees of contemporary music. In that year scores of eight of his Studies were published, and 1750 Arch Records began recording all the Studies thus far composed. He received his first commission that year. In 1981 he made his first trip to the United States since 1947, visiting San Francisco for a recorded performance of the Studies. The following year he was composer-in-residence at the Cabrillo Festival in Aptos, California, at which his early instrumental works were performed. That fall he toured Europe. It was a dramatic change from his reclusive life over the previous forty years. At his European appearances his manager played his tapes and Ligeti spoke about the music. It was also in 1982 that Nancarrow

received a letter informing him that he was the recipient of a $300,000 MacArthur Fellowship, "given in recognition of your accomplishments in Music which demonstrate your originality, dedication to creative pursuits, and capacity for self-direction."

With major commissions from the Arditti Quartet and pianist Ursula Oppens in 1988, Nancarrow returned to writing for live performers. In 1990 the New England Conservatory of Music gave him an honorary doctorate and the University of Mexico City presented a two-day celebration of his music, including performances on his player piano. Although he suffered a stroke in 1990, he continued to compose until 1993. He died at his home in Mexico City.

[See Kyle Gann, *The Music of Conlon Nancarrow* (1995); James R. Greeson and Gretchen B. Gearhart, "Conlon Nancarrow: An Arkansas Original," *AHQ* 54 (Winter 1995): 457–69; and Conlon Nancarrow, *Complete Studies for Player Piano,* 5 vols. WER 60166/67–50, WER 6168/9–2, WER 60165-50. Wergo 1988–91.]

GRETCHEN GEARHART

NEAL, FRANCES POTTER (Oct. 27, 1905–July 30, 1990), librarian, was born in Strong, Union County, Arkansas. She was the oldest of three daughters of Finis Potter and Lucy Letitia Richardson. She attended the University of Arkansas in Fayetteville for two years and returned to Union County to teach in the elementary school system. In 1931 she married Karl Neal, a cotton buyer, and moved with him to Warren, Bradley County, Arkansas. They had no children, but she had four nephews and one niece, all of whom she loved dearly.

She taught in the Warren public school system and worked after hours with other teachers, school board members, the Parent Teachers Association, and parents to establish libraries in the local elementary schools. She did summer work at the University of Arkansas in Fayetteville to finish her degree in elementary education.

In 1947 the Neals moved to Little Rock, where she became circulation librarian for the Arkansas Library Commission. At that time there were few tax-supported public libraries in Arkansas and most of the rural population had no local library service.

The state library laws allowed citizens with no local library to borrow books directly from the Arkansas Library Commission by mail. Some people knew of this and were taking advantage of the opportunity. Neal established a publicity program which increased awareness of the service, and many more people in the most untraveled parts of the state became regular readers. Later, when library taxes came up for a vote, they were among the strongest supporters.

Loans of books were made not only to individuals but also to family groups, clubs, churches, PTA's, and country stores. Any group could receive a large collection of books to read and pass around; when they returned them in three months, they could receive a new collection. Reading became very popular in the good old days before television.

In 1949 Neal took a year-long leave to attend the University of Denver in Colorado where she earned a master's degree in library science. On returning to Arkansas, she was appointed acting librarian of the Arkansas Library Commission while the librarian was on leave.

In 1952 Neal was appointed state librarian and executive secretary of the Arkansas Library Commission, a position she held until her retirement in 1978. She set a goal for herself of a tax-supported library in each county. True, there were already several such libraries, but with seventy-five counties in the state, there was still plenty of work to do. Through the years she wrote hundreds of letters, visited county officials, spoke at meetings of men's and women's clubs, junior chambers of commerce, PTA's and school boards, and church groups, as well as to individuals who visited library booths at county fairs.

At each biennium, one or more counties passed a library tax. Some had to try more than once but that just called for more work in the next two years.

When federal money was first granted to states for library service, a bookmobile was purchased and stocked with books. Neal's plan was for the bookmobile to be driven through the back roads to country stores and crossroad communities so people could visit and see a room full of books on all subjects. A librarian was there to explain the use of the bookmobile and answer questions. Many counties purchased bookmobiles because of this demonstration.

Later federal grants were matched with state funds to use for enlarging or remodeling libraries or for erecting new ones. Each year there was a waiting list of tax-supported libraries applying to receive these funds.

Neal died in Little Rock. She had made great progress toward her goal: all but three counties had passed a library tax and each of these three had a tax-supported city public library in the county seat.

Frances Potter Neal held offices in state, regional, and national library associations and was recognized and respected throughout the library world. She received many awards and citations for her constant effort in spreading the written word, among them a citation in 1956 from the Arkansas Junior Chamber of Commerce for exceptional work in public library promotion; a 1957 woman-of-the-year citation for outstanding and useful service to rural people by the *Progressive Farmer;* a certificate of recognition for service and deeds to citizens of Arkansas from David Pryor, governor of Arkansas; a certificate of appreciation from the Cooperative Office of Education Program for offering career opportunities to young people; and the Governor's Volunteer Excellence Award in 1984 in recognition of outstanding volunteer service to the people of Arkansas.

JACQUELINE POE

NEWBERRY, FARRAR CLAUDIUS (July 7, 1887–July 31, 1968), historian, businessman, was born in Gurdon, Arkansas. Little is known about his parents, but they appear to have been of moderate means. They placed a high value on education and always tried to provide the best possible for their children. In 1894 the family moved seventeen miles to the flourishing river town of Arkadelphia.

Arkadelphia, in addition to its public school system, boasted a church-sponsored educational institution called Arkadelphia Methodist College, which had grades from kindergarten through college. Newberry went to school there until his graduation with a bachelor of arts in history in 1906. By then Arkadelphia Methodist College had changed its name to Henderson-Brown College.

Newberry spent two years at Vanderbilt University, emerging with a master of arts in history and a Phi Beta Kappa key. He taught briefly at the Union City Training School in Tennessee. The siren call of Arkansas was too great, though, and he returned to Arkadelphia in 1909, accepting a position on the faculty of his alma mater. While teaching at Henderson, Newberry developed an interest in the study of law. He took a one-year position on the history faculty of the University of Arkansas at Fayetteville, taking law courses in his spare time.

He finished his law studies back in Arkadelphia in the offices of Calloway and Huie, then the most prominent attorneys in Arkadelphia. Upon their recommendation he was admitted to the bar in 1912. He set up a law practice in Arkadelphia, but soon was taken with politics. He was elected to the Arkansas General Assembly. Apparently that experience was sufficient to rid him of the political bug, and he did not stand for reelection. That year he married Lila Lee Thompson of Little Rock.

Shortly after his marriage, Newberry made the connections which would provide him with his lifelong career. Southwest Arkansas has long provided the larger part of the state's timber production. The area had long been a fruitful hunting ground for the Woodmen of the World, a nonprofit fraternal benefit life insurance society. In addition to life insurance, the society, founded in 1890, provided its members with social and recreational programs and supports community service, the study of American history, and conservation of natural resources. Newberry took a position with them in 1914 and rose quickly through the ranks. In 1915 he was promoted to the rank of "Head Consul" of the jurisdiction of Arkansas. In 1918 he became state manager of the organization.

This necessitated a move from his beloved Arkadelphia to Little Rock. For the next seventeen years he labored as state manager with excellent results; in 1935 he was brought to the head office in Omaha, Nebraska. Over the next eight years he progressed steadily up the corporate ladder, achieving the presidency in 1943. He held this position until his retirement twelve years later. During this period he also served as president of the board of regents of the University of Omaha, president of the National Fraternal Congress of America, and president of the Omaha Chamber of Commerce. He most enjoyed his membership in the International Concatenated Order of the Hoo Hoo, a secret fraternity of men who worked in the timber industry which had its headquarters in Gurdon, Arkansas.

On retirement his first objective was to return to Arkadelphia. He and his wife built a spacious house, modeled after George Washington's Mount Vernon and situated directly across the street from Henderson College. On his death the house was donated to Henderson. It became the president's house.

Newberry's retirement was an active one. He wrote three books and contributed numerous articles on Clark County history to the local newspapers. He was affectionately known by Arkadelphians as the unofficial historian of Clark County. His greatest passion, though, was the study of the lives of the American presidents. He achieved a reputation throughout the south as an authority on the subject and was much in demand as a speaker.

Farrar Newberry died in Arkadelphia, leaving his wife and two sons, Farrar Newberry Jr. and Nick T. Newberry.

[A collection of Newberry's papers is in the archives of Henderson State University, including newspaper articles and privately published books by Newberry, correspondence, and photographs. A guide to the collection is available from the archives.]

J. ROBERT GREENE

NUTTALL, THOMAS (Jan. 5, 1786–Sept. 10, 1859), naturalist and ornithologist, was born in Yorkshire, England, to James Nuttall and Margaret Hardacre. At fourteen years of age Thomas was apprenticed as a printer to an uncle in Liverpool. He developed an interest in botany, which he learned on his own. In 1808, following seven years of apprenticeship, he shunned a business offer from his uncle and sailed from Liverpool to Philadelphia, Pennsylvania.

Upon his arrival he searched for a copy of Benjamin Smith Barton's *Elements of Botany* and eventually secured one directly from the author. Barton, professor of botany at the University of Pennsylvania, immediately accepted Nuttall as his protégé. Through Barton, Nuttall established a relationship with the famous collector of plants and animals of the South, William Bartram.

Barton and other leaders of Philadelphia's scientific community took great interest in Nuttall and directed his study and training. In 1810 Barton outfitted Nuttall's first expedition, which collected botanical species on a route from Philadelphia to Lake Michigan and on to Fort Mandon on the upper Missouri River.

This first trek was in the company of one of the expeditions of Manuel Lisa, a fur trader and explorer. Nuttall made abundant scientific collections. Much to the amusement of his fellow voyagers, he frequently got lost and had to be rescued. In preparation for a possible Indian raid, his party checked his rifle and found it filled with dirt; he had used it to dig plants.

After a successful two-year adventure, he returned

to England when the War of 1812 began. During the war years he prepared the six-hundred-page *Genera of North America Plants,* highlighting 834 genera and including many species new to science.

In October 1818, having returned to the United States, Nuttall left Philadelphia on a two-year trek which became one of the first scientific expeditions in Arkansas. Traveling primarily on the Ohio and Mississippi Rivers, he reached the White River cutoff to the Arkansas River on January 12, 1819. He eventually arrived at Arkansas Post, where he took residence with Dr. Robert McKay. The settlement's lack of culture and overall roughness distressed him. He described the post inhabitants as "French, above all they are chiefly renegade Americans who have fled honest society." After several weeks he departed in a large skiff on the Arkansas River. He described the land along the river as inhabited by few families and scattered villages of Quapaws.

Near Little Rock Nuttall met Nathaniel Pryor, sergeant of the Lewis and Clark expedition. He proceeded no further than the settlement of Dardanelle in the Cherokee lands. From April 9 until April 20 Nuttall stayed at the house of a chief of the Cherokee acting as an Indian trader, "possessing a decently furnished and well-provided house, and several Negro slaves."

Nuttall arrived in Fort Smith on April 24, 1818. He considered the mountains as large as the Alleghenies. The surgeon at the fort, Dr. Thomas Russell (1793–1826), and the commandant of the garrison, Major William Bradford, set out for the Red River with a detachment to order white settlers off land granted to the Osage Indians. Nuttall was invited to accompany the party and surveyed a large tract of country in the present state of Oklahoma. He remained for three weeks, captivated by the plant and bird life of the flowering prairies.

During his explorations in Arkansas, Nuttall had numerous encounters with the Osage. He made observations on their character and customs, which he recorded in his journal along with tales of cruel barbarism inflicted on white men.

Nuttall wanted to reach the Rocky Mountains, but on the third day of the journey from Fort Smith he suffered a relapse of a mountain fever and became desperately ill. For weeks he hovered near death, and finally he and his traveling companion determined to turn back. They encountered an encampment of Osage who charged them and grabbed their meager supplies and belongings. As the Osage became more hostile, Nuttall retreated to the river and escaped.

The unfortunate expedition lasted five weeks before Nuttall returned to Fort Smith. For a month he slowly recovered. Finally on October 16 he left Fort Smith with his precious collections. He was still desperately ill and took six weeks to reach Arkansas Post.

In January 1820, after a year of waiting for the boat, Nuttall found an opportunity to descend the river to New Orleans. He was disappointed not to have reached the Rockies, but he had survived illness, Indians, and renegade whites and collected a few hundred new species in the Southwest.

In 1821 he published *A Journal of Travels into the Arkansa Territory.* From 1822 to 1834 he served as curator of the botanical garden at Harvard University. At Harvard he was known for his attic, accessible by a rope ladder which he would pull up in order to work without interruption. In 1832 he wrote *A Manual of the United States and Canada,* which established his preeminence in this field.

In 1842 Nuttall was bequeathed his uncle's estate, "Nutgrove," near Liverpool. There he spent the last sixteen years of his life.

[See Thomas Nuttall, *A Journal of Travels into the Arkansa Territory during the Year 1819* (1821) (Arkansas is spelled "Arkansa" by Nuttall); Jeannette E. Graustein, *Thomas Nuttall, Naturalist: Explorations in America 1808–1841* (1967); and Howard Ensign Evans, *Pioneer Naturalists* (1995).]

DAN THIEL

OTTENHEIMER, GUS (July 17, 1897–Mar. 16, 1985), industrialist and philanthropist, was born in Little Rock to Hannah Berger and Daniel Phillip Ottenheimer, a businessman. Family members had come to Arkansas in the 1850s; Gus's grandfather Phillip and his great uncle Abraham had served in the Confederate army. Phillip and Abe were joined by their brother Daniel in Little Rock after the war, and the three opened Ottenheimer Brothers, which became a large carpet and dry-goods enterprise. The Ottenheimer clan were members of Congregation B'nai Israel of Little Rock throughout their lives.

Gus Ottenheimer was the fourth and last of his parents' children; the others were Leonard, Ruth, and Gladys. When D. P. Ottenheimer died in 1908, Leonard dropped out of school and became the family's bread-winner. In 1915 he helped Gus off to Washington and Lee University School of Law, where Gus had to work for his tuition and board. Gus's desire for higher education and the price paid for it—his own hard work and Leonard's sacrifice—had a lasting effect on them.

After he returned to Little Rock, Gus worked for a short time in the law firm of Mehaffy, Reid, and Mehaffy. From 1922 until 1926, he worked in Providence, Rhode Island. Meanwhile, Leonard launched a jobbing company of ladies' ready-to-wear at 108 East Markham, Little Rock. He acquired a New York office that enabled him to give Arkansas merchants better merchandise and prices. In August 1926 Gus joined the company, and they revived with pride the old family name of "Ottenheimer Brothers."

To survive after the 1929 stock-market crash, such firms as theirs had to either liquidate or become manufacturers. The brothers chose the latter option and in January 1933 began a manufacturing operation on the upper floors of their building. With six sewing machines and several seamstresses, copying styles from photos, they learned the business in what they called "the hunt and peck" method. To their surprise their efforts flourished; by June they had some fifty workers, and a local newspaper boasted that it was "refreshing to ears and soothing syrup to morale to begin hearing of 'going' concerns rather than 'gone' ones." Later the brothers concentrated almost exclusively on moderately priced cotton garments. From the beginning of their effort until they sold their company in the 1970s, they made pleasant working conditions for their employees one of their top goals. After their sister Gladys married Joseph Hirsch of Dallas in 1944, the newlyweds joined the family venture.

The Ottenheimer brothers made economic and racial history in the South when in 1943 they opened a unit, the Rocket Plant, to black employees. So successful was their effort that it was publicized nationwide, and other factories in the South began following suit.

In 1948 the Ottenheimers began selling their products exclusively to Sears, Roebuck, and when Leonard, Gus, and Gladys retired in 1955, Sears bought the company, renaming it the Kellwood Company. The Ottenheimer brothers built a large new plant in southwest Little Rock and leased it to Sears. A division of the plant was located at Lonoke, Arkansas, and named for the Ottenheimers. Sears honored the Ottenheimers in 1978, and Kellwoood's president acknowledged the brothers' "vision, practical planning, and respect for human resources."

Gus Ottenheimer became known nationwide through his work with the National Association of Manufacturers. He promoted Arkansas's and Pulaski County's industrial growth. His influence extended worldwide through his work with the Rotary International's Institute of International Understanding and its Ventures of International Friendship, whose programs introduced students to Rotary's values and America's free enterprise system. Gus was outspoken in his denunciation of collective controls of the economy and wage controls. He fought efforts to remove the state's Freedom to Work law (right to work) and the antiviolence law.

Gus and Leonard promoted real estate in Little Rock. In the late 1950s they and other investors developed the Cloverdale addition in the city's southwest. The addition became Little Rock's fastest-growing section and was incorporated as part of the metropolitan area.

Gus Ottenheimer is remembered for his work in higher education. In the 1950s and 1960s he headed efforts to improve Little Rock Junior College and saw it grow to a four-year institution, then merge with the University of Arkansas System. The Ottenheimers also remembered the students. Gus never took his college degree for granted (he was seldom seen without his Washington and Lee Law School lapel pin), nor did Leonard forget that his education was cut short. In 1965 they incorporated the Ottenheimer Brothers Foundation for educational and charitable purposes. The bachelor brothers felt they had failed their forebears in not leaving progeny, and Gus explained the foundation was created so that their name and that of their forebears would not be forgotten. In fact, no one with the Ottenheimer name remained in Arkansas after their deaths. In 1980 they established Ottenheimer Brothers Tuition Scholarships at the University of Arkansas, Little Rock, enabling ten students annually to attend its Law School. They also established an endowed scholarship fund at Washington and Lee School of Law. By 1994 the foundation had paid or pledged more than $4 million to educational, religious, and charitable institutions or organizations. Gus, Leonard, Gladys, and Joe Hirsch all died in Little Rock in the 1980s.

[The Ottenheimer Papers are at the Ottenheimer Foundation, Little Rock. See Carolyn Gray LeMaster, *The Ottenheimers of Arkansas* (1995), and *A Corner of the Tapestry: A History of the Jewish Experience in Arkansas: 1820s–1990s* (1994).]

CAROLYN GRAY LEMASTER

OVERTON, WILLIAM RAY (Sept. 19, 1939–July 14, 1987), United States district judge, was born in Hot Spring County, Arkansas, to Elizabeth Ford and Odis Ray Overton, a mine foreman at Magnet Cove. His mother, who taught in public schools, was a master of the English language; Overton joked that he got a little learning in language by osmosis. His father died when Overton was sixteen years old. His stepfather, James Kimzey, was an educator and a history buff.

Overton graduated from the University of Arkansas at Fayetteville and its Law School. He served as editor of the law review, an honor reflecting his scholarship, writing ability, and the confidence of the faculty.

On January 25, 1964, he and Susan Linebarger were married. They had two sons, Ford and Warren.

After law school Overton joined the Wright, Lindsey and Jennings law firm in Little Rock, becoming a full partner after only two years. From 1964 until he became a judge, his law practice generally involved representing defendants in civil litigation (car wreck cases, product liability cases, and so on). He was considered a top-flight trial lawyer and legal scholar. His legal papers were highly regarded in the profession but attracted little public attention.

During his Law School days, Overton and David Pryor, later governor and United States senator, became fast friends. In 1979 President Jimmy Carter, at the request of Senator Pryor, appointed Overton, then thirty-nine years old, to the United States district bench for the Eastern District of Arkansas.

Overton is best known for his decision in *McLean v. Arkansas Board of Education* (January 5, 1982), which attracted worldwide attention. The case challenged the constitutionality of a state law, Act 590 of 1981, which required Arkansas public schools to give "balanced treatment" to creation science and to the theory of evolution. The challenge came from a biology teacher, clergy of several denominations, and organizations including the American Jewish Congress, the Arkansas Education Association, and the National Association of Biology Teachers.

The constitutional issue centered on the First Amendment's prohibition of the establishment of religion. Overton found that the statute violated this clause and stated that "it is in the area of the public schools that these values must be guarded most vigilantly." He traced the origins of the Act to fundamentalist Christian organizations that "consider the introduction of creation science into the public schools part of their ministry." The evidence for creation science, witnesses had testified, was to be found solely in the biblical book of Genesis; the dual approach required by the statute "has no scientific factual basis or legitimate educational purpose," Overton stated. Defining science by five essential characteristics, he concluded that "creation science . . . is simply not science." Therefore "the evidence is overwhelming that both the purpose and the effect of Act 590 is the advancement of religion in the public schools." Pointing out that "evolution is the cornerstone of modern biology," he concluded, "No group, no matter how large or small, may use the organs of government, of which the public schools are the most conspicuous and influential, to foist its religious beliefs on others."

After this opinion was filed, Overton received thousands of letters, some praising him for protecting religious freedom and others accusing him of doing the devil's work. The world scientific community applauded the decision. *Science,* the leading journal of American professional science, published the decision verbatim. A few years later, Stephen J. Gould, zoologist and paleontologist, wrote in *Natural History:* "As I was writing this essay, I learned of the untimely death from cancer . . . of Federal Judge William R. Overton of Arkansas. Judge Overton presided and wrote the decision in *McLean v. Arkansas* (January 5, 1982) . . . he struck down the Arkansas law mandating equal time for 'creation science' . . . Judge Overton's brilliant and beautifully crafted decision is the finest legal document ever written about this question—far surpassing anything that the Scopes trial generated . . . Judge Overton's definitions of science are so cogent and clearly expressed that we can use his words as a model for our own proceedings."

The economist John Kenneth Galbraith wrote to Overton: "Years ago I learned that a judge . . . should never be thanked for a decision. Justice, I was told, is what is normal and right. But no rule prevents me from saying how literate, interesting and informative I found your 'Memorandum Opinion.'"

Overton was noted for his ability to get to the heart of the matter, and he insisted that lawyers do so. His written opinions are crisp and were rendered quickly. He handed down several other important opinions during his short tenure.

A case which attracted much attention was *Donovan v. Tony and Susan Alamo Foundation*, 567 F. Supp, 556 (1982). The Alamos operated several commercial enterprises staffed primarily by young followers of a quasi-religious group who were compensated only by free room and board. Overton held that the Alamos were subject to the Fair Labor Standards Act and required to pay their employees the going rate.

In another decision showing his concern with the separation of church and state, *Arkansas Day Care Ass'n, Inc. v. Clinton* (577 F.Supp.388 1983), he held unconstitutional a statute which exempted religious child-care facilities from state licensing standards.

To say that Overton was good company is a serious understatement. He was a delightful raconteur and loved a good joke, whether told by him or someone else. He had a finely tuned, self-deprecating sense of humor.

The Arkansas Bar Foundation established a scholarship in Judge Overton's name.

[See the *New York Times*, July 15, 1987 (obituary) and the *Arkansas Gazette*, July 17, 1987. The text of Judge Overton's judgment, injunction, and opinion enjoining the Arkansas Board of Education from implementing the Balanced Treatment of Creation Science and Evolution Science Act is in *Science*, 215 (1982): 934–42.]

WILLIAM R. WILSON JR.

OWEN, EZRA (Mar. 17, 1770–Oct. 11, 1859), pioneer patriarch, was born in Halifax County, Virginia. He was apparently a neighbor and friend of Daniel Boone, with whom he was allied in protecting frontier settlements from the Indians. During a sojourn in Georgia, he married Lydia Vance on July 16, 1793. Owen was twenty-three when he married, Lydia only thirteen. Tradition has it that Owen sent his child bride to school to finish her education. Before 1800 they moved to Kentucky.

In 1809 Owen and his young family moved to Kaskaskia in the newly formed Illinois Territory. During his years there, he was active in county, territorial, and state government, and served as an Illinois Ranger and, during the War of 1812, as a spy and a courier. In 1811 he earned the rank of major in the Illinois militia, a title he appended to his name for the rest of his long life.

By January 1826 Owen and his now extended family had migrated to yet another frontier town, Little Rock, in the Territory of Arkansas. Ten of the eleven children of Owen and Lydia, with their own growing families, accompanied their father to Arkansas. Major Owen quickly became involved in politics. He was elected a trustee of the town of Little Rock in January 1826, a position he resigned less than six months later, possibly because he had already located lands outside of the city. He secured an appointment as a Pulaski County magistrate from Saline Township in 1828, and he was doorkeeper for the Arkansas Territorial House of Representatives for the 1829 and 1831 sessions.

By the summer of 1826 Owen and his sons and son-in-law were engaged in buying and selling land in what was in later times identified as the exact geographical center of the state (a monument now marks the site), along the Military Road or Southwest Trail, in Section 14, Township 1 South, Range 14 West of the Fifth Principal Meridian, at that time a part of Saline Township, Pulaski County. In 1829 Ezra Madison Owen, one of Owen's sons, established a post office there, originally named Dogwood Springs.

In the entrepreneurial spirit of the Jacksonian Era, Owen and his family engaged in land speculation and town development and made use of political patronage to further their fortunes. For example, Ezra Madison Owen, the most political of Owen's offspring, served as magistrate of Pulaski County, juror on a superior court grand jury investigating the problem of selling whiskey to Indians, sheriff of Saline County, captain of the company of patrols in his home area, clerk of Saline County, and postmaster of Dogwood Springs (later Collegeville).

When the new county of Saline was carved out of western Pulaski County in 1835, it encompassed the Owen family lands. From the beginning, Major Owen was involved in county politics. When the county was divided into townships, the one including the Owen lands was designated "Owen Township"; the creek running through the area was named "Owen Creek"; the place of holding elections in the township was Owen's house; and the overseer of roads in the neighborhood was Ezra Owen himself.

On June 12, 1838, Owen was listed as "owner and proprietor" on a "Bill of Assurances" filed at the Saline County Courthouse along with a plat of his proposed town of Collegeville. The plat laid off the town into thirty-six blocks, each with four lots. Owen hoped to establish a state college in his town. Legend insists that he almost succeeded in making it the state capital, but it seems unlikely that this was ever more than an entrepreneur's hope.

From the time Owen arrived during the territorial period to the time he left for Texas in 1846, he and his family increased their wealth considerably, mostly in land and improvements, such as a sawmill. When neighboring Texas became a part of the Union in 1845, Owen must have heard once again the call of the frontier. In 1846 he and most of his extended family were "gone to Texas," where his grandson, David O. Dodd, "Boy Martyr of the Confederacy," was born in November of 1846. The court records from Saline County for the next few years contain numerous actions for foreclosures and creditors' bills against Owen and other family members; it seems they practically abandoned their Arkansas lands and dreams to push on to another opportunity.

Owen died in Lavaca County, Texas. His obituary called him archetypal of "American energy, bravery and patriotism."

[Sources include "Application for Military Bounty Land, #250 161-Ezra Owen," 1857, and "Application for Pension-Ezra Owen," Burleson County, Texas, Probate Court; *Arkansas Advocate, Arkansas Gazette,* and the *Little Rock True Democrat,* 1826–59; Arkansas State Land Office Records, Roll 27, Book 85 (mf); Clarence Edwin Carter, ed., *The Territorial Papers of the United States* (1950); David O. Dodd Manuscript Collection, General Microfilm File, Arkansas History Commission, Little Rock; Eddie G. Landreth, ed., *Saline County, Arkansas Chancery Court Book A: 1841–1871* (1989); William A. Meese, "Illinois and Randolph County," *Journal of the Illinois State Historical Society* 2 (July 1918); and U.S. Census Records: Arkansas, Texas, Illinois, Louisiana, Mississippi, 1820–1880.]

CAROLYN EARLE BILLINGSLEY

OWENS, FREEMAN HARRY (Jan. 20, 1890– Dec. 9, 1979), photographer and inventor, was born in Pine Bluff to Charles Owens and Christabel Owens (maiden name unknown). Freeman Owens became interested in show business early in his life; his father was manager of the Trulock Hotel, where performers with traveling theater companies stayed. When he was in high school he designed and constructed a motion picture camera, ordered film, and photographed Pine Bluff scenes which were shown in local movie houses.

The camera he constructed is on display at the Jefferson County Museum.

Owens had a boyhood chum, Max Aaronson, who also grew up in the shadow of historic Trinity Episcopal Church. Aaronson, whose professional name was Gilbert Anderson, became a popular movie actor and a founder of Essanay Studios, a successful movie company in Chicago. When Owens was ready to try his wings professionally, all he had to do was contact his old friend for a job at Essanay, where he began his career as a cameraman.

But in time studio work became tame for Owens. He began a photographic project that was the forerunner of the newsreels which were so popular in the 1930s and 1940s. He photographed the stockyards fire at Chicago and a hurricane at Charleston, South Carolina. He began to be written up in newspapers across America as "the fearless young cameraman, ready for any assignment." He went to Alaska in 1911 and filmed the wonders of the area. He covered an extended trout-fishing excursion with Grantland Rice and other sportswriters of the era. The *Cincinnati Times-Star* featured a picture of Owens inside a cage at the zoo facing a water buffalo which was glaring back with a jaundiced eye. "Risking his life to get 'movies' at the Cincinnati Zoological Garden," was the caption under the photograph.

His next photographic project surely placed his life in jeopardy. America had entered World War I, and Owens enlisted as a marine corps combat cameraman. He photographed the western front, made some remarkable aerial scenes, and covered President Wilson and the League of Nations.

Back in America after the war, Owens picked up where he had left off. He filmed the great Babe Ruth in slow motion and was promptly sued by the Sultan of Swat for revealing to the public his secret of hitting home runs.

Later Owens began to work for photographic research laboratories and started his career as an inventor. Before he retired he held patents to approximately two thousand improvements in photography. The plastic lens which does such a good job with the family Kodak is probably the same plastic lens design formulated by Owens.

Around 1930 the movie industry cranked up its ballyhoo machines to inundate America with the idea, "The Movies Talk!" Well, in many cases, they didn't talk, they squawked. Sound would become unsynchronized with images on the screen, and interruptions were frequent as theater projectionists struggled to get things back in harmony. It remained for Owens to stabilize Hollywood's talking movies.

But he did not profit from this work; instead, he became involved in a dispute with Lee de Forest, the celebrated "Father of Radio." The controversy ended up in lengthy and bitter litigation. According to Owens, he perfected the system of sound on film, the same sound-tracking technique used in present-day motion picture production.

When he attempted to secure a patent on the system, de Forest sued. Owens won decisions in the lower courts, but the United States Supreme Court, in a landmark decision, reversed the lower courts and Owens lost all claim and right to his work. The Court did not say Owens lifted de Forest's ideas. It merely held that once a person worked for a research company, the fruits of his labor, whether on company time or his own time, belonged to the research company. For the rest of his life, Lee de Forest was not one of Owens's favorite subjects. But, without a doubt, Owens contributed much to the American art form which we know as the "movies."

[Sources include a Freeman Owens scrapbook in the Pine Bluff/Jefferson County Library. Boxes of original Owens records are on file with the Jefferson County Historical Museum at Pine Bluff. This article is also based on conversations between Owens and the author held over a period of years.]

Dave Wallis

PACAHA (?–?), Native American chief, was probably born in northeast Arkansas sometime in the early 1500s. He is known solely from the four accounts of the Hernando de Soto expedition, which visited northeast Arkansas in the summer of 1541. One of the accounts refers to him as "Capaha," but this is probably an author's mistake.

Pacaha lived in a fortified village near the Mississippi River. The town was surrounded by a water-filled moat and a log palisade wall, with guard towers and loopholes in the wall. Archeologists believe that the town may have been located in what is now Crittenden County. Pacaha controlled a number of smaller fortified towns in the region and may have had political power over some adjacent Native American groups.

At the time of de Soto's arrival, Pacaha was at war with a neighboring chief named Casqui. This war had been going on for a long time, possibly generations. Hernando de Soto succeeded in establishing a fragile peace between the warring groups, but it probably did not last after de Soto left northeast Arkansas.

Pacaha's first meeting with the de Soto expedition was far from peaceful. De Soto had first made contact with Pacaha's mortal enemy, Casqui, and when the Spanish expedition approached Pacaha's town, Casqui's people followed. Assuming they were coming to attack, Pacaha and the residents of his town fled in terror to an island or better-fortified village nearby. Many of his people drowned while trying to escape. Meanwhile, Casqui's people sacked the town, stealing everything they could carry off and desecrating temples and religious relics.

De Soto finally convinced Pacaha that his intentions were peaceful and prepared to help Pacaha attack Casqui to punish him for ransacking the village. But when Casqui realized this, he apologized and returned the items stolen from Pacaha's people. A special dinner was held, at which de Soto arranged peace between the two rivals. As a token of esteem, Pacaha presented de Soto with one of his wives, one of his sisters, and another woman from the tribe. In part, this was to upstage Casqui, who had given one of his daughters to de Soto. These "marriages" were meant to establish a lasting alliance between each chief and de Soto.

The de Soto expedition stayed at Pacaha for as long as forty days, during which exploratory parties were sent to the north to continue searching for gold and to help decide which way to travel next. Unfortunately, the accounts do not tell us much more about Pacaha during this time. From some of the statements made by Pacaha, Casqui, and de Soto, it is clear that Pacaha was younger than Casqui, but ruled over more people and probably a larger area. But on the other hand, Pacaha was generally afraid of attacks by Casqui, and Pacaha had never been into Casqui's territory. This may indicate that Casqui was the aggressor in the war between the two chiefs.

The de Soto accounts are the only written record of Pacaha and his people. We do not know what befell them after de Soto moved on to explore more of Arkansas.

[Information on Pacaha is included in the accounts of the Hernando de Soto expedition, fully translated and published in *The De Soto Chronicles: The Expedition of*

Hernando de Soto to North America in 1539–1543, edited by Lawrence A. Clayton, Vernon James Knight Jr., and Edward C. Moore (1993). Archeological information on the probable locations of Pacaha's and Casqui's towns and their territories is included in "The Parkin Archeological Site and Its Role in Determining the Route of the de Soto Expedition" by Phyllis A. Morse in *The Expedition of Hernando de Soto West of the Mississippi, 1541–1543*, edited by Gloria A. Young and Michael P. Hoffman (1993).]

Jeffrey M. Mitchem

PARKER, ISAAC CHARLES (Oct. 15, 1838–Nov. 17, 1896), once called "one of the greatest American trial judges," was born in Belmont County, Ohio, the son of Joseph Parker and Jane Shannon. He spent his early life working on the family farm, attending school, and later teaching. In 1859 he was admitted to the Ohio bar and then moved to St. Joseph, Missouri.

Parker's professional life began in Missouri. From 1861 to 1864 he served as city attorney in St. Joseph. During the Civil War, he became a corporal in the state militia. As a presidential elector in 1864, he cast his vote for Abraham Lincoln and thereafter adhered to the Republican Party. He married a native of St. Joseph, Mary O'Toole; they had two sons, Charles and James.

In 1870 Parker was elected to the United States House of Representatives where he served as chairman of the Committee on Expenditures of the Navy Department and as a member of the Committee on Territories and Appropriations. When he lost a bid for a Senate seat in 1874, President Ulysses S. Grant appointed him chief justice of the Territory of Utah. Parker successfully petitioned Grant for the judgeship of the Western District of Arkansas, which included the Indian Territory (present-day Oklahoma). Arkansas was closer to family in Missouri, and he had developed an interest in Indian affairs.

The jurisdiction encompassed all or parts of the Indian Territory until 1896. Cherokees, Chickasaws, Choctaws, Creeks, and Seminoles, removed from their homelands by the United States Government during the 1830s, lived there. New treaties in 1866 brought additional Indian tribes to the territory, but there was increasing pressure from whites to open the lands to settlement. The treaties granted the railroads access, enhancing the possibility of profits in cattle, lumber, and mining. With competing interests and the vast land that made avoiding justice easy, the Indian Territory became a chaotic refuge for the lawless.

Parker's job was to oversee the enforcement of federal law. Because the court handled cases involving anyone not a member of any tribe, it compiled an enormous criminal docket. Between 1875 and 1896 Parker's court handled over twelve thousand criminal cases with nearly nine thousand convictions. Only 160 were guilty verdicts in capital (murder or rape) cases and warranted the mandatory sentence of death by hanging. Seventy-nine of these resulted in execution. Today, Parker is best remembered as the "hanging judge," but his views on death as punishment were more complex than the stereotype allows: "I favor the abolition of capital punishment ... provided there is a certainty of punishment, whatever that punishment may be. In the uncertainty of punishment following crime lies the weakness of our 'halting crime.'"

Parker believed that reform was the ultimate goal of the criminal justice system: "The whole system of punishment is based on the idea of reform, or it is worse than nothing." The object of the punishment was "to lift the man up; to stamp out his bad nature and wicked disposition." He demanded that prison conditions support firm, but not severe, discipline and education in reading and arithmetic. He investigated the prisons where he sent the convicted and found that only those at Detroit and Chester, Illinois, met his standards.

Parker believed the purpose of the federal court in Fort Smith was to allow tribal governments to operate without the harmful influence of American citizens illegally entering Indian Territory. He viewed himself as a defender of Indian rights. In Congress he had argued: "Do not let us add another chapter to a century of dishonor by breaking up their local government ... Their local governments are better than any Territorial system that we, as a government, can establish over them." He often publicly commented on the chaos resulting from white intruders: "[Indians] are a religiously inclined, law-abiding, authority-respecting people. The Indian race is not one of the criminals."

In 1889 Congress established a circuit court of appeals for the district and gave persons convicted of capital offenses the right to appeal their cases to the United States Supreme Court. During the 1890s the Supreme Court reviewed forty-four death-sentence convictions from the Western District and reversed thirty-one of them. Parker was criticized for allowing inflammatory evidence, prejudicial remarks from prosecutors, and jury instructions that implied the guilt of defendants.

Parker felt that the appellate process contributed to increasing crime: "[T]he greatest cause of the increase of crime is the action of the appellate courts ... They make most strenuous efforts ... to see not when they can affirm but when they can reverse a case." He advocated remodeling the appellate court system into courts of criminal appeals focusing on guilt or innocence and not on legal technicalities.

Shortly before his death he revealed his guiding principles to a newspaper reporter: "I have ever had the single aim of justice in view ... 'Do equal and exact justice,' is my motto." Though the realities of enforcing law in the Indian Territory did not always permit this, the judge strove for justice in twenty-one years of service.

Judge Parker served on the Fort Smith School Board and as the first president of St. John's Hospital (today Sparks Regional Medical Center). He died of Bright's disease and is buried in the Fort Smith National Cemetery.

[See G. Byron Dobbs, "Murder in the Supreme Court: Appeals from the Hanging Judge," *Arkansas Law Review* (Spring 1975): 47–70; Fred Harvey Harrington, *Hanging Judge* (1951; rpt. 1996); Glenn Shirley, *Law West of Fort Smith: A History of Frontier Justice in the Indian Territory, 1834–1896* (1957); Mary M. Stolberg, "The Evolution of Frontier Justice: The Case of Judge Isaac Parker," *Prologue* (Spring 1988): 7–23; Roger H. Tuller, "'The Hanging Judge' and the Indians: Isaac C. Parker and the U.S. Indian Policy, 1871–1896," M.A. thesis, Texas Christian University, 1993.]

JULIET L. GALONSKA

PARKS, WILLIAM PRATT (fl. 1861–1892), was a Confederate soldier and officer and a leader of the Greenback Party in Arkansas.

The first appearance of William Pratt Parks in history is as a private in the Pulaski County Field Artillery Battery, formed in May 1861 under the command of Captain William E. Woodruff. This unit, part of the Arkansas state forces, served with distinction at the Battle of Wilson's Creek, southwest of Springfield, Missouri, on August 10, 1861. Afterward, the battery was disbanded along with the rest of the Arkansas state troops to prevent their being pressed into the Confederate states' army. When Captain Woodruff formed a new battery, Parks's name was not on its roster.

In October 1861 Parks signed up with Company D, Fourth Arkansas Infantry Battalion. On December 3 he was appointed a first lieutenant of that unit. Soon afterward, Company D was detached from the Fourth Battalion to serve in the heavy artillery. The unit was transferred from the Arkansas service to that of Tennessee. The first recorded action fought by this unit, Hoadley's Heavy Artillery Battery commanded by Captain Frederick W. Hoadley, was in the New Madrid-Island No. 10 Campaign in February–April 1862. Hoadley's Battery was armed with three pieces, one of which was rifled. On April 7 the Confederates left their position at the New Madrid Bend and abandoned their heavy artillery pieces. During the ensuing flight there was a severe loss of men and equipment, and Hoadley's Battery was severely mauled.

During May and June of 1862, the Tennessee heavy artillery units stationed at Vicksburg were reorganized as the First Tennessee Heavy Artillery Regiment. The remainder of Hoadley's Battery was merged with the remnants of two Tennessee batteries and part of another. As for Hoadley, he was promoted to the position of regiments major. This left open the captaincy of the new heavy artillery battery, and on May 10 Parks was chosen the new captain. At about this time Parks was serving as a volunteer aboard the Confederate ship, CSS *Arkansas*. Through the summer and fall of 1862, Parks's Battery, known as Battery B, First Tennessee Heavy Artillery Regiment, periodically exchanged fire with the Union fleet on the Mississippi River. As of October 31, Battery B's armament consisted of two rifled 32-pounder heavy artillery pieces, one 32-pounder heavy artillery piece, one 32-pounder, and one 42-pounder smoothbore.

Although Parks's career was on the rise, his health did not keep pace. During November and December, he was frequently ill. In January 1863 he was relieved of command of Battery B. By March 14, he was back on active duty as a Confederate army quartermaster at Vicksburg, Mississippi. He also was in charge of the supply lines for the Confederacy between Vicksburg and Yazoo City. He was serving on active duty when Vicksburg surrendered on July 4. On July 8 he signed his parole form, stating that he would never take up arms against the United States Government again. He did not fully live up to that agreement, however, as he subsequently took part of Battery B across the Mississippi River even though that unit's men had not yet been formally exchanged. At this point, Captain William P. Parks dropped out of sight of accessible recorded history for over a decade.

Parks next appears as a leader of the discontented farmers against the Democratic Party elite. He was now a lawyer and a farmer living near Lewisville, Lafayette County, Arkansas. One vehicle for this agrarian protest was the Greenback Party, which advocated the use of paper currency known as "greenbacks" to artificially increase the money supply and create an inflation that would make it easier for farmers to pay off their debts. In 1880 Parks was the Greenback nominee for governor of Arkansas. He received the endorsement of the Arkansas Republican Party, but he won only a third of the vote even though the Republicans did not run any candidates of their own. In 1882 Parks traveled to southern Arkansas campaigning for Greenbackers, although he does not seem to have been a candidate.

In 1884 he entered the newspaper business with the purchase of an interest in the *Hope Dispatch,* a radical farmer newspaper. In 1892 he returned to the political fray as the Populist Party nominee for state attorney general. In 1896 Parks was a member of the Populist Party state convention's committee on resolutions and was a delegate to the Populist national convention. Thereafter, Parks returned to the mists of time and nothing more is known about his activities.

[See the *Columbia Banner* (Magnolia, Arkansas), Apr. 8 and Sept. 9, 1880; July 27, Aug. 3, Oct. 5, and Oct. 12, 1882; May 31, 1883; Sept. 4, 1884; June 4, 1885; Sept. 1 and Sept. 8, 1892; and the *Lonoke Weekly Democrat,* July 23, 1896. Sources also include Parks's service record, Fourth Arkansas Infantry Battalion, Arkansas History Commission, Little Rock, and First Tennessee Heavy Artillery Regiment, National Archives, Washington, D.C.; and William E. Woodruff, *With the Light Guns in '61-'65: Reminiscences of Eleven Arkansas, Missouri and Texas Light Batteries, in the Civil War* (n.d.).]

CHARLES J. RECTOR

PARNELL, HARVEY (Feb. 28, 1880–Jan. 16, 1936), governor of Arkansas, was born in Orlando, Cleveland County, Arkansas, to William Robert Parnell, a farmer, and Mary Elizabeth Martin. Parnell's early career as a small business owner and farmer informed his later career as a political progressive. In 1902 he married Mabel Winston and settled on a large farm near Crooked Bayou in Chicot County, where he raised two daughters and several thousand acres of cattle. His rapid ascent from the lower chambers in the state capitol into the governor's chair was due as much to fortuity as to political pluck.

The Democrat from Chicot County first entered politics in 1919 as a member of the House of Representatives. His was a silent but consistent vote in the forty-second general assembly that endorsed mainstream reform measures adopted by the national Democratic Party. Dubbed "progressives," these legislators rallied behind women's suffrage, the child labor amendment, and prohibition. It was after his election to the state senate in 1923 that Parnell blended his reform zeal and business acumen, joining genteel politicos across the South in the 1920s whose metier was "business progressivism." He believed that improving state services, building roads, and modernizing public schools would attract the manufacturing and industry needed to broaden the economic horizon of a state where 80 percent of the population listed farmer as occupation. As Parnell explained it, "all manufacturing establishments are in states with good school systems." He also believed that the state's responsibility to expand and improve public services carried with it the power to raise the revenue for them. He introduced and fought hard for the passage of luxury and license taxes, as well as the state's first income tax that provided millions of dollars annually for roads and schools. Later on, as governor, he filled a vacant United State Senate seat with the appointment of Hattie Caraway, who became the first woman elected to that chamber.

In 1926 the state supreme court settled a constitutional dispute, declaring that the office of lieutenant governor had been created in an earlier state election; *ipso facto*, a prominent government post was vacant. In an auspicious political gambit, Parnell announced his candidacy and later that year became the first lieutenant governor of Arkansas. He presided over the state senate and the passage of Governor Martineau's roadbuilding legislation. Ground had yet to be broken in this ambitious program when Martineau accepted a federal appointment. Parnell quickly filled this vacancy, fielding his next election prospects from the governor's mansion. The southern version of Tammany Hall, the local party bosses, county patronage rolls, and courthouse gangs that powered state politics became known as "the Parnell machine" in the Arkansas gubernatorial elections of 1928 and 1930. His campaign epithet, the merchant-turned-farmer, seemed promising to rural voters and indeed, the farm to market roads that were paved in his first term as governor became the campaign trail for a second term.

The overwhelming impact of the stock-market crash in 1929, followed by a devastating drought in 1930, turned Parnell's administration into irony: an income tax for a generation that had just lost income; highway construction financed by a banking system on the verge of collapse; elaborate government reorganization for a state too poor to convene a constituional convention. Parnell insisted that self-help and private charities would bring economic recovery, but by the end of 1932, the worst of the Great Depression, Arkansas had exhausted the resources of the Reconstruction Finance Corporation (RFC) and the Red Cross. Amid charges that his administration was ineffective, if not outright corrupt, Parnell salvaged a few items from his reform agenda. In the spate of emergency relief legislation was the long-awaited compulsory school attendance law. Arkansas embraced the New Deal in 1933 and Parnell retired from politics. He traveled the state as an appraiser for the RFC until his death in Little Rock.

[See Pamela Webb Salamo, "Harvey Parnell, 1928–1933," in *The Governors of Arkansas: Essays in Political Biography,* Timothy P. Donovan, Willard B. Gatewood Jr., and Jeannie M. Whayne, eds., 2d ed. (1995).]

PAMELA SALAMO

PATTERSON, RUTH POLK (Aug. 10, 1930–1988?), teacher and author, was born in Howard County, Arkansas, the daughter of Mattie Ann Bullock and Arthur Polk, a farmer. Her background included American-Indian, African-American, and white lineage traceable to the 1830s in southwest Arkansas. She graduated from Childress High School in Nashville, Arkansas, in 1949 and married her high-school principal, Thomas Edward Patterson. After giving birth to three children, she enrolled at Arkansas AM & N College in Pine Bluff and graduated *cum laude* in 1958.

In 1962 Patterson and her husband moved to Little Rock where he became executive director of the Arkansas Teachers' Association and she taught at Horace Mann High School. She later received a master's degree in English from the University of Arkansas at Fayetteville, but not before she gave birth to her fourth child in 1965.

Patterson became involved in African and African-American education in the public schools when she began doctoral studies at Emory University. Her dissertation was a proposal for an African-American studies program which she eventually initiated and implemented in the Little Rock School District, where she was supervisor of minority studies. She received her Ph.D. in American studies from Emory in 1977.

Between 1974 and 1980 Patterson served as coordinator of Afro-American studies and supervisor of minority studies with the Little Rock School District. In 1975 she traveled to West Africa, where she studied African culture at the University of Ghana at Legon. She returned to Africa in 1979 to study at Fourah Bay University at Freetown, Sierra Leone. During this period she published articles in such journals as the *English Journal,* the *Bulletin of the Arkansas Teachers Association,* and *Approaches to the Study of West African Culture.* By 1984 she was back in the classroom teaching English, her supervisory position having been phased out by budget cuts.

Meanwhile, with a grant from the Arkansas Humanities Council, Patterson began work on a pioneering family history, *The Seed of Sally Good'n.* The book centers on the Spencer Polk homestead in rural southwestern Arkansas at Muddy Fork in Pike County. Here Spencer Polk, Patterson's grandfather, was the patriarch of a numerous and energetic family.

Spencer Polk's father, Taylor Polk, was the son of white settlers in the Arkansas Territory who were distantly related to President James Knox Polk. In the 1820s Taylor Polk purchased a slave named Sally; eventually he had three children with her. He built a cabin for Sally and her children near his own house in Montgomery County and provided for the children's schooling alongside his white sons. Sally was sold around 1838, evidently because Taylor believed she had been unfaithful to him. "It was an act as cruel and final as death," Patterson says. Sally's children remained on the Polk homestead. Taylor Polk moved his family and twelve slaves to Pike County in 1849 or 1850.

Patterson's work on the Polk family history included an archeological survey of Spencer Polk's homestead. The family house was large enough for an extended family, a traditional African family organization, as contrasted to the nuclear European organization. Spencer Polk's log house "contained two or more families at all times." Numerous outbuildings—smokehouse, stables, corncrib, barn, cowsheds, corral, sorghum mill, beehives, and so on—suggest a family of considerable worth.

Spencer Polk "made his living as a subsistence

farmer, albeit on a grand scale." He owned several hundred acres and surrounded "his family with an aura of southern 'cornbread' aristocracy." He was famous for cordial hospitality; his door was always open to travelers through the isolated backwoods of the county.

Patterson portrays her family "as actors in the drama of life in pioneer Arkansas." She explores the complexities of the family's sense of identity, its "two-mindedness" about its black and white heritage. When Spencer's son Jimmy is murdered, Patterson relates his death to the larger context of the rampant lynchings of 1910–20.

Reviews of the book praised it as thoughtful, moving, "a courageous book that never flinches from facing ... painful contradictions ... a salutary corrective of stereotyped images of black life." After its publication in 1985 Patterson continued to write and lecture about the African-American experience in Arkansas while struggling with cancer. She died three years later.

[*The Seed of Sally Good'n: A Black Family of Arkansas, 1833–1953* is in print in 1998. Patterson's papers are in the Special Collections Division, University of Arkansas Libraries, Fayetteville.]

Lou Ann Norman

PAYNE, MILTON SAM (Aug. 1, 1883–Sept. 3, 1963), town marshal and killer, was born in Black Rock, Arkansas, on the western side of the Black River in Lawrence County. He was the son of R. P. and V. M. Payne, and he had two brothers and four sisters. Their neighbors considered the Payne family friendly and law-abiding citizens.

Payne was convicted of killing five men and was given three life sentences, serving in Arkansas prisons for over twenty years. He bragged that he never robbed a bank, was never convicted of stealing anything, never led a prison escape, was never charged with child abuse. But his domineering and abusive personality made him a target of controversy.

In February 1904 he married eighteen-year-old Mandy Dunlap. On July 1 he was accused of stealing a hog but was found not guilty. His next encounter with the law was in 1911 when he sued the St. Louis and San Francisco Railway Company for fifty dollars for hitting his "blue speckled dog." He was awarded thirty-five dollars. He was elected marshal of Black Rock, and acting in his official capacity, he killed an African American, Gus Brown. He was never arrested or tried for killing Brown.

Payne used his "railroad money" to hire an attorney to defend him for assaulting Marvin Angle. At the trial Payne and several witnesses testified that Angle, a member of the Black Rock "aristocracy," had been cheating at cards. Payne said: "I was awful mad, I guess I was all to pieces ... he called me a damn liar, after he done stole my money, he then wanted to give me a cussing over it ... I didn't have no intention to kill Marvin. I know that Marvin is a better man than me. I thought I would wound him and keep him from whipping me." He was found guilty and sentenced to three years in the Arkansas Penitentiary. Twenty-one months later Governor George Hays pardoned him.

Having survived the brutality of Arkansas Penitentiary, Payne had the "credentials" and respect to become a lawman. He was hired as marshal of Walnut Ridge. Acting as marshal, he shot a man named Dan Tolson five times in the back for Tolson's refusal or neglect to observe the new stock law. Payne was sentenced to life imprisonment for the Tolson murder.

When he returned to the penitentiary, he was thirty-four years old, stood five feet eight inches tall, weighed 134 pounds, wore a size-six shoe, and had finished the sixth grade. He had a "very noticeable flat nose" and "three gold teeth upper left." Three weeks after returning to the prison, Payne, now a trusty guard, killed a prisoner who was attempting to escape. For such meritorious duty Superintendent J. T. Burkett recommended that Payne's life sentence be reduced. Payne was also rewarded by being made the "day yardman," the most powerful trusty position at Camp No. 2 of Tucker farm.

In May 1919 he killed twenty-one-year-old David Smith, another trusty guard. He was tried and given a life sentence, but since he still had fifteen years to serve for the Tolson killing, he became depressed and thought a prison official "had it in for him."

Payne escaped from Tucker farm in January 1920 and for seventeen months lived in the Pacific Northwest and Canada. In June 1921 he surrendered to Governor Thomas McRae in Little Rock. Three months later, as trusty guard, he stopped Tom Slaughter, a notorious bank robber and killer, and prevented Slaughter's escape. Payne was lauded by prison officials and his "life sentences" were commuted to twenty-one years by Governor McRae. He was given an "indefinite furlough" on December 16, 1924.

In 1926 Payne shot at O. S. Davis, a Black Rock

acquaintance. Governor Thomas Terrell revoked his parole, and he was returned to prison. But the next year he was furloughed again.

In January 1928 Fred Brandon, a Black Rock man with whom Payne had quarreled openly, was found slain. Payne was quickly arrested and charged with first-degree murder. He vehemently denied killing Brandon. He was convicted and appealed his conviction to the Arkansas Supreme Court, but it was upheld. He was paroled for the Brandon conviction in 1933 or 1934.

On May 2, 1935, he was again elected marshal of Black Rock and served in this capacity for many years. He enforced town ordinances, ran in the whiskey men and gamblers, and assisted in chasing the robbers of the First National Bank of Black Rock.

In an *Arkansas Gazette* article Payne said: "I have never been accused of bank robbery, theft or any crimes . . . All of my trouble has been trying to enforce the law." Superintendent J. T. Burkett said that Payne "had repeatedly offered his life to prevent riots and escapes and has recaptured more of our escapees while acting as trusty than any other man ever confined in the Penitentiary."

Payne lived the last thirty years of his life outside of prison. His wife of fifty-nine years, Mandy Dunlap Payne, buried him in Oak Forest Cemetery in Black Rock.

[Sources include Lawrence County Circuit Court indictment, July 1, 1904; Justice of the Peace Court of Black River Township, proceedings July 3, 1913, and June 25, 1926; Lawrence County Circuit Court, eastern district, proceedings, March 1928, all in the Lawrence County Historical Society archives, Powhatan, Arkansas; and Arkansas State Penitentiary document Jan. 22, 1917, Pine Bluff, Arkansas Department of Correction. Also see the *Arkansas Gazette*, Nov. 2, 1916, May 24, 1919, and June 12, 1921.]

JERRY D. GIBBENS

PETER, LILY (June 2, 1891–July 26, 1991) farmer, author, and patron of the arts, was born in Phillips County, Arkansas, at the confluence of Big Creek and Big Cypress Bayou. Her father, William O. Peter, was a descendant of missionaries, among whom was the early American composer Johan Friedrich Peter. Her mother, Florence Mowbray, was widowed after seventeen years but managed to see her five children educated.

Lily was reared deep in the wetlands of eastern Arkansas and was taught at home until she was ten. An etching of Hernando de Soto in one of her schoolbooks inspired her to learn Spanish so that she could read from the original documents of his explorations. She eventually wrote an epic poem on the topic, *The Great Riding.*

When she finished the eighth grade, her parents determined that she should have further schooling by going to live with her father's sister Mary in Ohio. In the spring of her first year there, her father was thrown from a wagon and died of his injuries. Word of the tragedy from her mother included instructions for Lily to remain in Ohio and finish school. Lily's earnings as a teacher would be needed since Will Peter left little but a mortgaged farm. When she came home she was hired as a teacher, beginning a forty-year career in the Phillips County schools. Later she attended West Tennessee State Normal School, Columbia University, and Vanderbilt University, where she earned a master's degree in English.

Lily's brother, Jesse, became a farmer; however, it was as if he and she were partners. She loved the land, and from the time she started teaching, she supplied money for his annual "furnishes" of seed and other essential items to their tenant farmers, keeping him out of serious debt. They accumulated land and eventually owned some four thousand acres in Phillips and Monroe Counties.

When Jesse died in 1956, he willed half the land to Lily and the other half to his other three siblings. Lily bought them out and took over management of the farms. She hired competent managers and selected her tenants astutely. She studied soils, fertilization, and cultivation. She studied the weather and sometimes was able to avoid losing crops by her understanding of air currents.

By 1960 Lily Peter was a wealthy woman and turned to philanthropy. Many educational institutions in Arkansas received contributions from her to their libraries, arts and science departments, and scholarships for students.

Peter is perhaps best known as the lady who brought the Philadelphia Orchestra to Arkansas. As a member of the committee for the Arkansas sesquicentennial celebration, she conceived of commissioning a symphonic work and inviting the Philadelphia Orchestra to play it. At the same time she commissioned a work adapted from chamber music by Johan Peter, a distant relative. She mortgaged farm acreage to pay for the composition by Norman Della Joio and for two performances in Little

Rock in 1969 by the Philadelphia Orchestra conducted by Eugene Ormandy. The story of her largess appeared in newspapers nationwide. The event is considered a milepost in the establishment of a solid base of support for the Arkansas Symphony.

She led a drive to fund the building of an auditorium for the Phillips County Community College, which was named for her and dedicated in December 1972 with a concert by the Arkansas Symphony Orchestra. She saw to it that the auditorium was acoustically excellent and had a state-of-the-art stage. She gave the school an Allen concert organ and financed a series of organ concerts dedicated to the memory of her mother, as well as the salary of a competent organ teacher for a period of time.

In the early seventies she read Rachel Carson's *Silent Spring*. She had observed enough damage to the environment from overuse of chemical fertilizers, herbicides, and pesticides in her immediate vicinity to be aware of the truths of Carson's claims. Lily set aside acreage and began experimenting to prove that farmers could make money while becoming less dependent on chemicals. For instance, she utilized the insect food chain to combat boll weevils. The cartoonist George Fisher depicted her as a tiny lady in a sunbonnet pitted against a giant representing the chemical industry.

Later she took on a battle against farmers who perceived channelization as the answer to flooding and the United States Corps of Engineers which proposed channelization of Big Creek, near Peter's home. Lily knew the value of flooding for replenishment of soil and the value of a snaking channel for mitigating erosion. She organized a contingent of citizens and led a successful movement to stop the Corps.

Lily Peter never married. When asked why, she replied: "Oh my Dear, I do so regret that I am past the age to have children. I would have been perfectly happy to submit myself to the man I loved and who loved me in return, but ones I loved didn't ask me and the ones who asked me I didn't love." She wanted no identification with feminism. She believed that women had their "places" and should stay in them. She believed the same of blacks; she was never comfortable with them in social situations, and she said she wished politicians and social workers would not support them in their effort toward integration. However, she paid the cost of sending a number of her tenants, both black and white, or their children to school.

Lily Peter died about two miles from her birthplace in Phillips County.

[Books by Peter include *The Great Riding* (1966; rpt. 1983); *The Green Linen of Summer* (1964); *In the Beginning: Myths of the Western World* (1983); and *The Sea Dream of the Mississippi* (1973). The Jaggers Papers at the University of Central Arkansas Archives contain taped interviews with Peter, photos, newspaper articles, and other materials. See AnnieLaura M. Jaggers, *A Nude Singularity: Lily Peter of Arkansas* (1993).]

ANNIELAURA M. JAGGERS

PIKE, ALBERT (Dec. 29, 1809–Apr. 2, 1891), lawyer, soldier, and author, was born in Boston, Massachusetts, the son of Benjamin Pike and Sarah Andrews. He attended school at Byfield, Newburyport, and Framingham, and he claimed to have attended Harvard for a year. Well versed in classical and contemporary literature, he wrote poems in his youth and continued to do so through most of his life.

In 1831 Pike left Massachusetts looking for new opportunities in the West. He went to Santa Fe, then traveled with an expedition into the Staked Plains, winding up at Fort Smith, Arkansas, in 1833. He settled in Pope County, where he taught school and contributed letters in support of Robert Crittenden, the Whig candidate for the Territory's delegate to Congress, to the *Arkansas Advocate*, the party's newspaper at Little Rock. At Crittenden's urging, the editor hired Pike, who moved to Little Rock to work for the paper. He also worked as a clerk in the legislature. On October 10, 1834, he married Mary Ann Hamilton; they had six children. With his wife's financial assistance he purchased an interest in the *Advocate*. In 1835 he became sole proprietor of the paper and continued its publication until he sold it in 1837.

In 1837 he passed the Arkansas bar and began to practice law. His practice ranged from district courts to the United States Supreme Court, before which he was admitted to practice in 1842. In 1843 he was named a receiver for the failed Arkansas State Bank, and his work trying to collect the debts of that institution helped him to make a fortune. From 1840 to 1845 he served as the first reporter of the Arkansas Supreme Court and he published the *Arkansas Form Book* in 1842.

When the Mexican War began in 1845 Pike helped raise the Little Rock Guards, a company that became a part of the Arkansas cavalry regiment, and was elected its captain. From Mexico he carried out a letter-writing campaign against what he considered the incompetence of the regiment's senior officers. Among his harshest attacks was his criticism of Lieutenant Colonel John Selden Roane's role in the Battle of Buena Vista, published in the *Arkansas Gazette*. Roane demanded an apology or satisfaction. The two fought a duel on a sandbank of the Arkansas River at Fort Smith, but neither was hit in two exchanges and their seconds persuaded them that honor had been satisfied.

After the war Pike returned to Little Rock where he became involved in railroad promotion. In 1853 he moved to New Orleans. Returning to Little Rock in 1857, he became involved more deeply in national politics, remaining with the Whig Party until its demise and then embracing the American (or Know-Nothing) Party that succeeded it. He was motivated in part by his concern with the growing sectional crisis. He had come to sympathize with the plantation South on the issue of slavery. In the American Party convention of 1856 he led a walkout by southern delegates when the new party failed to produce a strong platform in support of slavery.

In 1850 he became a Mason and entered the Scottish Rite in 1853. He was elected Grand Commander of the Supreme Council, Southern Jurisdiction of the United States of the Scottish Rite in 1859.

When Arkansas seceded from the Union, the state convention sent Pike to the Indian Territory as its commissioner with the authority to negotiate treaties with the various tribes. As a result of his experience with the Indians, Pike was appointed brigadier general in the Confederate army on August 15, 1861, and in the following November was placed in command of the Department of Indian Territory.

Pike encouraged the formation of Indian regiments for Confederate service. From the beginning his view of his responsibilities in the Indian Territory conflicted with that of his superiors. He had believed that Indian troops would be used only for the defense of Indian Territory. When he was ordered to join the forces of General Earl Van Dorn in northwestern Arkansas in March 1862 and they were used at Elkhorn Tavern on March 7–8, 1862, he protested. He also opposed later efforts by General Thomas C. Hindman to exercise any authority in the Territory. In July 1862 he printed a circular airing his differences with Hindman. Pike was not supported by the government at Richmond in the dispute, and on July 12 he resigned in anger. For the rest of the war Pike remained relatively inconspicuous.

After the war he moved to New York. In August 1865 he received a presidential pardon. He returned for a time to Arkansas, but by 1867 he had moved to Memphis, Tennessee, where he practiced law and edited the *Memphis Appeal*. In 1868 he moved his legal practice to Washington, D.C., and from 1868 to 1870 edited the *Patriot*. He never returned to Arkansas. He continued to serve as the Grand Commander of the Masonic Lodge until 1889, and he spent years rewriting the rituals of the Scottish Rite Masons. He died at the Scottish Rite Temple in Washington.

[Pike's publications include *Prose Sketches and Poems Written in the Western Country* (1834), *Morals and Dogma of the Ancient and Accepted Scottish Rite of Free Masonry* (1872), and posthumously published poems: *General Albert Pike's Poems* (1900), *Hymns to the Gods and Other Poems* (1916), and *Lyrics and Love Songs* (1916). He contributed several biographies to John Hallum's *Biographical and Pictorial History of Arkansas* (1887). See Walter L. Brown, *A Life of Albert Pike* (1997).]

CARL H. MONEYHON

PITTMAN, MARGARET (Jan. 20, 1902–Aug. 19, 1995), microbiologist, was the daughter of James Pittman, a country doctor, and Virginia Alice McCormick. In 1909 the family moved to the village of Cincinnati in northwest Arkansas, where Margaret sometimes helped her father with administering anesthesia and vaccinating children. After James Pittman's early death in 1919, Virginia Pittman took her three children to Conway, where she helped support their studies at Hendrix College by sewing and by canning fruits and vegetables at home.

After graduating *magna cum laude* from Hendrix in 1923, Margaret Pittman attended the University of Chicago, where she studied bacteriology. The offer of a fellowship to continue her studies for a Ph.D. was "an opportunity undreamed of," she said.

Bacteriology was a relatively new science. In the late nineteenth century rapid progress was made in the discovery of the causes of infectious diseases. Even so, in the early twentieth century many diseases—typhoid fever, diphtheria, pneumonia, whooping cough, scarlet fever, and others—could not be prevented. The year 1918 saw the worst outbreak of infectious disease in modern times, the "Spanish flu" pandemic in which twenty-three million people died worldwide, half a million or more in the United States. Pittman began her career in the aftermath of the Spanish flu when society was dedicating great resources to the control of disease by public health measures. In fact, one of her first assignments was to investigate whether *Haemophilus influenzae* causes influenza.

From 1928 to 1934 Pittman did postgraduate work at the Rockefeller Institute for Medical Research in New York. Here she discovered that certain types of influenza bacteria have a capsule which allows them to enter the bloodstream readily and overcome natural defenses. One of the encapsulated types she discovered causes a form of meningitis. In all, Pittman found six encapsulated strains of *Haemophilus influenzae*. These discoveries, together with several publications on pneumo-coccus pneumonia, and other research papers, won her an international reputation before she was thirty years old.

During the Great Depression she joined the National Institute of Health, winning a job by placing among the top three candidates on a Civil Service test. Her research career there was spent primarily in the production, testing, and standardization of vaccines to prevent typhoid, cholera, and pertussis (whooping cough). She promoted the concept that the effectiveness of a vaccine is related to its potency, as determined by laboratory tests, and she became well known for developing methods for testing the potency of antisera and vaccines.

During World War II Pittman worked on developing standards for blood plasma. Great amounts of plasma were used to treat the wounded, but blood transfusions sometimes caused severe fever and chills. Working with colleagues, she developed requirements for assuring the safety of plasma.

In 1943 she began work on a vaccine for pertussis, a devastating childhood disease. She and a colleague developed a technique for testing the safety and efficacy of the vaccine. Her work became the basis for an international potency requirement. Within five years of the establishment of the requirement, there was a dramatic drop in the death rate. She said that "despite the problems that have occurred with the pertussis vaccine ... I consider this work one of my best accomplishments."

Pittman was chief of the Laboratory of Bacterial Products, Division of Biologics Standards, from 1957 until 1971, the first woman to head a laboratory at the National Institutes of Health. She was known as a blunt, straight-to-the-point sort of person, systematic and energetic. She was always seeking and embracing the new and could recognize new opportunities in new technologies.

She was involved in cholera research in Pakistan with the Southeast Asia Treaty Organization and served as NIH project director of cholera research for about five years. She also served as consultant to the World Health Organization in formulating a proposed requirement for cholera vaccine.

After her retirement at age seventy, she continued by invitation as an unpaid guest worker at NIH, served as a consultant in Cairo, Madrid, Teheran, and Glasgow, and published twenty scientific papers. Creativity did not desert her in old age. In 1976 she was struggling with the question of why pertussis vaccine had a number of toxic side effects. As she paced the floor, "suddenly it came to me that pertussis had a true exotoxin [a protein toxin excreted by bacteria], like diphtheria or cholera toxin, that caused the harmful effects." "No one paid attention" until 1978, when her idea was accepted by fellow scientists. Her concept of pertussis as a toxin-mediated disease contributed to the development of a safer vaccine. She said it was "satisfying to have changed the direction of work on pertussis vaccine."

Among her honors was the Federal Women's Award which stated that "her ability to identify problems, stimulate research and evaluate results have made her an unusually effective leader." She was recognized by the American Academy of Pediatrics for her "efforts in improving the health and welfare of children." The Margaret Pittman Lectureship at the National Institutes of Health honors her research accomplishments there.

Pittman loved to garden and maintained a garden at the apartment house where she lived. She enjoyed traveling and was active in the Mount Vernon United Methodist Church of Washington, D.C. She died in Cheverly, Maryland.

[See Margaret Pittman, "A Life with Biological Products," *Annual Review of Microbiology* 44 (1990): 1–25; Elizabeth Moot O'Hern, *Profiles of Pioneer Women Scientists* (1985); Gail McBride, "Margaret Pittman: Down to a Forty-Hour Work-Week," *Medicine on the Midway*, Bulletin of the Medical Alumni Association, University of Chicago (Spring 1987); Victoria A. Harden, "Reflections of Fifty Years at NIH: An Interview with Margaret Pittman," *NIHAA Update* (Spring 1989); and Harry F. Dowling, *Fighting Infection: Conquests of the Twentieth Century* (1977). There is an obituary in the *Northwest Arkansas Times*, Sept. 1, 1995.

This entry is based also on interviews with Dr. Harry Meyer, Nov. 14, 1997, and Dr. Victoria A. Harden, Dec. 16, 1997.]

NANCY A. WILLIAMS

POPE, JOHN (Feb. 1773–July 12, 1845), territorial governor, was born in Prince William County, Virginia, the eldest son of Colonel William and Penelope Pope. The family moved to Louisville, Kentucky, in 1779. Pope's earliest education came under the supervision of his parents. After an accident necessitated amputation of the boy's arm, his father determined to prepare him for a profession. John Pope received a classical education at Dr. James Priestley's school in Bardstown, Kentucky. He studied law under George Nicholas in Lexington and established a practice in Shelbyville, Kentucky.

In 1798 Pope won a seat in the Kentucky General Assembly representing Shelby County. Following this early success he held either elective or appointed political office almost continuously until 1844. As a contemporary and sometimes bitter rival of Henry Clay, Pope ranked as one of the most prominent political figures in early nineteenth-century Kentucky. Throughout his career, Pope earned a reputation for refusing to alter his beliefs once he studied an issue and decided his position. During his only term in the United States Senate this characteristic cost him reelection after he opposed United States entry into the War of 1812.

Despite his sometimes controversial beliefs, Pope also knew how to gain important political contacts. Having known Andrew Jackson since 1819, Pope enthusiastically supported Jackson's 1828 presidential candidacy. He hoped to be rewarded with the United States attorney generalship, but instead he received an appointment as the territorial governor of Arkansas (succeeding the recently deceased George Izard in the spring of 1829). Despite his initial disappointment, he approached his new office with zeal.

He arrived in Arkansas in May 1829, the first governor to move his family to the territory. Early in his first term he expressed a vision for Arkansas, that it might become "by a wise and just course of policy, the enterprise, public spirit, intelligence, and elevated character of the people, a bright star in the political constellation." He also addressed a series of issues that he hoped would make that vision a reality.

Upon receipt of census returns, Pope determined that the number of representatives in the legislature should be increased and equitably distributed; accordingly, he raised the number from nine to twenty-three and devised a plan for their distribution. Deciding that the territorial mail service was inefficient, Pope recommended a weekly Little Rock-Memphis-New Orleans river route, via steamship. The legislature adopted a slightly altered plan, a weekly Little Rock-Memphis overland route across the newly constructed Military Road. In October 1829 Pope also expressed the Jacksonian belief in extended democracy by making many of the territory's offices elective rather than appointed. He believed that these policies would increase migration to the territory and diminish its reputation as a place of violence and corruption.

Pope's most persistent and belligerent opponent during his tenure in Arkansas was Robert Crittenden, another former Kentuckian. Fortunately for Pope, he gained the powerful allegiance of Colonel Ambrose Sevier and the *Arkansas Gazette;* both shared his vision of Arkansas as a land ripe for positive improvements. These allies proved valuable during the peak of Crittenden's criticisms. Pope's encounters with the Crittenden faction were at the center of most of the governor's difficulties during his two terms in office. Pope's earlier rivalry with Henry Clay had been one of honest ideological difference expressed with anger and passion, but also respect, by men of intelligence and eloquence who happened to hold differing opinions on policy issues. The rivalry with Crittenden, by contrast, was founded on spite and jealousy, and fought by way of bitterly partisan journalism rather than open and direct debate. The Crittenden faction's purpose was to discredit and embarrass Pope in the eyes of his supporters. It had little, if any, effect on Pope's reputation.

Pope's tenure in Arkansas ended sooner than he would have liked. By 1834 his personal political convictions were increasingly at odds with the anti-bank, anti-tariff policies of the Jackson administration. He made the mistake of making these differences known to Jackson in a private letter. As a result, he was not appointed to a third term as territorial governor in 1835. He was succeeded in that office by William S. Fulton. Although Pope was not governor when Arkansas became a state in 1836, his vision of organization and reform and the policies that gave shape to that vision clearly set the stage for that achievement. Pope County, Arkansas, is named in his honor.

Pope returned to Kentucky, where he was elected to the United States House of Representatives and served from 1837 to 1842. He is buried on Cemetery Hill in Springfield, Kentucky, next to his third wife, Frances Walton Pope.

[The John Pope Papers are at Filson Club Historical Society, Louisville, Kentucky. See Orval W. Baylor, *John Pope: Kentuckian* (1943); George T. Blakley, "Rendezvous with Republicanism: John T. Pope vs. Henry Clay in 1816," *Indiana Magazine of History* 62:3 (Sept. 1966): 233–50; and the Pope County Historical Association, *History of Pope County, Arkansas* (1979).]

ROBERT PATRICK BENDER

POTTS, KIRKBRIDE (Mar. 24, 1803–Nov. 27, 1879), was a master builder, agent for the Bureau of Indian Affairs, postmaster, cattle drover, and operator of an inn. He was born in Pennsylvania to Joshua Potts, wheelwright, and Mary Bunting, both descendants of prominent land-holding families of Pennsylvania and New Jersey.

In 1828 Potts moved from Pennsylvania by way of Missouri to what is now Pottsville, Arkansas, bringing with him a train of four Conestoga wagons holding his furniture and two slave families. He purchased one hundred and sixty acres of dense woods, cane brakes, and grasses along Galla Creek where he built a two-story log house. On February 10, 1829, he married Pamelia Allison Logan, daughter of a prominent politician and member of the first Arkansas legislature. Shortly afterward, he wrote to a sister in New Jersey, saying he was doing well with a good start in this world, and referring to his wife as "a fine and agreeable person." While living in the log structure, he and Pamelia became the parents of Sara, Joseph, Joshua, Lizzie, Richard, Thomas, James, John, and Charles.

Kirkbride Potts operated his farm, served as a U.S. Government agent for the removal of Cherokee and Choctaw "wards" to the Cherokee Nation, kept the Galla Creek post office, and hosted an inn on the Military Road. Along with these activities he made three trips to California, one in pursuit of gold, and two to push herds of cattle to feed the miners. In a letter to his sister Ann he said a five-month trip by wagon to the great Salt Lake and the remainder by mule pack was "a long and fateagueing [sic] trip and well calculated to wear out the patience of almost anyone." In another letter, from Red Bluffs, California, to the *Arkansas Gazette and Democrat* in 1857, Potts said he was delayed almost a year to "bring his cattle to market" in good condition.

Shortly before, or during these trips to California, Potts began building a stately home in keeping with his status in the community. He patterned it after the Classical Revival homes he knew in Pennsylvania and constructed it primarily by slave and local free labor, using native materials. Lumber for siding and trim, bricks for chimneys, and laths for plastered walls were designed and created on site. Only windows, mantels, and glass panes were factory made and shipped up the Arkansas River.

The new structure, built to serve as both a home and an inn, was two-story, with four large rooms on each floor, and a one-story kitchen to the rear. Each room of the main building, as well as the kitchen, had a large fireplace and an artistically designed mantel. A stairway with wide treads, easy risers, and polished rail led from one floor to the next. Entrance to the building was by way of a two-story portico supported by hand-made columns.

The building, completed in 1858, served as an inn, an overnight Butterfield Stage stop, a post office, a home, and a gathering place for literary and social events. It also provided entertainment and rest for writers, politicians, and Arkansas's prominent people. Albert Pike stayed there when traveling from Little Rock to Fort Smith, and Persis Lovely of the renowned Lovely family died in the Potts' home shortly before the new building was finished. Other notables made it a point to reach the Potts' place to spend the night: lawyers "riding the circuit" from one court to another, military officers, Indian chiefs, and governors.

With the coming of the Civil War in 1861 the Butterfield Overland Stage closed, and Potts Inn ceased operating as a stage line station. Kirkbride Potts adjusted to changing conditions and converted the inn to a hotel. With his experience and good physical facilities, he furnished high-class accommodations to surveyors and engineers working for the newly established Little Rock and Fort Smith Railway Company.

According to the *Russellville Democrat*, Potts died at his home, leaving a history of service to his community, state, and nation. A host of descendants have followed his example of leadership and service.

Even though much of the current information on Kirkbride Potts comes from oral history, one legacy endures visible and sturdy, the stately building he designed and constructed in the 1850s. It stands on a rise overlooking Pottsville and the lands of Galla Creek. The walls are plumb, the wide board floors level, and plaster clings smooth and tight to the handmade laths. The chimneys retain their original bricks and mortar, and the watertight roof remains straight and true. A stairway of wide treads, easy risers, a polished hand rail, and a generous landing rises from the first floor as it did the first time Pamelia Potts ascended it in 1858.

Kirkbride and Pamelia are buried on a plot in the nearby Potts cemetery. Potts descendants sold the inn to the Pope County Historical Foundation in 1970.

[A genealogy of the Potts family (1910) is in the Pope County Library, Russellville, Arkansas. "Potts Family Letters, 1825–1852," are in the Small Manuscript Collection, Box 43, no. 19, Arkansas History Commission. Few written records remain. This account relies in part on the author's conversations with George Kirkbride Potts, Sept. and Oct. 1993 and Apr. 1994. See George Turrentine, "Potts Station on Galla Creek," *Arkansas Valley Historical Papers* 13 (1956), in the Pope County Library. Sources also include an obituary for Persis Lovely, *Arkansas Gazette*, Feb. 16, 1842; *Arkansas Gazette and Democrat*, June 25, 1857; and Potts's obituary, *Russellville Democrat*, Nov. 28, 1879.]

LOIS LAWSON MORRIS

POWELL, RICHARD EWING (Nov. 14, 1904–Jan. 2, 1963), actor, director, and producer, was born in Mountain View, Arkansas, to Ewing Powell and Dolly Thompson.

Powell, who was known as Dick Powell, began his career as a big band singer and concluded it as a film director and producer. Although his parents displayed no musical talent, the youth and his two brothers, Howard and Luther, were natural singers. They were all probably influenced by George R. "Dick" Case of Mountain View, the man for whom Dick Powell was named. Case had one of the few pianos in the village and willingly taught young Powell to play it. At age five the "prodigy" sang in public for the first time, rendering "Casey Jones," then a new song. The family moved to Berryville and later to Little Rock while Powell was a child.

In the capital city he sang in a church choir and at funerals while studying, singing, and earning his living working for a telephone company. In the mid-1920s he went into radio work and about the same time married Mildred Maund, his hometown sweetheart. This proved to be an unhappy union primarily because Maund dis-

approved of her husband's show business aspirations, and the couple divorced in 1933.

In 1927 Powell joined Charlie Davis's orchestra as a vocalist and later that same year made his first record. On November 30, 1927, he recorded "Time Will Tell" and "Beautiful" for the Gennett label. The next month he recorded "Beautiful" for Vocalian; this version became his first issued recording. Powell's subsequent records and broadcasting work led to a screen test and, ultimately, to Hollywood stardom. His first film appearance was in a nonspeaking role in *Street Scene*. In 1932 he had his first musical role, in the Warner Brothers movie, *Blessed Event*, in which he played a band leader and sang "I'm Making Hay in the Moonlight." That same year his role in *Forty-second Street* made him an overnight star. Several other musical films followed, and in 1935 and 1936 Powell was in the box office top ten. However, he was tiring of musicals and protested, "I'm not a kid any more, but I'm still playing boy scouts." Even so, it was several years before he abandoned musicals and changed his screen image.

In 1936 Powell married actress Joan Blondell, and over the next several years, he appeared with her in a number of films, including *I Want a Divorce* (1940). The couple divorced in 1945. Powell then married the actress June Allyson and remained with her until his death.

In 1944, the year before he married Allyson, Powell changed his screen image by playing Raymond Chandler's hard-boiled detective, Philip Marlowe, in *Murder, My Sweet*, also known as *Farewell, My Lovely*. Despite the wishes of many fans, Powell never returned to singing.

During the 1930s and 1940s, Powell was very active on radio. In 1934 he starred on the Old Gold radio show with Ted Fio Rito's orchestra. In 1934–37 he headlined "Hollywood Hotel" with the singer Frances Langford, a show that has an important niche in radio history. When this program first aired in 1934, New York and Chicago were the major production centers; the success of "Hollywood Hotel" helped make Hollywood an origination point for major radio programs. In 1937–38 Powell hosted "Your Hollywood Party" which helped launch Bob Hope to stardom. Powell's other radio shows include "Tuesday Night Party" (1939), "American Cruise" (1941), and "Dick Powell Serenade" (1942–43). From the mid-1940s to the early 1950s, he starred on several mystery and private-eye radio dramas, of which the best remembered is "Richard Diamond: Private Detective" which first aired on NBC in 1949.

In the early 1950s Powell entered television, becoming an important performer, director, and producer. He and June Allyson were part of Four Star Productions, originally with Charles Boyer, Rosalind Russell, and Joel McCrea. Russell and McCrea later dropped out and were replaced by Ida Lupino and David Niven. Four Star produced many early television dramas. In 1954 Powell had his last important film role in *Susan Slept Here*, which co-starred Debbie Reynolds. Thereafter, he worked in movies primarily as a director. It was while working in this capacity on *The Conqueror* (1956) that, many film historians believe, Powell contracted the cancer that claimed his life. This motion picture about Genghis Khan was filmed near an atomic test site, and several of those connected with the project, John Wayne, Agnes Moorehead, and Powell, among others, died of cancer. Some believe the movie's location was directly responsible for those deaths.

Powell's son Dick Powell Jr. portrayed him briefly in the movie *Day of the Locust* (1975). On November 12–13 the first of what promised to be an annual Dick Powell Music and Film Festival was held at Powell's birthplace in Mountain View. At that time a marker was erected designating his home as a historical site.

[Sources include W. K. McNeil, *Dick Powell Music and Film Festival Program Book* (1993); and Tony Thomas, *The Dick Powell Story* (1993). Bigraphical dictionaries for Hollywood figures of the period contain information about him.]

W. K. MCNEIL

PRICE, FLORENCE BEATRICE SMITH (Apr. 9, 1888–June 3, 1953), composer, performer, and teacher, was born in Little Rock to Dr. James H. Smith, a dentist, and Florence Gulliver, a teacher before her marriage in 1876. The Smiths were prominent in Little Rock during the latter part of the nineteenth century and once entertained the abolitionist Frederick Douglass as a house guest.

Florence received instruction in music from her mother, and appeared in a concert featuring her own compositions when she was only four years old. She graduated as valedictorian of the class of 1903 at Capitol Hill School in Little Rock. She attended the New England Conservatory of Music in Boston, and in 1906 received her soloist's diploma in organ and a teacher's

diploma in piano. She returned to Arkansas and took teaching positions at Cotton Plant-Arkadelphia Academy in Cotton Plant, and at Shorter College in North Little Rock. In 1910 she moved to Atlanta to accept a position as head of the music department at Clark University.

She returned to Little Rock and married Thomas Jewell Price on September 25, 1912. Thomas Price was a law partner with Scipio Africanus Jones, who played a role in the successful defense of twelve men sentenced to death in the Elaine (Arkansas) race riot of 1919. Thomas Price participated in the initial appeal of this case. While Thomas practiced law, Florence established a private music studio. She taught piano lessons and began writing teaching pieces for piano, an activity she pursued throughout her career.

She was the mother of two daughters, Florence Louise, born July 6, 1917, and Edith C., born March 29, 1921. A son, Tommy, died in childhood.

In spite of her credentials, Price was denied membership into the Arkansas State Music Teachers' Association because of her race. In 1925 and 1927 she won prize money for her compositions in competitions sponsored by *Opportunity* magazine, which supported the work of African-American composers and performers. By 1927 the Price family had moved to Chicago, a cosmopolitan city which could offer more professional opportunities for Price's career.

Price gradually established herself in the Chicago area as a teacher, composer, pianist, and organist. She continued music studies at various institutions, including the American Conservatory of Music and Chicago Musical College.

In 1928 G. Schirmer, a major publisher, accepted one of her short piano pieces, "At the Cotton Gin." This character piece and such others as "Arkansas Jitter," "Bayou Dance," and "Dance of the Cotton Blossoms," have their origins, in part, in dance, particularly the Juba, and in plantation songs. Her piano teaching pieces were later accepted for publication.

Price's ability to write in larger forms was demonstrated in such works as the Symphony in E Minor (1931–32) and Piano Sonata in E Minor (1932), both of which won awards in competitions sponsored by the Rodman Wanamaker Foundation. The Symphony in E Minor was first performed by the Chicago Symphony Orchestra on June 15, 1933, with Frederick Stock conducting. It marked the first performance by a major

American symphony orchestra of a work written by a black woman composer. The symphony was later performed at the Century of Progress Exhibition at the Chicago World's Fair of 1933, where Price also appeared as soloist in one of her piano concertos.

These larger instrumental works reflect Price's synthesis of European classical models and the influence of African-American melodic and rhythmic idioms. Her work may be characterized as conservative and attractive. In the 1930s her symphonic works were performed by the orchestras of Chicago, Detroit, Pittsburgh, and Brooklyn, a distinction she shared with such contemporaries of hers as Aaron Copland, William Grant Still, William Dawson, Roy Harris, and George Gershwin. Her music was also performed in England and France.

She composed chamber music and music for radio in addition to her solo pieces for piano and organ. Her songs and spiritual settings were performed by famous singers including Marian Anderson, who included Price's setting of "My Soul's Been Anchored in de Lord" in a concert attended by some seventy-five thousand people on Easter Sunday, April 9, 1939, at the Lincoln Memorial, Washington, D.C.

Price returned to Little Rock in 1935 as a "noted musician of Chicago" to present a recital of her compositions at Dunbar High School, sponsored by the Alumni Association of Philander Smith College. She continued to compose and teach in Chicago after Thomas's death in 1942. She was making plans for a European trip when she died in Chicago. In 1964 a Chicago elementary school was named in her honor, a tribute to an Arkansas musician who made her own distinctive mark in American music.

[A collection of Price's papers and scores is in Special Collections Division, University of Arkansas Libraries, Fayetteville. See Barbara Garvey Jackson, "Florence Price, Composer," in *The Black Perspective in Music* 5:1 (Spring 1977); Margaret Bonds, "A Reminiscence," *International Library of Negro Life and History* (1967); and articles in *Pan Pipes* 46 (Jan. 1954) and 47 (Jan. 1955); *American Music Teacher* 19:4 (Feb.–Mar. 1970) and 40:1 (Aug.–Sept. 1990); *Etude* (Nov. 1936); *School Musician* 41 (Mar. 1970). Ph.D. dissertations include work by Rae Linda Brown, Yale University, 1987; Mildred Green, University of Oklahoma, 1975; and Lisa Sawyer, University of Missouri, Kansas City, 1990. Discussions of Price's work appear in Christine Ammer, *Unsung: A History of Women in American Music* (1980); Samuel A. Floyd, ed., *Black Music in the Harlem*

Renaissance: A Collection of Essays (1990); and Jane Frasier, *Women Composers: A Discography* (1983).

Price's discography includes compact disc reissues of spiritual arrangements recorded by Marian Anderson, "The Lady from Philadelphia" (Pearl GEMM CD 9069) and "He's Got the Whole World in His Hands" (RCA Victor 09026-61960-2), and Leontyne Price (RCA Victor Gold Seal 09026-68157-2). Several of Price's art songs are featured in compact disc recordings by Yolanda Marcoulescou-Stern (Gasparo Records GSCD 287) and Pamela Dillard (Koch International Classics KIC 7247). Price's Piano Sonata in E Minor, "Dances in the Canebrakes," and several other short pieces are featured on "Black Diamonds: Althea Waites Plays Piano Music by African-American Composers" (Cambria CD 1097). "Fantasie Negre," performed by pianist Helen Walker-Hill, is included in "Kaleidoscope: Music by African-American Women" (Leonarda Productions LE 339). "Deserted Garden" for violin and piano is featured on "Here's One" (4-Tay 4005).]

DAN DYKEMA

PRYOR, SUSAN HAMPTON NEWTON (Nov. 9, 1900–Feb. 14, 1984), mother, community leader, and writer, was born in Camden, Arkansas, to Robert D. Newton and Cornelia Ellen Newton. Her father was sheriff of Ouachita County, as was his father. Both of her grandfathers were veterans of the Civil War. Her brother Robert was an All-American at the University of Florida in 1923.

After graduation from Camden High School, "Susie" Newton attended the University of Arkansas at Fayetteville, but returned home due to her mother's illness. Later, she attended a business course in Hot Springs, learning typing, shorthand, and bookkeeping and becoming a "thoroughly modern" woman. She secured a position at the Stout Lumber Company in Thornton and later was employed by the South Arkansas Grocery Company and Gaughan and Stifford law firm in Camden. She left the law firm upon her appointment as a deputy circuit clerk of Ouachita County. In 1926 she became one of the first women to run for political office in Arkansas when she ran for the circuit clerk's office in the Democratic primary, losing the primary to a World War I veteran by only two hundred votes. Then she went to work as the bookkeeper at the Bensberg Music Shop.

She married W. Edgar Pryor, an automobile dealer of Camden, on April 6, 1927. The Camden newspaper said the marriage was "particularly interesting because of the prominence of both the bride and bridegroom." Four children were born to the marriage: William Edgar Pryor Jr., a Presbyterian minister; David Hampton Pryor, governor, United States representative and senator; Mary Cornelia Pryor Lindsey and Elinor Pryor Ozment, wives and mothers. A letter written by her son Bill in 1975, when Pryor was nominated as the Arkansas Woman of the Year, describes her role as mother: "My mother is a most remarkable woman. In relationship to her four children perhaps her greatest gift was plenty of rope anchored to a secure mooring . . . She did a good job of parenting."

Motherhood, however, could not occupy all of her energy. Don Harrell, a family friend, once wrote of her, "Susie keeps a number of projects in the air at once." Her hobbies included painting in oils and watercolor, photography, sewing, and music, including playing the piano and guitar and twenty-five years of singing in the church choir.

She was also a writer of fiction and essays. When her son David began a weekly newspaper, the *Ouachita Citizen*, Pryor wrote two columns, "Food Fair" and "Items of Friendly Interest," from 1957 to 1960. She kept notebooks and scrapbooks and wrote frequent letters to many people, all expressing her love of people and life and her strong belief in good and God. At age sixty she enrolled in a writing correspondence course. When she died, she and a friend were working on a cookbook.

In the midst of the Great Depression, Pryor was instrumental in starting Community House in South Camden. This was a place that provided a library, learning activities, and much more to those impoverished by the economic times. Once during those hard times, Pryor walked into a Camden bank, handed the banker one thousand dollars and asked him to make loans at no interest to people who needed them and as the money was repaid to lend it again. She was one of the first women in Arkansas to run for and secure a seat on a school board to help promote education.

One of the founding members of the Ouachita Historical Society, Pryor had an avid interest in history. She was instrumental in one of the first historical restoration projects in Arkansas, the Chidester House, and later rescued the Tuft House from destruction by buying it, moving it to her property, restoring and living in it. She also presented programs on Camden history at schools and clubs. Her passion for history is memorialized by the endowment of the Susie Pryor Award, established in 1985 by the Arkansas Women's History Institute. The award offers a prize every year for the best unpublished essay concerning Arkansas women's history.

W. Edgar Pryor died in September 1952. Susie Pryor had always been deeply involved in the programs of her church, the First Presbyterian, and in 1957 after her last child had gone to college, she received an invitation to travel to British Guiana to tutor the children of missionaries there. For five months she lived with the missionaries among the Indians. Her family and friends urged her not to go, but she quoted one of her favorite sayings, "The only really safe place to be is in the will of God," and went.

Pryor died at eighty-three. Her children and grandchildren have described her variously as "independent," "strong," "a haven," "fun," and "determined." According to the memorial sermon delivered by her son Bill, the only adjective Susie used was "perfectly." Pryor herself once wrote, "To be remembered by those you love is never to have died." It certainly seems to be true of her.

[The following materials are housed at the Arkansas History Commission and Archives: *Patterns: A Social History of Camden*, vol. 2; Camden School Writing Project (1988): 90–93; the *Ouachita Citizen*, 1957–1960; the *Arkansas Democrat*, Apr. 23, 1978; and the *Arkansas Gazette*, Feb. 15, 1984. See also the *Arkansan*, May 1979.]

JANICE BUFFORD EDDLEMAN

RANDOLPH, VANCE (Feb. 23, 1892–Nov. 1, 1980), folklorist, was born in Pittsburg, Kansas, to John Randolph, an attorney and Republican politician, and Theresa Gould, a librarian. A child of genteel, upper-middle-class parents, he was even as a boy attracted to the fringes of that staid society, to the ethnic diversity of southeastern Kansas mining camps and the socialist politics of the *Appeal to Reason*, published in nearby Girard. His most vivid childhood memories centered on the visits to Pittsburg of flamboyant figures like Buffalo Bill Cody and Carrie Nation. Despite dropping out of high school—he never did graduate—he flirted with an academic career on at least two occasions, completing an M.A. in Psychology at Clark University (where he wrote a thesis on Freudian dream analysis) in 1915, seeking without success to obtain Franz Boas's support for graduate work in anthropology at Columbia (he wanted to study Ozark mountain people), and finally enrolling in the doctoral program in psychology at the University of Kansas in 1921.

But these were all false starts. Randolph's real work would take place, as he had proposed to Boas, in the Ozarks, but it would be done without institutional support by a man without academic credentials. Randolph made his living as a hack writer, but he made his name as a student of traditional Ozark lifeways. He became a man of many pseudonyms, writing for money under a host of fanciful monikers—"Anton S. Booker" when he wanted to sound sophisticated and "foreign," "William Yancey Shackleford" when he was passing as a man of the south and west, "Belden Kittredge" when he wanted a scholarly tone. When he was writing for love, doing Ozark folklore (and mostly not getting paid for it), he called himself Vance Randolph.

His first scholarly efforts were in dialect studies and folk belief, the latter subject providing the material for his first *Journal of American Folklore* article in 1927, while the former led to numerous publications in *American Speech* and *Dialect Notes* in the 1920s and 1930s. He would eventually produce major, book-length works in both fields: *Ozark Superstitions* (later reissued as *Ozark Magic and Folklore*) was published by Columbia University Press in 1947, while *Down In the Holler: A Gallery of Ozark Folk Speech* appeared in 1953 from the University of Oklahoma Press. Before this, however, he had produced *The Ozarks* in 1931 and *Ozark Mountain Folks* in 1932; at the time they were ignored by most academic reviewers (and sometimes resented by Ozarkers themselves for their celebration of "backward" elements in the region's culture), but more recent students have recognized them as pioneering examples of what are now called folklife studies.

Randolph collected steadily throughout the 1930s and 1940s, even as he supported himself with everything from articles for sporting magazines to various works for juvenile readers—*The Camp on Wildcat Creek* (1934), *The Camp-Meeting Murders* (1936)—and many books for the Little Blue Books series published by Emanuel Haldeman-Julius. Most of the latter dealt with scientific topics or western history, but a few pseudonymous titles (*Autobiography of a Booze-Fighter*) demonstrate once again the author's versatility. Randolph also published an attempt at a serious novel (*Hedwig*, 1935) and a collection of short fiction (*From An Ozark Holler*, 1933). But his important work, once more, was the work that did not pay.

He had been collecting traditional music since the 1920s, when he sought to contact potential singers through a column in the weekly Pineville, Missouri, newspaper, but *Ozark Folk Songs*, the enormous collection issued by the State Historical Society of Missouri, may be his single most impressive work. It appeared in four volumes between 1946 and 1950. The 1950s also saw the publication of five volumes of Ozark folk tales, beginning with *We Always Lie to Strangers* in 1951, followed by *Who Blowed Up the Church House?* (1952), *The Devil's Pretty Daughter* (1955), *The Talking Turtle* (1957), and *Sticks in the Knapsack* (1958). A collection of Ozark jokes and jests, *Hot Springs and Hell*, appeared in 1965, and the massive *Ozark Folklore: A Bibliography* followed in 1972. A collection of bawdy folk tales, *Pissing in the Snow*, was published in 1978; it became far and away the most popular of his books.

In 1978 Randolph was elected a Fellow of the American Folklore Society, an honor which pleased him immensely. A supplement to his Ozark folklore bibliography, edited by Gordon McCann, appeared posthumously in 1987, followed in 1992 by two more volumes of bawdy materials edited by longtime Randolph admirer Gershon Legman, *Roll Me in Your Arms* and *Blow the Candle Out* (1985).

Robert Cochran

RAY, JOE (1855–?), was a slave whose life story was recorded by the Federal Writers' Project. In the 1930s the project, under the Works Progress Administration, sent workers to record the reminiscences of former slaves. The slave narratives were compiled state by state by interviewers who wrote down the interviews in the presumed dialect of the narrator. The following excerpt is an account by Joe Ray, an ex-slave born in Fulton, Arkansas, who was eighty-three years old when the interview was recorded. The interviewer is unknown.

> My folks was shipped from Africa across the waters and fetched a good price on the slave market at New Orleans where my pappy stayed for a long time helping with the fresh Negroes that come over on the slave boats.
>
> His name was John and my mammy's name was Rhoda. She belonged to Jim Hawkins who had a plantation at Fulton, Arkansas, down in Hempstead County. When she met my pappy old master Hawkins sold her to pappy's master, name of Ray, so's dey could stay together.
>
> Dere at Fulton I was born in 1855. I was eight year old when Vickburg give up to the Yankees and an old

slave man dere looked at the lines on my hand and said I was eight year old.

Some of the slaves was moved around all over the south during the War. Me and pappy was at Vicksburg when the Rebels stuck their swords in the ground to give up. But dem Yanks had a terrible time whipping us. The Yank soldiers dug holes in the ground and put in kegs of powder. Den dey blowed up the land down by the river and almost turned the river [Mississippi] around!

Master Ray sold mammy, me and my twin sister and two brothers to Enoch Smith, and he was the last master we had. Some of my folks stayed with him a long time after they was free—doing the washings, ironings and cooking. The boys tend to his horses and work in the fields.

His house was made of sawed cedar logs from a close-by mill, and the beds had round legs of cedar posts, with rope slats made diamond fashion. When the ropes was drawn up it made the bottom tight as a dollar bill.

The slaves lived in log huts, mostly one room, with a tar roof. Dere was no beds like the master had. Just a kind of bunk with corn shuckings stuck in a cotton bag for to lay on. After working in the fields all day, sometimes without anything to eat for dinner, the slaves come to the cabins a night, cook their supper of white salt meat and talk awhile before going to sleep. Dey had to get sleep early and get up early; nobody sleep late, even Sunday.

Dere was two overseers on the place and dey carried a bull whip all the time. Dey didn't whip the girls; the old master pinch their ears if dey get mean and not mind. But I saw a slave man whipped until his shirt was cut to pieces! Dey whipped dem like horses, but the master didn't want dem beat to death. If dey whip dem too hard the old master shake his head and say, "Dat's too much money to kill!"

The auction sales brought the master lots of money. One man sold for $1,500. The slaves stand bare to the waist, men and women alike, the buyers feeling of dem to see if dey had been mean enough for whippings.

The master give each slave family about 4-pounds of fat meat every week, with a quart of molasses, a peck of corn meal and som bran for flour. When dat run out you was just out until Saturday night come around again.

The clothes was all home spun, made of cotton and when I was a little boy the master give me pair of red shoes. In dem days I wore a charm for sharp luck. It was [a] needle with a blue velvet string through the eye, but when I do something mean that [charm] didn't keep the master's whip off my back!

After freedom one time I worked at the old Peabody hotel in Memphis. [Lots] of gamblers around dere den; dey come down the river and have some big gambling games. I done some gambling too, but not like dem white folks who paid me a dollar for a cigar after dey have a streak of big winnings.

Lincoln was a great man, but dis country needs a king.

Folks call me a prophet, because I tell dem things dat comes true. Now I been telling dem dat slavery is coming back and it ain't far away. Maybe dey wont believe it—but slavery is coming soon.

[The Joe Ray narrative is in the Archives and Manuscripts Division of the Oklahoma Historical Society, Oklahoma City, in unpublished Works Progress Administration Records, slave narratives.]

APRIL L. BROWN

READ, LESSIE STRINGFELLOW (Jan. 3, 1891–June 21, 1971), newspaper editor and spiritualist, was born Mabel Staples in Temple, Texas. The daughter of William and Lillian Staples, her forebears included a Supreme Court justice and two signers of the Declaration of Independence. She was adopted at age two, upon the death of both parents, by the renowned horticulturist Henry Martyn Stringfellow and his wife, Alice.

The Stringfellows had lost their only child, a nineteen-year-old boy named Leslie, to malaria in 1886. According to Alice Stringfellow, Leslie made himself known to them after his death by means of spirit communication. Leslie encouraged them, she writes, to adopt "a little dependent human being who will arouse your energies and give you an increased interest in life." She continues: "Her name when we found her was Mabel, but at the request of both herself and her spirit 'brover' it was afterwards changed to 'Lessie' which she lisped in trying to name our boy whom she heard us talk to nightly." Spirit communications were not discussed outside the family and had little effect on their lives outside the home.

Lessie was raised in San Antonio, Galveston, and later Lampassas, Texas, where she was selected "Lampassas Fire Queen" of 1908. In a lavish society wedding she married James Read, a young Lampassas businessman. In 1911 the couple moved with the Stringfellows to Fayetteville, Arkansas, where a few years later James Read disappeared from Lessie's life permanently.

Without the responsibilities of a wife but retaining the married status that allowed her to move unimpeded in society, Read began to make her presence felt in Arkansas. By 1915 at twenty-four she was involved in the women's suffrage movement. A founder of the Washington County Women's Suffrage Association and president of the Fayetteville Equal Suffrage Association, she was named national press chairman in 1916 for the largest international women's organization of that time, the General Federation of Women's Clubs. She was also editor of the organization's *General Federation News.* From 1916 through 1926 she served as press director for national conventions of the GFWC, and in that capacity met and spoke with national figures of her day: Thomas Edison, John D. Rockefeller, Mrs. Herbert Hoover, John Gould Fletcher, Luther Burbank, Jane Addams of Hull House, and suffragist Carrie Chapman Catt.

She studied at the University of Arkansas and was working as a journalist for the *Fayetteville Democrat* in 1918 when its editor, J. D. Hurst, resigned to join the American forces in World War I. She became editor of the paper. When he returned from the war, she offered to resign in his favor, but Hurst declined, choosing instead to work as the newspaper's business manager. For the next twenty-seven years Read was editor of the *Fayetteville Democrat.*

In *A Fulbright Chronicle* Allan Gilbert notes: "Lessie's style was strong on 'famous resident' and 'famous visitor' stories. Her scoops tended toward the exotic. She loved arts and crafts, and homespun writers, and lavished attention on them." During her years with the paper, Read worked in an unconventionally feminine atmosphere: she was the editor, Roberta Fulbright was the owner, and Maude Gold was the paper's only full-time reporter. A man wrote the sports page, but the tone and intellectual content of the *Fayetteville Daily Democrat* were set by women.

This was the situation in 1933 when the newspaper became embroiled in a battle with a corrupt political machine that had operated in Washington County for years. Officials in the county government were involved in poll-tax fraud, automobile theft, and a protection racket for producers of "moonshine." Since the machine included the sheriff and members of the local judiciary, the newspaper represented the citizens' only means of redress. The paper galvanized the county's churches and civic organizations into forming the Good Govern-ment League, which ultimately forced out the corrupt officials and voted in its own candidates. During this troubled era, threats were received at the newspaper and one of Roberta Fulbright's employees began carrying a gun, but Fulbright, Read, and Gold did not back down.

Read was a correspondent for the *St. Louis Post-Dispatch,* the *Houston Chronicle,* the *Memphis Commercial Appeal,* the Associated Press, and various news syndicates. She wrote for *Good Housekeeping, Delineator, Southern Women's Magazine, Country Gentleman, Woman Citizen,* and *Saturday Evening Post.* She published the work of Arkansas poet George Ballard, and Alice Stringfellow's *Leslie's Letters to His Mother,* and edited a book of poetry by Roberta W. Fulbright, with whom she shared a close friendship. She also assisted Vance Randolph with collecting original folk tales in the Arkansas Ozarks for the Library of Congress.

Read never apologized for her spiritualism. She showed remarkable candor in publishing her adoptive mother's writings. She may have been influenced by her correspondence with Sir Arthur Conan Doyle, author of the Sherlock Holmes stories and the best known spiritualist of his time, who read Alice's manuscript and encouraged her to publish it. Read was a member of the Rosicrutians, an international spiritualist organization whose local meetings were held regularly in her home until 1966. "Miss Lessie" conducted her career from the mansion Henry Martyn Stringfellow built at 329 Washington Avenue in Fayetteville.

[The Lessie S. Read Papers are in the Special Collections Division, University of Arkansas Libraries, Fayetteville. She edited Alice Stringfellow's *Leslie's Letters to His Mother* (1926); *Ozark Ballads* by George Ballard (1928); and, with Walter Lemke, *Ninety-Seven Years* (1943). Sources also include the author's telephone interview with Dwain Manske on August 3, 1993, and a series of interviews with Maude Gold Hawn during September 1993.]

STEPHEN CHISM

RECTOR, HENRY MASSIE (May 1, 1816–Aug. 12, 1899), planter and the first Civil War governor of Arkansas, was born at Fountain Ferry, Kentucky, near Louisville, the only child surviving to maturity of Elias Rector and Fannie Bardella Thurston. Elias Rector, a land surveyor and speculator, acquired considerable land, including claims to large tracts in Arkansas.

Henry Rector received the rudiments of an education from his mother; beginning in 1833 he attended a school in Louisville, Kentucky, for two years.

In 1835 he moved to Arkansas and assumed the management of the landholdings he had inherited from his father. He pressed his claims to the famous Hot Springs, but after lengthy litigation the government confirmed individual claims to land around the springs but reserved the springs for public use. In October 1838 he married Jane Elizabeth Field of Louisville. They had four sons, Frank N., William, Henry Jr., and Elias W., and four daughters, Ann Baylor, Julia Sevier, Fanny Thurston, and Ada E. His wife died in 1857 and he married Ernestine Flora Linke three years later. They had one child, Ernestine Flora.

In 1841 he moved to a plantation near Collegeville in Saline County where he farmed and read law. In 1842 President John Tyler appointed him United States marshall for the district of Arkansas. In 1848 he was elected to the state senate representing the district composed of Perry and Saline Counties. He devoted considerable attention to questions relating to the state penitentiary and acquired a reputation as a skilled debater. In 1852 he was chosen a Democratic presidential elector.

In 1853 Rector became United States surveyor general for Arkansas, a post he held until 1857. In 1854 he moved to Little Rock where he practiced law and carried on extensive farming operations along the Arkansas River. He was elected to one term in the general assembly to represent Pulaski County as a Democrat. In 1859 the general assembly elected him to the state supreme court.

Although Rector was related to members of the Johnson-Conway-Sevier dynasty (also known as the Family), which dominated antebellum politics in Arkansas, he secured their enmity after Representative Thomas Carmichael Hindman of Phillips County persuaded him to run against the Dynasty candidate for governor, Richard H. Johnson, in 1860. Hindman had launched an anti-Dynasty movement two years earlier. Running as an independent candidate in a campaign that focused on Johnson's close ties to the banks and his place in the state political machine, Rector became the sixth governor of the state when he polled 31,518 votes to Johnson's 28,662.

Rector's election coincided with that of Republican Abraham Lincoln as president. Because of Lincoln's views on the expansion of slavery, the sectional crisis intensified. Although Rector's inaugural address did not call for Arkansas's immediate secession, he approved the general assembly's provision for a special election to be held on February 15, 1861, to elect delegates to a convention to decide whether or not Arkansas should secede. When the delegates met on March 4, 1861, the antisecessionists elected David Walker as chairman of the convention. Walker blocked a decision to secede immediately but approved calling an election on August 5 to allow a vote of the people to determine the issue.

Although Rector was not willing to lead the state out of the union, he condoned the actions of eastern Arkansas extremists who seized the federal arsenal in Little Rock on February 8, 1861. He then sent the state militia to seize the Fort Smith arsenal. When President Lincoln called for volunteers after the fall of Fort Sumter, Rector refused. David Walker reconvened the secession convention in Little Rock on May 6, 1861, and it voted to secede and join the Confederacy.

Rector presided over the mobilization of the state. While he was commander-in-chief of the state militia and chairman of the state war board, the secession convention, dominated by the Family, played a key role in the mobilization. By the end of 1861 Arkansas had 21,500 men enrolled for military service. When wartime inflation and profiteering ran unchecked, Hindman, who had become a general in command of the Confederate army in Arkansas, blamed Rector and declared martial law. The clash resulted in Hindman's replacement. But Rector's undoing originated with the secession convention. After ushering the state out of the union in May, the convention wrote a new state constitution and secured a constitutional provision that shortened the governor's term to two years. On October 6, 1862, Harris Flanigan, the Family candidate, defeated Rector in his bid for reelection by a vote of 18,187 to 7,419. When the new general assembly met on November 3, 1862, Rector reported on conditions in the state and resigned. After his application for a commission in the Confederate army was rejected, he volunteered in the state reserve corps for the duration of the war.

Rector returned to farming after the war and hauled cotton in wagons from his plantations in Hempstead, Garland, and Pulaski Counties to Little Rock. He waged many court battles over his Hot Springs claims and was a delegate to the constitutional convention in 1874 from Garland County. He died in Little Rock and was buried in Mount Holly Cemetery.

JEANNIE M. WHAYNE

REED, ROSE PEARL (1868–1925), was born in Rich Hill, Missouri, the first child of Myra Maebelle Shirley, the woman who became known as the "bandit queen" Belle Starr. Pearl's father was Jim Reed, a known thief and murderer.

Growing up, Pearl was subject to the upheaval caused by her parents' lives of crime. Immediately after Pearl's birth, Belle took her to Scyene, Texas, near Dallas, where they lived with Belle's parents while Reed roamed Indian Territory. Belle at this time was working as a horse dealer and saloon entertainer. In 1870–71, after Reed killed two men in Evansville, Arkansas, the family moved to California and settled in Los Nietos, east of Los Angeles. By 1872 Reed was recognized as a wanted man, and he fled back to Indian Territory. Belle took Pearl and an infant son, Edwin, back to Texas by ship around Cape Horn.

On August 6, 1874, when Pearl was six, her father was shot and killed by a friend hoping to collect a five-thousand-dollar reward. At the same time, pressure was building in Scyene against Belle and her outlaw friends. In 1875 a Dallas grand jury indicted Belle for arson. Later an indictment was issued for horse theft and Belle was jailed. The charges were dropped, but the pressure had done its job. In 1876 she went to Kansas and sent Pearl and Eddie to live with their grandmother Reed in Missouri.

In 1880 Pearl, age twelve, and Eddie, age nine, rejoined Belle, with her new husband, Sam Starr, at Younger's Bend, Indian Territory. Two years later Belle and Sam were arrested, tried for horse theft, and sentenced to one year in prison. Once again the children were separated from their mother, and Pearl stayed either with a neighbor close to Younger's Bend or with friends in Kansas.

In 1886 Pearl became pregnant with her first child. In April 1887 a daughter was born in Siloam Springs, Arkansas, and left in the care of Pearl's Aunt Mamie. Later the baby was left with an orphanage in Wichita, Kansas. Some thirty-seven years later mother and daughter were reunited, after Pearl asked the orphanage for help in locating her daughter.

At the age of twenty-one, after losing her father, her child, and her stepfather, Pearl lost her mother. On February 3, 1889, Belle Starr was shot and killed by an unknown assailant. Pearl left Indian Territory after the murder and established herself as a prostitute in Van Buren, Arkansas. Capitalizing on the dime novel fame of Belle, she changed her name to Pearl Starr.

After securing enough money, Pearl moved across the river to Fort Smith and established her own bordello. The house was located on "the Row," a street of gambling houses, saloons, and bordellos, and was clearly identified with a bright red star surrounded by lighted pearls. The parlor featured a talented piano player, good whiskey, and the "most beautiful girls west of the Mississippi." Business prospered, and Pearl purchased additional houses and invested in saloons and other property.

Her first husband was Charles Kaigler, a Fort Smith businessman, with whom she had a daughter, Ruth. In 1897 Pearl married Count Arthur E. Erbach, from the German region of Hesse. With him she had a son, who lived less than a year. The count himself lived only a few weeks after the baby's birth. On May 5, 1902, Pearl, being four months pregnant, married Dell Andrews, a gambler. On November 8, 1902, Jennette Andrews was born. In 1908, Pearl filed for divorce from Andrews and for custody of their daughter.

Pearl was concerned that her livelihood would harm her children. In Fort Smith she built a two-story home at 501 South 19th Street, far from the activities of "the Row," and hired housekeepers to take care of her daughters. When they got older, she purchased a home in Winslow, Arkansas, and hired a couple to look after them. She enrolled the girls as Ruth Kaigler and Jennette Andrews in the Winslow schools so as to keep her own identity a secret. She remained in Fort Smith to attend to business but visited the children as often as possible, coming up to Winslow by train.

The only time Pearl was implicated in a crime was in 1911. After a burglary at a general merchandise store in Fort Smith, police found several of the stolen items hidden at Pearl's Winslow home. She was found guilty of robbery and sentenced to a year in the Arkansas State Penitentiary. Posting two thousand dollars bail, her attorneys appealed the case to the Arkansas Supreme Court, which overturned the verdict.

In 1916 the city of Fort Smith began enacting ordinances making prostitution illegal. For a few years Pearl's activities were overlooked, but eventually she was arrested. The charges were dropped with the understanding that she would leave the community. In 1921, at age fifty-three, Pearl left Fort Smith for Bisbee, Arizona. She operated the Starr Hotel there and invested in a copper mine. She also acquired a boardinghouse known as the Savoy Hotel in Douglas, Arizona. She died in Arizona.

[See Edwin P. Hicks, *Belle Starr and Her Pearl* (1963); Glenn Shirley, *Belle Starr and Her Times: The Literature, the Facts and the Legends* (1982); and Phillip W. Steele, *Starr Tracks: Belle and Pearl Starr* (1992).]

JULIET L. GALONSKA

REEVES, BASS (c. 1840–1910), deputy United States marshal, was born a slave near Paris, Lamar County, Texas. On the plantation of Colonel George Reeves, Bass lived with his mother, Perlalee, and sister, Jane. According to family history, he was his master's "companion," serving as valet, bodyguard, coachman, and butler.

The circumstances under which Bass Reeves achieved his freedom remain sketchy. An often repeated account holds that he fled across the Red River into Indian Territory (present-day Oklahoma) after a fight with Colonel Reeves during a card game. Another version relates that Reeves served his master as a body servant in the Confederate army and fled sometime during the war. He may have fought with the Union forces as a member of the Indian Home Guards or simply remained in Indian Territory as a civilian. Either way, he gained a mastery of firearms and fluency in Seminole, Creek, and Cherokee.

During the post–Civil War years Reeves began his celebrated career as a deputy United States marshal. The federal court for the Western District of Arkansas, with its seat in Fort Smith, held jurisdiction over all or parts of Indian Territory until 1896. Any crime involving a person other than a tribal member fell to its administration. The law enforcement agency working in Indian Territory was integrated, having its share of Indian and African members. The use of these officers was an effective way of carrying out the work of the federal court because of the multicultural population in the jurisdiction. As one historian has noted, "A deputy's authority to a great extent depended on his being accepted and respected by the Indians." African-American deputies held an advantage because of the Five Tribes' history of slaveholding. Many African-American officers had lived with Indians, understood local customs, and knew tribal languages.

At six feet, two inches, weighing 180 to 200 pounds, Reeves had the physical strength and presence to make an imposing officer. His experience with firearms and hunting and tracking, coupled with his knowledge of Indian Territory, made him an excellent choice as a deputy. Family history holds that he was one of the first deputies Judge Isaac C. Parker hired to enforce federal law in the territory.

Making arrests often took ingenious methods. Once Reeves disguised himself as a tramp and walked twenty-eight miles to the home of two outlaws. Although they were not home at the time, Reeves convinced their mother to let him spend the night. When the sons returned, they shared a room with Reeves, who handcuffed them while they slept and transported them to Fort Smith.

Reeves was also known for his memory. Lacking the ability to read or write was a formidable obstacle, considering that legal writs and subpoenas required proper service. Reeves studied the paperwork until he could associate the symbols of a written name with the sounds of the name as spoken. He also used his memory to associate names with specific subpoenas or writs. When he located the suspects or witnesses, Reeves selected the correct documents by matching the symbols. Then he would have the person read the paper aloud. Only if the person could not read was Reeves forced to find someone who could.

The financial reward for making arrests was adequate, but usually not more than five hundred dollars per year. A deputy received two dollars for making an arrest and could receive six cents per mile for going to the place of arrest and ten cents per mile for himself and a prisoner returning to court. If a deputy failed to make an arrest, he received no payment. If he killed a suspect while attempting an arrest, he had to bury the dead man at his own expense unless he could find relatives to claim the body. Serving subpoenas, finding witnesses, and other routine court business earned fifty cents per service.

This was little reward for a profession that constantly placed one's life at risk. Bass Reeves reportedly killed fourteen men in his career, but proved self-defense in each case. The most sensational of these incidents involved the death of Reeves's cook, William Leech, in 1884. Three years later Reeves was brought to trial accused of Leech's murder. Testimony established that Reeves's rifle misfired while he was cleaning it, the bullet striking Leech in the neck, and the jury found Reeves not guilty.

Reeves had to arrest his son, Benjamin, who had killed his wife in a domestic dispute. According to the *Muskogee Phoenix*, January 13, 1910, "Marshal Bennett said that perhaps another deputy had better be sent to arrest [Benjamin]. [Bass] was in the room at the time, and with a devotion of duty equalling that of the old Roman, Brutus, whose . . . love for his son could not sway him from justice, he said, 'Give me the writ,' and went out and arrested his son."

Reeves worked as a deputy marshal until 1907, serving the Fort Smith and Muskogee federal courts. With Oklahoma statehood, he moved to local law enforcement, finishing his career at Muskogee. He died of Bright's disease. The location of his burial remains unknown.

[See Paul L. Brady, *A Certain Blindness: A Black Family's Quest for the Promise of America* (1990); Arthur T. Burton, *Black, Red and Deadly: Black and Indian Gunfighters of the Indian Territory 1870–1907* (1991); Daniel F. Littlefield and Lonnie E. Underhill, "Negro Marshals in the Indian Territory," *Journal of Negro History* (April 1971): 77–87; and Nudie E. Williams, "*United States vs. Bass Reeves:* Black Lawman on Trial," *Chronicles of Oklahoma* (Summer 1990): 154–67.]

JULIET L. GALONSKA

REMMEL, HARMON LIVERIGHT (Jan. 15, 1852–Oct. 14, 1927), political leader and businessman, was born in Stratford in Fulton County, New York, to Godlove Remmel and Henrietta Bever, who had emigrated from Cologne, Germany. He attended Fairfield Seminary in Fairfield, New York.

In 1876 opportunity of abundant timber resources lured him to Arkansas. He settled in Newport, and with his brother Augustus Caleb established the Remmel Brothers Lumber Company. He earned the reputation of business developer and was elected to the village council. A Republican, he received the federal appointment of postmaster of Newport in 1877. On March 13, 1878, he married Laura Lee Stafford of Staunton, Virginia.

In 1884 he was selected to the Arkansas Republican state central committee. He received the Republican nomination for congress from the Newport district, losing to the Democratic candidate. In 1886 he was elected to the state legislature. In 1892 he served as a delegate to the Republican national convention, and did so at every national convention through 1924.

In 1894 and 1896 he ran for governor, losing both races to Democrats. In 1896 he moved to Little Rock. Facing strong political opponents there, he retained his representation in the Jackson County Republican organization. He became manager for Arkansas of the

Mutual Life Insurance Company of New York, continuing in this capacity for twenty-six years. In 1897 he was a delegate to the Monetary Conference in Indianapolis, serving on its executive committee.

In 1897 he was selected to represent Arkansas in the Republican National League. Arkansas's Republican boss, Powell Clayton, appointed ambassador to Mexico, turned the conduct of the state Republican Party over to Remmel and Henry M. Cooper, who received federal appointments from President William McKinley. Remmel was made the state's collector of internal revenue, and Cooper received the post of United States marshal for the Eastern District of Arkansas. Because the marshal post received a much higher salary, Remmel protested to Clayton; as a compromise, Cooper and Remmel split the difference between the two salaries.

In 1900 Remmel ran for governor, losing to Democrat Jeff Davis. He also became the chairman of the state Republican central committee. In 1902 he organized the Mercantile Trust Company, where he served as president until 1912. But he suffered a major setback when political enemies informed President Theodore Roosevelt of the deal between Remmel and Cooper to split their salaries. Roosevelt forced both men to resign.

Remmel was nominated for United States senator in 1903, but again lost to a Democrat. Then in 1905, with the intervention of Powell Clayton, Roosevelt appointed Remmel United States marshal for the Eastern District of Arkansas. In return, Remmel agreed to resign as chairman of the state Republican central committee.

In 1909 he was appointed to the state capitol commission, which oversaw the construction of Arkansas's new capitol building. In 1910 he became chairman of the Arkansas Good Roads Association, president of the Little Rock Board of Trade, and resumed the chairmanship of the state Republican central committee. With the retirement of Powell Clayton in 1913, Remmel became Arkansas's member of the Republican National Committee. He helped organize the Bankers' Trust Company in Little Rock.

In October 1913 Laura Remmel died. Remmel married Elizabeth I. Cameron of Fort Covington, New York, in 1915.

Turmoil erupted in 1914 when members of Pulaski County's Republican organization moved to exclude African Americans from participation in the local party. Remmel denounced their actions, blocking the Lily Whites' maneuvers at the state convention.

Remmel's position on the Lily Whites remains a topic of contention among historians. At the 1916 state convention he supported the seating of the Lily White delegation from Pulaski County. But at the same convention he formed an alliance with black Republican leader Elias Camp Morris of Helena, and supported including an African American in the delegation to the national convention.

With America's entry into World War I in 1917, he joined other prominent Arkansans in promoting the war effort. He was appointed to the Arkansas State Council of Defense, and served as chairman of the state's Four-Minute Men, so-called for their brief patriotic speeches.

In 1920 the split between white and black Republicans continued, resulting in a walkout by black delegates at the state convention. Remmel remained with the Lily Whites in preference to joining a hastily convened Black and Tan convention. Despite his determination to reconcile the differences between black and white Republicans, turmoil again marred the state convention of 1924. Afterward, Remmel worked out a compromise with black Republican leader Scipio A. Jones, resulting in a grudgingly united Republican Party.

Remmel promoted new industries and the harnessing of the state's natural resources and advocated the development of the light and power industry. His advocacy was recognized when the state's first hydroelectric dam, near Hot Springs, was named Remmel Dam.

He was a member of the Methodist Episcopal Church, South and a temperance advocate. He had one son, Harmon Liveright Remmel Jr., and an adopted daughter Elizabeth C. Remmel. He died in Hot Springs.

[The Harmon Liveright Remmel Papers, and the Republican Party, Arkansas, State Committee Records, 1882–1956, are in the Special Collections Division, University of Arkansas Libraries, Fayetteville. See Todd E. Lewis, "'Caesars Are Too Many': Harmon Liveright Remmel and the Republican Party of Arkansas, 1913–1927," *AHQ* 56 (Spring 1997): 1–25; and Marvin F. Russell, "The Rise of a Republican Leader: Harmon L. Remmel," *AHQ* 36 (Autumn 1977): 234–57.]

TODD E. LEWIS

REYNOLDS, DANIEL HARRIS (Dec. 14, 1832–Mar. 14, 1902), Confederate brigadier general, lawyer, was born in Hillian Township, Knox County, Ohio, the fourth of ten children of Amos Reynolds and Sophia Houck. Daniel Reynolds attended Ohio Wesleyan University but did not graduate. While enrolled there, he befriended Otho Strahl, who also became a Confederate brigadier general. Reynolds then moved to Somerville, Tennessee, where he studied law under private tutelage. He passed the bar in 1858. He relocated to Lake Village, Chicot County, Arkansas, where he established a thriving legal practice, and he remained there until the outbreak of hostilities in April 1861.

Reynolds's familial connections and personal sympathies were southern. Therefore, with the outbreak of the Civil War, Reynolds organized a cavalry company known as the "Chicot Rangers" for service in the Confederate army. This unit entered Confederate service as Company A, First Arkansas Mounted Rifles, with Reynolds elected as captain in June 1861. Reynolds's service with this command began in the Trans-Mississippi Department, where they participated in the Battle of Wilson's Creek, Missouri (August 10, 1861). Following the Battle of Pea Ridge, Arkansas (March 7–8, 1862), Reynolds and his regiment transferred east of the Mississippi River, where they served dismounted as infantry for the rest of the war.

Reynolds's abilities as an effective field commander earned him steady promotion within the First Arkansas. Reynolds was promoted to major in April 1862 and advanced to lieutenant colonel in May. Due to his praiseworthy performance at what he called "the great fight" at Chickamauga, Georgia (September 19–20, 1863), Reynolds earned promotion to colonel.

The only blemish on his wartime record occurred late in the winter of 1864, when he was briefly arrested by order of Major General Samuel French. This incident seems to have resulted from Reynolds initiating a petition of protest against a general review of officers' competence by an examining board, ordered in January of 1864. It serves as an illustration of the divisive personal feuds that tore apart the upper levels of the Confederate command in the West during the second half of the war. The "frivolous" charges were soon dropped and, ironically, Reynolds was soon after promoted to brigadier general. For the remainder of the war, he commanded "Reynolds' Arkansas Brigade," composed of the 1st and 2nd Arkansas Mounted Rifles (serving dismounted) and the 4th, 9th, and 25th Arkansas Infantry regiments.

During the Atlanta campaign Reynolds served as

chief Confederate commander on the field during the battle of Lovejoy's Station, Georgia (August 20, 1864), where he defeated the Union cavalry under command of Major General Judson Kilpatrick. This victory against a federal force significantly larger than that under his command prevented the destruction of the Macon and Western Railroad, a vital link in Confederate efforts to supply Lieutenant General John Bell Hood's forces in Atlanta, and earned Reynolds the praise of the normally abrasive Hood. As a result of this battle, Union major general William T. Sherman was forced to alter his strategy regarding the capture of Atlanta, reverting to his original plan of making a grand left wheel around the city.

The war effectively ended for Reynolds in March 1865, when he was wounded by artillery fire while positioning his troops at the battle of Bentonville, North Carolina. This wound resulted in the amputation of his left leg. Local citizens helped nurse Reynolds during his recovery, which lasted beyond the surrender of the Army of Tennessee by General Joseph E. Johnston to General Sherman in April.

Reynolds returned to Lake Village after the war, reestablished his law office, and began acquiring real estate in the Chicot County area. He married Martha Jane Wallace in 1868; three daughters and two sons were born to this union. Reynolds served as a state legislator during the 1866–67 term, prior to the disfranchisement of former Confederates during Radical Reconstruction. He remained an active participant in veterans' affairs for the rest of his life, and the Lake Village chapter of United Confederate Veterans was named in his honor.

Reynolds was one of twenty-nine Arkansans to achieve the rank of brigadier general in the Confederate army during the Civil War and, with the exception of Major General Patrick Cleburne, saw more combat duty than any other Arkansas general. He died in Lake Village and is buried in Lake Village Cemetery.

[The Daniel Harris Reynolds Papers are in the Special Collections Division, University of Arkansas Libraries, Fayetteville. Other sources include David Evans, *Sherman's Horsemen: Union Cavalry Operations in the Atlanta Campaign* (1996); James Lee McDonough and James Pickett Jones, *War So Terrible: Sherman and Atlanta* (1987); Ezra J. Warner, *Generals in Gray: Lives of the Confederate Commanders* (1959); Robert H. Dacus, *Reminiscences of Company "H," First Arkansas Mounted Rifles* (1897); and

the Ohio Wesleyan Historical Collection, Ohio Wesleyan University.]

ROBERT PATRICK BENDER

RIDDLE, ALMEDA JAMES (Nov. 21, 1898–June 30, 1986), balladeer and folk song collector, was born in Cleburne County, Arkansas, to J. L. James, a timberman, grocer, and singing-school teacher, and Martha Frances Wilkerson, whose father, the only grandparent Riddle ever knew, was a Confederate soldier. Riddle was a teenager before she learned she was related to the outlaws Frank and Jesse James.

She was the fifth of eight children born, one of four girls who lived to adulthood. She lived her entire life in the foothills of the Ozarks in Cleburne and White Counties.

She was educated by her parents. Her dad taught her to read music before she could read words. He also taught her principles of harmony and how to play the violin. She learned her first song, "The Blind Child's Prayer," at age six from her mother, who also helped her learn to read and taught her "women's work," crocheting, knitting, and quilting. When the family moved to a farm, Riddle became a "farm boy."

As a child she began collecting written texts of old songs, called "ballets," pronounced "ballad." When the family bought a store near the railroad, she became acquainted with the workers and learned every song she could from them about dying soldiers, cowboys, graveyards, railroads, and parted lovers.

In 1916, after three years of "steady courting," she married H. Price Riddle. Four children were born, but her husband and the baby died of injuries from a tornado in 1926. Her "ballet" and poetry collections were also destroyed. From 1926 to 1949, she raised her three children alone. Until they were grown, she had no time to sit and write from memory all the songs she had learned earlier.

In 1952 John Quincy Wolf, a folklorist from Memphis, advertised for anyone who knew old songs. A neighbor introduced Riddle to Dr. Wolf, who arranged for her first public concert. He introduced her to Alan Lomax, who recorded Riddle's songs in 1959.

By 1960 urban interest in folk music had become a full-fledged revival, and Riddle was sought out for folk festivals throughout the nation. After her mother's death she took her father's advice to "go where you want to go, and do what you need to do." As she traveled to Newport, UCLA, Harvard, Minneapolis, and Boston to sing, she also participated in clinics, workshops, and seminars. Her aim was to teach as many of the old songs as possible to the younger generation, whom she likened to "children begging for bread." She became a personal link with history for Americans seeking their own roots.

In 1964 she served on the faculty at the Idyllwild Arts Foundation in California. In 1966 she made a film for NET'S ninety eastern outlets and tapes for Dr. Wolf and the Library of Congress. In 1967 she sang in Washington, D.C., at the National Festival of American Folklife. Studios recording her songs during this time were Atlantic, Prestige, Folkways, Rounder, and Vanguard, prompting critics Nat Henthoff, Godfrey John, and Maury Bernstein to praise her singing techniques. Her last trip was to Washington, D.C., in June 1983 to accept a plaque from the National Endowment for the Arts.

Her singing style was described as "feathering." At the end of phrases was a yodel-like rise, a slight vocal flick resembling a built-in sob or catch in her voice, effectively conveying anguish in the lyrics of old songs of lost love and family tragedy. She sang without accompaniment, keeping the pulse with her hands down by her side, which she moved, palms down, back and forth in a slight arc.

She considered herself a balladeer and educator, not an entertainer. She abhorred the idea of "performing" a song: "A singer should not get in the way of the song but just stand back and present it." She was more than a human storehouse of valuable antiques; she favored only those songs which contained a message or lesson. Her exceptional memory, strong voice, and natural musicianship set her apart from many equally authentic folk singers. She preferred to shun innovation and commercial success rather than to risk losing the purity of the ballad form, which originated during the Middle Ages and was rooted in Ireland, Scotland, and England. It is believed she possessed a larger repertoire of such songs, over six hundred, than any other American. Some of her favorites were "Lady Margaret," "The House Carpenter's Wife," and "Four Marys."

She was a devout, self-effacing woman with a sense of humor and a passion for her songs, endearing her to those who knew her. Riddle's last public appearance was at the Ozark Folk Center in Mountain Home, Arkansas, and the last song on that program dealt with how "time and age has laid her hand on me." She dreaded pain, pills, and nursing homes, but spent her final eighteen months in just that situation. At her death she was survived by two children, eight grandchildren, and twelve great-grandchildren.

[Roger Abrahams edited *A Singer and Her Songs* (1970). Reproductions of the ballet book and songs used in Abraham's book are on deposit at the Archives of the Center for Intercultural Studies in Folklore and Oral History, University of Texas, Austin. Album notes for a companion recording, "Ballads and Hymns from the Ozarks," Rounder #0017, are extensive. An unpublished manuscript of Abraham's 1985 revision of the book resides in the Resource Center, Ozark Folk Center, Mountain View, Arkansas.

Field tapes by Dr. Wolf are in the Regional Cultural Center, Lyon College, Batesville; tapes made by Alan Lomax are at Hunter College, City College of New York. George West produced a documentary film, *Arkansas Portraits: Almeda Riddle* (1986).

See the *Arkansas Gazette*, Mar. 21, 1965, Oct. 8, 1967, Dec. 25, 1972, June 13, 1982; *Arkansas Democrat*, Feb. 24, 1980; and *HiFi Stereo Review*, Mar. 1965.

This biography is based also on the author's correspondence with Riddle, Apr. 24 and June 20, 1984, and on privately owned scrapbooks.]

PATRICIA LASTER

ROANE, JOHN SELDEN (Jan. 8, 1817–Apr. 8, 1867), governor of Arkansas, was born in Lebanon, Wilson County, Tennessee, and moved to Arkansas in 1837. He settled in Pine Bluff and studied law under his older brother, Samuel Calhoun Roane, a leading jurist and owner of one of Arkansas's largest plantations. With his elder brother's influence and patronage, John Roane moved easily and comfortably into the frontier aristocracy. In 1840, with the help of his brother, he went to Van Buren as the first prosecuting attorney of the newly created Second Judicial District. In late 1842 he returned to Jefferson County and was elected a representative to the Fourth Arkansas General Assembly. In 1844 he went back to Van Buren and was elected to serve in the Fifth General Assembly, which convened in November of that year. The assembly, by a vote of thirty-six to thirty-two, elected him speaker.

Roane probably would have run for another term had it not been for the Mexican War. He raised a company of mounted infantry from Van Buren and took them to Washington, Arkansas, where they became part of the First Arkansas Mounted Rifles. The men elected Roane lieutenant colonel, and the regiment set off for Mexico. The unit, led by men with almost no military experience, was poorly trained and performed badly at the Battle of Buena Vista on February 22–23, 1847. The performance of the regiment became the subject of heated controversy and eventually led to a duel between one of its captains, Albert Pike, and Roane. Fortunately neither man was hurt.

Roane returned to Pine Bluff after the war and occupied himself with overseeing a newly acquired plantation and practicing law. He remained in private life until 1849, when the impending resignation of Governor Thomas Stevenson Drew lured him back into politics. The Democratic caucus, which began meeting on December 8, 1848, nominated Roane on the fifth ballot by a vote of forty-four to twenty-four. Roane was not especially popular with rank-and-file Democrats outside the caucus, but serious opposition failed to coalesce in support of an alternative Democratic candidate. In the March 14, 1849, special election he barely outpolled his opponent by a vote of 3,290 to 3,228.

As governor, Roane supported internal improvements, the establishment of a state college, and the recruitment of immigrants to Arkansas. He hoped to finance his program by using the proceeds from the sale of federal lands that were turned back to the states, but the general assembly passed a series of distribution bills which gave the money to pet projects in the districts that the legislators represented. Roane, like his predecessor, knew that Arkansas's most serious challenge was to find a way to get enough revenue to restore the state's financial credit. The general assembly responded to the very real crisis by ignoring Roane's proposals. It further undermined the financial stability of the state by lowering the tax base, failing to force the collection of individual overdue loans owed to the State Bank, and refusing to repeal the distribution laws.

On national issues Roane sympathized with the southern radicals, believing that the states were sovereign bodies, that slaves were property, and that any state had the right to leave the Union. The Arkansas General Assembly had so frustrated Roane's efforts to deal with the serious financial crisis in the state that he chose not to seek reelection in 1852. He returned to his plantation in Pine Bluff and never held public office

again. On July 5, 1855, Roane married Mary Kimbrough Smith; they had five children.

Roane was in Pine Bluff at the beginning of the Civil War, but he did not enter the service for almost a year. On March 20, 1862, he finally received a commission as a brigadier general in the Confederate army. He commanded a brigade at the Battle of Prairie Grove on December 7, 1862, and served on garrison and detached duties in Arkansas, Louisiana, and Texas. He showed little talent for military service and was not well liked by his superiors or the men he led. After the war Roane returned to Pine Bluff, where he died suddenly. He is buried in Oakland Cemetery in Little Rock.

[See Bobby Roberts, "John Seldon Roane, 1849–1852," in *The Governors of Arkansas: Essays in Political Biography,* Timothy P. Donovan, Willard B. Gatewood Jr., and Jeannie M. Whayne, eds., 2d ed. (1995).]

BOBBY ROBERTS

ROBINSON, JOHN MARSHALL (July 31, 1879– July 19, 1970), physician, African-American Democratic leader, was born in Pickens, Mississippi, the son of Amos G. and Isabell Robinson. John attended Rust College in his home state and Meharry Medical College in Nashville, Tennessee.

While in Nashville Robinson met and married India Cox; in 1903 a son was born to them, John Marshall Jr., apparently Robinson's only child. India died in 1921, and in 1923 Robinson married Myrna Hayes of Camden.

Although his studies had not been completed, Robinson passed the qualifications set by the Arkansas Board of Medical Examiners and spent three years practicing in Newport, Arkansas. In 1904 he finished his education at Knoxville Medical College in Tennessee, after which he returned to Newport.

In April 1905 he and Dr. John G. Thornton of Little Rock founded the Pulaski County Medical, Dental and Pharmaceutical Association. Robinson moved to Little Rock in 1906. Because no hospital for African Americans existed in Little Rock, he had to conduct surgery in his office. Shortly after its founding, the Medical, Dental and Pharmaceutical Association attempted to alleviate poor working conditions by establishing a hospital, but this effort failed.

Then in 1911 an affair with a married woman had dire consequences for Robinson when he fatally shot the woman's husband. He received a seven-year sentence in the state penitentiary, of which he served two years.

After his release from prison, Robinson directed his energies to serving the African-American community. In 1918 he was one of fifty founders of a branch of the National Association for the Advancement of Colored People in Little Rock. In 1918 he joined three other physicians in establishing Bush Memorial Hospital, named for John E. Bush, recently deceased community leader and founder of the Mosaic Templars. Robinson served as chief surgeon of the hospital until about 1927–29, when financial problems caused it to close. He also served as an assistant surgeon at the Missouri-Pacific Hospital in 1919–30. After Bush Memorial Hospital closed, he became chief surgeon of the Royal Circle of Friends Hospital, a position he held in 1929–33. Finally, in 1933 he became chief surgeon of the Lena Jordan Hospital, specializing in the care of crippled children, a post he retained for over twenty years.

Robinson turned his attention to politics in the late 1920s. Never a member of the established black Republican leadership, he founded the Arkansas Negro Democratic Association in 1928. He justified the creation of the association on the grounds that long-term black loyalty to the Republican Party had yielded little reward. Arkansas's white supremacist state Democratic Party welcomed Robinson's organization at arm's length, inviting black Democrats to a celebration in honor of Democratic vice presidential candidate Joseph Taylor Robinson of Arkansas, but refusing to allow blacks to participate in the state Democratic Party primary held in August 1928. When black Democrats were not allowed to vote in the Little Rock Democratic primary in November, Robinson filed a lawsuit which was heard by the Arkansas Supreme Court on March 17, 1930. In *Robinson v. Holman* the court upheld the state Democratic Party's right to exclude black voters. The United States Supreme Court refused to hear the case.

Following this disappointment, the Arkansas Negro Democratic Association became dormant, reemerging in 1940 when Robinson petitioned Arkansas's Democratic State Committee to allow blacks to vote in primary elections. No substantive action was taken on the petition. Then in May 1941, the United States Supreme Court rendered a decision in a Louisiana case that made primary elections subject to federal regulation. Encouraged by the decision, Robinson announced in

July 1942 that members of his organization intended to vote in the upcoming Democratic primary election. Again, state Democratic Party officials refused to allow black Democrats to vote. Robinson therefore decided to take his case before a federal court. However, a United States Supreme Court decision in April 1944, *Smith v. Allwright,* made such action unnecessary; blacks could not be denied the right to participate in primary elections.

Despite rumors that they would be barred from voting on the grounds of insufficient loyalty to the Democratic Party, black Arkansans voted in the July 1944 Democratic primary. However, white Democratic leaders sought other ways to exclude them. Robinson's right to vote was challenged on the grounds of his criminal conviction. He responded by striking a deal with Governor Homer M. Adkins: Robinson would resign as president of the Arkansas Negro Democratic Association and retire from politics in exchange for a pardon; he received his pardon in November 1944, but later resumed his involvement with the association.

Robinson became the first vice president of the Southern Council of Negro Democrats, and in 1949 was named the man of the year by the *Arkansas State Press.* However, after 1950 his influence began to wane. A new organization, the Young Negro Democratic Association, usurped the position of Robinson's association, and he retired from politics.

Robinson was one of the first African-American physicians to become a member of the Pulaski County Medical Society, admitted in 1953, and he received a Certificate of Merit from the Arkansas Medical Society in 1960. He also served on the staffs of Arkansas Baptist Medical Center, St. Vincent Infirmary, and Memorial Hospital.

His community service earned him the Community Chest Bronze Oscar Award in 1939. He also remained active in Bethel African Methodist Episcopal Church. He died in Little Rock.

[Sources include the *Arkansas Democrat,* July–Aug. 1928, and obituary July 21, 1970; the *Arkansas Gazette,* Feb. 1911, July–Aug. 1942, Apr.–July, Sept., 1944, obituary, July 21, 1970; and the *Arkansas State Press,* Nov. 17, 1944. Sources also include correspondence 1917–25, 1928–32, National Association for the Advancement of Colored People, text-film, University of Arkansas Libraries, Fayetteville.

See John Kirk, "Dr. J. M. Robinson, the Arkansas Negro Democratic Association and Black Politics in Little Rock,

Arkansas, 1928–1952," *Pulaski County Historical Review* 41 (Spring 1993): 2–26; and "Dr. J. M. Robinson, the Arkansas Negro Democratic Association and Black Politics in Little Rock, Arkansas, 1928–1952," *Pulaski County Historical Review* 41 (Summer 1993): 39–47. See also C. Calvin Smith, "The Politics of Evasion: Arkansas' Reaction to *Smith v. Allwright,* 1944," *Journal of Negro History* 67 (Spring 1982): 40–51; and Dale Lya Pierson, "John M. Robinson, M.D., 1879–1970," *Pulaski County Historical Review* 41 (Winter 1993): 91–93.]

TODD E. LEWIS

ROBINSON, JOSEPH TAYLOR (Aug. 28, 1872–July 14, 1937), politician, majority leader of the United States Senate, was born in Concord Township, Lonoke County, to James Madison Robinson, a doctor and farmer from New York, and Matilda Jane Swaim of Tennessee. He attended the University of Arkansas for a year before returning to Lonoke upon his father's death in 1892. There he studied law with Thomas C. Trimble, a judge and political leader.

In 1894 Robinson defeated a Populist candidate for state representative, and became the youngest member of the general assembly at age twenty-two. He introduced a bill to create a commission, similar to the Interstate Commerce Commission, to regulate state railroad rates. The bill was defeated, but in the next legislature a similar bill was passed as an amendment to the state constitution and sent to the voters, who approved it overwhelmingly in 1898.

In 1895 Robinson married Ewilda "Billie" Grady Miller.

With a growing law practice providing needed income, Robinson re-entered politics. In 1902 he won a seat in the U.S. House of Representatives, a position he held for a decade. With the Democrats in the minority and unable to pass their own bills, Robinson supported such progressive Republican legislation as railroad regulation, the Pure Food and Drug Act, campaign contribution restrictions, the graduated income tax, and the direct election of senators.

Robinson's career took many rapid turns in 1912. He announced he would run for the Senate against the incumbent Jeff Davis, but after assaying Davis's strength, he changed his mind. He ran for governor instead, and bested George W. Donaghey by nearly a two-to-one margin. But before Robinson's inauguration, the recently reelected Davis died of a heart attack. Robinson won a close vote for Davis's Senate seat. In March 1913 he resigned the governorship and headed for Washington.

In the Senate Robinson became a politician of national stature. He stood by President Woodrow Wilson, leading fights for progressive legislation, such as a proposal to end child labor, and for wartime measures, such as the arming of merchant ships and the declaration of war against Germany in 1917. After the war he helped direct the unsuccessful battle for ratification of the Versailles Treaty, earning a reputation as a master tactician and excellent parliamentarian. In recognition of his efforts, he was chosen the permanent chairman of the 1920 Democratic National Convention.

His fame and power grew throughout the 1920s. In 1923 he became the Democratic leader of the Senate. Then in 1924 he was one of many "favorite son" candidates nominated for president. As the convention deadlocked through 102 ballots, the *New York Times* announced Robinson the "obvious compromise candidate." Instead, the delegates chose Wall Street lawyer John W. Davis.

In 1928 Robinson made headlines again when, on the floor of the Senate, he attacked the anti-Catholic religious bigotry of Alabama senator Tom Heflin and the venomous hatred of the Ku Klux Klan. Because of his courageous stand against intolerance, he was again chosen to serve as the permanent chairman of the Democratic National Convention.

Al Smith selected him as his running mate in the presidential election of 1928. Robinson thus became the first southerner nominated for national office after the Civil War. Herbert Hoover won, however, in an election filled with slurs against Smith's Catholic faith and anti-prohibitionist views. The next year Hoover named Robinson as the only Democratic delegate to the London Naval Disarmament Conference. And, upon his return, he secured enough Democratic votes for the treaty to ensure its passage.

As the Great Depression of the 1930s grew, so did Robinson's prestige. After the 1932 election, with the Democrats in control of the federal government, Robinson became the majority leader of the Senate. From this position he pushed President Franklin Roosevelt's New Deal legislation through a sometimes reluctant Senate. In 1933 he guided the Emergency Banking Act through the Senate (in less than nine hours), introduced and pushed to passage the Civilian Conservation Corps, the Federal Emergency Relief Act, the Work Relief Act, the Home Owners Loan Act and the Railroad Coordination Act. In a hard fight, he steered the Agricultural Adjustment Act through rough waters.

After 1933 he continued to support Roosevelt's program, in both foreign and domestic battles. In 1935 he led an unsuccessful attempt to bring the United States into the World Court. He supported other Roosevelt measures, such as the Social Security Act and the Rural Electrification Act, even while pushing through the Robinson-Patman Anti-Price Discrimination Act to protect small retailers from large chain stores, without administration support.

Robinson's career came to an end in 1937 during one of the most heated Senate conflicts of the twentieth century—Roosevelt's plan to enlarge the Supreme Court. In June 1937 Roosevelt offered Robinson a seat—if he could get four other justices approved. For the next month a bitter battle ensued in the hot Senate chamber with Robinson leading the floor fight. Suddenly on July 14, 1937, the skirmish ended when Robinson died, apparently the victim of a heart attack. He was laid to rest in Little Rock. He had no children.

[The Joseph Taylor Robinson Papers are in the Special Collections Division, University of Arkansas Libraries, Fayetteville. Other sources include the U.S. Congress, *Congressional Record*, 1903–1937; and Franklin D. Roosevelt, Official Files, and President's Personal Files, Franklin D. Roosevelt Library, Hyde Park, New York.

See Cecil Edward Weller Jr., *Joe T. Robinson: Always a Loyal Democrat* (1998), which has an extensive bibliography.]

CECIL EDWARD WELLER JR.

ROCKEFELLER, WINTHROP (May 1, 1912–Feb. 22, 1973), governor, was born in New York. The grandson of Standard Oil founder John D. Rockefeller, Winthrop was the fifth child of John D. Rockefeller Jr. and Abby Aldrich. After three years at Yale, he went to work in the Texas oil industry where he first became involved in civil rights, an interest he pursued his entire life, including participation in the National Urban League.

In 1941 Rockefeller enlisted as a private in the army. He fought in Guam and the Phillipines and left the army as a lieutenant colonel in October 1946. Returning to the oil industry in New York, he resumed his various philanthropic activities.

Winthrop Rockefeller and Barbara "Bobo" Sears married on February 14, 1948. They had one son, Winthrop Paul Rockefeller. Winthrop and Barbara divorced August 3, 1954. On June 11, 1956, he married Jeanette Edris.

Rockefeller moved to Arkansas in 1953, cutting his ties with New York. He probably moved so that he could build something from the ground up, rather than administer an established family business. He bought some nine hundred acres of land atop Petit Jean Mountain near Morrilton, and built Winrock, a Santa Gertrudis cattle-breeding ranch.

In 1955 Governor Orval Faubus appointed Rockefeller the first chairman of the Arkansas Industrial Development Commission. Rockefeller's name and wealth helped the AIDC claim credit for 12,521 new jobs in 1956.

A lifelong Republican, Rockefeller had no trouble working for the Democratic Faubus until 1960, when Rockefeller began working to build Arkansas's Republican Party. In May 1961 the Republican State Committee elected Rockefeller their national committeeman. By 1962 Faubus was indirectly endorsing efforts by the Arkansas General Assembly to legislate Rockefeller out of a job. Rockefeller's popularity helped him remain chairman of the AIDC until he resigned April 1, 1964. Three days later, he announced his candidacy for governor of Arkansas.

Rockefeller's efforts to build the Republican Party in 1960 took the guise of the "Committee for the Two-Party System." The Republican Party in Arkansas was dominated by a small group of "post office Republicans," lawyers and businessmen whose main concern was not electoral success but dispensing federal patronage. These Old Guard Republicans were both unwilling to surrender control of the party and unable to accept Rockefeller's more moderate brand of Republicanism. A feud erupted between 1962 and 1964, with Rockefeller's faction taking control of the party by June 1964. But Rockefeller's inability to reconcile some Arkansas Republicans to his view of the party's goals would make it impossible for him to achieve his goal of building an electorally viable Republican organization in the state.

By most accounts Rockefeller became a reluctant gubernatorial candidate in 1964, joining the race because he believed he was the only candidate who could defeat Faubus. In the end, however, Faubus's hold on the state was too powerful. Rockefeller lost, 43 percent to Faubus's 57 percent. But for a Republican in Arkansas, 43 percent was remarkable.

Rockefeller's 1966 campaign for governor began the day after the 1964 election. Rockefeller and his staff expected a rematch with Faubus. But in January the governor announced that he would not seek a seventh term. Rockefeller's Democratic opponent was James D. "Justice Jim" Johnson, a hard-core segregationist. The 1966 campaign was nasty and bitter, with a clear choice available between the two candidates. Rockefeller won with 54.4 percent of the vote.

When he was inaugurated on January 10, 1967, he became Arkansas's first Republican governor since 1874. But he had to deal with an Arkansas General Assembly composed of thirty-five Democrats in the senate and ninety-seven Democrats and three Republicans in the house. Considering these odds, Rockefeller's reform agenda fared remarkably well.

During the regular session of the Sixty-sixth General Assembly (January 9–March 31, 1967), thirty-nine administration-sponsored bills became law. They included bills to improve education, the creation of a new administration department designed to streamline state government, and highway safety bills. These passed despite tensions between Rockefeller and the state senate over gubernatorial appointments.

Rockefeller called two special sessions in 1968, the first in February aimed at nonfiscal reform measures. Administration-sponsored prison bills and Arkansas's first minimum wage passed in this session. The second special session, held in May, focused on a series of tax increases, but the governor's program failed. Politics was the culprit; the Democratic primaries were only a month away.

During Rockefeller's term the condition of Arkansas's prisons often took center stage. A 1966 Arkansas State Police report was a horror story of filth, torture, and corruption. In February Rockefeller hired Tom Murton as assistant superintendent of the Arkansas State Penitentiary. During the year he spent in Arkansas, Murton improved the living and dietary conditions of prisoners. But he found it impossible to get along with other state officials and was fired in March 1968, after his highly publicized digging for the bodies of allegedly murdered inmates at Tucker and Cummins Prisons.

Rockefeller's primary achievement in civil rights was to give African Americans a voice in state government, hiring or appointing them whenever possible. For example, prior to 1967, no black had ever served on a local draft board in the state. By 1968, 80 percent of Arkansas's black population was under the influence of integrated draft boards.

When Dr. Martin Luther King Jr. was assinated in April 1968, riots flared up in 110 cities across the United States. Violence was avoided in Little Rock largely because Rockefeller, at his wife's suggestion, proposed a prayer service on the steps of the state capitol. The governor stood hand-in-hand with black leaders singing "We Shall Overcome," the only southern governor to publicly eulogize King.

Rockefeller's reelection in 1968 was not a foregone conclusion. Democrats considered his 1966 election a fluke. Marion Crank, an eighteen-year veteran of the Arkansas House of Representatives, became Rockefeller's opponent. It was a close election, but Crank's ties to the Faubus machine and revelations that his entire family was on the state payroll gave Rockefeller a narrow victory.

The regular session of the Sixty-seventh General Assembly was the longest in history, lasting ninety-three days. The cornerstone of Rockefeller's legislative agenda, a $90 million tax program, failed, with the legislature passing taxes totaling approximately $20 million. The governor's only significant achievement was a bill permitting the sale of mixed drinks in those counties where it was approved by the voters.

He ran for a third term in 1970 because he believed his Democratic opponent would be Faubus. But his victories had forced the Democratic Party to reform, and a newcomer, Dale Bumpers, defeated Faubus in a primary runoff. Bumpers's program for Arkansas was very similar to Rockefeller's. With no ties to the old Faubus machine, Bumpers was a very tough opponent. Liberal urban Democrats, who had made Rockefeller's two victories possible, turned in droves to the Democratic nominee. Bumpers won, 375,648 votes to Rockefeller's 197,418.

Rockefeller had one last significant contribution to make before leaving office. An opponent of the death penalty, he commuted the death sentences of the fifteen men awaiting execution in Arkansas.

Following Rockefeller's defeat, the more conservative members of the party regained control. Rockefeller retained his position as national committeeman until his death, but after 1970 his contributions to the party dropped dramatically.

Winthrop and Jeannette Rockefeller divorced on April 30, 1971. In September 1972 Rockefeller was diagnosed with cancer. He died in Palm Springs, California.

[The Winthrop Rockefeller Collection in the archives at the University of Arkansas at Little Rock contains the official papers of Rockefeller's governorship. Although his personal papers are not yet available to researchers, the official papers of Record Groups III and IV contain some information on Rockefeller's relations with the Republican Party prior to his election. The Rockefeller Family Archives at the Rockefeller Archive Center in North Tarrytown, New York, contain what little documentation is available concerning Rockefeller's life before his move to Arkansas.

Rockefeller wrote several articles, the most significant of which is "Executive Clemency and the Death Penalty," *Catholic University Law Review* 21 (Fall 1971): 94–102. See John Ward, *The Arkansas Rockefeller* (1978); Orval Eugene Faubus, *Down from the Hills*, vol. 2 (1986); Cathy Kunzinger Urwin, *Agenda for Reform: Winthrop Rockefeller as Governor of Arkansas, 1967–71* (1991); Alvin Moscow, *The Rockefeller Inheritance* (1977); and John Ensor Harr and Peter J. Johnson, *The Rockefeller Century* (1988).]

CATHY KUNZINGER URWIN

ROGERS, BETTY BLAKE (Sept. 9, 1879–June 21, 1944), author and wife of humorist and film star Will Rogers, was born at Silver Springs (later called Monte Ne), Arkansas, to James Wyeth and Amelia Crowder Blake. After Mr. Blake's death in 1882, the family moved a few miles north to Rogers. Betty was seventh in a family of seven girls and two boys. Mrs. Blake supported her large family through dressmaking. The Blake home was a social center, and Betty was a popular young lady whose social life included singing and acting at the local opera house.

Betty Blake met Will Rogers while she was recovering from typhoid at her sister Cora's home in the small town of Oolagah, Indian Territory (today Oklahoma). Her brother-in-law was the local railroad agent, and she met Rogers when he came to the depot to pick up a package. Betty and Will were both twenty years old, and they soon became friends. Their shared sense of humor and love of music proved to be a lasting bond between them.

After Betty returned to Rogers the couple corresponded for several years. Betty saw Will only occasionally during this time since he was performing with a traveling show. While Will traveled and began to make a name for himself, Betty worked at H. L. Stroud Mercantile Company in Rogers, at the *Rogers Democrat*, and at the Frisco Railroad station in Jenny Lind, Arkansas, near Fort Smith.

In 1906 Will suddenly proposed marriage, but Betty refused him because of her qualms about a life in show business. A year and a half later, Will returned to Rogers and proposed again, promising that after a final tour they would settle down in Oklahoma.

Betty and Will married on November 25, 1908, in a small ceremony at her mother's home in Rogers. They honeymooned in New York, where Will's performances took only a small part of each day. As Will was offered better jobs, Betty began to have second thoughts about her husband's career. Soon she was encouraging him to continue.

Until Will Jr. was born in 1911, Betty and Will traveled everywhere together. After her son was born Betty began to return to Rogers for long visits. Her daughter Mary was born there in 1913. Mary was followed by two more children, James in 1914 and Fred, who died at age two in 1920.

Occasionally Betty would leave the children with her mother and join Will on the road. Sometimes she would take an apartment in New York, where her sister Theda helped care for the children. In addition to her roles as wife and mother, Betty also managed the family finances, a chore complicated by Will's growing success and his generous and extravagant nature.

She was also a partner in Will's career. It was Betty who first convinced Will to begin talking as he performed rope tricks, and it was Will's talk which brought him fame. Betty encouraged Will to start on the lecture circuit and helped him choose scripts after he began making movies.

In 1919, as Will's film career began to flourish, the family moved to Beverly Hills, California. But they never really felt at home there and soon bought a ranch in the Santa Monica hills. Will's popularity continued to grow, and tours often kept him on the road. Betty never became much involved in civic affairs, remaining focused on her family.

Will Rogers was a great promoter of airplane travel and was a good friend of aviator Wiley Post. On August 15, 1935, Rogers and Post were killed in a plane crash in Alaska. After Will's death Betty worked to further his reputation. She was responsible for the development of the Will Rogers State Historical Park at the Santa Monica ranch and was instrumental in the creation of the Will Rogers Memorial in Claremore, Oklahoma, dedicated in 1938. She wrote a biography of Will, published in 1941, in which she revealed her intelligence, humor, and strength, though she characteristically talked little about herself.

In 1944 she made the decision to move Will's body to Claremore, near his Oklahoma birthplace. She died at Santa Monica and was buried in Claremore next to her husband.

[The research library at Rogers Historical Museum includes an unpublished study by Lois Snelling: "One of the Blake Girls: The Story of Betty Blake (Mrs. Will Rogers) and Her Benton County Family." The library also contains files of clippings, correspondence and other materials.

Betty Rogers's book is *Will Rogers: His Wife's Story* (rpt. 1979). Reba Collins, *Will Rogers: Courtship and Correspondence, 1900–1915* (1992), includes Will's letters to Betty and to his family. The papers from which these letters are drawn are at the Will Rogers Memorial, Claremore, Oklahoma. See also Will Rogers, *The Autobiography of Will Rogers* (1949). An obituary is in the *Rogers Daily News*, June 22, 1944.]

GAYE KELLER BLAND

ROGERS, JOHN HENRY (Oct. 9, 1845–Apr. 16, 1911), a congressman and United States district court judge, was born in Bertie County, North Carolina, the son of Absolom Rogers, a planter and slaveholder. When John was seven years old, the family relocated to Madison County, Mississippi, where Absolom Rogers either acquired or operated a cotton plantation. In 1861, when he was fifteen years old, John Rogers became the drillmaster for a company of home guards, and in March 1862 was mustered into Company H, Ninth Regiment, Mississippi Volunteers, as a private soldier. He served in the same regiment throughout the war until it was surrendered at Greensboro, North Carolina, on May 1, 1865.

The young soldier saw a considerable amount of action. He was awarded a battlefield commission for gallantry at Franklin, Tennessee, in 1864.

At the end of the war, when Johnston's army surrendered at Greensboro, North Carolina, Rogers walked some thousand miles back to his family's home in Mississippi. After graduating from the University of Mississippi in 1868, he studied law on his own initiative and was admitted to the bar. In 1869 he moved to Fort Smith, Arkansas, and began practicing law. Soon after he arrived, he was invited to occupy desk space in the law office of Judge William Walker.

Rogers entered into a partnership with Walker which lasted until 1874, when the two agreed to separate. Rogers continued to practice in Fort Smith until 1877 when the Twelfth Judicial Circuit was created. Rogers was elected circuit judge. He served until 1882, when he resigned, citing health reasons.

Either Rogers's health dramatically improved, or the health reasons were simply a cover for his political plans, because he immediately announced his intention to run for Congress. He was elected to the Forty-eighth Congress and served in the United States House of Representatives from 1883 until March 1891. After his second term he became a member of the Judiciary Committee. He participated in writing and securing passage of an act reforming federal criminal procedure and claimed credit for a statutory reform granting the writ of error to persons convicted of federal felonies. On the civil side, Rogers was a proponent of the creation of the United States Circuit Court of Appeals.

As a Confederate war hero and a man of imposing demeanor, Rogers became a spokesman for the white southern point of view. He was a vigorous opponent of the Speaker of the House, Thomas B. Reed of Maine, and worked to defeat a bill intended to protect the rights of black voters. The bill passed in the House, only to be defeated in the Senate.

In March 1891 Rogers announced that he would retire from Congress and resume his law practice in Fort Smith. He led the Arkansas delegation to the Democratic national convention in 1892. He became a president of the Fort Smith Board of Education and in December of 1894 was elected permanent chairman of the Arkansas Convention of Mayors. In 1895 Center College in Danville, Kentucky, awarded Rogers an honorary degree.

He was appointed to the district bench on November 27, 1896. Judge Isaac Parker, his predecessor, had sentenced sixty-nine defendants to hang. That record must be seen in the context of his court's jurisdiction over the Indian Territory and the lack of any right to appeal. On average about two thousand criminal cases per year were disposed of in Judge Parker's court.

When Rogers took the bench, criminal cases from Indian Territory were heard in the new federal courts for the territory. In the first full year of Rogers's tenure, the number of criminal cases declined by nearly two-thirds to 548. In 1902, the last year for which summaries are available from the National Archives, only twenty criminal cases are recorded for Judge Rogers's court. Unlike Parker, Rogers was not a "hanging" judge.

He was a popular speaker. His keynote address, delivered in New Orleans in 1903 to a convention of United Confederate Veterans, was so well received that the organization published it in a pamphlet titled "The South Vindicated." The forty-page pamphlet featured a portrait of Judge Rogers, along with a sketch of his life.

The thrust of his oration, which must have taken two hours to deliver, was that the secession of the Confederate states was lawful under the Constitution and that no blame should be attached to the southern states. He said the result of the war was beyond question and the South was fully reconciled to the Union. He spoke of Reconstruction as the true "lawless" period in the history of the war.

In April 1911 Judge Rogers traveled to Little Rock to hear cases for Judge Jacob Trieber. Rogers had been on a hunting trip with friends in Oklahoma; the weather was nasty, and the judge came down with a bad cold. On the morning of Monday, April 17, 1911, Judge Rogers was due in court at 9:30; when he did not appear, Judge Trieber and others went to Rogers's hotel room and found him dead, apparently of a heart attack. Rogers's wife, Mary Gray Rogers, and four children survived him.

[This biography is based on the record "In Memoriam: John Henry Rogers, 1845–1911" (Fort Smith, Arkansas: Calvert-McBride Co., 1912).]

MORTON GITELMAN

ROOTS, LOGAN HOLT (Mar. 26, 1841–May 30, 1893), banker and businessman, was the third of four children of Benajah Guernsey Roots, an educator, and Martha Sibley Holt. He was born at Locust Hill, near Tamaroa, Illinois.

His early academic interest turned toward mathematics. At age fifteen he worked with an engineering corps engaged in railroad construction. When he was seventeen, he enrolled in the Illinois Normal University. He taught school for a year and then returned to the university where he graduated valedictorian in 1862. According to family accounts he paid for most of his expenses at school by buying produce in central Illinois, shipping it to southern Illinois, and selling it at a profit. This attention to business and profit remained a Roots characteristic.

After graduation he joined the Union army. Because of his business abilities, he was assigned to the commissary department. He was in charge of all the supplies for General William Sherman's troops on the march from Atlanta to the sea. Roots attained the rank of colonel, was a member of Sherman's staff in the grand review at Washington in May 1865, and came west with Sherman where he was assigned to Arkansas and formed a military attachment for the state.

Roots remained in Arkansas after the Civil War. He invested in mining interests in Nevada with his brother Philander Keep Roots (P. K.) and acquired a cotton plantation near DeValls Bluff. He was active in Republican Party politics, campaigned for the state constitution of 1868, and was elected to Congress from Arkansas's First District in 1868. As a congressman he was a key supporter of railroad development, introducing the first bill to create the Texas Pacific Railway Company. He supported other internal developments, such as levies and water gauges on rivers.

P. K. and his wife, Fanny, moved to Arkansas to help Roots run for reelection in 1870. Defeated in that election, Roots was appointed marshal for the United States Court for the Western District of Arkansas in 1871. As a marshal Roots vigorously pushed his Republican Party agenda in Fort Smith. By that time, however, the state Republican Party had split, which made intra-party rivalries as bitter as those between Democrats and Republicans. Politics and charges of scandal in the business dealings of the marshal's office led to the removal of Roots in 1872.

In August 1871 Roots married Emily Margaret Blakeslee of New York at DeValls Bluff. They had seven children; all four sons died in infancy.

Following Roots's removal from the marshalship, he and Emily moved to Little Rock where he assumed the presidency of Merchant's National Bank, later renamed the First National Bank of Little Rock.

Even though Roots did not seek public office again, he was a delegate to several national party conventions. He was best known as a banker, financier, and investor. He was appointed a vice president of the National Bankers' Association in 1880. The next year, he and P. K. became two of the three stockholders in the newly formed Southwestern Telegraph and

Telephone Company, where he also served as president. Soon after the company was formed it acquired properties in Galveston and Houston. Roots was also a director of the Texas and St. Louis Railroad and treasurer of the Texas and California Stage Company. He was a stockholder of the Citizens' Street Railway Company and of S. B. Kirby's sewing machine company, both in Little Rock. He helped draft a charter to reform Little Rock city government and was appointed to the city board of public affairs that was created to solve a financial crisis in 1885. He also joined former governor Powell Clayton in the Eureka Springs Railroad and Improvement Company, which developed the Crescent Hotel in Eureka Springs.

Roots was an Arkansas booster. He promoted the state to investors and immigrants and was the first president of the state board of immigration. To tout the state, he attended national expositions, where his speeches received wide press coverage. He supported education and institutions for people with handicaps. For many years he was treasurer of the Episcopal Diocese of Arkansas, and he also held the highest offices among the state Masons. One of his last contributions was to negotiate a property trade between the federal government and the city of Little Rock. As a result of the transactions, the federal government transferred the arsenal grounds, now McArthur Park, to the city. In return, the state legislature ceded one thousand acres across the river to the federal government, which named the facilities on this land in honor of Logan H. Roots. A diabetic, Roots died at the age of fifty-two after a brief illness.

[The Logan Holt Roots Letters are in Archives and Special Collections, Ottenheimer Library, University of Arkansas at Little Rock. The "Letters of Logan Roots, 1840–1887" are held by the Arkansas History Commission. An obituary appears in the *Arkansas Gazette*, May 31, 1893. Roots's public life is well documented in the *Gazette*.]

FRANCES MITCHELL ROSS

ROSE, URIAH MILTON (Mar. 5, 1834–Aug. 12, 1913) lawyer, judge, ambassador, was born in Bradford, Kentucky, to Joseph Rose, a physician, and Nancy Simpson.

In 1853, five years after being orphaned, Uriah graduated from Transylvania Law School at Lexington, Kentucky, and married Margaret T. Gibbs of Lebanon, Kentucky. A few months later they moved to Batesville, Arkansas, where, after taking a year to prepare himself, he began his practice of law. Several years after arriving in Arkansas, he was appointed by Governor Conway as chancellor of Pulaski County, which required him to travel to Little Rock regularly.

When the Confederate state government moved from Little Rock to Washington, Arkansas, Rose also moved his family there from Batesville. While living in Washington with few judicial duties, he was appointed Confederate state historian with the rank of major, and traveled to Richmond, Virginia, to record the name of each Arkansan serving in the Confederate army. Returning through Jackson, Mississippi, he left his records in a warehouse for safekeeping, intending to return after the war to retrieve them. When Union forces overran the city, the warehouse was burned, destroying the records.

After the war, Rose and his family moved to Little Rock, where he set up a law practice in partnership with George C. Watkins, former chief justice of the state supreme court. The partnership was successful, and Rose and Watkins became the state's premier lawyers, with other lawyers around the state turning to them for appeals to the state supreme court. The firm continued in Little Rock into the twentieth century as Rose, Hemingway, Cantrell, and Loughborough (including George B. Rose, his son) and in 1997 continues as the Rose Law Firm.

In 1874, in the midst of an armed conflict to decide the proper governor of the state which became known as the Brooks-Baxter war, U. M. Rose went to President Ulysses S. Grant to advocate Baxter's case directly. After Rose's presentation, the president declared Baxter the governor of Arkansas, ending the "war."

On at least two occasions Rose was proposed in the state legislature as United States senator. He asked that his name be withdrawn on both occasions. He did agree to serve the state in 1877 as a member of a three-man commission appointed by the governor to bring the state's finances out of the chaos created before the war with the issuance of various bonds.

Rose was courteous, slender, tall, and diplomatic. His son said, "It seemed impossible for him to do an ungraceful act, as it was impossible for him to utter an unbecoming speech." He was much sought after as a speaker; his speeches were cerebral, but also witty, amusing, and eloquent. His legal practice was various; it included jury trials and several dozen cases appealed to the United States Supreme Court.

His reputation as the state's ablest lawyer spread very quickly, and he was asked to present talks across the country. He appeared on many occasions before the United States Supreme Court during the last quarter of the nineteenth century. Supreme Court justice Stanley Matthews, when asked who was the ablest lawyer appearing before the court one year, replied: "The ablest lawyer ... was U. M. Rose of Arkansas." United States Supreme Court justice Felix Frankfurter described Rose as "one of the luminaries of our profession—not merely a very distinguished practitioner but a highly cultivated, philosophical student of civilization and of the role of law and the lawyers in progress of civilization ... [who] inspired me in my formative years as a lawyer."

In 1878 a group of attorneys from twenty-one states, including U. M. Rose as the only member from Arkansas, founded the American Bar Association. In 1901 he was elected the association's twenty-fourth president. Before and after his tenure as president, he was a very active and highly regarded member.

After the creation of the American Bar Association, several attorneys met in 1882 in the office of Judge Rose "for the purpose of providing for the organization of a State Bar Association." Rose was asked to make all necessary arrangements for holding an initial convention at which he was elected chairman of the executive committee.

In October 1905 President Theodore Roosevelt heard Rose present a toast to the president on behalf of the state at a luncheon in Roosevelt's honor. As a result of that meeting and Rose's stature and reputation in the national legal community, Roosevelt appointed Rose as one of three United States ambassadors to the Second Hague Peace Conference in April 1907, where he served with distinction.

By act of Congress each state is entitled to place statues of two of its citizens in the United States Capitol. In 1915 the Arkansas legislature, "because of the distinguished civic services and the eminent virtues and abilities of the late U. M. Rose" decided it was proper that his statue be erected there in size "not less than life."

Rose died at home in Little Rock. A tireless reader, especially of history, memoirs, and poetry, he left a library of over eight thousand volumes, which was donated to the Little Rock public library at his death. On the day of his funeral, all of the state, county, and city public offices were closed in his honor. He is buried at Oakland Cemetery in Little Rock next to his wife.

[Sources include U. M. Rose, *U. M. Rose: Memoirs and Addresses*, ed. George I. Jones (1914); John M. Harrell, *The Brooks and Baxter War: A History of the Reconstruction Period in Arkansas* (1893); Calvin DeArmond Davis, *The United States and the Second Hague Peace Conference* (1975); and George B. Pugh, "U. M. Rose: Twenty-fourth President," *American Bar Association Journal*, vol. 14, no. 1 (1928): 13–17.]

ALLEN W. BIRD II

RUST, JOHN DANIEL (Sept. 6, 1892–Jan. 20, 1954), inventor of the first practical spindle cotton picker, was born near Necessity, Stephens County, Texas, to Benjamin Daniel Rust, a farmer and schoolteacher, and Susan Minerva Burnett, a homemaker. As a youngster John did farm work and displayed an aptitude for mechanical tinkering. His parents died when he was sixteen, and he drifted around Texas, Oklahoma, and Kansas. In the early 1920s, while working in Kansas City, he bought a drafting board and enrolled in a correspondence course to learn mechanical drafting.

Rust was intrigued with the challenge of building a mechanical cotton picker. Other inventors had used a spindle with barbs, which twisted the fibers onto the spindle and pulled the cotton lock from the boll. But the spindle soon became clogged with cotton. How could the cotton be stripped off the barbs? Rust suddenly hit on the answer: use a smooth, moist spindle. As he recalled later: "The thought came to me one night after I had gone to bed. I remembered how cotton used to stick to my fingers when I was a boy picking in the early morning dew. I jumped out of bed, found some absorbent cotton and a nail for testing. I licked the nail and twirled it in the cotton and found that it would work."

He went back to Texas to live with a sister in Weatherford. He assembled the first working model in her garage, and tested it on ten artificial stalks set up on a board. The machine picked ninety-seven out of a hundred locks of cotton.

He continued testing with funds invested by family and friends. In 1928 his brother Mack, who held a degree in mechanical engineering from the University of Texas, joined him. Rust was issued his first patent in 1933. Eventually, he and his brother owned forty-seven patents.

During the Great Depression the Rust brothers began a migration in search of financial support. As a young man, John Rust had pondered the socialist ideas that circulated in the Southwest. In 1930 they moved to Louisiana's Newllano cooperative community, which invested in their project. After two years John and Mack moved on to New Orleans, where they chartered the Southern Harvester Company; next they went to Lake Providence, where local planters financed their experiments.

From 1924 to 1927 John was married to Faye Pinkston; they had two children. In 1933 he and Thelma Ford of Leesville, Louisiana, married. They had no children.

In 1934, still in pursuit of financial backers, the Rust brothers relocated to Memphis, Tennessee, the center of the Cotton South, and founded the Rust Cotton Picker Company, successor to the Southern Harvester Company. On August 31, 1936, the Rust picker was demonstrated at the Delta Experiment Station in Stoneville, Mississippi. Though the demonstration attracted national press coverage, it produced mixed results. The machine knocked cotton to the ground and accumulated bits of leaves and stems in the staple it picked, lowering the grade and of course the price. But it did pick cotton, and the Rust Cotton Picker Company hoped to have five hundred machines ready for the picking season in 1937.

The Rust machine sent a shock wave through the country. The reality of a machine that would actually pick cotton loomed over the South, potentially eliminating jobs and raising the specter of social convulsions in the midst of the depression. The sharecropper–crop lien system which had been in place since the end of slavery would certainly collapse. Millions of black sharecroppers would surely migrate to northern cities in search of employment that did not exist.

The Rust Cotton Picker Company, however, lacked financing for commercial production. The Rust brothers could build a few prototypes, but the production of thousands of machines required the resources of a large company. In addition, Rust was not convinced that his machine possessed the durability required in a commercial product. The brothers' partnership dissolved, and Mack Rust moved to Arizona.

As the Rust company slipped into bankruptcy, International Harvester Corporation of Chicago, Illinois, announced in 1942 that it had a production-ready model of a mechanical cotton picker. International Harvester (IH) had spent $5.25 million over two decades to develop a spindle-type picker. Unlike Rust's, their picker used a barbed spindle, which improved its affinity for cotton fibers. However, the scarcity of steel during World War II delayed production. In 1948 International Harvester opened a new manufacturing plant in Memphis, and became the first company to produce commercially a mechanical cotton picker.

Though bankruptcy left Rust nothing but his drafting board, he set out in 1943 to redesign his spindle device in order to make it more reliable. At last his efforts paid off in two contracts. After the war, the Allis-Chalmers Manufacturing Company of Milwaukee, Wisconsin, began the manufacture of pickers in Gadsden, Alabama, using the Rust patents. In 1949 Rust entered into another agreement with the Ben Pearson Company of Pine Bluff, Arkansas, a company known for archery equipment. Rust moved to Pine Bluff to act as engineering consultant. Pearson went on to market Rust pickers internationally.

The Rust cotton picker was finally a commercial success, and Rust, after years of hardship, became a wealthy man. He repaid his sponsors, established scholarships at colleges in Arkansas and Mississippi, and toyed with a universal language which he called "Plaantauk." His death occurred at Pine Bluff just as the use of mechanical cotton pickers moved the South into a revolutionary new era of agribusiness.

[The University of Memphis Library has a small collection of Rust Papers. Rust told his own story in "The Origin and Development of the Cotton Picker," *West Tennessee Historical Society Papers* 7 (1953): 38–56. See also Donald Holley, "The Second Great Emancipation: The Rust Cotton Picker and How It Changed Arkansas," *AHQ* 52 (Spring 1993): 44–77.

Contemporary accounts include Oliver Carlson, "The Revolution in Cotton," *American Mercury* 34 (Sept. 1935): 129–36; Robert Kenneth Straus, "Enter the Cotton Picker: The Story of the Rust Brothers' Invention," *Harpers* 173 (Sept. 1936): 386–95; "Mr. Little Ol' Rust," *Fortune* 46 (Dec. 1952): 150–52, 198–205. See also James H. Street, *The New Revolution in the Cotton Economy: Mechanization and Its Consequences* (1957); and Tom Honeycutt, "The Second Great Emancipator: Eccentric Inventor John Rust Changed the Face of Modern Agriculture," *Arkansas Times* 11 (Feb. 1985): 76–78, 81–82.]

DONALD HOLLEY

SAMUELS, ROBERT G. (middle name unknown) (1846?–?), a leader of the Republican Party, was born to a family in bondage to Nick Trammell, a member of an outlaw gang led by John Murrell. After Trammell, a slave trader, tired of the outlaw life, he moved to Washington, Arkansas. Here he traded Robert and his mother and sister to a merchant and planter named David Block in return for some land. Robert's mother married a slave, Richard Samuels, who belonged to the Jett family.

Bob Samuels grew up under the slave regime to become, in the words of Judge Alfred H. Carrigan, "one of the most noted slaves of Hempstead County." This appears to have been because of his intelligence and education. His mother was Block's chief housekeeper, and his stepfather was a skilled blacksmith. Together, they probably had some influence in securing him an education.

Following the end of the Civil War, the Samuels family prospered. Richard Samuels was elected as a delegate to the Arkansas Constitutional Assembly in 1867 and as a member of the Arkansas General Assembly in 1868, and he served as sheriff and clerk of Hempstead County.

During this time Robert Samuels gained prominence to the point that he became respected by both the black and the white people of Hempstead County. Realizing that racial strife could work to the detriment of black people, he used his influence, in the words of historian Charlean Moss Williams, to do a "noble part in holding back insurrections among the disgruntled Negroes of the county and used his influence effectively on many an occasion when riot seemed inevatable [sic]."

Samuels struggled for civil rights through peaceful means. In 1912 he was one of the leaders of the Hempstead County Suffrage League that successfully opposed the adoption of the proposed constitutional Amendment Eleven, the "Grandfather Clause," which, if adopted, would have prevented black citizens from voting in Arkansas.

Samuels was also a member of the Republican Party in Hempstead County. For many years he was the county party's secretary as well as a delegate to many state party conventions. He was especially active in fighting the "Lily-Whites," who wished to expel all of the blacks from the state GOP. In 1914 when the Lily-Whites were victorious in Pulaski County, Samuels and his associates were able to hold the fort in Hempstead County. However, in 1916 the Lily-Whites held a county convention and sent a delegation that was seated by the state convention. This led to the blacks being frozen out of the county GOP. But Samuels fought on, and by 1930 Lily-Whitism was eliminated from the county and state GOP.

In addition to these pursuits, Samuels was a farmer in Ozan Township, Hempstead County. According to historian Llewellyn W. Williamson, Samuels "served as a fountain of information for white and black in Washington for more than a half century."

His wife's name was Sarah (maiden name unknown), and they had two sons and three daughters.

In light of Robert Samuels's accomplishments and his prominence as one of the leading black Republicans in Arkansas, it is surprising to find that practically nothing has been written about him. He deserves to be remembered.

[Alfred H. Carrigan's assessment of Samuels is in Scrapbook 4, Hempstead County, in the Southwest Arkansas Regional Archives in Washington, Arkansas. These archives also contain the Charlean Moss Williams Collection, folder 43, "Samuels, Robert G.," and copies of the *Washington Telegraph* for June 12, 1908, Apr. 12 and May 3, 1912, July 9, 1914, and Aug. 25, 1916.

The Hempstead County 1880 census book is in the Arkansas History Commission.

Other sources are Llewellyn W. Williamson, *Black Footsteps around Hempstead County* (1977); and George P. Rawick, ed., *The American Slave: A Composite Autobiography*, vol. 10, *Arkansas Narratives*, pt. 6 (1972).]

CHARLES J. RECTOR

SANDERS, IRA E. (May 6, 1894–Apr. 9, 1985), rabbi and social activist, son of Daniel and Pauline Sanders, was born at Rich Hill, Missouri. From his earliest training he was given a love of all things Jewish. He admired the writings of the Hebrew prophets, especially in the words, "He hath showed thee, O Man, what is good; and what doth the Lord require of thee, but to do justly and to love mercy, and to walk humbly with thy God?" (Micah 6:8). After his graduation from the (Reform) Hebrew Union College in Cincinnati, he received a master's degree from Columbia University and was ordained to the rabbinate in 1919. He immediately began serving as rabbi of Congregation Keneseth Israel in Allentown, Pennsylvania, then served as an associate rabbi for two years at Temple Israel in New York City. From there he was selected to become spiritual leader of Congregation B'nai Israel in Little Rock. He married Selma Loeb in 1922, and they had one child, Flora.

The prophets' teaching of justice and mercy was translated by Sanders into a lifelong interest in social action. When he came to Arkansas in 1926, he immediately worked toward the establishment of a school of social work. Through his efforts the Little Rock School of Social Work, the forerunner of the University of Arkansas School of Social Work, opened in 1927 with Sanders as its first dean. He taught sociology at the University of Arkansas for sixteen years. As America entered the Great Depression, many of the students he had trained filled the ranks of social workers needed for relief programs. His circle of influence widened as he served as the second president of the Little Rock Council of Social Agencies and as the first chairman of the Pulaski County Public Welfare Commission (later part of the federal Works Progress Administration). He was a founder and president of the Arkansas Human Betterment League and a founder of the Urban League of Greater Little Rock. He helped found the Arkansas Lighthouse for the Blind and the Arkansas Eugenics Association (later called the Planned Parenthood Association).

Part of his responsibility as rabbi was to prepare the children of his congregation for their confirmations at age fifteen. Several young men of B'nai Israel were later ordained as rabbis. Sanders not only was respected by his own congregation, but he also won veneration among non-Jews. His gift of oratory was exceptional; congregants and visitors were often mesmerized by his eloquent voice as he forcefully, yet beautifully, delivered the prophets' messages. He became a sought-after speaker in Arkansas. He debated the well-known lawyer Clarence Darrow in 1930 on the subject "Is Man Immortal?" before an overflow crowd. Though no winner was declared, many of those who attended gave the debate to Sanders, who approached the subject philosophically, whereas Darrow had appealed to the audience personally and emotionally. Sanders's defense of man's immortality was remembered for years.

Shortly after coming to Little Rock, he first encountered the South's "Jim Crow" laws on a bus ride from the temple to his home. From that time forward until his death, he worked toward improving race relations. He was outspoken in favor of the integration of Central High School in 1957, appearing before the state legislature to urge compliance in Arkansas regarding the United States Supreme Court's 1954 *Brown v. Board of Education* school desegregation decision.

He served for forty-one years on the Little Rock Public Library Board. He was on the boards of the Arkansas Tuberculosis Association and the Arkansas Association for Mental Health. He was a member of the national executive board of the Union of American Hebrew Congregations (Reform), and he helped found the Jewish Welfare Fund in Arkansas and the Arkansas Jewish Assembly, an umbrella group which from 1932 to 1951 sought to bring together and spiritually nourish the scattered Jews of Arkansas.

During the 1960s Sanders helped establish the Arkansas Council on Brotherhood of the National Conference of Christians and Jews. He assisted in nineteen bond drives for the State of Israel. In 1967 the deputy director general of Israel's Ministry of Foreign Affairs presented him with an award for service to Israel.

Sanders wrote numerous articles and, with Rabbi E. E. Palnick, wrote the centennial history of Congregation B'nai Israel. An avid reader, he was dismayed when he lost his eyesight during the last few years of his life. Several of his congregants came and read to him regularly, and he found comfort in recorded books on tape. He was working on his autobiography at the time of his death in Little Rock.

[Sources include the *Arkansas Democrat,* June 3, 1951 (Sunday Magazine), and Apr. 9, 1985; "Testimonial Dinner Honoring Rabbi Ira E. Sanders," program, June 11, 1951; the *Arkansas Gazette,* Feb. 21, 1954, June 12, 1983, Apr. 9, 1985; Carolyn Gray LeMaster, *A Corner of the Tapestry: A History of the Jewish Experience in Arkansas, 1820s–1990s* (1994); and Mark K. Bauman and Berkley Kalin, eds., *The Quiet Voices: Southern Rabbis and Black Civil Rights, 1880s to 1990s* (1997).]

CAROLYN GRAY LEMASTER

SARASIN (variously Saracen, Sarrasin, Sarasin) (?–1832?), Quapaw war chief, is believed to be a descendant of François Sarasin, a French interpreter at Arkansas Post during the eighteenth century, but his parents are unknown.

Sarasin became a legend among Arkansas settlers for rescuing white children captured by Indians raiding in the territory. Many versions of this story in Arkansas folklore, probably not all true, indicate the high regard in which Sarasin was held by his white neighbors.

One story containing the basic elements of the legend concerns the capture of a trapper's two little children, taken from their home by a Chickasaw raiding party. Sarasin went to the children's mother and vowed to rescue them. He rowed down the river until he came upon the Chickasaw camp near Arkansas Post. In the middle of the night, he went into the camp and saw the children. He lifted up his tomahawk and gave the Quapaw war cry. The Chickasaws, fearing that Quapaw warriors were upon them, fled. Sarasin returned the children unharmed to their mother.

White friendship for Sarasin did not extend to the Quapaw nation. Settlers and territorial officials, coveting valuable Quapaw land on the Arkansas River, began to call for the removal of the Quapaws in the 1820s. In the tragic ordeal which followed, Sarasin made his greatest contribution to his people.

In the treaty of 1824, the Quapaws ceded their land, which extended from the mouth of the Arkansas River to Little Rock and southwest to the Ouachita River, to the United States. In return they received land among the Caddos on the Red River and a two-thousand-dollar annual annuity. The treaty also reserved land along the Arkansas River for eleven mixed-blood Quapaws, including Sarasin, who received eighty acres.

The Quapaws moved to the Caddo country in early 1826, but met with disaster. Floods destroyed crops; starvation killed sixty people, including members of Sarasin's family; and bureaucratic confusion undermined the Quapaws' confidence in the government's agents. After six months there, Sarasin broke with Heckaton, the principal chief, and led one-fourth of the nation back to the land reserved for him on the Arkansas River.

Sarasin and other leaders of the Arkansas band met in council on January 28, 1827, and signed a letter to President John Quincy Adams. They claimed that starvation and the resulting divisions among the Quapaws had forced them to return to Arkansas. The federal Indian agent, they charged, had acted like a tyrant and denied them their part of the annuity. The council expressed the desire to remain in Arkansas and asked the president to protect them from further threat of removal. They also requested that the young men be taught to plow and the women to spin and weave.

The federal government responded by awarding one-fourth of the Quapaws' annuity to the Arkansas band. This was done despite the protests of the Indian agent, who claimed Sarasin had been appointed war chief without the consent of the Quapaws. Sarasin, the agent charged, had overreached his authority and challenged the leadership of Heckaton, though the majority of the nation opposed Sarasin. Sarasin and the other leaders accused the agent of allowing the illegal sale of liquor among the Quapaws and the Caddos.

The federal government, in hopes of persuading Sarasin and his band to leave Arkansas again, prohibited them from using the annuity money to buy land. Many Quapaws became squatters on land near Pine Bluff, farming and hiring themselves out to pick cotton and hunt game for white families. Sarasin used the money to lay the foundation for a Quapaw future in Arkansas. He persuaded George Izard, the governor of Arkansas Territory, to buy agricultural implements with the annuity. He arranged with Izard to send ten Quapaw boys to school. Sarasin recognized that the Quapaws had to overcome their dependency on whites, who provided them with manufactured goods and repaired their implements.

By the 1830s most of the Quapaws had returned to Arkansas. Heckaton abandoned the Red River settlements and led the remnant of the nation back to the Arkansas River. Sarasin rejected government suggestions that his people join the Cherokees or the Osages. (The latter he considered enemies of the Quapaws.) He and Heckaton pleaded with federal and territorial officials to allow the Quapaws to remain in Arkansas. Sarasin was promised only that he could remain in the territory.

In 1832 the Quapaws finally received annuity payments that had been denied them for years. It was too little and too late. Unable to buy land, many Quapaws were pushed off their farms by white settlers, and some found refuge only in the swamps. With their situation becoming more tenuous, the Quapaws signed the treaty of 1833 by which they agreed to move to the northeastern corner of Indian Territory.

To the chagrin of government officials, Sarasin did not go to the new reservation. Instead, he led three hundred Quapaws back to the Red River. He soon returned to Arkansas and lived in Jefferson County until his death. His gravestone records that he died in 1832; other evidence suggests that he lived beyond that date. His body was later buried in the cemetery of St. Joseph's Church in Pine Bluff under the inscription: "Friend of the Missionaries. Rescuer of captive children."

[See the *Arkansas Gazette;* Clarence Carter, ed., *The Territorial Papers of the United States,* vols. 20–21 (1953); and David W. Bizzell, ed., "A Report on the Quapaw: The Letters of Governor George Izard to the American Philosophical Society, 1825, 1827," *Pulaski County Historical Review* 29 (Winter 1981): 66–79.

See also W. David Baird, *The Quapaw Indians: A History of the Downstream People* (1980); Samuel D. Dickinson, "The Quapaw Journey to Red River," *Pulaski County Historical Review* 34 (Spring 1986): 14–23; Velma Seamster Nieberding, *The Quapaws (Those Who Went Downstream)* (1976); and Fred W. Allsopp, *Folklore of Romantic Arkansas,* vol. 1 (1931).]

JOSEPH PATRICK KEY

SAWYER, SOPHIA (May 5, 1792–Feb. 22, 1854), educator and missionary to the Cherokee, was born in Fitchburg, Massachusetts, to parents who are remembered only for their extreme poverty. Sophia never married.

Some innate quality, probably intelligence combined with determined ambition, brought Sawyer to the attention of Dr. Seth Payson of Rindge, New Hampshire, a Congregational clergyman, who took her into his household as a housemaid and sent her to school. With the support of Payson and a family named Raymond, she graduated from Reverend Joseph Emerson's female seminary at Byfield, Massachusetts. Sawyer had experience teaching while living with the Payson family and now had the academic qualifications to teach primary school. She did not have the funds to continue her education, but she did have religious zeal, a desire to prove worthy of those who had provided her education, and an ambition to achieve moral and religious perfection. She also believed that God intended this ambitious and eccentric woman to learn humility.

By 1823 she was teaching in a Cherokee Indian mission school in Georgia, supported by the American Board of Missions. For the next fourteen years she taught in Brainerd, New Echota, and Running Water. She ran afoul of Georgia authorities, breaking a law against teaching slaves by tutoring two young Negro pupils, the sons of Cherokee slaves. She refused to be intimidated and, after praying over the matter, informed the soldiers that she was on Indian territory and would obey Indian laws. Other missionaries had been jailed for refusing to obey Georgia laws, but not Sawyer.

In 1837 Sawyer returned to New Hampshire to visit friends and relatives and to recover from an illness. She had taught the children of John Ridge, a Cherokee leader, in Georgia, and he asked her to accompany his family when they were removed to new Indian territory in Oklahoma. In the fall of 1837 she joined the Ridge family. Ridge was not destined to find peace in his new home; he was murdered by enemies in the Cherokee Nation for collaborating with the United States Government by signing treaties allowing the Indians to be removed from the eastern United States to Oklahoma Territory.

Sawyer had established a school at the Ridge home in Honey Creek near present-day Southwest City, Missouri. After Ridge was slain, Sawyer considered maintaining her school, but became concerned that his widow, Sarah, was "sinking under the weight of sorrow." Sawyer joined Sarah and her children when they fled to Fayetteville, Arkansas. They arrived in Fayetteville on July 1, 1839, and Sawyer immediately set about to establish a new school. Her first pupils were fourteen Cherokee girls, daughters of prominent Indian families.

Classes were held first in a log hut and next on the second floor of a retail store. Legend has it that a thespian society rented the lower floor of the building. Sawyer's normally diligent supervision of her charges was intensified lest they become corrupted by the morals of the actors on the first floor. By October 1840 Sawyer was held in such high regard locally that Judge David Walker and his wife, Jane, deeded her a tract of land on which to construct permanent school buildings. Attendance had grown to fifty pupils, which included young boys as day students. Sawyer still reported to the American Board of Missions, but her school was financially self-sustaining.

The Fayetteville Female Seminary was considered an excellent school. Sawyer taught the primary grades, but hired other teachers for advanced subjects. The Reverend Cephus Washburn, a fellow missionary to the Cherokee and the founder of Dwight Mission, was among the instructors hired by Sawyer. In 1848 Governor Thomas S. Drew was a guest at the commencement ceremonies.

Sawyer took such a personal interest in her students that when they were sick she would nurse them herself at the respectable homes where they boarded. This is not to imply that Sawyer was a soft-hearted pushover. The daughter of a former student described her as "so dignified and reserved that no one thought of approaching her with the slightest familiarity." Her dress was puritanical, and her white lace cap served to reinforce her severity by its contrast with her prim face.

Sawyer died in Fayetteville from tuberculosis. She was first buried on her school grounds, but later became the first recorded burial in Fayetteville's Evergreen Cemetery. Five years after her death the seminary was incorporated. It was used as an infirmary after the Battle of Prairie Grove and was partially burned later in the Civil War. In 1923 a remaining building became a stable.

[See C. T. Foreman, "Miss Sophia Sawyer and Her School," *Chronicles of Oklahoma* 32 (Winter 1954–55); Mrs. A. G. Little, *Noted Daughters of Arkansas,* transcript of a paper read at the Charlevoix Chapter, D.A.R., Blytheville, Arkansas, Mar. 8, 1947; W. S. Campbell's *One Hundred Years of Fayetteville* (1928); "Standards High at City Seminary" in the *Northwest Arkansas Times* sesquicentennial edition, July 16, 1978; "Fayetteville Female Seminary Was City's Top Girls' School," *Northwest Arkansas Times* centennial edition, June 14, 1960; Margaret Ross, "Chronicles of Arkansas" in the *Arkansas Gazette,* Apr. 12, 1959; "Death of Miss Sawyer," Clara Bertha Eno Papers (Folder 4, item 32), Special Collections Division, University of Arkansas Libraries, Fayetteville; and Sophia Sawyer Papers (1814–1833), William L. Clements Library, University of Michigan.]

CASSANDRA MCCRAW

SCOTT, ANDREW HORATIO (Aug. 6, 1789–

Mar. 13, 1851), lawyer and judge, was born in Hanover County, Virginia, to Andrew Scott and Ellisabeth Ferguson. He grew up on the ragged edges of the westward expansion in Pennsylvania, Vincennes, Indiana Territory, and Ste. Genevieve, Territory of Missouri.

After floating down the Ohio River through perilous country to the French settlement of Ste. Genevieve shortly after the turn of the century, he read law under his brother John. Andrew followed in his brother's footsteps into jurisprudence and politics. He served two terms as clerk in the Missouri territorial legislature.

He moved a short distance to the west to an old Spanish iron-mining community, Potosi, where he worked for higher education standards. His efforts in the legislature resulted in the establishment of an academy in Potosi. In 1817 he was appointed a trustee of the school. Before leaving Potosi, he helped run one of the town's earliest mercantile businesses, Scott and Bates.

In March 1819 Scott was commissioned as sheriff of the newly formed Jefferson County in the Territory of Missouri. That same month, President James Monroe appointed him as a superior court judge in the newly created Territory of Arkansas. He reported to Arkansas Post for duty by July 4, 1819. He put into operation the first government at the territorial capital.

Before the capital moved to Little Rock in 1821, Scott was involved in a duel which resulted in the death of another superior court member, Judge Selden. Several years after his move to Little Rock, Scott, a small man of about 130 pounds, was involved in another incident which resulted in the death of 250-pound Edmund Hogan. Having acted in self-defense, Scott was absolved of all charges.

Scott, possibly the man who had more "firsts" to his name than anyone else in the area, was elected territorial circuit judge for the First District in 1827.

In the spring of 1829, he relocated his family northwest of Little Rock, to land previously held by the Cherokee Indians. He laid out a town which he named Scotia and helped to create the county of Pope the same year. Scotia was named the first county seat. Scott served as the first county judge of Pope County and also served as a representative in the territorial legislature from Pope County. Additionally, he was a delegate at the Constitutional Convention at Little Rock in 1936, in preparation for statehood that same year.

Both Andrew Scott and his brother John had counties named in their honor, Scott County, Arkansas, and Scott County, Missouri.

Andrew Scott and his wife, Eliza Jones, had eight children. He died unexpectedly at Norristown, Arkansas, a year after he completed his last official act, the enumeration of the 1850 U.S. Census for Pope County. He was first buried in the Dover Cemetery, but was reinterred in the Oakland Cemetery at Russellville, Arkansas. The vigor of his mind and clearness exhibited in his judicial opinions, published in the supreme court reports, give him prominence with the bar and bench of the state forever.

[See Russell P. Baker, *Township Atlas of Arkansas* (1984); Gregory Carrera, *The Founding of Arkansas Post, 1868* (1968); Clarence Edwin Carter, *The Territory of Arkansas, 1891–1825,* Superintendent of Documents, vol. 19, Washington, D.C.; Louis Houck, *A History of Missouri* (1908); James Logan, *Obits and Biographical Notes from Arkansas Newspapers, 1819–1845,* vol. 3; Bill McCuen,

Historical Report of the State of Arkansas (1986); William F. Pope, *Early Days of Arkansas* (1895); Margaret Ross, *Arkansas Gazette, The Early Years, 1819–1866* (1969); Firman A. Rozier, *The History of the Early Settlement of the Mississippi Valley* (1890).]

WANDA NEWBERRY GRAY

SEARCY, RICHARD (1792–Dec. 25, 1832), judge, proprietor of Batesville, was probably born in Granville County, North Carolina, to Polly and Reuben Searcy, a Revolutionary War veteran and circuit court clerk. However, Richard spent most of his early and formative years in Sumner County in north-central Tennessee.

In 1816 Searcy moved to Davidsonville in the Missouri Territory, where he became the Lawrence County court clerk under Judge Stephen F. Austin. While establishing himself in this huge county (thirty-two present counties include land once in Lawrence County), Searcy held several other important posts: postmaster, president of the board of commissioners of Davidsonville, and justice of the peace for Spring River Township. By the end of 1820, he had become not only a prominent civil servant but a significant landowner as well, owning over two thousand acres. His newly developed regional importance revealed itself in his appointment as secretary of the first Arkansas Territorial Legislature at Arkansas Post in February 1820. He was selected clerk-in-chief of the October 1821 session of the general assembly.

In this position Searcy witnessed the assembly granting Robert Bean and others "full and ample powers" to find the most appropriate place in the newly minted Independence County for a courthouse and a jail. The next day, Searcy, along with Joseph Hardin, Samuel Hall, and Charles Kelly, offered bonds of $250 each to become owners of the land and proprietors of the Independence County town that became Batesville. Their investment began to pay off almost immediately. The land was platted and ready for sale by 1821, and the courthouse and jail were indeed located there. The adjacent White River provided commercial and transportation advantages, and the new town began to grow.

Searcy did not confine his activities to land speculation, however. In 1821, with his law license in hand, he began a five-year stint as Second Circuit Court judge, a tenure that the *Arkansas Democrat* described in his obituary as one "characterized by sound judgment, unwavering fidelity, and correct decision." He stepped down from the bench on November 5, 1825, to "practice LAW in the several counties composing the second circuit, and in the Supreme Court of the Territory of Arkansas."

He spent the remaining seven years of his life as an attorney in Batesville. The fact that he could afford the only privately owned brick building in town as well as ten slaves speaks to his success in collecting fees, yet differing opinions existed over his personal style and speaking ability. According to John Hallum, Searcy was "a good writer, a fine advocate before a jury, a good lawyer before a court, and a pleasing, effective speaker to the people," but a critic claimed Searcy displayed "awkward gestures when pleading and a disagreeable delivery when speaking."

Even if Searcy did possess "awkward" physical and verbal habits they did not greatly impede him because he also possessed important and powerful friends. He was an attorney in Batesville for Robert Crittenden, secretary of Arkansas Territory and a Whig political power. Searcy conducted numerous transactions for Crittenden. He was also one of Joseph Hardin's representatives in Little Rock. Hardin was one of the four original proprietors of Little Rock, and he empowered Searcy to protect his "interest and claim in a certain pre-emption right situate at the Little Rock in the County of Pulaski—and more particularly to the making of the partition of said claim."

Searcy's most prominent legal undertaking also involved land disposition, this time on an even larger scale. In 1827 the Arkansas Superior Court faced 117 claims regarding Spanish land grants predating the Louisiana Purchase. Many prominent men had purchased land from James Bowie without proof of validity and, fearful of losing their money, had "every reputable lawyer in the territory, except Richard Searcy ...on one side of the case, and Sam Roane alone on the other." Roane asked Searcy to assist him, and together they asked for a continuance so they could learn Spanish and Spanish law and gather evidence in Louisiana. This motion was denied, and despite a relevant precedent in their favor, they lost their cases in 1827. However, in the end they received vindication when Congress, in 1831, overturned all 117 decisions.

In the interim, Searcy had a heated and very public falling out with his judicial successor, James Bates, over the particulars of a case Searcy argued before Bates, *Hawthorn v. Hightower*, and over different political allegiances. The feud cost Searcy dearly in the following years, effectively thwarting his political ambitions. After Robert Crittenden killed Congressman Robert Conway in a duel in 1827, he backed Searcy to run as a Whig for Conway's seat against Ambrose Sevier. With Bates actively campaigning against him, Searcy lost the special election to fill the vacant seat and also the regular 1829 election.

In the winter of 1830 Searcy fell ill. Hoping warm weather would reinvigorate him, he wintered in Cuba and later jouneyed to Texas. In the fall of 1832 in Batesville, Searcy contracted measles and died, leaving no survivors.

[Sources include Marion Stark Craig's transcriptions of the Lawrence County Circuit Court Minute Books (1816–1826) and the Lawrence County Deed Books (1815–1827) in the Lyon College library, Batesville. Many of Searcy's transactions are recorded in the Independence County Deed Books, particularly Books "A" and "B" in the Independence County Courthouse, Batesville. See the *Arkansas Gazette*, Dec. 18, 1827, Jan. 23, 1828, and an obituary Feb. 7, 1833. A reprint of a *Gazette* article, "Gazette Account of County Creation by Territorial Legislature, 1820," is in the *Independence County Chronicle* 1 (Autumn 1960): 39. The Stroud Collection in the Lyon College library holds several Searcy family papers. Searcy's will is in the Independence County Courthouse, and his probate records are in box 56 of the Independence County Chancery Court. See also *Batesville News Review* (Fall 1951); A. C. McGinnis, "Independence County Reaches 150th Year in 1970," *Independence County Chronicle* 12 (Spring 1970); William Pope, *Early Days in Arkansas* (1894); and "Early Settlers of Arkansas" in *The Spirit of the Times* (Dec. 22, 1849).]

BRAD AUSTIN

SEVIER, AMBROSE HUNDLEY (Nov. 10, 1801–Dec. 31, 1848), territorial delegate to Congress, United States senator, was born in Greene County, Tennessee, to John Sevier and Susannah Conway. He was the grandnephew of John Sevier, a Revolutionary War hero and the first governor of Tennessee. His cousins were leaders in Arkansas politics: Henry Wharton Conway founded the Democratic Party in Arkansas; James Sevier Conway was Arkansas's first state governor; and Elias Nelson Conway became the fifth governor.

Sevier came to Little Rock in late October 1820 to live with his cousin Henry Conway. In the second territorial legislature of 1821, the first assembly in the new capital of Little Rock, Sevier became clerk of the territorial House of Representatives. Two years later he was admitted to the bar and elected to the territorial lower house from Pulaski County. In 1827 his colleagues elevated him to the speakership.

On September 26, 1827, Sevier married Juliette E. Johnson, the eldest daughter of Superior Judge Benjamin Johnson. With this marriage, Sevier entered into another powerful political family. Judge Johnson's older brother, Richard Mentor Johnson of Kentucky, served in both Houses of Congress and as Martin Van Buren's vice president. From Sevier's union with Juliette came four children: Annie M., Mattie J., Elizabeth, and Ambrose H. Jr. Juliette Johnson's brother, Robert Ward Johnson, represented Arkansas in both Houses of Congress and in the Confederate Congress. Related by blood with the Conway family and through marriage with the Johnson family, Sevier became the central figure of a dynasty which dominated Arkansas politics from 1833 to 1860. Between the 1820s and the 1860s members of these families and their relations held offices for an aggregate number of 190 years.

Sevier assumed leadership of "the Dynasty" after the death in 1827 of territorial delegate Henry Conway, who was mortally wounded in a duel. (Sevier himself had fought a duel with future Whig congressman Thomas W. Newton two months earlier, but neither combatant was injured.) Conway had won election as territorial delegate in December; Sevier took his seat in Congress on February 13, 1828. He aligned himself with Andrew Jackson, and his group became the state Democratic Party. More than any other politician, Sevier was the one who secured Arkansas's statehood. President Jackson signed the legislation on June 15, 1836. Arkansas's first state legislature rewarded Sevier by electing him to a full six year term in the United States Senate.

Now at the pinnacle of his power within Arkansas, Sevier became an important figure in the Senate. According to one writer: "Sevier entered the Senate in this, its age of glory, and conquered it . . . He alone of Arkansas' pre-Civil War senators achieved any prominence in the chamber." During his twelve-year tenure Sevier chaired two major committees, Indian Affairs and Foreign Relations. His policies, in many ways, were those of a frontier senator. He eagerly supported Jackson's Indian removal policy, worked unsuccessfully to give free land in the West, and strongly backed efforts to secure all of Oregon for the United States. Sevier's expansionist views were quite popular with newly elected president James Polk and with the Democratic Party. He was chair of the Foreign Relations Committee between 1845 and 1848. During that time he ushered the Oregon Treaty through the Senate and supported the adminstration's war with Mexico.

As Sevier's power in the Senate waxed, his control over affairs back home waned a bit. Since the Democrats controlled the General Assembly in 1842, Sevier easily defeated his Whig opponent, yet within weeks the same legislature censured him for financial malfeasance regarding bonds associated with a failed Arkansas Real Estate Bank. Personal tragedy struck him when his wife died in 1845. In March 1848 Sevier resigned his seat at the behest of President Polk, who appointed him a peace commissioner in Mexico. There Sevier became ill and had to resign his commission in June. He recovered enough to return to Washington by July and returned to Little Rock by the end of August, but his health still suffered. Meanwhile, Solon Borland, his replacement in the Senate, built support for his own candidacy. Borland, the editor of the Democratic Party's main newspaper, was supposed to keep the seat only until Sevier could reclaim it. In November 1848 Borland surprised Sevier by upending him by only four votes in the legislature. Sevier died by year's end. He is buried on his plantation in Pulaski County.

[See Brian Walton, "Ambrose Hundley Sevier in the United States Senate, 1836–1848," *AHQ* 32 (Spring 1973): 25–60; and James M. Woods, *Rebellion and Realignment: Arkansas's Road to Secession* (1987).]

JAMES M. WOODS

SHAVER, DOROTHY (July 29, 1893–June 29, 1959), business executive, was born at Center Point, Howard County, Arkansas, the daughter of James Shaver and Sally Borden. Her maternal grandfather was Benjamin Borden, editor of the *Arkansas Gazette*. Her paternal grandfather, Robert G. Shaver, was a Confederate commander. Her family moved from Howard County in 1898, for her father wanted to take advantage of the booming economy of the newly created railroad town of Mena. James Shaver became a prominent lawyer and citizen in Mena. Dorothy Shaver attended the University of Arkansas for two years, then returned to Mena to teach school. In 1914 she was one of the four young female teachers not rehired by the Mena School Board,

evidently because they attended a local dance. She taught at Prescott during 1914–15, then returned to the Mena schools for the 1915–16 school year. She then resigned, and with her sister Elsie left Arkansas for good to go to Chicago.

By 1919 the Shaver sisters were living in New York City, and the *Mena Star* reported they were having great success with Elsie's creation of the "Five Little Shaver Dolls," which were "unusually artistic and charming rag dolls." Elsie did the designing, and Dorothy did the marketing. Dorothy Shaver's marketing skills proved to be the catalyst for her career. In 1921 the fashionable Lord and Taylor specialty store hired Shaver as a comparison shopper. Her rise was "rapid and brilliant." She organized a bureau of fashion in 1924 and soon Lord and Taylor set the pace of style in New York. In 1927 Shaver was elected to the board of directors. In 1931 she became a vice president.

She challenged Parisian domination of fashion by encouraging and developing American designing talent, creating a one-thousand-dollar award system to honor American designers. Sixty young designers were promoted by Lord and Taylor, among them Adrian Potter, Merry Hill, Nettie Rosenstein, Anne Fogarty, Rose Marie Reid, Pauline Trigère, and Lilly Daché.

In 1937 Dorothy became first vice president. She now directed the entire advertising, fashion promotion, public relations, and display programs connected with Lord and Taylor. The store's advertising "took on an elusive feminine quality . . . with an artistic taste in window display and in advertising." Among her innovations were the Lord and Taylor Christmas windows, featuring animated figures and holiday music rather than merchandise. She became known as a woman "sizzling with ideas, not only with design, but about politics and the world in general." During the war years the United States Quartermaster Corps consulted Shaver in the selection of merchandise and the design of women's uniforms.

In December 1945 Dorothy was elected president of the store with its ten-story building on Fifth Avenue housing eighty-three departments. The press recognized her appointment as a landmark for women and praised her "shrewd insight," her "revolutionary thinking," and her "outstanding record in merchandising." She initiated a new concept of establishing suburban branch stores. Sales rose from $30 million in 1945 to $100 million in 1959. The Associated Press voted

Shaver as the outstanding woman in business in 1946 and 1947, praising her "distinguished leadership and taste in fashion."

She served on numerous civic, national, and industrial boards and commissions. A fellow of the Metropolitan Museum of Art, she helped establish its Costume Institute. A grateful Society of New York Dress Designers honored her for support of American design in 1953. She was a trustee of the Parsons School of Design.

Dorothy Shaver died at Hudson, New York, following a stroke. A funeral service was held in New York; she was buried Texarkana, Arkansas, in the family plot. Her estate amounted to a little over one million dollars, most of which she left to her sister Elsie.

[See Eleanor Clyner and Lillian Erlich, *Modern American Career Women* (1959), and *Notable American Women: The Modern Period* (1980), Barbara Sicherman and Carol Hurd Green, eds. See also Harold Coogan, "Dorothy Shaver: Mena to Fifth Avenue," in the *Mena Star,* Sept. 13, 1987; and the *Arkansas Gazette,* Nov. 3, 1946. This entry is also based on interviews with Faith Kirsch, June 8, 1986, and Agnes Shaver, Jan. 8, 1987, and correspondence with Agnes Shaver, June through Dec. 1986.]

HAROLD COOGAN

SHAVER, ROBERT GLENN (Apr. 18, 1831–Jan. 13, 1915), Confederate commander, was born at Acadia Post Office in Sullivan County, fourteen miles southwest from Bristol, exactly on the line between Virginia and Tennessee. After attending Law School at Emory and Henry College, he moved with his parents in 1850 to Arkansas, about twenty miles east of Batesville, in what was then Lawrence, now Sharp County. He married Adelaide Louise Ringgold June 10, 1856.

When the Civil War erupted in 1861, Shaver received orders from the Military Board of Arkansas to raise a regiment. In response to his call, enough volunteers showed up to create thirty-two companies, of which ten companies were organized into the Seventh Arkansas Regiment. Shaver was chosen unanimously as colonel. He became known as "Fighting Bob" by his men, who recognized his strong personality which was characterized by a strong intellect and a genial disposition.

The Seventh Arkansas Regiment became known as "Shaver's Regiment." Swett's artillery battery of Shaver's unit fired the first artillery shots in the pivotal battle at Shiloh, Tennessee, in 1862. During this battle Shaver was seriously wounded in the head and in his left side by an exploding shell. He lay unconscious for several hours, and he suffered from these wounds until the end of his life.

After the Union victory at Shiloh, Shaver's troops saw action in Arkansas. Shaver was a commander at the Battle of Prairie Grove in northwestern Arkansas. In 1864 General Tappan mentioned Shaver in his battle report for "gallantry and faithful service" for his role in the clash at Jenkin's Ferry in southern Arkansas. As the war was nearing its conclusion in 1865, Shaver received orders in March to report to Texas to take command of Galveston. Reaching Marshall, Texas, with his troops, he received news of General Lee's surrender at Appomattox. Shaver took his command to Shreveport, Louisiana, and surrendered to General Herron. Shaver's surrender was the last organized Confederate force to surrender. Shaver's troops came mainly from north Arkansas. He procured from Herron a large steamboat, eight months of rations, a supply of seed potatoes, and took his men to Jacksonport, Arkansas, arriving there June 20, 1865.

Living at Jacksonport, Shaver soon found himself getting caught up in the problems of postwar Arkansas. He later claimed to be the state commander of the Klu Klux Klan, a claim modern historians dispute. By 1868 he was indicted on charges of murder, arson, treason, and robbery. He fled Arkansas to British Honduras, his family eventually joining him. After Elisha Baxter had been elected governor of Arkansas in 1872, Shaver returned and all charges were dropped. He was appointed sheriff of newly created Howard County in western Arkansas. He lived at Center Point until 1900, when he joined his son James, who was an attorney in the newly created railroad town of Mena.

He had a full life of reminiscences. He was appointed commander of the state guard and the reserve militia, receiving the rank of general that had eluded him during the war. He also served as commander of the Arkansas Division of United Confederate Veterans. He was interviewed by newspapers, and he traveled to Confederate reunion camps across the state. In March 1910 the Arkansas Division of the United Daughters of the Confederacy selected Shaver to dedicate a monument at Shiloh Battlefield to all the Arkansas men who fought and died there. Shaver selected the site, known as the "Hornet's Nest," and the dedication took place in September 1911. By 1914 he was in failing health and by

December was living with a daughter at Foreman, Arkansas, where he died. His widely attended funeral and burial was held at Center Point, where he was buried in uniform next to his wife and two small children. Three of his children are buried at Mena's White Oak Cemetery, and one son is buried at Texarkana.

[See the *Mena Star,* Apr. 17, 1907, Oct. 5, 1907, June 26, 1909, Apr. 9, 1914, Jan. 14, 1915, and Jan. 16, 1915; the *Arkansas Gazette,* Mar. 3, 1897; the *Mena Weekly Star,* May 30, 1907; the *Polk County Democrat,* Sept. 11, 1911; and the *Independence County Chronicle* 19 (July 1978): 70–74. See also John Dimitry and John M. Harrell, *Confederate Military History: Louisiana and Arkansas,* Clement A. Evans, ed. (1899); and Harold Coogan, "Robert Glenn Shaver," *Mena Star,* Nov. 23, 1987.]

HAROLD COOGAN

SHEPPERSON, CARRIE LENA FAMBRO STILL (c. 1868–1927), teacher and mother of William Grant Still, the composer and musician, was born in rural Georgia near Milledgeville to Anne Fambro, a freedwoman. Family tradition averred that her father was a white man, possibly a Spaniard who was a landowner in Florida.

Encouraged by her mother to pursue her education, Carrie Fambro graduated from Atlanta University in 1886. In 1893, while teaching at Alabama State Agricultural and Mechanical College, she met William Grant Still, a colleague and 1892 graduate of Alcorn Agricultural and Mechanical College at Lorman, Mississippi. The couple married and settled in Woodville, Mississippi, in 1894. On May 11, 1895, their son, William Grant Still Jr., was born at Piney Woods. The elder Still died that year at the age of twenty-four.

After her husband's death Carrie Still moved to Little Rock, where her mother lived with her sister Laura. In 1896 she secured a position teaching English at Union School, built in 1877 as Little Rock's first school for black children. Carrie lived with her son and her mother in a house in an integrated neighborhood. In 1904 she married Charles B. Shepperson, a railway postal clerk, and he joined the household. Their union survived until his accidental drowning; the date is unknown.

Shepperson taught English in Little Rock for thirty years, at Union, Capital Hill, and at M. W. Gibbs High School.

Still Shepperson's unpaid public work provided an additional forum for her race work. The city school sys-

tem replaced Union School with Capital Hill, but inadequate funding did not provide for a library. (This was the Progressive/Jim Crow era of Governor Jeff Davis and his white man's government.) Still Shepperson organized and staged a school-sponsored and student-performed public program. The proceeds were donated to the school to establish a library at the new site. The benefit production was so successful that she inaugurated a series of annual productions at Capital Hill and later at Gibbs High School.

Up to 1917 Still Shepperson staged the programs in the school auditorium. But in 1918 she reserved the Kempner Theater in downtown Little Rock, a segregated venue in which blacks were restricted to the balcony. She secured both levels for two nights, Friday and Saturday. The shows sold out for both performances, in part because black people wanted to sit on the first floor.

Shepperson's race uplift in staging annual school productions reflected a sense of racial obligation or socially responsible individualism characteristic among black women engaged in community building. The annual programs provided a vehicle with which to mentor black youth and encouraged creative expression and academic skills among the students.

Shepperson was a leader of the Lotus Club, whose members met regularly to discuss books, current events, and research. At her death she had completed a manuscript. The topic is unknown; it was never published.

She was a teacher for over forty years, over thirty in Little Rock. At her death she was teaching at Gibbs High School.

[See the William Grant Still Collection, Special Collections Division, University of Arkansas Libraries, Fayetteville; Verna Arvey, *In One Lifetime* (1984); and Fon Louise Gordon, "Black Women in Arkansas," *Pulaski County Historical Review* 35 (Summer 1987): 26–37. See also Stephanie J. Shaw, *What a Woman Ought to Be and to Do* (1996), and Darlene Clark Hine, *Hine Sight: Black Women and the Re-Construction of American History* (1994).]

FON LOUISE GORDON

SHREVE, HENRY MILLER (Oct. 21, 1785–Mar. 6, 1851), steamboat captain and inventor, was born in Burlington County, New Jersey, to Israel Shreve and Mary Cokely. In 1788 Israel Shreve headed a wagon train to western Pennsylvania, where he settled his family a few miles from the town of Brownsville. Henry Shreve spent his youth in the area between the Youghiogheny and Monongahela Rivers, absorbing the sights and sounds of river life. He bought his first keelboat in 1807 and initiated a flourishing fur trade between St. Louis and Pittsburgh. In 1810 he set out for the lead mines run by the Sauk and Fox Indians on the Galena River. The first American to pilot a keelboat so far up the Mississippi system, Shreve struck a deal with the Indians and returned lead from that source to New Orleans.

Shreve watched with interest as the Fulton-Livingston group inaugurated steamboat trade on the Mississippi. Convinced that the design of their steamboat, the *New Orleans,* was inferior, Shreve invested in a steamboat designed for inland rivers by Daniel French, a Brownsville inventor. The *Enterprise* made its first voyage to New Orleans in 1814, just in time for Shreve to assist Andrew Jackson in that city's defense during the War of 1812. The *Enterprise* brought supplies to the troops, and Jackson assigned it to transport troops and munitions, most notably to Fort St. Philip south of the city. Shreve also convoyed a group of dawdling keelboats loaded with supplies to New Orleans from Natchez, and he transported a group of women and children fifty miles upriver to safety just before the main battle erupted. During the battle, he manned a twenty-four-pound gun.

In 1815 Shreve took the *Enterprise* all the way to Cairo, Illinois, something no steamboat had yet accomplished. His success encouraged him to design a steamboat better adapted to the Mississippi. The *Washington* had a low, shallow hull, two decks, and twin smokestacks. Despite an early explosion that resulted in several deaths, the *Washington* proved its utility, and Shreve's design became the standard on inland waters.

On January 2, 1827, Shreve was named superintendent of western river improvements by President John Quincy Adams. He began clearing obstructions from the Mississippi and Ohio Rivers, using the *Heliopolis,* a steam snagboat of his own design, twin hulls connected by beams and fitted with numerous contraptions for ramming embedded trees or hoisting snags. He cleared the Arkansas River of obstructions in the early 1830s, and by 1833 steamboats were docking regularly as far inland as Little Rock, Fort Smith, and Fort Gibson in eastern Oklahoma.

Shreve's battle with the Great Red River Raft brought him the most renown. Beginning in 1833 Shreve labored to clear approximately two hundred miles of obstructions, which hindered the settlement of southwest Arkansas and the upper Red River valley. He began somewhere between the Mississippi River and present-day Alexandria and worked his way northwestward toward present-day Shreveport. "The Raft," as it was known locally, consisted of tightly compacted dead trees that had fallen into the river during the frequent cave-ins following spring rains. In many places the Red was closed to navigation, and boats had to leave the river and navigate through a maze of bayous.

"I find public opinion much against the probability of removing the raft," Shreve reported to Charles Gratiot, secretary of war, in the spring of 1833, "but I am of a different opinion, and believe that I shall succeed." He spent the winter and spring months of the next few years slowly clearing the Great Raft, unable to work through the hot, humid summers. The raft was so solid in places that new trees grew from the driftwood accumulated in the middle of the riverbed. A congressional report later stated that one snag raised by the *Heliopolis* contained sixteen hundred cubic feet of timber, and could not have weighed less than sixty tons.

Shreve was working on the Raft in northern Louisiana in 1836 when local entrepreneurs incorporated a new town on the banks of the now free-flowing Red. In gratitude for his work they named the new town Shreveport.

He was relieved of his appointed office in 1841 by the new Whig administration of John Tyler. These changing political currents brought his work on the Great Raft to an end at Shreveport. Not until the 1870s was the Raft permanently conquered. At the end of his term Shreve was in charge of five snagboats, the last of which was named the *Henry M. Shreve.* Moving to St. Louis, Shreve spent his remaining years developing a three-hundred-acre farm and continuing to press the federal government for compensation for his invention of the snagboat. His work had saved the government hundreds of thousands of dollars, but Congress never appropriated adequate compensation.

After the death of his wife, Mary, in 1845, Shreve married Lydia Rodgers of Boston. He and his first wife had three children, and he and Lydia had two daughters. He is buried in Bellefontaine Cemetery in St. Louis, where his tombstone is in view of the Mississippi River he loved. Henry Miller Shreve in 1986 became one of the first inductees into the National River Hall of Fame in Dubuque, Iowa.

[See Henry Miller Shreve Letters, 1827–1841, Louisiana State University-Shreveport Archives; Edith McCall, *Conquering the Rivers: Henry Miller Shreve and the Navigation of America's Inland Waterways* (1984); U.S. Congress, House Report 383, 24th Congress, 1st session, 1836; Caroline S. Pfaff, "Henry Miller Shreve: A Biography," *Louisiana Historical Quarterly* 10 (Apr. 1927): 192–240; Edith McCall, *Mississippi Riverboatman: The Story of Henry Miller Shreve* (1986); Walter Havighurst, *Voices on the River: The Story of the Mississippi Waterways* (1964).]

JANET G. BRANTLEY

SLAUGHTER, TOM (Dec. 25, 1896–Dec. 9, 1921), bank robber and killer, was born in Bernice, Louisiana, but lived in Dallas, Texas, as a child. When he was fourteen years old, he was sent to live with an uncle in Pope County, Arkansas. There he stole a calf, was caught, and was sentenced to a year in the Arkansas Boys' Industrial Home. He escaped a few months later, returned to Russellville, and paraded before Sheriff Oates, who put him in jail. He escaped the next night. From then on Slaughter rarely failed to escape any jail he was in.

In 1916 he was arrested for a series of automobile thefts in Dallas. He escaped from the Dallas County jail, "one of the ... most strongly built in the Southwest— liberating seven other prisoners at the same time." Sentenced to six years in the Texas penitentiary, he escaped in July 1917, knocking out a guard with a shovel.

He formed a gang and terrorized the Southwest, robbing banks throughout the region. In 1917 he was caught and jailed in Nowata, Oklahoma, but he overpowered the jailer and fled. In 1918 Slaughter and his brother Dave were arrested in Oklahoma but escaped custody in Texas. Slaughter was apprehended and returned to the Huntsville, Texas, penitentiary, where he took a "pin and pricked hundreds of holes in his face and body, covered them with croton oil, which brought out a rash, ate two cakes of soap to bring about a fever and reported to the sick bay." Hospital officials diagnosed smallpox and isolated Slaughter, and again he escaped.

In 1919 the Slaughter gang stole twenty-four thousand dollars in a noon-day bank robbery in Petty, Texas. Slaughter and Fulton Green, a member of his gang, killed the cashier of a bank in Pennsylvania. Slaughter liked theatrics. In September 1920 he and his gang robbed a bank at Graham, Texas, on a Saturday afternoon when the town was filled with citizens.

In October Slaughter, accompanied by four men and two women, arrived in Hot Springs, Arkansas, where the group went on a drinking spree, disturbing the peace. Hot Springs police went to investigate, a gunfight followed, and Slaughter and Green killed Sheriff Row Brown and wounded officer Bill Wilson.

They fled to Oklahoma, formed a gang, and went to southern Kansas where they planned robberies at Sedan and Cedarville. Always flamboyant, Slaughter bought expensive clothes in Sedan, but he dropped a wad of money with the Nowata Bank's name on it. The store owner notified police, and Slaughter was arrested.

Meanwhile, citizens of Garland County, Arkansas, had made up a reward of five thousand dollars for the capture of Slaughter and Green. When their arrest was announced, Arkansas officials began extradition proceedings. Kansas officials did not want to release them, but the Hot Springs sheriff and the police chief used the reward money to bribe the Sedan sheriff, who transported the pair to Oklahoma, making extradition to Arkansas possible. At the trial both men pleaded not guilty, but were sentenced to life at hard labor.

Officials feared Slaughter's buddies. Guards revealed they had received threatening letters during the trial. A prison trusty claimed he had been approached about wrecking a passenger train behind the prison walls to distract officials while Slaughter escaped. An official of the Texas State Penitentiary warned: "[E]xpect nothing but trouble from him, he has lots of desperate friends, and a wide acquaintance of notorious desperate criminals."

While living at the "walls" in Little Rock, Slaughter asked for a minister to visit him. The Reverend W. B. Hogg of Winfield Memorial Methodist Church responded, and Slaughter was converted and baptized into the church by Reverend Hogg.

In January 1921 Slaughter was sent to Tucker farm. Warden Dee Horton set about to break Slaughter, who irritated him with his swaggering independence. Slaughter, six feet tall with blue eyes, massive arms, hairy chest, and full head of sandy brown hair, was ruggedly handsome. He had a reputation as a lady's man, and three women—Myrtle Slaughter of El Dorado, Arkansas; Nora Brooks of Ponca City, Oklahoma; and Mable Slaughter of Joplin, Missouri— claimed to be his wife.

On September 18, 1921, Slaughter, attempting to escape, killed inmate Bliss Atkinson. He was tried in Pine Bluff for the killing and sentenced to die. He was transported to Little Rock, guarded around the clock. He was cooperative and meek; but one week before his scheduled electrocution, he feigned illness, overpowered two guards, unlocked the stockade, and invited everyone who wished to make a break.

Slaughter marched the nurse, Miss Cumbie, ahead of himself and walked to Warden Dempsey's apartment where he took the warden and his family as prisoners and locked them in the death cells. For five hours Slaughter paraded around the prisoners he had "freed," taking their money and valuables. Slaughter, with Jack Howard, an inmate from Garland County, and five African-American prisoners fled in an automobile.

Alerted, the police at Benton, Arkansas, set up a road block. One hour after their escape, the group was spotted. Later, Howard and two African Americans appeared at a farmhouse in Benton and said that Slaughter had been shot. Jack Howard had shot Slaughter three times in the back. Slaughter's body was taken to Benton where "thousands stormed the Healey and Roth funeral home."

In death Slaughter was a celebrity. The Palez Floral Shop in Benton received "several very expensive" orders from Hot Springs and towns all over Oklahoma and Texas. Three ministers, including Reverend Hogg, officiated at the funeral, and the crowd was estimated "at more then 5,000." The funeral was a bizarre admixture of tent revival, political rally, burlesque show, and county fair. Slaughter, despite his three wives and numerous girlfriends, left no child to mourn him. He was buried in Oakland Cemetery in Little Rock.

[Sources include prison records in the Texas penitentiary in Huntsville, Texas, and the Arkansas Department of Corrections, Pine Bluff; articles in the *Arkansas Gazette;* and Jerry D. Gibbens, "The Short Violent Life of Tom Slaughter: Con Man, Killer, Celebrity," *Garland County Record* (1993).]

JERRY D. GIBBENS

SMITH, ALFRED EDGAR (Dec. 2, 1903–May 26, 1986), federal official, newsman, and columnist, was born in Hot Springs, Arkansas, to Jesse R. Smith and Mamie Johnson, who managed Crystal Baths, a spa for African Americans. They died when Smith was young. He worked his way through Langston High School and later worked as a night bellhop for the Eastman and Arlington Hotels and as an exercise boy at Oaklawn race track. He was a member of a choir that sang spirituals for famous visitors to Hot Springs. With four other boys he formed a basketball team, sometimes allowing the Langston girls to play. He went to Howard University in Washington, D.C., attending only when he had saved enough money to pay the fees.

He had no trouble with English and social studies, but he needed help with trigonometry, algebra, calculus, and astronomy, and he hired a West Indian student to tutor him. He observed that West Indian students were discriminated against on the campus. W. E. B. Dubois, then editor of *Crisis* magazine, encouraged Smith to write about this. The essay, "West Indian on the Campus," was published in the Urban League's *Opportunity* magazine.

He received a bachelor's and a master's degree from Howard in 1928 and 1932 at the beginning of the Great Depression when jobs were difficult to find. He worked as a substitute teacher and as a postal worker for awhile. He worked with the Emergency Relief Program of the Works Progress Administration (WPA), and wrote articles for the WPA, including "Negroes under WPA" and "The Negro and Relief," and he prepared a documentary film, "We Work Again," produced by Pathé News.

Around 1938 some twenty government agencies employed African Americans in executive positions. These appointees organized the Federal Council on African-American Affairs, known as the Black Cabinet. As a council member, Smith wrote messages to black organizations for President Franklin D. Roosevelt, commented on projects affecting black workers, and was a source of information on blacks for government agencies. He warned these agencies about the use of derogatory terms such as "you people."

The Black Cabinet worked and lobbied by day; at night they walked the Negro Alliance picket lines to open employment, theaters, and government cafeterias to African Americans. The group had to make sure that no laws were broken, walking a narrow path between federal restrictions, activism, blandishment, and communist infiltration.

Smith worked as Washington correspondent, columnist, and feature writer for the *Chicago Defender, Ebony,* the *Negro Digest,* and the *Chicago Globe.* From 1940 to 1949 he wrote a weekly column for the

Chicago Defender called "National Grapevine." Writing as Charley Cherokee, man about town in "spats, cane, gloves, velour, carnations and all," he observed the Washington scene as an insider. Entertaining but sparing no one, Charley's subjects ranged from in-fighting at Howard University to race discrimination in the defense industry and the armed services ("these blasted Negro youths who insist on fighting for their right to fight"), to the foibles of politicians. Charley tweaked "best friend" Eleanor Roosevelt for cautioning African Americans against too much demanding: "Really, Eleanor, you shouldn't write when you're tired."

In 1942 Smith founded the Capital Press Club as a professional organization for black journalists in Washington, D.C., in reaction to the National Press Club's policy of excluding blacks. He served as its first president and held other offices, including another term as president. In 1948 he received the club's "newsman of the year" award. Smith knew that African-American newsmen were poorly paid, had little respect, and were excluded from not only the National Press Club, but also the White House and congressional press associations. The Capital Press Club was seen by some publishers as a union demanding higher pay and other rights. During the club's first few years, restaurant owners demanded large guarantees before club meetings could be held in their establishments.

In 1961 Smith was public relations officer for the secretary of labor, Arthur Goldberg, under President John F. Kennedy. Among his correspondents were Arkansas senator Hattie Caraway and I. Van Meter, editor of *Time*.

Talking about his successes with his wife, Lula, Smith said, "I'm an Ozark hillbilly—if slightly off color—lean and mean and tough as a ten-penny nail."

[The Alfred Edgar Smith Papers are in the Special Collections Division, University of Arkansas Libraries, Fayetteville. "An Outline of the World History of the Negro in a Thousand Words" is available at the Moorland Spingarn Research Center, Howard University. Other sources include Ralph J. Bunche, *The Political Status of the Negro in the Age of FDR* (1973); Langston Hughes, Milton Meltzer, and C. Erick Lincoln, *A Pictorial History of Black Americans* (1963); and Norman Hodges, *Black History* (1971).]

IZOLA PRESTON

SMITH, GERALD LYMAN KENNETH (Feb. 27, 1898–Apr. 15, 1976), political crusader and minister, was born in Pardeeville, Wisconsin, to Lyman Z. Smith, a traveling salesman and farmer, and Sarah Smith (maiden name unknown), a teacher and housewife. Gerald had one sister, Barbara, born in 1888. He came from four generations of Republicans and three generations of circuit-riding Disciples Of Christ ministers. He worked his way through Valparaiso University, earning a degree in biblical studies in 1918. He became a minister, serving increasingly larger churches in the Midwest.

In 1929 Smith became minister of the King's Highway Christian Church in Shreveport, Louisiana, where he increased the membership and led successful fund drives. Shortly after moving to Shreveport, he met Huey P. Long, governor and subsequently United States senator, and the political boss of Louisiana. Smith was converted to Long's program after the senator saved some of Smith's congregants' homes from mortgage foreclosure. The association with Long cost Smith his position as pastor because many members of his church distrusted Long's policies and disliked his personality. Smith flirted with joining the Silver Shirt movement of pro-fascist demagogue William Dudley Palley but instead joined Long as the national organizer of his Share-Our-Wealth Society. He was at Long's side when "the Kingfish" was assassinated on September 8, 1935, and pronounced his eulogy to 150,000 mourners.

Working with Long, Smith discovered his gift as a speaker blessed with a mellifluous voice that could move the masses. Journalist H. L. Mencken considered Smith the greatest public speaker he had heard. For the next decade Smith's career was lifted up on the wings of his sonorous phrases. He became associated with Dr. Francis E. Townsend, a physician with a plan to mitigate the Great Depression by providing generous pensions to the elderly. In 1936 Townsend, Smith, and Father Charles E. Coughlin, the radio priest, created the Union Party. The party nominated North Dakota congressman William Lemke to challenge Franklin D. Roosevelt for the presidency. The campaign failed miserably and Townsend and Coughlin severed their relationships with Smith.

Smith founded the Committee of One Million in New York to fight communism, liberalism, Jews, and organized labor. In 1939 he moved to Detroit. He established the Christian Nationalist Crusade in 1942 and began publishing a hatespewing monthly, *The Cross and the Flag*. He created the isolationist America First Party and ran for the United States Senate. Polling more than 100,000 votes in the Republican primary, he nonetheless lost the contest. He ran for president in 1944, 1948, and 1956 as the candidate of the Christian Nationalist Party. By the latter campaign his supporters had diminished to the lunatic fringe. After 1956 he concentrated on writing rather than public speaking.

Smith's great hatred was for Jews, and it is as an anti-Semite that he will be remembered. He blamed Jews for the Crucifixion and claimed Jesus was a Gentile. However, according to Smith, Roosevelt was a Jew, as were Truman and Eisenhower. Hitler was a Bolshevik and a tool of the Jews. Communism was a Jewish invention, and most Jews were Bolsheviks. Jews provoked blacks to begin the civil rights movement that disrupted the tranquil status quo. Smith himself, he claimed, was persecuted because he had the courage to discuss the Jewish question. Like Hitler, he was a misunderstood man.

Smith came to Arkansas in 1964. He purchased Penn Castle, a Victorian mansion in Eureka Springs, and remodeled it as his summer home. In June 1965 he broke ground for a seven-story-high statue of Jesus. The "Christ of the Ozarks" was dedicated on June 15, 1966, and became a major tourist attraction. Smith soon added a Christ Only Art Museum and a Bible Museum. In 1968 Smith began staging a Passion Play in an outdoor amphitheater seating three thousand, soon expanded to six thousand, making it the largest outdoor pageant in the nation. The play was performed on a four-hundred-foot reproduction of a street of old Jerusalem and included live animals and local people miming crowd scenes. The actors' words were projected via a stereophonic sound system. Smith's "Sacred Projects" transformed Eureka Springs from a dying town to a thriving tourist center, but not all residents approved of his influence in their community. At the time of his death in California, Smith was planning a Disney-like replica of the Holy Land in Eureka Springs, to be called the "New Holy Land." He is buried at the foot of his "Christ of the Ozarks" statue.

[The Gerald L. K. Smith Papers, consisting of more than one hundred cubic feet dating to Smith's boyhood, are in the Bentley Historical Library at the University of Michigan. The Huey P. Long Papers, the T. Harry Williams Papers, and the Huey P. Long Scrapbooks at Louisiana State University include information on Smith. The chief biography of Smith is Glen Jeansonne, *Gerald L. K. Smith: Minister of Hate* (1988; rpt. 1997), which offers an extensive bibliography.]

GLEN S. JEANSONNE

SMITH, THOMAS (July 17, 1808–Aug. 17, 1885), first superintendent of public instruction in Arkansas, was born in Lancaster, Pennsylvania. His parents' names are unknown. When he was twenty he married Martha McKay and started teaching school. After eight years his wife died, leaving four children. Smith began studying medicine and graduated with honors from medical school in Cincinnati when he was forty years old.

In 1861 at the age of fifty-three, he entered the Union army as surgeon for the Eleventh Missouri Regiment, volunteers. Eight months later his strength was exhausted; he resigned his commission and returned home to St. Louis. His second wife died there in 1862. He signed up again, in the Thirty-third Regiment, Missouri volunteers, served in the camps at Helena, Arkansas, and resigned to return home in 1863. In 1864 he was hired by wealthy cotton planters near Helena to be their family physician. He and his third wife, Susan Hoffman of St. Louis, made their home in Helena.

Smith was a delegate to the state constitutional convention of 1868. For the next several years he devoted his life to establishing public education in Arkansas. He wrote the constitutional "clause" upon which Arkansas's state school system was established. He became the first state superintendent of public instruction, and in that office directed the first systematic count of school-age children and organized the school system under the law. He launched the first educational magazine ever published in the state and edited it for three years. He started a state professional association of teachers. He was ex-officio chairman of the board of trustees that established the University of Arkansas, selected its first president, caused its curriculum to emphasize the preparation of teachers, and opened its doors to its first students. Comparing Smith to other state officers under Reconstruction, John Gould Fletcher wrote, "none was uncorrupt except the superintendent of schools, who unobtrusively began to put into effect the laws establishing an efficient system of free public education."

In his biennial official reports and his editorials in the *Arkansas Journal of Education*, Smith told what the situation was like when he began work: "The circumstances under which our public school system was inaugurated were peculiar. The people had just emerged from a severe civil strife, the country was impoverished, and a new class of pupils hitherto shut off from the means of education was to be provided for." He said that "two thirds of the adult population cannot read the Lords' prayer or write their own names," in Arkansas in 1868. "The lack of education among the masses . . . has long been felt among the intelligent classes to be a great hindrance to the upbuilding of the material, social and moral interests of the commonwealth."

Smith expressed faith in the public schools: "The great superiority of public schools over all others is that they furnish to the rich and poor alike the benefits of an education. The orphan and the friendless have here an equal opportunity with the most opulent of the land." He said, "All intelligent persons know that general education will promote general prosperity."

Inevitably serious obstacles arose: "At first, many opposed and refused their cooperation in establishing schools . . . and . . . much embarrassment and delay were experienced in our first efforts." It was not easy to set up schools and conduct them, for "in many parts of the country, schools were to be organized for the first time and the people were consequently without experience."

Smith brought trained teachers from states where the educational system was further advanced and established pilot schools: "The work was steadily pushed forward . . . and a few good schools were opened at different points throughout the state. The people were thus afforded an opportunity of witnessing the results . . . and their prejudices began to give way, and it was not long before the better class of citizens in every county were ready to give their influence in favor of free schools." As a result, "While the burden of taxation is felt to be very heavy, there are but few who are not willing to be taxed."

At the end of his first two years in office, more than two thousand teachers had been hired and about 108,000 children were attending school. But by 1873 Smith saw everything he had built up collapse: the magazine, the teachers' association, and the school system itself. Difficult conditions, opposition, and graft played their parts in the debacle. The worst problem was that teachers were paid with depreciated scrip so that they received only a half or a third of the contract amount. Teachers left the state en masse, and Smith became so discouraged that he left, too.

But the cause of public education took on a life of its own, and before long Arkansas began its long struggle to build a system of free education. Smith returned to Little Rock in 1881, where he practiced medicine for the rest of his life. He died in Little Rock.

[This entry is taken from Clare B. Kennan, "Dr. Thomas Smith, Forgotten Man of Arkansas Education," *AHQ* 20 (Winter 1961): 303–17. —*Editor.*]

SMITHEE, JASPER NEWTON (Jan. 11, 1842–July 4, 1902), journalist and chairman of the Arkansas Democratic Party, was born in Sharp County to a poor Scottish-Irish farming family whose names are unknown. His formal education consisted of three months in a country school until he was apprenticed at age twelve to the *Des Arc Citizen,* where he learned the printing trade.

When he was eighteen he bought half-ownership in the *Prairie County Democrat* and used it to support the Southern Democratic presidential ticket in 1860. When South Carolina seceded from the Union in December of that year, Smithee sold his interest in the paper to work for the secessionist cause in Arkansas. Following the state's secession in 1861, Smithee enlisted as a private in the field artillery and worked up to the rank of first lieutenant in the Confederate States Army.

After the Civil War he worked as a typesetter in Memphis. He returned to Little Rock in 1866 as a foreman at the *Arkansas Gazette*'s printing office.

He and Annie E. Cowgill, a great-granddaughter of Benjamin Harrison, a signer of the Declaration of Independence, married on January 1, 1867. They had six sons.

At the *Gazette* Smithee became city editor, managing editor, and then owner. In 1873 he became the charter president of the Arkansas Press Association; he served in that capacity for three terms. In 1874 he sold the *Gazette.*

He served in the Brooks-Baxter war as a colonel in the forces supporting the claims of Elisha Baxter to the governorship of Arkansas. For this service he was appointed commissioner of state lands. When he took charge of the office, it was losing twenty-five thousand dollars per year. He made it self-sufficient and was reelected in 1874 and 1876. In 1878 he founded the *Arkansas Democrat* newspaper. He also became chairman of the Arkansas Democratic Party that year, a position he held for four years. A year after founding it, he sold the *Democrat* to enter the real estate business. In 1880 he ran unsuccessfully for the Democratic gubernatorial nomination.

In 1885 Smithee was appointed by President Grover Cleveland as a special federal agent of the general land office for Colorado and New Mexico with his headquarters in Santa Fe. Five years later he was back in the newspaper business, holding an editorial position at the *Rocky Mountain News* in Denver. There he became acquainted with the pro-silver wing of the Democratic Party. Led by William Jennings Bryan, this group advocated the use of silver-backed currency to artificially increase the money supply and create an inflation that would make it easier for farmers to pay their debts. It would also stimulate business for the silver mining industry in Colorado.

Following the purchase of the *Arkansas Gazette* by a New York investor, John R. Dos Passos, Smithee became its editor in 1896. His new tenure as editor was fraught with disappointment. He helped William Jennings Bryan carry Arkansas by a large margin in the presidential election of 1896. But he failed to persuade the state Democratic Party to embrace his brand of populism. Several other pro-silver Democratic editors locked horns with him over railroad regulation. In 1897 a state senator from Yell County, R. D. McMullen, whom Smithee had attacked in an editorial, shot at him but missed. In early 1899 Smithee resigned as editor of the *Gazette.*

After enduring several months of illness, Smithee committed suicide in a Little Rock hotel room.

[Sources include the *Arkansas Gazette,* Sept. 18, 1880, July 5, 1902; *Baxter Bulletin,* July 11, 1902; *Columbia Banner,* Mar. 25, 1880, Sept. 8, 1881, June 8, 1882, Nov. 27, 1889; *Helena Weekly World,* Dec. 4, 1895, June 9, 1897, July 6, 1898; *Pine Bluff Semi-Weekly Graphic,* June 6, 1896, July 9, 1902; *Pine Bluff Weekly Commercial,* May 23, 1896, Dec. 4, 1897; *Pine Bluff Weekly Press Eagle,* Jan. 9, 1896–Feb. 7, 1899; and *Wheeler's Independent,* Apr. 7, 1880. See also Deborah Halter, "We Haven't Really Come so Far in the Newspaper Business," *Arkansas Democrat-Gazette,* June 26, 1994.]

CHARLES J. RECTOR

SOTO, HERNANDO DE (1500?–May 21, 1542),

explorer, was born in the Extremadura region of western Spain, the second son of Francisco Méndez de Soto and Leonor Arias Tinoco. He was probably raised in the town of Jerez de los Caballeros. Although his family was of noble heritage, de Soto was poor, and he borrowed money to travel to the New World in 1514. He became a soldier and participated in raids and expeditions in Panama, Nicaragua, and Peru. By 1536, he had gained fame as a cruel but successful military leader in the conquest of Indian groups in Central and South America and had become wealthy from his involvement in the sale of Indian slaves.

He returned to Spain in 1536, married Isabel de Bobadilla, and petitioned the Spanish king for a governorship in Central America. His request was turned down, but he was offered instead the opportunity to explore and conquer La Florida, which consisted of much of what is now the southern United States. He was also offered the governorship of Cuba, which would serve as his base for the conquest. De Soto accepted the offer and began gathering an army of mercenaries and making other preparations in 1537.

In May 1539 de Soto set out from Cuba with approximately six hundred men, plus horses, pigs, and equipment. His contract required him to establish settlements and forts as well as to explore the region. After landing somewhere on the west coast of Florida, the expedition traveled through many southeastern states before crossing the Mississippi River into Arkansas on June 18, 1541.

The members of the de Soto expedition were the first Europeans to set foot in what is now Arkansas. Many of the pigs they brought escaped, and most of the wild hogs in Arkansas and the South today are descended from the ones brought by de Soto. The four existing accounts of the expedition describe the people they met as they traveled through the state during the next two years. Scholars debate the details of the actual route, but archeologists have discovered small brass bells and other Spanish artifacts at a handful of archeological sites, tantalizing evidence of the expedition's presence.

After traveling around the state for almost a year, de Soto led his expedition back to the Mississippi River, somewhere in southeastern Arkansas. By this time, he and most of the expedition members were disillusioned and tired of the almost constant battles with native peoples. The gold and other riches they had sought were not to be found, and almost half of the original six hundred men had been killed since they began in 1539.

None was more disillusioned than de Soto himself, and he sent an exploratory party down the Mississippi to see if it was feasible to build boats and sail to Mexico. When the men returned a week later, having failed to find the Gulf of Mexico, de Soto fell ill. He was apparently afflicted with some kind of fever, dying at a place called Guachoya.

De Soto's death presented a dilemma to the surviving Spaniards, because he had represented himself to the native people as Hijo del Sol, or "Son of the Sun." After telling them that de Soto had risen into the sky, the soldiers secretly buried his corpse under cover of darkness. A day or two later, it became obvious that the Indians had noticed the freshly dug soil and didn't believe that de Soto had merely gone to visit his fellow gods. Fearing desecration of his corpse and the possible repercussions of the Indians' discovery of de Soto's mortality, the soldiers dug up the body at night, weighted it down, and quietly dumped it in the Mississippi River from a canoe.

A little over a year later, the surviving Spaniards built barges and sailed from Arkansas down the Mississippi, after first trying to travel to Mexico overland. We are fortunate to have narratives of the expedition, three written by survivors, and one written forty or fifty years later from interviews with survivors. Although these accounts are biased, together they give us a fairly complete picture of Hernando de Soto the man. When he first arrived in Arkansas, he still saw himself as a gallant conqueror, but by the time of his death his spirit was broken.

The most valuable aspect of the expedition accounts is their portrayal of the native groups encountered by de Soto. His relations with most native Arkansans were relatively cordial, but de Soto and his soldiers thought nothing of torturing and killing native people who refused to cooperate by providing food, guides, interpreters, bearers, and concubines. His primary aim was the gaining of riches, and the descendants of the Native American Arkansas residents understandably view him as an evil murderer.

[The best source for information about de Soto and his expedition is the two-volume *The De Soto Chronicles: The Expedition of Hernando de Soto to North America in 1539–1543*, edited by Lawrence A. Clayton, Vernon James Knight Jr., and Edward C. Moore (1993). A collection of papers on historical and archeological studies of de Soto in Arkansas and surrounding states is in *The Expedition of Hernando de Soto West of the Mississippi, 1541–1543*, edited by Gloria A. Young and Michael P. Hoffman (1993).

The Arkansas Archeological Survey and the Arkansas Department of Parks and Tourism cooperate in research and interpretation at the Parkin Archeological State Park, where museum exhibits and archeological excavations reveal evidence that the de Soto expedition visited the nearby native settlement of Casqui.]

JEFFREY M. MITCHEM

STEELE, FREDERICK (Jan. 14, 1819–Jan. 12, 1868), United States Volunteers major general and commander of the Department of Arkansas in the Civil War, was born in Delhi, New York, the son of Nathaniel Steele III and his second wife, Dameras Johnson. Little is known of Frederick's early years; he entered West Point in 1839.

A friend and classmate of Ulysses S. Grant, he graduated in 1843 and was commissioned a second lieutenant. He served in the Mexican War from 1847 to 1848, then in California, Pennsylvania, and various posts in the West until the Civil War.

Appointed a major with the Eleventh Infantry May 14, 1861, he commanded a brigade in operations in Missouri, including action at Dug Springs and the Battle of Wilson's Creek. He was commissioned as a brigadier general with the United States Volunteers on January 29, 1862.

He commanded the First Division, Army of the Southwest, which occupied Helena, Arkansas, from July to August 1862. Union forces under the command of General Samuel R. Curtis had moved down into Arkansas from southern Missouri in the spring of 1862, meeting only light opposition. Taking Helena instead of Little Rock, then retreating because of supply problems and guerrilla activity, Curtis left Steele and his men in Helena to be resupplied by riverboat.

In late 1862 and early 1863, two documents were circulated which made accusations against Steele. The first reached President Lincoln, accusing Steele of returning freed slaves to their owner. Steele claimed his purpose was to break up a house of prostitution. Testimonials from Grant and General William T. Sherman helped refute the charges. The second, in the form of court-martial papers, apparently did not circulate as widely; it accused Steele of being so drunk at the Battle of Vicksburg as to be unable to carry out his duty and of issuing passes and safeguards to three Confederate generals. No action was taken on the court martial.

During the first half of 1863, Steele commanded an army corps that took part in the expedition to the Yazoo River, the assault on Chickasaw Bluffs, and the capture of Arkansas Post January 11, 1863. Forces under Steele also participated in the Vicksburg campaign, the attack on Jackson, Mississippi, May 14, 1863, and the siege of Vicksburg. In July 1863 he was given command of the Army of Arkansas.

Union forces under Steele took Fort Smith on September 1, 1863, and Little Rock on September 10. Steele was surprised by the ease of his victory. Occupying the Little Rock home of Confederate general Chester Ashley, he set up his quarters and office as commander of the Department of Arkansas.

Until his reassignment December 22, 1864, the only significant military action that Steele led was the Red River expedition. The objective was to defeat Confederate general Edmund Kirby Smith and consolidate Union control of the trans-Mississippi territory. Forces from the Fort Smith garrison under General John M. Thayer joined with those of the Seventh Army Corps under Steele at Camden, but they were unable to link up with forces out of Shreveport under General Nathaniel Banks. Hampered by supply problems and guerrilla activity, Steele retreated to Little Rock rather than be surrounded by Confederates, fighting battles at Jenkin's Ferry and Mark's Mill in which the Third Division received heavy losses.

Lincoln also assigned Steele a political mission in Arkansas in which he had as much success as he did in the Red River campaign. The mission entailed working with Arkansas Unionists to reorganize loyal state government and to send a congressional delegation to Washington that the Republican Congress would accept. A conservative Democrat who opposed emancipation, Steele showed little enthusiasm for the task.

Elections were held for a new legislature and executive officials. They met in Little Rock to begin restoring civil government, but Governor Isaac Murphy, the military commander of the district of Little Rock General John Wynn Davidson, and United States senator-elect William Meade Fishback together opposed what a Unionist Little Rock newspaper called Steele's "conciliatory policy." Steele actively encouraged his men to fraternize with the civilian population. He also sponsored the conservative *National Democrat* newspaper, which extolled the virtues of slavery and endorsed a gubernatorial candidate, a planter named Anthony Rogers.

Steele described the publisher as a "pimp for my headquarters." His behind-the-scenes political actions undercut the Unionist movement in the state and prevented him from realizing Lincoln's goal of restoring loyal government.

After the Red River campaign, Union political and military authority outside of the garrison towns of Fort Smith, Little Rock, and Helena, always weak, was further diminished. This coupled with the rejection of the credentials of the Arkansas congressional delegation in the summer of 1864 led Lincoln to remove Steele from his command.

Steele went on to command forces in Alabama, Florida, and Louisiana during the rest of the war. From December 1865 to November 1867, he commanded the Department of the Columbia (Pacific Northwest). While on leave of absence in San Mateo, California, he died, apparently of a stroke.

[Information can be found in the *Fort Smith New Era*, 1863–64; *National Democrat* (Little Rock), 1863–1864; *Unconditional Union* (Little Rock), 1863–64; *The War of the Rebellion: A Compilation of the Official Records of the Union and Confederate Armies, 1880–1901*; the *Frederick Steele Papers*, microfilm edition; and Patricia J. Palmer, *Frederick Steele: Forgotten General* (1971).]

BEN BOULDEN

STEPHENS, CHARLOTTE ANDREWS (May 9, 1854–Dec. 17, 1951), the first black teacher in the Little Rock public schools, was born into slavery in Little Rock. Her parents were William Wallace Andrews, a mulatto slave to Chester Ashley, United States senator, and Caroline Williams Andrews, a slave to the Noah Badgett family.

Both of Stephens's parents had what she termed "peculiar privileges" which set her own life to great advantage. The Ashley family taught Wallace Andrews to read and encouraged his education and his religious interests at a time when such practices were illegal in other southern states. A second advantage was the custom of slaves "hiring their time." In this way Caroline Andrews worked as laundress and was able to support her family in a home provided for them by the Ashleys at Tenth and Broadway. In 1854 the Ashleys gave land at Eighth and Broadway for a church that Wallace Andrews headed. There he secretly taught his parishioners and his two young children to read, write, and spell.

Emancipation came to Little Rock slaves in September 1863 when federal troops occupied the city. Andrews immediately opened a private school for blacks in his church. Within a few months, Quaker missionaries (the Society of Friends) came to Arkansas to educate freedmen and used this church for their school. Stephens recalled, "They were a part of that noble band who came with the Bible in one hand and the spelling book in the other, to help the newly emancipated race escape from the shackles of ignorance, which were more cruel than physical slavery." By 1867 the Quakers built the Union School at Sixth and State.

In 1868 Little Rock organized its first public school system, part of the Reconstruction program advocating economic progress and public education. In the 1860s about 30 percent of whites and 95 percent of blacks were unable to read and write. Though the statewide system featured trained leaders and a standard curriculum, it was segregated. Little Rock bought the Union School from the Quakers. Lottie Stephens was fifteen years old and the brightest student in her class in 1869. For this reason, she was appointed to fill out the term of her white teacher, who had become ill. The following fall, three more black women were hired to teach for the district.

After a year of teaching and saving money, Stephens enrolled at Oberlin (Ohio) College. She recalled that Oberlin was like heaven to her. Her intellect was hungry for the study of Latin, geometry, the history of Rome, music, and biblical antiquities. Three years later she returned to Little Rock to teach, and here she taught for seventy years. After teaching at Union School she taught at First Ward School until 1877, then at Capital Hill School, Gibbs High School, and finally Dunbar High School and Junior College. She served twice as a school principal. She taught first grade through eighth grade, sometimes with as many as ninety children in her room. At the high-school level she devoted thirty-four years to English, Latin, and science. In her final years she served as a librarian at Dunbar School.

In 1910 a new elementary school was to be named. The all-white board chose between her name and that of Booker T. Washington. Stephens Elementary at Eighteenth and Maple was thus named and remained for half a century the only school in Little Rock named for a woman. In 1950 a modern school building replaced the original at the same site. Stephens attended and spoke at the dedication ceremony of her "name school": "I am thankful to the Heavenly Father for permitting me to work for years in the field of public education for a race so needy and so hungry for knowledge." That second building, now removed, will be replaced by a third Charlotte Stephens School with a planned opening for fall 2000.

In 1877 she married John Herbert Stephens. She said he was a "teacher but knew the carpenters trade," and it was by that trade that he helped to support their children, six of whom lived to adulthood. In the era after the Civil War, when blacks had more opportunities to serve in public life, Stephens recalled that her husband served as a deputy sheriff and deputy constable. "He was with me for years before his death: we raised a family of six children and gave each one a college education." In addition to her long career in teaching, Stephens was active in the civic life of the black community. When she died in Little Rock, she was survived by two of her children.

[See George P. Rawick, ed., *The American Slave: A Composite Autobiography*, vol. 10, *Arkansas Narratives*, pt. 6 (1972): 226–33; the *Arkansas Democrat*, Mar. 11, 1951; Adolphine Fletcher Terry, *Charlotte Stephens* (1973); Clara B. Kennan, "The First Black Teacher in Little Rock," *AHQ* 9 (Autumn 1950): 194–204; Fon Louise Gordon, "Black Women in Arkansas," *Pulaski County Historical Review* 25 (1977): 26–28; the *Arkansas Gazette*, Dec. 19, 1951; and the *Arkansas Democrat*, Dec. 18, 1951.]

SONDRA GORDY

STEPHENS, WILTON ROBERT (Sept. 14, 1907–Dec. 2, 1991), investor and utility executive, was the second of six children of Albert J. Stephens and Ethel Pumphrey. He was born and reared on a farm near Prattsville in central Arkansas. From boyhood he was called "Witt." His roots were deep in the Saline River bottoms of Grant County, where his father settled in 1902 and his mother's family had lived for three generations. His maternal grandfather, Nathan Pumphrey, owned a plantation near Prattsville before the Civil War. His paternal grandfather, Dow Stephens, fought with General Fremont's Union Cavalry, and came to Arkansas in 1879. Land and family commanded Witt Stephens's loyalties throughout his life.

As a boy he worked the fields on his father's farm. At seven he was shelling peanuts at night and selling them in Sheridan, the county seat, on Saturdays. From the start his passion was making money. He left school before graduation and began selling fancy belt buckles on commission for a costume jewelry company. Swiftly he became the regional representative for the firm, touring the Southwest. He returned home in 1933 and took a job in Little Rock as a bond salesman. Three months later, with fifteen thousand dollars borrowed from friends, he established the W. R. Stephens Investment Company, the foundation of what was to become a great fortune. His specialty was buying and selling Arkansas's defaulted municipal bonds.

In 1935 he married Joy Summers of Little Rock, who died in 1954.

In 1943 the state government made Arkansas municipal bonds redeemable at face value. It was Stephens's first triumph as an investment banker. In 1947 he brought his brother Jackson T. Stephens into the firm and changed its name to Stephens Inc. Over decades the company invested in a great sweep of enterprises, serving in the start-up or expansion of Wal-Mart, Systematics, Federal Express, and Tyson Foods, among others. In the 1940s Witt Stephens acquired substantial holdings in several Arkansas banks; this acquisition continued, and in the 1980s Witt and Jack bought a significant interest in Worthen Bank, one of the largest in Arkansas.

Sometime in the forties Witt Stephens had made his first million. In 1945 he moved into utilities and natural gas production, acquiring a small utility, the Arkansas Oklahoma Gas Company at Fort Smith, and exploring its reserves. In 1954 Stephens acquired control of a large utility, Arkansas Louisiana Gas Company. Two years later he became president of the company, called Arkla, and his brother Jack took charge of Stephens Inc.

In 1956 he married Anna Bess Chisum of Little Rock. They had three children: Elizabeth, Pamela, and Witt Jr.

From 1956 to 1972 Arkla expanded its operations and acquired vast natural gas reserves while moving into related manufactures, from fertilizer to appliances. Meantime, Witt Stephens bought thousands of acres of land around his old home place and established a farm and cattle ranch. As early as 1959 *Fortune Magazine* estimated his personal worth at $19 million. In 1972 he retired from Arkla and for two decades concentrated on his favorite interests—politics, buying and selling bonds, and entertaining groups of ten at daily luncheons in his suite in the Stephens Building. On weekends he went to the farm.

His luncheons, which were in effect a salon, sparkled with unconventional, sometimes brilliant, conversation. His guest lists featured celebrated figures from politics, business, finance, law, church, theater, academe, sports, and journalism. His understanding of people was both intuitive and cultivated. As his nephew Ray Thornton wrote, his ability "to recognize patterns of behavior … was not limited to financial forecasting but was useful in understanding the currents of politics as well as the continuum of history."

Witt Stephens was engaged in politics for half a century. He was a prodigious fund-raiser, backing and sometimes launching candidates at every level. He served two terms himself in the Arkansas House of Representatives; however, he chose not to continue in public office on the advice of his father. He was an important figure in financing the campaigns of a succession of governors, from Homer Atkins (1941–45) to Sid McMath (1949–53) to Orval Faubus (1955–67) to Bill Clinton (1979–81 and 1983–93). He was close to Atkins and Faubus. Shortly before his death, he was backing the Clinton presidential campaign, eager to have an Arkansan as president.

He had a voice like gravel. His favorite opening in conversation was, "Are you interested in making some money today?" He made money for many friends and clients and for himself. In 1991 *Forbes* magazine, in its annual report on the four hundred richest Americans, estimated the combined fortunes of Witt and Jack Stephens and their families at $900 million. No one knows the full value of the Stephens natural gas reserves.

Witt Stephens's work in business and finance had the touch of genius. His philanthropies leaned toward the personal, as in his founding a Grant County museum at Sheridan. He was a Baptist by religious conviction, kept a Bible on his desk, and loved to debate biblical issues with visiting clergymen, although he didn't spend much time in church. He was in bad health for the last decade of his life, but he was hard at work at his office and held his last luncheon on the day he was stricken and hospitalized, seventeen days before his death. He was buried at Prattsville.

[The basis of this entry is the author's fifteen years of conversations with Witt Stephens and interviews with Vernon Giss, Pat Webb, and Ray Thornton. Other sources include Ray Thornton's *A. J. Stephens as Remembered by His Family* (1983); the *Arkansas Gazette*, Sept. 25 and 26, 1988;

Arkansas Business, Dec. 9 and 16, 1991; *Arkansas Democrat-Gazette*, Dec. 5, 1991; *Fortune*, Oct. 1959; *Forbes*, Oct. 1991; and the Congressional Record, excerpts assembled by Ray Thornton.]

JAMES O. POWELL

STERN, JANE RITA ELLENBOGEN (Aug. 2, 1918–Dec. 16, 1989), environmentalist and naturalist, was born in Little Rock to Leonard E. Ellenbogen, who owned a real-estate firm, a clothing store, and a laundry at various times, and Birdie Burger. Jane Ellenbogen attended Little Rock Junior College (now University of Arkansas, Little Rock). After a three-year courtship, she and Dr. Howard S. Stern married on March 26, 1940. They were parents of two children, Arthur M. (1944) and Ellen C. (1946).

The family moved to Pine Bluff in 1948, where Stern was the leader of her daughter's Girl Scout troop from 1954 to 1964.

Stern's love for the outdoors developed on excursions to rivers or forests with her husband, an award-winning photographer. One of his prints, "The Morning's at Seven, the Hillside's Dew-pearled" (1939), shows Jane walking in grass in the early morning light.

Her interest in birds started when her son was obtaining his Boy Scout nature badge. He hung a bird feeder outside his window, and his mother became intrigued. She became a charter member of the Jefferson County Audubon Society. The step from "birding" to studying the environment started when she visited places only to find that the birds, along with the woods they inhabited, had vanished. Harold Alexander, a wildlife biologist with the Arkansas Game and Fish Commission, was an early mentor of hers.

Always shunning leadership roles, Stern preferred to accumulate data and work with people one to one. Her approach was to state her position with flashing, steady, dark-brown eyes and a slight smile as she loosed her barrage on her adversary. She gained the respect of her opponents, especially the United States Army Corps of Engineers. When the Corps began the Pine Bluff Urban Water Management Study, Stern was asked to serve as chairman of the citizens' advisory committee and to select other members. The study's purpose was to develop a comprehensive flood protection and flood plain management plan for the Pine Bluff urban area.

Stern campaigned with Dr. Neil Compton to stop the damming of the Buffalo River. In 1968 she rallied opponents of a dam the Corps had planned on the Saline River at Benton. In July 1975 the Corps canceled the project, saying the dam could not be justified on a cost-to-benefit ratio. When the Cache River-Bayou Deview Channelization Project was proposed by the Memphis District of the Army Engineers, Stern was a founding member of the Citizens Committee to Save the Cache River Basin. The Corps abandoned the project, a historic victory for conservationists nationwide protecting an important habitat of migratory birds.

Stern participated in the opposition to channelization of Bayou Meto and Bayou Bartholomew. These projects, too, were abandoned by the Corps. In August 1971 the Arkansas Wildlife Federation presented her with its Water Conservationist award.

She was a leader in the Audubon Society's move to outlaw the killing of hawks and owls. John Heuston, a columnist for the *Arkansas Democrat,* once wrote an article promoting the killing of hawks and owls to protect other wildlife. He came to work the following Monday and found Jane Stern perched on his desk. "When she finally retracted her verbal talons from my quivering body, I knew all about the Audubon Society, and a thousand good reasons why hawks and owls were beneficial. I never shot another hawk."

David Perdue, duck hunter and conservationist, wrote, "Amazingly, she realized that hunting and fishing interests were the key to protecting the environment in Arkansas."

In search of the habitat of the traill, or willow flycatcher, Stern was directed to the virgin Konecny Prairie and Grove near Slovak in Prairie County by Raymond C. McMasters, director of the White River Wildlife Refuge. After visiting the prairie in 1969, Stern began a movement to preserve it for future generations. In 1976 it became Arkansas's first conservation easement.

Stern discovered a new plant species on the prairie, the *Mespilus canescens,* a shrub in the rose family, whose common name is Stern's medlar. After nineteen years her find was accepted by the nation's botanists in 1988. The Arkansas Native Plant Society presented Stern with the Carl R. Amason Conservation Award in 1989.

At the annual meeting of the Arkansas Wildlife Federation in 1978, Stern reluctantly accepted the Conservationist of the Year award (she felt that others deserved it more). In 1990 the Shugart Red-Cockaded Woodpecker Conservation Award was presented to

Stern posthumously by the Arkansas Audubon Society. It commemorated the hours she had spent convincing timber growers to stop the rapid disappearance of the endangered woodpecker's habitat.

Steve N. Wilson Jr., director of the Arkansas Game and Fish Commission and her friend for over twenty years, received a call from her only two months before her death regarding the condition of Lake Pine Bluff, continuing her long fight to get the commission to clean up the lake.

Stern died in Pine Bluff. Her contributions to environmental protection are visible in the remaining free-flowing streams and clean lakes, the prairies, the birds, and the wildlife, and are remembered by the people she touched with her passion for conservation.

[The Jane Stern Collection is in the Arkansas Archives, Torreyson Library, University of Central Arkansas. See the *Pine Bluff Commercial*, June 29, 1969, Mar. 2, 1975, Dec. 17, 18, 19, and 20, 1989; and the *Pine Bluff News*, Aug. 10, 1978, and Dec. 21, 1989. This entry is also based on interviews with Ellen Stern, May 7, 21, and 23, 1996; Howard Stern, May 10, 1996; Jane McNulty Powell, May 30, 1996; and Nesbitt Bowers, June 6, 1996.]

JAMES W. LESLIE

STEVENSON, MARIA TONCRAY WATKINS

(May 13, 1793–Mar. 21, 1874), pioneer, was born in Williamsport, Maryland, to Daniel Toncray and Hulda Tracy, who emigrated from England.

On January 31, 1815, Maria (pronounced Ma-RYE-ah) married Isaac Watkins, who had served in the War of 1812. He may have introduced himself as "Major" Watkins because he was not called Mr. Watkins. They had a plantation in Shelbyville, Kentucky. Because he had signed a note for a friend who could not repay, he had to sell property to cover the loan. Arkansas Territory had just been opened to settlement, and the decision was made to begin a new life in new territory. The couple with their five-year-old son George traveled by steamboat on the Ohio and Mississippi Rivers, then by keelboat to Arkansas Post, living in a log cabin on their boat. Accompanying them was a slave, thought to be the first to come to Arkansas.

From Maria's diary: "Left Shelbyville Kentucky on Sunday 31st December 1820 . . . O, the sorrow of my heart I felt at parting with my sister's children, who are dear to me as my own—farewell, dear ones . . . Arrived at mouth of White River on Wednesday, February 7th.

We stayed at Squire Patty's who . . . showed us all the kindness possible . . . I met with a widow woman. She appeared to sympathize with me in leaving dear ones behind and coming to this wilderness of sorrow . . . arrived at Post of Arkansas on Sunday evening, stayed at Judge Hamilton's . . . and had our boat repaired. They were very kind to us, but I discovered great discord or uneasiness in the mind of Mrs. Hamilton. I endeavored to converse with her on the subject of religion, but found she was a stranger to the happy influence . . . proceeded on our way to the Rock, very slowly and many times my heart is put to task.

"On our way, my son George Claiborne fell overboard and remained quite sick and pale during the day. I again was constrained about my son, one that has been the child of many prayers.

"At last we have arrived at Little Rock . . . Oh, the disappointment to me, only one house and few cabins, but two decent families . . . I endure many privations in this place, the sound of the Gospel of Jesus is not heard in this village."

The family had a log house built on land now called Little Rock blocks 4 and 5, which is at present-day Fifth and Cumberland. Isaac established the first tavern in Little Rock. He also had a horse-drawn gristmill and a farm. The first Baptist church in Little Rock was organized in the Watkins home in 1824 by the Reverend Silas Toncray, Maria's brother.

From Maria's diary: "The first year we endured much sickness in the family . . . the Lord was pleased to take my little son, Henry Conway to himself. Oh, what a trying year to me. It was blessed for the good of my son, I trust.

"Oh, my dear little Catherine, my afflicted infant, when she was born, bid fair for health and vigor, but to my grief, she never grew any or appeared to have one days health, and in the midst of this great affliction, there was a greater one at hand.

"My husband was assassinated on 13th December, 1827. He left home after dinner as pleasant as ever I saw him in my life. At dinner, he seemed to gaze over me as if he could not put his eyes definitely on me. He walked up to town as was common after dinner and was sitting in a store way . . . when,—awful to tell—a villain took deliberate aim and pierced a rifle ball into his right breast, which deprived him of mortal life . . . When I saw him pale and lifeless, the bleeding wound exposed, my reason and all, was gone and for a moment I knew nothing, but that God who near my soul has always stood, restored and supported me. My poor little afflicted Catherine now seems to be a comfort to me, but a short time after her father died, it pleased Him to remove her to some happier clime."

The murderer, whom Major Watkins had accused of stealing pigs, jumped on his horse and escaped to the Republic of Texas and was never caught.

Left with two of her four children, George and Mary Eliza, Maria ran a boardinghouse, leased the farmland to tenants, rented the gristmill, and sold other businesses Isaac had begun. As there were no public or private schools she taught the children. She continued to make her home available for Sunday worship and other religious services.

She made a trip back to Kentucky: "March, 1829: The time is arrived for me to set out on my long anticipated journey to Kentucky. Left Little Rock, March 28th, morning at nine o'clock, in company with Mr. Hitchcock and Mr. Washburn in a skiff, arrived safely at White River on Saturday ... Embarked on board steamboat 'Huntress' at daylight, next morning. We have had a safe passage which is great cause for gratitude to my heavenly Father...."

She married the Reverend William W. Stevenson on March 29, 1831. They had one child, Robert Watkins Stevenson, who became a police judge and later participated in the California gold rush. Mr. Stevenson organized a Campbellite congregation, now First Christian Church, Disciples of Christ, Little Rock.

Mary Eliza Watkins married John J. Clendennin, an associate justice of the Arkansas Supreme Court. George Watkins served a term as attorney general and became third chief justice of the Supreme Court of Arkansas in 1853–54.

Maria is buried at Little Rock in Mount Holly Cemetery in the Watkins plot, her name in the upper corner of a medium-sized monument, "In memory of MARIA, 2nd wife of ISAAC WATKINS" above the dates of her birth and death.

[Sources include Maria's diary in the Arkansas History Commission; the *Arkansas Gazette* for 1903; F. Hampton Roy and Charles Witsell, *How We Lived: Little Rock as an American City* (1964): 19; and the Mount Holly Burial Index.]

ANNE FULK

STILL, WILLIAM GRANT (May 11, 1895–Dec. 9, 1978), composer, was born in Woodville, Mississippi, to William Grant Still Sr. and Carrie Lena Fambro, both schoolteachers. After the mysterious death of the elder Still in 1895, Carrie Still and her son moved to Little Rock to live with her mother. Carrie taught in the public schools. Still later recalled a home life made comfortable with books, musical instruments, and phonograph records.

In 1904 Carrie Still married Charles Benjamin Shepperson, a railway postal clerk, who encouraged Still in his musical interests. Still enrolled at Wilberforce College where he studied medicine and music and performed on the violin, oboe, and clarinet.

On October 4, 1915, he married Grace Bundy. They had four children, William, Gail, June, and Caroline.

In the summer of 1916 Still was in Memphis, Tennessee, where he worked as an arranger and performer for W. C. Handy's band, absorbing the sights and sounds along Beale Street. He entered the Oberlin Conservatory of Music in 1917, but left for service in the United States Navy during World War I. After the war he returned to Oberlin, but left without a degree to go to Harlem.

In New York, in the midst of the Harlem Renaissance, Still worked for the Pace and Handy Music Publishing Company and performed in Handy's band. He studied with George Whitefield Chadwick, director of the New England Conservatory of Music, and with Edgard Varese.

His compositions were performed by the International Composers Guild and George Barrere's Little Symphony orchestra. These early works include *Africa, From the Black Belt, From the Land of Dreams, From the Journal of a Wanderer, Death Song,* and *Levee Land.* He also produced arrangements and orchestrations, most notably for Paul Whiteman and Willard Robison.

Still's first major orchestral composition, the *Afro-American Symphony,* completed in 1930, was first performed in 1931 by the Rochester (New York) Philharmonic Orchestra with Howard Hanson conducting. This marked the first time that a major orchestra played the complete score of a work by an African-American composer. Before the end of World War II, his symphony was performed in New York, Los Angeles, San Francisco, Chicago, Berlin, London, and Paris. Still and Hanson became close professional associates, and many of Still's works were first performed in Rochester.

In 1934 Still moved to Los Angeles and met Verna Arvey, an accomplished pianist and one of his keen admirers, who became a close professional associate. In the fall of 1934, his ballet, *La Guiablesse,* was performed to critical acclaim by the Chicago Grand Opera Company at the Chicago Civic Opera House.

Still was guest conductor for a Los Angeles Philharmonic concert at the Hollywood Bowl in 1936. Two excerpts from his own work were performed: "Land of Romance" from *Africa* and the "Scherzo" from the *Afro-American Symphony.* The music critic for the *Los Angeles Times* wrote: "Dignity, sincerity, and a certain pride characterize Still's writing."

In December 1937, the Philadelphia Symphony, with Leopold Stokowski as conductor, performed Still's Symphony in G Minor, entitled *Song of a New Race.* The critic for the *Philadelphia Inquirer* wrote that it "was of absorbing interest ... ranging from the exuberance of jazz to brooding wistfulness."

In 1938 Still was chosen to write the theme music for the "City of Tomorrow" at the 1939–40 New York World's Fair. His composition, *Song of a City,* was recorded and played for the duration of the fair.

Still composed theme music for films, including *Lost Horizon* in 1935, *Pennies from Heaven* in 1936, and *Stormy Weather* in 1943. He resigned in protest from the latter because, he claimed, the film and the studio, Twentieth-Century Fox, "degraded colored people." Later he wrote music for television productions including "Gunsmoke," "Have Gun, Will Travel," and the original "Perry Mason."

Still's awareness of social and racial injustice is reflected in his writings, including articles and letters to the editors of major newspapers, as well as in his musical compositions. He set to music "And They Lynched Him to a Tree," a poem by Katherine Garrison Chapin, first performed by the New York Philharmonic Orchestra in 1940. He also wrote the music for "In Memoriam: The Colored Soldiers Who Died for Democracy," a poem by Verna Arvey, first performed in 1943 at Carnegie Hall by the New York Philharmonic.

The New York City Opera Company, under the direction of Laszlo Halasz, presented the premiere performance of Still's opera *Troubled Island* in 1949. Langston Hughes wrote the libretto, based on the story of the rise to power and tragic ending of Jean Jacques Dessalines, the first emperor of Haiti. Still was demoralized by negative reviews but gained the distinction of being the first African American to have an opera performed by a major company in the United States.

He was a strong advocate for American music and criticized orchestras and conductors for featuring the works of foreign composers. During the anti-Communist hysteria of the early 1950s, he openly railed against communism in music to a degree beyond his own best interests.

Still received numerous honors and awards, including the following: a Harmon Award in 1928; Guggenheim fellowships in 1934, 1935, and 1938; a Rosenwald fellowship in 1939, renewed the following year; the Cleveland Symphony Orchestra's Fynette H. Kulas American Composers' Fund Commission in 1944, which he used to compose "Poem for Orchestra"; the Golden Jubilee Season Composition Competition prize from the Cincinnati Symphony Orchestra in 1944 for "Festive Overture"; the National Association for American Composers and Conductors Citation in 1949 for outstanding service to American music; the George Washington Carver Award from Phi Beta Sigma in 1953; a Freedoms Foundation Award in 1953 for "To You America!"; a Distinguished Achievement Award from the National Negro Opera Company Foundation in 1955; the National Federation of Music Clubs and the Aeolian Music Foundation Prize in 1961 for "The Peaceful Land," which was dedicated to the United Nations; the National Association of Negro Musicians Trophy in 1968; and the Mississippi Institute of Arts and Letters Music Award in 1981 for "A Bayou Legend," the institute's first award issued posthumously. He received nine honorary degrees.

In 1932 Still and Grace Bundy separated, and they divorced on February 6, 1939. Two days later Still and Verna Arvey, the daughter of Russian Jewish immigrants, married in Mexico (interracial marriages were illegal in California at the time). They had two children, Duncan and Judith.

Arvey was influential in the life and career of Still. She performed many of his works and wrote magazine articles and newspaper features about him. She collaborated with him in composing music. She was his most fervent admirer and supporter and closest confidante for over forty years.

Still wrote nearly two hundred compositions, including symphonies, ballets, operas, chamber music pieces, works for solo instruments, and art songs. His hundreds of arrangements and orchestrations received critical acclaim, but many have not survived. His music drew deeply from his background in the blues, spirituals, and jazz, as well as his formal study and his knowledge of folk music.

After spending nearly three years in a convalescent home, Still died in Los Angeles. His body was cremated, and the ashes were scattered in the Pacific Ocean.

[The William Grant Still and Verna Arvey Papers are in the Special Collections Division, University of Arkansas Libraries, Fayetteville. They include music scores, manuscripts, correspondence, diaries, scrapbooks, audio recordings, and photographs.

Biographical material includes Verna Arvey, *In One Lifetime* (1984), and Still's own account, "My Arkansas Boyhood," *AHQ* 26 (Autumn 1967): 285–92.

See also Gail Murchison, "'Dean of Afro-American Composers' or 'Harlem Renaissance Man': *The New Negro* and the Musical Poetics of William Grant Still," *AHQ* 53 (Spring 1994): 42–74; John Michael Spencer, "The William Grant Still Reader: Essays on American Music," a special issue of *Black Sacred Music: A Journal of Theomusicology* (1992); Judith Anne Still, Celeste Anne Headlee, and Lisa M. Headlee-Huffman, eds., *William Grant Still and the Fusion of Cultures in American Music*, 2d ed. (1995); and Judith Anne Still, Michael J. Dabrishus, and Carolyn L. Quin, *William Grant Still: A Bio-Bibliography* (1996).]

MICHAEL J. DABRISHUS

STONE, EDWARD DURELL

STONE, EDWARD DURELL (Mar. 9, 1902–Aug. 6, 1978), architect, was born in Fayetteville, the son of Benjamin Hicks Stone and Ruth Johnson. His grandfather was a businessman whose prosperity allowed his descendants to be well educated and comfortable. One of Stone's childhood playmates was J. William Fulbright, later United States senator.

After discovering a talent for design at the University of Arkansas, Stone joined his older brother, James Hicks Stone, an architect in Boston. There, Edward Stone studied evenings at the Boston Architectural Club and attended Harvard University and the Massachusetts Institute of Technology.

In 1927 he won the Rotch Traveling Scholarship which provided a stipend for two years of travel and study in Europe, where he found the world of art in transition. The traditional eclecticism dictated by the French École des Beaux Arts was being challenged by the austere "machine aesthetic" based upon construction with iron, steel, and glass and later dubbed the International Style. Although he studied and sketched the traditional monuments of architecture, Stone was also impressed by the new work of such Internationalists as Le Corbusier, Mies van der Rohe, and Walter Gropius.

Returning in 1929 Stone found the country in financial disarray and work in architecture all but nonexistent. Settling in New York City he found employment as a designer on the Waldorf Astoria Hotel and later with the consortium of architects designing Rockefeller Center. In that complex he is credited with the design of Radio City Music Hall, still one of the showplaces of the city.

He opened his own small firm in 1933, where he was "literally on the streets" and "doing odd jobs, designing advertising layouts or lighting fixtures." As economic conditions improved, he achieved a reputation as a designer within the newly imported Internationalist idiom. His work was widely published and included the highly visible Museum of Modern Art in New York City, with architect Philip Goodwin.

In 1931 he and Orlean Vandiver married. Two sons were born to them: Edward Durell Stone Jr. and Robert Vandiver Stone.

In 1942 Stone entered World War II as a major in the Army Air Forces and designed air bases throughout the United States.

Soon after reestablishing his office in New York City at the war's end, he designed the El Panama Hotel in Panama City, which renewed his reputation and generated international acclaim.

During the 1940s and 1950s, he was a leader among East Coast "modernist" artists and designers including painters, sculptors, architects, and furniture and textile designers. His associates included architects Alvar Aalto, Buckminister Fuller, and Frank Lloyd Wright, sculptors Alexander Calder and Isamu Noguchi, and furniture designers Hans and Florence Knoll. The integration of all the arts was a hallmark of the time, and many of Stone's projects, such as the University of Arkansas Fine Arts Center in 1949, bear out that philosophy.

Stone became disillusioned with the austere Internationalist philosophy: "Much of our present architecture lacks that intangible quality of permanence, formality and dignity. It bears more resemblance to the latest automobile, depending upon shining, metallic finishes—doomed to an early obsolescence." He began to seek an architecture of warmth and graciousness and ultimately developed an entirely personal approach to design.

In 1954 he designed the United States Embassy complex in New Delhi, India, a milestone expressing the ideal which he had begun to hold dear: an interpretation of classical elegance, with its dignity, simple geometry, and flowing and generous spaces. The harsh Indian climate was the setting for the development of his fascination with patterned and filtered sunlight, which had begun when he worked in the tropics. The embassy complex was widely applauded and laid the foundation for most of his future work.

His marriage having been dissolved, he and Maria Elena Torchio married in 1954; a son, Benjamin Hicks Stone III, and a daughter, Maria Francesca Stone, were born to the marriage.

During the next twenty years offices bearing the name "Edward Durell Stone, Architect" were established in California, Palo Alto and Los Angeles, in Chicago and, as the need arose, in Florida and Arkansas, Saudi Arabia and Pakistan. Projects such as the Stuart Pharmaceutical Company in Pasadena were closely akin to the New Delhi Embassy while others, such as the Huntington Hartford Gallery of Modern Art in New York City, explored new directions. All conformed to Stone's affinity for formal planning, rich colors, textured surfaces, and filtered sunlight.

Notable projects include the Kennedy Center for the Performing Arts in Washington, D.C.; the General Motors Building in New York City; the Standard Oil Building in Chicago; the United States Pavilion at the Brussels World's Fair; and the Busch Memorial Stadium in St. Louis.

His international practice included such works as the Phoenicia Hotel and a campus for International College in Beirut, Lebanon; airports at Jeddah and Riyadh in Saudi Arabia; and the Governmental Complex, Presidential Estate, and Institute of Nuclear Sciences and Technology at Islamabad, Pakistan. (For an accounting of the several hundred projects executed by the firm, see the sources listed below.)

Divorced in 1966, he was married in 1972 to Violet Campbell Moffat; they had a daughter, Fiona Campbell Stone.

Stone returned to Arkansas frequently, and during the late 1940s and early 1950s, while designing the University of Arkansas Fine Arts Center in Fayetteville and the University Medical Center in Little Rock, he developed a strong association with the University of Arkansas School of Architecture. Other projects within the state include the Pine Bluff Civic Center; the Arkansas First National Bank in Hot Springs; and residences in Little Rock, Pine Bluff, Harrison, McGehee, and Fayetteville.

He taught as a visiting design critic at Yale, Princeton, and Cornell Universities, the Massachusetts Institute of Technology, and the University of Arkansas. He was a Fellow of the American Institute of Architects, the American Academy of Arts and Sciences and the British Royal Society of Arts, and received the Medal of Honor from the New York Chapter, AIA, and two Gold Medals from the New York Architectural League.

The design idiom for which his buildings are noted reflects his character and way of life. Articles invariably describe him as warm, courtly, expansive, and gracious, all terms which could describe his architecture: "I try to find an architecture that is timeless and free from the mannerisms of the moment. Architecture should follow a grander and more ageless pattern ... the inspiration for a building should be the accumulation of history." *Time*'s cover story spoke of him as "a pioneer modernist, undoubtedly the profession's freest spirit and by general consensus the most versatile designer of his generation."

[The Edward Durell Stone Papers (written and graphic) are in Special Collections Division, University of Arkansas Libraries, Fayetteville. The best accounts of Stone and his work are his autobiography, *The Evolution of an Architect* (1962); his later volume on the firm's work, *Edward Durell Stone, Recent and Future Architecture* (1967); Paul Heyer, *Architects on Architecture* (1966); Ian McCallum, *Architecture USA* (1959); *Contemporary Architects*, Muriel Emanuel, ed. (1980); *American Art Journal*, vol. 17, no. 3 and vol. 20, no. 3; and *Time*, Mar. 31, 1958. Articles of interest were published in *Architectural Forum*, *Architectural Record*, and *Progressive Architecture*, and in *Time*, *Life*, *House Beautiful*, and *House and Garden*. See the obituaries in the *Arkansas Gazette*, Aug. 8, 1978, and in major newspapers and professional journals.]

ERNEST E. JACKS

STUART, RUTH MCENERY (Feb. 19, 1852–May 6, 1917), writer and platform speaker, was born Mary Routh McEnery in Marksville, Louisiana, to Mary Routh Stirling and James McEnery, who was at that time mayor of Marksville. The McEnery family was prominent in Louisiana politics; two of Routh's uncles served as governor and one was a United States senator and a justice of the Louisiana Supreme Court. Some time before 1860 the family moved to New Orleans where James had an appointment at the United States Customs House.

Routh taught at the Loquet-LeRoy Institute in New Orleans before she and Alfred Oden Stuart were married in 1879. They moved to Washington, Arkansas, where A. O. had farm property and was a partner in the mercantile establishment of Stuart and Holman. Routh was well liked in Washington for her hospitality; she organized the Dear Old Town Club and sponsored social gatherings and a book club.

After A. O. died in 1883, Routh and her infant son, Stirling, returned to her family home in New Orleans; she began to think of a career as a writer. After the publication of two of her stories and acceptance of two others in 1888, she moved to New York. She also discarded the family spelling of her name for the more familiar "Ruth." When she began to succeed as a writer, she asked her sister Sarah to live with her and help with the care of her child and home.

In 1893 Harper and Brothers published *A Golden Wedding and Other Tales,* a collection of eleven of her short stories and two poems. "The Woman's Exchange of Simpkinsville," included in this collection, is set in an imaginary Arkansas town modeled after Washington. The success of this story led her to include some of its characters in her later Arkansas fiction. She became associated with the "Harper Set" of writers published by that magazine and worked temporarily as an editor of *Harper's.*

Between 1888 and 1917 Stuart published more than seventy-five stories in addition to dialect verse. These works appeared in major magazines of the day, including *Harper's Bazaar, Harper's New Monthly Magazine, Century Magazine, New Princeton Review, Delineator,* the *Outlook,* and *Lippincott's Magazine.* They were collected in twenty-three volumes.

In academic terms Stuart belongs to the school of American local color, writing that emphasizes regional characteristics in the landscape, way of life, and language. Her works drew on three main threads of her experience, the white plain folk of Washington, the immigrants and aristocrats of New Orleans, and southern black people. Stuart's stories provide details of the natural and man-made environment, cultural, religious, and family values, and, most noticeably, the idiosyncrasies of the southern regional dialect. She peopled her imaginary Simpkinsville with genteel farmers and their wives, elderly spinsters, country doctors, preachers, and storekeepers. The "Arkansas Prophet" is a "queer, half-luney" black man who, since he is also the "shorest shot in the State" manages to rescue a mistreated Simpkinsville girl from the clutches of a man from the North. Deuteronomy Jones is the garrulous old narrator of her "Sonny" stories, which recount Sonny's life from his birth on Christmas night through "Sonny's Christening," "Sonny's Diploma," down to "Weddin' Presents." The heroine of "Queen o' Sheba's Triumph" is a black woman who leaves Arkansas to start a new life in New York.

Stuart also developed a reputation as a platform entertainer and traveled widely in the United States. Some of her works were apparently written for oral presentation, such as the collection *Moriah's Mourning and Other Half-Hour Sketches.* She was also known in England where she was invited to become a member of the Lyceum Club in 1904.

After her only child died in a fall in 1905, Stuart lost some creative momentum. Recurrent bouts of illness and a change in literary fashion diminished her literary output, but she continued to give readings and to travel. In 1915 Tulane University awarded her an honorary degree of Doctor of Letters. Her grave is in New Orleans, near her son's.

One of Stuart's characters spoke for many readers of the time when she said, "I never would read a book thet didn't end right; in fact, I don't think the law ought to allow sech to be printed." The elements that made Stuart a popular writer in her lifetime diminished her appeal to later readers. They saw her as sentimental and condescending in her treatment of African Americans and women. However, in the latter decades of the twentieth century, women's studies have brought Stuart back into the curriculum, if not the canon, of American literature, giving her credit for her strong female characters, her sympathetic humor, and her skillful use of irony.

[Sources include the A. O. Stuart Family File, Southwest Arkansas Regional Archives, Old Washington State Park, Arkansas, and the Ruth McEnery Stuart Papers, McKeldin Library, Tulane University, New Orleans. For a list of Stuart's published works, see Ethel C. Simpson, ed.,

Simpkinsville and Vicinity: Arkansas Stories of Ruth McEnery Stuart (1983; rpt. 1999).]

ETHEL C. SIMPSON

TATUM, REECE (May 3, 1921–Jan. 18, 1967), professional basketball player who became an international star as the "clown prince" of the Harlem Globetrotters, was born at El Dorado. His parents' names are unknown; his father was a farmer and a part-time preacher.

At the peak of his popularity in the early 1950s, "Goose" Tatum earned in excess of fifty thousand dollars a year, a fabulous sports salary for the times and especially so in light of the Globetrotters' tight fiscal policies. Abe Saperstein, a white man who formed the Globetrotters at Chicago in 1927, had his pick of talented black basketball players until 1950, when the National Basketball Association started scouting and signing black players.

Tatum grew up in an era when unofficial but rigid segregation existed in professional baseball, football, and basketball. He played high-school basketball, but attracted more attention in baseball. He played for the Indianapolis Clowns and the Birmingham Black Barons in baseball's Negro Leagues before joining the Globetrotters in 1942. Almost immediately he was drafted into the air force. Stationed at Lincoln, Nebraska, for three years, he played "straight" basketball for the base team and spent additional hours in the gym, perfecting and expanding routines the Globetrotters had showed him. He blossomed as their chief attraction after World War II.

Like many other great clowns, Tatum rarely induced laughter between shows. He could be melancholy and temperamental. "It was amazing," former Globetrotter teammate Leon Hillard said. "You'd see Goose out on the floor, laughing and playing tricks, but as soon as he was inside the clubhouse, he just turned it off, like an electric switch. He was like two people."

A hook-shot artist at six feet, three inches with an eighty-four-inch arm span, Tatum scored fifty-four points in one game. He could be a serious competitor when the Globetrotters felt they had a point to prove. In March of 1951 he dominated an eighteen-game tour against a team of college all-stars, and started it by scoring thirty points in Madison Square Garden.

Over the years, tension built between Tatum and team management over his habit of failing to show up for some games. It came to a head in 1955 when Saperstein tracked him down by telephone in Arkansas, after Tatum had been missing from the tour for several games, and told him he was suspended. Soon Tatum left the Globetrotters and struck out on his own. He organized the Harlem Road Kings and went on touring, Globetrotter style, sticking with the South for the most part, staying closer to his wife and two children.

His later years were neither happy nor profitable. Injuries and illness curtailed his playing time, and he was essential to the show. In 1959 he was hit with a bill for $118,000 in back income taxes. In 1966 he was hospitalized for a liver ailment.

On January 18, 1967, he planned to fly from his home in El Paso, Texas, to Dallas and perhaps play a few minutes in a game that night. Instead, he became ill and was rushed to a hospital, where he died of an apparent heart attack.

In 1974 he became the first black athlete inducted by the Arkansas Sports Hall of Fame.

[Sources include George Vecsey, Harlem Globetrotters (1974); and Arkansas Gazette files, 1955–56, 1959, 1961, 1967, and 1974.]

JIM BAILEY

TAYLOR, CHARLES EDWARD (Sept. 15, 1868–Jan. 11, 1932), Progressive reform mayor of Little Rock, was born in Austin, Tunica County, Mississippi, the son of William Arbuckle Taylor and Mary Perkins. During the mid-1870s the Taylors moved to eastern Arkansas and then to Little Rock. After graduation from high school Taylor worked first at a hardware store, then as a traveling salesman. In 1901 he became secretary-treasurer of the Arkansas Brick and Manufacturing Company. He lived at 2312 Broadway with his wife, Belle Blackwood Taylor, whom he married on October 15, 1895, and their four children. He was a member of Little Rock's Second Baptist Church, where he served as Sunday School superintendent for sixteen years, and was a member of many fraternal and community organizations.

When Taylor announced his candidacy for mayor in November 1910, he had never held public office before. Even though there was no true political machine in Little Rock, as existed in other cities during this period, Taylor ran as a reform candidate and was supported by the Young Men's and the Traveling Men's Good Government Clubs. He campaigned as an experienced businessman, not a politician, and promised more efficient, "business-like" government, city growth, expanded and improved city services, a healthier environment, and an improved moral climate—in general "a bigger, better, cleaner and more progressive city."

The election results showed John Tuohey the winner by thirty-eight votes. Taylor challenged the count, charging 250 illegal votes had been cast, forcing a runoff, which he won by 229 votes. Even though Taylor used the popular jargon of progressivism as a campaign tool, it was not empty rhetoric. He and the city council assumed many new responsibilities for city government and directed a wide range of reforms which transformed Little Rock from a nineteenth century river town into a modern municipality.

When Taylor took office in April 1911, he set about to rid the city of its "wide-open town" image, improve public health, which was threatened by a typhoid epidemic, and modernize the fire department, which had been ineffective against recent, devastating downtown fires. In tackling social problems such as gambling, drinking, and prostitution, Taylor, a true progressive, believed that these problems wasted human potential and that it was society's responsibility to provide everyone with the opportunity to become a healthy, productive citizen. He and his police chief began to enforce the laws against gambling; Taylor led two raids himself. They regulated saloons more closely (state prohibition went into effect in 1916) and, on the recommendation of the vice commission in 1913, set about to eliminate the "red light district" in Little Rock.

In his effort to improve the city's public health, Taylor and the city council replaced the board of health with a full-fledged health department; instituted sanitary regulations and inspections of dairies, slaughterhouses, and other food supply services; began garbage collection; monitored drinking water; and expanded the sewer system. All these reforms contributed to the decrease in the city's death rate from typhoid and other diseases.

To improve the fire department Taylor replaced horse-drawn wagons with new, motorized fire equipment, including an aerial truck, that was much more effective in a city with tall buildings and a growing population. The city council also enacted comprehensive building, electrical, and plumbing codes.

During his four terms, Taylor added to the city's inventory of such "modern" conveniences as paved streets, sewer lines, water mains, water hydrants, electric street lights, and fire stations. The community of Pulaski Heights was annexed in 1916. His leadership was evident in the formation of the United Charities, a forerunner of the United Way, and in the Parkways Association plan to provide Little Rock with parks, parkways, and shaded streets. He tried to implement plans for a badly needed new city hospital and for a city auditorium, though neither of these nor the park plan was funded.

Taylor recognized that the chief obstacle to city improvements was the state constitution's prohibition against cities issuing bonds. In 1911–12 he initiated a statewide campaign for an amendment to allow such funding, but neither it nor two more attempts during his tenure were successful. Little Rock's increasing indebtedness was one problem Taylor was not able to solve and which his opponents used against him.

After eight years in office, Taylor decided to end his political career and reenter the business world. He was involved in the initial stages of an automobile manufacturing company and then an oil lease business, neither of which proved profitable. In 1923 he became secretary-manager of the Pine Bluff Chamber of Commerce until his retirement in 1931. Taylor died of a heart attack in Pine Bluff.

During the second decade of the twentieth century, the capital city took on what the *Arkansas Gazette* described as "a new municipal life." A large part of the credit for this new spirit must be given to Taylor and his vision of a progressive city.

[Charles E. Taylor's personal papers and scrapbook are in the possession of the Taylor family. A Taylor campaign brochure, "Plain Facts about Our City," was printed by the *Arkansas Gazette*, Dec. 6, 1914. See the *Arkansas Gazette*, Dec. 6, 1916, and Jan. 12, 1932; and the *Arkansas Democrat*, Mar. 20–31, 1919. Obituaries are in the *Arkansas Gazette*, Jan. 12, 1932, and the *Pine Bluff Commercial*, Jan. 11, 1932. See articles by Martha Williamson Rimmer in the *Pulaski County Historical Review* 25 (Sept. 1977): 49–60; 25 (Dec. 1977): 65–72; and 31 (Spring 1983): 10–14; and an M.A. thesis, University of Arkansas, Fayetteville, 1977.]

MARTHA WILLIAMSON RIMMER

TERRAL, THOMAS JEFFERSON (Dec. 21, 1882– Mar. 9, 1946), governor of Arkansas, was born in Union Parish, Louisiana, the son of George W. and Celia G. Terral. He attended public schools in Louisiana and Mississippi and studied at the University of Kentucky.

He earned a law degree at the University of Arkansas in 1910. After admittance to the Arkansas bar, he practiced law in Little Rock. On February 25, 1914, he married Eula Terral, a Pine Bluff resident and probably a distant relative. The couple had no children.

Thomas Terral was active in Arkansas politics well before he served the state as governor. During the 1911, 1913, and 1915 sessions of the general assembly, he was either the assistant secretary or the secretary of the Arkansas State Senate. When the assembly was not in session, he served as deputy state superintendent of public instruction. In 1916 Terral ran for secretary of state in the Democratic primary. He won the nomination easily, as he did the later general election. Two years later, Terral won a second term as secretary of state. However, a bid for governor in 1920 ended in failure.

Four years later he ran for governor again. Like others in the race for the Democratic nomination, he hoped to gain an advantage by winning the endorsement of the Ku Klux Klan. The Arkansas Klan denied him membership on a technicality, however, and endorsed one of his opponents. Later "naturalized" (inducted) by the Louisiana Klan, Terral won the Democratic nomination by some twelve thousand votes. In the general election, he easily defeated the Republican contender.

He assumed the office of governor on January 13, 1925. His legislative agenda was modest. He wanted laws that would punish bootleggers and "pistol toters"; by enacting a luxury tax, he proposed to double the amount of state money invested in public education; he recommended a revolving loan fund for the benefit of higher education; and he advocated an additional one-cent-per-gallon tax on gasoline to fund road construction. A strong proponent of governmental efficiency, Terral proposed the abolition of most honorary boards and commissions, to be replaced by a limited number of new departments run by professional staff. He urged the creation of Arkansas's first state park at Petit Jean Mountain.

The legislature proved receptive to much of Terral's program relating to governmental efficiency. It balked, however, at levying an additional gasoline tax, and it also refused to abolish the fish and game commission. Terral retaliated by vetoing legislative proposals to legalize Sunday baseball and to license physicians who did not meet requirements of medical examining boards.

Terral believed that the record of his first term in office justified his reelection. Arkansas's voters thought differently. In 1926 he lost the Democratic nomination to John E. Martineau by sixteen thousand votes in a particularly ugly primary. Thereafter, Terral practiced law in Little Rock until his death twenty years later. He was buried in Roselawn Memorial Park.

[See W. David Baird, "Thomas Jefferson Terral, 1925–1927," in *The Governors of Arkansas: Essays in Political Biography,* Timothy P. Donovan, Willard B. Gatewood Jr., and Jeannie M. Whayne, eds., 2d ed. (1995).]

W. DAVID BAIRD

TERRY, ADOLPHINE FLETCHER (Nov. 3, 1882–July 25, 1976), social and political activist, was born in Little Rock. Her father, John Gould Fletcher, a captain in the Confederate army, worked in the cotton business and in banking and served terms as sheriff of Pulaski County and mayor of Little Rock. Her mother was Adolphine Krause Fletcher. Adolphine was the oldest child; her brother was the poet John Gould Fletcher; her sister Mary was a suffragist.

When Adolphine was not quite sixteen, she attended Vassar College in Poughkeepsie, New York. After graduating, she returned home, and in 1910 she married David D. Terry, a lawyer who served as U.S. congressman from 1933 to 1942. The couple raised a family of five children: David D. Terry Jr., Mary, Sally, William, and Joseph.

Adolphine Terry became a community leader with particular interest in education and the well-being of children. She helped establish the first juvenile court system in Arkansas and a free, statewide library system. She led efforts as early as 1908 to consolidate school districts, appoint professional county superintendents, and provide school transportation for rural children. She formed the first School Improvement Association in Arkansas, forerunner of the Parent Teacher Association. "I believe in prayer," she said, "but I also believe in action and less conversations."

Terry's oldest daughter Mary was born with a rare bone disease that crippled her for life. In 1938 Terry published *Courage,* recounting her struggle to accept her daughter's condition. "I planned my life through the years, quite sure of myself . . . a little scornful of those who did not have all that I possessed—wonderful health, a pleasant home, and an interesting life. I was not a modest person. I was intellectual without being spiritual."

Terry compensated for her daughter's physical problems by building up her mental acuity. She took Mary to concerts, lectures, shops, church, and picture shows. When Mary was eight, her diagnosis worsened, and doctors predicted she would not live past her fifteenth birthday. At that point Terry decided to accept her daughter as she was and determined to give her child as full a life as possible. She adopted a boy, Joseph, whom Mary befriended. She took her children, including Mary, on long trips to Arizona and New Mexico. Despite predictions, Mary lived a long life, earned a college degree, traveled, and worked in psychological testing. Terry said caring for Mary led to a spiritual awakening in which she found "in some measure the spiritual meaning of life, a sense of real achievement and peace."

When Terry learned in September 1957 that Governor Orval Faubus had used troops to prevent black students from attending Central High School in Little Rock and that a white mob had terrorized the students, she wrote, "For days, I walked about unable to concentrate on anything, except the fact that we had been disgraced by a group of poor whites and a portion of the lunatic fringe ... Where had the better class been while this was being concocted? Shame on us."

When Faubus ignored a U.S. Supreme Court ruling to integrate the schools, Terry, who was seventy-five years old, and two friends, Vivion Brewer and Velma Powell, formed the Women's Emergency Committee. The women, about fifty of them, held their first meeting on September 16, 1958, at Terry's home, becoming the first organized white group to oppose Faubus and demand the reopening of the high schools. Their interest was primarily peace and order, not integration. Terry wrote, "Of course no one really wants integration. There are too many problems. But it is here and it is right."

These well-to-do white women filled a void in leadership. Terry wrote to the governor suggesting that he could be a second Abraham Lincoln if he would lead the South into a future where desegregation was the moral standard. Later, when running for a fourth term, Faubus called her "the strongest integrationist you ever saw." Terry replied that at age seventy-seven she was not interested in becoming a campaign issue. She said Faubus had chosen "to be recorded in history, not as a great leader, but as a Talmadge, a Bilbo, a demagogue."

In the months following its formation, the Women's Emergency Committee worked to persuade the public to reopen Little Rock's four high schools, which had been closed by an act of the state legislature in August 1958. WEC members became targets of hate mail and harassment; Terry said one woman threatened to burn her house down. But the group attracted support and interested prominent men in the cause. Its membership grew, and its volunteers and resources were used to strengthen other groups, including Stop This Outrageous Purge, which supported teachers who were pro-integration or moderates.

In May 1959, along with STOP and black voters, the WEC campaigned successfully to recall three school board members who were segregationists. The recall election was the first full-scale loss for Faubus and the segregationists. To secure public support, the WEC produced a study documenting the negative effect the school crisis was having upon the Little Rock economy. Their efforts altered the course of public action and helped in reopening the schools in 1959. Terry wrote of those years, "We are living through the most exciting time of the world, because the soul of man everywhere is demanding more rights and more recognition—and, most of all, more human dignity."

In other efforts Terry helped form the local chapter of the American Association of University Women and was instrumental in starting the Pulaski County Tuberculosis Association and the Community Chest, the forerunner of the United Way. She was active in historic preservation and the arts. In later years she worked to make the city auditorium accessible to older people and the handicapped.

Terry died at ninety-three. She and her sister willed the Fletcher home to the city of Little Rock to be "enjoyed by the people of Arkansas." The 1839 mansion, where Terry had lived since childhood, became the Arkansas Arts Center's Decorative Arts Museum.

[Sources include the Fletcher-Terry Papers, Archives and Special Collections, University of Arkansas Libraries, Little Rock; and articles in the *Arkansas Gazette* on July 8, 1960, May 27, 1966, and Apr. 28, 1990. This entry is based also on a taped interview with Bill and Betty Terry on Mar. 25, 1993. *Courage* was published in 1938 under the pen name Mary Lindsey; Terry's other books are *Cordelia, a Member of the Household* (1967), and *Charlotte Stephens, Little Rock's First Black Teacher* (1973).]

PEGGY HARRIS

THACH, JOHN S. (Apr. 11, 1906–Apr. 15, 1981), aviator, admiral, was born in Pine Bluff to James H. Thach and Jo Bocage and was raised in Fordyce. He followed his older brother, James Harmon Thach Jr., to the United States Naval Academy, graduating in 1927. After serving briefly with battleships, John transferred into naval aviation.

By the 1930s Thach had a reputation as one of the navy's best aviators as a member of one of its most famous units, Fighting One, the "High Hat" squadron. Known for their aerobatic stunts, Thach and the High Hats performed all the stunt work for Clark Gable's 1931 movie "Hell Divers." A versatile pilot, Thach set an endurance record by flying an XP2H seaplane from Norfolk, Virginia, to Panama in twenty-five hours, fifteen minutes.

Thach is best known for a single air combat tactic, the Thach Weave. At the outbreak of the Second World War, Thach held test-pilot status and was commander of the "Felix-the-Cat" Fighter Three squadron. He knew from intelligence reports that the latest Japanese fighter plane, the Mitsubishi A6M Reisen, called the "Zero," was extremely maneuverable and had exceptional range. The Zero put America's 1941-vintage fighters at a serious disadvantage.

Thach set out to neutralize the Zero's agility by bringing to bear the generally superior firepower of the slower American aircraft. In the months before the United States entered World War II, in consultation with Edward J. "Butch" O'Hare, the naval air hero for whom Chicago's airport is named, Thach developed the technique of veering back and forth, which came to be known as the Thach Weave.

Traditional American combat tactics called for flights of three aircraft in combat. Thach abandoned convention, designing his tactic for two-plane elements. The two airplanes flew side by side until attacked, then turned toward each other. This resulted in the attacker losing a clear closing shot because it presented a diminishing target with an increasing angle of deflection. Meanwhile, the aircraft not under attack was afforded an almost head-on shot at the aggressor as the two friendly aircraft continued to turn and cross each other's tails. The aggressor was forced to pull up and expose his underside to attack or dive away to save himself.

Worked out on Thach's kitchen table with match-sticks, the maneuver had its first test at the Battle of the Coral Sea in May 1942. With twenty Japanese fighters attacking the carrier Lexington, Fighting Three used the weave to shoot down nineteen aircraft. One member of Thach's squadron scored five kills. The Thach Weave proved itself to be not merely a fluke a month later when Fighting Three employed it again with great success. This time they used it flying from the deck of the carrier Yorktown at the Battle of Midway, June 3–7, 1942.

After Midway Thach's tactical skill was deemed too valuable to risk in combat. Transferred stateside, Thach taught combat tactics at Jacksonville, Florida, and returned to the movie business for the navy, this time in the form of training films. He returned to battle as operations officer for Vice Admiral John S. McCain's fast-carrier task force at the end of the Second World War. He was promoted to captain, and in the summer of 1950 commanded the escort carrier Sicily at the outset of the Korean conflict. Among his commands was the aircraft carrier Franklin D. Roosevelt. He was promoted to rear admiral in 1955 and became an advocate for naval power in the missile age.

He became one of the navy's top antisubmarine warfare experts. As deputy chief of naval operations for air, he played a key role in the adoption of the A-7 Corsair II for carrier use and in defeating Secretary of Defense Robert McNamara's plan to force the F-111 on the navy. In 1965 he was made commander in chief of U.S. naval forces in Europe. He retired in 1967 after forty years of active duty.

He and his brother James simultaneously held the rank of full admiral on active duty, among the few pairs of brothers ever to do so. Not an aviator, James served with distinction in the Pacific and was captain of the battleship Missouri from 1948 to 1949.

John Thach and his wife, Madalynn, had four children. He died in Coronado, California, and is buried at Point Loma Military Cemetery in San Diego.

[Sources include the John Thach File, Arkansas Aviation Historical Association Archives, Little Rock, Arkansas; and Thomas F. Gates, "'Keep Your Planes Together, Fight as a Team': Felix the Cat, Part Two," *Hook*, vol. 8, no. 3. Obituaries are in the *Arkansas Gazette*, Apr. 17, 1981, and in *Navy Times*, May 25, 1981. There is also an article in the *Arkansas Gazette*, Nov. 11, 1981.]

WILLIAM M. SMITH, JR.

THADEN, LOUISE MCPHETRIDGE (Nov. 12, 1905–Nov. 9, 1979), aviation pioneer, was born in Bentonville, the daughter of Roy and Edna McPhetridge. She was raised in the small northwest Arkansas town, graduating from Bentonville High. She attended the University of Arkansas in Fayetteville between 1921 and 1925, majoring in journalism and physical education. She left college after her junior year and in 1927 pursued a job as a salesperson with Travel Air Corporation, an aircraft manufacturer based in Wichita, Kansas. The company sent her to its sales office in San Francisco.

In the Bay Area on June 19, 1928, she married Herbert Thaden, a former U.S. Army pilot and engineer working on the development of the first American all-metal aircraft. She also started flying lessons, soloing in 1927 to earn her pilot's certificate. She received certificate No. 74, signed by Orville Wright. Within two years, she became the fourth woman in America to hold a transport pilot rating.

Thaden shared the spotlight with Amelia Earhart during the golden age of aviation. Thaden was the first woman to win major flying events and awards, and she set world performance records. Although history has remembered Earhart from the publicity of her over-water flights and her mysterious death, during the 1930s Thaden was her equal in both skill and celebrity.

Her first world record was the women's altitude mark of 20,260 feet set on December 1, 1928. She followed it with a women's endurance mark of 22 hours, 3 minutes, 12 seconds on March 17, 1929.

She defeated both Earhart and Pancho Barnes to win the first Women's Air Derby, a transcontinental race from Santa Monica, California, to the site of the 1929 National Air Races in Cleveland, Ohio. On August 19 she took off from Santa Monica and reached Cleveland on August 27 after almost twenty-five hundred miles of flying. Her notable competition met with ignoble outcomes. Earhart damaged her Lockheed Vega aircraft with a ground loop accident in Yuma, Arizona. Barnes first became lost and veered into Mexico, then tore the right wing from her Travel Air when she hit a Chevrolet in Pecos, Texas. Blanche Noyes had an in-flight fire over west Texas, then suffered a ground loop at Pecos. By the time Thaden reached Fort Worth, Texas, she had control of the race.

In 1930 she and Earhart formed the Ninety-Nines, an international organization for women pilots which continues to the present day. Thaden refused the lead-ership role, insisting Earhart become president. Thaden served as the group's treasurer from 1930 to 1934, and as vice president from 1934 to 1936.

In 1936 she and copilot Noyes captured the Bendix Cup race, winning the New York to Los Angeles event in the first year women were eligible to compete. Her win with Noyes in a standard factory edition Beech Staggerwing C17R stunned the aviation world. The victory also set a new east-to-west record of 14 hours, 54 minutes. As a result, Thaden received aviation's highest honor, the Harmon Trophy, in 1936. "We had to prove that women were good pilots," Thaden said. "In an age where some men didn't think a woman should drive a horse and buggy, much less drive an automobile, it was a job to prove that females could fly."

Along with Frances Marsalis, Thaden set a new endurance record by flying a Curtiss Thrush biplane for 196 hours over Long Island, New York. During the eight days, Thaden made seventy-eight air-to-air refueling contacts and occasionally made live radio broadcasts to a national audience. The two pilots received food, water, and fresh clothing lowered by rope from another airplane during the record-setting event.

During the height of her aviation achievements, she bore a son, Bill, in 1930 and daughter, Pat, in 1933. In 1935 she worked for the Bureau of Air Commerce promoting the marking of airfields and landmarks nationwide. She retired from full-time competition in 1938 to devote more time to her family. In the same year she published her memoirs, *High, Wide and Frightened*. Active in the Civil Air Patrol during the Second World War, she reached the rank of lieutenant colonel. The Bentonville, Arkansas, airport was renamed Louise Thaden Field in 1951, and a building at the National Staggerwing Museum in Tullahoma, Tennessee, was named in her honor in 1974. She died of a heart attack in High Point, North Carolina.

[See the Louise Thaden File, Arkansas Aviation Museum, Fayetteville, Arkansas; Louise Thaden, *High, Wide and Frightened* (1938); Kathleen Brooks-Pazmany, *United States Women in Aviation, 1919–1929* (1991); "Louise Thaden in Retrospect," *Sport Aviation*, Sept. 1990; and the *Arkansas Gazette*, Nov. 4, 1980.]

WILLIAM M. SMITH JR.

THARPE, ROSETTA (Mar. 20, 1915–Oct. 9, 1973), was born Rosetta Nubin in Cotton Plant, Arkansas, but grew up in Chicago. There she debuted at age six as

"Little Sister," singing "I Looked Down the Line and I Wondered" to an audience reportedly numbering a thousand. Her first musical influence was her mother, Katie Bell Nubin, a dynamic singer of spirituals, with whom Rosetta later recorded several excellent vocal duets. Other chief musical influences included the ecstatic religion of the Sanctified Church and the blues guitar. Eventually she developed a style of playing guitar that some critics have compared favorably with that of blues artist Memphis Minnie.

After gaining a following in Chicago as a singer-evangelist Rosetta moved to Harlem where she achieved even greater success, scoring with both gospel and secular audiences. Her electrifying church performances were so well received that they led to her appearing in the 1938 "From Spirituals to Swing" concerts at Carnegie Hall. She also performed with the orchestras of Cab Calloway, Benny Goodman, and Count Basie and made recordings with Lucky Millinder. Most of her recordings were made for Decca, but she also recorded for the Diplomat, Mercury, Verve, and Savoy labels.

Tharpe's first recording session provided a glimpse of what was to come from her. She performed a very spirited version of Thomas A. Dorsey's "Hide Me in Thy Bosom" under the secularized title "Rock Me," a number she sang in both theaters and churches. Her repertoire borrowed heavily from traditional sources. For example, two of her most popular songs with audiences were "That's All," a number first recorded by Washington Phillips in 1927 and later reworked by white guitarist Merle Travis, and "This Train," a novelty piece that later became a staple with folk music enthusiasts of the 1960s. Tharpe moved between church and secular audiences in ways that few gospel singers, black or white, had ever done before. This accomplishment was given mainstream media attention when in 1939 *Life* ran a feature story on her success in appealing to both religious and pop audiences.

Tharpe's greatest success came in the 1940s. With the boogie-woogie pianist Sammy Price and his trio she recorded "Strange Things Happening Every Day," a number that made the race-record top ten in 1945. In 1946 she joined forces with Marie Knight, a gospel shouter from Newark; over the next few years the duo recorded many outstanding vocal duets. Knight's relatively unadorned shouting style perfectly complemented Tharpe's flamboyant approach and, beginning with "Up above My Head," the two had several recordings on the *Billboard* race charts. Their 78s also brought them numerous engagements in churches, theaters, and clubs. Then, the two split up. Knight began performing as a blues singer. Tharpe didn't like the blues and returned to the church, only to find that she was suddenly *persona non grata* for many on this circuit. Apparently her venture into singing blues caused many to regard her as "selling out."

Losing much of her traditional church audience, she went to Europe, touring England in 1957 with Chris Barber's Jazz Band. Then in the 1960s she made two European tours, both arranged by French jazz critic Hugues Panassie. Tharpe headlined a 1960 Apollo Theatre show and in 1967 was booked at the Newport Folk Festival. Her appearance there must have been memorable, because she showed up dressed in mink. She also remained active in the recording studio—one of her late 1960s albums earned a Grammy nomination. Her first love, however, remained the church, and near the end of her life she was booked solid in small country churches in areas where big name singers rarely appeared and where her old records were fondly recalled. It was pleasing to her to be back on the church circuit, even if it was a smaller circuit than the one where she achieved her initial fame.

[See Viv Broughton, *Black Gospel: An Illustrated History of the Gospel Sound* (1985), and Tony Heilbut, *The Gospel Sound: Good News and Bad Times* (1971; rpt. 1975).]

W. K. MCNEIL

THOMAS, DAVID YANCEY (1872–1943), historian, grew up on a farm in southwest Kentucky, the youngest of nine children. During the 1890s he earned degrees from Emory, Vanderbilt, and Columbia Universities; afterward, he taught at Hendrix College intermittently from 1898 until 1903. He and Sarah Janney married in 1905; they had two children, Mary Elizabeth and Albert.

He was on the University of Arkansas faculty from 1907 until 1940. For most of that time he was chairman of the history and political science department. He had a long list of publications to his credit, including forty-three articles and eight books.

He was a forceful, and often singular, advocate for the preservation of Arkansas archival materials. He helped to found the Arkansas Historical Association and was the first editor of its journal, the *Arkansas*

Historical Quarterly. Whenever he turned to an Arkansas topic, he had to dig for materials to support his research. He wrote scores of letters asking for information from Arkansas governors, congressmen, and other prominent people or their families and pleaded with them to deposit their papers in the university library. In the 1930s, George Donaghey, a former governor of Arkansas, became interested in the problem and helped to set up a special fund so that Thomas could buy old Arkansas newspapers and documents from private collectors for the university library.

Thomas was a social critic, speaking out frequently and forcefully on the issues of the day. In one of his many public speeches, he set out his view that an educator had an obligation to society to point out problems in the world and to work toward their solution. In the period before and after the First World War, he represented Arkansas on the University Committee on Southern Race Questions, a regional coalition organized to call attention to racial problems in the South. On behalf of the committee, he condemned lynching in Arkansas and, in 1919, investigated the Elaine Race Riots in the Arkansas Delta.

During World War I, Thomas prepared special classes on war aims and European history for soldiers taking officer's training at the university. In 1920 he published a lesson plan for a course designed to teach civics to women preparing to vote for the first time. He was active in the interwar peace movement, giving strong support to one national group working to outlaw adherence to the World Court. He argued for public ownership of utilities; and, at one point, scolded both the Daughters of the American Revolution and the American Legion over issues relating to academic freedom.

Thomas's public positions on controversial questions pleased some people but seriously displeased many others. In 1939 one of his statements on contemporary Arkansas politics appears to have irritated Governor Carl Bailey. The university board of trustees, apparently responding to pressure from Governor Bailey, forced Thomas to retire from the university in 1940. He was sixty-seven years old at the time, but he was not yet financially prepared for retirement. He had to find work elsewhere and ended up moving to Austin to take a job teaching international relations at the University of Texas, where he remained from 1941 until he died in 1943.

In 1940 the temporarily unemployed Thomas found that he had time to turn to a project he had been considering for years: the establishment of a statewide organization to support the publication of an Arkansas history journal. After months of preparation by Thomas and others, the Arkansas Historical Association (AHA) was organized in February 1941. Even though he had moved to Austin, Thomas agreed to be editor of the AHA's quarterly journal.

Finding the material and the money to publish the first issues of the *Arkansas Historical Quarterly* was a great challenge. Dr. Thomas had to beg people for articles, and he did a lot of writing and rewriting himself. He also had to worry constantly about funding. Revenue from memberships was the sole source of money for the project, and there was always a question as to whether the association could afford the next issue. One way or another, he managed to get out the first four issues in 1942 and had started on volume two of the *Quarterly* before he died.

[The David Yancey Thomas Papers are in the Special Collections Division, University of Arkansas Libraries, Fayetteville.]

Bob Besom

THOMPSON, CHARLES LOUIS (Nov. 16, 1868–Dec. 30, 1959), architect, was born in Danville, Illinois, to James C. Thompson and Henrietta Lighter. He did not receive formal architectural training, but began as a draftsman under the supervision of an established architect: "I got my structural education from bricklayers, carpenters, plasterers, plumbers." At the age of fourteen, after the deaths of his parents, he quit school to help support his brothers and sisters.

He came to Arkansas in 1886. According to one account, he chose Little Rock over New York or New Orleans because it was "the farthest in the wilderness." After placing "position wanted" advertisements, he accepted a job with Benjamin J. Bartlett, who was among the first professionally trained architects in the state. Thompson became a full partner with Bartlett in 1888.

In July 1889 Thompson married Lillian McGann, who contracted tuberculosis and died in 1904, leaving three children. In 1908 Thompson married Mary Watkins, from a well-known Little Rock family, and had with her two daughters and a son.

Thompson was noted for public service. In 1909 Governor George Donaghey appointed him to a special commission to supervise completion of the new state capitol building, then a controversial project. In 1925 Thompson helped establish the Little Rock Chamber of Commerce and served as its first president. Two years later he helped raise funds for the victims of the 1927 flood. During the Great Depression he led efforts to provide relief for the state's citizens. He also initiated and led efforts to improve the water distribution system in the city of Little Rock. In 1931 the *Arkansas Gazette* said that Thompson could be "called upon in any big emergency."

He was committed to the professionalization of architecture. With Bartlett and others he established the Arkansas Society of Engineers, Architects, and Surveyors. In 1921 he helped organize the Arkansas chapter of the American Institute of Architecture. During the 1930s he helped establish the Arkansas Board of Architects to register and certify architects.

Thompson began his career when architects moved frequently to take advantage of new opportunities. In 1890 Benjamin Bartlett moved away, leaving Thompson sole proprietor of his own office at the age of twenty-two. In 1891 Thompson formed a partnership with a civil engineer, Fred J. H. Rickon. The firm of Rickon and Thompson, Architects and Civil Engineers, completed a variety of projects, including many residences and two significant structures which no longer stand, the Rector Bath House in Hot Springs (1895) and the B'Nai Israel Temple (1897) in Little Rock. The firm was dissolved in 1897.

For nearly the next twenty years Thompson was the sole proprietor of his own firm. Thomas Harding Jr., the son of a Little Rock architect, joined Thompson in 1898 at the age of fourteen and eventually became a partner in 1916, making the firm Thompson and Harding, Architects. In 1925 Harding left, and the partnership was dissolved.

Today, Thompson's reputation is based, in part, on the sheer number of buildings he designed. He and his firm designed fifteen courthouses in Arkansas. Among the best known are the Washington County Courthouse (1905) in Fayetteville, the Cleveland County Courthouse (1910) in Rison, and the Monroe County Courthouse (1911) in Clarendon. He designed the Little Rock City Hall (1907) and the Arkadelphia City Library (1900). St. Edwards Catholic Church (1901) in Little Rock featured Gothic details and was perhaps his best-known church design.

Thompson also earned many residential commissions around the state. One of the best known is the "new" Peter Hoetze House (1905) in Little Rock, built in the Colonial Revival Style on a very large scale. Situated on a corner lot at 1619 South Louisiana Street in Little Rock, the house has a hipped roof, three roof dormers, with the central dormer having a broken pediment, and a balustraded roof deck, sometimes referred to as a "widow's walk." The entrance has double ionic columns extending the full height of the two floors. A broken pediment, repeating the central roof dormer, is above the front door. There is a curved portico on the north entrance.

One of Thompson's more unusual designs, the John R. Fordyce House (1904), was Little Rock's only house in the Egyptian revival style. It features pylons with capitals resembling papyrus leaves at the front entrance, slightly inward sloping exterior walls, and a hipped roof. The plantation house Marlsgate (1904), another large-scale, classical revival design, was originally constructed for the Dortch family in Scott. The foregoing examples, except as noted, are standing in 1996.

In 1927 Thompson formed a new partnership with the already established firm of Ginocchio and Sanders. Some years later his son-in-law, Edwin B. Cromwell, joined the firm, which evolved into Cromwell, Truemper, Levy, Parker, and Woodsmall, and is in 1996 one of the ten oldest such firms in the United States.

Thompson retired from architecture in 1938 after fifty-two years. He was prolific and a master of the fashionable styles of his time from Queen Anne to Craftsman to Prairie School. His success was based on his talent as a designer, his skill in business, and his commitment to public service. He died in Little Rock.

[The most comprehensive biography of Thompson is F. Hampton Roy, *Charles L. Thompson and Associates, Arkansas Architects* (1982). An obituary appeared in the *Arkansas Gazette*, Dec. 31, 1959. Calvin R. Ledbetter Jr. discusses the controversy surrounding the construction of the 1912 state capitol building in *Carpenter from Conway: George Washington Donaghey as Governor of Arkansas, 1909–1913* (1993).

The Old State House Museum, Little Rock, holds a collection of Thompson's drawings. The Arkansas Historic Preservation Program of the Department of Arkansas Heritage holds a copy of a nomination to the National Register of Historic Places, "Structures in Arkansas Represented by the Charles L. Thompson Design Collection —a Thematic Group."]

STEPHEN L. RECKEN

THOMPSON, GREEN WALTER (1848?–Mar. 20, 1902), political leader and businessman, was prominent in Little Rock from the end of the Civil War until his untimely death. He was born a slave on the Robert Elliott farm, Ouachita County, Arkansas. We know he grew up on a prosperous farm, but nothing is known of his family. Since the 1880 census records him as a "mulatto," it is likely Thompson was fathered by a white man. His mother eventually married a slave named Thompson, and Green Elliot took his stepfather's name.

While still a teenage slave, Green Elliott married a slave named Dora Hildreth; they were soon the parents of a baby girl. He left Ouachita County shortly after Christmas in 1865 and set out to build a new life in the capital, leaving behind his wife and newborn child.

The muddy streets of Little Rock were filled with thousands of freedmen at the end of the Civil War. Green Thompson prospered in this new environment. By 1871 he was in the grocery business. Soon he opened a saloon and later a feed store. Like others of the city's emerging black elite, Thompson invested in real estate; by 1895 he owned a real-estate company. One of his major assets was Thompson Hall, a large brick building with a public meeting hall, the scene of black social and political events.

His "before the war" family did not prevent Thompson from getting married and starting a family in Little Rock. By 1880 he was married to Darthulia W. Thompson and the father of two sons, the firstborn named Green Walter Thompson Jr. This child apparently died at an early age; Darthulia died in 1896. A year and a half later the forty-eight-year-old widower married twenty-year-old Mary Fairchild.

Thompson was no more than twenty-seven years old when he sought and won his first elective office. In 1875 he was elected the Sixth Ward alderman on the Little Rock City Council. For the next eighteen years he served on the council, setting a record tenure for blacks that was not broken for almost one hundred years.

The twenty years following the Civil War was an exciting time for black voters. A few years earlier these electors were slaves, not citizens; now they were a political force in Little Rock. This was especially true in the Sixth Ward, where Green Thompson lived. Derisively referred to as the "Bloody Sixth" by the race-baiting *Arkansas Gazette,* it had a heavily black population.

Once elected, Little Rock aldermen usually found themselves occupied with mundane matters. City government, hamstrung by the same state constitution that shackles local government today, dealt mostly with the delivery of basic services. A certain egalitarian informality prevailed among council members, allowing for a relatively free exchange of ideas. Occasionally partisan confrontations occurred. In 1878 the white Democratic majority on the council convened in a court of impeachment in an attempt to remove incumbent Republican police judge W. J. Warwick, who was charged with embezzlement. Though Thompson and fellow black Republican Isaac Gillam fought the effort, the judge was removed from office. In April 1878 Thompson suffered a more painful setback when he nominated a black political ally, William Rector, for city sanitary policeman. Both Thompson and Gillam supported Rector and managed to recruit the votes of two white Democratic aldermen, but eventually a white candidate was selected.

In 1888 Thompson accepted his party's nomination for the state House of Representatives from Pulaski County. With the country caught in a prolonged agricultural depression and political orthodoxy under challenge, the election of 1888 was a great event in Arkansas political history. The incumbent Democratic Party fought desperately to stave off defeat, and voting irregularities were common throughout the state. The results in Pulaski County were so tainted that a recount was undertaken and over one thousand false ballots were discovered. In February 1889, after a public outcry, the local Pulaski County Democratic incumbents resigned, and Green Thompson and the other Republicans were seated. Thompson did not run for reelection, but in 1890 he was the unsuccessful Union-Labor Party nominee for state senator.

As the Gilded Age gave way to the more strident decade of the 1890s, Thompson and other black politicians found themselves battling the dogs of discrimination, segregation, and, finally, disfranchisement. The warm relationship between blacks and the Republican Party slowly degenerated as the party of Abraham Lincoln and Charles Sumner became the party of Mark Hanna and William McKinley.

In 1891 the Arkansas legislature passed new election laws that consolidated the voting process in the hands of the Democratic Party. These "reforms" curtailed the number of blacks who voted in 1892. Still, the Democrats realized that the 1891 election law would not be enough to purge the black aldermen from the

"Bloody Sixth Ward." Thus, in 1893 the city eliminated the ancient system of electing aldermen by ward and implemented citywide at-large elections. Green Thompson waged a vigorous campaign for reelection, but it was hopeless: Democrats swept into every position on the city council. No other black citizen won election to the Little Rock City Council until 1969.

Political impotence must have been bitter for Green Thompson, a man of the people who relished the test of the ballot box. Even after the advent of Jim Crow, he maintained his interest in politics. At least he had business interests to divert his mind from the turn of political events.

Thompson died at the hands of a murderer on March 20, 1902. He was returning home from a meeting about midnight, when an assailant killed him with an ax as he stabled his horses. Although family members were initially charged, no one was ever convicted for the murder.

[The papers of Green Thompson do not survive. His tenure as an alderman can be traced through the Little Rock City Council minute books as well as the pages of the *Arkansas Gazette*. His probate records are located in the Arkansas History Commission.]

Том W. Dillard

TONTY, HENRY DE (1650–1704), explorer, trader, and founder of Arkansas Post, was probably born in Paris, the eldest son of Lorenzo di Tonti and Isabelle de Liette. His family fled to Paris from Naples after taking part in an insurrection. He joined the French armed forces when he was eighteen. While in military service he lost his right hand in a grenade explosion. When he replaced the hand with one made of metal, he became known as "the man with the iron hand."

At the age of twenty-eight, de Tonty was introduced to Robert Cavalier, Sieur de la Salle, whom he joined on an expedition to North America. Once in Canada de Tonty was given the task of building the *Griffon,* the first sailing vessel on the Great Lakes. Together, La Salle and de Tonty explored much of what is now Michigan and Illinois and built forts in that territory. In the spring of 1680 de Tonty was left in charge of the Illinois Territory and was to oversee completion of a fort they had begun on Lake Peoria. This task became impossible when his men deserted, and an Iroquois war party raided the area. He and five others escaped and made their way back to Green Bay. After recovering from his wounds, he and La Salle returned to Illinois to build Fort Saint Louis.

De Tonty had a feudal loyalty to La Salle and was his courageous lieutenant. He saw La Salle for the last time in 1683, when La Salle went back to France to prepare for the colonization of the Louisiana Territory. In 1689 de Tonty set out for the Mississippi River valley in search of La Salle, whom he believed to be in the area. His efforts to find him were unsuccessful. It would be four years before he learned the fate of La Salle's expedition, which had ended in disaster on the Spanish Texas coast in 1687.

Failing to find La Salle, de Tonty led his party to some land granted to him by La Salle on the Arkansas River. He ordered ten of his men to build a trading post there. The exact location of Poste de Arkansea is not known. It was on the north bank of the river, estimated at eighteen to forty-five miles from its mouth, near a Quapaw village called Osotouy. De Tonty and the rest of his men returned to Illinois. The men left at the post, led by Coutoure Charpenter, built a French-style cabin and awaited trappers and traders.

A few men from La Salle's expedition reached the post and were overjoyed to find other Frenchmen there. The survivors, led by Henri Joutel, told of their misfortunes and the death of La Salle, who had been killed by some of his own men. When de Tonty heard this news, he set out to recover La Salle's body, but this adventure failed when some of his men decided it was not worth risking their lives for a man's body, even La Salle's.

De Tonty evidently had some hopes for Arkansas Post. In 1689 he granted land there to Jesuit priests for their use in teaching "the mysteries of our Holy Religion" to the "Savages who are Upon our River of Akanzea." Settlement by Jesuits would be important in maintaining good relations with the Indians. De Tonty pledged to provide support for a missionary and to build a mission house for the Indians. But the Jesuits did not take up the land grant, and nothing came of these plans.

After only a few years the post was languishing. Its commander deserted it in 1687, and de Tonty was more interested in the possibilities of settlement on the Gulf Coast. Arkansas Post was never the primary object of his interest in trade on the lower Mississippi and his efforts to extend French power there.

In 1700 de Tonty went to Louisiana Territory near the mouth of the Mississippi and settled, serving the

French crown on Indian matters. He died at Mobile, most likely of yellow fever. He had spent most of his life dealing with Indians and trappers. He was a courageous explorer and an effective administrator, well respected by Indians, missionaries, and the French aristocracy. He laid some of the groundwork for French Louisiana.

In 1898 a sizable group of Italians, led by an Italian priest named Pietro Bandini, migrated from Sunnyside Plantation in Chicot County to northwestern Arkansas to escape conditions of servitude at Sunnyside. They named their new settlement Tontitown in honor of their countryman, who had explored what is now Arkansas two hundred years before.

[See Roger Coleman, "The Arkansas Post Story," *Southwest Cultural Resources Center Professional Papers* 12 (1987): 12; Norman W. Caldwell, "Tonty and the Beginning of Arkansas Post," *AHQ* 8 (Autumn 1949): 189–205; Dr. and Mrs. T. L. Hodges, "Possibilities for the Archaeologist and Historian in Eastern Arkansas," *AHQ* 2: 2 (1943): 141–59; and Dumas Malone, ed., *Dictionary of American Biography*, vol. 9 (1943).]

SHANE LIND

TOWNSEND, WALLACE (Aug. 20, 1882–Jan. 7, 1979), lawyer and leader in the Republican Party, was born in DeWitt, Iowa, the son of John R. Townsend and Italia James. He moved to Little Rock with his family in November 1894 and received his B.A. from Hendrix College in 1902. He managed the Hendrix baseball team and was business manager of the college monthly publication, the *Hendrix Mirror*. He taught at Clarendon High School and was principal of the Kramer School.

His most noteworthy service as an educator was his tenure as principal of Little Rock High School in the years 1906 to 1910, when the school earned its first accreditation. In fact, the school progressed so much under his tenure that private academies in Little Rock closed because their students left them for the public high school.

In 1906 Townsend was awarded a LL.B. at the University of Arkansas and began his law career in 1910. His law practice was chiefly concerned with revenue bonds.

Townsend began his participation in partisan politics as the Republican Party nominee for state superintendent of public instruction in 1910. This race and his subsequent service as the state Grand Old Party's legal counsel brought him into the party's ruling circles at a time when Lily-Whitism was an important issue. Townsend advocated a Lily-White position, and in 1914 the Lily-White faction, under the leadership of Townsend and Pulaski County GOP chairman Augustus C. Remmel, was swept into power in the Republican Party.

Lily-Whitism was a recurring issue within the Arkansas Republican Party since the formation of a Lily-White faction in 1888. The Lily-Whites believed the reason for the weakness of the Arkansas GOP was that the vast majority of blacks were affiliated with it, alienating racist white southerners from the party. Their prescription for southern Republican victories, then, was for the black members of the party to be placed in a subordinate position or expelled altogether. Eventually, Lily-Whitism received support within the national GOP structure, especially among the Progressives. This development helped galvanize Lily-Whitism in the Arkansas GOP.

Following the 1914 Lily-White victory, Townsend rose further within the state party to become the Lily-White nominee for governor. Despite the Lily-White success in maintaining their control over the Arkansas GOP, they were unable to make electoral gains. Part of the reason for this was the inconsistent manner in which the Lily-Whites treated black party members. Unlike the Lily-Whites in other southern Republican parties, in Arkansas blacks were not expelled wholesale or placed in a subordinate position. Instead, the Lily-Whites prevented the blacks from participating in the local parties in roughly a dozen of the counties with the largest black populations. The Arkansas Lily-Whites apparently wished to make the state GOP acceptable to the racist whites and at the same time keep the black vote. Eventually, the Lily-Whites lost heart, and by 1928, a reconciliation between the blacks and the Arkansas GOP was reached. Even so, the once strong bonds between the black electorate and the state party were broken, and Lily-Whitism contributed in a major way to the eventual black defection to the Democratic Party.

Townsend served in a variety of Arkansas Republican Party offices. He attended every Republican National Convention during the years 1912–1960. From 1914 to 1916 he served as an at-large member of the Arkansas Republican State Committee, and from 1916 to 1962, he served on the state party's executive committee. He was the state party's vice chairman during 1920–28 and the Republican national committeeman from Arkansas from 1928 through 1961. Townsend received patronage rewards for his party service, including the office of register of the U.S. land office at Little Rock during 1922–24 and the position of United States attorney for the Eastern District of Arkansas during 1930–34.

Townsend also served as a leader within a number of private organizations such as the Little Rock Chamber of Commerce and the Little Rock Boys' Club. In 1962 he married Bess Voss, who died in 1958. In 1962 he married Floy Smith Plunkett. He retired from his law practice in 1974. He was survived by his wife, two daughters, six grandchildren, and two great-grandchildren.

[The Wallace Townsend Papers are in the Archives and Special Collections Department, UALR Library, University of Arkansas at Little Rock. Obituaries were published in the *Arkansas Democrat* and the *Arkansas Gazette* on Jan. 8, 1979.]

CHARLES J. RECTOR

TRENT, ALPHONSO (Oct. 24, 1902–Oct. 14, 1959), jazz pianist and band leader, was born in Fort Smith, Arkansas, the son of E. O. Trent and Hattie Smith. His father, one of the first black graduates of Ohio State University, was principal of Lincoln High School in Fort Smith. Alphonso began performing as a pianist in his early teens.

In 1923 he attended Shorter College in Little Rock, where he began working with a group led by Eugene Crooke called the Syncho Six. The group featured Trent on piano, Crooke on banjo, trumpeter Edwin Swayzee, saxophonist James Jeter, vocalist John Fielding, and drummer A. G. Godley. Another early addition to the band was the legendary jazz trombonist Leo "Snub" Mosley, then only fifteen years old.

In 1925 the band set out for Texas, playing on street corners for nickels and dimes. Now known as the Alphonso Trent Orchestra, the group arrived in Dallas and played low-paying dance jobs at first. Finally, they were booked into the elegant Adolphus Hotel, where their two-week engagement stretched into eighteen months. It was just the break they needed. They not only found steady work, but also gained exposure on broadcasts over radio station WFAA. The broadcasts from the Adolphus were a first for a black orchestra in the Southwest, and reached an audience throughout the central United States and Canada.

The long engagement at the Adolphus provided the band with a chance to rehearse and refine their musical identity. Right from the start, the band, which had grown to eleven musicians, had been founded as a co-op unit. All members received the same pay and were expected to contribute ideas to the development of the musical arrangements. Although Trent bought arrangements and hired arrangers, the most musically exciting orchestrations came from the band members' own collective efforts.

Trent was the inspirational leader of the band. His musical training served as the cornerstone for the construction of their elaborate arrangements. His emphasis on good tone quality and intonation helped them achieve a sophistication and finesse rare among bands of the Southwest.

During the Adolphus engagement, Trent married Dallas native Essie Mae Grissom, whom he met at a party held in the band's honor.

In the summer of 1926 the band left the Adolphus and toured major hotels throughout Texas, playing at such notable hotels as the Galvez in Galveston and the Rice in Houston. They opened a new hotel in San Antonio and performed at the inaugural ball of governor Miriam A. Ferguson.

Then in October of 1927, Trent took his orchestra on their first eastern tour. He had encouragement from the great orchestra leader Paul Whiteman, who heard the Alphonso Trent Orchestra in Dallas and thought they should head for the larger markets in the East, including New York City. However, Trent seemed satisfied playing the lucrative but less prestigious ballrooms of the Midwest. For the next two years the band played long engagements in Cincinnati, Louisville, Lexington, and Buffalo, among other cities.

During this time the band made its first recordings, four songs for the Gennett Company in Richmond, Indiana. Also during this period the violinist Leroy "Stuff" Smith joined the band. In 1928 they played aboard the steamer *St. Paul* at St. Louis, where they engaged in a "battle of the bands" with Louis Armstrong. The Trent band was involved in many such battles against the top bands in the country, including the Fletcher Henderson band and the McKinney Cotton Pickers.

The summer of 1929 was spent performing at a resort in Port Stanley, Ontario. At the close of the engagement, the band headed for its one and only date in New York City, a week at the Savoy Ballroom. Afterward, they were offered a contract at the Arcadia, the number-two ballroom in New York, but Trent refused. The reason seems to have been his fear of losing sidemen to more established band leaders. He opted instead for a more lucrative job at the Plantation Club in Cleveland, Ohio.

During that engagement a fire consumed the club and destroyed the band's instruments and library. Several versions of the story have been told, and all include reference to gangsters and arson. The band was stranded in Cleveland without instruments until Trent's family came to the rescue, purchasing new instruments. By this time, however, the Great Depression had begun, jobs were scarce, and the band hobbled back to Fort Smith. Trent kept his musicians busy, using his hometown as a base of operations. They rehearsed at the Trent home on 9th Street, and several of the musicians married young women from the area.

The Alphonso Trent Orchestra made one last road trip in the winter of 1932–33, but by this time Trent was no longer with them. He had returned to Fort Smith ostensibly to attend to family matters, but he must have been disheartened, too. It was not long, however, before he had another band on the road, a small group touring the Dakotas, Wyoming, Colorado, and Texas. He continued to offer opportunities to young musicians, including the immortal jazz guitarist Charlie Christian.

After World War II he settled in Fort Smith to manage the family's real-estate holdings and the city's first housing project. He remained active in the music business, but restricted his performances to local nightclubs. He died of a heart attack in Fort Smith.

[See Henry Q. Rinne, "A Short History of the Alphonso Trent Orchestra," *AHQ* 45 (Autumn 1986): 228–49. Two songs, "Black and Blue Rhapsody" and "Nightmare," are on Historical Records: "Territory Bands," HLP-24, and "Rare Bands of the Twenties," HLP-3.]

HENRY Q. RINNE

TRIEBER, JACOB (Oct. 6, 1853–Sept. 17, 1927), banker and judge, son of Morris Trieber and Blume Brodeck, was born in Raschkow, Prussia, and came to America with his family in 1866. They lived in St. Louis for two years before settling in Helena, Arkansas, where Morris Trieber opened a dry-goods store. Jacob helped keep the store's books and in 1873 began studying law with former Arkansas Supreme Court justice Marshall

L. Stephenson. Trieber learned English well but retained a heavy German accent throughout his life. He was admitted to the Arkansas bar in 1876 and formed a partnership with Marshall Stephenson's brother, L. C. Stephenson, then later with Marshall himself.

In 1885 Trieber and several friends organized the First National Bank of Helena, with Trieber serving as its first president. He became proficient in banking law and in 1913 was a moving force in the establishment of a state banking law. He became a member of the Republican Party in 1874 and was elected to Helena's city council in 1882. He was named superintendent of the state census in 1890, elected treasurer of Phillips County in 1892, and was appointed as United States district attorney for the Eastern District of Arkansas in 1897.

Jacob Trieber married Ida Schradski in 1882, and the couple had two children, Harry and Bess. The family was Jewish (Reform) and affiliated with Congregation Beth El in Helena and, later, Congregation B'nai Israel of Little Rock.

President William McKinley appointed Trieber a federal judge for the Eastern District of Arkansas in 1900; Trieber thus became the first Jewish federal judge in the United States. His appointment was "a miracle of no small proportions," considering he was an immigrant with a heavy German accent, of modest means, with no formal college or Law School training, and came from a small town in rural Arkansas. Yet he became known nationwide for his judicial abilities and astuteness at law. He presided over cases involving bankruptcy, litigation of Indian land disputes, violation of liquor laws on Indian reservations, labor issues, problems with the railroads, bootlegging, and racial prejudice. During his twenty-seven years as federal judge he handled thousands of cases, kept his docket current, and also served as a judge in the Western District of Arkansas, Eastern and Western Districts of Missouri, and the Southern District of New York.

As a child in Prussia, Trieber he had seen firsthand the results of racism and intolerance against his own people. He was touched by the lynching of blacks in Arkansas and felt such tragedies affected not only blacks, but all of the state's citizens. In a letter to Colonel H. L. Remmel, president of the Arkansas Board of Trade, in 1901, he wrote that "people wouldn't know there is anything in Arkansas except murder and demagoguery." While the country was "growing by leaps and bounds ... Arkansas is asleep ... despite her great natural resources." Job discrimination against blacks also troubled him, as well as intimidation by "white-cappers" (Ku Klux Klan members) that could lead to mob rule.

Because Arkansas's judicial system seemed unable or unwilling to prevent violence and racism, Trieber used his federal authority against such injustices. Two of his rulings in 1903 involved the whitecappers. *United States v. Hodges* dealt with whitecappers' efforts to have black workers fired at a sawmill at White Hall, Arkansas. *United States v. Morris* was a case involving terrorism by whitecappers in Cross County. In *Hodges* Trieber instructed jurors to consider whether a person should be permitted to employ whom he pleased or whether he could be compelled by others. In *Morris,* he held that "the rights to lease lands and to accept employment for hire are fundamental rights, inherent in every free citizen," regardless of race or color. In 1906 the United States Supreme Court overruled *Hodges,* reasoning that the ability to earn a living was not a fundamental right of citizens protected by the Thirteenth Amendment.

The Supreme Court's decision on *Hodges* led to more tragedy. Judge Gerald Heaney wrote in 1985, "[F]or almost fifty years ... the *Hodges* case ... became the rod and staff of those who denied that the federal government had the authority to intervene in race relations." It was not until the Civil Rights Act of 1964 that comprehensive protection against racial discrimination in employment was established. And in 1968 the Supreme Court overruled its 1906 ruling of *Hodges,* which had nullified Judge Trieber's opinion. Thus, "Judge Trieber's interpretation of the Thirteenth Amendment and the Civil Rights Act of 1866 was at last vindicated." The Court also adopted Trieber's reasoning in *Morris* "and held that the Civil Rights Act of 1866 by authority of the Thirteenth Amendment, reached private, racially-motivated interference with fundamental rights."

Trieber, known for his lucid, concise opinions and the ability to clear dockets quickly, was invited to New York in 1927 at the suggestion of Chief Justice William Howard Taft to help ease the congested docket of the federal courts there. The work was strenuous, and the weather was hot; he died while there. Some of his rulings, such as those regarding the regulatory rights of Congress that helped establish present-day migratory bird laws, have had permanent effects.

[Sources include the Judge Jacob Trieber Papers, courtesy J. Marshall Trieber; Honorable Gerald Heaney, "Jacob Trieber: Lawyer, Politician, Judge," *UALR Law Journal,* vol. 8 (1985–86); *Arkansas Banker,* vol. 11 (1927); and Carolyn Gray LeMaster, *A Corner of the Tapestry: A History of the Jewish Experience in Arkansas, 1820s–1900s* (1994).]

CAROLYN GRAY LEMASTER

TURNER, JESSE (Oct. 3, 1805–Nov. 22, 1894), lawyer, politician, was born in Orange County, North Carolina, to James Turner and Rebecca Clendenin, and was raised and educated at Salem. At age eighteen Jesse taught school for a year and began reading law. He received his license in 1825 and practiced law for several years at Waynesboro. In April 1830 Turner moved to Jackson County, Alabama. In May 1831 he arrived in Arkansas; he spent some time in Van Buren and Fayetteville and settled near the Crawford County Court, then located about eighteen miles southeast of Van Buren. In 1838, after Crawford County was divided to create Franklin County and the court was permanently established, Turner moved to Van Buren, where he lived for the rest of his life.

Turner and Violet P. Drennan of Pittsburgh, Pennsylvania, a niece of John Drennan, an early settler of Van Buren, married in the fall of 1842; she died in September 1843. In June 1855 he and Rebecca Allen (1823–1917) of Pittsburgh married. They had one son, Jesse Turner Jr.

Turner practiced law, following the circuit court, and he took an interest in both national and local politics. During his sixty-plus years in Arkansas, he knew and corresponded with most of the politically powerful individuals in the state, including Absalom Fowler, Robert Crittenden, Albert Pike, David Walker, and Augustus Garland. In *Biographical and Pictorial History of Arkansas* (1887), John Hallum recounts several anecdotes concerning Turner, including an unfought duel and some of Turner's more colorful legal cases. Hallum characterized Turner "as the soul of honor ... and with it he has a rich vein of eccentricity, supplemented liberally with what we call absentmindedness." He often forgot his saddlebags and once rode off on his friend's horse instead of his own without realizing it.

In 1832 Turner found himself in a duel with another lawyer, Matthew Leeper, after the latter grossly insulted him in open court sessions. Adjourning to Indian Territory to face off with pistols, Leeper apologized to

Turner for his unjustified language just before the duel commenced. Angry that the duel had been averted, Judge S. G. Sneed, Leeper's second, shot at Turner, but the gun failed.

Turner was elected to the state legislature in 1838. He served as president of the Whig state party convention in 1840 and ran as a candidate for presidential elector on the Whig ticket in 1848. During the 1840s and early 1850s, he campaigned throughout the state for presidential candidates William H. Harrison, Zachary Taylor, and Millard Fillmore.

Secretary of War John Bell appointed Turner in 1841 to serve on the board of visitors that examined West Point cadets. In 1851 Congress created the Western District of Arkansas, its jurisdiction extending into what is now New Mexico. The federal court was located at Van Buren, and President Fillmore appointed Turner United States district attorney for the district, a position that he held until the Civil War.

Turner was a strong supporter of internal improvements, particularly the building of railroads to reduce western Arkansas's dependence on the Arkansas River. In 1854 he was one of a group to charter the Little Rock and Fort Smith Railroad; he served as president from 1857 until 1868 when the company was reorganized. He continued to be one of the directors and a vice president through the 1880s.

In 1861 he served as delegate from Crawford County to the Secession Convention, where he opposed secession as illegal and ruinous to the South. Turner, along with David Walker, was one of the northern and western Arkansas leaders in opposing secession. After Fort Sumter, yielding to popular sentiment in Van Buren and the majority will, the convention reassembled and Turner voted for secession. He continued to be a Union man, returned to Van Buren, and did not take part in the Civil War.

After the war, in 1866–67, he was elected to represent Crawford and Franklin Counties in the state senate, serving as chairman of the judiciary committee. He opposed the Reconstruction Acts and supported public education and the incorporation of new railroads. Turner was again elected to the state senate in 1874, served another term as chairman of the judiciary committee, and was a strong supporter of Governor Augustus Garland's administration.

During the 1870s he served as a delegate-at-large to the 1876 national Democratic convention. He was appointed associate justice of the state supreme court in 1878, filling out David Walker's unexpired term. Periodically, Turner also served as a special judge when justices were disqualified from hearing certain cases. His judicial opinions are reported in the 32d through 35th volumes of *Arkansas Reports*.

In writing the majority opinion for the court, he was meticulous in his documentation of issues. Although some of his opinions concern appeals on criminal law, most relate to administration of estates and probate law, including issues related to married women and property law. In another instance, the court struck down a legislative act, and Turner's opinion detailed the general assembly's failure to follow constitutional requirements.

After his son's graduation from Law School and admission to the bar in 1879, the two set up a law practice together. Turner continued to practice law until his death. He died at the Fort Smith Opera House during a lecture on the life of Davy Crockett.

[The Jesse Turner Papers, 1778–1929, are at Duke University Durham, North Carolina. A microfilm copy of this collection is held at the University of Arkansas at Little Rock Archives, which also holds the Turner Family Papers, 1847–1935, and the Rebecca Allen Turner Papers, 1840–1895.

See also Clara Eno, *History of Crawford County, Arkansas* (195?): 181–86; *Encyclopedia of the New West*, William S. Speer and John Henry Brown, eds. (1881); and John Livingston, *Sketches of Eminent Americans* (n.d.).]

LINDA R. PINE

TYLER, T. TEXAS (June 20, 1916–Jan. 23, 1972) was born in Mena and was christened David Luke Myrick. Tyler, who had a "growl in his voice and a million friends," initiated a distinctive country/western music style which established him in the top levels of stardom in the recording industry and on the performance stage in the 1940s, 1950s, and on into the 1960s.

His recording "Deck of Cards" became a best seller in 1948 and set the pattern for such future country stars as "Red" Sovine, Jimmy Dean, Tex Ritter, "Whispering" Bill Anderson, and others. "Deck of Cards" tells the story of a soldier who is admonished by his commanding officer for playing cards during a church service, and the soldier explains why the deck of cards is his almanac, diary, and Bible. Tyler ends the song with, "And Ah know that story's true, 'cause Ah *was* that soldier boy."

Myrick's childhood years were difficult, with few comforts. His parents did menial jobs for their livelihood. Myrick later commented often, "I was born and I was raised poor." His school years were confined to the elementary grades. Some of his hometown people insist, and it cannot be confirmed, that he spent some time in a reformatory. Parents admonished their children to stay away from the Myrick boy.

Somewhere in all of this growing up he became interested in music. Teaching himself on a Sears, Roebuck guitar, he was soon performing in local talent shows and at dances. He left home in 1932, heading east. He appeared on the popular "Major Bowes Amateur Hour" radio program. His rendition of "Silver Haired Daddy" won him top honors and kicked his career in gear. He soon appeared live on radio stations in Rhode Island, Virginia, and West Virginia. By 1941 he was in California using "Tex Tyler" for a stage name.

After serving in the army during World War Two, Tyler returned to California and organized a band. He signed a contract with a small record label, Four Star Records. Accompanied by brash, honky-tonk instrumentation, every song featured Tyler's distinctive growl. His 1948 "Deck of Cards" topped the country/western charts. His next big hit, "Daddy Gave My Dog Away," revealed an expanded stage name. Introduced one night by an announcer as the "teasing singer, T. Texas Tyler," his permanent stage name was now set.

Tyler soon had his own Los Angeles television show. He was voted by disc jockeys in 1950 as the most popular country/western performer. Country/western magazines voted his television show as "Best Country/Western Music Show of the Year" in 1950. He performed in Carnegie Hall, was cast in western films, and appeared often on the "Grand Ole Opry," "Louisiana Hayride," and on "Country Jamboree." The "Man with a Million Friends" continued with hits like "Remember Me," which became his theme song, "Filipino Baby," "Divorce Me C.O.D.," and "Those Oklahoma Hills." He recorded a number of hits for Decca, Capitol, King, and Starday.

Tyler visited often in Mena where his mother was confined to a rest home. By 1964 he had a religious experience and thereafter recorded only religious music and conducted revivals. Stricken with cancer in 1971, Tyler died at Springfield, Missouri. His burial was in Huntington, West Virginia. The *Arkansas Gazette* and his hometown paper, the *Mena Star,* carried short obituaries. There were no memorial services held in his hometown, but today Tyler's memory has been revived by organizers of the annual "T. Texas Tyler Religious Jamboree" held in Mena every May.

[See the *Mena Star,* July 5, 1938, Jan. 24, 1972, June 14, 1987; the *Arkansas Gazette,* Jan. 26, 1972; the *Looking Glass* (Polk County) vol. 5, no. 9 (Dec. 1979) and vol. 12, nos. 7, 8, 9 (1986). See also Allen Eyles, *The Western* (1975). Sources include the following interviews: Glen Cole, Zeke Cummings, Lamar Cummings, and Jane Long, Jan. 1987; Robert Jennings, Mar. 1987; Marie Williams, Apr. 1987, all of Mena; and Mrs. Austin Rogers, Apr. 1987 (Texarkana).]

HAROLD COOGAN

UMSTED, SIDNEY ALBERT (Nov. 22, 1876–Nov. 3, 1925), timber man and father of the Smackover Oil Field, was born in Houston County, Texas, to Albert Umsted and Caroline Pearson. Albert abandoned the family, and Caroline's brother, John Pearson, went to Texas and brought Caroline and her two sons back to Chidester, Arkansas. Caroline married Harrison Bratton in 1892 when Sidney was sixteen, and they moved to Bernice, Louisiana, to farm. Sidney, who had no formal education, soon left home and began making the sawmill circuit in northern Louisiana, working at Bernice, Farmerville, Dubach, Homer, and Junction City. By his early twenties, he had his own sawmill.

On December 31, 1902, he and Edna Sedalia Edwards, a daughter of Albert and Mary Wertham Edwards of Junction City, Arkansas, married. Three years later the couple moved to Smackover, Arkansas, where they built a house. Umsted set up a sawmill north of town near Smackover Creek in an area connected to the Old Camden Road by a logging trace. He soon knew the forest from Smackover Creek north to the Ouachita River like the back of his hand. He used the knowledge about timber that he had acquired in Louisiana and became very successful in Arkansas. Within fifteen years, his mill was the primary source of employment in this undeveloped part of Arkansas.

He began purchasing and leasing large tracts of land in Ouachita County and in the Snow Hill/Standard Umsted areas of Union County. Oil had been discovered in Louisiana on some of the property he had cruised and cut. He recognized that the Arkansas topography was similar to that in Louisiana where successful oil fields had been discovered and had confidence that oil was located in this area.

He selected a well site less than a mile south of the Ouachita River on land he had leased from a black farmer named Charlie Richardson. He and four other businessmen formed a partnership. Umsted reserved the majority of the investment for himself; the other partners and the V. K. F Drilling Company owned the rest. On July 29, 1922, the well blew in at a little below 2,000 feet, starting the famous Smackover Oil Field. This well began the boom in the Smackover area.

After the discovery well, Umsted began exploration at other sites on property that he had already leased for his sawmill. His first activities were confined to the Smackover area, where he promoted many successful oil companies. Later he became a power throughout the southern oil fields. He became one of the wealthiest men in Arkansas as he continued investing in oil properties locally and in Louisiana, Texas, Mississippi, and Oklahoma.

In May 1924 he moved with his wife and three daughters to Camden, where he had built a fine residence, a Mediterranean-style home which is now on the National Register of Historic Places.

Sidney Umsted lived only six years after oil was discovered on his property. He died in the Baptist Hospital in Memphis, Tennessee, from pneumonia contracted as a result of injuries received in the wreck of the Sunnyland, a fast St. Louis-San Francisco passenger train, near Victoria, Mississippi. He was only forty-nine. At the time of his death he was the largest royalty owner in the Smackover district, receiving royalties from more than a hundred producing wells, in addition to owning several wells outright.

Umsted was a benefactor to the small towns in the area. His land, money, and influence helped create the Standard-Umsted and Smackover schools. People admired and respected him. T. J. Gaughan, a lawyer in Ouachita County and Umsted's close friend, said, "His personality was his greatest asset. His disposition was for fair dealing and straight business. His finest trait was loyalty."

[The Arkansas Oil and Brine Museum at Smackover maintains a research file on Umsted which includes clippings and photographs. See A. R. Buckalew and R. B. Buckalew, "The Discovery of Oil in South Arkansas, 1920–1924," AHQ 33 (Autumn 1974): 195–238; and the El Dorado News-Times, Aug. 14, 1994.]

JEANNE CLEMENTS

UPHAM, DANIEL P. (1827?–Nov. 1882), was an entrepreneur and an early Republican politician. Little is known about his life prior to his arrival in Arkansas in 1865. We know that he was a merchant in New York City. A business was sold to him by Brigadier General Alexander Shaler at the beginning of the Civil War. Upham apparently was in debt. Shaler was in a good position to help Upham as he was in command of the Union troops at DeValls Bluff, Arkansas.

At DeValls Bluff, Upham used Shaler's influence to secure several licenses to operate saloons, engage in the steamboat trade on the White River, and lease a two-thousand-acre cotton plantation. He made these deals without spending his own money, finding others to invest the necessary funds. In the course of making his deals, Upham was able to secure shares of these enterprises. These were profitable enough so that he was able to return to New York, pay off his debts, and return to Arkansas with his wife, Lizzie (maiden name unknown), and his brother Henry.

During the ensuing years, both Daniel and Henry Upham prospered and invested heavily in land to become two of the largest landowners in Woodruff County. Daniel P. Upham entered politics and was elected as a Republican state representative from Woodruff County in March 1868. He was one of the leading "radicals" in the state legislature and helped to pass Governor Powell Clayton's agenda into law.

Upham's activities earned him the hatred of the recently organized Ku Klux Klan. On October 2, 1868, the Klan attempted to assassinate him. This incident was part of the KKK's reign of terror in eastern and southern Arkansas.

Governor Clayton instituted martial law in that part of the state on November 4, 1868, in order to combat the lawlessness. Upham was commissioned a brigadier general in the Arkansas militia despite his lack of prior military experience, and in November 1868 he was assigned to the command of the district of northeastern Arkansas. His force originally consisted of 120 poorly armed men who were greatly outnumbered by the KKK. Even so, Upham's command was able to capture Augusta and hold out there until reinforcements arrived. But Upham was unable to prevent the KKK from occupying his own plantation and capturing his overseer. Following the arrival of reinforcements, Upham took the offensive. His force, eventually numbering over one thousand men, thrashed the Klan in northeastern Arkansas in a series of skirmishes. By late January 1869 his command completed its task and was disbanded. During the course of operations, Upham's militia was accused of ruthless and malicious conduct. An investigation by Governor Clayton cleared Upham and his men of wrongdoing.

Following the end of the so-called "Militia War," Upham returned to Woodruff County where he devoted himself to his business and family. He remained an officer in the militia, and during the Brooks-Baxter war of 1874, he was on the side of Joseph Brooks. In the summer of 1876 Upham was appointed United States marshal for the Western District of Arkansas, a controversial appointment. The September 8, 1876, *Western Wheelers Independent* called Upham an "efficient officer" whose "business in his department will meet promptness and dispatch." By contrast, the *Independent Arkansian* called him "as grand a rascal as ever went unhung." The August 4, 1876, *Hot Springs Daily Telegraph* accused him as "a man whose services are available for any dirty work."

As marshal at Fort Smith, Upham executed his duties efficiently yet without glamour. In 1880 he was removed from his duties by the machinations of a political enemy, Stephen Dorsey. Despite his failing health, Upham spent the next year and a half fighting to regain his position. In a letter to Stephen Wheeler, clerk of the United States Court for the Western District of Arkansas, Upham blamed his former benefactor Powell Clayton for his failure. In November of that year Upham passed away in Oxford, Massachusetts, at the age of either fifty-five or fifty-six. He was survived by his wife, Lizzie, and an adopted daughter.

[The D. P. Upham Collection is in Archives and Special Collections, University of Arkansas, Little Rock. See the *Arkansas Gazette*, Jan. 22, 1869, and Nov. 22, 1882; Powell Clayton, *The Aftermath of the Civil War in Arkansas* (1915); and John I. Smith, *Forward from Rebellion: Reconstruction and Revolution in Arkansas, 1868–1874* (1983).]

CHARLES J. RECTOR

WALLWORTH, PAUL (Apr. 22, 1890–Jan. 6, 1955), pioneer rice farmer, was born in Warren, Wisconsin. The names of his parents could not be verified.

"Just for one year, just to see how it goes," Wallworth said to his wife back in 1918, as he planted rice on his Arkansas County farm. Thirty-seven years later when he died, he was known as a leader in the rice industry who perfected new and revolutionary procedures still being used in 1999.

In January 1956, the *Rice Journal* printed this information: "In earning the title of Pioneer, Mr. Wallworth gets credit for bringing into the area the first pull-type combine in 1927, the first self-propelled combine, shipped in from Toronto, Canada in 1936, the first successfully to plant rice in water, the first to use a plane for seeding, the first to dry rice, the first to use overflow gates which were originally wooden—though later steel gates were made for him in Houston, Texas, and activity in one of the first successful dryers in this territory."

Wallworth's farm, which was located directly north of the University of Arkansas Rice Branch Experiment Station, contained 1,740 acres. This included a 340-acre reservoir which, when built in 1942, was the deepest reservoir on the Grand Prairie. Wallworth was constantly experimenting, working out procedures that would make farming easier and more profitable. For instance, he found out that the deeper the water in his reservoir the less the evaporation; in other words, shallow water spread over a large area makes for greater loss. He experimented until he learned that seven gallons of water evaporate per acre per minute and that during the growing season twenty-six inches of water per acre will evaporate. Prior to the construction of the reservoir, eight deep wells were needed to irrigate his rice.

The farm was two and three-quarter miles long and one mile wide with a canal running through the middle of the entire length of the farm. Every half mile a graded road crossed, cutting the farm into plots of one hundred and fifty acres. Each had its own water gate from the canal, and each was accessible from three sides.

A local farmer recalled that Paul Wallworth not only made rice his livelihood, he also made it his hobby. He constantly pioneered new developments in seed, farm machinery, and scientific research designed to secure greater production and efficiency.

In 1944 Wallworth was one of the group which organized the Stuttgart Grain Drying Cooperative. Elected its first president, he held that office until 1954, when failing health compelled him to retire from the post.

While still young he went to Texas. He married Vivian Roach at Blessing, Texas, on June 10, 1914, and they moved to Arkansas County, Arkansas, four years later. They had three daughters. Paul Wallworth died in Stuttgart, Arkansas.

Wallworth was quoted in a local paper as saying, "Success can only be attained after many reverses and good farming practices come, not only from study, but also from hard work." His innovative ideas, ingenuity, and hard work laid the foundation for modern-day successful Arkansas rice farming.

[See the *Rice Journal* (Jan. 1956): 10–12; the *Stuttgart Arkansas Standard*, Feb. 22 and Mar. 1, 1973; and J. M. Spicer's *Beginnings of the Rice Industry* (1964; rpt. 1993). Wallworth's obituary appeared in the *Stuttgart Arkansas Daily Leader*, Jan. 8, 1955. Information also came from interviews with Paul Wallworth and with Kathryn Wallworth Lookadoo.]

BENNIE FROWNFELTER BURKETT

WALTON, SAMUEL MOORE (Mar. 29, 1918–Apr. 5, 1992), founder of Wal-Mart discount stores, was born in Kingfisher, Oklahoma, to Thomas Gibson Walton, a banker and farmer, and Nancy Lee Lawrence. Walton showed signs of an entrepreneurial gift early, selling magazine subscriptions starting "probably as young as seven or eight years old." He worked his way through college delivering newspapers, earning four to five thousand dollars a year. He earned a degree in business in 1940 from the University of Missouri.

His first job was with J. C. Penney. In January 1942 he went to work for a duPont gunpowder plant at Claremore, Oklahoma. There he met Helen Robson, daughter of a prominent local attorney. Walton was inducted into military service in July 1942. On February 14, 1943, he and Helen Robson married. The couple moved to Salt Lake City, where he served with Company A, 777th Military Police Battalion. He was discharged from the military in 1945. The family's military experience led Helen Walton to determine that she would never again move to a town larger than ten thousand people. A first child, Rob, was born in 1944; John, Jim, and Alice followed.

The couple purchased a Ben Franklin five-and-dime franchise in Newport, Arkansas, a small river town. Here Walton began to develop his discount marketing concept: "Here's the simple lesson we learned ... by cutting your price, you can boost your sales to a point where you earn far more at the cheaper retail price than you would have by selling the item at the higher price.

In retailer language, you can lower your markup but earn more because of the increased volume." The store was so successful that the landlord did not renew Walton's lease, but instead, leased the store to his son.

The Waltons moved on, arriving in Bentonville, a small agricultural town in northwest Arkansas, on May 1, 1950. By May 9, with the help of his father-in-law, Walton had bought the Harrison Variety Store; it was open for business by July 29. It was the third self-service variety store in the nation and the first in the state. Discount marketing requires a large customer base, problematic in a town of three thousand people. Walton's answer was to open stores in other small towns. In 1952 he opened a Ben Franklin franchise in Fayetteville, twenty-five miles south of Bentonville. Shortly thereafter, he opened another. By now his brother Bud was on board, helping Walton launch and manage the stores. By the early 1960s the Waltons owned a chain of sixteen Ben Franklin stores in Arkansas, Missouri, and Kansas, the largest chain of independently owned variety stores in the nation.

To supervise his multiple stores in isolated small towns, Walton learned to fly: "We never could have maintained the operating controls or communications without having the ability to get into our stores on a consistent basis." He also scouted for new store locations from the air.

Walton was committed to the discount concept. In Rogers, Arkansas, he opened the first Wal-Mart in November 1962. Continuing expansion and the success of the marketing idea created a need for fresh capital. In 1969 Wal-Mart was incorporated, and in March 1970 the company offered 300,000 shares of public stock. By January 1970 Sam and Bud Walton owned eighteen Wal-Mart Stores and fourteen Ben Franklins. By 1976 Walton had closed all his Ben Franklin stores, and by the end of 1980 330 Wal-Marts were in operation. By 1990 there were 1,528, doing $25.8 billion in annual sales. In 1991 Wal-Mart became the nation's largest retailer, with 1,700 stores. In 1997 the company surpassed $100 billion in sales. Wal-Mart associates, as the employees are called, were offered stock options as part of their employment package. Anecdotes of longtime hourly workers with six-figure retirement accounts were common.

David Glass became chief executive officer in 1988, but Walton remained chairman until his death. Walton became a management guru, his autobiography reaching number four on *Publishers Weekly*'s hardcover non-fiction bestseller list. At his death his wealth was estimated at twenty-one to twenty-three billion dollars.

Though Walton was generally admired, his success was not without its critics. Many consumers, particularly in the South, were grateful to Wal-Mart for serving small rural markets, but others feared for the survival of their local economies. The editor of the Jackson, Mississippi, *Clarion-Ledger* wrote on June 3, 1990, "Is it really worth saving a few bucks to virtually destroy the heart and soul of our small town business community?" A study published in *Economic Development Review* revealed the impact of Wal-Marts in thirty-four small communities. According to the report, towns which had a Wal-Mart enjoyed increased overall retail sales of 53.6 percent in the first year and 43.6 percent in subsequent years, much of that increase going to Wal-Mart itself. But small businesses in those towns suffered cumulative sales declines of 25.4 percent after five years. Towns which did not have a Wal-Mart lost 12.9 percent general merchandise sales in the first year a Wal-Mart opened in a neighboring town, as shoppers would drive to the Wal-Mart towns. Other studies suggest that the increased cost of roads, water, sewage, telephone, and other services installed in Wal-Mart locations exceed the sales and property tax revenues collected from new stores.

Wal-Mart boosters applaud Walton for bringing discount marketing to rural America. Its detractors vilify him for precisely the same thing. Walton himself, late in life, remained "absolutely convinced that the only way we can improve one another's quality of life . . . is through what we call free enterprise."

Walton was awarded the Medal of Freedom by President George Bush. He went quail hunting with Jimmy Carter. But he remained, as they used to say in Newport, "common as anybody." He died in Little Rock.

[See Walton's autobiography (with John Huey), *Sam Walton: Made in America* (1992); Sandra Vance and Roy V. Scott, *Wal-Mart: A History of Sam Walton's Retail Phenomenon* (1994); Bob Ortega, *In Sam We Trust: The Untold Story of Sam Walton and How Wal-Mart is Devouring America* (1998); and Vance Trimble, *Sam Walton: The Inside Story of America's Richest Man* (1990). The Wal-Mart Visitors Center in Bentonville has additional information.]

KIM I. MARTIN

WASHBURN, CEPHAS (July 25, 1793–Mar. 17, 1860), missionary to the Cherokee Indians and founder of Dwight Mission, was born in Randolph, Vermont. His parents' names are not known.

Washburn graduated from the University of Vermont in 1816. He was licensed to preach in January 1818 by a committee of the Royalton (Congregational) Association. He began his career as a preacher in the destitute towns of Vermont. He married Abigail Woodard of Randolph, Vermont, in October 1818. The couple had four sons and two daughters.

In October 1818 Washburn moved to Savannah, Georgia, where he served as an agent for one year with the Savannah Missionary Society. In 1819 the American Board of Commissioners for Foreign Missions sent him to Arkansas to begin a mission among the Cherokees. He was joined by his brother-in-law, the Reverend Alfred Finney, who was to aid in establishing the mission.

Washburn's party left Brainerd, Georgia, in November 1819 headed for Arkansas in covered wagons. They reached Elliot, Georgia, in January. On May 16, 1820, Washburn and Finney left their families at Elliot and began the treacherous journey to the wilderness of Arkansas. They met with cold, snow, and ice. They found areas that were too wet to pass through and areas of quicksand. Others joined them at Arkansas Post, and the group reached Little Rock in July 1820. Washburn preached a sermon on July 4. This is thought to be the first sermon ever preached in Little Rock.

Washburn met with Cherokee leaders in July 1820 and was given permission to select a site for their mission. The missionaries decided on a location four miles north of the Arkansas River along the west side of the Illinois Creek near present-day Russellville in Pope County.

They set out to establish the mission immediately. By October, with the aid of two hired men, they had built two cabins. They went back to Elliot to get their families and returned to the mission in May 1821. The first public worship was held on Sunday, May 13, 1821. Four or five Cherokees were present, but without an interpreter they could not understand what was said. A good number of whites and some blacks from the settlement on the south side of the river were also there.

The mission was named Dwight Mission in honor of Reverend Timothy Dwight, president of Yale College, and first corporate member of the American Board of Commissioners for Foreign Missions.

The missionaries built, expanded, and rendered increased services to the Cherokee Indians. The devotion of Washburn and the others kept them there through many hardships. Their physical labor was hard: they had to build a school, a church, and houses, and produce their own food. To persuade the Cherokees to accept Christianity was not an easy task. The Cherokees were suspicious and fearful. The missionaries could communicate with them only through interpreters, and the interpreters were not always honest. Washburn's character and devotion were admirable. He was described by another missionary as "a strict, straight-laced Calvinist with Puritan ideals and character beyond reproach." His concern for the welfare of the Indians and their salvation was visible in his efforts and in the success he achieved. He exercised skill, patience, and understanding in preaching to the Cherokees. He kept his teachings simple. Hundreds of Indians were converted to Christ.

The first function of the mission was to convert, but the second function was to educate the Cherokees. Their school opened January 1, 1822, under Washburn's guidance, with eighteen children enrolled. By May the school was well established with an enrollment of fifty.

Just when so much progress was being made, a new treaty was signed, and in 1828 the Cherokees were moved to what is now northeastern Oklahoma. Washburn asked to establish a mission there. The federal government agreed to reimburse the mission for the value of the Dwight buildings on the condition that the funds be used to build a new mission. The mission moved early in 1829 to a location on Sallisaw Creek in what is now Sequoyah County. In May 1830 school began with sixty students enrolled. By 1838 enrollment had grown to 113, to Washburn's delight.

In June 1840 Washburn asked to be discharged from Dwight Mission. He took his family to Benton, Arkansas. There he preached and taught school. He established the Far West Seminar, which became the first college in Arkansas. A fire in 1845 destroyed the school, and the project ended.

In 1847 Washburn moved to Fort Smith where he was a Presbyterian minister for five years. From there he went to Norristown in Pope County and organized a church at Dardanelle and one at Galley Rock.

Washburn's last year was spent as an evangelist

under the Synod of Arkansas. He traveled the state and set up many churches. On the way to preach in Helena in early 1860, he stopped in Little Rock. He developed pneumonia while there and died at the home of Dr. R. L. Dodge, an old friend. He was buried in Mount Holly Cemetery in Little Rock. In 1937 the Presbyterian Synods erected a monument at his grave site.

[A collection of Washburn family papers is at the Arkansas History Commission. See Cephas Washburn, *Reminiscences of the Indians* (c. 1869; rpt. 1971); O. B. Campbell, *Mission to the Cherokee Indians* (1973); Dorsey D. Jones, *Cephas Washburn and his Works in Arkansas* (1900?); Fred W. Allsopp, *Folklore of Romantic Arkansas*, vol. 2 (1931); W. J. Lemke, *The Washburns: Father and Son* (1955).]

MELISSA A. TURNER

WATKINS, CHARLES LEE (Aug. 10, 1879–Aug. 29, 1966), first parliamentarian of the United States Senate, was born in Mount Ida, Arkansas, the oldest of seven children of Nancy Rebecca Smith and John A. Watkins. In 1899 he took a stenographic and typing test for a job with Arkansas attorney general Jeff Davis. Since the test was drawn from the Arkansas Code of Laws, which Watkins had read in his uncle's law office, he reproduced the text half from shorthand and half from memory. He was hired, and when Davis became governor, Watkins continued to work for him. On the side, Watkins studied law at the University of Arkansas Law School in Little Rock. In 1903 he and Martha Heard Walker married. Their only child, Charles Owen Watkins, was born in 1905. Martha Watkins died in 1923. In 1944 Charles and Barbara Laura Sandmeier were married.

On December 1, 1904, Watkins went to Washington as stenographer for Arkansas senator James P. Clarke. He would remain on the Senate staff for almost sixty years. After the Democrats won the Senate majority in 1912, Clarke was elected president *pro tempore* and made Watkins a bill clerk in the office of the secretary of the Senate. When Clarke died in 1916, Watkins switched to the patronage of Arkansas senator Joseph T. Robinson, whose rise to the Democratic floor leadership assured his continued tenure on the Senate staff. In 1919 Watkins was appointed minute and journal clerk of the Senate, to record minutes of the daily legislative proceedings for the *Senate Journal.* Impressed with Watkins's grasp of the Senate rules, Senator Robinson brought him to the White House in an unsuccessful effort to persuade President Woodrow Wilson of the need to compromise to win passage of the Treaty of Versailles.

As journal clerk, Watkins learned parliamentary procedure from assistant secretary of the Senate Henry Rose, who sat beside him at the front desk in the Senate chamber and advised the presiding officer. When Rose became incapacitated by illness in 1923, Watkins assumed his duties. Vice President Charles G. Dawes observed that the "modest young man" seated in front of him had mastered the Senate rules. In 1928, anticipating a battle over procedural maneuvers to authorize construction of Boulder Dam, Watkins produced a detailed statement on precedents that convinced both sides and prevented a clash. The vice president commented that "by indefatigable work almost every minute of the day and most of the night he has made himself the actual parliamentarian of the Senate and its highest authority on the precedents." In 1935, with the pace of legislation increasing during the New Deal, the Senate designated Watkins as "parliamentarian and journal clerk." Two years later senators separated those functions to make him their first parliamentarian.

The lanky, slow-talking Watkins sat immediately below the presiding officer. He would tilt his chair backward to whisper advice, which the presiding officer would then repeat aloud in making rulings. Reporters called him the Senate's ventriloquist.

The abundant precedents of the Senate far outnumber its formal rules. To better equip himself, Watkins read through the past records and compiled massive volumes on procedural actions. When questions arose during a debate, senators would sometimes call for a quorum to suspend business so that he could rush to his office and consult his notes. More often, there was no time for research, and Watkins depended upon his phenomenal memory to recall specific precedents. (Later parliamentarians have resorted to computers to provide information.)

Watkins described himself as a registered Arkansas Democrat, but as parliamentarian he advised all senators and staff regardless of party. When Republicans took the majority in the Senate in 1947 and 1953, they kept Watkins at his post. Before offering legislation, senators consulted him about parliamentary obstacles they might encounter. Freshmen turned to him for instruction. Even those with experience in the House of Representatives needed help understanding the vast differences between House and Senate rules. Watkins frequently entertained them with stories of the great debates and famous senators he had observed.

In 1945 he took a leave of absence to serve as parliamentarian of the first United Nations conference in San Francisco; otherwise, he devoted his attention exclusively to the Senate. When he reached his seventies, the Senate provided him with assistants to spell him on the Senate floor, especially during lengthy filibusters.

Still working at eighty-five, Watkins retained his long-term memory but began forgetting things said or done more recently. This caused mounting confusion on the Senate floor. At the end of the session in 1964, Democratic leader Mike Mansfield and Republican leader Everett Dirksen informed Watkins that it was his last night. President (and former majority leader) Lyndon B. Johnson sent a telegram saying that it would be "hard to imagine the Senate without Charlie Watkins." When Watkins died in Washington, the Senate adjourned in his memory.

[Vice President Charles G. Dawes published his observations of Watkins in *Notes as Vice President, 1928–1929* (1935). Floyd M. Riddick, Watkins's successor, discussed the evolution of the office of Senate Parliamentarian in oral history interviews for the Senate Historical Office (1978–1979), deposited in the Library of Congress and the National Archives. Watkins's extensive notes were edited and published as *Senate Procedure: Precedents and Practices,* 84th Cong. (1958); and 88th Cong., Senate Doc. 44 (1964). Senators paid their respect to him in *Tributes to Charles L. Watkins, the First Parliamentarian of the Senate,* 89th Cong., lst sess., Senate Doc. 6 (1965).

Watkins was the subject of newspaper articles in the *Washington Evening Star,* June 26, 1950, May 25, 1952, Aug. 11, 1962, and Oct. 30, 1964, and the *New York Times,* Mar. 7, 1960, and Dec. 31, 1964. Obituaries appeared in the *Arkansas Gazette, Washington Evening Star,* and *Washington Post,* Aug. 30, 1966.]

DONALD A. RITCHIE

WATSON, HARRIET LOUISE GERTRUDE RUTHERFORD (Nov. 23, 1885–Nov. 1974), teacher and librarian, was born in Rome, Georgia, the elder of two children of Samuel W. Rutherford and Mary Anne Lemon. Known as "Hattie," she attended elementary school in Atlanta and graduated from Spelman Seminary secondary school. She matriculated as the only college graduate in the September class of 1907. On September 25, 1907, she married John Brown Watson, a graduate of Brown University. The couple settled in Atlanta and both taught at Morehouse College for several years. In 1928 the American Baptist Home Mission Society (ABHMS) selected her husband as president of tiny Leland College in Baker, Louisiana. After five years there, he accepted the presidency of Arkansas AM & N College at Pine Bluff. Hattie Rutherford Watson's corollary position, as the wife of the president and first lady at the state's black federally funded land-grant institution, aided in the state's participation in the regional and national context of the New South and the New Deal in American history.

Pledged to black education, Watson served on the boards of trustees of three black private institutions: alumnae member of the Spelman College board, Morehouse College, and Atlanta University (her tenure coincided with that of James Weldon Johnson). Her "socially responsible individualism" informed her participation in the organization of the Neighborhood Union in Atlanta in 1908 and her partnership with her husband in the reorganization of Leland College. It was her tenure at AM & N College, however, that represented the flourishing of her self-definition of black womanhood to include first lady, librarian, trustee, teacher, and mentor.

In her capacity as first lady Watson maintained social and community-building relationships in Pine Bluff. Her activities included membership in the Social and Art Club (NACW); the Delta Omega Omega chapter of Alpha Kappa Alpha (AKA) Sorority; Jack and Jill; the Pine Hill Community Club; and the PTA. She was a member of St. Paul Baptist Church for over forty years; and established the John Brown Watson Sunday School at AM & N College. She participated in the professionalization of her work with membership in the American Library Association and the Arkansas State Library Association. Her professional contributions to the college also included cofounding and co-editing the *Arkansawyer,* the official college newspaper.

In 1936 Mary McLeod Bethune, director of the Negro Division of the National Youth Administration (NYA), selected Watson as administrator of one of five NYA-sponsored educational camps for young black women in the country. The camps provided academic and paid vocational training and adequate material conditions as well as race-consciousness and opportunities for individual and collective responsibility for unmarried black women, ages eighteen to twenty-five. Located at AM & N College, NYA Camp Bethune enjoyed two sessions in 1937: February 1 through June 30; and July 1 through September 30. The sessions enrolled sixty-two and fifty-eight campers, respectively.

Watson's administration also provided employment for a small cadre of black teachers and professionals: the staff for the second session was five women and two men, including a camp nurse and a camp physician. In addition to the NYA course Watson's pedagogy included a camp newspaper, student government association, plenary sessions, and group activities. She proved to be an effective teacher and mentor to the young women.

After the close of NYA Camp Bethune, Watson established the Free Baby Clinic on campus in 1939 as part of the WPA nursery school established five years earlier. In April of the same year Watson and her husband adopted their only child, an infant daughter, Marion Anderson Watson. John Brown Watson died in 1942, and Watson maintained residence in Pine Bluff and continued as assistant librarian at the college. She completed a master of science degree in library science at Atlanta University in 1956. A WPA library, completed in 1939, was dedicated and renamed in honor of John Brown Watson in 1958. Watson retired from the college library in 1962; she resigned from the Spelman College board the following year. She died at Pine Bluff.

[See the John Brown Watson Papers, John Hay Library, Brown University, Providence, Rhode Island; Spelman College Archives, Spelman College, Atlanta, Georgia; Stephanie J. Shaw, *What a Woman Ought to Be and to Do: Black Professional Women Workers during the Jim Crow Era* (1996); and Darlene Clark Hine, *Hine Sight: Black Women and the Re-Construction of American History* (1994).]

FON LOUISE GORDON

WILLIAMS, THOMAS JEFFERSON (June 4, 1811–Feb. 12, 1865), pioneer, clergyman, and Civil War Unionist, was born in Caswell County, North Carolina, the son of Nathan Williams, a farmer, and Rebecca Jackson, a Cherokee Indian. In the 1820s the family (Williams had four brothers and three sisters) moved to Franklin County, Tennessee, where Williams received some rudimentary education. He was one of the few members of his family who could read and write. In 1832 he married Margaret Hill, and the couple had thirteen children.

In the spring of 1838 Williams and two of his brothers formed part of a Tennessee militia company which "escorted" several hundred Cherokee Indians west to Indian Territory. These part-Cherokee men took the last party west before the larger and more famous Trail of Tears procession began later that year. Following the Arkansas River to Fort Smith, Williams had his first look at Arkansas. Upon the death of his father in 1844, he packed up his family and, together with the families of at least five of his brothers and sisters, migrated to Arkansas.

One of the first settlers in the northern part of Conway County near the present community of Center Ridge, Williams farmed 160 acres, ran a small cotton gin, and served as preacher for a congregation of the Christian Church (Disciples of Christ). He supported the Whig Party in the 1850s, even naming two of his sons Daniel Webster and Henry Clay. Shortly after Lincoln's election in 1860, he was a leader in the county meeting at Springfield which took a stand against secession, but upheld the right of citizens to own slaves. Williams himself owned one slave in 1860.

He remained devoted to the Union even after Arkansas seceded and the war began. With the Confederate Conscription Act of April 1862, pressure to enlist in the Rebel army became intense in Arkansas. Williams led a band of several dozen men from Conway and Van Buren Counties, most of them Williams's family and neighbors, who left their homes to hide out in the bush to avoid conscription. In May a large Union force under General Samuel Curtis made its way from Missouri to Batesville, Arkansas. Williams's band traveled through dangerous rebel territory and joined Curtis's army in Batesville, enlisting for six months in what would be designated Company B of the First Arkansas Infantry Battalion. The company elected Williams as captain and his son Nathan as second lieutenant.

In July the company marched with Curtis's men from Batesville to Helena, where they remained camped during the summer and fall of 1862. With twenty thousand men crowded into Helena during the hot malarial months of late summer, disease took its toll. Almost half of Williams's company died of camp diseases, including his two brothers, nephew, and a brother-in-law. Williams became so debilitated by diarrhea that the camp surgeon and his commanding officer judged him unfit for service and discharged him in September. He refused, however, to leave his men. To save the remnant of the battalion, the commander sent Williams and his men upriver to Benton Barracks in St. Louis, where they remained until they mustered out in December 1862.

Williams and the survivors of his company feared they would be killed if they returned to their homes in rebel territory. They made their way instead to Springfield, Missouri, where they scouted for the Union army, occasionally making forays into northern Arkansas. In late summer 1863 Union forces took Little Rock and moved up the Arkansas River to Fort Smith. Williams's band moved with Union troops back to central Arkansas and home. In September General Frederick Steele authorized the Union men of Conway County to form an independent company to protect themselves from rebel threats. During the following seventeen months, Captain Williams led his men in a vicious guerrilla war against roving rebel bands in north-central Arkansas. Called variously Williams's Raiders or Williams's Company of Scouts and Spies, the independent company scouted for the Third Arkansas Union Cavalry led by Colonel Abraham Ryan garrisoned on the Arkansas River at Lewisburg (near Morrilton).

In 1864 Williams's brother and nephew, William Day Williams and his son John Frank Williams, were captured by the Confederates marching northeast on the Dover-Clinton road. They took the pair to Batesville where they killed William and sent his son back to Conway County with a message for his uncle: stop spying for the Union army or be killed. Soon thereafter, rebels made good on their threat. Colonel A. R. Witt led a band of ragtag Confederate guerrillas based at Quitman, twenty miles to the east of Williams's farm. Just after Williams had come home to visit his family on the night of February 12, 1865, about sixty of Witt's band surrounded the Williams's house. Calling him out, the rebels shot and killed him as he opened the door, gun in hand. Williams's sons gave chase to the rebels and ruthlessly exacted retribution.

The personal grudges and political violence between Union and rebel settlers in Conway County outlasted the Civil War. It would be resurrected later during Reconstruction in the struggle between the Ku Klux Klan and the Republican militia.

[Information can be found in the federal pension applications of Williams's widow and his sons, Leroy and

Morton Williams, National Archives, Washington, D.C.; *War of Rebellion: A Compilation of the Official Records of the Union and Confederate Armies* (Washington, 1880–1901); James W. Demby, *Mysteries and Miseries of Arkansas* (1863); Albert Webb Bishop, *Report of the Adjutant General* in 39th Congress, 2d Sess., Senate Misc. Doc., no. 53; and interviews with Polly Church, John B. Mason, Thelma Hensley, Arlie Williams, and Lonnie Maxwell. An obituary appears in the Little Rock *Home Aegis and Monthly Review* 9 (1865): 209.]

KENNETH C. BARNES

WILLIAMS, VIRGINIA ANNE RICE (Oct. 27, 1919–June 16, 1970), biochemist, was born in North Little Rock to Roderic J. Rice, a banker, and Mattie Thurman. As a high-school student trying to decide on a career, Virginia was torn between music and science, two disciplines in which she excelled. Her teachers urged her to pursue music, fearing she lacked the temperament for science. However, Williams later explained, she felt she "lacked the talent and desire to pursue the long and difficult road to the concert stage." And so she opted for what became a distinguished career in science.

Virginia Williams performed pioneering research that led to breakthroughs in science's understanding of enzymes. Her studies of certain agricultural products, particularly vitamin B in rice, contributed to the development of more nutritious grains, and she was one of the first researchers to recognize the role of biotin, a water-soluble vitamin, in the breakdown of fatty acids.

After attending public schools, Virginia enrolled at Hendrix College at Conway, from which she graduated with a degree in chemistry in 1940. Two years later, she married fellow chemist Hulen B. Williams, and the couple moved to Baton Rouge, Louisiana, where the bride enrolled as a graduate student at Louisiana State University. In 1947 she was awarded a doctorate in biochemistry. She would continue to work as a researcher and professor at LSU for the rest of her life.

In the early 1940s, when Williams began her career with studies on the effect of milling on rice, little was known about the cellular function of vitamins. As a researcher on the staff of the Louisiana Agricultural Experiment Station, where she worked from 1942 to 1962, she began studying the makeup of enzymes, substances produced by living cells. Enzymes act as catalysts, causing or accelerating chemical changes within the animal or plant that produces them. These early studies of enzymes and rice served as the basis for her lifelong interest in the ways foods interact with the human body.

Williams's husband, whose career paralleled hers, noted that she "had a rare sense of those things that are important and worth doing in research." He explained that "most enzymes have a key-and-lock type function. What they did not understand at the time was that lock-and-key concept. It was still to be unraveled, and that's where Virginia chose to focus."

As her research continued, and with it, her publication of scientific papers, Williams became internationally known in the field of enzymology. In 1954, as a result of her work on vitamin B, nutrition, and the metabolism of bacteria, Williams became the first LSU faculty member to be elected to the American Society of Biological Chemists.

In 1955 she was one of twenty-eight American scientists awarded grants from the National Science Foundation to attend the Third International Congress of Biochemistry in Brussels, Belgium. At that conference she presented a paper on *bacterium cadaveris*, an enzyme obtained from animal tissues. She was one of the first scientists to report on the enzyme's relationship to the then poorly understood mechanisms of human metabolism.

Over the next several years, Williams continued her investigation of *bacterium cadaveris* in hopes of learning how its use of proteins and carbohydrates helped it adapt and survive. That work also helped scientists find new ways of controlling the bacteria.

In 1967 Williams again reported on her work, this time at the Seventh International Congress of Biochemistry in Tokyo. That same year she coauthored with her husband, Hulen, an introductory textbook titled *Basic Physical Chemistry for the Life Sciences*. The *Journal of Chemical Education* cited the book, with its emphasis on thermodynamics, enzyme kinetics, and macromolecules, as one of the best such texts in the field.

By 1969 Williams's research had attracted the attention of the United States Department of Health, Education and Welfare, which awarded her a three-year stipend for the study of the two enzymes, histidase and aspartase, and the roles they were believed to play in causing certain human diseases, including leukemia and liver damage. That same year, she was honored by her university with a Distinguished Faculty Fellowship Award.

Williams died of complications following surgery for cancer. She was survived by her husband, a son, and a daughter.

She wrote more than sixty scientific papers, many of which helped lay the foundation for an improved understanding of enzymes and their functions. She gained prominence for her creative application of principles from the mathematical and physical sciences to her own field of biochemistry. She is best remembered among biochemists, though, for early work on biotin, which offered the first evidence that the substance played a role in the synthesis of fatty acids. As a result, she has been credited with laying the foundation for research that led to breakthroughs in human understanding of an essential biochemical process.

Throughout her career Williams remained a highly regarded lecturer at LSU. Today, the Virginia Rice Williams Library and Classroom Building at Baton Rouge is named in her honor, the only academic building in the LSU system commemorating the achievements of a woman.

[Sources include press releases, faculty and staff biographical data forms, and a memorial from Media Services, Louisiana State University, Baton Rouge; an unpublished biographical sketch by Hulen B. Williams; and a telephone interview with Hulen B. Williams in June 1993. See also the *Baton Rouge State-Times*, Nov. 5, 1963.]

MARA LEVERITT

WILLIAMSON, SONNY BOY (Dec. 5, 1912– May 25, 1965), blues musician, was born in Glendora, Mississippi, the son of Millie and James Miller. His name, the first of many, seems to have been Aleck (or Alex) Miller, though he may have been known as Rice (perhaps in recognition of his appetite for it). He taught himself to play harmonica as a very young child, and by the age of six was performing at church events, apparently billing himself as Reverend Blue. Soon thereafter he left home, and for more than three decades he lived the precarious life of an itinerant musician, working as a solo act and in association with a host of other now-famous bluesmen, especially Sunnyland Slim, Elmore James, Robert Johnson, Howlin' Wolf, and Robert Jr. Lockwood. He traveled throughout the south, working carnivals and lumber camps as well as juke joints and street corners in Mississippi, Arkansas, and Tennessee.

He almost certainly played in New Orleans in the 1920s, and on the radio in southern Illinois in the late 1930s, but his claim to a 1930s appearance on the "Grand Ole Opry" in Nashville has never been documented. Additional names also crop up during this period— he was known both as Willie Miller and as Willie Williamson, among other names and nicknames.

In November 1941 he began playing with Robert Jr. Lockwood on the now-famous "King Biscuit" radio show on Helena's KFFA, where he starred on and off for more than twenty years. It was on this show, apparently, that he first unveiled his "Sonny Boy Williamson" moniker, initiating enormous confusion among later blues scholars since another Sonny Boy Williamson, a harmonica player named John Lee Williamson, from Tennessee, had already established himself in Chicago. The show was an immediate success, and Williamson himself became its most famous performer. Its sponsor, the Interstate Grocery Company, was soon marketing a Sonny Boy Corn Meal, with the harmonica-wielding singer displayed on every bag, seated on a giant ear of corn. Despite these successes, Williamson did not record until 1951, when Lillian McMurry's newly established Trumpet label in Jackson, Mississippi, issued "Eyesight to the Blind," "Mighty Long Time," "Nine Below Zero," and "Mr. Down Child," among others. These first recordings, long since recognized as classics of the genre, show him at the very top of his form, a laconic, often mordant vocalist, and an absolutely masterful instrumentalist. In 1954 his contract was purchased by the Chess label, in Chicago, and he soon moved north, playing club dates in Detroit, St. Louis, Milwaukee, and Philadelphia. His several hits in the late 1950s and early 1960s ("Fattening Frogs for Snakes," "Don't Start Me to Talkin'," "Your Funeral and My Trial," "One Way Out," "99") were followed by successful European tours in 1963 and 1964. On his passport he was "Sonny Boy" Williams, and he was often billed in Europe as Sonny Boy Williamson II.

He greatly enjoyed the appreciation of European blues fans—he toured in Denmark, Germany, and Poland, and performed in several English concerts with the Animals and the Yardbirds. He seriously considered settling permanently in England, but returned instead to Helena, where he again appeared on the "King Biscuit" show. His death, in fact, was discovered by drummer "Peck" Curtis when Williamson failed to arrive at the station for a performance.

His fame, in the years since his death, has only increased. Scores of well-known musicians credit his influence on their work; a prominent blues festival held every year in Helena celebrates his fame; no blues harmonica player is more widely appreciated. Williamson is buried in Tutwiler, Mississippi, where the birth date on his tombstone is almost certainly incorrect and his death date is wrong beyond any doubt. Several names are listed, but Aleck Miller is given precedence. He is a prodigious musical presence, but the man behind the harmonica remains as enigmatic and elusive as ever, just as he seems to have planned it.

[Williamson's music is readily available, most completely in a boxed set, *The Chess Years*, on the Charly label. Chess reissues of *Down and Out Blues* (Chess 31272), *The Real Folk Blues* (Chess 9272), and *More Real Folk Blues* (Chess 9277) are also valuable. Biographical sketches of uneven reliability are found in the standard blues reference works—Sheldon Harris's *Blues Who's Who* (1979) and Gérard Herzhaft's *Encyclopedia of the Blues* (1992). Among the most valuable treatments are Paul Oliver's liner notes to *Sonny Boy Williamson: "King Biscuit Time"* (Arhoolie 2020) and Robert Palmer's discussion of Williamson in *Deep Blues: A Musical and Cultural History of the Mississippi Delta* (1981). William Donoghue's *Don't Start Me to Talkin'* is haphazardly punctuated and almost comically unfocused, but it is nevertheless an unusually thorough treatment of the problems facing would-be biographers of Williamson. Among its several virtues are the identification of specific areas of uncertainty and the attribution of varying accounts to their sources.]

ROBERT COCHRAN

WILSON, CHARLES MORROW (June 16, 1905–Mar. 1, 1977), writer, was born in Fayetteville to Joseph Dickson Wilson and Martha Maude Morrow. He received a B.A. degree from the University of Arkansas in 1926 and studied agriculture and history in England. In the middle 1930s he was married to a New York photographer, Iris Woolcock. The marriage ended in divorce.

Wilson began his career at the University of Arkansas working as a reporter for the *St. Louis Post Dispatch*. In 1930 he moved to New York City where he worked part-time as a reporter for the *New York Times* and began writing the first of a prodigious number of books and magazine articles. He frequently worked for institutions, governments, and corporations as a publicist.

In 1939 he married Martha Lois Starr of Fayetteville. They had three sons: Morrow, James, and Joseph. He had established his residence in Putney, Vermont, in the mid-1930s and in 1939 settled there with his family. The home was partly a working farm where he experimented with fruit trees and food crops. In 1974 he told the *Brattleboro Reformer* that feeding the world's population was of intense interest to him. He believed the problem could be solved by increasing the number of edible plants. He found fruits "the most interesting area of feeding people," at a time when "we're only beginning to find out what will grow in the world."

In 1936 the Atlas Corporation sent him to Cuba to investigate the sugar trade. Later he was retained by United Fruit Company as a journalist for several company projects. In 1940 he was appointed special assistant to United Fruit Company's president, Samuel Zemmuray. In 1941 Wilson served as the director of the company's Middle America Information Bureau. He was also associated with the Firestone Plantation Company beginning in 1945. That work took him to Africa, where he became a consultant to the president of Liberia, William V. S. Tubman. Wherever Wilson traveled, he gathered information for his books and articles.

He was sent by United Fruit to a Maya site, Bonampak, in the jungles of Chiapas on the Mexican-Guatemalan border. Bonampak (c. A.D. 700) was discovered by the western world in 1946. The Lacondone people there were "unquestionably the purest descendants of the ancient Mayas." They worshiped in ruined temples which contained collectively some twelve hundred feet of well-preserved, colored frescos depicting battles, ceremonies, and processions. Wilson accompanied an expedition in 1947 organized by the Carnegie Institute and financed by United Fruit. Later he published articles on Bonampak in the *St. Louis Post-Dispatch*, *Natural History*, and *Nature Magazine*, and wrote an unpublished novel about the Lacondones.

Still, foreign travel did not pull Wilson entirely away from his first loves, the Ozarks and rural America. He said in 1955 that his ambition was "to write good books of Americana." Representative of these are *Backwoods America* (1936), a rather standard work honoring the "peasants" of the Southern mountains, and *Bodacious Ozarks* (1959), which includes essays about his family, Ozark language, and Orval Faubus. *Rudolf Diesel: Pioneer of the Age of Power* (1965) is a good example of his biographical work. His novel *A Man's Reach* (1945) was reviewed as "a robust novel based on the life of a rootin', tootin', fightin' legislative pioneer by name of Archibald Yell, an early governor of Arkansas."

One of Wilson's novels, *Acres of Sky* (1930), achieved regional significance when he helped composer Arthur Kreutz and librettist Zoe Schiller adapt it for the stage as a musical drama, the first production of the University of Arkansas's new Fine Arts Theatre in 1955. It received good reviews after a sellout opening night, but the production did not make it to the New York stage as Wilson and his collaborators had hoped. The novel, with its overblown language and melodramatic plot, was received with less fanfare. Nonetheless, *Acres of Sky* can be compared favorably with other 1930s works of Arkansas literature that extol the beauties and quaint citizenry of places like "Hawg Eye," "Weddington," and War Eagle.

Wilson's career illustrates how a basic living could be made writing for American magazines from the 1930s to the 1970s. Among the dozens of magazines that printed his pieces were *Saturday Review of Literature* and *Reader's Digest*. His subjects ranged from American railroads and rural life, to rubber and banana plantations, to Governor Orval Faubus.

Wilson was sometimes a caustic and demanding personality, but he constantly sought knowledge of people and their environments. He kept up a massive correspondence with acquaintances, publishing houses, editors, magazines, newspapers, public officials, and businesses and corporations. He was awarded a Distinguished Alumnus Citation from the University of Arkansas in 1947, a citation for contributions to inter-American relations from the University of Florida in 1960, and a doctor of letters degree from North American University (Arizona) in 1970.

He remained proud of his Fayetteville family. In a 1953 autobiographical note, he called his grandfather, Alfred McElroy Wilson, a state representative and American Indian arbiter, his "beacon and lighthouse." He worked with the city of Fayetteville to secure family land for the present Wilson Park.

His last years were spent in Putney and, occasionally, Cedar Key, Florida. He died in Hanover, New Hampshire, and was buried in Putney.

[The Charles Morrow Wilson Papers at the Special Collections Division, University of Arkansas Libraries, Fayetteville, consist of personal and professional corre-spondence, family documentation, literary manuscripts and fragments, reviews, bibliographies and biographical notes, printed material, and photographs. Of related interest are the Alfred McElroy Wilson Papers.

Other sources include the *Arkansas Democrat*, Nov. 17, 1950; the *Arkansas Traveler*, Nov. 1950; and the *Brattleboro Reformer* (Vermont), May 11, 1974. An obituary is in the *Northwest Arkansas Times*, Mar. 21, 1977.

Among Wilson's forty-six books are *Backwoods America* (1936); *Central America* (1941); *Trees and Test Tubes* (1944); *Tropics, World of Tomorrow* (1950); *Roots, Miracle Below* (1961); and *Empire in Green and Gold: The Story of the American Banana Trade* (1978).]

ELLEN COMPTON SHIPLEY

WILSON, ROBERT EDWARD LEE (Mar. 5, 1865–Sept. 27, 1933), planter, land developer, and business-man, was born in Frenchman's Bayou in Mississippi County. Few figures have so influenced the development of a community and region as he. Even today, his legacy casts a long shadow over Mississippi County and particularly the community named for him, Wilson, Arkansas.

He was the son of Josiah Lee Wilson and Martha Parson. His maternal grandfather was the great British reformer Robert Owen. His father died when Wilson was five years old; Martha Wilson moved the family to Memphis. Martha died in 1878 during a yellow fever epidemic, leaving Wilson an orphan at the age of thirteen. Placed in the guardianship of his uncle, he was sent off to the log schoolhouse of Judge Byers in Covington, Tennessee.

Byers often sent his students out on surveying expeditions. Wilson later credited this experience as the one that awakened his interest in agriculture and led him back to Arkansas. The man who became "Boss Lee" returned to Arkansas in 1880 as a wage laborer on a farm near Bassett, where he earned ten dollars a month plus his board. The following year he made a one-mule, twenty-acre crop. Over the next three years he managed to save $150, which he used to buy a small sawmill. He then traded a portion of his cleared land for 2,100 acres of hardwood timber.

As his prospects improved, he decided to farm the 160 acres of cleared land he inherited from his father, plus 120 acres on an adjoining farm, "just to get a home for my bride." His bride was Elizabeth Adams Beall, the daughter of Socrates A. Beall, a recent arrival from Pennsylvania. "Lizzie" and Wilson married in 1885.

Wilson's marriage led directly to a logging partnership with Socrates Beall. They opened sawmills at Golden Lake and Armorel. From these humble beginnings, Wilson extended his logging operations deeper into the forest. Around the logging camps grew company stores and towns. One of those towns was Wilson, founded in 1886.

Most lumbering companies sold their freshly cut timberlands. Wilson chose to clear and drain his properties. Over many centuries, constant flooding had laid down some of the richest alluvial soil in the world. On these deep black, fertile lands Wilson began to plant cotton.

Draining these swampy areas was an essential part of turning Mississippi County into the state's most heavily agricultural county. Wilson played a crucial role in the organization of the county's drainage districts, despite serious, and sometimes dangerous, opposition from many of the county's tax-weary, cash-strapped landowners, who did not recognize the long-term economic advantages of draining the swamplands.

Wilson's work ethic and eye for business opportunities made him one of the largest landowners in Arkansas. Though he, too, suffered under the strains that all southern agriculture felt in the early twentieth century, Wilson practiced a strategy that made Lee Wilson and Company an extremely profitable operation through the rest of the century: diversification. In addition to cotton, Wilson's farms produced corn, wheat, soybeans, and alfalfa. He invested heavily in mercantile establishments, banking, railroads, manufacturing, cotton ginning, education, and, at one time, the production of electricity.

Wilson believed strongly in the value of education. He donated the land and paid for much of the construction of the Wilson elementary and high-school building in 1920. He served on the board of trustees of Hendrix College and what was then A & M College in Jonesboro. The student health center and the old administration building on the Arkansas State University campus in Jonesboro bear Wilson's name today. He directed his trustees to set aside a portion of his estate to be used for educational purposes throughout Arkansas.

Wilson died in Memphis, Tennessee. By the time of his death, his estate included sixty-five thousand acres in addition to most of the businesses and all of the residences in Wilson, Arkansas, and other real property in five Mississippi County towns. All of these properties were included under the umbrella of Lee Wilson and Company and passed down, in trust, to his son, Robert E. Lee Wilson Jr. ("Roy") and longtime employee James H. Crain. In the sixty-six years since "Boss Lee's" death, Lee Wilson and Company has become a cornerstone of the prosperity and economic development of Mississippi County and the lives of its citizens.

[See the *Arkansas Democrat*, July 6, 1986; the *Osceola Times*, Sept. 24, 1970; the *Blytheville Courier News*, July 1, 1936; and *Fortune*, Aug. 1964. See also Mabel F. Edrington, *History of Mississippi County, Arkansas* (1962); John A. Fox, *Mississippi County, Arkansas: Through the Years* (1986); Lee Wilson and Company, *Growing Prosperity: The Story of the South's Best Known Farmer* (1930); and Deanna Snowden, *Mississippi County, Arkansas: Appreciating the Past, Anticipating the Future* (1986).]

J. WAYNE JONES

WILSON, TRIPHENIA FANCHER (Nov. 10, 1855 –Apr. 30, 1897), survivor of the Mountain Meadows Massacre, was born in (then) Boone County to Alexander Fancher, a farmer, and Eliza Ingram. When she was two years old she witnessed one of the most horrible crimes in American history, the slaughter in southwestern Utah of some 120 people from Arkansas.

Her father was the leader of an emigrant wagon train that left northwest Arkansas in late April or early May 1857 bound for California. The Fancher party consisted of thirty to forty families (the exact number is not known), mostly farmers, many related by kinship or friendship, who planned to settle in California. They were prosperous people who had with them nine hundred head of cattle, a large number of horses and mules including a prize stallion, several carriages, and much household property.

By early August they reached Salt Lake City and camped on the Jordon River to replenish supplies and repair equipment. It was a bad time for them to be there. Tensions were high between the Church of Jesus Christ of Latter-Day Saints, which governed the Utah Territory, and the United States Government over issues of sovereignty, polygamy, and the territorial ambitions of the church. The Mormons, as the Latter-Day Saints were called, wanted a kingdom "free and independent of all other kingdoms." In July President James Buchanan appointed a new set of federal officials for Utah, including a governor to replace the Mormon leader Brigham Young. In the same month a military expedition set out from Fort Laramie, Wyoming, headed toward Utah. The Mormons began preparations to resist a military "invasion" by the hated "gentiles." They armed the Indians in the territory, including the Yannawant, Puavant, and Santa Clara Indians in the southwest.

The Fancher party was crossing the territory as tensions escalated. From Salt Lake City they took a southern route; along the way the Mormons refused to sell grain to them, being under orders from Brigham Young to conserve it in case of invasion. In early September the party reached Mountain Meadows in extreme southwestern Utah, a well-known stopping place on the old Spanish Trail, where there was ample grass for their cattle. They camped near a large spring at the end of a narrow valley.

On September 6 or 7 they were attacked. The first gunfire killed several Arkansans and wounded about seventeen. The party circled their wagons and returned fire. For at least four days they put up a stubborn fight. At some point they must have discovered that they were fighting white men as well as Indians.

On September 11 a man named Bateman, under the orders of John D. Lee, a field commander for Mormon and Indian forces, approached the besieged Arkansans under a white flag and offered to help them. He convinced them that in order to save themselves they must give up their arms and follow him to safety. He said that he and his men would protect them from the Indians and lead them to a safe place.

The sick and wounded and the children came out first in wagons. Then followed the women and older children. The men came last, walking single file, guarded by armed men alongside them. At a prearranged signal the Mormon "protectors" turned on the men and shot them dead. At the same moment the Indians attacked the women and older children. The sick and wounded at the head of the column were killed by Lee and his aides. It took perhaps an hour to shoot, club, and stab to death some one hundred and twenty defenseless men, women, and children. About eighty-six members of the Church of Jesus Christ of Latter-Day Saints were present on the meadow that day; twenty-four of them participated in the slaughter. They and the Indians carried off all the property the Arkansans had owned, including the clothes they were wearing, and left their bodies on the ground for animals to consume.

Of thirteen members of the Fancher family, only Triphenia and her older brother Christopher (Kit) survived. They were among seventeen surviving children who were taken into the homes of Mormon families in the area. It took several months for officials of the federal government to reach the children. By June 1858 the children had been found. Reports about their health were contradictory, but they seem to have been in good condition, though poorly dressed. One report noted that they had not "made any developments" living with the Mormons, evidently meaning normal development toward growth and maturity.

Arrangements were made by the slow federal bureaucracy to transport the children back to Arkansas. They left Salt Lake City in June 1859 for Fort Leavenworth, Kansas, escorted by three men, five women, and a major of the army, and guarded by a company of heavily armed cavalrymen. The children were met at Fort Leavenworth and fifteen were brought to Carrollton, Arkansas, more than two years after they had left for California. The other two children went on to Washington, D.C., to tell authorities what they knew of the massacre before coming home to Arkansas.

Triphenia and Kit Fancher grew up in the home of their cousin Hampton Bynum Fancher at the Osage community near Harrison, Arkansas. Kit died in his twenties. Triphenia married James C. Wilson on July 9, 1871, and with him she had nine children. She is buried at Rule in Carroll County.

[Sources include Ray W. Irwin, "The Mountain Meadows Massacre," *AHQ* 9 (Spring 1950); Juanita Brooks, *The Mountain Meadows Massacre* (1950; rpt. 1991); Jim Lair, *The Mountain Meadows Massacre: An Outlander's View* (1986); a series of articles by J. K. Fancher in the *Harrison Daily Times*, Mar. 16, 1989–Sept. 6, 1991; and interviews with J. K. Fancher, Feb. 2 and June 3, 1998.]

NANCY A. WILLIAMS

WITTLAKE, EUGENE BISHOP (Aug. 14, 1912– June 30, 1988), paleobotanist and museum director, was born in Sheridan, Wyoming, to Elmer Albert Wittlake, an office supervisor, and Emma Alice Beeney(?). He earned a bachelor of arts degree from Augustana College, Illinois, and a master of science from the State University of Iowa. He and Elizabeth Grundy married in 1947 and had one son, Eugene Louis.

Wittlake taught biology at the University of Arkansas in Fayetteville from 1946 until 1951, when he enrolled at the University of Kansas to earn a doctorate in botany/biology with an emphasis in plant morphology. In 1956 he returned to Arkansas as associate professor of botany at what is now Arkansas State University.

He immediately joined the faculty museum Committee, an advisory group for the Arkansas State College Museum. At the urging of Jean R. Williams, museum director, he also assisted with archeological digs in eastern Arkansas. He later said, "There was some urgency in our mission. We wanted to obtain the artifacts before they were all gone, and they were disappearing rapidly at the time." Elizabeth Wittlake said, "I went along on the digs as cook, secretary and jack-of-all-trades; no matter if I liked it or not." Their teamwork built collections which serve scholars, students, and tourists.

In May 1959 Dr. Carl R. Reng, president of Arkansas State, asked Wittlake to become director of the museum while continuing to teach. Mrs. Wittlake served the museum as a volunteer. In 1961 Dr. Reng gave her a title, curator of history. In 1972, after thirteen years of service, she was added to the payroll as assistant director.

When the Dean B. Ellis Library was completed in 1964, Wittlake was offered "the east end of the basement to house the museum's growing collection." This provided space for exhibit preparation, conservation, storage, records, and exhibits. The number of objects increased sixfold during Wittlake's tenure through donations, purchases, and trades.

Each year the Wittlakes took to the road. Buying trips were their vacations; they visited nine hundred museums in ten years. Buyers in various parts of the country identified objects for possible acquisition. Nettie Wheeler of Muskogee, Oklahoma, helped them locate American Indian objects. The collaboration with Wheeler developed collections of items from the Quapaw, Caddo, Osage, Cherokee, Choctaw, and Chickasaw who lived in what is now Arkansas: garments made from skins, beading, baskets, household goods, toys, and documents such as land records. For comparative study, the Wittlakes also acquired Sioux, Hopi, Pueblo, Navajo, and Apache collections. Their exhibits won recognition from the *National Geographic*.

Wittlake not only acquired significant collections, he also documented artifacts, designed and built cases,

painted backgrounds, taught students multiple skills, and twice packed up all the collections to move into expanded space. Both Wittlakes gave countless talks and conducted tours for civic, professional, and school groups.

Wittlake outfitted a utility trailer on a truck bed and took his son, friends, and students on fossil-finding excursions, discovering rich caches in Arkansas, Kansas, and Wyoming. He published the results of his research in paleobotony (the study of fossil plants) in monographs and professional journals throughout mid-America.

He helped to organize the Arkansas Museums Association and served as its first president in 1964. He was a charter member and the second president of the Craighead County Historical Society, director of the Arkansas Junior Science and Humanities Symposium, president of the Arkansas Academy of Science, and a member of honor societies in geology, botany, and bryology (the study of mosses).

The Wittlakes won accreditation for the museum from the American Association of Museums in 1973. Eugene Wittlake retired from the university in 1979 and was made professor emeritus in the College of Arts and Sciences. A plaque in the museum pays tribute to Eugene and Elizabeth Wittlake and their work.

Wittlake died in Jonesboro, survived by his wife and son.

[This biography is based on the author's interviews with Eugene L. Wittlake, June 9, 13, and 16, 1997; on materials from the Arkansas State University Museum archives; and family records held by Eugene L. Wittlake. See also the *Arkansas Gazette*, Mar. 11, 1980, and the *Jonesboro Sun*, Nov. 25, 1960.

Wittlake's research was published in such journals as the *Bryologist, University of Iowa Studies*, the *American Midland Naturalist*, and the *Ohio Journal of Science*.]

CHARLOTT A. JONES

WOMACK, HENRY MCCOY (Aug. 13, 1882– Jan. 18, 1953), blacksmith, was born to Joel Franklin and Lucinda Walls Womack in New Site, Alabama. The family migrated to Arkansas when Henry Womack, called Tobe, was old enough to recall being scared as they forded the Arkansas River at Little Rock. He remembered, too, the cries of wolves and panthers as the family traveled by ox-drawn wagon to Kirby, Arkansas. There his father opened "Womack & Son,

Blacksmiths" to serve the loggers and farmers of Pike County. In time three siblings joined the family: Ruby, Etta, and Joel Franklin Jr.

Tobe spent his boyhood in Kirby, starting early to work in his father's shop learning the trade. He attended the one-room schoolhouse and hunted and fished nearby forests and streams for food and recreation. He established a reputation as a skilled woodsman and blacksmith "who sang while he worked . . . could tame and shoe the crankiest horses and at a fair price." He made fast growth physically, becoming a strikingly tall adult with black hair and gray eyes.

On February 2, 1904, he married Minnie Vesta Taylor, a teacher and daughter of a Baptist circuit-rider preacher, who performed their marriage ceremony. Of thirteen children born to them, eight lived to maturity.

With the beginning of family responsibilities, Womack began looking toward Clark County with its rich Caddo River bottomland, its cotton, grain, and vegetable farms, and its logging and milling as a more favorable site for his own blacksmith shop. He moved his family to Amity where he established Womack's Blacksmith Shop behind the merchandise and hardware stores that made up one side of Amity's town square. He worked in the squatty, soot-covered shop as farrier, iron and steel worker, and, as time passed, coffin maker and miller. A chinaberry tree, suggesting Longfellow's spreading chestnut, stood near the shop, where farmers gathered to pitch horseshoes and shoot the breeze.

One of some twenty-four hundred blacksmiths in Arkansas during the 1920s and 1930s, Tobe Womack repaired wagons, buggies, farm implements, hardware and household utensils, and firearms, but his special skill was making and fitting horseshoes. He fitted the horses' shoes according to the weather and the work they performed. He knew that a typical horseshoe meets the road in three places, a bar on the toe and a one-inch square calk on each heel, and that road horses, in contrast to field horses, need sharp calks at each of the three points. Sometimes a horse had to be fastened in stocks, which held the leg rigid while the foot was being shod, or occasionally turned onto its back and tied to the chinaberry tree.

Womack added several sidelines to his "way with horses." Wooden pegs on the wall near the forge held wagon wheel rims in all sizes to be shaped into scythes. Three-pronged gigs—heavy forks of steel mounted on long canes or wooden poles—were a source of income, as night fishing for frogs was popular with his customers. Frog legs often graced the family's dinner table, since part of the blacksmith's pay was always in produce and catch. Other walls held work benches with iron vises for metal or wood articles being worked on, along with tool racks for hammers, from tack hammers to great sledge hammers.

He combined his expertise with metal and wood to make iceboxes of seasoned pine, lined with hammered and fitted tin, with a hole in the bottom for a drain. Eventually, a gristmill occupied part of the shop. Farmers brought their corn to be ground and the miller/blacksmith was paid "by the share in cornmeal," half to the farmer, half to Womack, who frequently traded some of his own half to the village grocer for "bolted meal" or other "boughten victuals."

Gimbels and chisels and shiny draw knives were for sale in the shop, and nails of all "penny," at that time an expression of how many nails one could buy for a penny. The smallest nails, not much thicker than a pin, were kept in a compartment with lace, thinnest nainsook, muslin, and satin, all covered with bright wrapping paper and string to protect them from the grime of the shop. These items were used for yet another "money maker," coffins for infants. Made of green pine slabs and trimmed with these fancy fabrics nailed into ruffles and frills, the baby coffins became a necessary service Womack performed for his community.

Minnie Vesta died on Pearl Harbor Day, December 7, 1941. One of his sons signed up for military service, and his daughters joined the war work force. The time seemed right to close the shop and join the rush to the west coast shipyards. But this venture was not a success for Womack, and he returned to Amity, where he died several years after the war.

An estimated two hundred blacksmiths, mostly farriers with portable equipment, operate in Arkansas in the 1990s. There is said to be a blacksmithing renaissance under way where folk handicrafts and art are treasured.

[See Nell Womack Evans, *Mama Wanted to Teach* (1990), and "His Tools Were Fire and Steel," *Ozarks Mountaineer* (1967). The Arkansas History Commission provided figures on the number of blacksmiths in the state.]

NELL WOMACK EVANS

WOODRUFF, WILLIAM EDWARD (Dec. 24, 1795–June 19, 1885), founder and editor of the *Arkansas Gazette*, was born in Fire Place, Long Island, New York, to Nathaniel Woodruff and Hannah Clarke. When Woodruff's father died, his mother moved her family of five boys to live with her mother in Brookhaven, New York. In 1810 William Woodruff began a six-year apprenticeship with a Sag Harbor printer named Alden Spooner, who provided him with food, lodging, a little formal education, and training in almost every aspect of the newspaper business.

In 1818 Woodruff traveled to Nashville, Tennessee, where he worked for Thomas G. Bradford at the *Clarion and Tennessee State Gazette*. In 1819 Congress created the Arkansas Territory. In the fall of that year, Woodruff purchased a used wooden printing press and traveled by keelboat and canoe to the territory's capital at Arkansas Post. He probably hoped to become the territory's official printer.

On November 20, 1819, Woodruff published the first issue of the *Arkansas Gazette*, which was the first newspaper in the territory and one of the first newspapers established west of the Mississippi River. He published it every Saturday on four pages and offered subscription rates at three dollars per annum in advance or four dollars to be paid at the end of the year. In the first issue he reprinted articles from American and European newspapers, thanked his readers for their support, and announced that day's territorial elections.

In 1820 he was, indeed, appointed the official printer for the territory. When the territorial capital moved to a more central location, Little Rock, in 1821, Woodruff followed.

Three years later he started the Arkansas Military Land Agency, managing land owned by people living outside of the territory. His position as public printer and editor of the *Gazette* lent him the prestige to attract business for his agency. He began buying and selling property across central Arkansas and by the mid-1830s owned thousands of acres. His agency and land speculation produced most of his wealth.

On November 14, 1827, William Woodruff and Jane Eliza Mills married; they raised eight children to maturity. Woodruff purchased a larger home for his family, kept his office there, and built a large garden to the side. He owned three slaves by 1830 and fourteen slaves in 1860. Presumably the slaves worked in domestic capacities; however, *Gazette* advertisements suggest that he hired them out as well.

Woodruff was a storekeeper, selling books, seed, and hymnals from his office. He opened a circulating library, invested in a salt manufactory, and purchased a ferry business and a small steamboat on the Arkansas River. He called for investment in Arkansas manufacturing and supported the construction of a railroad line from Memphis to Little Rock.

As *Gazette* editor Woodruff took stands against dueling and drinking. Dueling, he said, "is neither sanctioned by the laws of God or [the] country, and ... ought to be discountenanced by every well regulated community." On the issue of race Woodruff did not transcend his time or place. He argued that southern slaves were better off than northern free Negroes and supported legislation to remove free blacks from Arkansas.

He remained politically neutral in the paper's early years but by the late 1820s increasingly took the side of the Democratic Party. He became embroiled in political debates and often drew the ire of his opponents. In 1833 he was elected to the town council. A year later he served as town treasurer and territorial auditor. He supported statehood in 1836, became Arkansas's first state treasurer, and served as Little Rock postmaster in 1845.

In 1838 Woodruff sold the *Gazette* to his foreman and business associate, Edward Cole. Woodruff became the sole owner of the *Gazette* again in December 1841, but sold it to a Whig named Benjamin Borden on January 4, 1843. Woodruff founded the *Arkansas Democrat* (not the progenitor of the twentieth-century *Arkansas Democrat*) for political reasons in 1846, and re-purchased the *Gazette* in 1850. Finally, in 1853, he retired from the newspaper business to enjoy "employments better suited to my taste and disposition."

During the Civil War the Arkansas legislature honored Woodruff by creating a new county in his name. While his older sons were fighting for the Confederacy, he stayed in Little Rock with his family. During the federal occupation of the capital city, he was expelled for writing a letter to a friend voicing pro-Confederate sentiments. With his daughter Evelina he traveled to Washington, Arkansas, and Louisville, Kentucky. His wife and young children remained in their Little Rock home, which they shared with federal officers and an army hospital.

After the war Woodruff returned and continued to trade in land but stayed out of the public eye. When he died, his family hired fourteen carriages for the funeral procession which, according to the *Arkansas Gazette*, stretched "about half a mile long and embraced representatives of the most distinguished families in the city." Governor Simon Hughes served as a pallbearer. Woodruff was interred in Mount Holly Cemetery.

[The Arkansas History Commission in Little Rock holds a large collection of Woodruff's papers and letters, 1810–1882, Guidebooks 5 and 18. His estate records are there under Pulaski County, Arkansas, Loose Probate Records. For land records, see Pulaski County tax records and deeds; for census data, see 1830 Population Schedule for Pulaski County and the 1860 Slave Census Schedule for Pulaski County, all at the history commission.

See the *Arkansas Gazette,* June 20, 1885 (obituary), and June 21, 1885; and a *Gazette* publication, *Supplement Commemorating the Founding of Arkansas' First Newspaper,* 1919.

See also Margaret Ross, *Arkansas Gazette: The Early Years, 1819–1866, A History* (1969); Jessie Ryon Lucke, "Correspondence concerning the Establishment of the First Arkansas Press," *AHQ* 14 (Summer 1955): 161–71; Richard W. Griffin, "Pro-Industrial Sentiment and Cotton Factories in Arkansas, 1820–1863," *AHQ* 15 (Summer 1956): 125–39; John W. Payne, "Samuel Preston Moore's Letters to William E. Woodruff," *AHQ* 15 (Autumn 1956): 228–48; and John Lewis Fergeson, "William E. Woodruff and the Territory of Arkansas, 1819–1836," Ph.D. dissertation, Tulane University, 1961.]

Ted J. Smith

YELL, ARCHIBALD (1797?–Feb. 23, 1847), governor and congressman, probably was born in Jefferson County, Tennessee, although both Kentucky and North Carolina have been claimed. The date is also uncertain; 1799 appears in some sources. His father, Moses Yell, and his third wife, Jane Curry, settled in the Duck River region of Tennessee, where their son Archibald received a very limited education. Archibald Yell was alleged to have participated in the major engagements in the Creek War, but archival evidence of his being a "boy captain" is missing. He carried the rank of sergeant in the War of 1812, participating in the Battle of New Orleans, where he received a favorable notice from General Andrew Jackson. He served as a first lieutenant in the Seminole War.

After studying law, Yell settled in Shelbyville (Bedford County), Tennessee, in partnership with his former teacher, William Gilchrist. Yell entered politics, defeating an Anti-Mason state legislator. His Tennessee career ended in a brawl. In 1830 President Andrew Jackson appointed Yell receiver of public monies at Little Rock. This first Arkansas stay was cut short by malaria, and he returned to Tennessee to recover. In 1835 he came back as a territorial circuit judge. He made his home in Fayetteville, where he built a fine Greek Revival house, Waxhaws. Yell helped organize northwest Arkansas Masons.

In 1836, when Arkansas began drafting a state constitution, Yell, the leading Jacksonian Democrat of the great Northwest, endorsed equal white male suffrage. Plantation area leaders favored a "three-fifths" system which gave them additional voting weight determined by the number of slaves they owned. They inserted a residency requirement that excluded Yell from running for governor. Yell instead ran for Congress, defeating Whig William Cummins and arriving in Washington at the end of the session. When President Martin Van Buren called a special session, Yell was forced to run again and shortly thereafter ran yet again in the 1837 regular general election, defeating Whig John Ringgold.

Yell did not seek reelection to Congress in 1838 but was elected governor in 1840. Faced with the collapse of the state-financed banking system, Yell failed to get state control over the banks' liquidation. Although he supported public schools and the abolition of imprisonment for debt, Yell vetoed a married women's property rights bill and refused on the grounds of economy to appoint a state geologist.

Yell resigned his gubernatorial seat in 1844 to run again for Congress. Opposed by his law partner, David Walker, Yell charmed the voters and ignored the issues, displaying his charismatic character to the fullest, in a race long remembered in Arkansas, as Yell out-sang and out-shot his Whig opponent.

At the onset of the Mexican War, Yell returned to Arkansas to enroll as a private in Captain Solon Borland's company of Arkansas volunteers. Elected regimental colonel, Yell attempted to keep his House seat and also indicated he wanted elevation to the Senate, but a hostile legislature forced him to resign his congressional seat and the Senate seat went to Chester Ashley. Yell's troubles continued when General John E. Wool, judging the Arkansas troops poorly disciplined, assigned them the worst camping sites. Yell was soon at odds with his former ally Borland as well as Whig captain Albert Pike. At the Battle of Buena Vista, "Col. Yell's Mounted Devils" were assaulted by a large number of Mexican lancers. In the melee that followed, some Arkansas soldiers ran away, and Yell fell at the forefront of the fighting, pierced by Mexican lances, while trying to rally the men. First buried at Saltillo, his body was later removed to a family plot at Waxhaws and then in 1872 was relocated to the Evergreen Cemetery in Fayetteville.

Although Yell was Arkansas's best example of a charismatic Jacksonian Democrat, he was also a land speculator, involved in the purchase of Mississippi River lands with federal judge Benjamin Johnson and David Walker; he invested in Red River lands with friend and future president James Knox Polk, and engaged in local speculations, notably the Franklin County town of Ozark, with his law colleague and political opponent David Walker. The strongest evidence of his Jacksonian Democracy was to be found in his appealing political style, his hard-money economic policies, and the remarkably poor spelling and grammar of his surviving correspondence. Opponents called him the man who spelled Congress with a *K*.

Yell was three times married. In Tennessee in 1821 he and Mary Scott, a planter's daughter, married. She died in 1823 in childbirth, together with one of the twin children. The surviving child, Mary Scott, was raised by her maternal grandparents. In 1827 he and Ann Jordan Moore married; they had three daughters: Artemesia, Jane Rochester, and Elizabeth Lawson, and a son, DeWitt Clinton. His third wife was a widow, Mary Ficklin from Lawrence County.

[See Michael B. Dougan, "Archibald Yell, 1840–1844," in *The Governors of Arkansas: Essays in Political Biography,* Timothy P. Donovan, Willard B. Gatewood Jr., and Jeannie M. Whayne, eds., 2d ed. (1995).]

MICHAEL B. DOUGAN

GENERAL INDEX

Aaronson, Max. *See* Anderson, Gilbert Maxwell
Abolitionists, 41
Adkins, Homer Martin, **5–6**, 15, 53, 113, 243, 273
Adler, Simon, 6–7, *il*
Adventurers. *See* Explorers and adventurers
Aerospace industry, 188–89
African Americans
    Catholic, 103, 205–6
    as civil rights activists (*see* Civil rights activists)
    civil rights of (*see* Civil rights in Arkansas)
    as composers, 229–30, 276–78
    education of, 61–62, 73–74, 130–31, 192, 220, 304
    free, in 19th-century Arkansas, 57–58, 128–29
    labor unions of, 140–41, 155
    Little Rock school integration and (*see* Little Rock school
        integration crisis of 1957)
    in manufacturing, 212
    public health services for, 127–28, 242–44
    Quaker, 61
    as slaves (*see* Slaves and former slaves)
    voting rights, 21, 28, 36, 108, 175, 243
Agricultural Adjustment Administration, 116, 145, 198
Agriculture. *See also* Farmers and planters
    cotton breeding, 201–3
    grape cultivation, 16
    Greenback Party and, 219
    research and education in, 8, 44–45
    rice farming, 299–300
    sharecropper's and tenant's union, 116–17, 197–98
Alexander, Harold Edward, 7–8
Alexander Road Improvement Act, 136
Ali, Muhammad, 169
Allen, Henry J., 141
Allen, John E., 176
Almanac Singers, 138
Alphonso Trent Orchestra, 293–94
Altheimer, Ben J[oseph?], 8–9
Ambassadors
    S. Borland, 32–33
    P. Clayton, 66–67
    U. M. Rose, 250–51
America First Party, 267
American Arts and Crafts Movement, 148–49
American Baptist Association (Missionary Baptists), 30
American Bar Association, 251
American Board of Missions, 256
American Civil Liberties Union, 165
American Cryptogram Association, 117
American (Know-Nothing) Party, 33, 51, 68, 198
Anderson, Gilbert Maxwell, **9–10,** 215
Anderson, James A., 191
Anderson, Marian, 230
Anti-Saloon League, 191
Anti-Semitism, 206, 267
Archeologists, S. C. Dellinger, 80–82
Architects
    E. D. Stone, 278–79
    C. L. Thompson, 288–89

Aretz, Winand, 119
Argenta, Arkansas, 101, 102
Arkadelphia, Arkansas, 209
Arkadelphia Methodist College, Arkadelphia, 209
Arkansas
    capitol building, 288–89
    constitution (*see* Constitution, Arkansas state)
    economic-development advocates in, 95–96
    geology of, 34–35
    mapping of, 196, 197
    state flag, 96–97
    state flower, 96
    statehood, 259
    Territory (*see* Arkansas Territory)
    World War II industry in, 5
Arkansas Advancement Association, 43
Arkansas Advocate (newspaper), 223
Arkansas Agricultural Wheel, 204
Arkansas Aircraft Company, 70
Arkansas AM & N College, 304
Arkansas Banner (newspaper), 32
Arkansas Baptist (newspaper), 30
Arkansas College, 170–71, 176
Arkansas Conference of the Methodist Episcopal Church, 166
Arkansas Democrat (newspaper), 12, 28, 199, 268, 269, 314
Arkansas Department of Health, 86, 127
Arkansas Department of Public Welfare, 116
Arkansas Eugenics Association, 74–75
Arkansas Federation of Women's Clubs (AFWC), 96
Arkansas Game and Fish Commission, 7, 8
Arkansas Gazette (newspaper), 25, 33, 199, 226, 268, 269
    founding of, 314–15
    Little Rock school integration crisis and editorials of, 10–11, 21
    J. N. Heiskell as editor of, 139–40
Arkansas General Assembly, representatives to, 42, 101, 102, 152,
    175–76, 179, 203, 206, 210, 219, 241, 253, 273, 283, 290
Arkansas Historical Association, 146, 287–88
Arkansas Historical Quarterly, 145, 287–88
Arkansas Home and Hospital for Crippled Negro Children (Lena
    Jordan Hospital), 156, 243
Arkansas Industrial Development Commission, 245
Arkansas Industrial Development Tours, 95
Arkansas Industrial University Medical Department, 184
Arkansas Library Commission, 208–9
Arkansas Live Stock Association, 20
Arkansas Methodist, 191
Arkansas Military Land Agency, 314
Arkansas Museums Association, 312
Arkansas Native Plant Society, 274
Arkansas Natural Gas Corporation, 20
Arkansas Natural History Museum, 12, 13
Arkansas Negro Democratic Association, 243
Arkansas Post, 18, 57, 144, 211, 258, 275
    founding of, 291
Arkansas Power and Light Company, 76
Arkansas Republican (newspaper), 28, 73
Arkansas River, clearing obstructions in, 263
Arkansas Sentinel (newspaper), 201

Pope, John, 226–27
Populist Party, 203, 204–5, 219
Populists and populism
    W. S. Morgan, 204–5
    J. N. Smithee, 268–69
Post colonies, 132
Pottery, art, 148–49
Potts, Kirkbride, 227–28
Pottsville, Arkansas, 227
Pound, Ezra, 107
Powell, Richard Ewing "Dick," 228–29
Powell, Velma, 284
Prairie County Democrat (newspaper), 268
Prairie Grove, Arkansas, Civil War battle at, 142, 144, 261
Price, Florence Beatrice Smith, 229–30, *il*
Prison system in Arkansas, 24–25
    convict leasing, 87
    reform of, 246
Progressive Farmers and Household Union, 140–41, 155
Prohibition, 136, 191
Promoters
    C. H. Brough, 43
    L. Ellison, 95–96
    S. W. Fordyce, 110–11
    M. L. Harrison, 131–33
    W. H. Harvey, 133–34
    L. H. Roots, 249–50
Pryor, David, 213, 231
Pryor, Nathaniel, 211
Pryor, Susan Hampton Newton, 230–31
Psychiatrists, I. J. Brooks, 40–41
Public health, 127–28
Publishers
    L.C. Bates, 20–21
    V. M. D. Duncan, 89–90
    O. Faubus, 100
    R. W. Fulbright, 114–15
    M. W. Gibbs, 121–22
    J. N. Heiskell, 139–40
    A. C. Millar, 190–91
    J. N. Smithee, 268–69
    W. E. Woodruff, 314–15
Pulaski County Medical, Dental, and Pharmaceutical Association,
    242
Pyle, Ernie, 65

Quakers, 61, 272
Quapaw cotton, 202
Quapaw Indians, 18–19, 254–56
Quinine, 59

Race riots. *See* Elaine Race Riot of 1919, Phillips County
Radio, 38, 39, 146
    "King Biscuit" program, 307
Radio personalities
    B. Burns, 47–48
    J. H. Dean, 79–80
    R. E. Powell, 228–29
Raidler, William, 88
Railroads, 24, 76, 132, 153, 154, 204, 224, 244, 296
    S. W. Fordyce and development of, 110
    routes and terminus locations of 19th century, 71–72
    state commission on, 64

Randolph, Vance, 231–32
Rangel, Rodrigo, 57
Ray, Joe, 232–33
Razorback Stadium, Fayetteville, 18
Read, Lessie Stringfellow, 233–34, *il*
Reagan, Ronald, 23
Real Estate Bank, 72, 260
Reconstruction Finance Corporation (RFC), 76, 183, 220
Reconstruction in Arkansas, 22, 28, 122–23, 152, 272, 296
    Brooks-Baxter War (*see* Brooks-Baxter War (1874))
    officials of, 65–66, 67
Rector, Henry Massie, 35, 104, 142, **234–36**
Rector Antitrust Act, 79, 154
Rector family. *See* Dynasty, The (Johnson-Conway-Sevier families)
Red River War (1874-1875), 97
Reed, Rose Pearl "Pearl Starr," 236–37
Reeves, Bass, 237–38
Remmel, Augustus C., 292
Remmel, Harmon Liveright, 238–39
Reng, Carl R., 312
Representatives. *See* Congressional Representatives, U.S.
Republican Party in Arkansas, 22, 27–28, 42, 49–50, 121, 122–23,
    203, 238–39, 249, 294
    Brindletail faction, 22, 42
    Brooks-Baxter War (*see* Brooks-Baxter War (1874))
    leaders of, 134–35, 238–39, 245–46, 253, 292–93, 298
    Lily-white faction, 50, 155, 239, 253, 292
    Minstrels faction, 22
    Reconstruction officials from, 65, 67
Revenue Stabilization Law, 165
Reynolds, Daniel Harris, 239–40
Rice farming, 299–300
Rickenbacker, Eddie, 70
Rickon, Fred J. H., 289
Riddle, Almeda James, 240–41
Ridge, John, 256
Ringgold, John, 176
Roane, John Selden, 241–42
Roane, Sam, 258
Robinson, John Marshall, 242–44
Robinson, Joseph Taylor, 15, 64, 87, 97, 181, 182, 191, 243, **244–45**, *il*
Rockefeller, Winthrop, 166, **245–47**
Rogers, Arkansas, 159, 300
Rogers, Betty Blake, 247–48
Rogers, John Henry, 248–49
Rogers, Roy, 247–48
Roman Catholics in Arkansas, 16–17, 51–52, 103–4, 105–6, 205–6
Roots, Logan Holt, 249–50, *il*
Roots, Philander Keep (P. K.), 249
Rose, Uriah Milton, 250–51, *il*
Rose law firm, 171, 250–51
Rotenberry, A. L., 30
Rothwell, Richard P., 35
Russell, Thomas, 211
Russellville, Arkansas, 144–45
Rust, Albert, 179
Rust, John Daniel, 251–52
Rust Cotton Picker Company, 252
Ryan, Abraham, 305

St. Bernard's Hospital, Jonesboro, 103
St. Edward's Hospital, Fort Smith, 103
St. Edward's School, Little Rock, 119

INDEX OF CONTRIBUTORS